Big Book of IP Telephony RFCs

LIMITED WARRANTY AND DISCLAIMER OF LIABILITY

ACADEMIC PRESS ("AP") AND ANYONE ELSE WHO HAS BEEN INVOLVED IN THE CREATION OR PRODUCTION OF THE ACCOMPANYING CODE ("THE PRODUCT") CANNOT AND DO NOT WARRANT THE PERFORMANCE OR RESULTS THAT MAY BE OBTAINED BY USING THE PRODUCT. THE PRODUCT IS SOLD "AS IS" WITHOUT WARRANTY OF MERCHANTABILITY OR FITNESS FOR ANY PARTICULAR PURPOSE.

IN NO EVENT, WHETHER AS A RESULT OF BREACH OF CONTRACT, WARRANTY, OR TORT (INCLUDING NEGLIGENCE), WILL AP OR ANYONE WHO HAS BEEN INVOLVED IN THE CREATION OR PRODUCTION OF THE PRODUCT BE LIABLE TO PURCHASER FOR ANY DAMAGES, INCLUDING ANY LOST PROFITS, LOST SAVINGS OR OTHER INCIDENTAL OR CONSEQUENTIAL DAMAGES ARISING OUT OF THE USE OR INABILITY TO USE THE PRODUCT OR ANY MODIFICATIONS THEREOF, OR DUE TO THE CONTENTS OF THE CODE, EVEN IF AP HAS BEEN ADVISED ON THE POSSIBILITY OF SUCH DAMAGES, OR FOR ANY CLAIM BY ANY OTHER PARTY.

SOME STATES DO NOT ALLOW LIMITATION ON HOW LONG AN IMPLIED WARRANTY LASTS, NOR EXCLUSIONS OR LIMITATIONS OF INCIDENTAL OR CONSEQUENTIAL DAMAGE, SO THE ABOVE LIMITATIONS AND EXCLUSIONS MAY NOT APPLY TO YOU. THIS WARRANTY GIVES YOU SPECIFIC LEGAL RIGHTS, AND YOU MAY ALSO HAVE OTHER RIGHTS WHICH VARY FROM JURISDICTION TO JURISDICTION.

THE RE-EXPORT OF UNITED STATES ORIGINAL SOFTWARE IS SUBJECT TO THE UNITED STATES LAWS UNDER THE EXPORT ADMINISTRATION ACT OF 1969 AS AMENDED. ANY FURTHER SALE OF THE PRODUCT SHALL BE IN COMPLIANCE WITH THE UNITED STATES DEPARTMENT OF COMMERCE ADMINISTRATION REGULATIONS. COMPLIANCE WITH SUCH REGULATIONS IS YOUR RESPONSIBILITY AND NOT THE RESPONSIBILITY OF AP.

Big Book IP Telephony RFCs

Compiled by Pete Loshin

Morgan
Kaufmann

An Imprint of ACADEMIC PRESS
A HARCOURT SCIENCE AND TECHNOLOGY COMPANY
San Diego San Francisco New York Boston
London Sydney Tokyo

ACADEMIC PRESS
A Harcourt Science and Technology Company
525 B Street, Suite 1900, San Diego, CA 92101-4495 USA
http://www.academicpress.com

Academic Press
Harcourt Place, 32 Jamestown Rd., London NW1 7BY, UK

Morgan Kaufmann
A Harcourt Science and Technology Company
340 Pine Street, Sixth Floor, San Francisco, CA 94104-3205
http://www.mkp.com

Library of Congress Catalog Number: 00-112075
International Standard Book Number: 0-12-455855-0

Printed in the United States of America
00 01 02 03 IP 9 8 7 6 5 4 3 2 1

Dedication

This book is dedicated to the members of the Internet Engineering Task Force.

Table of Contents

Preface

The vast majority of this book is available online, free for the downloading. If you know what you're looking for, you can very easily download all the RFCs in this book, along with any RFCs that have been released since this book was published. You can even go to my web site, www.Internet-Standard.com, and download them from there.

That's what I had always done when I needed to look up something about an Internet standard, specification, or protocol. I found myself downloading many of the same RFCs, over and over. And depending on what project I might be working on, I'd even print out some of those RFCs, for easy reference or for taking notes—which could be time-consuming and generally just a nuisance.

I realized that there must be other networking professionals who had the same problem—and when I started asking them about it, my suspicions were confirmed.

The full copyright statement now included at the end of all RFCs specifies (among other things) that:

> *This document and translations of it may be copied and furnished to others, and derivative works that comment on or otherwise explain it or assist in its implementation may be prepared, copied, published and distributed, in whole or in part, without restriction of any kind, provided that the above copyright notice and this paragraph are included on all such copies and derivative works....*

The goal is to distribute RFCs as widely as possible, and the IETF puts only the most minimal restrictions on those who wish to redistribute them. After all, the more aware people (and vendors) are of the specifications, the more likely they are to build implementations that conform to them—or to do experiments to see if there is a better solution.

So, why buy this book? If you are looking for answers about Internet specifications for IP telephony, you can do what I've already done:

- Search out relevant, and current, RFCs on IP telephony, Voice-over IP (VoIP) and other telecommunications and voice network issues. I usually start with the RFC archives maintained by the RFC Editor's search page at www.rfc-editor.org/rfcsearch.html, but there are several others that I use. Not to mention searches of offline literature and just plain asking around.
- Read through all of them, decide which ones to print out, and then print them out. I've estimated the cost—in paper, toner, and electricity—of printing out 500 pages of RFCs yourself at about \$10–\$15. With a high-capacity, high-speed, highly reliable printer, you could print them all out in a few minutes. With a personal laser printer like the one I use it might take half an hour or even more to print them all out.
- Write up summaries of each RFC, so you can quickly find what you're looking for just by skimming the summaries instead of reading through each one.
- Get the whole thing indexed, so you can find any term you need, across all the RFCs.

Or, you can just go ahead and buy the book. Included here are summaries of the current RFCs published on telecommunications and the Internet. This means you'll have a good introduction to IP telephony from first-hand sources.

The RFCs included in this book were selected so as to provide the most complete reference of the topic in a reasonably sized book. Marginally relevant RFCs have been left out, but everything else you need (and nothing else) has been included. If you need to know more than what is in this book, you'll probably have to get in touch with the people who wrote the RFCs.

You should also realize that this is far from the last word on IP telephony: new RFCs will be coming out, and older ones (such as those reproduced here) are being obsoleted quite frequently. Think of this as Volume 1 of the *Big Book of IP Telephony RFCs*—we may need to publish Volume 2 in just a few years.

Finally, one of the best things about having it all in a book is that you can read the IP telephony RFCs without your computer, without Internet access, even without any electricity (as long as the sun is out). And you can read it on the plane, even during takeoff and landing, and no one will ask you to turn it off.

For more information about RFCs and the Internet Standards process in general, as well as updated information about IP telephony specifications, see my web site:

www.Internet-Standard.com

If you have any comments, complaints, or suggestions about this or any book in the *Big Book of RFC* series, please contact me at:

loshin@Internet-Standard.com

Hearing from readers, whatever they have to say, is always one of the highlights of my day.

Introduction

What exactly is IP telephony? For the purposes of this collection, it refers to any application by which the Internet can be used for transport of telecommunications data (voice or fax) that might otherwise be carried solely across a telephone network. That includes the integration of telephone numbers (telephony addresses) with Internet addresses (whether web or e-mail), as well as the mechanisms necessary to make it possible for a device connected only to an IP network to set up a telephone connection with a device connected only to a circuit-switched telephone network.

IP telephony is almost an oxymoron: IP networking is by its nature connectionless, whereas telephony is connection-oriented; IP is packet-switched and telephony is circuit-switched; IP transmissions provide no service guarantees, whereas telephony depends on quality of service and bandwidth guarantees. Thus, creating usable IP telephony is one of the greatest technical networking challenges facing us as we enter the 21st century.

The benefits of solving this problem are great, however: large organizations stand to save considerable sums if they are able to consolidate their voice and data networks, making it possible to maintain only one infrastructure for both types of data rather than bearing the expense of two infrastructures. Enabling the Internet as a practical medium for telecommunication also promises great savings for consumers, particularly as broadband access to the home becomes increasingly available.

The IETF has been working on defining usable standards for Voice-over IP and IP telephony for several years, but only in the past few years have these specifications matured to the point of becoming Proposed Standards. It may be several more years before all the protocols for successfully doing IP telephony are complete, and perhaps even longer before they are widely and interoperably implemented, but the documents in this book provide an excellent introduction to the fundamental challenges facing IP telephony implementers.

What's In This Book

IP telephony is still a work in progress as of the end of 2000; there are many Internet drafts still working their way through the process of becoming RFCs, and, in many cases, getting on the Standards track.

This book, like others in this series covering subject areas that are still in development, should be considered Volume 1 of the *Big Book of IP Telephony RFCs* rather than a definitive and complete stand-alone reference.

The RFCs

As of November 2000, the following documents comprise the full selection of IP telephony-related RFCs.

RFC 1889: RTP: A Transport Protocol for Real-Time Applications
Telephony is fundamentally a real-time application: it is supremely sensitive to fluctuations in both network bandwidth and network latency, both of which often seem to be fundamental attributes of the Internet. RTP, the real-time transport protocol (it is not defined as an acronym), is defined in this Proposed Standard RFC to add features such as payload type identification, sequence numbering, timestamping, and delivery monitoring, to be used by applications such as voice and video transmitted over the Internet.

RFC 2303: Minimal PSTN address format in Internet Mail
This Proposed Standard specification describes a *minimal* addressing mechanism to encode PSTN—Publicly-Switched Telephone Network—addresses (also known as telephone numbers) into e-mail addresses. The purpose is to enable e-mail users to access PSTN services via e-mail, as well as to enable PSTN-over-e-mail services that could use the existing e-mail infrastructure to transmit voice.

RFC 2458: Toward the PSTN/Internet Inter-Networking—Pre-PINT Implementations
This Informational RFC is a key foundational document for Internet telephony. It defines the basic services that can be expected from the interface of the Internet with the publicly switched telephone network (PSTN), hence the IETF working group name PINT, for PSTN/Internet Inter-Networking. This RFC also describes the basic approaches used by early implementers (pre-PINT) including AT&T, Lucent, Siemens, and Nortel.

RFC 2543: SIP: Session Initiation Protocol
This Proposed Standard RFC defines the Session Initiation Protocol (SIP). According to the RFC's abstract, SIP "is an application-layer control (signaling) protocol for creating, modifying and terminating sessions with one or more participants." Making and breaking connections like this is fundamental to any type of telephony, and SIP is key for IP telephony as well as for multimedia conferencing and distribution, both for unicast and for multicast.

RFC 2658: RTP Payload Format for PureVoice™ Audio
The Qualcomm PureVoice CODEC is defined as a standard for wireless CDMA terminals (phones and other mobile devices), and this Proposed Standard specification describes how PureVoice audio data can be formatted to be carried via RTP (defined in RFC 1889).

RFC 2705: Media Gateway Control Protocol (MGCP) Version 1.0
A media gateway is defined as a device connecting two dissimilar networks and providing media mapping and transcoding functions (if necessary) between those networks; for example, the Internet (or other IP networks) with the publicly switched telehpone network (PSTN). This Informational RFC defines a protocol to be used to control these media gateways remotely; for example, to set up telephone calls.

RFC 2719: Framework Architecture for Signaling Transport
This Informational RFC "defines an architecture framework and functional requirements for transport of signaling information over IP." Signaling is a key component of IP telephony, and this document defines "encapsulation methods, end-to-end protocol mechanisms, and IP capabilities" that make it possible for signaling to be done transparently over IP networks.

RFC 2804: IETF Policy on Wiretapping
This Informational RFC is jointly authored by the IAB and the IESG to establish the official position of the primary Internet Standards bodies on the issue of considering the need to perform wiretaps on Internet transmissions. In short, the policy is that such requirements would not be considered when creating and maintaining standards. This document explains why wiretapping is out of the scope of the IETF/IESG/IAB charters; it also includes a formal definition of wiretapping. It is instructive not just for IP telephony but for those interested in how the IETF functions as an international standards body.

RFC 2805: Media Gateway Control Protocol Architecture and Requirements
This Informational RFC defines an architecture for the protocol that controls media gateways (MGCP) defined in RFC 2705. It provides an overview to the

functions and features that media gateways must provide as well as defining how the protocol fulfills those requirements.

RFC 2806: URLs for Telephone Calls
This Proposed Standard RFC defines three new schemes for URLs: tel, fax, and modem. A scheme defines a URL format for a network resource to be accessed through web client software, much as HTTP and FTP define schemes for Hypertext Transport Protocol and File Transfer Protocol resources.

RFC 2824: Call Processing Language Framework and Requirements
The abstract to this Informational RFC reads:

> *A large number of the services we wish to make possible for Internet telephony require fairly elaborate combinations of signaling operations, often in network devices, to complete. We want a simple and standardized way to create such services to make them easier to implement and deploy. This document describes an architectural framework for such a mechanism, which we call a call processing language. It also outlines requirements for such a language.*

After defining terminology, the authors continue with scenarios for using a call processing language (CPL) as well as discussion about how such a language would be created and would work to enable telephony signaling.

RFC 2833: RTP Payload for DTMF Digits, Telephony Tones, and Telephony Signals
This Proposed Standard RFC defines two RTP payload formats, one for dual-tone multifrequency (DTMF) digits and other events (such as dial tone, ringing tone, and so on), and the other for multifrequency tones such as the actual sounds transmitted to correspond to a dial tone, phone ringing, and so on.

RFC 2846: GSTN Address Element Extensions in E-mail Services
This Proposed Standard RFC expands on the specification for telephony addressing set out in RFC 2303 and defines a more comprehensive discussion of how to incorporate globally switched telephone network (GSTN) addresses (basically these are telephone numbers as the GSTN is pretty much the same as the publicly switched telephone network or PSTN). Though the RFC focuses on e-mail, the specification can be extended to other types of addresses (such as URLs) that might incorporate phone numbers.

RFC 2848: The PINT Service Protocol: Extensions to SIP and SDP for IP Access to Telephone Call Services
Generic PINT, or PSTN/Internet Interworking, services follow this scenario, from this Proposed Standard RFC:

1. An IP host sends a request to a server on an IP network.
2. The server relays the request into a telephone network.
3. The telephone network performs the requested call service.

For example, vendors can set up a service that allows a customer to request, via the Internet, a callback direct to his or her telephone. This RFC defines the PINT Service Protocol (version 1.0), a protocol that makes it possible to invoke telephone services like this through an IP network. This version provides very basic functions including the ability to place calls, send/receive faxes, and receive Internet content over the telephone.

RFC 2871: A Framework for Telephony Routing over IP
This Informational RFC describes the framework for Telephony Routing over IP (TRIP), the "discovery and exchange of IP telephony gateway routing tables between providers." Essentially, the problem is that an IP telephony calling device—a device connected to an IP network—attempting to complete a telephone call to an endpoint on a circuit-switched telephone network (such as the PSTN) must figure out how to reach that network. The calling device must have some mechanism to identify a route for the call, and TRIP provides a framework and a protocol that makes IP telephony gateway routing possible.

RFC 2976: The SIP INFO Method
This Proposed Standard RFC documents a proposed extension to the Session Initiation Protocol (SIP), itself defined in RFC 2543. The INFO method described in this RFC makes it possible for hosts to share session control information that is generated during the actual session. In particular, the INFO method can be used to exchange information about ISDN control signaling messages during IP telephony exchanges.

Network Working Group
Request for Comments: 1889
Category: Standards Track

Audio-Video Transport Working Group
H. Schulzrinne
GMD Fokus
S. Casner
Precept Software, Inc.
R. Frederick
Xerox Palo Alto Research Center
V. Jacobson
Lawrence Berkeley National Laboratory
January 1996

RFC 1889

RTP: A Transport Protocol for Real-Time Applications

Status of this Memo

This document specifies an Internet standards track protocol for the Internet community, and requests discussion and suggestions for improvements. Please refer to the current edition of the "Internet Official Protocol Standards" (STD 1) for the standardization state and status of this protocol. Distribution of this memo is unlimited.

Abstract

This memorandum describes RTP, the real-time transport protocol. RTP provides end-to-end network transport functions suitable for applications transmitting real-time data, such as audio, video or simulation data, over multicast or unicast network services. RTP does not address resource reservation and does not guarantee quality-of-service for real-time services. The data transport is augmented by a control protocol (RTCP) to allow monitoring of the data delivery in a manner scalable to large multicast networks, and to provide minimal control and identification functionality. RTP and RTCP are designed to be independent of the underlying transport and network layers. The protocol supports the use of RTP-level translators and mixers.

Table of Contents

1. Introduction

This memorandum specifies the real-time transport protocol (RTP), which provides end-to-end delivery services for data with real-time characteristics, such as interactive audio and video. Those services include payload type identification, sequence numbering, timestamping and delivery monitoring. Applications typically run RTP on top of UDP to make use of its multiplexing and checksum services; both protocols contribute parts of the transport protocol functionality. However, RTP may be used with other suitable underlying network or transport protocols (see Section 10). RTP supports data transfer to multiple destinations using multicast distribution if provided by the underlying network.

Note that RTP itself does not provide any mechanism to ensure timely delivery or provide other quality-of-service guarantees, but relies on lower-layer services to do so. It does not guarantee delivery or prevent out-of-order delivery, nor does it assume that the underlying network is reliable and delivers packets in sequence. The sequence numbers included in RTP allow the receiver to reconstruct the sender's packet sequence, but sequence numbers might also be used to determine the proper location of a packet, for example in video decoding, without necessarily decoding packets in sequence.

While RTP is primarily designed to satisfy the needs of multi-participant multimedia conferences, it is not limited to that particular application. Storage of continuous data, interactive distributed simulation, active badge, and control and measurement applications may also find RTP applicable.

This document defines RTP, consisting of two closely-linked parts:

- o the real-time transport protocol (RTP), to carry data that has real-time properties.

- o the RTP control protocol (RTCP), to monitor the quality of service and to convey information about the participants in an on-going session. The latter aspect of RTCP may be sufficient for "loosely controlled" sessions, i.e., where there is no explicit membership control and set-up, but it is not necessarily intended to support all of an application's control communication requirements. This functionality may be fully or partially subsumed by a separate session control protocol, which is beyond the scope of this document.

RTP represents a new style of protocol following the principles of application level framing and integrated layer processing proposed by Clark and Tennenhouse [1]. That is, RTP is intended to be malleable to provide the information required by a particular application and will often be integrated into the application processing rather than being implemented as a separate layer. RTP is a protocol framework that is deliberately not complete. This document specifies those functions expected to be common across all the applications for which RTP would be appropriate. Unlike conventional protocols in which additional functions might be accommodated by making the protocol more general or by adding an option mechanism that would require parsing, RTP is intended to be tailored through modifications and/or additions to the headers as needed. Examples are given in Sections 5.3 and 6.3.3.

Therefore, in addition to this document, a complete specification of RTP for a particular application will require one or more companion documents (see Section 12):

- o a profile specification document, which defines a set of payload type codes and their mapping to payload formats (e.g., media encodings). A profile may also define extensions or modifications to RTP that are specific to a particular class of applications. Typically an application will operate under only one profile. A profile for audio and video data may be found in the companion RFC TBD.

- o payload format specification documents, which define how a particular payload, such as an audio or video encoding, is to be carried in RTP.

A discussion of real-time services and algorithms for their implementation as well as background discussion on some of the RTP design decisions can be found in [2].

Several RTP applications, both experimental and commercial, have already been implemented from draft specifications. These applications include audio and video tools along with diagnostic tools such as traffic monitors. Users of these tools number in the thousands. However, the current Internet cannot yet support the full potential demand for real-time services. High-bandwidth services using RTP, such as video, can potentially seriously degrade the quality of service of other network services. Thus, implementors should take appropriate precautions to limit accidental bandwidth usage. Application documentation should clearly outline the limitations and possible operational impact of high-bandwidth real-time services on the Internet and other network services.

2. RTP Use Scenarios

The following sections describe some aspects of the use of RTP. The examples were chosen to illustrate the basic operation of applications using RTP, not to limit what RTP may be used for. In these examples, RTP is carried on top of IP and UDP, and follows the conventions established by the profile for audio and video specified in the companion Internet-Draft draft-ietf-avt-profile

2.1 Simple Multicast Audio Conference

A working group of the IETF meets to discuss the latest protocol draft, using the IP multicast services of the Internet for voice communications. Through some allocation mechanism the working group chair obtains a multicast group address and pair of ports. One port is used for audio data, and the other is used for control (RTCP) packets. This address and port information is distributed to the intended participants. If privacy is desired, the data and control packets may be encrypted as specified in Section 9.1, in which case an encryption key must also be generated and distributed. The exact details of these allocation and distribution mechanisms are beyond the scope of RTP.

The audio conferencing application used by each conference participant sends audio data in small chunks of, say, 20 ms duration. Each chunk of audio data is preceded by an RTP header; RTP header and data are in turn contained in a UDP packet. The RTP header indicates what type of audio encoding (such as PCM, ADPCM or LPC) is contained in each packet so that senders can change the encoding during a conference, for example, to accommodate a new participant that is connected through a low-bandwidth link or react to indications of network congestion.

The Internet, like other packet networks, occasionally loses and reorders packets and delays them by variable amounts of time. To cope with these impairments, the RTP header contains timing information and a sequence number that allow the receivers to reconstruct the timing produced by the source, so that in this example, chunks of audio are contiguously played out the speaker every 20 ms. This timing reconstruction is performed separately for each source of RTP packets in the conference. The sequence number can also be used by the receiver to estimate how many packets are being lost.

Since members of the working group join and leave during the conference, it is useful to know who is participating at any moment and how well they are receiving the audio data. For that purpose, each instance of the audio application in the conference periodically multicasts a reception report plus the name of its user on the RTCP (control) port. The reception report indicates how well the current speaker is being received and may be used to control adaptive encodings. In addition to the user name, other identifying information may also be included subject to control bandwidth limits. A site sends the RTCP BYE packet (Section 6.5) when it leaves the conference.

2.2 Audio and Video Conference

If both audio and video media are used in a conference, they are transmitted as separate RTP sessions RTCP packets are transmitted for each medium using two different UDP port pairs and/or multicast addresses. There is no direct coupling at the RTP level between the audio and video sessions, except that a user participating in both sessions should use the same distinguished (canonical) name in the RTCP packets for both so that the sessions can be associated.

One motivation for this separation is to allow some participants in the conference to receive only one medium if they choose. Further explanation is given in Section 5.2. Despite the separation, synchronized playback of a source's audio and video can be achieved using timing information carried in the RTCP packets for both sessions.

2.3 Mixers and Translators

So far, we have assumed that all sites want to receive media data in the same format. However, this may not always be appropriate. Consider the case where participants in one area are connected through a low-speed link to the majority of the conference participants who enjoy high-speed network access. Instead of forcing everyone to use a lower-bandwidth, reduced-quality audio encoding, an RTP-level relay called a mixer may be placed near the low-bandwidth area. This mixer resynchronizes incoming audio packets to reconstruct the constant 20 ms spacing generated by the sender, mixes these reconstructed audio streams into a single stream, translates the audio encoding to a lower-bandwidth one and forwards the lower-bandwidth packet stream across the low-speed link. These packets might be unicast to a single recipient or multicast on a different address to multiple recipients. The RTP header includes a means for mixers to identify the sources that contributed to a mixed packet so that correct talker indication can be provided at the receivers.

Some of the intended participants in the audio conference may be connected with high bandwidth links but might not be directly reachable via IP multicast. For example, they might be behind an application-level firewall that will not let any IP packets pass. For these sites, mixing may not be necessary, in which case another type of RTP-level relay called a translator may be used. Two translators are installed, one on either side of the firewall, with the outside one funneling all multicast packets received through a secure connection to the translator inside the firewall. The translator inside the firewall sends them again as multicast packets to a multicast group restricted to the site's internal network.

Mixers and translators may be designed for a variety of purposes. An example is a video mixer that scales the images of individual people in separate video streams and composites them into one video stream to simulate a group scene. Other examples of translation include the connection of a group of hosts speaking only IP/UDP to a group of hosts that understand only ST-II, or the packet-by-packet encoding translation of video streams from individual sources without resynchronization or mixing. Details of the operation of mixers and translators are given in Section 7.

3. Definitions

RTP payload: The data transported by RTP in a packet, for example audio samples or compressed video data. The payload format and interpretation are beyond the scope of this document.

RTP packet: A data packet consisting of the fixed RTP header, a possibly empty list of contributing sources (see below), and the payload data. Some underlying protocols may require an encapsulation of the RTP packet to be defined. Typically one packet of the underlying protocol contains a single RTP packet, but several RTP packets may be contained if permitted by the encapsulation method (see Section 10).

RTCP packet: A control packet consisting of a fixed header part similar to that of RTP data packets, followed by structured elements that vary depending upon the RTCP packet type. The formats are defined in Section 6. Typically, multiple RTCP packets are sent together as a compound RTCP packet in a single packet of the underlying protocol; this is enabled by the length field in the fixed header of each RTCP packet.

Port: The "abstraction that transport protocols use to distinguish among multiple destinations within a given host computer. TCP/IP protocols identify ports using small positive integers." [3] The transport selectors (TSEL) used by the OSI transport layer are equivalent to ports. RTP depends upon the lower-layer protocol to provide some mechanism such as ports to multiplex the RTP and RTCP packets of a session.

Transport address: The combination of a network address and port that identifies a transport-level endpoint, for example an IP address and a UDP port. Packets are transmitted from a source transport address to a destination transport address.

RTP session: The association among a set of participants communicating with RTP. For each participant, the session is defined by a particular pair of destination transport addresses (one network address plus a port pair for RTP and RTCP). The destination transport address pair may be common for all participants, as in the case of IP multicast, or may be different for each, as in the case of individual unicast network addresses plus a common port pair. In a multimedia session, each medium is carried in a separate RTP session with its own RTCP packets. The multiple RTP sessions are distinguished by different port number pairs and/or different multicast addresses.

Synchronization source (SSRC): The source of a stream of RTP packets, identified by a 32-bit numeric SSRC identifier carried in the RTP header so as not to be dependent upon the network address. All packets from a synchronization source form part of the same timing and sequence number space, so a receiver groups packets by synchronization source for playback. Examples of synchronization sources include the sender of a stream of packets derived from a signal source such as a microphone or a camera, or an RTP mixer (see below). A synchronization source may change its data format, e.g., audio encoding, over time. The SSRC identifier is a randomly chosen value meant to be globally unique within a particular RTP session (see Section 8). A participant need not use the same SSRC identifier for all the RTP sessions in a multimedia session; the binding of the SSRC identifiers is provided through RTCP (see Section 6.4.1). If a participant generates multiple streams in one RTP session, for example from separate video cameras, each must be identified as a different SSRC.

Contributing source (CSRC): A source of a stream of RTP packets that has contributed to the combined stream produced by an RTP mixer (see below). The mixer inserts a list of the SSRC identifiers of the sources that contributed to the generation of a particular packet into the RTP header of that packet. This list is called the CSRC list. An example application is audio conferencing where a mixer indicates all the talkers whose speech was combined to produce the outgoing packet, allowing the receiver to indicate the current talker, even though all the audio packets contain the same SSRC identifier (that of the mixer).

End system: An application that generates the content to be sent in RTP packets and/or consumes the content of received RTP packets. An end system can act as one or more synchronization sources in a particular RTP session, but typically only one.

Mixer: An intermediate system that receives RTP packets from one or more sources, possibly changes the data format, combines the packets in some manner and then forwards a new RTP packet. Since the timing among multiple input sources will not generally be synchronized, the mixer will make timing adjustments among the streams and generate its own timing for the combined stream. Thus, all data packets originating from a mixer will be identified as having the mixer as their synchronization source.

Translator: An intermediate system that forwards RTP packets with their synchronization source identifier intact. Examples of translators include devices that convert encodings without mixing, replicators from multicast to unicast, and application-level filters in firewalls.

Monitor: An application that receives RTCP packets sent by participants in an RTP session, in particular the reception reports, and estimates the current quality of service for distribution monitoring, fault diagnosis and long-term statistics. The monitor function is likely to be built into the application(s) participating in the session, but may also be a separate application that does not otherwise participate and does not send or receive the RTP data packets. These are called third party monitors.

Non-RTP means: Protocols and mechanisms that may be needed in addition to RTP to provide a usable service. In particular, for multimedia conferences, a conference control application may distribute multicast addresses and keys for encryption, negotiate the encryption algorithm to be used, and define dynamic mappings between RTP payload type values and the payload formats they represent for formats that do not have a predefined payload type value. For simple applications, electronic mail or a conference database may also be used. The specification of such protocols and mechanisms is outside the scope of this document.

4. Byte Order, Alignment, and Time Format

All integer fields are carried in network byte order, that is, most significant byte (octet) first. This byte order is commonly known as big-endian. The transmission order is described in detail in [4]. Unless otherwise noted, numeric constants are in decimal (base 10).

All header data is aligned to its natural length, i.e., 16-bit fields are aligned on even offsets, 32-bit fields are aligned at offsets divisible by four, etc. Octets designated as padding have the value zero.

Wallclock time (absolute time) is represented using the timestamp format of the Network Time Protocol (NTP), which is in seconds relative to 0h UTC on 1 January 1900 [5]. The full resolution NTP timestamp is a 64-bit unsigned fixed-point number with the integer part in the first 32 bits and the fractional part in the last 32 bits. In some fields where a more compact representation is appropriate, only the middle 32 bits are used; that is, the low 16 bits of the integer part and the high 16 bits of the fractional part. The high 16 bits of the integer part must be determined independently.

5. RTP Data Transfer Protocol

5.1 RTP Fixed Header Fields

The RTP header has the following format:

```
 0                   1                   2                   3
 0 1 2 3 4 5 6 7 8 9 0 1 2 3 4 5 6 7 8 9 0 1 2 3 4 5 6 7 8 9 0 1
+-+-+-+-+-+-+-+-+-+-+-+-+-+-+-+-+-+-+-+-+-+-+-+-+-+-+-+-+-+-+-+-+
|V=2|P|X|  CC   |M|     PT      |       sequence number         |
+-+-+-+-+-+-+-+-+-+-+-+-+-+-+-+-+-+-+-+-+-+-+-+-+-+-+-+-+-+-+-+-+
|                           timestamp                           |
+-+-+-+-+-+-+-+-+-+-+-+-+-+-+-+-+-+-+-+-+-+-+-+-+-+-+-+-+-+-+-+-+
|           synchronization source (SSRC) identifier            |
+=+=+=+=+=+=+=+=+=+=+=+=+=+=+=+=+=+=+=+=+=+=+=+=+=+=+=+=+=+=+=+=+
|            contributing source (CSRC) identifiers             |
|                             ....                              |
+-+-+-+-+-+-+-+-+-+-+-+-+-+-+-+-+-+-+-+-+-+-+-+-+-+-+-+-+-+-+-+-+
```

The first twelve octets are present in every RTP packet, while the list of CSRC identifiers is present only when inserted by a mixer. The fields have the following meaning:

version (V): 2 bits
    This field identifies the version of RTP. The version defined by this specification is two (2). (The value 1 is used by the first draft version of RTP and the value 0 is used by the protocol initially implemented in the "vat" audio tool.)

padding (P): 1 bit
    If the padding bit is set, the packet contains one or more additional padding octets at the end which are not part of the

payload. The last octet of the padding contains a count of how many padding octets should be ignored. Padding may be needed by some encryption algorithms with fixed block sizes or for carrying several RTP packets in a lower-layer protocol data unit.

extension (X): 1 bit
If the extension bit is set, the fixed header is followed by exactly one header extension, with a format defined in Section 5.3.1.

CSRC count (CC): 4 bits
The CSRC count contains the number of CSRC identifiers that follow the fixed header.

marker (M): 1 bit
The interpretation of the marker is defined by a profile. It is intended to allow significant events such as frame boundaries to be marked in the packet stream. A profile may define additional marker bits or specify that there is no marker bit by changing the number of bits in the payload type field (see Section 5.3).

payload type (PT): 7 bits
This field identifies the format of the RTP payload and determines its interpretation by the application. A profile specifies a default static mapping of payload type codes to payload formats. Additional payload type codes may be defined dynamically through non-RTP means (see Section 3). An initial set of default mappings for audio and video is specified in the companion profile Internet-Draft draft-ietf-avt-profile, and may be extended in future editions of the Assigned Numbers RFC [6]. An RTP sender emits a single RTP payload type at any given time; this field is not intended for multiplexing separate media streams (see Section 5.2).

sequence number: 16 bits
The sequence number increments by one for each RTP data packet sent, and may be used by the receiver to detect packet loss and to restore packet sequence. The initial value of the sequence number is random (unpredictable) to make known-plaintext attacks on encryption more difficult, even if the source itself does not encrypt, because the packets may flow through a translator that does. Techniques for choosing unpredictable numbers are discussed in [7].

timestamp: 32 bits
The timestamp reflects the sampling instant of the first octet in the RTP data packet. The sampling instant must be derived

from a clock that increments monotonically and linearly in time to allow synchronization and jitter calculations (see Section 6.3.1). The resolution of the clock must be sufficient for the desired synchronization accuracy and for measuring packet arrival jitter (one tick per video frame is typically not sufficient). The clock frequency is dependent on the format of data carried as payload and is specified statically in the profile or payload format specification that defines the format, or may be specified dynamically for payload formats defined through non-RTP means. If RTP packets are generated periodically, the nominal sampling instant as determined from the sampling clock is to be used, not a reading of the system clock. As an example, for fixed-rate audio the timestamp clock would likely increment by one for each sampling period. If an audio application reads blocks covering 160 sampling periods from the input device, the timestamp would be increased by 160 for each such block, regardless of whether the block is transmitted in a packet or dropped as silent.

The initial value of the timestamp is random, as for the sequence number. Several consecutive RTP packets may have equal timestamps if they are (logically) generated at once, e.g., belong to the same video frame. Consecutive RTP packets may contain timestamps that are not monotonic if the data is not transmitted in the order it was sampled, as in the case of MPEG interpolated video frames. (The sequence numbers of the packets as transmitted will still be monotonic.)

SSRC: 32 bits

The SSRC field identifies the synchronization source. This identifier is chosen randomly, with the intent that no two synchronization sources within the same RTP session will have the same SSRC identifier. An example algorithm for generating a random identifier is presented in Appendix A.6. Although the probability of multiple sources choosing the same identifier is low, all RTP implementations must be prepared to detect and resolve collisions. Section 8 describes the probability of collision along with a mechanism for resolving collisions and detecting RTP-level forwarding loops based on the uniqueness of the SSRC identifier. If a source changes its source transport address, it must also choose a new SSRC identifier to avoid being interpreted as a looped source.

CSRC list: 0 to 15 items, 32 bits each

The CSRC list identifies the contributing sources for the payload contained in this packet. The number of identifiers is given by the CC field. If there are more than 15 contributing sources, only 15 may be identified. CSRC identifiers are inserted by mixers, using the SSRC identifiers of contributing sources. For example, for audio packets the SSRC identifiers of all sources that were mixed together to create a packet are listed, allowing correct talker indication at the receiver.

5.2 Multiplexing RTP Sessions

For efficient protocol processing, the number of multiplexing points should be minimized, as described in the integrated layer processing design principle [1]. In RTP, multiplexing is provided by the destination transport address (network address and port number) which define an RTP session. For example, in a teleconference composed of audio and video media encoded separately, each medium should be carried in a separate RTP session with its own destination transport address. It is not intended that the audio and video be carried in a single RTP session and demultiplexed based on the payload type or SSRC fields. Interleaving packets with different payload types but using the same SSRC would introduce several problems:

1. If one payload type were switched during a session, there would be no general means to identify which of the old values the new one replaced.

2. An SSRC is defined to identify a single timing and sequence number space. Interleaving multiple payload types would require different timing spaces if the media clock rates differ and would require different sequence number spaces to tell which payload type suffered packet loss.

3. The RTCP sender and receiver reports (see Section 6.3) can only describe one timing and sequence number space per SSRC and do not carry a payload type field.

4. An RTP mixer would not be able to combine interleaved streams of incompatible media into one stream.

5. Carrying multiple media in one RTP session precludes: the use of different network paths or network resource allocations if appropriate; reception of a subset of the media if desired, for example just audio if video would exceed the available bandwidth; and receiver implementations that use separate processes for the different media, whereas using separate RTP sessions permits either single- or multiple-process implementations.

Using a different SSRC for each medium but sending them in the same RTP session would avoid the first three problems but not the last two.

5.3 Profile-Specific Modifications to the RTP Header

The existing RTP data packet header is believed to be complete for the set of functions required in common across all the application classes that RTP might support. However, in keeping with the ALF design principle, the header may be tailored through modifications or additions defined in a profile specification while still allowing profile-independent monitoring and recording tools to function.

- o The marker bit and payload type field carry profile-specific information, but they are allocated in the fixed header since many applications are expected to need them and might otherwise have to add another 32-bit word just to hold them. The octet containing these fields may be redefined by a profile to suit different requirements, for example with a more or fewer marker bits. If there are any marker bits, one should be located in the most significant bit of the octet since profile-independent monitors may be able to observe a correlation between packet loss patterns and the marker bit.

- o Additional information that is required for a particular payload format, such as a video encoding, should be carried in the payload section of the packet. This might be in a header that is always present at the start of the payload section, or might be indicated by a reserved value in the data pattern.

- o If a particular class of applications needs additional functionality independent of payload format, the profile under which those applications operate should define additional fixed fields to follow immediately after the SSRC field of the existing fixed header. Those applications will be able to quickly and directly access the additional fields while profile-independent monitors or recorders can still process the RTP packets by interpreting only the first twelve octets.

If it turns out that additional functionality is needed in common across all profiles, then a new version of RTP should be defined to make a permanent change to the fixed header.

5.3.1 RTP Header Extension

An extension mechanism is provided to allow individual implementations to experiment with new payload-format-independent functions that require additional information to be carried in the RTP data packet header. This mechanism is designed so that the header extension may be ignored by other interoperating implementations that have not been extended.

Note that this header extension is intended only for limited use. Most potential uses of this mechanism would be better done another way, using the methods described in the previous section. For example, a profile-specific extension to the fixed header is less expensive to process because it is not conditional nor in a variable location. Additional information required for a particular payload format should not use this header extension, but should be carried in the payload section of the packet.

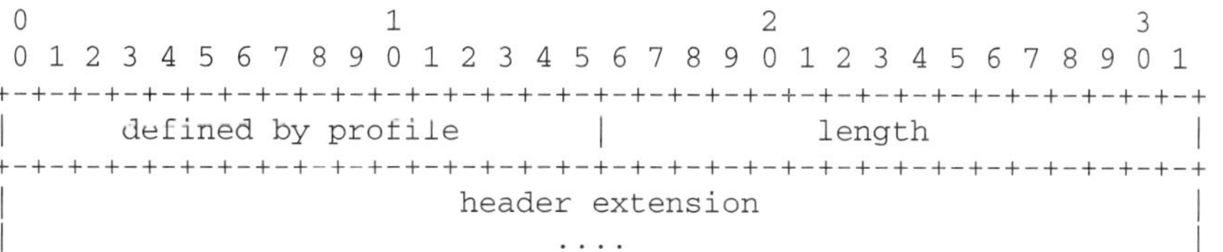

If the X bit in the RTP header is one, a variable-length header extension is appended to the RTP header, following the CSRC list if present. The header extension contains a 16-bit length field that counts the number of 32-bit words in the extension, excluding the four-octet extension header (therefore zero is a valid length). Only a single extension may be appended to the RTP data header. To allow multiple interoperating implementations to each experiment independently with different header extensions, or to allow a particular implementation to experiment with more than one type of header extension, the first 16 bits of the header extension are left open for distinguishing identifiers or parameters. The format of these 16 bits is to be defined by the profile specification under which the implementations are operating. This RTP specification does not define any header extensions itself.

6. RTP Control Protocol -- RTCP

The RTP control protocol (RTCP) is based on the periodic transmission of control packets to all participants in the session, using the same distribution mechanism as the data packets. The underlying protocol must provide multiplexing of the data and control packets, for example using separate port numbers with UDP. RTCP performs four functions:

1. The primary function is to provide feedback on the quality of the data distribution. This is an integral part of the RTP's role as a transport protocol and is related to the flow and congestion control functions of other transport protocols. The feedback may be directly useful for control of adaptive encodings [8,9], but experiments with IP

multicasting have shown that it is also critical to get feedback from the receivers to diagnose faults in the distribution. Sending reception feedback reports to all participants allows one who is observing problems to evaluate whether those problems are local or global. With a distribution mechanism like IP multicast, it is also possible for an entity such as a network service provider who is not otherwise involved in the session to receive the feedback information and act as a third-party monitor to diagnose network problems. This feedback function is performed by the RTCP sender and receiver reports, described below in Section 6.3.

2. RTCP carries a persistent transport-level identifier for an RTP source called the canonical name or CNAME, Section 6.4.1. Since the SSRC identifier may change if a conflict is discovered or a program is restarted, receivers require the CNAME to keep track of each participant. Receivers also require the CNAME to associate multiple data streams from a given participant in a set of related RTP sessions, for example to synchronize audio and video.

3. The first two functions require that all participants send RTCP packets, therefore the rate must be controlled in order for RTP to scale up to a large number of participants. By having each participant send its control packets to all the others, each can independently observe the number of participants. This number is used to calculate the rate at which the packets are sent, as explained in Section 6.2.

4. A fourth, optional function is to convey minimal session control information, for example participant identification to be displayed in the user interface. This is most likely to be useful in "loosely controlled" sessions where participants enter and leave without membership control or parameter negotiation. RTCP serves as a convenient channel to reach all the participants, but it is not necessarily expected to support all the control communication requirements of an application. A higher-level session control protocol, which is beyond the scope of this document, may be needed.

Functions 1-3 are mandatory when RTP is used in the IP multicast environment, and are recommended for all environments. RTP application designers are advised to avoid mechanisms that can only work in unicast mode and will not scale to larger numbers.

6.1 RTCP Packet Format

This specification defines several RTCP packet types to carry a variety of control information:

SR: Sender report, for transmission and reception statistics from participants that are active senders

RR: Receiver report, for reception statistics from participants that are not active senders

SDES: Source description items, including CNAME

BYE: Indicates end of participation

APP: Application specific functions

Each RTCP packet begins with a fixed part similar to that of RTP data packets, followed by structured elements that may be of variable length according to the packet type but always end on a 32-bit boundary. The alignment requirement and a length field in the fixed part are included to make RTCP packets "stackable". Multiple RTCP packets may be concatenated without any intervening separators to form a compound RTCP packet that is sent in a single packet of the lower layer protocol, for example UDP. There is no explicit count of individual RTCP packets in the compound packet since the lower layer protocols are expected to provide an overall length to determine the end of the compound packet.

Each individual RTCP packet in the compound packet may be processed independently with no requirements upon the order or combination of packets. However, in order to perform the functions of the protocol, the following constraints are imposed:

- Reception statistics (in SR or RR) should be sent as often as bandwidth constraints will allow to maximize the resolution of the statistics, therefore each periodically transmitted compound RTCP packet should include a report packet.

- New receivers need to receive the CNAME for a source as soon as possible to identify the source and to begin associating media for purposes such as lip-sync, so each compound RTCP packet should also include the SDES CNAME.

- The number of packet types that may appear first in the compound packet should be limited to increase the number of constant bits in the first word and the probability of successfully validating RTCP packets against misaddressed RTP data packets or other unrelated packets.

Thus, all RTCP packets must be sent in a compound packet of at least two individual packets, with the following format recommended:

Encryption prefix: If and only if the compound packet is to be encrypted, it is prefixed by a random 32-bit quantity redrawn for every compound packet transmitted.

SR or RR: The first RTCP packet in the compound packet must always be a report packet to facilitate header validation as described in Appendix A.2. This is true even if no data has been sent nor received, in which case an empty RR is sent, and even if the only other RTCP packet in the compound packet is a BYE.

Additional RRs: If the number of sources for which reception statistics are being reported exceeds 31, the number that will fit into one SR or RR packet, then additional RR packets should follow the initial report packet.

SDES: An SDES packet containing a CNAME item must be included in each compound RTCP packet. Other source description items may optionally be included if required by a particular application, subject to bandwidth constraints (see Section 6.2.2).

BYE or APP: Other RTCP packet types, including those yet to be defined, may follow in any order, except that BYE should be the last packet sent with a given SSRC/CSRC. Packet types may appear more than once.

It is advisable for translators and mixers to combine individual RTCP packets from the multiple sources they are forwarding into one compound packet whenever feasible in order to amortize the packet overhead (see Section 7). An example RTCP compound packet as might be produced by a mixer is shown in Fig. 1. If the overall length of a compound packet would exceed the maximum transmission unit (MTU) of the network path, it may be segmented into multiple shorter compound packets to be transmitted in separate packets of the underlying protocol. Note that each of the compound packets must begin with an SR or RR packet.

An implementation may ignore incoming RTCP packets with types unknown to it. Additional RTCP packet types may be registered with the Internet Assigned Numbers Authority (IANA).

6.2 RTCP Transmission Interval

```
if encrypted: random 32-bit integer
 |
 |[------- packet -------][----------- packet -----------][-packet-]
 |
 |             receiver reports          chunk        chunk
 V                                    item  item     item  item
--------------------------------------------------------------------
|R[SR|# sender #site#site][SDES|# CNAME PHONE |#CNAME LOC][BYE##why]
|R[  |# report #  1 #  2 ][    |#             |#         ][   ##   ]
|R[  |#        #    #    ][    |#             |#         ][   ##   ]
|R[  |#        #    #    ][    |#             |#         ][   ##   ]
--------------------------------------------------------------------
|<------------------  UDP packet (compound packet) --------------->|

#: SSRC/CSRC
```

Figure 1: Example of an RTCP compound packet

RTP is designed to allow an application to scale automatically over session sizes ranging from a few participants to thousands. For example, in an audio conference the data traffic is inherently self-limiting because only one or two people will speak at a time, so with multicast distribution the data rate on any given link remains relatively constant independent of the number of participants. However, the control traffic is not self-limiting. If the reception reports from each participant were sent at a constant rate, the control traffic would grow linearly with the number of participants. Therefore, the rate must be scaled down.

For each session, it is assumed that the data traffic is subject to an aggregate limit called the "session bandwidth" to be divided among the participants. This bandwidth might be reserved and the limit enforced by the network, or it might just be a reasonable share. The session bandwidth may be chosen based or some cost or a priori knowledge of the available network bandwidth for the session. It is somewhat independent of the media encoding, but the encoding choice may be limited by the session bandwidth. The session bandwidth parameter is expected to be supplied by a session management application when it invokes a media application, but media applications may also set a default based on the single-sender data bandwidth for the encoding selected for the session. The application may also enforce bandwidth limits based on multicast scope rules or other criteria.

Bandwidth calculations for control and data traffic include lower-layer transport and network protocols (e.g., UDP and IP) since that is what the resource reservation system would need to know. The application can also be expected to know which of these protocols are in use. Link level headers are not included in the calculation since the packet will be encapsulated with different link level headers as it travels.

The control traffic should be limited to a small and known fraction of the session bandwidth: small so that the primary function of the transport protocol to carry data is not impaired; known so that the control traffic can be included in the bandwidth specification given to a resource reservation protocol, and so that each participant can independently calculate its share. It is suggested that the fraction of the session bandwidth allocated to RTCP be fixed at 5%. While the value of this and other constants in the interval calculation is not critical, all participants in the session must use the same values so the same interval will be calculated. Therefore, these constants should be fixed for a particular profile.

The algorithm described in Appendix A.7 was designed to meet the goals outlined above. It calculates the interval between sending compound RTCP packets to divide the allowed control traffic bandwidth among the participants. This allows an application to provide fast response for small sessions where, for example, identification of all participants is important, yet automatically adapt to large sessions. The algorithm incorporates the following characteristics:

- Senders are collectively allocated at least 1/4 of the control traffic bandwidth so that in sessions with a large number of receivers but a small number of senders, newly joining participants will more quickly receive the CNAME for the sending sites.

- The calculated interval between RTCP packets is required to be greater than a minimum of 5 seconds to avoid having bursts of RTCP packets exceed the allowed bandwidth when the number of participants is small and the traffic isn't smoothed according to the law of large numbers.

- The interval between RTCP packets is varied randomly over the range [0.5,1.5] times the calculated interval to avoid unintended synchronization of all participants [10]. The first RTCP packet sent after joining a session is also delayed by a random variation of half the minimum RTCP interval in case the application is started at multiple sites simultaneously, for example as initiated by a session announcement.

o A dynamic estimate of the average compound RTCP packet size is calculated, including all those received and sent, to automatically adapt to changes in the amount of control information carried.

This algorithm may be used for sessions in which all participants are allowed to send. In that case, the session bandwidth parameter is the product of the individual sender's bandwidth times the number of participants, and the RTCP bandwidth is 5% of that.

6.2.1 Maintaining the number of session members

Calculation of the RTCP packet interval depends upon an estimate of the number of sites participating in the session. New sites are added to the count when they are heard, and an entry for each is created in a table indexed by the SSRC or CSRC identifier (see Section 8.2) to keep track of them. New entries may not be considered valid until multiple packets carrying the new SSRC have been received (see Appendix A.1). Entries may be deleted from the table when an RTCP BYE packet with the corresponding SSRC identifier is received.

A participant may mark another site inactive, or delete it if not yet valid, if no RTP or RTCP packet has been received for a small number of RTCP report intervals (5 is suggested). This provides some robustness against packet loss. All sites must calculate roughly the same value for the RTCP report interval in order for this timeout to work properly.

Once a site has been validated, then if it is later marked inactive the state for that site should still be retained and the site should continue to be counted in the total number of sites sharing RTCP bandwidth for a period long enough to span typical network partitions. This is to avoid excessive traffic, when the partition heals, due to an RTCP report interval that is too small. A timeout of 30 minutes is suggested. Note that this is still larger than 5 times the largest value to which the RTCP report interval is expected to usefully scale, about 2 to 5 minutes.

6.2.2 Allocation of source description bandwidth

This specification defines several source description (SDES) items in addition to the mandatory CNAME item, such as NAME (personal name) and EMAIL (email address). It also provides a means to define new application-specific RTCP packet types. Applications should exercise caution in allocating control bandwidth to this additional information because it will slow down the rate at which reception reports and CNAME are sent, thus impairing the performance of the protocol. It is recommended that no more than 20% of the RTCP bandwidth allocated to a single participant be used to carry the additional information. Furthermore, it is not intended that all SDES items should be included in every application. Those that are included should be assigned a fraction of the bandwidth according to their utility. Rather than estimate these fractions dynamically, it is recommended that the percentages be translated statically into report interval counts based on the typical length of an item.

For example, an application may be designed to send only CNAME, NAME and EMAIL and not any others. NAME might be given much higher priority than EMAIL because the NAME would be displayed continuously in the application's user interface, whereas EMAIL would be displayed only when requested. At every RTCP interval, an RR packet and an SDES packet with the CNAME item would be sent. For a small session operating at the minimum interval, that would be every 5 seconds on the average. Every third interval (15 seconds), one extra item would be included in the SDES packet. Seven out of eight times this would be the NAME item, and every eighth time (2 minutes) it would be the EMAIL item.

When multiple applications operate in concert using cross-application binding through a common CNAME for each participant, for example in a multimedia conference composed of an RTP session for each medium, the additional SDES information might be sent in only one RTP session. The other sessions would carry only the CNAME item.

6.3 Sender and Receiver Reports

RTP receivers provide reception quality feedback using RTCP report packets which may take one of two forms depending upon whether or not the receiver is also a sender. The only difference between the sender report (SR) and receiver report (RR) forms, besides the packet type code, is that the sender report includes a 20-byte sender information section for use by active senders. The SR is issued if a site has sent any data packets during the interval since issuing the last report or the previous one, otherwise the RR is issued.

Both the SR and RR forms include zero or more reception report blocks, one for each of the synchronization sources from which this receiver has received RTP data packets since the last report. Reports are not issued for contributing sources listed in the CSRC list. Each reception report block provides statistics about the data received from the particular source indicated in that block. Since a maximum of 31 reception report blocks will fit in an SR or RR packet, additional RR packets may be stacked after the initial SR or RR packet as needed to contain the reception reports for all sources heard during the interval since the last report.

The next sections define the formats of the two reports, how they may be extended in a profile-specific manner if an application requires additional feedback information, and how the reports may be used. Details of reception reporting by translators and mixers is given in Section 7.

6.3.1 SR: Sender report RTCP packet

```
 0                   1                   2                   3
 0 1 2 3 4 5 6 7 8 9 0 1 2 3 4 5 6 7 8 9 0 1 2 3 4 5 6 7 8 9 0 1
+-+-+-+-+-+-+-+-+-+-+-+-+-+-+-+-+-+-+-+-+-+-+-+-+-+-+-+-+-+-+-+-+
|V=2|P|    RC   |   PT=SR=200   |             length            | header
+-+-+-+-+-+-+-+-+-+-+-+-+-+-+-+-+-+-+-+-+-+-+-+-+-+-+-+-+-+-+-+-+
|                         SSRC of sender                        |
+=+=+=+=+=+=+=+=+=+=+=+=+=+=+=+=+=+=+=+=+=+=+=+=+=+=+=+=+=+=+=+=+
|              NTP timestamp, most significant word             | sender
+-+-+-+-+-+-+-+-+-+-+-+-+-+-+-+-+-+-+-+-+-+-+-+-+-+-+-+-+-+-+-+-+ info
|             NTP timestamp, least significant word             |
+-+-+-+-+-+-+-+-+-+-+-+-+-+-+-+-+-+-+-+-+-+-+-+-+-+-+-+-+-+-+-+-+
|                         RTP timestamp                         |
+-+-+-+-+-+-+-+-+-+-+-+-+-+-+-+-+-+-+-+-+-+-+-+-+-+-+-+-+-+-+-+-+
|                     sender's packet count                     |
+-+-+-+-+-+-+-+-+-+-+-+-+-+-+-+-+-+-+-+-+-+-+-+-+-+-+-+-+-+-+-+-+
|                      sender's octet count                     |
+=+=+=+=+=+=+=+=+=+=+=+=+=+=+=+=+=+=+=+=+=+=+=+=+=+=+=+=+=+=+=+=+
|                 SSRC_1 (SSRC of first source)                 | report
+-+-+-+-+-+-+-+-+-+-+-+-+-+-+-+-+-+-+-+-+-+-+-+-+-+-+-+-+-+-+-+-+ block
| fraction lost |       cumulative number of packets lost       |   1
-+-+-+-+-+-+-+-+-+-+-+-+-+-+-+-+-+-+-+-+-+-+-+-+-+-+-+-+-+-+-+-+
|           extended highest sequence number received           |
+-+-+-+-+-+-+-+-+-+-+-+-+-+-+-+-+-+-+-+-+-+-+-+-+-+-+-+-+-+-+-+-+
|                      interarrival jitter                      |
+-+-+-+-+-+-+-+-+-+-+-+-+-+-+-+-+-+-+-+-+-+-+-+-+-+-+-+-+-+-+-+-+
|                         last SR (LSR)                         |
+-+-+-+-+-+-+-+-+-+-+-+-+-+-+-+-+-+-+-+-+-+-+-+-+-+-+-+-+-+-+-+-+
|                   delay since last SR (DLSR)                  |
+=+=+=+=+=+=+=+=+=+=+=+=+=+=+=+=+=+=+=+=+=+=+=+=+=+=+=+=+=+=+=+=+
|                 SSRC_2 (SSRC of second source)                | report
+-+-+-+-+-+-+-+-+-+-+-+-+-+-+-+-+-+-+-+-+-+-+-+-+-+-+-+-+-+-+-+-+ block
:                               ...                             :   2
+=+=+=+=+=+=+=+=+=+=+=+=+=+=+=+=+=+=+=+=+=+=+=+=+=+=+=+=+=+=+=+=+
|                  profile-specific extensions                  |
+-+-+-+-+-+-+-+-+-+-+-+-+-+-+-+-+-+-+-+-+-+-+-+-+-+-+-+-+-+-+-+-+
```

The sender report packet consists of three sections, possibly followed by a fourth profile-specific extension section if defined. The first section, the header, is 8 octets long. The fields have the following meaning:

version (V): 2 bits
Identifies the version of RTP, which is the same in RTCP packets as in RTP data packets. The version defined by this specification is two (2).

padding (P): 1 bit
If the padding bit is set, this RTCP packet contains some additional padding octets at the end which are not part of the control information. The last octet of the padding is a count of how many padding octets should be ignored. Padding may be needed by some encryption algorithms with fixed block sizes. In a compound RTCP packet, padding should only be required on the last individual packet because the compound packet is encrypted as a whole.

reception report count (RC): 5 bits
The number of reception report blocks contained in this packet. A value of zero is valid.

packet type (PT): 8 bits
Contains the constant 200 to identify this as an RTCP SR packet.

length: 16 bits
The length of this RTCP packet in 32-bit words minus one, including the header and any padding. (The offset of one makes zero a valid length and avoids a possible infinite loop in scanning a compound RTCP packet, while counting 32-bit words avoids a validity check for a multiple of 4.)

SSRC: 32 bits
The synchronization source identifier for the originator of this SR packet.

The second section, the sender information, is 20 octets long and is present in every sender report packet. It summarizes the data transmissions from this sender. The fields have the following meaning:

NTP timestamp: 64 bits
Indicates the wallclock time when this report was sent so that it may be used in combination with timestamps returned in reception reports from other receivers to measure round-trip propagation to those receivers. Receivers should expect that the measurement accuracy of the timestamp may be limited to far less than the resolution of the NTP timestamp. The measurement uncertainty of the timestamp is not indicated as it may not be known. A sender that can keep track of elapsed time but has no notion of wallclock time may use the elapsed time since joining

the session instead. This is assumed to be less than 68 years, so the high bit will be zero. It is permissible to use the sampling clock to estimate elapsed wallclock time. A sender that has no notion of wallclock or elapsed time may set the NTP timestamp to zero.

RTP timestamp: 32 bits
Corresponds to the same time as the NTP timestamp (above), but in the same units and with the same random offset as the RTP timestamps in data packets. This correspondence may be used for intra- and inter-media synchronization for sources whose NTP timestamps are synchronized, and may be used by media-independent receivers to estimate the nominal RTP clock frequency. Note that in most cases this timestamp will not be equal to the RTP timestamp in any adjacent data packet. Rather, it is calculated from the corresponding NTP timestamp using the relationship between the RTP timestamp counter and real time as maintained by periodically checking the wallclock time at a sampling instant.

sender's packet count: 32 bits
The total number of RTP data packets transmitted by the sender since starting transmission up until the time this SR packet was generated. The count is reset if the sender changes its SSRC identifier.

sender's octet count: 32 bits
The total number of payload octets (i.e., not including header or padding) transmitted in RTP data packets by the sender since starting transmission up until the time this SR packet was generated. The count is reset if the sender changes its SSRC identifier. This field can be used to estimate the average payload data rate.

The third section contains zero or more reception report blocks depending on the number of other sources heard by this sender since the last report. Each reception report block conveys statistics on the reception of RTP packets from a single synchronization source. Receivers do not carry over statistics when a source changes its SSRC identifier due to a collision. These statistics are:

SSRC_n (source identifier): 32 bits
The SSRC identifier of the source to which the information in this reception report block pertains.

fraction lost: 8 bits
The fraction of RTP data packets from source SSRC_n lost since the previous SR or RR packet was sent, expressed as a fixed

point number with the binary point at the left edge of the field. (That is equivalent to taking the integer part after multiplying the loss fraction by 256.) This fraction is defined to be the number of packets lost divided by the number of packets expected, as defined in the next paragraph. An implementation is shown in Appendix A.3. If the loss is negative due to duplicates, the fraction lost is set to zero. Note that a receiver cannot tell whether any packets were lost after the last one received, and that there will be no reception report block issued for a source if all packets from that source sent during the last reporting interval have been lost.

cumulative number of packets lost: 24 bits
The total number of RTP data packets from source SSRC_n that have been lost since the beginning of reception. This number is defined to be the number of packets expected less the number of packets actually received, where the number of packets received includes any which are late or duplicates. Thus packets that arrive late are not counted as lost, and the loss may be negative if there are duplicates. The number of packets expected is defined to be the extended last sequence number received, as defined next, less the initial sequence number received. This may be calculated as shown in Appendix A.3.

extended highest sequence number received: 32 bits
The low 16 bits contain the highest sequence number received in an RTP data packet from source SSRC_n, and the most significant 16 bits extend that sequence number with the corresponding count of sequence number cycles, which may be maintained according to the algorithm in Appendix A.1. Note that different receivers within the same session will generate different extensions to the sequence number if their start times differ significantly.

interarrival jitter: 32 bits
An estimate of the statistical variance of the RTP data packet interarrival time, measured in timestamp units and expressed as an unsigned integer. The interarrival jitter J is defined to be the mean deviation (smoothed absolute value) of the difference D in packet spacing at the receiver compared to the sender for a pair of packets. As shown in the equation below, this is equivalent to the difference in the "relative transit time" for the two packets; the relative transit time is the difference between a packet's RTP timestamp and the receiver's clock at the time of arrival, measured in the same units.

If Si is the RTP timestamp from packet i, and Ri is the time of arrival in RTP timestamp units for packet i, then for two packets i and j, D may be expressed as

$$D(i,j)=(Rj-Ri)-(Sj-Si)=(Rj-Sj)-(Ri-Si)$$

The interarrival jitter is calculated continuously as each data packet i is received from source SSRC_n, using this difference D for that packet and the previous packet i-1 in order of arrival (not necessarily in sequence), according to the formula

$$J=J+(|D(i-1,i)|-J)/16$$

Whenever a reception report is issued, the current value of J is sampled.

The jitter calculation is prescribed here to allow profile-independent monitors to make valid interpretations of reports coming from different implementations. This algorithm is the optimal first-order estimator and the gain parameter 1/16 gives a good noise reduction ratio while maintaining a reasonable rate of convergence [11]. A sample implementation is shown in Appendix A.8.

last SR timestamp (LSR): 32 bits
The middle 32 bits out of 64 in the NTP timestamp (as explained in Section 4) received as part of the most recent RTCP sender report (SR) packet from source SSRC_n. If no SR has been received yet, the field is set to zero.

delay since last SR (DLSR): 32 bits
The delay, expressed in units of 1/65536 seconds, between receiving the last SR packet from source SSRC_n and sending this reception report block. If no SR packet has been received yet from SSRC_n, the DLSR field is set to zero.

Let SSRC_r denote the receiver issuing this receiver report. Source SSRC_n can compute the round propagation delay to SSRC_r by recording the time A when this reception report block is received. It calculates the total round-trip time A-LSR using the last SR timestamp (LSR) field, and then subtracting this field to leave the round-trip propagation delay as (A- LSR - DLSR). This is illustrated in Fig. 2.

This may be used as an approximate measure of distance to cluster receivers, although some links have very asymmetric delays.

6.3.2 RR: Receiver report RTCP packet

```
   [10 Nov 1995 11:33:25.125]           [10 Nov 1995 11:33:36.5]
   n                 SR(n)              A=b710:8000 (46864.500 s)
   ---------------------------------------------------------------->
                      v                 ^
   ntp_sec =0xb44db705 v               ^ dlsr=0x0005.4000 (    5.250s)
   ntp_frac=0x20000000  v             ^  lsr =0xb705:2000 (46853.125s)
     (3024992016.125 s)  v           ^
   r                      v         ^ RR(n)
   ---------------------------------------------------------------->
                          |<-DLSR->|
                           (5.250 s)

   A     0xb710:8000 (46864.500 s)
   DLSR -0x0005:4000 (    5.250 s)
   LSR  -0xb705:2000 (46853.125 s)
   -------------------------------
   delay 0x   6:2000 (    6.125 s)
```

Figure 2: Example for round-trip time computation

```
 0                   1                   2                   3
 0 1 2 3 4 5 6 7 8 9 0 1 2 3 4 5 6 7 8 9 0 1 2 3 4 5 6 7 8 9 0 1
+-+-+-+-+-+-+-+-+-+-+-+-+-+-+-+-+-+-+-+-+-+-+-+-+-+-+-+-+-+-+-+-+
|V=2|P|    RC   |   PT=RR=201   |             length            | header
+-+-+-+-+-+-+-+-+-+-+-+-+-+-+-+-+-+-+-+-+-+-+-+-+-+-+-+-+-+-+-+-+
|                     SSRC of packet sender                     |
+=+=+=+=+=+=+=+=+=+=+=+=+=+=+=+=+=+=+=+=+=+=+=+=+=+=+=+=+=+=+=+=+
|                 SSRC_1 (SSRC of first source)                 | report
+-+-+-+-+-+-+-+-+-+-+-+-+-+-+-+-+-+-+-+-+-+-+-+-+-+-+-+-+-+-+-+-+ block
| fraction lost |       cumulative number of packets lost       |   1
+-+-+-+-+-+-+-+-+-+-+-+-+-+-+-+-+-+-+-+-+-+-+-+-+-+-+-+-+-+-+-+-+
|           extended highest sequence number received           |
+-+-+-+-+-+-+-+-+-+-+-+-+-+-+-+-+-+-+-+-+-+-+-+-+-+-+-+-+-+-+-+-+
|                      interarrival jitter                      |
+-+-+-+-+-+-+-+-+-+-+-+-+-+-+-+-+-+-+-+-+-+-+-+-+-+-+-+-+-+-+-+-+
|                         last SR (LSR)                         |
+-+-+-+-+-+-+-+-+-+-+-+-+-+-+-+-+-+-+-+-+-+-+-+-+-+-+-+-+-+-+-+-+
|                   delay since last SR (DLSR)                  |
+=+=+=+=+=+=+=+=+=+=+=+=+=+=+=+=+=+=+=+=+=+=+=+=+=+=+=+=+=+=+=+=+
|                 SSRC_2 (SSRC of second source)                | report
+-+-+-+-+-+-+-+-+-+-+-+-+-+-+-+-+-+-+-+-+-+-+-+-+-+-+-+-+-+-+-+-+ block
:                               ...                             :   2
+=+=+=+=+=+=+=+=+=+=+=+=+=+=+=+=+=+=+=+=+=+=+=+=+=+=+=+=+=+=+=+=+
|                  profile-specific extensions                  |
+-+-+-+-+-+-+-+-+-+-+-+-+-+-+-+-+-+-+-+-+-+-+-+-+-+-+-+-+-+-+-+-+
```

The format of the receiver report (RR) packet is the same as that of the SR packet except that the packet type field contains the constant 201 and the five words of sender information are omitted (these are the NTP and RTP timestamps and sender's packet and octet counts). The remaining fields have the same meaning as for the SR packet.

An empty RR packet (RC = 0) is put at the head of a compound RTCP packet when there is no data transmission or reception to report.

6.3.3 Extending the sender and receiver reports

A profile should define profile- or application-specific extensions to the sender report and receiver if there is additional information that should be reported regularly about the sender or receivers. This method should be used in preference to defining another RTCP packet type because it requires less overhead:

- o fewer octets in the packet (no RTCP header or SSRC field);
- o simpler and faster parsing because applications running under that profile would be programmed to always expect the extension fields in the directly accessible location after the reception reports.

If additional sender information is required, it should be included first in the extension for sender reports, but would not be present in receiver reports. If information about receivers is to be included, that data may be structured as an array of blocks parallel to the existing array of reception report blocks; that is, the number of blocks would be indicated by the RC field.

6.3.4 Analyzing sender and receiver reports

It is expected that reception quality feedback will be useful not only for the sender but also for other receivers and third-party monitors. The sender may modify its transmissions based on the feedback; receivers can determine whether problems are local, regional or global; network managers may use profile-independent monitors that receive only the RTCP packets and not the corresponding RTP data packets to evaluate the performance of their networks for multicast distribution.

Cumulative counts are used in both the sender information and receiver report blocks so that differences may be calculated between any two reports to make measurements over both short and long time periods, and to provide resilience against the loss of a report. The difference between the last two reports received can be used to estimate the recent quality of the distribution. The NTP timestamp is included so that rates may be calculated from these differences over the interval between two reports. Since that timestamp is independent of the clock rate for the data encoding, it is possible to implement encoding- and profile-independent quality monitors.

An example calculation is the packet loss rate over the interval between two reception reports. The difference in the cumulative number of packets lost gives the number lost during that interval. The difference in the extended last sequence numbers received gives the number of packets expected during the interval. The ratio of these two is the packet loss fraction over the interval. This ratio should equal the fraction lost field if the two reports are consecutive, but otherwise not. The loss rate per second can be obtained by dividing the loss fraction by the difference in NTP timestamps, expressed in seconds. The number of packets received is the number of packets expected minus the number lost. The number of packets expected may also be used to judge the statistical validity of any loss estimates. For example, 1 out of 5 packets lost has a lower significance than 200 out of 1000.

From the sender information, a third-party monitor can calculate the average payload data rate and the average packet rate over an interval without receiving the data. Taking the ratio of the two gives the average payload size. If it can be assumed that packet loss is independent of packet size, then the number of packets received by a particular receiver times the average payload size (or the corresponding packet size) gives the apparent throughput available to that receiver.

In addition to the cumulative counts which allow long-term packet loss measurements using differences between reports, the fraction lost field provides a short-term measurement from a single report. This becomes more important as the size of a session scales up enough that reception state information might not be kept for all receivers or the interval between reports becomes long enough that only one report might have been received from a particular receiver.

The interarrival jitter field provides a second short-term measure of network congestion. Packet loss tracks persistent congestion while the jitter measure tracks transient congestion. The jitter measure may indicate congestion before it leads to packet loss. Since the interarrival jitter field is only a snapshot of the jitter at the time of a report, it may be necessary to analyze a number of reports from one receiver over time or from multiple receivers, e.g., within a single network.

6.4 SDES: Source description RTCP packet

```
 0                   1                   2                   3
 0 1 2 3 4 5 6 7 8 9 0 1 2 3 4 5 6 7 8 9 0 1 2 3 4 5 6 7 8 9 0 1
+-+-+-+-+-+-+-+-+-+-+-+-+-+-+-+-+-+-+-+-+-+-+-+-+-+-+-+-+-+-+-+-+
|V=2|P|    SC   |  PT=SDES=202  |             length            | header
+=+=+=+=+=+=+=+=+=+=+=+=+=+=+=+=+=+=+=+=+=+=+=+=+=+=+=+=+=+=+=+=+
|                          SSRC/CSRC_1                          | chunk
+-+-+-+-+-+-+-+-+-+-+-+-+-+-+-+-+-+-+-+-+-+-+-+-+-+-+-+-+-+-+-+-+   1
|                           SDES items                          |
|                              ...                              |
+=+=+=+=+=+=+=+=+=+=+=+=+=+=+=+=+=+=+=+=+=+=+=+=+=+=+=+=+=+=+=+=+
|                          SSRC/CSRC_2                          | chunk
+-+-+-+-+-+-+-+-+-+-+-+-+-+-+-+-+-+-+-+-+-+-+-+-+-+-+-+-+-+-+-+-+   2
|                           SDES items                          |
|                              ...                              |
+=+=+=+=+=+=+=+=+=+=+=+=+=+=+=+=+=+=+=+=+=+=+=+=+=+=+=+=+=+=+=+=+
```

The SDES packet is a three-level structure composed of a header and zero or more chunks, each of of which is composed of items describing the source identified in that chunk. The items are described individually in subsequent sections.

version (V), padding (P), length:
As described for the SR packet (see Section 6.3.1).

packet type (PT): 8 bits
Contains the constant 202 to identify this as an RTCP SDES packet.

source count (SC): 5 bits
The number of SSRC/CSRC chunks contained in this SDES packet. A value of zero is valid but useless.

Each chunk consists of an SSRC/CSRC identifier followed by a list of zero or more items, which carry information about the SSRC/CSRC. Each chunk starts on a 32-bit boundary. Each item consists of an 8-bit type field, an 8-bit octet count describing the length of the text (thus, not including this two-octet header), and the text itself. Note that the text can be no longer than 255 octets, but this is consistent with the need to limit RTCP bandwidth consumption.

The text is encoded according to the UTF-2 encoding specified in Annex F of ISO standard 10646 [12,13]. This encoding is also known as UTF-8 or UTF-FSS. It is described in "File System Safe UCS Transformation Format (FSS_UTF)", X/Open Preliminary Specification, Document Number P316 and Unicode Technical Report #4. US-ASCII is a subset of this encoding and requires no additional encoding. The presence of multi-octet encodings is indicated by setting the most significant bit of a character to a value of one.

Items are contiguous, i.e., items are not individually padded to a 32-bit boundary. Text is not null terminated because some multi-octet encodings include null octets. The list of items in each chunk is terminated by one or more null octets, the first of which is interpreted as an item type of zero to denote the end of the list, and the remainder as needed to pad until the next 32-bit boundary. A chunk with zero items (four null octets) is valid but useless.

End systems send one SDES packet containing their own source identifier (the same as the SSRC in the fixed RTP header). A mixer sends one SDES packet containing a chunk for each contributing source from which it is receiving SDES information, or multiple complete SDES packets in the format above if there are more than 31 such sources (see Section 7).

The SDES items currently defined are described in the next sections. Only the CNAME item is mandatory. Some items shown here may be useful only for particular profiles, but the item types are all assigned from one common space to promote shared use and to simplify profile-independent applications. Additional items may be defined in a profile by registering the type numbers with IANA.

6.4.1 CNAME: Canonical end-point identifier SDES item

```
 0                   1                   2                   3
 0 1 2 3 4 5 6 7 8 9 0 1 2 3 4 5 6 7 8 9 0 1 2 3 4 5 6 7 8 9 0 1
+-+-+-+-+-+-+-+-+-+-+-+-+-+-+-+-+-+-+-+-+-+-+-+-+-+-+-+-+-+-+-+-+
|    CNAME=1    |     length    | user and domain name         ...
+-+-+-+-+-+-+-+-+-+-+-+-+-+-+-+-+-+-+-+-+-+-+-+-+-+-+-+-+-+-+-+-+
```

The CNAME identifier has the following properties:

- o Because the randomly allocated SSRC identifier may change if a conflict is discovered or if a program is restarted, the CNAME item is required to provide the binding from the SSRC identifier to an identifier for the source that remains constant.

- o Like the SSRC identifier, the CNAME identifier should also be unique among all participants within one RTP session.

- o To provide a binding across multiple media tools used by one participant in a set of related RTP sessions, the CNAME should be fixed for that participant.

o To facilitate third-party monitoring, the CNAME should be suitable for either a program or a person to locate the source.

Therefore, the CNAME should be derived algorithmically and not entered manually, when possible. To meet these requirements, the following format should be used unless a profile specifies an alternate syntax or semantics. The CNAME item should have the format "user@host", or "host" if a user name is not available as on single-user systems. For both formats, "host" is either the fully qualified domain name of the host from which the real-time data originates, formatted according to the rules specified in RFC 1034 [14], RFC 1035 [15] and Section 2.1 of RFC 1123 [16]; or the standard ASCII representation of the host's numeric address on the interface used for the RTP communication. For example, the standard ASCII representation of an IP Version 4 address is "dotted decimal", also known as dotted quad. Other address types are expected to have ASCII representations that are mutually unique. The fully qualified domain name is more convenient for a human observer and may avoid the need to send a NAME item in addition, but it may be difficult or impossible to obtain reliably in some operating environments. Applications that may be run in such environments should use the ASCII representation of the address instead.

Examples are "doe@sleepy.megacorp.com" or "doe@192.0.2.89" for a multi-user system. On a system with no user name, examples would be "sleepy.megacorp.com" or "192.0.2.89".

The user name should be in a form that a program such as "finger" or "talk" could use, i.e., it typically is the login name rather than the personal name. The host name is not necessarily identical to the one in the participant's electronic mail address.

This syntax will not provide unique identifiers for each source if an application permits a user to generate multiple sources from one host. Such an application would have to rely on the SSRC to further identify the source, or the profile for that application would have to specify additional syntax for the CNAME identifier.

If each application creates its CNAME independently, the resulting CNAMEs may not be identical as would be required to provide a binding across multiple media tools belonging to one participant in a set of related RTP sessions. If cross-media binding is required, it may be necessary for the CNAME of each tool to be externally configured with the same value by a coordination tool.

Application writers should be aware that private network address assignments such as the Net-10 assignment proposed in RFC 1597 [17] may create network addresses that are not globally unique. This would lead to non-unique CNAMEs if hosts with private addresses and no direct IP connectivity to the public Internet have their RTP packets forwarded to the public Internet through an RTP-level translator. (See also RFC 1627 [18].) To handle this case, applications may provide a means to configure a unique CNAME, but the burden is on the translator to translate CNAMEs from private addresses to public addresses if necessary to keep private addresses from being exposed.

6.4.2 NAME: User name SDES item

```
 0                   1                   2                   3
 0 1 2 3 4 5 6 7 8 9 0 1 2 3 4 5 6 7 8 9 0 1 2 3 4 5 6 7 8 9 0 1
+-+-+-+-+-+-+-+-+-+-+-+-+-+-+-+-+-+-+-+-+-+-+-+-+-+-+-+-+-+-+-+-+
|     NAME=2    |     length    | common name of source        ...
+-+-+-+-+-+-+-+-+-+-+-+-+-+-+-+-+-+-+-+-+-+-+-+-+-+-+-+-+-+-+-+-+
```

This is the real name used to describe the source, e.g., "John Doe, Bit Recycler, Megacorp". It may be in any form desired by the user. For applications such as conferencing, this form of name may be the most desirable for display in participant lists, and therefore might be sent most frequently of those items other than CNAME. Profiles may establish such priorities. The NAME value is expected to remain constant at least for the duration of a session. It should not be relied upon to be unique among all participants in the session.

6.4.3 EMAIL: Electronic mail address SDES item

```
 0                   1                   2                   3
 0 1 2 3 4 5 6 7 8 9 0 1 2 3 4 5 6 7 8 9 0 1 2 3 4 5 6 7 8 9 0 1
+-+-+-+-+-+-+-+-+-+-+-+-+-+-+-+-+-+-+-+-+-+-+-+-+-+-+-+-+-+-+-+-+
|    EMAIL=3    |     length    | email address of source      ...
+-+-+-+-+-+-+-+-+-+-+-+-+-+-+-+-+-+-+-+-+-+-+-+-+-+-+-+-+-+-+-+-+
```

The email address is formatted according to RFC 822 [19], for example, "John.Doe@megacorp.com". The EMAIL value is expected to remain constant for the duration of a session.

6.4.4 PHONE: Phone number SDES item

```
 0                   1                   2                   3
 0 1 2 3 4 5 6 7 8 9 0 1 2 3 4 5 6 7 8 9 0 1 2 3 4 5 6 7 8 9 0 1
+-+-+-+-+-+-+-+-+-+-+-+-+-+-+-+-+-+-+-+-+-+-+-+-+-+-+-+-+-+-+-+-+
|    PHONE=4    |     length    | phone number of source       ...
+-+-+-+-+-+-+-+-+-+-+-+-+-+-+-+-+-+-+-+-+-+-+-+-+-+-+-+-+-+-+-+-+
```

The phone number should be formatted with the plus sign replacing the international access code. For example, "+1 908 555 1212" for a number in the United States.

6.4.5 LOC: Geographic user location SDES item

```
 0                   1                   2                   3
 0 1 2 3 4 5 6 7 8 9 0 1 2 3 4 5 6 7 8 9 0 1 2 3 4 5 6 7 8 9 0 1
+-+-+-+-+-+-+-+-+-+-+-+-+-+-+-+-+-+-+-+-+-+-+-+-+-+-+-+-+-+-+-+-+
|     LOC=5     |     length    | geographic location of site ...
+-+-+-+-+-+-+-+-+-+-+-+-+-+-+-+-+-+-+-+-+-+-+-+-+-+-+-+-+-+-+-+-+
```

Depending on the application, different degrees of detail are appropriate for this item. For conference applications, a string like "Murray Hill, New Jersey" may be sufficient, while, for an active badge system, strings like "Room 2A244, AT&T BL MH" might be appropriate. The degree of detail is left to the implementation and/or user, but format and content may be prescribed by a profile. The LOC value is expected to remain constant for the duration of a session, except for mobile hosts.

6.4.6 TOOL: Application or tool name SDES item

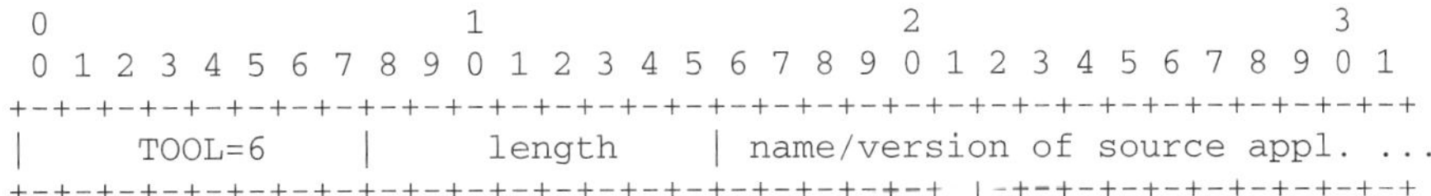

```
 0                   1                   2                   3
 0 1 2 3 4 5 6 7 8 9 0 1 2 3 4 5 6 7 8 9 0 1 2 3 4 5 6 7 8 9 0 1
+-+-+-+-+-+-+-+-+-+-+-+-+-+-+-+-+-+-+-+-+-+-+-+-+-+-+-+-+-+-+-+-+
|     TOOL=6    |     length    | name/version of source appl. ...
+-+-+-+-+-+-+-+-+-+-+-+-+-+-+-+-+-+-+-+-+-+-+-+-+-+-+-+-+-+-+-+-+
```

A string giving the name and possibly version of the application generating the stream, e.g., "videotool 1.2". This information may be useful for debugging purposes and is similar to the Mailer or Mail-System-Version SMTP headers. The TOOL value is expected to remain constant for the duration of the session.

6.4.7 NOTE: Notice/status SDES item

```
 0                   1                   2                   3
 0 1 2 3 4 5 6 7 8 9 0 1 2 3 4 5 6 7 8 9 0 1 2 3 4 5 6 7 8 9 0 1
+-+-+-+-+-+-+-+-+-+-+-+-+-+-+-+-+-+-+-+-+-+-+-+-+-+-+-+-+-+-+-+-+
|     NOTE=7    |     length    | note about the source        ...
+-+-+-+-+-+-+-+-+-+-+-+-+-+-+-+-+-+-+-+-+-+-+-+-+-+-+-+-+-+-+-+-+
```

The following semantics are suggested for this item, but these or other semantics may be explicitly defined by a profile. The NOTE item is intended for transient messages describing the current state of the source, e.g., "on the phone, can't talk". Or, during a seminar, this item might be used to convey the title of the talk. It should be used only to carry exceptional information and should not be included routinely by all participants because this would slow down the rate at which reception reports and CNAME are sent, thus impairing the performance of the protocol. In particular, it should not be included as an item in a user's configuration file nor automatically generated as in a quote-of-the-day.

Since the NOTE item may be important to display while it is active, the rate at which other non-CNAME items such as NAME are transmitted might be reduced so that the NOTE item can take that part of the RTCP bandwidth. When the transient message becomes inactive, the NOTE item should continue to be transmitted a few times at the same repetition rate but with a string of length zero to signal the receivers. However, receivers should also consider the NOTE item inactive if it is not received for a small multiple of the repetition rate, or perhaps 20-30 RTCP intervals.

6.4.8 PRIV: Private extensions SDES item

```
 0                   1                   2                   3
 0 1 2 3 4 5 6 7 8 9 0 1 2 3 4 5 6 7 8 9 0 1 2 3 4 5 6 7 8 9 0 1
+-+-+-+-+-+-+-+-+-+-+-+-+-+-+-+-+-+-+-+-+-+-+-+-+-+-+-+-+-+-+-+-+
|     PRIV=8    |     length    | prefix length | prefix string...
+-+-+-+-+-+-+-+-+-+-+-+-+-+-+-+-+-+-+-+-+-+-+-+-+-+-+-+-+-+-+-+-+
...             |                  value string               ...
+-+-+-+-+-+-+-+-+-+-+-+-+-+-+-+-+-+-+-+-+-+-+-+-+-+-+-+-+-+-+-+-+
```

This item is used to define experimental or application-specific SDES extensions. The item contains a prefix consisting of a length-string pair, followed by the value string filling the remainder of the item and carrying the desired information. The prefix length field is 8 bits long. The prefix string is a name chosen by the person defining the PRIV item to be unique with respect to other PRIV items this application might receive. The application creator might choose to use the application name plus an additional subtype identification if needed. Alternatively, it is recommended that others choose a name based on the entity they represent, then coordinate the use of the name within that entity.

Note that the prefix consumes some space within the item's total length of 255 octets, so the prefix should be kept as short as possible. This facility and the constrained RTCP bandwidth should not be overloaded; it is not intended to satisfy all the control communication requirements of all applications.

SDES PRIV prefixes will not be registered by IANA. If some form of the PRIV item proves to be of general utility, it should instead be assigned a regular SDES item type registered with IANA so that no prefix is required. This simplifies use and increases transmission efficiency.

6.5 BYE: Goodbye RTCP packet

```
 0                   1                   2                   3
 0 1 2 3 4 5 6 7 8 9 0 1 2 3 4 5 6 7 8 9 0 1 2 3 4 5 6 7 8 9 0 1
+-+-+-+-+-+-+-+-+-+-+-+-+-+-+-+-+-+-+-+-+-+-+-+-+-+-+-+-+-+-+-+-+
|V=2|P|    SC   |   PT=BYE=203  |             length            |
+-+-+-+-+-+-+-+-+-+-+-+-+-+-+-+-+-+-+-+-+-+-+-+-+-+-+-+-+-+-+-+-+
|                           SSRC/CSRC                           |
+-+-+-+-+-+-+-+-+-+-+-+-+-+-+-+-+-+-+-+-+-+-+-+-+-+-+-+-+-+-+-+-+
:                              ...                              :
+=+=+=+=+=+=+=+=+=+=+=+=+=+=+=+=+=+=+=+=+=+=+=+=+=+=+=+=+=+=+=+=+
|     length    |               reason for leaving             ... (opt)
+-+-+-+-+-+-+-+-+-+-+-+-+-+-+-+-+-+-+-+-+-+-+-+-+-+-+-+-+-+-+-+-+
```

The BYE packet indicates that one or more sources are no longer active.

version (V), padding (P), length:
As described for the SR packet (see Section 6.3.1).

packet type (PT): 8 bits
Contains the constant 203 to identify this as an RTCP BYE packet.

source count (SC): 5 bits
The number of SSRC/CSRC identifiers included in this BYE packet. A count value of zero is valid, but useless.

If a BYE packet is received by a mixer, the mixer forwards the BYE packet with the SSRC/CSRC identifier(s) unchanged. If a mixer shuts down, it should send a BYE packet listing all contributing sources it handles, as well as its own SSRC identifier. Optionally, the BYE packet may include an 8-bit octet count followed by that many octets of text indicating the reason for leaving, e.g., "camera malfunction" or "RTP loop detected". The string has the same encoding as that described for SDES. If the string fills the packet to the next 32-bit boundary, the string is not null terminated. If not, the BYE packet is padded with null octets.

6.6 APP: Application-defined RTCP packet

```
 0                   1                   2                   3
 0 1 2 3 4 5 6 7 8 9 0 1 2 3 4 5 6 7 8 9 0 1 2 3 4 5 6 7 8 9 0 1
+-+-+-+-+-+-+-+-+-+-+-+-+-+-+-+-+-+-+-+-+-+-+-+-+-+-+-+-+-+-+-+-+
|V=2|P| subtype |   PT=APP=204  |             length            |
+-+-+-+-+-+-+-+-+-+-+-+-+-+-+-+-+-+-+-+-+-+-+-+-+-+-+-+-+-+-+-+-+
|                           SSRC/CSRC                           |
+-+-+-+-+-+-+-+-+-+-+-+-+-+-+-+-+-+-+-+-+-+-+-+-+-+-+-+-+-+-+-+-+
|                          name (ASCII)                         |
+-+-+-+-+-+-+-+-+-+-+-+-+-+-+-+-+-+-+-+-+-+-+-+-+-+-+-+-+-+-+-+-+
|                   application-dependent data                ...
+-+-+-+-+-+-+-+-+-+-+-+-+-+-+-+-+-+-+-+-+-+-+-+-+-+-+-+-+-+-+-+-+
```

The APP packet is intended for experimental use as new applications and new features are developed, without requiring packet type value registration. APP packets with unrecognized names should be ignored. After testing and if wider use is justified, it is recommended that each APP packet be redefined without the subtype and name fields and registered with the Internet Assigned Numbers Authority using an RTCP packet type.

version (V), padding (P), length:
As described for the SR packet (see Section 6.3.1).

subtype: 5 bits
May be used as a subtype to allow a set of APP packets to be defined under one unique name, or for any application-dependent data.

packet type (PT): 8 bits
Contains the constant 204 to identify this as an RTCP APP packet.

name: 4 octets
A name chosen by the person defining the set of APP packets to be unique with respect to other APP packets this application might receive. The application creator might choose to use the application name, and then coordinate the allocation of subtype values to others who want to define new packet types for the application. Alternatively, it is recommended that others choose a name based on the entity they represent, then coordinate the use of the name within that entity. The name is interpreted as a sequence of four ASCII characters, with uppercase and lowercase characters treated as distinct.

application-dependent data: variable length
Application-dependent data may or may not appear in an APP packet. It is interpreted by the application and not RTP itself. It must be a multiple of 32 bits long.

7. RTP Translators and Mixers

In addition to end systems, RTP supports the notion of "translators" and "mixers", which could be considered as "intermediate systems" at the RTP level. Although this support adds some complexity to the protocol, the need for these functions has been clearly established by experiments with multicast audio and video applications in the Internet. Example uses of translators and mixers given in Section 2.3 stem from the presence of firewalls and low bandwidth connections, both of which are likely to remain.

7.1 General Description

An RTP translator/mixer connects two or more transport-level "clouds". Typically, each cloud is defined by a common network and transport protocol (e.g., IP/UDP), multicast address or pair of unicast addresses, and transport level destination port. (Network-level protocol translators, such as IP version 4 to IP version 6, may be present within a cloud invisibly to RTP.) One system may serve as a translator or mixer for a number of RTP sessions, but each is considered a logically separate entity.

In order to avoid creating a loop when a translator or mixer is installed, the following rules must be observed:

- o Each of the clouds connected by translators and mixers participating in one RTP session either must be distinct from all the others in at least one of these parameters (protocol, address, port), or must be isolated at the network level from the others.

- o A derivative of the first rule is that there must not be multiple translators or mixers connected in parallel unless by some arrangement they partition the set of sources to be forwarded.

Similarly, all RTP end systems that can communicate through one or more RTP translators or mixers share the same SSRC space, that is, the SSRC identifiers must be unique among all these end systems. Section 8.2 describes the collision resolution algorithm by which SSRC identifiers are kept unique and loops are detected.

There may be many varieties of translators and mixers designed for different purposes and applications. Some examples are to add or remove encryption, change the encoding of the data or the underlying protocols, or replicate between a multicast address and one or more unicast addresses. The distinction between translators and mixers is that a translator passes through the data streams from different sources separately, whereas a mixer combines them to form one new stream:

Translator: Forwards RTP packets with their SSRC identifier intact; this makes it possible for receivers to identify individual sources even though packets from all the sources pass through the same translator and carry the translator's network source address. Some kinds of translators will pass through the data untouched, but others may change the encoding of the data and thus the RTP data payload type and timestamp. If multiple data packets are re-encoded into one, or vice versa, a translator must assign new sequence numbers to the outgoing packets. Losses in the incoming packet stream may induce corresponding gaps in the outgoing sequence numbers. Receivers cannot detect the presence of a translator unless they know by some other means what payload type or transport address was used by the original source.

Mixer: Receives streams of RTP data packets from one or more sources, possibly changes the data format, combines the streams in some manner and then forwards the combined stream. Since the timing among multiple input sources will not generally be synchronized, the mixer will make timing adjustments among the streams and generate its own timing for the combined stream, so it is the synchronization source. Thus, all data packets forwarded by a mixer will be marked with the mixer's own SSRC identifier. In order to preserve the identity of the original sources contributing to the mixed packet, the mixer should insert their SSRC identifiers into the CSRC identifier list following the fixed RTP header of the packet. A mixer that is also itself a contributing source for some packet should explicitly include its own SSRC identifier in the CSRC list for that packet.

For some applications, it may be acceptable for a mixer not to identify sources in the CSRC list. However, this introduces the danger that loops involving those sources could not be detected.

The advantage of a mixer over a translator for applications like audio is that the output bandwidth is limited to that of one source even when multiple sources are active on the input side. This may be important for low-bandwidth links. The disadvantage is that receivers on the output side don't have any control over which sources are passed through or muted, unless some mechanism is implemented for remote control of the mixer. The regeneration of synchronization information by mixers also means that receivers can't do inter-media synchronization of the original streams. A multi-media mixer could do it.

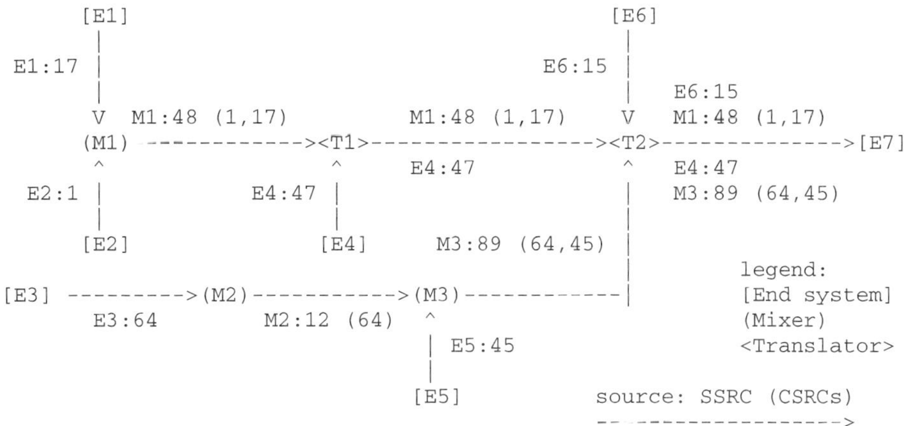

Figure 3: Sample RTP network with end systems, mixers and translators

A collection of mixers and translators is shown in Figure 3 to illustrate their effect on SSRC and CSRC identifiers. In the figure, end systems are shown as rectangles (named E), translators as triangles (named T) and mixers as ovals (named M). The notation "M1: 48(1,17)" designates a packet originating a mixer M1, identified with M1's (random) SSRC value of 48 and two CSRC identifiers, 1 and 17, copied from the SSRC identifiers of packets from E1 and E2.

7.2 RTCP Processing in Translators

In addition to forwarding data packets, perhaps modified, translators and mixers must also process RTCP packets. In many cases, they will take apart the compound RTCP packets received from end systems to aggregate SDES information and to modify the SR or RR packets. Retransmission of this information may be triggered by the packet arrival or by the RTCP interval timer of the translator or mixer itself.

A translator that does not modify the data packets, for example one that just replicates between a multicast address and a unicast address, may simply forward RTCP packets unmodified as well. A translator that transforms the payload in some way must make corresponding transformations in the SR and RR information so that it still reflects the characteristics of the data and the reception quality. These translators must not simply forward RTCP packets. In general, a translator should not aggregate SR and RR packets from different sources into one packet since that would reduce the accuracy of the propagation delay measurements based on the LSR and DLSR fields.

SR sender information: A translator does not generate its own sender information, but forwards the SR packets received from one cloud to the others. The SSRC is left intact but the sender information must be modified if required by the translation. If a translator changes the data encoding, it must change the "sender's byte count" field. If it also combines several data packets into one output packet, it must change the "sender's packet count" field. If it changes the timestamp frequency, it must change the "RTP timestamp" field in the SR packet.

SR/RR reception report blocks: A translator forwards reception reports received from one cloud to the others. Note that these flow in the direction opposite to the data. The SSRC is left intact. If a translator combines several data packets into one output packet, and therefore changes the sequence numbers, it must make the inverse manipulation for the packet loss fields and the "extended last sequence number" field. This may be complex. In the extreme case, there may be no meaningful way to translate the reception reports, so the translator may pass on no reception report at all or a synthetic report based on its own reception. The general rule is to do what makes sense for a particular translation.

A translator does not require an SSRC identifier of its own, but may choose to allocate one for the purpose of sending reports about what it has received. These would be sent to all the connected clouds, each corresponding to the translation of the data stream as sent to that cloud, since reception reports are normally multicast to all participants.

SDES: Translators typically forward without change the SDES information they receive from one cloud to the others, but may, for example, decide to filter non-CNAME SDES information if bandwidth is limited. The CNAMEs must be forwarded to allow SSRC identifier collision detection to work. A translator that generates its own RR packets must send SDES CNAME information about itself to the same clouds that it sends those RR packets.

BYE: Translators forward BYE packets unchanged. Translators with their own SSRC should generate BYE packets with that SSRC identifier if they are about to cease forwarding packets.

APP: Translators forward APP packets unchanged.

7.3 RTCP Processing in Mixers

Since a mixer generates a new data stream of its own, it does not pass through SR or RR packets at all and instead generates new information for both sides.

SR sender information: A mixer does not pass through sender information from the sources it mixes because the characteristics of the source streams are lost in the mix. As a synchronization source, the mixer generates its own SR packets with sender information about the mixed data stream and sends them in the same direction as the mixed stream.

SR/RR reception report blocks: A mixer generates its own reception reports for sources in each cloud and sends them out only to the same cloud. It does not send these reception reports to the other clouds and does not forward reception reports from one cloud to the others because the sources would not be SSRCs there (only CSRCs).

SDES: Mixers typically forward without change the SDES information they receive from one cloud to the others, but may, for example, decide to filter non-CNAME SDES information if bandwidth is limited. The CNAMEs must be forwarded to allow SSRC identifier collision detection to work. (An identifier in a CSRC list generated by a mixer might collide with an SSRC identifier generated by an end system.) A mixer must send SDES CNAME information about itself to the same clouds that it sends SR or RR packets.

Since mixers do not forward SR or RR packets, they will typically be extracting SDES packets from a compound RTCP packet. To minimize overhead, chunks from the SDES packets may be aggregated into a single SDES packet which is then stacked on an SR or RR packet originating from the mixer. The RTCP packet rate may be different on each side of the mixer.

A mixer that does not insert CSRC identifiers may also refrain from forwarding SDES CNAMEs. In this case, the SSRC identifier spaces in the two clouds are independent. As mentioned earlier, this mode of operation creates a danger that loops can't be detected.

BYE: Mixers need to forward BYE packets. They should generate BYE packets with their own SSRC identifiers if they are about to cease forwarding packets.

APP: The treatment of APP packets by mixers is application-specific.

7.4 Cascaded Mixers

An RTP session may involve a collection of mixers and translators as shown in Figure 3. If two mixers are cascaded, such as M2 and M3 in the figure, packets received by a mixer may already have been mixed and may include a CSRC list with multiple identifiers. The second mixer should build the CSRC list for the outgoing packet using the CSRC identifiers from already-mixed input packets and the SSRC identifiers from unmixed input packets. This is shown in the output arc from mixer M3 labeled M3:89(64,45) in the figure. As in the case of mixers that are not cascaded, if the resulting CSRC list has more than 15 identifiers, the remainder cannot be included.

8. SSRC Identifier Allocation and Use

The SSRC identifier carried in the RTP header and in various fields of RTCP packets is a random 32-bit number that is required to be globally unique within an RTP session. It is crucial that the number be chosen with care in order that participants on the same network or starting at the same time are not likely to choose the same number.

It is not sufficient to use the local network address (such as an IPv4 address) for the identifier because the address may not be unique. Since RTP translators and mixers enable interoperation among multiple networks with different address spaces, the allocation patterns for addresses within two spaces might result in a much higher rate of collision than would occur with random allocation.

Multiple sources running on one host would also conflict.

It is also not sufficient to obtain an SSRC identifier simply by calling random() without carefully initializing the state. An example of how to generate a random identifier is presented in Appendix A.6.

8.1 Probability of Collision

Since the identifiers are chosen randomly, it is possible that two or more sources will choose the same number. Collision occurs with the highest probability when all sources are started simultaneously, for example when triggered automatically by some session management event. If N is the number of sources and L the length of the identifier (here, 32 bits), the probability that two sources independently pick the same value can be approximated for large N [20] as 1 - exp(-N**2 / 2**(L+1)). For N=1000, the probability is roughly 10**-4.

The typical collision probability is much lower than the worst-case above. When one new source joins an RTP session in which all the other sources already have unique identifiers, the probability of collision is just the fraction of numbers used out of the space. Again, if N is the number of sources and L the length of the identifier, the probability of collision is N / 2**L. For N=1000, the probability is roughly 2*10**-7.

The probability of collision is further reduced by the opportunity for a new source to receive packets from other participants before sending its first packet (either data or control). If the new source keeps track of the other participants (by SSRC identifier), then before transmitting its first packet the new source can verify that its identifier does not conflict with any that have been received, or else choose again.

8.2 Collision Resolution and Loop Detection

Although the probability of SSRC identifier collision is low, all RTP implementations must be prepared to detect collisions and take the appropriate actions to resolve them. If a source discovers at any time that another source is using the same SSRC identifier as its own, it must send an RTCP BYE packet for the old identifier and choose another random one. If a receiver discovers that two other sources are colliding, it may keep the packets from one and discard the packets from the other when this can be detected by different source transport addresses or CNAMEs. The two sources are expected to resolve the collision so that the situation doesn't last.

Because the random identifiers are kept globally unique for each RTP session, they can also be used to detect loops that may be introduced by mixers or translators. A loop causes duplication of data and control information, either unmodified or possibly mixed, as in the following examples:

- o A translator may incorrectly forward a packet to the same multicast group from which it has received the packet, either directly or through a chain of translators. In that case, the same packet appears several times, originating from different network sources.

- o Two translators incorrectly set up in parallel, i.e., with the same multicast groups on both sides, would both forward packets from one multicast group to the other. Unidirectional translators would produce two copies; bidirectional translators would form a loop.

- o A mixer can close a loop by sending to the same transport destination upon which it receives packets, either directly or through another mixer or translator. In this case a source might show up both as an SSRC on a data packet and a CSRC in a mixed data packet.

A source may discover that its own packets are being looped, or that packets from another source are being looped (a third-party loop).

Both loops and collisions in the random selection of a source identifier result in packets arriving with the same SSRC identifier but a different source transport address, which may be that of the end system originating the packet or an intermediate system. Consequently, if a source changes its source transport address, it must also choose a new SSRC identifier to avoid being interpreted as a looped source. Loops or collisions occurring on the far side of a translator or mixer cannot be detected using the source transport address if all copies of the packets go through the translator or mixer, however collisions may still be detected when chunks from two RTCP SDES packets contain the same SSRC identifier but different CNAMEs.

To detect and resolve these conflicts, an RTP implementation must include an algorithm similar to the one described below. It ignores packets from a new source or loop that collide with an established source. It resolves collisions with the participant's own SSRC identifier by sending an RTCP BYE for the old identifier and choosing a new one. However, when the collision was induced by a loop of the participant's own packets, the algorithm will choose a new identifier only once and thereafter ignore packets from the looping source transport address. This is required to avoid a flood of BYE packets.

This algorithm depends upon the source transport address being the same for both RTP and RTCP packets from a source. The algorithm would require modifications to support applications that don't meet this constraint.

This algorithm requires keeping a table indexed by source identifiers and containing the source transport address from which the identifier was (first) received, along with other state for that source. Each SSRC or CSRC identifier received in a data or control packet is looked up in this table in order to process that data or control information. For control packets, each element with its own SSRC, for example an SDES chunk, requires a separate lookup. (The SSRC in a reception report block is an exception.) If the SSRC or CSRC is not found, a new entry is created. These table entries are removed when an RTCP BYE packet is received with the corresponding SSRC, or after no packets have arrived for a relatively long time (see Section 6.2.1).

In order to track loops of the participant's own data packets, it is also necessary to keep a separate list of source transport addresses (not identifiers) that have been found to be conflicting. Note that this should be a short list, usually empty. Each element in this list stores the source address plus the time when the most recent conflicting packet was received. An element may be removed from the list when no conflicting packet has arrived from that source for a time on the order of 10 RTCP report intervals (see Section 6.2).

For the algorithm as shown, it is assumed that the participant's own source identifier and state are included in the source identifier table. The algorithm could be restructured to first make a separate comparison against the participant's own source identifier.

```
IF the SSRC or CSRC identifier is not found in the source
   identifier table:
THEN create a new entry storing the source transport address
     and the SSRC or CSRC along with other state.
     CONTINUE with normal processing.

(identifier is found in the table)

IF the source transport address from the packet matches
   the one saved in the table entry for this identifier:
THEN CONTINUE with normal processing.

(an identifier collision or a loop is indicated)

IF the source identifier is not the participant's own:
THEN IF the source identifier is from an RTCP SDES chunk
        containing a CNAME item that differs from the CNAME
        in the table entry:
     THEN (optionally) count a third-party collision.
     ELSE (optionally) count a third-party loop.
     ABORT processing of data packet or control element.

(a collision or loop of the participant's own data)

IF the source transport address is found in the list of
  conflicting addresses:
THEN IF the source identifier is not from an RTCP SDES chunk
        containing a CNAME item OR if that CNAME is the
        participant's own:
```

```
        THEN (optionally) count occurrence of own traffic looped.
             mark current time in conflicting address list entry.
             ABORT processing of data packet or control element.
   log occurrence of a collision.
   create a new entry in the conflicting address list and
   mark current time.
   send an RTCP BYE packet with the old SSRC identifier.
   choose a new identifier.
   create a new entry in the source identifier table with the
     old SSRC plus the source transport address from the packet
     being processed.
   CONTINUE with normal processing.
```

In this algorithm, packets from a newly conflicting source address will be ignored and packets from the original source will be kept. (If the original source was through a mixer and later the same source is received directly, the receiver may be well advised to switch unless other sources in the mix would be lost.) If no packets arrive from the original source for an extended period, the table entry will be timed out and the new source will be able to take over. This might occur if the original source detects the collision and moves to a new source identifier, but in the usual case an RTCP BYE packet will be received from the original source to delete the state without having to wait for a timeout.

When a new SSRC identifier is chosen due to a collision, the candidate identifier should first be looked up in the source identifier table to see if it was already in use by some other source. If so, another candidate should be generated and the process repeated.

A loop of data packets to a multicast destination can cause severe network flooding. All mixers and translators are required to implement a loop detection algorithm like the one here so that they can break loops. This should limit the excess traffic to no more than one duplicate copy of the original traffic, which may allow the session to continue so that the cause of the loop can be found and fixed. However, in extreme cases where a mixer or translator does not properly break the loop and high traffic levels result, it may be necessary for end systems to cease transmitting data or control packets entirely. This decision may depend upon the application. An error condition should be indicated as appropriate. Transmission might be attempted again periodically after a long, random time (on the order of minutes).

9. Security

Lower layer protocols may eventually provide all the security services that may be desired for applications of RTP, including authentication, integrity, and confidentiality. These services have recently been specified for IP. Since the need for a confidentiality service is well established in the initial audio and video applications that are expected to use RTP, a confidentiality service is defined in the next section for use with RTP and RTCP until lower layer services are available. The overhead on the protocol for this service is low, so the penalty will be minimal if this service is obsoleted by lower layer services in the future.

Alternatively, other services, other implementations of services and other algorithms may be defined for RTP in the future if warranted. The selection presented here is meant to simplify implementation of interoperable, secure applications and provide guidance to implementors. No claim is made that the methods presented here are appropriate for a particular security need. A profile may specify which services and algorithms should be offered by applications, and may provide guidance as to their appropriate use.

Key distribution and certificates are outside the scope of this document.

9.1 Confidentiality

Confidentiality means that only the intended receiver(s) can decode the received packets; for others, the packet contains no useful information. Confidentiality of the content is achieved by encryption.

When encryption of RTP or RTCP is desired, all the octets that will be encapsulated for transmission in a single lower-layer packet are encrypted as a unit. For RTCP, a 32-bit random number is prepended to the unit before encryption to deter known plaintext attacks. For RTP, no prefix is required because the sequence number and timestamp fields are initialized with random offsets.

For RTCP, it is allowed to split a compound RTCP packet into two lower-layer packets, one to be encrypted and one to be sent in the clear. For example, SDES information might be encrypted while reception reports were sent in the clear to accommodate third-party monitors that are not privy to the encryption key. In this example, depicted in Fig. 4, the SDES information must be appended to an RR packet with no reports (and the encrypted) to satisfy the requirement that all compound RTCP packets begin with an SR or RR packet.

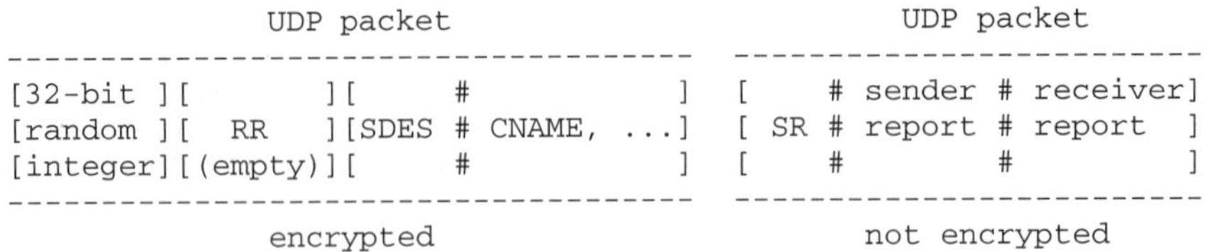

```
            UDP packet                            UDP packet
-------------------------------------  ------------------------
[32-bit ][       ][     #            ] [    # sender # receiver]
[random ][  RR   ][SDES # CNAME, ...] [ SR # report # report  ]
[integer][(empty)][     #            ] [    #        #         ]
-------------------------------------  ------------------------
            encrypted                         not encrypted
```

#: SSRC

Figure 4: Encrypted and non-encrypted RTCP packets

The presence of encryption and the use of the correct key are confirmed by the receiver through header or payload validity checks. Examples of such validity checks for RTP and RTCP headers are given in Appendices A.1 and A.2.

The default encryption algorithm is the Data Encryption Standard (DES) algorithm in cipher block chaining (CBC) mode, as described in Section 1.1 of RFC 1423 [21], except that padding to a multiple of 8 octets is indicated as described for the P bit in Section 5.1. The initialization vector is zero because random values are supplied in the RTP header or by the random prefix for compound RTCP packets. For details on the use of CBC initialization vectors, see [22]. Implementations that support encryption should always support the DES algorithm in CBC mode as the default to maximize interoperability. This method is chosen because it has been demonstrated to be easy and practical to use in experimental audio and video tools in operation on the Internet. Other encryption algorithms may be specified dynamically for a session by non-RTP means.

As an alternative to encryption at the RTP level as described above, profiles may define additional payload types for encrypted encodings. Those encodings must specify how padding and other aspects of the encryption should be handled. This method allows encrypting only the data while leaving the headers in the clear for applications where that is desired. It may be particularly useful for hardware devices that will handle both decryption and decoding.

9.2 Authentication and Message Integrity

Authentication and message integrity are not defined in the current specification of RTP since these services would not be directly feasible without a key management infrastructure. It is expected that authentication and integrity services will be provided by lower layer protocols in the future.

10. RTP over Network and Transport Protocols

This section describes issues specific to carrying RTP packets within particular network and transport protocols. The following rules apply unless superseded by protocol-specific definitions outside this specification.

RTP relies on the underlying protocol(s) to provide demultiplexing of RTP data and RTCP control streams. For UDP and similar protocols, RTP uses an even port number and the corresponding RTCP stream uses the next higher (odd) port number. If an application is supplied with an odd number for use as the RTP port, it should replace this number with the next lower (even) number.

RTP data packets contain no length field or other delineation, therefore RTP relies on the underlying protocol(s) to provide a length indication. The maximum length of RTP packets is limited only by the underlying protocols.

If RTP packets are to be carried in an underlying protocol that provides the abstraction of a continuous octet stream rather than messages (packets), an encapsulation of the RTP packets must be defined to provide a framing mechanism. Framing is also needed if the underlying protocol may contain padding so that the extent of the RTP payload cannot be determined. The framing mechanism is not defined here.

A profile may specify a framing method to be used even when RTP is carried in protocols that do provide framing in order to allow carrying several RTP packets in one lower-layer protocol data unit, such as a UDP packet. Carrying several RTP packets in one network or transport packet reduces header overhead and may simplify synchronization between different streams.

11. Summary of Protocol Constants

This section contains a summary listing of the constants defined in this specification.

The RTP payload type (PT) constants are defined in profiles rather than this document. However, the octet of the RTP header which contains the marker bit(s) and payload type must avoid the reserved values 200 and 201 (decimal) to distinguish RTP packets from the RTCP SR and RR packet types for the header validation procedure described in Appendix A.1. For the standard definition of one marker bit and a 7-bit payload type field as shown in this specification, this restriction means that payload types 72 and 73 are reserved.

11.1 RTCP packet types

abbrev.	name	value
SR	sender report	200
RR	receiver report	201
SDES	source description	202
BYE	goodbye	203
APP	application-defined	204

These type values were chosen in the range 200-204 for improved header validity checking of RTCP packets compared to RTP packets or other unrelated packets. When the RTCP packet type field is compared to the corresponding octet of the RTP header, this range corresponds to the marker bit being 1 (which it usually is not in data packets) and to the high bit of the standard payload type field being 1 (since the static payload types are typically defined in the low half). This range was also chosen to be some distance numerically from 0 and 255 since all-zeros and all-ones are common data patterns.

Since all compound RTCP packets must begin with SR or RR, these codes were chosen as an even/odd pair to allow the RTCP validity check to test the maximum number of bits with mask and value.

Other constants are assigned by IANA. Experimenters are encouraged to register the numbers they need for experiments, and then unregister those which prove to be unneeded.

11.2 SDES types

abbrev.	name	value
END	end of SDES list	0
CNAME	canonical name	1
NAME	user name	2
EMAIL	user's electronic mail address	3
PHONE	user's phone number	4
LOC	geographic user location	5
TOOL	name of application or tool	6
NOTE	notice about the source	7
PRIV	private extensions	8

Other constants are assigned by IANA. Experimenters are encouraged to register the numbers they need for experiments, and then unregister those which prove to be unneeded.

12. RTP Profiles and Payload Format Specifications

A complete specification of RTP for a particular application will require one or more companion documents of two types described here: profiles, and payload format specifications.

RTP may be used for a variety of applications with somewhat differing requirements. The flexibility to adapt to those requirements is provided by allowing multiple choices in the main protocol specification, then selecting the appropriate choices or defining extensions for a particular environment and class of applications in a separate profile document. Typically an application will operate under only one profile so there is no explicit indication of which profile is in use. A profile for audio and video applications may be found in the companion Internet-Draft draft-ietf-avt-profile for

The second type of companion document is a payload format specification, which defines how a particular kind of payload data, such as H.261 encoded video, should be carried in RTP. These documents are typically titled "RTP Payload Format for XYZ Audio/Video Encoding". Payload formats may be useful under multiple profiles and may therefore be defined independently of any particular profile. The profile documents are then responsible for assigning a default mapping of that format to a payload type value if needed.

Within this specification, the following items have been identified for possible definition within a profile, but this list is not meant to be exhaustive:

RTP data header: The octet in the RTP data header that contains the marker bit and payload type field may be redefined by a profile to suit different requirements, for example with more or fewer marker bits (Section 5.3).

Payload types: Assuming that a payload type field is included, the profile will usually define a set of payload formats (e.g., media encodings) and a default static mapping of those formats to payload type values. Some of the payload formats may be defined by reference to separate payload format specifications. For each payload type defined, the profile must specify the RTP timestamp clock rate to be used (Section 5.1).

RTP data header additions: Additional fields may be appended to the fixed RTP data header if some additional functionality is required across the profile's class of applications independent of payload type (Section 5.3).

RTP data header extensions: The contents of the first 16 bits of the RTP data header extension structure must be defined if use of that mechanism is to be allowed under the profile for implementation-specific extensions (Section 5.3.1).

RTCP packet types: New application-class-specific RTCP packet types may be defined and registered with IANA.

RTCP report interval: A profile should specify that the values suggested in Section 6.2 for the constants employed in the calculation of the RTCP report interval will be used. Those are the RTCP fraction of session bandwidth, the minimum report interval, and the bandwidth split between senders and receivers. A profile may specify alternate values if they have been demonstrated to work in a scalable manner.

SR/RR extension: An extension section may be defined for the RTCP SR and RR packets if there is additional information that should be reported regularly about the sender or receivers (Section 6.3.3).

SDES use: The profile may specify the relative priorities for RTCP SDES items to be transmitted or excluded entirely (Section 6.2.2); an alternate syntax or semantics for the CNAME item (Section 6.4.1); the format of the LOC item (Section 6.4.5); the semantics and use of the NOTE item (Section 6.4.7); or new SDES item types to be registered with IANA.

Security: A profile may specify which security services and algorithms should be offered by applications, and may provide guidance as to their appropriate use (Section 9).

String-to-key mapping: A profile may specify how a user-provided password or pass phrase is mapped into an encryption key.

Underlying protocol: Use of a particular underlying network or transport layer protocol to carry RTP packets may be required.

Transport mapping: A mapping of RTP and RTCP to transport-level addresses, e.g., UDP ports, other than the standard mapping defined in Section 10 may be specified.

Encapsulation: An encapsulation of RTP packets may be defined to allow multiple RTP data packets to be carried in one lower-layer packet or to provide framing over underlying protocols that do not already do so (Section 10).

It is not expected that a new profile will be required for every application. Within one application class, it would be better to extend an existing profile rather than make a new one in order to facilitate interoperation among the applications since each will typically run under only one profile. Simple extensions such as the definition of additional payload type values or RTCP packet types may be accomplished by registering them through the Internet Assigned Numbers Authority and publishing their descriptions in an addendum to the profile or in a payload format specification.

A. Algorithms

We provide examples of C code for aspects of RTP sender and receiver algorithms. There may be other implementation methods that are faster in particular operating environments or have other advantages. These implementation notes are for informational purposes only and are meant to clarify the RTP specification.

The following definitions are used for all examples; for clarity and brevity, the structure definitions are only valid for 32-bit big-endian (most significant octet first) architectures. Bit fields are assumed to be packed tightly in big-endian bit order, with no additional padding. Modifications would be required to construct a portable implementation.

```
/*
 * rtp.h  --  RTP header file (RFC XXXX)
 */
#include <sys/types.h>

/*
 * The type definitions below are valid for 32-bit architectures and
 * may have to be adjusted for 16- or 64-bit architectures.
 */
typedef unsigned char  u_int8;
typedef unsigned short u_int16;
typedef unsigned int   u_int32;
typedef          short int16;

/*
 * Current protocol version.
 */
#define RTP_VERSION    2

#define RTP_SEQ_MOD (1<<16)
#define RTP_MAX_SDES 255      /* maximum text length for SDES */

typedef enum {
    RTCP_SR   = 200,
    RTCP_RR   = 201,
    RTCP_SDES = 202,
    RTCP_BYE  = 203,
    RTCP_APP  = 204
} rtcp_type_t;

typedef enum {
    RTCP_SDES_END   = 0,
    RTCP_SDES_CNAME = 1,
```

```
        RTCP_SDES_NAME  = 2,
        RTCP_SDES_EMAIL = 3,
        RTCP_SDES_PHONE = 4,
        RTCP_SDES_LOC   = 5,
        RTCP_SDES_TOOL  = 6,
        RTCP_SDES_NOTE  = 7,
        RTCP_SDES_PRIV  = 8
    } rtcp_sdes_type_t;

    /*
     * RTP data header
     */
    typedef struct {
        unsigned int version:2;   /* protocol version */
        unsigned int p:1;         /* padding flag */
        unsigned int x:1;         /* header extension flag */
        unsigned int cc:4;        /* CSRC count */
        unsigned int m:1;         /* marker bit */
        unsigned int pt:7;        /* payload type */
        u_int16 seq;              /* sequence number */
        u_int32 ts;               /* timestamp */
        u_int32 ssrc;             /* synchronization source */
        u_int32 csrc[1];          /* optional CSRC list */
    } rtp_hdr_t;

    /*
     * RTCP common header word
     */
    typedef struct {
        unsigned int version:2;   /* protocol version */
        unsigned int p:1;         /* padding flag */
        unsigned int count:5;     /* varies by packet type */
        unsigned int pt:8;        /* RTCP packet type */
        u_int16 length;           /* pkt len in words, w/o this word */
    } rtcp_common_t;

    /*
     * Big-endian mask for version, padding bit and packet type pair
     */
    #define RTCP_VALID_MASK (0xc000 | 0x2000 | 0xfe)
    #define RTCP_VALID_VALUE ((RTP_VERSION << 14) | RTCP_SR)

    /*
     * Reception report block
     */
    typedef struct {
        u_int32 ssrc;             /* data source being reported */
        unsigned int fraction:8;  /* fraction lost since last SR/RR */
```

```
        int lost:24;              /* cumul. no. pkts lost (signed!) */
        u_int32 last_seq;         /* extended last seq. no. received */
        u_int32 jitter;           /* interarrival jitter */
        u_int32 lsr;              /* last SR packet from this source */
        u_int32 dlsr;             /* delay since last SR packet */
    } rtcp_rr_t;

    /*
     * SDES item
     */
    typedef struct {
        u_int8 type;              /* type of item (rtcp_sdes_type_t) */
        u_int8 length;            /* length of item (in octets) */
        char data[1];             /* text, not null-terminated */
    } rtcp_sdes_item_t;

    /*
     * One RTCP packet
     */
    typedef struct {
        rtcp_common_t common;     /* common header */
        union {
            /* sender report (SR) */
            struct {
                u_int32 ssrc;     /* sender generating this report */
                u_int32 ntp_sec;  /* NTP timestamp */
                u_int32 ntp_frac;
                u_int32 rtp_ts;   /* RTP timestamp */
                u_int32 psent;    /* packets sent */
                u_int32 osent;    /* octets sent */
                rtcp_rr_t rr[1];  /* variable-length list */
            } sr;

            /* reception report (RR) */
            struct {
                u_int32 ssrc;     /* receiver generating this report */
                rtcp_rr_t rr[1];  /* variable-length list */
            } rr;

            /* source description (SDES) */
            struct rtcp_sdes {
                u_int32 src;      /* first SSRC/CSRC */
                rtcp_sdes_item_t item[1]; /* list of SDES items */
            } sdes;

            /* BYE */
            struct {
                u_int32 src[1];   /* list of sources */
```

```
                /* can't express trailing text for reason */
            } bye;
        } r;
    } rtcp_t;

    typedef struct rtcp_sdes rtcp_sdes_t;

    /*
     * Per-source state information
     */
    typedef struct {
        u_int16 max_seq;        /* highest seq. number seen */
        u_int32 cycles;         /* shifted count of seq. number cycles */
        u_int32 base_seq;       /* base seq number */
        u_int32 bad_seq;        /* last 'bad' seq number + 1 */
        u_int32 probation;      /* sequ. packets till source is valid */
        u_int32 received;       /* packets received */
        u_int32 expected_prior; /* packet expected at last interval */
        u_int32 received_prior; /* packet received at last interval */
        u_int32 transit;        /* relative trans time for prev pkt */
        u_int32 jitter;         /* estimated jitter */
        /* ... */
    } source;
```

A.1 RTP Data Header Validity Checks

An RTP receiver should check the validity of the RTP header on incoming packets since they might be encrypted or might be from a different application that happens to be misaddressed. Similarly, if encryption is enabled, the header validity check is needed to verify that incoming packets have been correctly decrypted, although a failure of the header validity check (e.g., unknown payload type) may not necessarily indicate decryption failure.

Only weak validity checks are possible on an RTP data packet from a source that has not been heard before:

o RTP version field must equal 2.

o The payload type must be known, in particular it must not be equal to SR or RR.

o If the P bit is set, then the last octet of the packet must contain a valid octet count, in particular, less than the total packet length minus the header size.

o The X bit must be zero if the profile does not specify that the header extension mechanism may be used. Otherwise, the extension length field must be less than the total packet size minus the fixed header length and padding.

o The length of the packet must be consistent with CC and payload type (if payloads have a known length).

The last three checks are somewhat complex and not always possible, leaving only the first two which total just a few bits. If the SSRC identifier in the packet is one that has been received before, then the packet is probably valid and checking if the sequence number is in the expected range provides further validation. If the SSRC identifier has not been seen before, then data packets carrying that identifier may be considered invalid until a small number of them arrive with consecutive sequence numbers.

The routine update_seq shown below ensures that a source is declared valid only after MIN_SEQUENTIAL packets have been received in sequence. It also validates the sequence number seq of a newly received packet and updates the sequence state for the packet's source in the structure to which s points.

When a new source is heard for the first time, that is, its SSRC identifier is not in the table (see Section 8.2), and the per-source state is allocated for it, s->probation should be set to the number of sequential packets required before declaring a source valid (parameter MIN_SEQUENTIAL) and s->max_seq initialized to seq-1 s->probation marks the source as not yet valid so the state may be discarded after a short timeout rather than a long one, as discussed in Section 6.2.1.

After a source is considered valid, the sequence number is considered valid if it is no more than MAX_DROPOUT ahead of s->max_seq nor more than MAX_MISORDER behind. If the new sequence number is ahead of max_seq modulo the RTP sequence number range (16 bits), but is smaller than max_seq , it has wrapped around and the (shifted) count of sequence number cycles is incremented. A value of one is returned to indicate a valid sequence number.

Otherwise, the value zero is returned to indicate that the validation failed, and the bad sequence number is stored. If the next packet received carries the next higher sequence number, it is considered the valid start of a new packet sequence presumably caused by an extended dropout or a source restart. Since multiple complete sequence number cycles may have been missed, the packet loss statistics are reset.

Typical values for the parameters are shown, based on a maximum misordering time of 2 seconds at 50 packets/second and a maximum dropout of 1 minute. The dropout parameter MAX_DROPOUT should be a small fraction of the 16-bit sequence number space to give a reasonable probability that new sequence numbers after a restart will not fall in the acceptable range for sequence numbers from before the restart.

```
void init_seq(source *s, u_int16 seq)
{
    s->base_seq = seq - 1;
    s->max_seq = seq;
    s->bad_seq = RTP_SEQ_MOD + 1;
    s->cycles = 0;
    s->received = 0;
    s->received_prior = 0;
    s->expected_prior = 0;
    /* other initialization */
}

int update_seq(source *s, u_int16 seq)
{
    u_int16 udelta = seq - s->max_seq;
    const int MAX_DROPOUT = 3000;
    const int MAX_MISORDER = 100;
    const int MIN_SEQUENTIAL = 2;

    /*
     * Source is not valid until MIN_SEQUENTIAL packets with
     * sequential sequence numbers have been received.
     */
    if (s->probation) {
        /* packet is in sequence */
        if (seq == s->max_seq + 1) {
            s->probation--;
            s->max_seq = seq;
            if (s->probation == 0) {
                init_seq(s, seq);
                s->received++;
                return 1;
            }
        } else {
            s->probation = MIN_SEQUENTIAL - 1;
            s->max_seq = seq;
        }
        return 0;
    } else if (udelta < MAX_DROPOUT) {
        /* in order, with permissible gap */
        if (seq < s->max_seq) {
            /*
```

```
                 * Sequence number wrapped - count another 64K cycle.
                 */
                s->cycles += RTP_SEQ_MOD;
            }
            s->max_seq = seq;
        } else if (udelta <= RTP_SEQ_MOD - MAX_MISORDER) {
            /* the sequence number made a very large jump */
            if (seq == s->bad_seq) {
                /*
                 * Two sequential packets -- assume that the other side
                 * restarted without telling us so just re-sync
                 * (i.e., pretend this was the first packet).
                 */
                init_seq(s, seq);
            }
            else {
                s->bad_seq = (seq + 1) & (RTP_SEQ_MOD-1);
                return 0;
            }
        } else {
            /* duplicate or reordered packet */
        }
        s->received++;
        return 1;
    }
```

The validity check can be made stronger requiring more than two packets in sequence. The disadvantages are that a larger number of initial packets will be discarded and that high packet loss rates could prevent validation. However, because the RTCP header validation is relatively strong, if an RTCP packet is received from a source before the data packets, the count could be adjusted so that only two packets are required in sequence. If initial data loss for a few seconds can be tolerated, an application could choose to discard all data packets from a source until a valid RTCP packet has been received from that source.

Depending on the application and encoding, algorithms may exploit additional knowledge about the payload format for further validation. For payload types where the timestamp increment is the same for all packets, the timestamp values can be predicted from the previous packet received from the same source using the sequence number difference (assuming no change in payload type).

A strong "fast-path" check is possible since with high probability the first four octets in the header of a newly received RTP data packet will be just the same as that of the previous packet from the same SSRC except that the sequence number will have increased by one.

Similarly, a single-entry cache may be used for faster SSRC lookups in applications where data is typically received from one source at a time.

A.2 RTCP Header Validity Checks

The following checks can be applied to RTCP packets.

- o RTP version field must equal 2.
- o The payload type field of the first RTCP packet in a compound packet must be equal to SR or RR.
- o The padding bit (P) should be zero for the first packet of a compound RTCP packet because only the last should possibly need padding.
- o The length fields of the individual RTCP packets must total to the overall length of the compound RTCP packet as received. This is a fairly strong check.

The code fragment below performs all of these checks. The packet type is not checked for subsequent packets since unknown packet types may be present and should be ignored.

```
u_int32 len;        /* length of compound RTCP packet in words */
rtcp_t *r;          /* RTCP header */
rtcp_t *end;        /* end of compound RTCP packet */

if ((*(u_int16 *)r & RTCP_VALID_MASK) != RTCP_VALID_VALUE) {
    /* something wrong with packet format */
}
end = (rtcp_t *)((u_int32 *)r + len);

do r = (rtcp_t *)((u_int32 *)r + r->common.length + 1);
while (r < end && r->common.version == 2);

if (r != end) {
    /* something wrong with packet format */
}
```

A.3 Determining the Number of RTP Packets Expected and Lost

In order to compute packet loss rates, the number of packets expected and actually received from each source needs to be known, using per-source state information defined in struct source referenced via pointer s in the code below. The number of packets received is simply the count of packets as they arrive, including any late or duplicate packets. The number of packets expected can be computed by the receiver as the difference between the highest sequence number received (s->max_seq) and the first sequence number received (s->base_seq). Since the sequence number is only 16 bits and will wrap around, it is necessary to extend the highest sequence number with the (shifted) count of sequence number wraparounds (s->cycles). Both the received packet count and the count of cycles are maintained the RTP header validity check routine in Appendix A.1.

```
extended_max = s->cycles + s->max_seq;
expected = extended_max - s->base_seq + 1;
```

The number of packets lost is defined to be the number of packets expected less the number of packets actually received:

```
lost = expected - s->received;
```

Since this number is carried in 24 bits, it should be clamped at 0xffffff rather than wrap around to zero.

The fraction of packets lost during the last reporting interval (since the previous SR or RR packet was sent) is calculated from differences in the expected and received packet counts across the interval, where expected_prior and received_prior are the values saved when the previous reception report was generated:

```
expected_interval = expected - s->expected_prior;
s->expected_prior = expected;
received_interval = s->received - s->received_prior;
s->received_prior = s->received;
lost_interval = expected_interval - received_interval;
if (expected_interval == 0 || lost_interval <= 0) fraction = 0;
else fraction = (lost_interval << 8) / expected_interval;
```

The resulting fraction is an 8-bit fixed point number with the binary point at the left edge.

A.4 Generating SDES RTCP Packets

This function builds one SDES chunk into buffer b composed of argc items supplied in arrays type , value and length b

```
char *rtp_write_sdes(char *b, u_int32 src, int argc,
                     rtcp_sdes_type_t type[], char *value[],
                     int length[])
{
    rtcp_sdes_t *s = (rtcp_sdes_t *)b;
    rtcp_sdes_item_t *rsp;
```

```
    int i;
    int len;
    int pad;

    /* SSRC header */
    s->src = src;
    rsp = &s->item[0];

    /* SDES items */
    for (i = 0; i < argc; i++) {
        rsp->type = type[i];
        len = length[i];
        if (len > RTP_MAX_SDES) {
            /* invalid length, may want to take other action */
            len = RTP_MAX_SDES;
        }
        rsp->length = len;
        memcpy(rsp->data, value[i], len);
        rsp = (rtcp_sdes_item_t *)&rsp->data[len];
    }

    /* terminate with end marker and pad to next 4-octet boundary */
    len = ((char *) rsp) - b;
    pad = 4 - (len & 0x3);
    b = (char *) rsp;
    while (pad--) *b++ = RTCP_SDES_END;

    return b;
}
```

A.5 Parsing RTCP SDES Packets

This function parses an SDES packet, calling functions find_member() to find a pointer to the information for a session member given the SSRC identifier and member_sdes() to store the new SDES information for that member. This function expects a pointer to the header of the RTCP packet.

```
void rtp_read_sdes(rtcp_t *r)
{
    int count = r->common.count;
    rtcp_sdes_t *sd = &r->r.sdes;
    rtcp_sdes_item_t *rsp, *rspn;
    rtcp_sdes_item_t *end = (rtcp_sdes_item_t *)
                            ((u_int32 *)r + r->common.length + 1);
    source *s;

    while (--count >= 0) {
```

```
        rsp = &sd->item[0];
        if (rsp >= end) break;
        s = find_member(sd->src);

        for (; rsp->type; rsp = rspn ) {
            rspn = (rtcp_sdes_item_t *)((char*)rsp+rsp->length+2);
            if (rspn >= end) {
                rsp = rspn;
                break;
            }
            member_sdes(s, rsp->type, rsp->data, rsp->length);
        }
        sd = (rtcp_sdes_t *)
             ((u_int32 *)sd + (((char *)rsp - (char *)sd) >> 2)+1);
    }
    if (count >= 0) {
        /* invalid packet format */
    }
}
```

A.6 Generating a Random 32-bit Identifier

The following subroutine generates a random 32-bit identifier using the MD5 routines published in RFC 1321 [23]. The system routines may not be present on all operating systems, but they should serve as hints as to what kinds of information may be used. Other system calls that may be appropriate include

- o getdomainname() ,
- o getwd() , or
- o getrusage()

"Live" video or audio samples are also a good source of random numbers, but care must be taken to avoid using a turned-off microphone or blinded camera as a source [7].

Use of this or similar routine is suggested to generate the initial seed for the random number generator producing the RTCP period (as shown in Appendix A.7), to generate the initial values for the sequence number and timestamp, and to generate SSRC values. Since this routine is likely to be CPU-intensive, its direct use to generate RTCP periods is inappropriate because predictability is not an issue. Note that this routine produces the same result on repeated calls until the value of the system clock changes unless different values are supplied for the type argument.

```
/*
 * Generate a random 32-bit quantity.
 */
#include <sys/types.h>   /* u_long */
#include <sys/time.h>    /* gettimeofday() */
#include <unistd.h>      /* get..() */
#include <stdio.h>       /* printf() */
#include <time.h>        /* clock() */
#include <sys/utsname.h> /* uname() */
#include "global.h"      /* from RFC 1321 */
#include "md5.h"         /* from RFC 1321 */

#define MD_CTX MD5_CTX
#define MDInit MD5Init
#define MDUpdate MD5Update
#define MDFinal MD5Final

static u_long md_32(char *string, int length)
{
    MD_CTX context;
    union {
        char   c[16];
        u_long x[4];
    } digest;
    u_long r;
    int i;

    MDInit (&context);
    MDUpdate (&context, string, length);
    MDFinal ((unsigned char *)&digest, &context);
    r = 0;
    for (i = 0; i < 3; i++) {
        r ^= digest.x[i];
    }
    return r;
}                                /* md_32 */


/*
 * Return random unsigned 32-bit quantity. Use 'type' argument if you
 * need to generate several different values in close succession.
 */
u_int32 random32(int type)
{
    struct {
        int     type;
        struct  timeval tv;
        clock_t cpu;
```

```
            pid_t   pid;
            u_long  hid;
            uid_t   uid;
            gid_t   gid;
            struct  utsname name;
        } s;

        gettimeofday(&s.tv, 0);
        uname(&s.name);
        s.type = type;
        s.cpu  = clock();
        s.pid  = getpid();
        s.hid  = gethostid();
        s.uid  = getuid();
        s.gid  = getgid();

        return md_32((char *)&s, sizeof(s));
    }                               /* random32 */
```

A.7 Computing the RTCP Transmission Interval

The following function returns the time between transmissions of RTCP packets, measured in seconds. It should be called after sending one compound RTCP packet to calculate the delay until the next should be sent. This function should also be called to calculate the delay before sending the first RTCP packet upon startup rather than send the packet immediately. This avoids any burst of RTCP packets if an application is started at many sites simultaneously, for example as a result of a session announcement.

The parameters have the following meaning:

rtcp_bw: The target RTCP bandwidth, i.e., the total bandwidth that will be used for RTCP packets by all members of this session, in octets per second. This should be 5% of the "session bandwidth" parameter supplied to the application at startup.

senders: Number of active senders since sending last report, known from construction of receiver reports for this RTCP packet. Includes ourselves, if we also sent during this interval.

members: The estimated number of session members, including ourselves. Incremented as we discover new session members from the receipt of RTP or RTCP packets, and decremented as session members leave (via RTCP BYE) or their state is timed out (30 minutes is recommended). On the first call, this parameter should have the value 1.

we_sent: Flag that is true if we have sent data during the last two RTCP intervals. If the flag is true, the compound RTCP packet just sent contained an SR packet.

packet_size: The size of the compound RTCP packet just sent, in octets, including the network encapsulation (e.g., 28 octets for UDP over IP).

avg_rtcp_size: Pointer to estimator for compound RTCP packet size; initialized and updated by this function for the packet just sent, and also updated by an identical line of code in the RTCP receive routine for every RTCP packet received from other participants in the session.

initial: Flag that is true for the first call upon startup to calculate the time until the first report should be sent.

```
#include <math.h>

double rtcp_interval(int members,
                     int senders,
                     double rtcp_bw,
                     int we_sent,
                     int packet_size,
                     int *avg_rtcp_size,
                     int initial)
{
    /*
     * Minimum time between RTCP packets from this site (in seconds).
     * This time prevents the reports from `clumping' when sessions
     * are small and the law of large numbers isn't helping to smooth
     * out the traffic.  It also keeps the report interval from
     * becoming ridiculously small during transient outages like a
     * network partition.
     */
    double const RTCP_MIN_TIME = 5.;
    /*
     * Fraction of the RTCP bandwidth to be shared among active
     * senders.  (This fraction was chosen so that in a typical
     * session with one or two active senders, the computed report
     * time would be roughly equal to the minimum report time so that
     * we don't unnecessarily slow down receiver reports.) The
     * receiver fraction must be 1 - the sender fraction.
     */
    double const RTCP_SENDER_BW_FRACTION = 0.25;
    double const RTCP_RCVR_BW_FRACTION = (1-RTCP_SENDER_BW_FRACTION);
    /*
     * Gain (smoothing constant) for the low-pass filter that
```

```
     * estimates the average RTCP packet size (see Cadzow reference).
     */
    double const RTCP_SIZE_GAIN = (1./16.);

    double t;                   /* interval */
    double rtcp_min_time = RTCP_MIN_TIME;
    int n;                      /* no. of members for computation */

    /*
     * Very first call at application start-up uses half the min
     * delay for quicker notification while still allowing some time
     * before reporting for randomization and to learn about other
     * sources so the report interval will converge to the correct
     * interval more quickly.  The average RTCP size is initialized
     * to 128 octets which is conservative (it assumes everyone else
     * is generating SRs instead of RRs: 20 IP + 8 UDP + 52 SR + 48
     * SDES CNAME).
     */
    if (initial) {
        rtcp_min_time /= 2;
        *avg_rtcp_size = 128;
    }

    /*
     * If there were active senders, give them at least a minimum
     * share of the RTCP bandwidth.  Otherwise all participants share
     * the RTCP bandwidth equally.
     */
    n = members;
    if (senders > 0 && senders < members * RTCP_SENDER_BW_FRACTION) {
        if (we_sent) {
            rtcp_bw *= RTCP_SENDER_BW_FRACTION;
            n = senders;
        } else {
            rtcp_bw *= RTCP_RCVR_BW_FRACTION;
            n -= senders;
        }
    }

    /*
     * Update the average size estimate by the size of the report
     * packet we just sent.
     */
    *avg_rtcp_size += (packet_size - *avg_rtcp_size)*RTCP_SIZE_GAIN;

    /*
     * The effective number of sites times the average packet size is
     * the total number of octets sent when each site sends a report.
```

```
         * Dividing this by the effective bandwidth gives the time
         * interval over which those packets must be sent in order to
         * meet the bandwidth target, with a minimum enforced.  In that
         * time interval we send one report so this time is also our
         * average time between reports.
         */
        t = (*avg_rtcp_size) * n / rtcp_bw;
        if (t < rtcp_min_time) t = rtcp_min_time;

        /*
         * To avoid traffic bursts from unintended synchronization with
         * other sites, we then pick our actual next report interval as a
         * random number uniformly distributed between 0.5*t and 1.5*t.
         */
        return t * (drand48() + 0.5);
    }
```

A.8 Estimating the Interarrival Jitter

The code fragments below implement the algorithm given in Section 6.3.1 for calculating an estimate of the statistical variance of the RTP data interarrival time to be inserted in the interarrival jitter field of reception reports. The inputs are r->ts , the timestamp from the incoming packet, and arrival , the current time in the same units. Here s points to state for the source; s->transit holds the relative transit time for the previous packet, and s->jitter holds the estimated jitter. The jitter field of the reception report is measured in timestamp units and expressed as an unsigned integer, but the jitter estimate is kept in a floating point. As each data packet arrives, the jitter estimate is updated:

```
int transit = arrival - r->ts;
int d = transit - s->transit;
s->transit = transit;
if (d < 0) d = -d;
s->jitter += (1./16.) * ((double)d - s->jitter);
```

When a reception report block (to which rr points) is generated for this member, the current jitter estimate is returned:

```
rr->jitter = (u_int32) s->jitter;
```

Alternatively, the jitter estimate can be kept as an integer, but scaled to reduce round-off error. The calculation is the same except for the last line:

```
s->jitter += d - ((s->jitter + 8) >> 4);
```

In this case, the estimate is sampled for the reception report as:

```
rr->jitter = s->jitter >> 4;
```

B. Security Considerations

RTP suffers from the same security liabilities as the underlying protocols. For example, an impostor can fake source or destination network addresses, or change the header or payload. Within RTCP, the CNAME and NAME information may be used to impersonate another participant. In addition, RTP may be sent via IP multicast, which provides no direct means for a sender to know all the receivers of the data sent and therefore no measure of privacy. Rightly or not, users may be more sensitive to privacy concerns with audio and video communication than they have been with more traditional forms of network communication [24]. Therefore, the use of security mechanisms with RTP is important. These mechanisms are discussed in Section 9.

RTP-level translators or mixers may be used to allow RTP traffic to reach hosts behind firewalls. Appropriate firewall security principles and practices, which are beyond the scope of this document, should be followed in the design and installation of these devices and in the admission of RTP applications for use behind the firewall.

C. Authors' Addresses

Henning Schulzrinne
GMD Fokus
Hardenbergplatz 2
D-10623 Berlin
Germany

EMail: schulzrinne@fokus.gmd.de

Stephen L. Casner
Precept Software, Inc.
21580 Stevens Creek Boulevard, Suite 207
Cupertino, CA 95014
United States

EMail: casner@precept.com

Ron Frederick
Xerox Palo Alto Research Center
3333 Coyote Hill Road
Palo Alto, CA 94304
United States

EMail: frederic@parc.xerox.com

Van Jacobson
MS 46a-1121
Lawrence Berkeley National Laboratory
Berkeley, CA 94720
United States

EMail: van@ee.lbl.gov

Acknowledgments

This memorandum is based on discussions within the IETF Audio/Video Transport working group chaired by Stephen Casner. The current protocol has its origins in the Network Voice Protocol and the Packet Video Protocol (Danny Cohen and Randy Cole) and the protocol implemented by the vat application (Van Jacobson and Steve McCanne). Christian Huitema provided ideas for the random identifier generator.

D. Bibliography

[1] D. D. Clark and D. L. Tennenhouse, "Architectural considerations for a new generation of protocols," in SIGCOMM Symposium on Communications Architectures and Protocols , (Philadelphia, Pennsylvania), pp. 200--208, IEEE, Sept. 1990. Computer Communications Review, Vol. 20(4), Sept. 1990.

[2] H. Schulzrinne, "Issues in designing a transport protocol for audio and video conferences and other multiparticipant real-time applications", Work in Progress.

[3] D. E. Comer, Internetworking with TCP/IP , vol. 1. Englewood Cliffs, New Jersey: Prentice Hall, 1991.

[4] Postel, J., "Internet Protocol", STD 5, RFC 791, USC/Information Sciences Institute, September 1981.

[5] Mills, D., "Network Time Protocol Version 3", RFC 1305, UDEL, March 1992.

[6] Reynolds, J., and J. Postel, "Assigned Numbers", STD 2, RFC 1700, USC/Information Sciences Institute, October 1994.

[7] Eastlake, D., Crocker, S., and J. Schiller, "Randomness Recommendations for Security", RFC 1750, DEC, Cybercash, MIT, December 1994.

[8] J.-C. Bolot, T. Turletti, and I. Wakeman, "Scalable feedback control for multicast video distribution in the internet," in SIGCOMM Symposium on Communications Architectures and Protocols , (London, England), pp. 58--67, ACM, Aug. 1994.

[9] I. Busse, B. Deffner, and H. Schulzrinne, "Dynamic QoS control of multimedia applications based on RTP," Computer Communications , Jan. 1996.

[10] S. Floyd and V. Jacobson, "The synchronization of periodic routing messages," in SIGCOMM Symposium on Communications Architectures and Protocols (D. P. Sidhu, ed.), (San Francisco, California), pp. 33--44, ACM, Sept. 1993. also in [25].

[11] J. A. Cadzow, Foundations of digital signal processing and data analysis New York, New York: Macmillan, 1987.

[12] International Standards Organization, "ISO/IEC DIS 10646-1:1993 information technology -- universal multiple-octet coded character set (UCS) -- part I: Architecture and basic multilingual plane," 1993.

[13] The Unicode Consortium, The Unicode Standard New York, New York: Addison-Wesley, 1991.

[14] Mockapetris, P., "Domain Names - Concepts and Facilities", STD 13, RFC 1034, USC/Information Sciences Institute, November 1987.

[15] Mockapetris, P., "Domain Names - Implementation and Specification", STD 13, RFC 1035, USC/Information Sciences Institute, November 1987.

[16] Braden, R., "Requirements for Internet Hosts - Application and Support", STD 3, RFC 1123, Internet Engineering Task Force, October 1989.

[17] Rekhter, Y., Moskowitz, R., Karrenberg, D., and G. de Groot, "Address Allocation for Private Internets", RFC 1597, T.J. Watson Research Center, IBM Corp., Chrysler Corp., RIPE NCC, March 1994.

[18] Lear, E., Fair, E., Crocker, D., and T. Kessler, "Network 10 Considered Harmful (Some Practices Shouldn't be Codified)", RFC 1627, Silicon Graphics, Inc., Apple Computer, Inc., Silicon Graphics, Inc., July 1994.

[19] Crocker, D., "Standard for the Format of ARPA Internet Text Messages", STD 11, RFC 822, UDEL, August 1982.

[20] W. Feller, An Introduction to Probability Theory and its Applications, Volume 1 , vol. 1. New York, New York: John Wiley and Sons, third ed., 1968.

[21] Balenson, D., "Privacy Enhancement for Internet Electronic Mail: Part III: Algorithms, Modes, and Identifiers", RFC 1423, TIS, IAB IRTF PSRG, IETF PEM WG, February 1993.

[22] V. L. Voydock and S. T. Kent, "Security mechanisms in high-level network protocols," ACM Computing Surveys , vol. 15, pp. 135--171, June 1983.

[23] Rivest, R., "The MD5 Message-Digest Algorithm", RFC 1321, MIT Laboratory for Computer Science and RSA Data Security, Inc., April 1992.

[24] S. Stubblebine, "Security services for multimedia conferencing," in 16th National Computer Security Conference , (Baltimore, Maryland), pp. 391--395, Sept. 1993.

[25] S. Floyd and V. Jacobson, "The synchronization of periodic routing messages," IEEE/ACM Transactions on Networking , vol. 2, pp. 122-136, April 1994.

Network Working Group C. Allocchio
Request for Comments: 2303 GARR-Italy
Category: Standards Track March 1998

Minimal PSTN address format in Internet Mail

Status of this Memo

This document specifies an Internet standards track protocol for the Internet community, and requests discussion and suggestions for improvements. Please refer to the current edition of the "Internet Official Protocol Standards" (STD 1) for the standardization state and status of this protocol. Distribution of this memo is unlimited.

Copyright Notice

IESC NOTE

This memo describes a simple method of encoding PSTN addresses in the local-part of Internet email addresses, along with an extension mechanism to allow encoding of additional standard attributes needed for email gateways to PSTN-based services.

As with all Internet mail addresses, the left-hand-side (local- part) of an address generated according to this specification, is not to be interpreted except by the MTA that is named on the right-hand-side (domain).

1. Introduction

Since the very first e-mail to PSTN services gateway appeared, a number of different methods to specify a PSTN address as an e-mail address have been used by implementors. Two major objectives for this were

- enable an e-mail user to access these services from his/her e-mail interface;

- enable some kind of "PSTN over e-mail service" transport, to reduce the costs of PSTN long distance transmissions, and use the existing e-mail infrastructure.

RFC 2303 1

This memo describes the MINIMAL addressing method to encode PSTN addresses into e-mail addresses and the standard extension mechanism to allow definition of further standard elements. The opposite problem, i.e. to allow a traditional numeric-only PSTN device user to access the e-mail transport service, is not discussed here.

All implementations supporting this PSTN over e-mail service MUST support as a minimum the specification described in this document. The generic complex case of converting the whole PSTN addressing into e-mail is out of scope in this minimal specification: there is some work in progress in the field, where also a number of standard optional extensions are being defined.

In this document the formal definitions are described using ABNF syntax, as defined into [7]. We will also use some of the "CORE DEFINITIONS" defined in "APPENDIX A - CORE" of that document. The exact meaning of the capitalised words

"MUST", "MUST NOT", "REQUIRED", "SHALL", "SHALL NOT", "SHOULD", "SHOULD NOT", "RECOMMENDED", "MAY", "OPTIONAL"

is defined in reference [6].

2. Minimal PSTN address

The minimal specification of a PSTN address in e-mail address is as follows:

```
pstn-address = pstn-mbox  [ qualif-type1 ]

pstn-mbox = service-selector "=" global-phone

service-selector = 1*( DIGIT / ALPHA / "-" )
                   ; note that SP (space) is not allowed in
                   ; service-selector.
                   ; service-selector MUST be handled as a case
                   ; INSENSITIVE string by implementations.
```

Specifications adopting the "pstn-address" definition MUST define a unique case insensitive "service-selector" element to identify the specific messaging service involved.

These specifications MUST also define which minimal "qualif-type1" extensions, if any, MUST be supported for the specified service.

Implementations confirming to these minimal requirements specification are allowed to ingnore any other non-minimal extensions address element which can be present in the "pstn-address". However, conforming implementations MUST preserve all "qualif-type1" address elements they receive.

The generic "qualif-type1" element is defined as:

```
qualif-type1 = "/" keyword "=" string

keyword = 1*( DIGIT / ALPHA / "-" )
          ; note that SP (space) is not allowed in keyword

string = PCHAR
         ; note that printable characters are %x20-7E
```

As such, all "pstn-address" extensions elements MUST be defined in the "qualif-type1" form.

2.1 Minimal "global-phone" definition

We now define the minimal supported syntax for global-phone:

```
global-phone = "+" 1*( DIGIT , written-sep )

written-sep = ( "-" / "." )
```

The use of other dialling schemas for PSTN numbers (like private numbering plans or local dialling conventions) is also allowed. However, this does not preclude nor remove the minimal compulsory requirement to support the "global-phone" syntax as defined above.

Any non "global-phone" dialling schema MUST NOT use the leading "+" between the "=" sign and the dialling string. The "+" sign is strictly reserved for the standard "global-phone" syntax.

Note:
The specification of these different dialling schemas is out of scope for this minimal specification.

User specification of PSTN e-mail addresses will be facilitated if they can insert these separators between dial elements like digits etc. For this reason we allow them in the syntax the written-sep element.

Implementors' note:
Use of the written-sep elements is allowed, but not recommended. Any occurences of written-sep elements in a pstn-mbox MUST be ignored by all conformant implementations. User Agents SHOULD remove written-sep elements before submitting messages to the Message Transport System.

RFC 2303 3

2.2 Some examples of a minimal "pstn-address"

```
VOICE=+3940226338

FAX=+12027653000/T33S=6377

SMS=+33-1-88335215
```

3. The e-mail address of the I-pstn device: mta-I-pstn

An "I-pstn device" has an e-mail address, or to be more exact, a name which enables a mail system to identify it on the e-mail global system.

In Internet mail, this is the Right Hand Side (RHS) part of the address, i.e. the part on the right of the "@" sign. We will call this "mta-I-pstn"

```
mta-I-pstn = domain
```

For "domain" strings used in SMTP transmissions, the string MUST conform to the requirements of that standard's <domain> specifications [1], [3]. For "domain" strings used in message content headers, the string MUST conform to the requirements of the relevant standards [2], [3].

Note: in both cases, the standards permit use of "domain names" or "domain literals" in addresses.

4. The pstn-email

The complete structure used to transfer a minimal PSTN address over the Internet e-mail transport system is called "pstn-email". This object is a an e-mail address which conforms to RFC822 [2] and RFC1123 [3] "addr-spec" syntax, with some extra structure which allows the PSTN number to be identified.

```
pstn-email = ["/"] pstn-address ["/"] "@" mta-I-pstn
```

Implementors' note:
The optional "/" characters can result from other mail transport services gateways, where it is also an optional element. Implementations MUST accept the optional slashes but SHOULD NOT generate them. Gateways are allowed to strip them off when converting to Internet mail addressing.

It is essential to remind that "pstn-address" element MUST strictly follow the "quoting rules" spcified in the relevant standards [2], [3].

4.1 Multiple subaddresses

In case a particular service requires multiple subaddresses (in any form defined by the specific standard specification for that service), and these subaddresses need to be given on the same "pstn-mbox", multiple "pstn-email" elements will be used.

Implementors' note:
The UA could accept multiple subaddress elements for the same global-phone, but it must generate multiple "pstn-mbox" elements when passing the message to the MTA.

4.2 Some examples of "pstn-email"

VOICE=+3940226338@worldvoice.com

FAX=+1.202.7653000/T33S=6377@faxserv.org

/SMS=+33-1-88335215/@telecom.com

5. Conclusions

This proposal creates a minimal standard encoding for PSTN addresses within the global e-mail transport system and defines the standard extension mechanism to be used to introduce specific new elements.

The proposal requires no changes to existing e-mail software. Each specific PSTN service using this proposal MUST define its own "service-selector" specification and MUST define the eventual other "qualif-type1" elements to be supported for its minimal addressing specification. An example is in reference [13].

6. Security Considerations

This document specifies a means by which PSTN addresses can be encoded into e-mail addresses. As routing of e-mail messages is determined by Domain Name System (DNS) information, a successful attack on this service could force the mail path via some particular gateway or message transfer agent where mail security can be affected by compromised software.

There are several means by which an attacker might be able to deliver incorrect mail routing information to a client. These include: (a) compromise of a DNS server, (b) generating a counterfeit response to a client's DNS query, (c) returning incorrect "additional information" in response to an unrelated query. Clients SHOULD ensure that mail routing is based only on authoritative answers. Once DNS Security mechanisms [5] become more widely deployed, clients SHOULD employ those mechanisms to verify the authenticity and integrity of mail routing records.

7. Author's Address

Claudio Allocchio
Sincrotrone Trieste
SS 14 Km 163.5 Basovizza
I 34012 Trieste
Italy

RFC822: Claudio.Allocchio@elettra.trieste.it
X.400: C=it;A=garr;P=Trieste;O=Elettra;
S=Allocchio;G=Claudio;
Phone: +39 40 3758523
Fax: +39 40 3758565

RFC 2303 6

8. References

[1] Postel, J., "Simple Mail Transfer Protocol", STD 10, RFC 821, August 1982.

[2] Crocker, D., " Standard for the format of ARPA Internet text messages", STD 11, RFC 822, August 1982.

[3] Braden, R., "Requirements for Internet hosts - application and support", RFC 1123, October 1989.

[4] Malamud, C. and M. Rose, "Principles of Operation for the TPC.INT Subdomain: Remote Printing -- Technical Procedures", RFC 1528, October 1993.

[5] Eastlake, D. and C. Kaufman, "Domain Name System Security Extensions", RFC 2065, January 1997.

[6] Bradner, S., "Key words for use in RFCs to Indicate Requirement Levels", RFC 2119, March 1997.

[7] Crocker, D. and P. Overell, "Augmented BNF for Syntax Specifications", RFC 2234, November 1997.

[8] ITU F.401 - Message Handling Services: Naming and Addressing for Public Message Handling Service; recommendation F.401 (August 1992)

[9] ITU F.423 - Message Handling Services: Intercommunication Between the Interpersonal Messaging Service and the Telefax Service; recommendation F.423 (August 1992)

[10] ITU E.164 - Numbering plan for the ISDN era; recommendation E.164/I.331 (August 1991)

[11] ITU T.33 - Facsimile routing utilizing the subaddress; recommendation T.33 (July, 1996)

[12] ETSI I-ETS 300,380 - Universal Personal Telecommunication (UPT): Access Devices Dual Tone Multi Frequency (DTMF) sender for acoustical coupling to the microphone of a handset telephone (March 1995)

[13] Allocchio, C., " Minimal FAX address format in Internet Mail", RFC 2304, March 1998.

[14] Kille, S., "MIXER (Mime Internet X.400 Enhanced Relay): Mapping between X.400 and RFC 822/MIME", RFC 2156, January 1998.

9. Full Copyright Statement

Netowrk Working Group
Request for Comments: 2458
Category: Informational

H. Lu
Editor
M. Krishnaswamy
Lucent Technologies
L. Conroy
Roke Manor Research
S. Bellovin
F. Burg
A. DeSimone
K. Tewani
AT&T Labs
P. Davidson
Nortel
H. Schulzrinne
Columbia University
K. Vishwanathan
Isochrome
November 1998

Toward the PSTN/Internet Inter-Networking --Pre-PINT Implementations

Status of this Memo

This memo provides information for the Internet community. It does not specify an Internet standard of any kind. Distribution of this memo is unlimited.

Copyright Notice

Abstract

This document contains the information relevant to the development of the inter-networking interfaces underway in the Public Switched Telephone Network (PSTN)/Internet Inter-Networking (PINT) Working Group. It addresses technologies, architectures, and several (but by no means all) existing pre-PINT implementations of the arrangements through which Internet applications can request and enrich PSTN telecommunications services. The common denominator of the enriched services (a.k.a. PINT services) is that they combine the Internet and PSTN services in such a way that the Internet is used for non-voice interactions, while the voice (and fax) are carried entirely over the PSTN. One key observation is that the pre-PINT implementations, being developed independently, do not inter-operate. It is a task of the PINT Working Group to define the inter-networking interfaces that will support inter-operation of the future implementations of PINT services.

Table of Contents

1. Introduction

This document contains the information relevant to the development of the inter-networking interfaces underway in the Public Switched Telephone Network (PSTN)/Internet Inter-Networking (PINT) Working Group. It addresses technologies, architectures, and several (but by no means all) existing pre-PINT implementations of the arrangements through which Internet applications can request and enrich PSTN telecommunications services. The common denominator of the enriched services (a.k.a. PINT services) is that they combine the Internet and PSTN services in such a way that the Internet is used for non-voice interactions, while the voice (and fax) are carried entirely over the PSTN.

The organization of the document is as follows. First, the basic terminology and a short "intuitive" description of the PINT services are provided. The rest of the information deals, in one way or the other, with the pre-PINT support of these services where they are used as a benchmark. Thus, an architectural overview common to all present solutions is presented. The flow of the document then divides into two streams: one is dedicated to the Intelligent Network (IN)-based solutions; the other explores alternative means (i.e., CallBroker and Computer-Telephony Integration (CTI) approach). At this point, the emerging standards are explored, in particular, the Session Initiation Protocol (SIP), which promises an elegant solution to the PINT problem. Each of the above developments is addressed in a respective section. The final sections of the document contain the overall security considerations, conclusion, acknowledgments, appendix, and a set of references. The security section summarizes the PINT security requirements derived from the pre-PINT experiences and the appendix presents a tutorial on the PSTN, IN, and Call Center functions.

2. Terminology

This document uses the following terminology:

Authentication -- verification of the identity of a party.

Authorization -- determination of whether or not a party has the right to perform certain activities.

PINT Gateway -- the PSTN node that interacts with the Internet.

User or Customer -- the person who asks for a service request to be issued. In the context of PINT Services, this person will use an Internet host to make his or her request. The term "user" is also used to describe a host originating the PINT service request on behalf of this person.

3. PINT Services

This document addresses four services initially identified by the PINT Working Group and presently supported by pre-PINT implementations. These services are: click-to-dial-back, click-to-fax, click-to-fax-back and voice-access-to-content.

Note that the word "click" should not be taken literally. It is rather used to point out that initiation of the related services takes place on the Internet, where point and click are the most prevalent user actions. In other words, a service request could originate from any type of IP-based platforms. There is no implication that these services must be implemented by a device within the PSTN or the Internet running a Web server.

The common denominator of the PINT services is that they combine the Internet and PSTN services in such a way that the Internet is used for non-voice interactions, while the voice (and fax) are carried entirely over the PSTN. (An example of such a service is combination of a Web-based Yellow Pages service with the ability to initiate PSTN calls between customers and suppliers in a manner described in what follows.)

Some of the benefits of using the PSTN are high quality of the voice, an ability to route the call to different locations depending on pre-set criteria (for example, time of the day, day of the week, and geographic location), outstanding security and reliability, and access to flexible, low cost, and secure billing and charging systems. The benefits of using the Internet are the uniform, well-defined, and widely-used interfaces available anywhere, anytime.

Click-to-Dial-Back

With this service, a user requests (through an IP host) that the PSTN call be established between another party and himself or herself. An important pre-requisite for using this service is that the user has simultaneous access to both the PSTN and Internet.

One example of an application of this service is on-line shopping: a user browsing through an on-line catalogue, clicks a button thus inviting a call from a sales representative. Note that (as is the case with the all-PSTN Free-Phone, or "800", service) flexible billing arrangements can be implemented here on behalf of the service provider. In addition (and also similarly to the Free-Phone/800), the PSTN could route the call depending on the time of day, day of week, availability of agents in different locations, and so on.

Click-to-Fax

With this service, a user at an IP host requests that a fax be sent to a particular fax number. In particular this service is especially meaningful when the fax is to be sent to someone who has only a fax machine (but no access to the Internet). Consider, as an example, a service scenario in which a Web user makes a reservation for a hotel room in Beijing from a travel service page containing hotel information of major cities around the world. Suppose a specific Beijing hotel chosen by the user does not have Internet connection but has a fax machine. The user fills out the hotel reservation form and then clicks a button sending out the form to the travel service provider, which in turn generates a fax request and sends it together with the hotel reservation form to the PSTN. Upon receiving the request and the associated data, the PSTN translates the data into the proper facsimile format and delivers it to the Beijing hotel as specified in the fax request.

Click-to-Fax-Back

With this service, a user at an IP host can request that a fax be sent to him or her. (Consider the user of the previous example, who now requests the confirmation from the Beijing Hotel. Another useful application of the service is when size of the information that a user intends to get is so large that downloading it to the user's PC over the Internet will require a long time and a lot of disk space.)

Voice-Access-to-Content

With this service, a user at an IP host requests that certain information on the Internet be accessed (and delivered) in an audio form over the PSTN, using the telephone as an informational appliance. One application of this service is to provide Web access to the blind. (This may require special resources--available in the PSTN--to convert the Web data into speech.)

4. Architectural Overview

4.1 Public Switched Telephone Network

From an application perspective, Internet nodes are interconnected directly, as shown in Figure 1. When two machines are to communicate, they will have the address of the destination end system, and will send network level datagrams, assuming that the underlying infrastructure will deliver them as required.

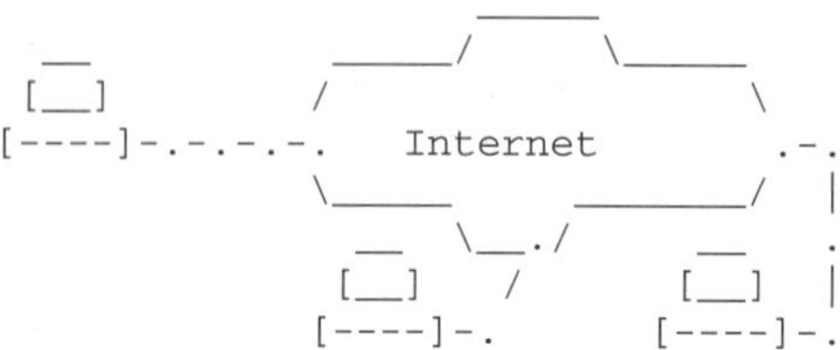

Figure 1

Where all nodes are on the same (broadcast) network, there is no need for intervening routers; they can send and deliver packets to one another directly. The Internet nodes are responsible for their own communications requests, and act as peers in the communication sessions that result.

This contrasts with the situation in the PSTN. There, the end systems are configured as shown in Figure 2. The end systems tend to be specific to a particular type of traffic, so that, for example, the majority of terminals are dedicated to carrying speech traffic (telephones) or to carrying facsimile data (fax machines). The terminals all connect to Central Offices (COs) via access lines, and these COs are interconnected into a network.

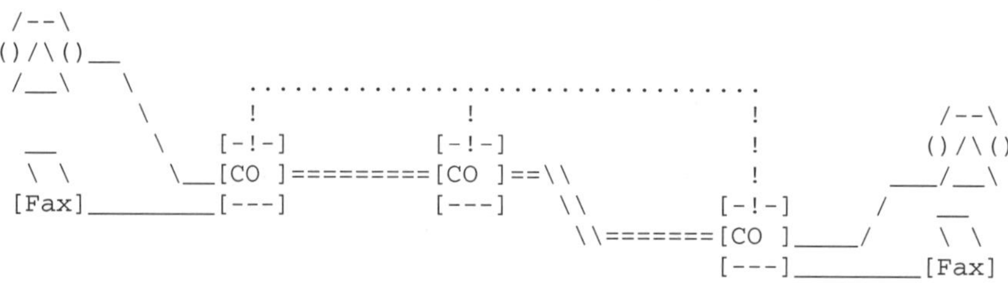

Key: ___ Access Lines
=== Trunk Links (inter-CO user data links)
... Inter-CO signaling network links
CO Central Office (Telephone Exchange)

Figure 2

Communications between the terminals are all "circuit switched", so a dedicated synchronous data path (or circuit) needs to be placed between the end terminals for carrying all communications. Arranging for such a circuit to be made or removed (cleared) is the responsibility of the Central Offices in the network. A user makes a request via his or her terminal, and this request is passed on to the "local" Central Office. The relationship between the terminals and the local Central Offices to which they are connected is strictly Client/Server.

The COs are interconnected using two different types of connections. One of these is called a trunk connection (shown as a double line in the above figure) and is used to carry the data traffic generated by the terminals. The other connection acts as part of a separate network (and is shown as a dotted line in the above figure). This is the signaling network, and is used by the Central Offices to request a connection to be made between themselves and the destination of the required circuit. This will be carried across the trunk link to the "next" Central Office in the path. The path, once in place through the PSTN, always takes the same route. This contrasts with the Internet, where the underlying datagram nature of the infrastructure means that data packets are carried over different routes, depending on the combined traffic flows through the network at the time.

The call set up process can be viewed as having two parts: one in which a request for connection is made, and the other in which the circuit is made across the PSTN and call data flows between the communicating parties. This is shown in the next pair of figures (3a and 3b).

```
      /--\
     ()  ()
       --____
      /++\   \
     /----\   \
        A      \    [-!-]
                \->[CO ]
                    [---]
     Time = 13:55
```

Figure 3a

```
Key: ___   Access Lines
     ===   Trunk Links (inter-CO user data links)
     ...   Inter-CO signaling network links
     CO    Central Office (Telephone Exchange)
```

RFC 2458 7

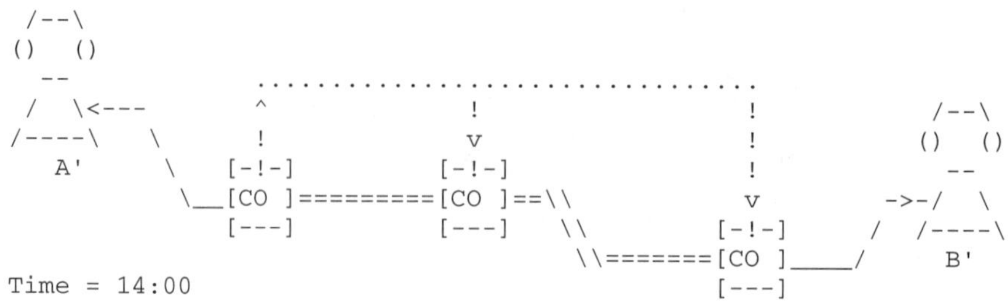

Figure 3b

Figure 3 shows a particular kind of service that can be provided; call booking. With this service, a request is sent for a connection to be made between the A and B telephones at a specified time. The telephone is then replaced (the request phase is terminated). At the specified time, the CO will make a connection across the network in the normal way, but will, first, ring the "local" or A' telephone to inform the user that his or her call is now about to be made.

For more complex services, the requesting telephone is often connected via its "local" CO to a Service Node (SN), where the user can be played prompts and can specify the parameters of his or her request in a more flexible manner. This is shown below, in Figures 4a and 4b. For more details of the operation of the Service Node (and other Intelligent Network units), see the Appendix.

When the SN is involved in the request and in the call setup process, it appears, to the CO, to be another PSTN terminal. As such, the initial request is routed to the Service Node, which, as an end system, then makes two independent calls "out" to A' and B'.

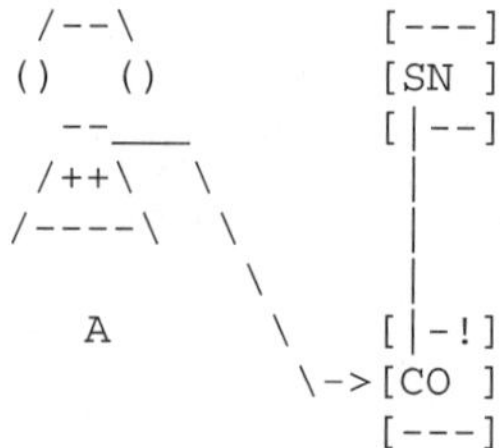

Figure 4a

```
Key: ___   Access Lines
     ===   Trunk Links (inter-CO user data links)
     ...   Inter-CO signaling network links
     CO    Central Office (Telephone Exchange)
     SN    Service Node
```

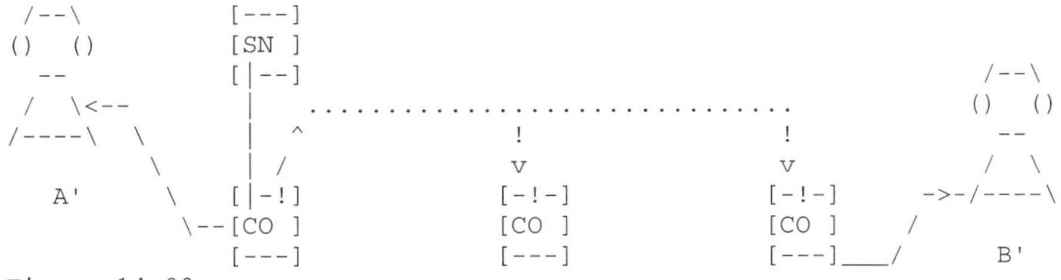

Figure 4b

Note that in both cases as shown in Figures 3 and 4 a similar service can be provided in which the B' telephone is replaced by an Intelligent Peripheral (or an Special Resource Functional entity within a Service Node), playing an announcement. This allows a "wake up" call to be requested, with the Intelligent Peripheral or Service Node Special Resource playing a suitable message to telephone A' at the specified time. Again, for more details of the operation of the Special Resources (and other Intelligent Network units), see the Appendix.

4.2 Pre-PINT Systems

Although the pre-PINT systems reported here (i.e., those developed by AT&T, Lucent, Siemens and Nortel) vary in the details of their operation, they exhibit similarities in the architecture. This section highlights the common features. Specific descriptions of these systems will follow.

All of the systems can be seen as being quite similar to that shown in the following diagram. In each case, the service is separated into two parts; one for the request and another for execution of the service. Figure 5 summarizes the process.

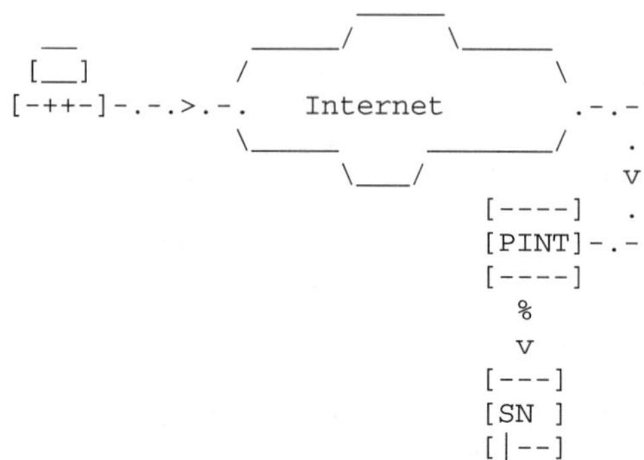

Figure 5a

Key: CO Central Office (Telephone Exchange)
SN Service Node
PINT PSTN/Internet Gateway
.-.-. Internet Access Link
%%% Gateway/Service Node Link
___ PSTN Access Lines
=== PSTN Trunk Links (inter-CO user data links)
... Inter-CO signaling network links

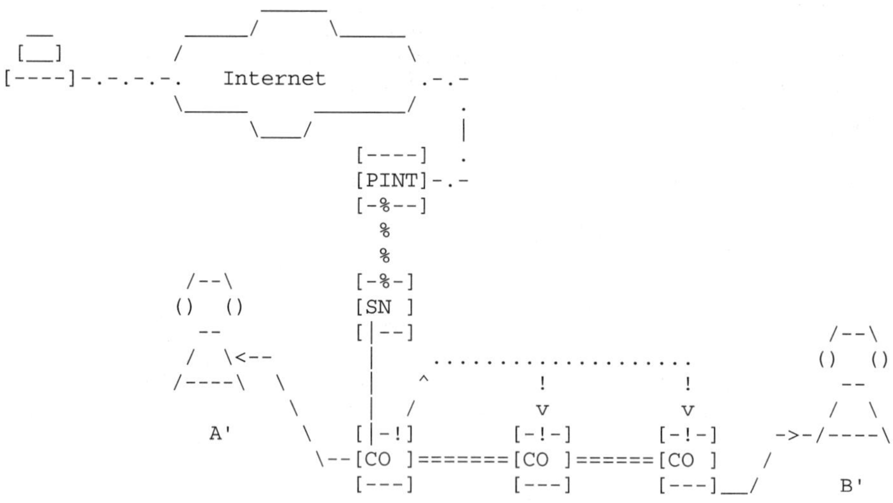

Figure 5b

Comparing Figure 4a with Figure 5a, the differences lie in the way that the information specifying the request is delivered to the Service Node. In the PSTN/IN method shown in the earlier diagram, the user connects to the SN from the telephone labeled A, with the connection being routed via the CO. In the latter case, the request is delivered from an Internet node, via the PINT gateway, and thence to the Service Node over a "private" link. The effect is identical, in that the request for service is specified (although the actual parameters used to specify the service required may differ somewhat).

The figures depicting the respective service execution phases (Figures 4b and 5b) show that the operation, from the IN/PSTN perspective, is again identical. The Service Node appears to initiate two independent calls "out" to telephones A' and B'.

The alternative systems developed by AT&T and by Nortel allow another option to be used in which the PINT Gateway does not have to connect to the PSTN via a Service Node (or other Intelligent Network component), but can instead connect directly to Central Offices that support the actions requested by the gateway. In these alternatives, the commands are couched at a "lower level", specifying the call states required for the intended service connection rather than the service identifier and the addresses involved (leaving the Intelligent Network components to coordinate the details of the service call on the gateway's behalf). In this way the vocabulary of the commands is closer to that used to control Central Offices. The difference really lies in the language used for the services specification, and all systems can use the overall architecture depicted in Figure 5; the only question remains whether the Intelligent Network components are actually needed in these other approaches.

The following diagram (Figure 6) shows the interface architecture involved in providing the kind of service mentioned above.

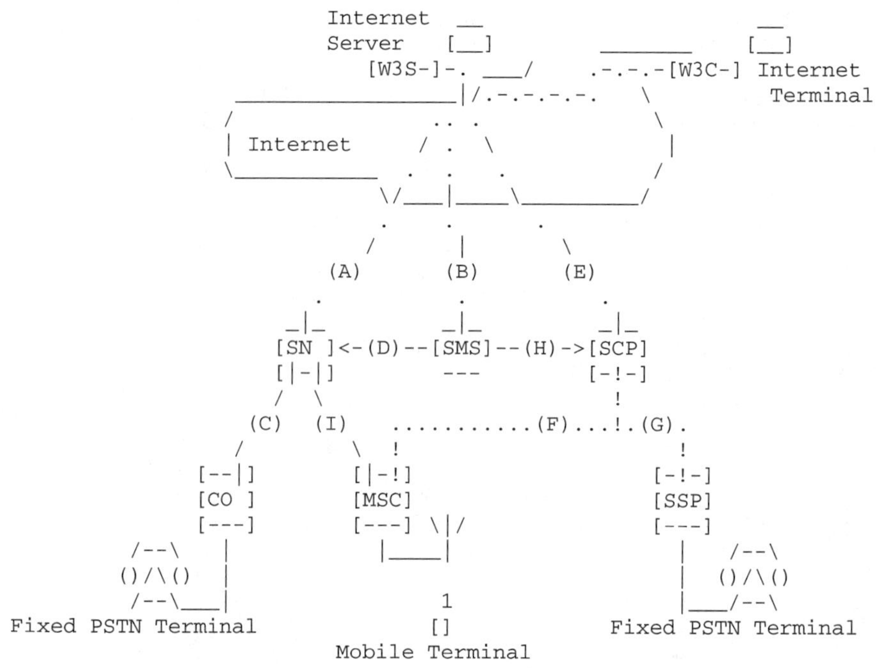

Key: W3S HTTP (Web) Server
W3C HTTP (Web) Client/Browser
CO Central Office (Telephone Exchange)
MSC Mobile Switching Center (Mobile Network Telephone Exchange)
SN Service Node
SSP Service Switching Point
SCP Service Control Point
SMS Service Management System
.-.-. Internet relationship
___ PSTN Access relationship
... PSTN "core" signaling relationship

Figure 6

The interfaces are:

A The interface over which Internet requests for service are delivered to the Service Node

B The interface over which Service Management requests are sent from the Internet to the Service Management System

C The interface over which the Service Node sends call control requests to a connected Central Office

D The interface over which the Service Management System manages the Service Node

E The interface over which Internet requests for service are delivered to the Service Control Point

F The interface over which the Service Control Point sends service call control requests to the Mobile Switching Center

G The interface over which the Service Control Point sends service control requests to the Service Switching Point

H The interface over which the Service Management System manages the Service Control Point

I The interface over which the Service Node sends service call control requests to the Mobile Switching Center

In practice, a number of the interfaces have very similar purposes to one another. The means by which these purposes are achieved differ, in that some of the interfaces (C and I) reflect access arrangements, whilst others (F and G) imply a "core" signaling relationship. However, it is possible to categorize them in terms of the "intent" of messages sent across the interfaces.

For example, Interfaces A and E are similar; one of the main aims of PINT work is to ensure that they are the same. Similarly, Interfaces D and H imply similar actions and are likely to carry similar messages. Interfaces C, F, G, and I are all used to request that a call be initiated, albeit via access or core signaling relationships.

The interfaces can also be viewed in terms of the kind of components that are involved and the bodies by which they are codified. Interfaces A, B, and E are all going to be realized as Internet Protocols. All of the others use existing protocols in the PSTN/IN. Traditionally, these have been codified by different groups, and this is likely to be the case in the PINT work.

The general arrangements for the different systems are shown below (Figures 7, 8, 9, and 10). They differ in the details of their configurations, but the main tasks they perform are very similar, and so the overall operation is similar to the generic architecture shown in Figures 5 and 6.

Key for following diagrams:

Components:

```
W3C     World Wide Web Client
W3S     World Wide Web Server
WSA     Web Server "Back End Program" Interface (CGI or Servlet
        interface)
Srvlt   Servlet "back end" program/objects
FS      Finger Server
SCTPC   Simple Computer Telephony Protocol Client
SCTPS   Simple Computer Telephony Protocol Server
CBC     CallBroker Client
CBS     CallBroker Server
SSTPC   Service Support Transport Protocol Client
SSF     Service Switching Function
SCF     Service Control Function
SRF     Special Resource Function
CO      Central Office/ Public Telephone Exchange
SSP     Service Switching Point
SCP     Service Control Point
SR/I.IP Special Resource/ "Internet" Intelligent Peripheral
SMS     Service Management System
INAPAd  Intelligent Network Application Part Adaptor
PktFlt  Packet Filter (Firewall)
SNMPAg  Simple Network Management Protocol Agent
```

Protocols:

```
P0    HyperText Transfer Protocol
P1    HTTP Server <-> "Back End Program" internal protocol
P2    CallBroker Client <-> CallBroker Server protocol (AT&T system),
   or SCTP Client <-> Server protocol (Nortel system)
P3    PINT User Agent <-> PINT Gateway protocol
P4    Intra-Intelligent Network protocol (e.g., INAP)
P5    Proprietary (INAP-based) Gateway-> I.IP protocol
P6    Finger protocol
P7    Digital Subscriber Signaling 1 protocol
P8    Simple Network Management Protocol
P9    SMS <-> Service Control Point/Service Node protocol
```

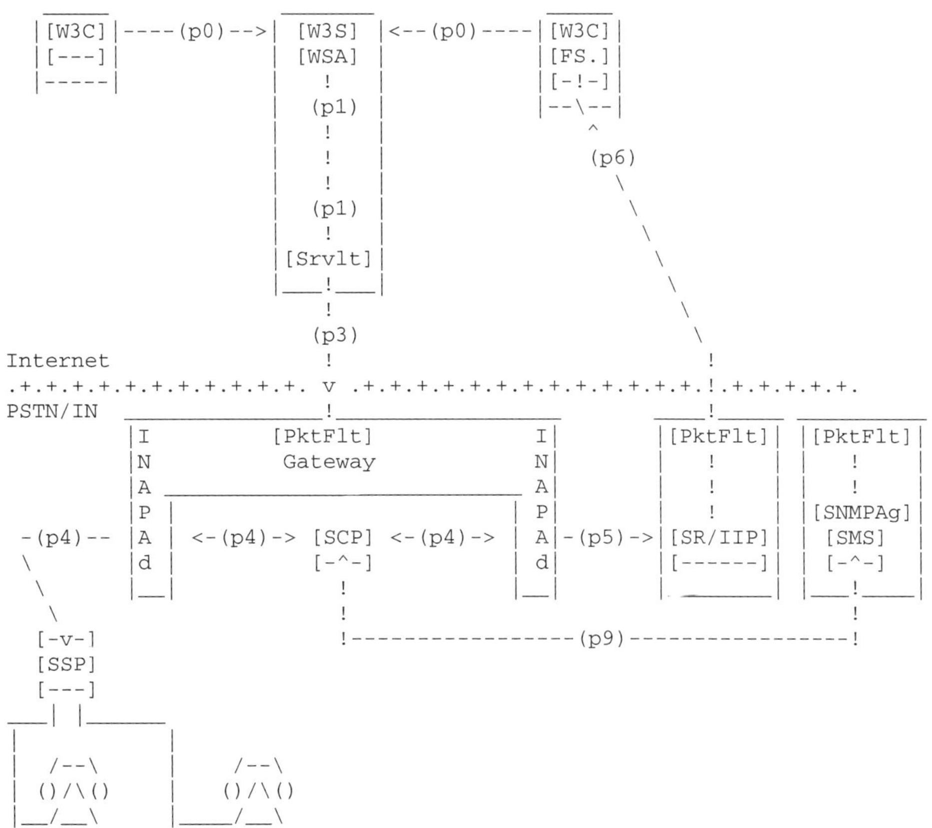

Figure 7: The Siemens Web Call Center

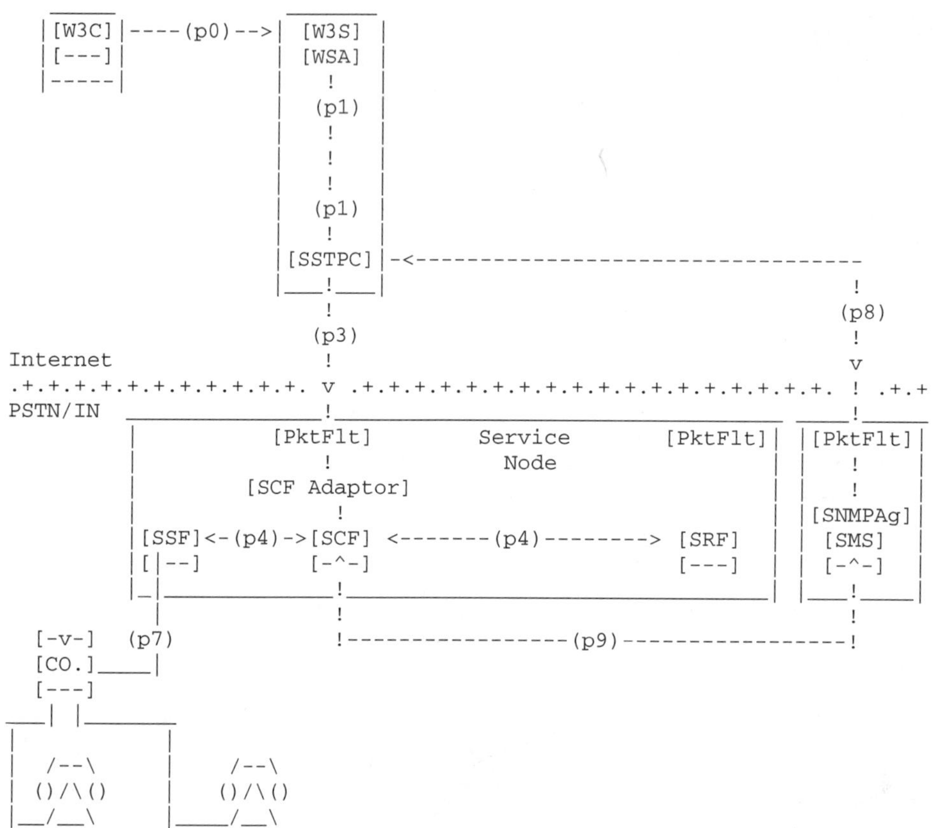

Figure 8: The Lucent System

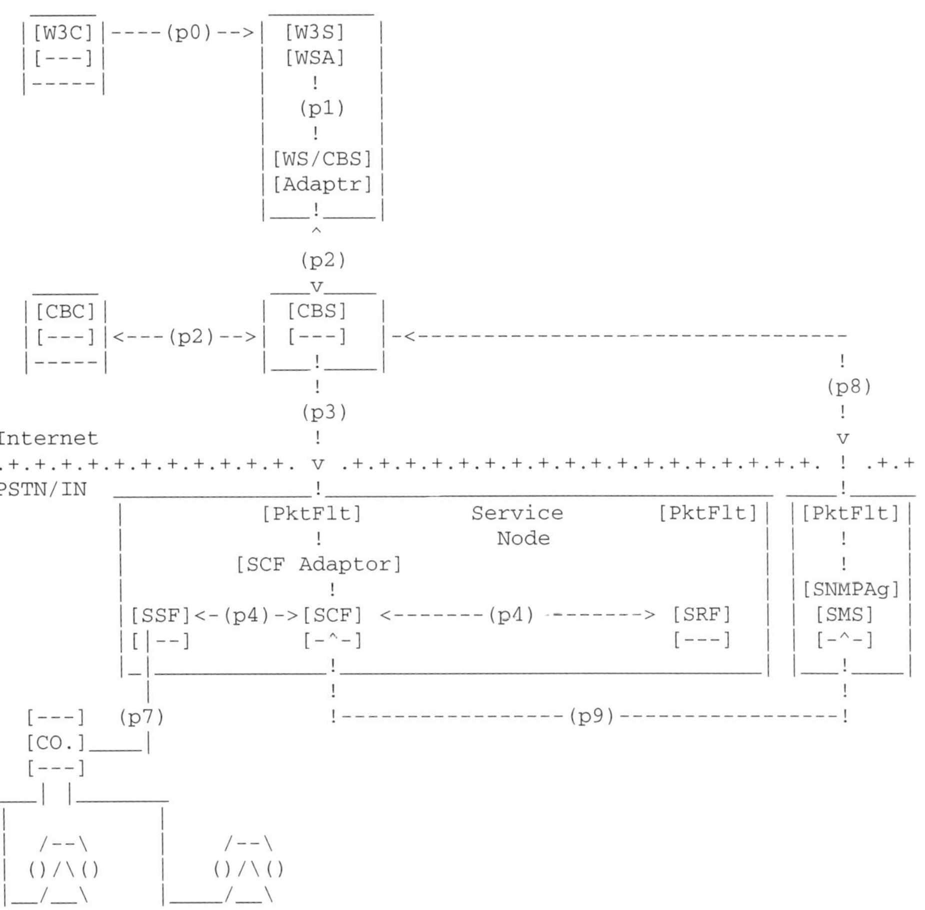

Figure 9: The AT&T System

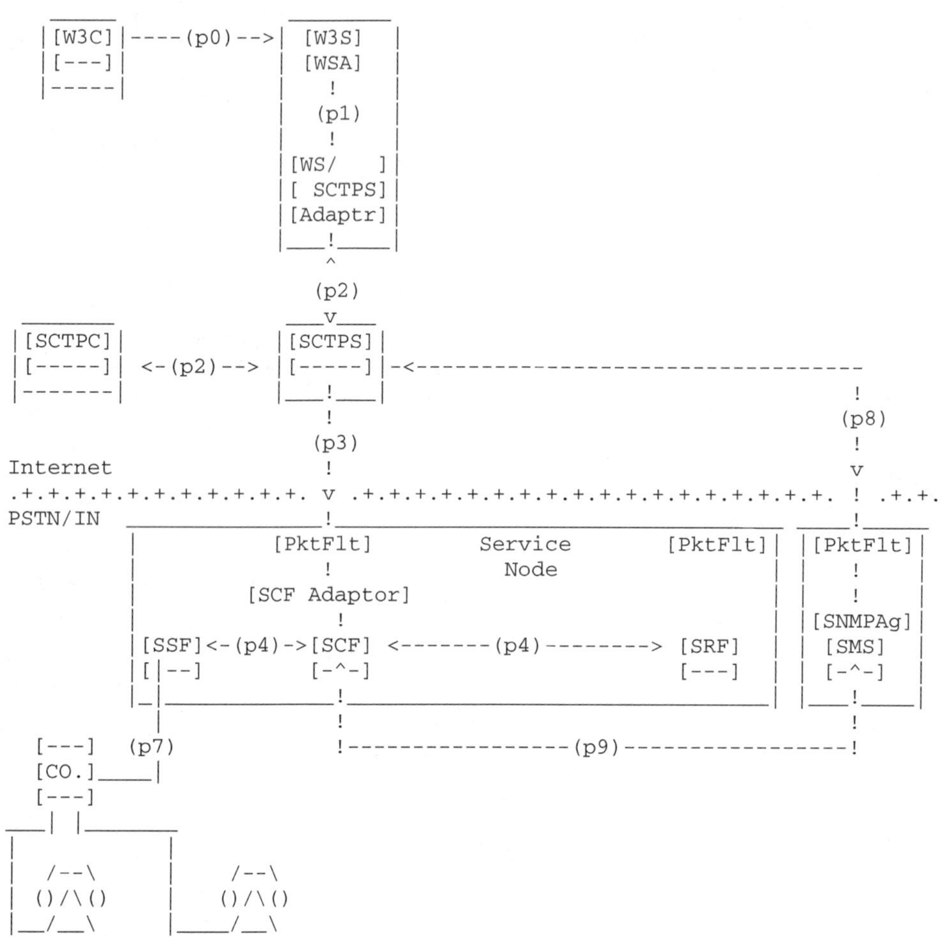

Figure 10: The Nortel System

As these are independent systems developed by different groups, the names of the components, unsurprisingly, don't match. Some features are offered by one of the systems, while they aren't by others. However, there are a number of common features. All of the systems provide a Web-based interface (at least as an option), using "back end" programs to construct protocols to pass onwards to the Intelligent Network system.

Several Intelligent Network Functional Entities are combined into a Service Node in the Lucent, AT&T , and Nortel systems, while in the Siemens scheme they are separate units. However, this is not particularly important for the provision of the services they offer.

The main difference lies in whether or not the SCF is "aware" of the Internet interface and has been modified to be "complicit" in supporting these Internet requests. The Siemens approach was to re-use an existing SCP, providing a gateway function to translate as needed. The Lucent system used a "lighter weight" SCF adapter to terminate the Internet protocols, as the SCF was modified to support the Internet interface directly.

The AT&T CallBroker and Nortel SCTP Servers introduce an intermediate protocol (labeled p2) that allows an alternative to the Web based interface supported by the others. This protocol matches the "CallBroker Client API", or the "SCTP Client API". These options provide for a bi-directional protocol, with indications sent from the Call Broker or SCTP Server to the Client as needed. This is not easily possible using an HTTP-based scheme (and in the Siemens case, a dedicated Finger client/server pair was used to emulate such an interface)

The protocol between the Internet server and the Intelligent Network (labeled p3 in the above diagrams) differs in each of the systems. One of the main aims of future work will be to develop a common protocol that will support the services offered, so that the p3 interface will allow different implementations to inter-operate. In the Lucent, Siemens, and Nortel systems, this was an "internal" protocol, as it was carried between entities within the Service Node or Gateway.

Other contrasts between the systems lie in the support for Internet access to Service Management, and access to the Internet by Special Resources. Internet Management access was most developed in the Lucent system, in which a Simple Network Management Protocol (SNMP) agent was provided to allow inter-operation with the SMS controlling the Service Node. In the Siemens scheme, the SMS had no direct Internet access; any management actions were carried out within the normal PSTN management activities. As for Internet access to special resources, this was only required by the Siemens system as part of its support for Call Center agent notification. Equivalent functionality would be provided in the AT&T and Nortel systems as mentioned above, and this would in turn be associated with event notifications being sent as part of their (p3) Internet/IN protocol. These differences reflect the different emphases in the products as they were developed; again, future work will have to ensure that common protocols can be used to support the chosen services fully.

5. IN-Based Solutions

5.1 The Lucent System

Figure 11 depicts the overall interconnection architecture of the Lucent prototype in support of the four PINT services. The IN-based architecture utilizes the Service Node and Service Management System in addition to the Web server, which enables Web-based access to the PINT services. This section summarizes the roles of these elements (complemented by a click-to-dial-back service scenario), outlines the interfaces of Web Server-Service Node and Web Server-Service Management System (i.e., the interfaces A & B), and addresses the common security concerns.

5.1.1 Roles of the Web Server, Service Node, and Service Management System

Web Server

The Web Server stores the profiles of content providers as well as pre-registered users. The content provider profile contains information such as content provider ID, telephone number, and fax number. In addition, the profile may also include service logic that specifies, for example, the telephone (or fax) number to be reached based on time of the day, day of the week, or geographical location of the user, and the conditions to accept the charge of the calls.

Similar to the content provider profile, the pre-registered user profile contains information such as user name, password, telephone number, and fax number. The last two pieces of information can also be linked to time of the day and day of the week so the user can be reached at the appropriate telephone (or fax) number accordingly.

Service Node

Situated in the PSTN, the SN, like the SCP, performs the service control function [1, 2, 3]. It executes service logic and instructs switches on how to complete a call. The SN also performs certain switching functions (like bridging of calls) as well as a set of specialized functions (like playing announcements, voice recognition and text-to-speech conversion).

Service Management System

The SMS performs administration and management of service logic and customer-related data on the SN. It is responsible for the replication of content provider profiles and provision of these data on the SN. These functions are non-real time.

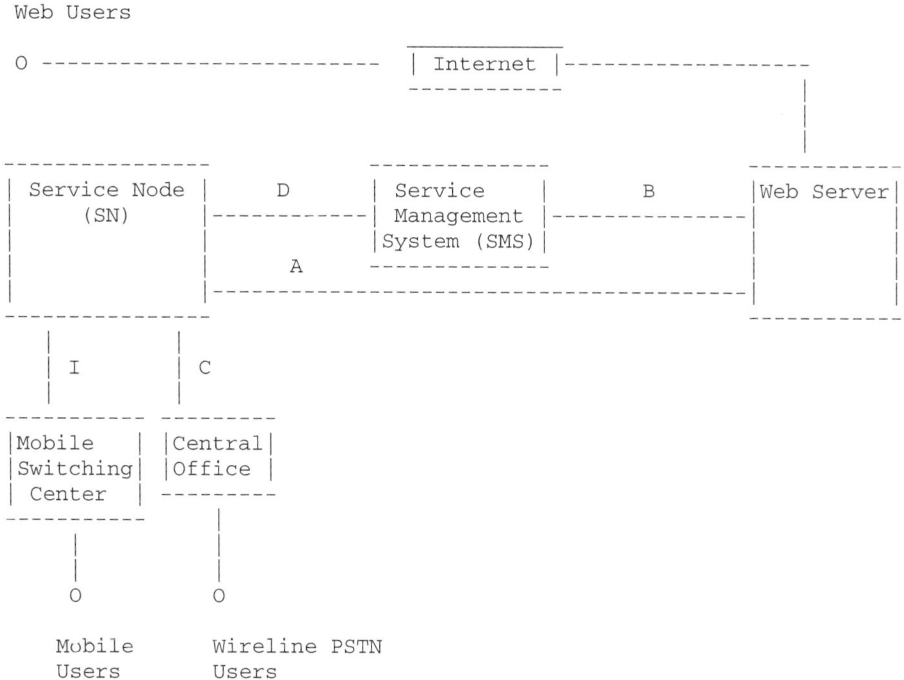

Figure 11: Overall Interconnection Architecture of the Lucent System

5.1.2 A Click-to-Dial-Back Service Scenario

A Web user, who has simultaneous access to the Web and telephone services (this can be achieved, for example, by having an ISDN connection), is browsing through a sales catalogue and deciding to speak to a sales representative.

When the Web user clicks a button inviting a telephone call from the sales office, the Web Server sends a message to the SN over the A interface, thus crossing the Internet-to-PSTN boundary. By matching the information received from the Web Server with the content provider profile that had been previously loaded and activated by the SMS over the D interface, the SN recognizes the signal.

At this point, the SN calls the Web user. The user answers the call, hears an announcement, e.g., "Please wait, while we are connecting you to the sale agent", and is waiting to be connected to the sale agent. Then the SN invokes service logic as indicated in the profile.

The execution of this logic selects an appropriate sales agent to call based on the time of the day. It is 8 P.M. in New York where the Web user is located, and the New York sales office has closed. The San Francisco office, however, is still open, and so the SN makes a call to an agent in that office. Finally, the SN bridges the two calls and establishes a two-party call between the sales agent and the Web user.

5.1.3 Web Server-Service Node Interface

Lucent developed the Service Support Transfer Protocol (SSTP) for communications between the SN and Web Server. SSTP is of a request/response type running on top of a reliable transport layer, such as TCP. The Web Server sends a request to the SN to invoke a service and the SN responds with a message indicating either success or failure. Note that SSTP engages only the service control function [1, 2, 3] of the SN.

5.1.3.1 Web Server to Service Node

In this direction, three kinds of messages may be sent: the Transaction Initiator message, the Data Message, and the End of Data message.

The latter two messages are needed if the service to be invoked involves data (such as the case in click-to-fax, click-to-fax-back and voice-access-to-content). This was so designed to handle the varying size of data and to ensure that the size of each stream is within the allowable size of the underlying transport packet data unit (imposed by some implementations of TCP/IP).

a. Transaction Initiator

This message provides all the necessary information but data for invoking a service. It includes the following information elements:

+ Transaction ID, which uniquely specifies a service request. The same transaction ID should be used for all the accompanying data-related messages, if the service request involves data. One way for generating unique transaction IDs is to concatenate the information: date, time, Web Server ID (uniquely assigned for each one connected to the SN), and transaction sequence number (a cyclic counter incremented for each service request).

+ Service ID, which specifies the service to be invoked. The service may be click-to-dial-back, click-to-fax, click-to-fax-back or voice-access-to-content.

+ Content Provider ID, which uniquely represents the content provider. This information is the key to accessing the content provider's service logic and data on the SN.

+ Content Provider Directory Number, which is the telephone or fax number of the content provider to be called through the PSTN.

+ User Directory Number, which is the telephone or fax number of the user requesting the service.

+ Billed Party, which specifies the party (either the user or content provider), to be billed.

In addition, optional parameters may be sent from the Web Server to the SN. For example, a retry parameter may be sent to specify the number of times the SN will attempt to complete a service request upon failure before the transport connection times out.

b. Data Message

This message provides the (encapsulated) user data part of a service request. For example, in the case of click-to-fax-back such data are the content to be faxed to the user. Each message is composed of the transaction ID and a data segment. The transaction ID must be the same as that of the transaction initiator part first invoking the service.

c. End of Data Message

This message contains the transaction ID and the end of data delimiter. The transaction ID is the same as that of the relevant transaction initiator message.

5.1.3.2 Service Node to Web Server

The SN must respond to a service request from the Web Server. The response message consists of the information elements:

transaction ID, service type, result, time, and error code.

+ Transaction ID, which is the same as that of the original service request.

+ Service Type, which is the same as that of the original service request.

+ Result, which is either success or failure.

+ Time, which indicates the time of the day completing the request.

+ Error Code, which gives the reason for failure. Possible reasons for failure are content provider telephone (or fax) busy, content provider telephone (or fax) no answer, user telephone busy, user refusal to complete, user no answer, nuisance control limit reached, and content provider telephone (or fax) not in the SN database.

5.1.3.3 Usage Scenarios: Click-to-Fax and Click-to-Fax-Back

For the click-to-fax and click-to-fax-back services, the Lucent system implemented only the case where the data to be sent as facsimile reside in the Web server. There are at least three messages that need to be sent from the Web server to the Service Node for these services.

The first message is the Transaction Initiator that identifies the service type as well as a unique Transaction ID. It also includes the sender/receiver fax number.

The next is one or more messages of the data to be faxed. Each message carries the same unique Transaction ID as the above.

Last comes the end of message. It consists of the Transaction ID (again, the same as that of the messages preceding it) and the end of data delimiter.

Upon receiving these messages, the Service Node, equipped with the special resource of a fax card, converts the data into the G3 format, calls the receiver fax, and sends back the result to the Web server immediately. Note that the receiver fax busy or no answer is interpreted as failure. Further, while the receiver fax answering the call is interpreted as success, it does not necessarily mean that the fax would go through successfully.

5.1.4 Web Server-SMS Interface and SNMP MIB

This interface is responsible for uploading the content provider profile from the Web Server to the SMS and for managing the information against any possible corruption. The SN verifies the Content Provider ID and the Content Provider Directory Number sent by the Web Server with the content provider profile pre-loaded from the SMS.

The content provider profile was based on ASN.1 [4] structure and SNMP [5] was used to set/get the object identifiers in the SMS database.

Following is an example of the simple MIB available on the SMS.

```
inwebContProviderTable OBJECT-TYPE
        SYNTAX          SEQUENCE OF InwebContProviderEntry
        MAX-ACCESS      not-accessible
        STATUS          current
        DESCRIPTION
                " A table containing Content Provider profiles "
        := { inweb 1}

inwebContProviderEntry OBJECT-TYPE
        SYNTAX          InwebContProviderEntry
        MAX-ACCESS      not-accessible
        STATUS          current
        DESCRIPTION
                " A conceptual row of the inweb. Each row
                        contains profile of one Content Provider"
        INDEX   { inwebSmsNumber }
        := { inwebContProviderTable 1 }

InwebContProviderEntry := SEQUENCE {
        inwebSmsNumber                    Integer32,
        inwebContentProviderId            Integer32,
        inwebContentProviderPhoneNumber Integer32,
        inwebContentProviderFaxNumber   Integer32
        }

inwebSmsNumber OBJECT-TYPE
        SYNTAX          Integer32
        MAX-ACCESS      read-only
        STATUS          current
        DESCRIPTION
                " Serial number of the SMS - used for SNMP indexing "
        := { inwebContProviderEntry 1 }

inwebContentProviderId OBJECT-TYPE
        SYNTAX          Integer32
        MAX-ACCESS      read-create
        STATUS          current
        DESCRIPTION
                " A number that uniquely identifies each Content
Provider "
        := { inwebContProviderEntry 2 }

inwebContentProviderPhoneNumber OBJECT-TYPE
        SYNTAX          Integer32
        MAX-ACCESS      read-create
        STATUS          current
```

RFC 2458 25

```
         DESCRIPTION
                 " Content Provider's Phone Number "
         := { inwebContProviderEntry 3 }

   inwebContentProviderFaxNumber OBJECT-TYPE
         SYNTAX         Integer32
         MAX-ACCESS     read-create
         STATUS         current
         DESCRIPTION
                 " Content Provider's Fax Number "
         := { inwebContProviderEntry 4 }
```

5.1.5 Security Considerations

The Lucent prototype addressed the security issues concerning the interface between the Web Server and the SN. Those concerning the interface between the Web Server and SMS, which was based in SNMP, were handled by the built-in security features of SNMP.

+ Secure Communication Links

If the Network Operator (PSTN provider) is also the Web Service provider, the Web Server and SN/SMS will communicate over a corporate intranet. This network is almost always protected by the corporation's firewall and so can be deemed secure. This was the case handled by the Lucent prototype.

Nevertheless, if different corporations serve as the Network Operator and the Web Service Provider, then it is likely that there may not exist a dedicated secure communication link between the Web Server and SN/SMS. This raises serious security considerations. One possible solution is to use Virtual Private Networks (VPN). VPN features support authentication of the calling and called parties and encryption of the messages sent over insecure links (such as those on the Internet).

+ Non-Repudiation

All transactions were logged on both the Web Server and the Service Node to account for all operations in case of doubt or dispute. The log information on the SN may also be used to generate bills.

+ Malicious Requests of Users

A user may make repeated requests to a content provider directory number maliciously. This scenario was handled by setting a Nuisance Control Limit (NCL) on either the SN or the Web Server or both. The NCL has two parameters: one defining the number of requests from a user and the other the period over which these requests takes place.

A user may also attempt to request a call from a directory number other than that of a content provider. This scenario was handled by verifying the directory number (and the content provider ID) against the database on the SN containing all the content provider information. If the directory number (or the content provider ID) was not in the database, the request would be rejected.

5.2 Siemens Web Call Center

5.2.1 Service Description

The Web Call Center is an Intelligent Network System that accepts requests from Internet nodes for services to be provided on the PSTN. As the name suggests, it was designed to support a cluster of services that, taken together, provide a subset of the features of a Call Center, with almost all user interactions provided via World Wide Web requests and responses. See the appendix for a background description of Call Center Features.

From an Intelligent Network perspective, there are a number of services that, when combined, provide the Call Center features. The Call Center features as implemented supported the scenario in which a customer makes a request to be called back by an agent at a time of the customer's choosing to discuss an item of interest to him or her. The agent will be selected based on his or her availability and expertise in this topic; the agent will be told whom he or she is calling and the topic of interest, and then the agent will be connected to the customer.

In addition, the individual services that were deployed to support this scenario provided support for management of the list of available agents as well. This involved allowing the agent to "log into" and "out of" the system and to indicate whether the agent was then ready to handle calls to the customer. The list of services, as seen from a user perspective, follows.

The services support:

i) Customer Request service - the customer explores a corporate Web site, selects a link that offers to request an agent to call the customer back and then is redirected to the Web Call Center server. This presents customer with a form asking for name, the telephone number at which he or she wishes to be called, and the time at which the call is to be made. Note will also be made of the page to which the customer was referred to when he or she was redirected. Once the form has been returned, the customer receives an acknowledgment page listing the parameters he or she has entered.

ii) Agent Registration/Logon - An agent requests a "login" page on the Web Call Center server. The service checks whether it has a record of an agent present at the Internet node from which th call is made. If not, then the caller will be sent a form allowing him or her to enter the service identity, the company's agent identifier and password. On return, the service identity and company agent identifier will be checked against a list of known identities. If found, the password will be checked, and if this matches the record held by the service then a new session record is made of this identity and the Internet node from which the call has been made.

NB: This is very similar to the Universal Personal Telecommunications (UPT) service feature "register for incoming calls". It implies that the identified person has exclusive use of the Internet node from that point onwards, so messages for them can be directed there.

iii) Agent Ready - an agent who has already logged on can indicate that he or she is ready by requesting an appropriate "ready" page on the Web Call Center Server. The service will match the agent by the Internet node Identifier and Agent Identity passed along with the Web request against its list of "active" agents. It will mark them as being ready to handle calls in its list of available agents (with their pre-defined skill set).

iv) Agent Not Ready - an agent can request an appropriate "ready" page on the Web Call Center Server to indicate that he or she is temporarily not ready to handle calls.

v) Agent Logoff - an agent can request an appropriate "Logout" page on the Web Call Center Server to indicate that he or she is no longer associated with a particular Internet node. The service will match the agent by the Internet Node Identifier and Agent Identity passed along with the Web request against its list of "active" agents. Once found, the session record for that agent is removed and the caller is notified of this with an acknowledgment page.

NB: This is very similar to the UPT "unregister" service feature.

vi) Call Center Agent Selection and Notification - When the time that the customer selected has arrived and an available agent with the right skills has been selected from the appropriate list, this service will send a notification to the Internet node associated with that agent. A dedicated server is assumed to be running on the agent's machine that, on receiving the notification, triggers the agent's browser into requesting a "Agent Call In" page from the Web Call Center Server. Once the agent's machine has made this request, he or she will be told that there is a customer to call.

NB: This is similar to a "Message Waiting" or "Wake Up Call" service.

Note: As implemented, the agent is led automatically into the following service (the returned Web page includes an automatic reload command).

vii) Agent Instruction - a selected agent makes a request of the "Customer Processing" page on the Web Call Center Server. The Internet node Identifier and Agent Identity the agent uses will be matched against a list of agents expected to handle calls, and the instructions for the calls will be returned to the agent.

NB: This is similar to a "Voice Mail Replay" message service, but in this case the message is automatically generated; there is no associated voice mail record feature accessible.

Note: As implemented, the instructions page will include a number of buttons, allowing the agent to view the page the customer was looking at when he or she made the request, and to trigger the customer callback (as described next).

ix) Agent/Customer Telephony Callback - the agent will make a request of a "dial-back" page on the Web Call Center Server. The Internet node Identifier and Agent Identity he or she uses will be matched against a list of agents expected to handle calls, and, when the appropriate records have been found, the service will make the telephone call through to the customer and then connect the agent to this telephone call (using the telephone number registered in the respective Call Center service record).

5.2.2 Implementation

5.2.2.1 Introduction

The Siemens Web Call Center used an existing IN system and service logic that supported Call Center features. The scenario it supports is very similar to the Siemens IN-based Call Center on which it was based; one of the goals was to minimize changes to the service offered. It is also virtually identical to the service "Internet Requested Telephony Dial-back" provided by the Lucent system.

As provided via the Internet, the services involved are mostly the same as those provided via the PSTN and IN alone. The main differences lie in the use of the World Wide Web as an interface to the services rather than a telephone, SSP, and Intelligent Peripheral. Also, the feature by which a telephone call is made between the agent and the customer is implemented within the IN system in a different way; this is the only element in which the PSTN is involved.

5.2.2.2 Web Call Center Configuration

The general arrangement for the Web Call Center system is shown in Figure 7. The components that were added to an existing IN system to deal with the Internet interface are described next.

In addition to the SCP, SSP and SMS that were part of the original IN-based system, another unit was included to send notification messages to agents; in the IN system the agents were sent "wake up" telephone calls when they were required to handle their next customers' call back. This unit is called the "Internet Intelligent Peripheral", and its use is described later under "Non-World Wide Web Interactions".

As there was a need to re-use as many of the existing IN components unchanged, a Gateway unit to deal with the interface between the Internet and the SCP was provided. This injected INAP (Intelligent Network Application Protocol) messages into the SCP, making it think that it had received an Initial DP trigger from an SSP. It also intercepted the "Connect To Resource" and "Prompt and Collect" INAP messages sent from the SCP, acting on these to return the parameters generated by the Internet users when they filled in the forms that triggered the service transaction. It also translated the "Play Announcement" message sent to the Intelligent Peripheral into a form that it could use. Finally, it passed on the INAP message used by the SCP to trigger SSP into making the telephone call back.

5.2.2.3 User Interaction

In the IN/PSTN-based system, the services have contact with the customers and agents via their telephones, SSPs, and Intelligent Peripherals programmed to play announcements to them and to capture their responses. These responses are indicated by DTMF tones sent by pressing keys on the telephones.

In this case, almost all interactions are provided via World Wide Web requests and responses. The sequence of announcements and responses for each service are "collapsed" into individual form filling transactions, and the requests are not limited to digits (or "star" and "hash"). The implications of the use of forms on service operation are covered in more detail later (under HTTP/IN Service mapping).

5.2.2.4 Service/Caller Identifiers

When provided via the IN/PSTN-based system, the services are passed the Calling Line Identity (CLI) of the caller and the number the caller dials (the DN). The CLI value is used extensively to identify the caller and (in the case of the agent) to index into service data tables to decide what to do next. While an equivalent value to the DN is passed to the Web-based transactions as the requested Universal Resource Locator (URL), the CLI cannot be given reliably. The nearest equivalent caller identifier is the IP Address of the customer or agent's machine. However, the use of HTTP proxies means that this "original" Internet node Address may not be available; if a proxy is used then its IP Address will be associated with the request.

In providing these Call Center features the customer only has one Web-based transaction; that of providing the initial request for a PSTN telephone callback. To do so he or she will have to fill in a form so as to specify not only the time to be called back, but also the telephone number to be reached. These values can be used if needed to identify the customer, and so the problem of originating Internet Node ambiguity is not relevant.

With the agents, however, there are sequences of coupled transactions, and the particular sequence must be identified. There will be a number of such transactions being carried out at once, and there needs to be some identifier to show which agent is being handled in each case.

Such an identifier is not part of a sequence of basic Web transactions. In a Web transaction, the HTTP Client/Web Browser makes a request, and the HTTP Server will respond to this, normally including some content in its reply message that will be processed by the browser, after which it closes the TCP connection. That's the end of the transaction; the HTTP client and server cannot normally maintain state information beyond this point. Any sequence is reduced to a set of unrelated transactions.

A result of this simple pattern is that any state information reflecting longer or more complex interactions must be stored (at least partially) in the client system. One approach is the use of cookies [6]. These can be set by HTTP servers as part of their response to a request, and will be sent back with all subsequent requests for appropriate URLs as extra HTTP headers. These cookies allow the HTTP server to identify the client in the following requests, so that it can continue an extended session with the client.

Cookies are used in providing the Internet Call Center. Persistent cookies are installed into the Web Browser on machines that are to be used by call center agents as a service management (pre-service) task. The cookie value is unique to the machine and is used to index into a list of machine IP addresses that is stored as part of the service data.

Also, a session cookie is stored onto the agent's machine when the agent registers, and is cleared when he or she de-registers. This is used to identify the agent and so the IP address of the node with which the agent is associated (and from which the agent's subsequent requests should originate). The services that interact with Call Center agents use the agent session cookie value as an identifier; in principle this is unnecessary but it does simplify the session data lookup procedure. The rest of the services use the persistent machine identifier in place of the CLI, indexing into their service data using it. Both cookies are sent with each agent request; if they are not present, then the request is redirected to other services (for example to the agent Logon service).

5.2.2.5 Mapping from HTTP Transactions to IN-Based Service Features

All of the client-initiated services require user interaction. With the IN/PSTN-based system, the majority of the services are typified by the callers being connected to an announcement unit that plays them a list of choices and captures their selection. The caller can pre-dial the digits needed; in this case the prompts are not needed and are not made.

The pattern of operation is somewhat different in the Internet case, as the initial HTTP request returns a response, after which the Web transaction has ended. Where that initial response returns a form to be filled in by the caller, subsequently submitting the form initiates a new HTTP transaction. This is all part of one instance of service, however. The service consists of two request/response pairs in tandem.

Although it is possible to design a service to handle this pair of Web transactions as a single unit, it may be better to reconfigure it. The design of a service that deals with two Web exchanges as a single extended transaction is quite complex. It must maintain state across the pair of Web exchanges, and it has to handle a number of failure cases including dealing with time-outs and "out of time" submission of forms. The alternative is to split the service into two sub-features. The first of these reflects the initial request and delivery of the form by return, with the second one dealing with processing of the submitted form and returning any confirmation by reply.

The services offered don't all require form-filling, and so can be treated as a single IN feature. There are two cases where forms are required. The first of these is the Customer Request service, while the other one is the "Agent Registration" service. In both cases the initial Web transaction (by which the form is requested and returned to the client) need not involve specific service logic processing; the initial delivery of the form to a customer or agent can be handled by a "normal" Web Server. In both cases the service logic is only triggered when the form is submitted; this means that, again, each of the services can be treated as a single IN feature.

The IN service logic that deals with these requests has a general pattern of action. An HTTP request is received, and this triggers the IN service logic into action. The service logic "sees" this as an Initial DP message and starts its processing as if it had been sent from an SSF. The SCF uses what appears to it to be an Intelligent Peripheral to collect the parameters of the request, and then to send back final announcements to the requesting entity.

The main difference, from the perspective of the IN service logic running on the SCF, is that the service does not need to instruct the SSF to make a temporary connection to the Intelligent Peripheral. It is as if this connection had already been made. Similarly, there is no need to close the service transaction by sending an explicit "Continue Execution" message to the SSF.

The sequence of "prompt/collect" instructions used to collect service parameters from a caller in an IN service maps quite well to a sequence of requests to extract a data value from the HTTP request, based on a tag. This is a fairly standard feature of Web Server CGI or Servlet processing. Using this mapping minimizes the changes to the service design, in that the service logic "sees" an Intelligent Peripheral to which it sends normal "Request Report Prompt & Collect" messages, and from which it receives data values in response.

All services have to fit in with the underlying HTTP interaction pattern, and so will be expected to send a final "Announce" instruction to the Intelligent Peripheral at the end of the service; this is done in many IN services anyway and in all of the service features described here. These announcements form the content returned to the Web Client.

5.2.2.6 Non-World Wide Web Interactions

There are two exceptions to the sole use of the World Wide Web for interaction. The first one occurs in the "Message Waiting"/"Wake Up Call" service by which the selected agent is informed of a callback request. World Wide Web transactions are very simple; the client browser makes a request for content associated with a particular HTTP URL, and the server sends a response, marking the end of the transaction. The server cannot make a spontaneous association with a client; it must be initiated by the client request.

While it would be possible for the server to defer closing an earlier transaction (by not sending back all of the content specified and leaving the TCP connection open) it was decided that an alternative scheme would be more convenient. The "wake up call" was arranged by an "Internet Intelligent Peripheral" sending a request to a daemon process running on the selected agent's machine, using the Finger protocol [7]. The daemon sent back a standard response, but in addition the Web Browser on the agent's machine was triggered into making a further HTTP request of the server. In this way the "Agent Instruction" transaction is started automatically, while still allowing it to use a normal HTTP request/response pattern.

The second exception occurs in the final "Agent/Customer Telephony Callback" service. While this transaction is initiated by the agent selecting a link on the "call instructions page" returned to them, and includes a "confirmation" page being sent back to them in an HTTP response, the purpose of this service is to make a telephone connection via the PSTN between the agent's telephone and the customer's telephone. It is the only service element that involves the PSTN directly. From an IN/PSTN perspective, the resulting telephone connection is different from that provided in the scheme using the IN and PSTN alone. In this case, a PSTN call is made out to the agent's telephone, another call is made out to the customer's telephone, and these calls are bridged. This differs from the earlier scheme, in which the agent originated a call to the voice mail replay system, and this call was redirected to a new destination (the customer's telephone). As this feature differs in purpose from the other services, and it requires a different implementation within the IN and PSTN system, it was organized as a separate service in this case.

5.2.2.7 Security Considerations

In the case of this system, assumptions were made that the interface presented to requesting agents and customers was provided via a fire wall to deal with most attacks on the IN components. The interface appeared as a Web Server, and there was no direct access to the HTTP documents served, nor to the servlets providing the service logic.

The Callback service was deemed to have simpler security requirements than other IN services as it was akin to a free phone "1-800" service access number; the agents work for the service subscriber and are not charged directly. Similarly, the requesting customer is not charged for his or her request, nor for the resulting call back. Service subscribers would be willing to pay the costs of telephone calls generated as a result of this cluster of services, and the costs of running the agent services could be charged directly to them. As such the authorization for service is defined by the contract between the service subscriber and the service provider.

Authentication of agents was seen as a problem. As an interim measure, cookies were used, but this scheme delivers the cookie data as a plain text item (a header of the Web request). Secure Socket Layer connections were required for communication with the agent services, and this had an impact on the performance of the IN system.

5.2.3 Derived Requirements/Lessons

Security is seen as a major issue. A firewall was used to control access to the IN Components. Similarly, SSL was used for communication with the Agents, so as to protect the cookie values that they were sending with their requests.

For other services, it is likely that the entity from which requests appear to originate will be charged for the service to be rendered. This has implications in terms of authentication and authorization of service provision at the time of the request. It is necessary for the service to be authorized in such a way that non-repudiation is ensured; this is likely to mean that a certificate of identity be provided from the person making the request, and that this can be tied in with a financial account that that person has with the service provider. The certificate can then be stored as part of the billing record. While the process of electronic commerce is outside of the scope of this work, the mechanism by which a request for confirmation of identity is passed out to the requesting user and is delivered back to the service logic must be considered.

When changing from a "pure" IN/PSTN system to one supporting requests via the Internet, the differences in the way that clients interacted with the services meant that the service logic had to be redesigned. It was realized that maintaining the state of a service during its processing was going to be a problem; this problem was side-stepped by re-engineering the services as form processors, allowing them to deal with fully specified requests as a single (Web) transaction. In addition, a "normal" Web Server was used to deliver the forms to the users. This is a change from the IN system, where the equivalent of the form (the prompts) were sent in sequence as part of the same service process.

The Call Center features provided suited this change. However, this may not be the case for other IN services. It is quite common for services to be designed such that the user is prompted for a response, and the service continues dependent on this response. The Web form presents all of the options at once, so this kind of variant prompt/collect sequence is not possible. From this, it is difficult to see how an IN service could be reused without some degree of modification.

An intermediate "gateway" system was provided to "cocoon" the service logic as far as possible from the details of the components with which it was working. Where needed, this unit translated calls from the service logic into commands that operated with the Internet (and the Web Server that acted as the interface). Our experience was that an SCP could be "spoofed" into thinking that it was operating with other IN components in the normal way. Within the limits of the service used, this proved simpler than was originally expected.

Selecting this simple approach still allows a considerable range of services to be provided while maintaining any investment in existing IN systems. Modification of existing IN service logic was also easier than feared. All of the services examined provided announcements at the end of the service transaction, and this could be used to trigger a Web response to be sent back to the requesting Internet user. The changes to the Call Center service logic turned out to be minor; it took as long to analyze the service and see how it could be arranged as a sequence of "form processing" transactions as it did to make the changes to the service logic.

In the Siemens Web Call Center, the "Internet Intelligent Peripheral" with which the service logic communicated was running as a separate program on the same node. Where more complex behavior is required of it (such as conversion of text to speech data and interface with the PSTN) then it would almost certainly be on a separate node. If data is transferred from the Internet in such a scheme, any intermediate gateway would be involved in relaying the data to this node.

6. Alternative Solutions

6.1 The AT&T System

AT&T developed a framework for controlling voice and voice-band data (e.g., fax) and for providing PINT services. Key to the framework is CallBroker, a logical entity that acts on behalf of a user to set up sessions and make requests for PSTN resources. The sessions typically include initiation of calls between two or more end points specified by the user. In addition to its interactions with the PSTN for call setup, the CallBroker is responsible for other functions, when necessary, such as authentication and usage recording.

This section briefly discusses the protocol at the two interfaces that need to be defined and the corresponding APIs to provide the above services. The two interfaces are (1) the one between the CallBroker (or Web Server) and the Service Control Function in the Service Node in the PSTN and (2) the one between the IP client and the CallBroker. The latter interface, in particular, will enable service providers to extend the architecture defined here to serve as a platform for other advanced/value-added services (to be identified later). In addition, the view taken here is that the IP client is more general, and implements a protocol for communication with the CallBroker that allows full two-way communications. For example, this is required for the cases where a called party hangs up and an indication may be necessary to be given to the IP Client about this status/progress. This is also necessary when conferencing to give an indication/status of various parties joining the call.

RFC 2458 37

6.1.1 High Level Architecture

A high level architecture depicting various logical entities and the Interfaces among these logical Entities and the IP Client is shown in Figure 12.

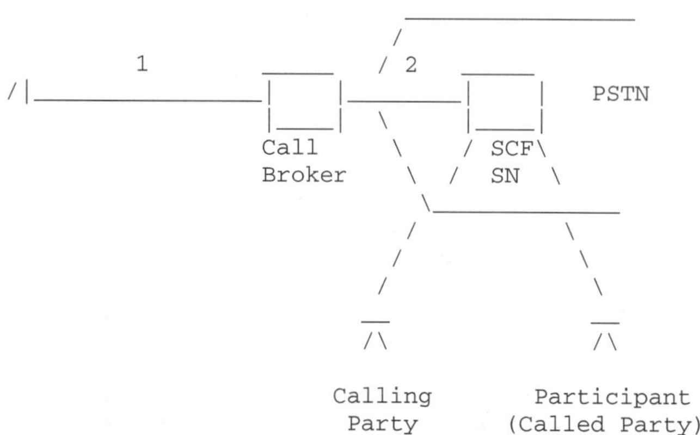

Figure 12: The CallBroker Architecture

The CallBroker, in addition to the initiation and control of calls on behalf of the user, performs additional functions. These functions include authenticating the IP Client, usage recording, and management of the session for the IP Client for the telephony call. The notion of the session requires that a client state machine be maintained in the CallBroker. This also helps in notifying the IP Client about the status/progress of the requests generated from the IP Client.

From the perspective of the IP Client, the logical entities needed for the above functions are within the CallBroker and are as shown in Figure 13 below. These correspond to the functions already discussed: Usage Recording Function, Session Management Function, Voice Bridge, and the Authentication Function. The fact that some of these functions may be physically separate from the CallBroker (such as the Voice Bridge being in the PSTN) is not inconsistent with the general view adopted here. Thus, the CallBroker Model mediates requests for network services and enables us to define various value added services in the future.

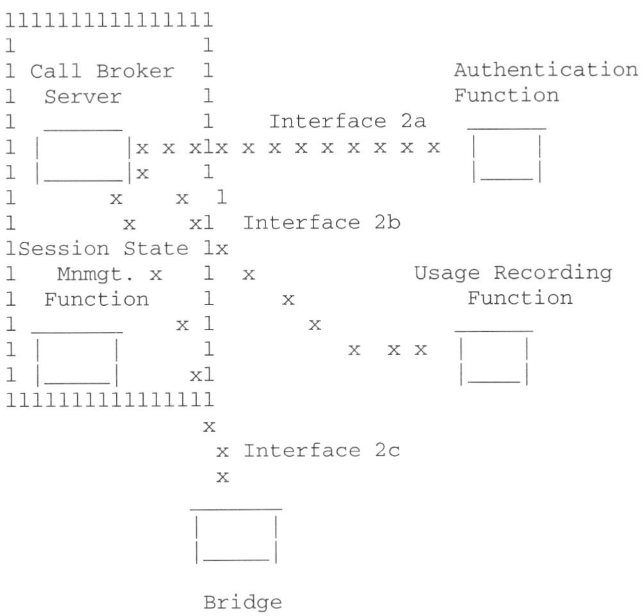

Figure 13: Functional Entities in the Call Broker

Various interfaces (i.e., 2a, 2b, 2c in Figure 13) between different functional entities in the CallBroker may also be standardized. The Session State Management Function may be physically realized as part of the CallBroker Server.

6.1.2 IP Client to CallBroker Interface

Communication on the IP Client to CallBroker Interface (Interface 1 in Figure 12) is a simple ASCII based protocol running directly on TCP. The messages on this interface are primarily requests from the client to the CallBroker, responses from the CallBroker to the IP client responding to the requests and unsolicited events from the CallBroker to the IP client. Since the communication is not strictly transaction oriented, traditional encapsulation protocols like HTTP cannot be used. There has been some ongoing work attempting to use multiple concurrent HTTP POST requests to support event delivery but, without too much difficulty, the ASCII protocol specified here can easily be mapped to the POST payload of the HTTP protocol.

6.1.3 Protocol

Basic Format

The basic format of the protocol is as follows:

```
[header]<<LF>
<<LF>
[body]<<LF>
<<LF>
<<LF>
```

The header and body of the protocol are separated by 2 line feed characters. The format of the header and the body is described below. Line feed characters in the header or body will be escaped using simple URL encoding.

Header

```
[session-id | 0]<<LF>
[message-id]<<LF>
[version-info]<<LF>
```

All CallBroker transactions are identified by sessions. A session does not necessarily correspond one-to-one to a TCP session. If the IP client is attempting to initiate a new session with the CallBroker the session-id field is populated with '0' to indicate session creation request. Every session request needs to be accompanied by sufficient information regarding authentication for the CallBroker to create the session.

Message-id represents the operation of the message.

Version-info contains optional version information of the protocol. This is to aid possible version mismatch detection and graceful error recovery.

Body

The body of the protocol messages consists of name value pairs. These name-value pairs are interpreted with reference to the message-id which signifies the operation to be performed by the CallBroker.

6.1.4 APIs Exposed to the IP Client

The APIs of the CallBroker exposed to the IP client are distinct and different from the APIs that the CallBroker uses from the different supporting subsystems including the authentication subsystem and the usage recording subsystem. The IP client APIs enable clients to effectively control voice conferencing.

6.1.5 Voice-Bridge Control API

The Voice Bridge Control API is used by CallBroker applications to access voice bridging functionality. The API distinguishes between sessions and calls. Calls represent actual voice calls placed from/to the voice bridge. These calls can be grouped together in sessions. All the calls that belong to a session are bridged. Calls have a significance outside the scope of sessions. Every call can be associated with multiple sessions with different weights at the same time. The advantage of this approach is the ability to support concepts like whispering in a conference call. Calls can also be dropped from a conference session and bridged together in a new session to give the notion of a sub-conference. These calls can later be re-added to the main conference session.

6.2 Simple Computer Telephony Protocol

6.2.1 Overview

The Simple Computer Telephony Protocol (SCTP) is a third party call control protocol and as such does not comply with the PINT charter. SCTP is described in this section to show how PINT services could be implemented using SCTP, and where SCTP fits into the PINT architecture.

In addition to third party call control, SCTP also provides subscriber (i.e., user) feature management (e.g., allows a user to set do not disturb, call forwarding parameters), and subscriber monitoring of terminal, line and address status. SCTP is strictly client/server-based. It has no provisions for peer to peer communications. SCTP runs as a TCP application protocol. It is ASCII-based and uses sockets. The SCTP Server is usually connected to a switch via a CTI (Computer-Telephony Integration) connection. Because of this, feature interactions are limited to those within the context of a single call, and not between PSTN services. The SCTP Server within a PINT Gateway could also be connected to an SN, or an SCP. See figures below. SCTP does NOT carry media.

6.2.2 How SCTP Fits in with the Reference PINT Services

SCTP Client as Part of a Web Server

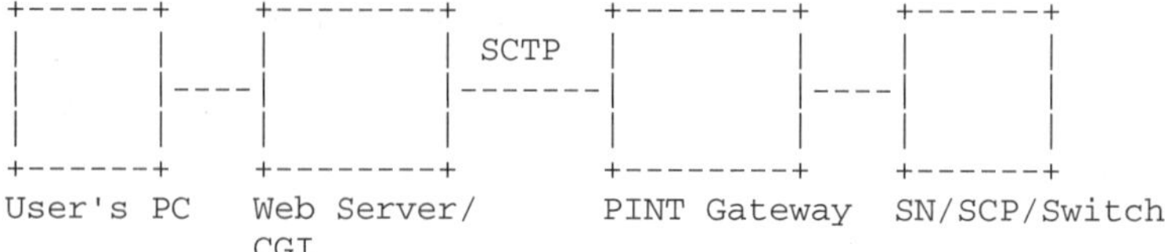

Figure 14: SCTP Client as Part of a Web Server

In this architecture, the SCTP Client is embedded in the Web Server. It is there for the specific purpose of initiating calls to the PSTN based on user requests. The SCTP Server is within the PINT Gateway. We go through the classic PINT examples:

Click-to-dial-back: The SCTP Client issues an SCTP MakeCall to the SCTP Server with the calling number supplied by Web page, and called number supplied by the user.

Click-to-fax-back: SCTP Client issues an SCTP MakeCall to the SCTP Server with called number set to user's fax machine, and calling number set to Web Server's fax machine, and treatment set to the URI for the file to be faxed. The SCTP Server takes the file and feeds it into the call just as a fax machine would.

Click-to-fax: SCTP Client issues an SCTP MakeCall with calling number set to user's fax machine, and called number set to Web Server's fax machine. How the file is supplied to the user's fax machine is outside the scope of SCTP.

Voice-access-to-content: SCTP Client issues an SCTP MakeCall with called number set to user's telephone number, and calling number set to Web Server and treatment set to a URI for the file of the particular Web page to be read to the called number. The SCTP Server takes care of the file to voice conversion and this is fed into the call as if it were voice.

In all of the above cases, the SCTP Client can generate a variety of different Web pages to send to the Web Server via CGI (Common Gateway Interface). The content of these pages is based on the call completion status of the CallMake SCTP action.

SCTP Client Running on the User's PC

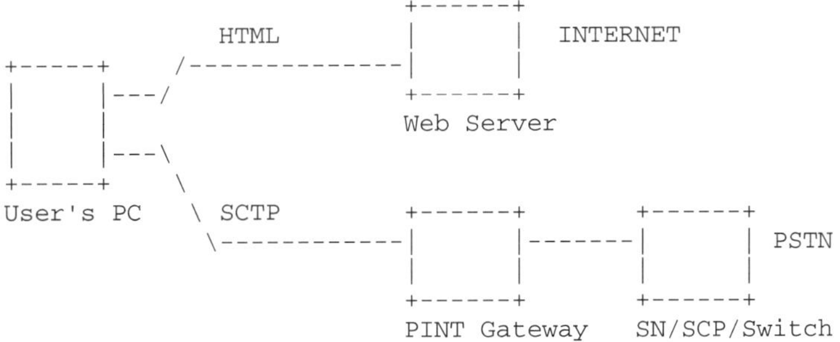

Figure 15: SCTP Client Running on the User's PC

In this architecture, the user has an SCTP Client co-located with it. If the user is using the telephone line for connection to a Web Server and there is an incoming call, then the SCTP Server in the PINT Gateway will post this event to thc SCTP Client. A window will pop up on the user's screen with options available to the user for handling of the incoming call. The user can choose to take the call, send it to voice mail, or send it to another number.

For the Fax back service, for example, if the user had a separate fax machine from his or her PC, then the SCTP Server would tell the SCTP Client there is an incoming fax. The user would end or suspend his or her Internet connection, the fax would come in, and the user could then resume the Internet connection.

7. Session Initiation Protocol--An Emerging Standard

7.1 Overview

SIP, the Session Initiation Protocol, is a simple signaling protocol for Internet conferencing and telephony. It is currently under development within the IETF MMUSIC (Multiparty Multimedia Session Control) Working Group.

SIP provides the necessary mechanisms to support the following services:

- call forwarding, including the equivalent of 700-, 800- and 900-type calls;
- call-forwarding no answer;

- call-forwarding busy;
- call-forwarding unconditional;
- other address-translation services;
- callee and calling "numbers" delivery, where the numbers can be of any (preferably unique) naming scheme;
- personal mobility, i.e., the ability to reach a called party under a single, location-independent address, even when the user changes terminals;
- terminal-type negotiation and selection: a caller can be given a choice of how to reach a party, e.g., via Internet telephony, mobile, phone, and an answering service;
- caller and callee authentication;
- blind and supervised call transfer;
- user location; and
- invitation to multicast conferences.

Extensions of SIP to allow third-party signaling (e.g., for click-to-dial-back services, fully meshed conferences and connections to Multipoint Control Units (MCUs), as well as mixed modes and the transition between those) have been specified.

SIP addresses (URLs) can be embedded in Web pages. SIP is addressing-neutral, with addresses expressed as URLs of various types such as SIP, H.323 or telephone (E.164). A purely representational example of a SIP URL might be sip:+12125551212@foo.example.com, where foo.example.com is the host serving as a gateway into the PSTN.

SIP is independent of the packet layer and only requires an unreliable datagram service, as it provides its own reliability mechanism. While SIP typically is used over UDP or TCP, it could, without technical changes, be run over IPX, or carrier pigeons, ATM AAL5 or X.25, in rough order of desirability.

SIP can set up calls "out-of-band". For example, while the SIP protocol exchanges use IP, plus UDP or TCP, the actual data transport can take place via the PSTN. This feature makes it possible to use SIP to control a PBX or send requests to a Service Control Point. The PINT services make use of this flexibility.

7.2 SIP Protocol

SIP is a textual client-server protocol, similar in syntax to HTTP and RTSP. Requests consist of a method (INVITE, BYE, ACK, or REGISTER), a list of parameter-value pairs describing the request and an optional request body. Parameters include the origin and destination of the call and a unique call identifier. They may indicate the caller's organization as well as the call's subject and priority. The request body contains a description of the call to be established or the conference to be joined. The description format is not prescribed by SIP; SDP is one possibility being standardized within the IETF. For the purposes of providing PINT services, an additional phone number address format is to be added to SDP.

Responses indicate whether a request is still being processed, was successful, can possibly be satisfied by another node or failed. When a call is redirected, the response indicates the name of the node to be tried. Unsuccessful calls may also return a better time to try again.

In a typical successful call, the caller sends an INVITE request to the callee. The callee accepts the call by returning a response code to the callee, which then confirms the receipt of that acceptance with an ACK request. Either side can terminate the call by sending a BYE request.

Requests can be authenticated using standard HTTP password and challenge-response mechanisms. Requests and responses may also be signed and encrypted.

7.3 SIP entities

SIP distinguishes three kinds of entities:

User agents receive and initiate calls and may forward the call.

A proxy server is an intermediary program that acts as both a server and a client for the purpose of making requests on behalf of other clients. Requests are serviced internally or by passing them on, possibly after translation, to other servers. A proxy must interpret, and, if necessary, rewrite a request message before forwarding it. A proxy server may, for example, locate a user and then attempt one or more possible network addresses.

Redirect server accepts a SIP request, maps the address into zero or more new addresses and returns these addresses to the client. Unlike a proxy server, it does not initiate its own SIP request. Unlike a user agent server, it does not accept calls.

Proxy and redirect servers may make use of location servers that determine the current likely location of the callee.

A PSTN gateway initiates phone calls between two parties. This may be a server that sends requests to an SCP in an IN environment or it may be a CTI-controlled PBX.

A SIP call may traverse one or more proxy servers.

The servers that control a PBX or an SCP act as user agents. A Web server may also act as a SIP user agent.

7.4 Providing Call Control Functionality

The SIP for PINT specification provides details on how to use SIP to initiate phone calls between two PSTN end points. (SIP can also initiate calls between Internet end points and between an Internet and PSTN end point, but this is beyond the scope of this document.)

It should be noted that the SIP client for initiating such phone calls can be either at the user's location (his/her workstation) or can be a Web server that calls up a SIP client via a CGI program. There is no difference in operation or functionality, except that the owner of the Web server may be legally responsible for the calls made.

A SIP client needs to convey two addresses to the PSTN gateway: the party making the call and the party to be called. (The party to be billed also needs to be identified; this can either be done by a SIP header or by having the server look up the appropriate party based on the two parties. This aspect is for further study.)

Described below are three ways these addresses can be conveyed in SIP. In the example, the address of party A is +1-212-555-1234 and that of party B is +1-415-555-1200. (The URL types in this and other examples are representational; they may but do not have to exist.)

(1) The two PSTN addresses are contained in the To header (and request-URI) and an Also header. For example:

```
INVITE sip:+1-212-555-1234@pbx.example.com SIP/2.0
To: phone:1-212-555-1234
From: sip:j.doe@example.com
Content-type: application/sdp
Call-ID: 19970721T135107.25.181@foo.bar.com
Also: phone:+1-415-555-1200

v=0
o=user1 53655765 2353687637 IN IP4 128.3.4.5
c=PSTN E.164 +1-415-555-1200
t=0 0
m=audio 0 RTP/AVP 0
```

In that case, the gateway first connects to party A and then party B, but without waiting for A to accept the call before calling B.

(2) Parties A and B are indicated by separate invitations. This allows the gateway to make sure that party A is indeed available before calling party B. After calling party A, the gateway could play an announcement indicating that the call is being connected using, for example, RTSP with appropriate Conference header indicating the call.

```
INVITE sip:+1-212-555-1234@pbx.example.com SIP/2.0
To: phone:1-212-555-1234
From: sip:j.doe@example.com
Content-type: application/sdp
Call-ID: 19970721T135107.25.181@foo.bar.com
...
INVITE sip:+1-415-555-1200@pbx.example.com SIP/2.0
To: phone:+1-415-555-1200
From: sip:j.doe@example.com
Content-type: application/sdp
Call-ID: 19970721T135107.25.181@foo.bar.com
...
```

(3) The two PSTN addresses are conveyed in the To header of the SIP request and the address in the SDP media description. Thus, a request may look as follows:

```
INVITE sip:+1-212-555-1234@pbx.example.com SIP/2.0
To: phone:1-212-555-1234
From: sip:j.doe@example.com
Content-type: application/sdp
Call-ID: 19970721T135107.25.181@foo.bar.com

v=0
o=user1 53655765 2353687637 IN IP4 128.3.4.5
c=PSTN E.164 +1-415-555-1200
t=0 0
m=audio 0 RTP/AVP 0
```

Here, pbx.example.com is the name of the PSTN gateway; the call will be established between 1-212-555-1234 and +1-415-555-1200.

Users can be added to an existing call by method (1) or (2).

8. Overall Security Considerations

Inter-networking of the Internet and PSTN necessitates the introduction of new interfaces (e.g., the A, B and E interfaces in Figure 6). To ensure that their use does not put the networks, in particular the PSTN, at additional security risk, these interfaces need to be designed with proper security considerations. Sections

5.1.5 and 5.2.2.7 describe how two of the pre-PINT implementations, the Lucent and Siemens systems, handle the security aspect, respectively.

Worth noting are the security requirements suggested by pre-PINT experiences. They are:

+Peer entity authentication to allow a communicating entity to prove its identity to another in the network (e.g., the requesting IP-host to the PINT gateway, and the PINT gateway to the PSTN node providing the service control function).

+Authorization and access control to verify if a network entity (e.g., the requesting IP-host) is allowed to use a network resource (e.g., requesting services from the PINT gateway).

+Non-repudiation to account for all operations in case of doubt or dispute.

+Confidentiality to avoid disclosure of information (e.g., the end user profile information and data) without the permission of its owner.

In the course of the PINT interface development, additional requirements are likely to arise. It is imperative that the resultant interfaces include specific means to meet all the security requirements.

9. Conclusion

This document has provided the information relevant to the development of inter-networking interfaces between the PSTN and Internet for supporting PINT services. Specifically, it addressed technologies, architectures, and several existing pre-PINT implementations of the arrangements through which Internet applications can request and enrich PSTN telecommunications services. One key observation is that the pre-PINT implementations, being developed independently, do not inter-operate. It is a task of the PINT Working Group to define the inter-networking interfaces that will support inter-operation of the future implementations of PINT services.

10. Acknowledgments

The authors would like to acknowledge Scott Bradner, Igor Faynberg, Dave Oran, Scott Petrack, Allyn Romanow for their insightful comments presented to the discussions in the PINT Working Group that lead to the creation of this document.

11. Appendix

11.1 PSTN/IN 101

11.1.1 Public Switched Telephone Network

What is normally considered as "the Telephone Network" consists of a set of interconnected networks. Potentially, each of these networks could be owned by a different Network Operator. The official name for such a network is Public Switched Telecommunications Network (PSTN). A simple PSTN consists of a set of Switches (called Central Offices or Telephone Exchanges) with links interconnecting them to make up the network, along with a set of access connections by which terminals are attached. The PSTN is used to deliver calls between terminals connected to itself or to other PSTNs with which it is interconnected. Calls on the PSTN are circuit switched; that is, a bi-directional connection is made between the calling and called terminals for the duration of the call. In PSTNs the connection is usually carried through the network in digital format occupying a fixed bandwidth; this is usually 56 or 64 Kbps. The overall configuration of the PSTN is shown in Figure 16.

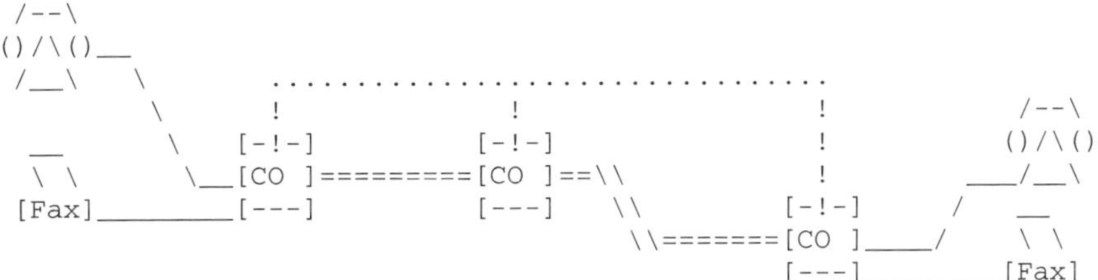


```
Key: ___   Access Lines
     ===   Trunk Links (inter-CO user data links)
     ...   Inter-CO signaling network links
```

Figure 16

Messages are sent between the Switches to make and dissolve connections through the network on demand and to indicate the status of terminals involved in a call; these "signaling" messages are carried over a separate (resilient) data network dedicated to this purpose. This signaling network is also known as the Common Channel Signaling (CCS) or Signaling System Number 7 (or SS7) network after the names of the signaling protocol suite used.

As yet, the majority of access connections to a PSTN carry analogue signals, with simple (analogue) telephones or Facsimile machines as terminals. Call requests are indicated to the Central Office to which a telephone is connected either by a sequence of pulses or tone pairs being sent. Notifications on the status of the request are sent back to the telephone in the form of tones. Indication from a Central Office that a call is being offered to a telephone is arranged by sending an alternating voltage down the access connection which in turn causes the ringer in the telephone to sound. These access lines have a unique address associated with them and can support a single call.

However, with analogue or digital multi-line connections, or Integrated Service Digital Network (ISDN) Basic or Primary Rate Interfaces (BRI or PRI), several concurrent calls are possible and a set of addresses are associated with them. The new ISDN access connections are designed so that data exchanged with the network is in multiplexed digital form, and there is an individual channel for each of the potential connections, together with a separate channel dedicated to sending and receiving call request and call alert data as well as carrying packet switched user data. These call request and call alert messages act as the equivalent of the pulses or tones that are sent when dialing, and the ringing signal that is sent to a telephone when a call is being made to it.

The operation of the call request is fairly simple in most cases and is shown in Figure 17.

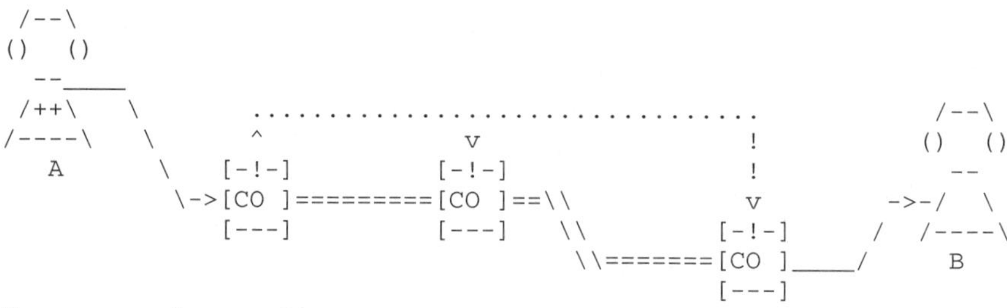

Key: ___ Access Lines
=== Trunk Links (inter-CO user data links)
... Inter-CO signaling network links
CO Central Office (Telephone Exchange)

Figure 17

The user presses a sequence of numbers on a telephone handset (labeled A), and the telephone passes a sequence of digits (either as pulses or tone pairs) to the Central Office via the access line. The Central Office contains a processor that will be notified that the user has made a request and the digit string that is the sole parameter of the request. This digit string is taken to be the unique address of an access line connected either to itself or to another Central Office. There is a hierarchical addressing scheme, so that the digit string can be parsed easily. A call request to a terminal (labeled B) connected to a remote Central Office can be routed by examining the digit string passed; the Central Office will extract the part of the passed address that corresponds to the remote Central Office in question, and can route the request onward, forming an inter-Switch call request and passing it via the signaling network. At the same time it will allocate one of its available transmission channels towards the remote Central Office.

11.1.2 Intelligent Network

This scheme has been used since the 1950s, and suffices for the majority of calls. However, there are a range of other services that can be (and have been) provided, enhancing this basic call processing. Freephone or Premium Rate services (1-800 or 1-900 services) are good examples of the supplementary services that have been introduced. Apart from the important feature that the cost of these calls is varied so that the caller does not pay for a free-phone call, or pays an extra charge for a premium rate call, they have the similarity that the number dialed must be translated to arrive at the "real" address of the destination terminal. They are known as number translation services, and make up the bulk of all supplementary services delivered today.

These were originally programmed into each Central Office, but the complexity of maintaining the data tables on each processor grew cumbersome, so a more general solution was sought. After a considerable gestation period, the eventual solution was the Intelligent Network. This takes the separation of Central Offices and the network links interconnecting them a stage further.

The Central Offices are considered to provide the Call Control Function (CCF). In addition, the Service Switching Function (SSF) is provided to "enhance" the operation of these Switches by detecting when a particular request has been made (such as by dialing 1-800). If this pattern is detected, the equipment implementing the SSF will send a specialized request message over the signaling network to a separate computer that implements the Service Control Function (SCF). This entity is responsible for querying service specific data (held in a unit providing the Service Data Function, or SDF), performing any digit translations necessary, and sending the details of how to proceed back to the SSF, where they are obeyed and the call is put through to the "real" destination. In many implementations, the SDF is closely coupled to the SCF. This configuration is shown in Figure 18.

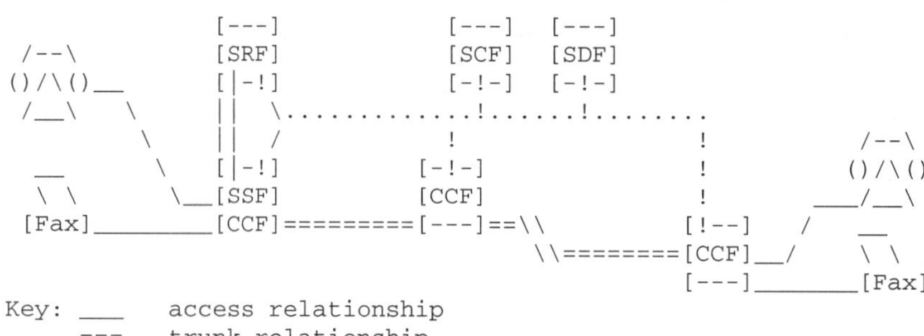

Key: ___ access relationship
=== trunk relationship
... signaling relationship

Figure 18

The advantage is that there can be a much smaller number of physical units dedicated to the SCF, and as they are connected to the signaling network they can be contacted by, and can send instructions back to, all of the units providing the SSF and thus the CCF.

In another enhancement, a separate entity called the Special Resource Function (SRF) was defined. Equipment implementing this function includes announcement units to play recorded messages (for example, prompts to enter digits) to callers. It will also include the tone decoders needed to capture any digits pressed by the caller in response to the prompts. It is connected to the rest of the PSTN usually via trunk data links. It will also include a signaling connection (directly or indirectly) back to the SCF, via the PSTN's core signaling network.

As an example of the way that these different functional entities interact, the SCF can ask an SSF handling a call to route the caller temporarily through to an SRF. In response to instructions sent to it from the SCF over the signaling network, the SRF can play announcements and can collect digits that the user presses on their terminal in response to prompts they are played. Once these digits have been collected they can be passed on to the SCF via a signaling message for further processing. In normal operation, the SCF would then ask the SSF to dissolve the temporary connection between the user's terminal and the SRF. This allows the collection of account numbers or passwords (or PINs) and forms the heart of many "Calling Card" services.

This pattern of user interaction is also used in a wide variety of other services where extra account information and PINs are needed. They are collected as just described and can be checked against the correct values stored in the service database prior to allowing the call to proceed.

The Intelligent Network functional entities can be realized as physical units in a number of different combinations. A common configuration is shown in Figure 19.

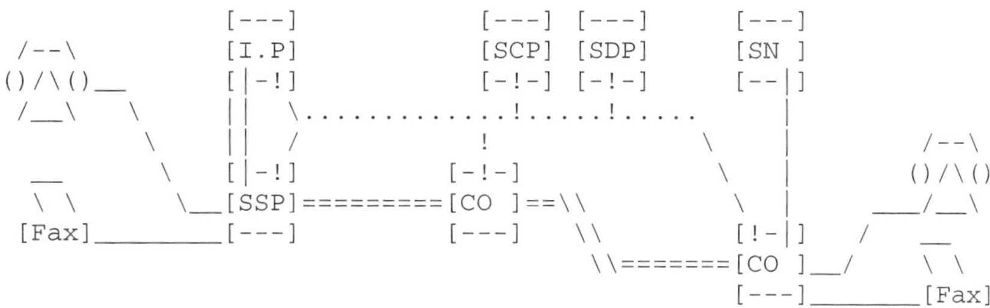


```
Key: ___  Access Lines
     ===  Trunk Links (inter-CO user data links)
     ...  Inter-CO signaling network links
     SSP  Service Switching Point - a unit that implements the
          Service Switching Function
     CCP  Call Control Point - a unit that performs call control
          functions.
          This is normally a kind of Central Office (shown as CO
          above)
     SCP  Service Control Point - a unit implementing the Service
          Control Function. NOTE that this is connected to the SS7
          Network and uses this connection for all of its
          communications.
     I.P  Intelligent Peripheral - a unit that contains specialized
          resources (like announcement units, tone decoders).
          In effect, it implements Special Resource Functions.
     SN   Service Node
```

Figure 19

This diagram also shows a unit called a Service Node, or SN. This contains components that realize all of the operational Intelligent Network functions (SSF, SCF, SDF, and SRF). It is sometimes more convenient to have all of these elements in one node (for example, for operations and maintenance reasons), particularly within smaller PSTNs or where there is a relatively low level of requests for particular services. Another difference is that, as they are all co-located, proprietary protocols can be used for internal communication, rather than the full Intelligent Network Application Part (INAP) protocol used over the core signaling network between discrete units. It also differs from the "unbundled" approach in that it is connected to the COs within a PSTN as a peripheral, having only an access connection to a Central Office; there is no connection to the core signaling network. Other than this, it operates in a similar way, and can provide the same kinds of services. Information on the specification of the Intelligent Network can be found in the ITU recommendations [1], while two books ([2] and [3]) describe the system, its history, operation, and the philosophy behind it.

11.2 Call Center Features

A Call Center is a system that allows a company to be organized with a group of similar individuals (agents), all of whom can either make calls to, or take calls from, customers. The system distributes incoming calls to the agents based on their availability and automates the placement of outgoing calls, selecting an agent to handle the call and routing the call to them only once the call request has been made of the PSTN.

The incoming call distribution feature ("automatic call distribution", or ACD) is usually coupled with a call queuing scheme. In this scheme, the callers are connected temporarily with an announcement unit that normally plays music. The calls are treated in sequence so that (once the caller is at the front of the queue) the ACD system selects the next available agent and routes the call through to them.

Another feature connects a customer making an incoming call to a unit that asks them for some information on the purpose of their call, selecting the agent to handle the call based on the particular area of expertise needed; to do this, the agents are further categorized by their knowledge (or "Skill Set"). If this skill set categorization is used then by implication there will be separate queues for each of the skill sets. This user selection scheme can be used independently of the others. For example these so-called "voice navigation systems" can be used to select a particular department extension number, based on the function required by the customer; as such, they can automate the job of company telephone receptionist in routing incoming calls.

Where possible, the information gleaned from the customer can be provided to the selected agent, usually via a separate networked computer connection. Similarly, if an outgoing call is being made to one of a list of customers, information on the customer and the purpose of the call can be provided to the agent selected to handle the call. Such configurations are generally called "Computer Telephony Integration" or CTI systems. Strictly, a CTI system can be arranged to handle routing of incoming calls and automation of outgoing calls only (also known as computer integrated telephony features), without the agents having access to a network of computers. However, the business case for combining the telephony functions of the call center with provision to the agents of computers with customer information can be compelling.

This is often further combined with a company's order and service processing computer system. In this case, a call is treated as part of a business transaction, with the information to be exchanged captured as fields of a computer form. While such a computer system is not, strictly, part of a call center, integrating the company computer system with the call center is very common. This allows the details of the call to be stored on a centralized database, allowing further automated order processing, for example. It also allows the call to be transferred from one agent to another where needed, ensuring that the new agent has the information already captured. This might be useful if someone with a different area of expertise were to be needed to handle the customer's requirements.

Traditionally, Call Centers have been used to support teams of agents working at a single site (or a small number of sites, with private telephony trunks interconnecting them). The site Private Automatic Branch eXchange (PABX) was integrated with a computer system to provide these features to people at that site. There can be a business case for provision of such features to distributed teams of workers as well. In particular, the possibility of providing support for people working from home has been seen as important. Some of the Call Center features have been incorporated into public telephone exchanges or Central Offices (COs) from many manufacturers as part of their "Centrex" service offerings.

There are practical limitations in providing such features on COs. Apart from the procedures needed to configure these features for any telephone line that is to use them, the basic requirement that every agent must have a connection to the supporting CO can limit its usefulness. Another approach is to provide Call Center features via the Intelligent Network. The features might thus be provided over a Telephone Operator's entire network, and would mean that the Call Center could be configured centrally while still allowing agents to be located anywhere within the telephone network. It also means that the supported company can pay for the Call Center features "as they go" rather than having a high "up front" cost.

12. References

[1] ITU-T Q.12xx Recommendation Series, Geneva, 1995.

[2] I. Faynberg, L. R. Gabuzda, M. P. Kaplan, and N. J. Shah, "The Intelligent Network Standards, their Application to Services", McGraw-Hill, 1996.

[3] T. Magedanz and R. Popesku-Zeletin, "Intelligent Networks: Basic Technology, Standards and Evolution", Intl. Thomson Computer Press, 1996.

[4] Information processing systems - Open Systems Interconnection - Specification of Abstract Syntax Notation One (ASN.1), International Organization for Standardization, International Standard 8824, December, 1987.

[5] McCloghrie, K., Editor, "Structure of Management Information for Version 2 of the Simple Network Management Protocol (SNMPv2)", RFC 1902, January 1996.

[6] Kristol, D. and L. Montulli, "HTTP State Management Mechanism", RFC 2109, February 1997.

[7] Zimmerman, D., "The Finger User Information Protocol", RFC 1288 December 1991.

Authors' Addresses

Steve Bellovin
AT&T Labs
Room E-215
180 Park Ave. Bldg. 103
Florham Park, NJ 07932-0000
USA

Phone: +1 973 360 8656
Fax: +1 973 360 8077
EMail: smb@research.att.com

Fred M. Burg
AT&T Labs
Room 1N-117
307 Middletown Lincroft Road
Lincroft, NJ 07738
USA

Phone: +1 732 576 4322
Fax: +1 732 576 4317
EMail: fburg@hogpb.att.com

Lawrence Conroy
Roke Manor Research Limited
IT&N-INIA Group
Roke Manor, Old Salisbury Lane,
Romsey, Hampshire SO51 0ZN
U.K.

Phone: +44 1794 833666
Fax: +44 1794 833434
EMail: lwc@roke.co.uk

Paul Davidson
Nortel
P.O.Box 3511 Station "C"
Mail Stop 242
Ottawa, Ontario, Canada K1Y 4H7

Phone: +1 613 763 4234
EMail: pauldav@nortel.ca

A. DeSimone
Lucent Technologies
Room 6H510
600-700 Mountain Avenue
Murray Hill, NJ 07974-0636
USA

Phone: +1 908 582 2382
Fax: +1 908 582 1086
E-Mail:tds@lucent.com

Murali Krishnaswamy
Bell Laboratories
Lucent Technologies
Room 2G-527a
101 Crawfords Corner Road
Holmdel, NJ 07733-3030
USA

Phone: +1 732 949 3611
Fax: +1 732 949 3210
EMail: murali@bell-labs.com

Hui-Lan Lu
Bell Laboratories
Lucent Technologies
Room 4K-309
101 Crawfords Corner Road
Holmdel, NJ 07733-3030
USA

Phone: +1 732 949 0321
Fax: +1 732 949 1196
EMail: hui-lan.lu@bell-labs.com

Henning Schulzrinne
Dept. of Computer Science
Columbia University
New York, NY 10027
USA

Phone: +1 212 939 7042 (@Bell Labs: 732 949 8344)
Fax: +1 212 666 0140
EMail: schulzrinne@cs.columbia.edu

Kamlesh T. Tewani
AT&T Labs
Room 1K-334
101, Crawfords Corner Rd.
Holmdel, NJ 07733
USA

Phone: +1 732 949 5369
Fax: +1 732 949 8569
EMail: tewani@att.com

Kumar Vishwanathan
Isochrone
EMail: kumar@isochrone.com

Full Copyright Statement

Network Working Group M. Handley
Request for Comments: 2543 ACIRI
Category: Standards Track H. Schulzrinne
Columbia U.
E. Schooler
Cal Tech
J. Rosenberg
Bell Labs
March 1999

SIP: Session Initiation Protocol

Status of this Memo

Copyright Notice

IESG Note

The IESG intends to charter, in the near future, one or more working groups to produce standards for "name lookup", where such names would include electronic mail addresses and telephone numbers, and the result of such a lookup would be a list of attributes and characteristics of the user or terminal associated with the name. Groups which are in need of a "name lookup" protocol should follow the development of these new working groups rather than using SIP for this function. In addition it is anticipated that SIP will migrate towards using such protocols, and SIP implementors are advised to monitor these efforts.

Abstract

The Session Initiation Protocol (SIP) is an application-layer control (signaling) protocol for creating, modifying and terminating sessions with one or more participants. These sessions include Internet multimedia conferences, Internet telephone calls and multimedia distribution. Members in a session can communicate via multicast or via a mesh of unicast relations, or a combination of these.

SIP invitations used to create sessions carry session descriptions which allow participants to agree on a set of compatible media types. SIP supports user mobility by proxying and redirecting requests to the user's current location. Users can register their current location. SIP is not tied to any particular conference control protocol. SIP is designed to be independent of the lower-layer transport protocol and can be extended with additional capabilities.

Table of Contents

1 Introduction

1.1 Overview of SIP Functionality

The Session Initiation Protocol (SIP) is an application-layer control protocol that can establish, modify and terminate multimedia sessions or calls. These multimedia sessions include multimedia conferences, distance learning, Internet telephony and similar applications. SIP can invite both persons and "robots", such as a media storage service. SIP can invite parties to both unicast and multicast sessions; the initiator does not necessarily have to be a member of the session to which it is inviting. Media and participants can be added to an existing session.

SIP can be used to initiate sessions as well as invite members to sessions that have been advertised and established by other means. Sessions can be advertised using multicast protocols such as SAP, electronic mail, news groups, web pages or directories (LDAP), among others.

SIP transparently supports name mapping and redirection services, allowing the implementation of ISDN and Intelligent Network telephony subscriber services. These facilities also enable personal mobility. In the parlance of telecommunications intelligent network services, this is defined as: "Personal mobility is the ability of end users to originate and receive calls and access subscribed telecommunication services on any terminal in any location, and the ability of the network to identify end users as they move. Personal mobility is based on the use of a unique personal identity (i.e., personal number)." [1]. Personal mobility complements terminal mobility, i.e., the ability to maintain communications when moving a single end system from one subnet to another.

SIP supports five facets of establishing and terminating multimedia communications:

User location: determination of the end system to be used for communication;

User capabilities: determination of the media and media parameters to be used;

User availability: determination of the willingness of the called party to engage in communications;

Call setup: "ringing", establishment of call parameters at both called and calling party;

Call handling: including transfer and termination of calls.

SIP can also initiate multi-party calls using a multipoint control unit (MCU) or fully-meshed interconnection instead of multicast. Internet telephony gateways that connect Public Switched Telephone Network (PSTN) parties can also use SIP to set up calls between them.

SIP is designed as part of the overall IETF multimedia data and control architecture currently incorporating protocols such as RSVP (RFC 2205 [2]) for reserving network resources, the real-time transport protocol (RTP) (RFC 1889 [3]) for transporting real-time data and providing QOS feedback, the real-time streaming protocol (RTSP) (RFC 2326 [4]) for controlling delivery of streaming media, the session announcement protocol (SAP) [5] for advertising multimedia sessions via multicast and the session description protocol (SDP) (RFC 2327 [6]) for describing multimedia sessions. However, the functionality and operation of SIP does not depend on any of these protocols.

SIP can also be used in conjunction with other call setup and signaling protocols. In that mode, an end system uses SIP exchanges to determine the appropriate end system address and protocol from a given address that is protocol-independent. For example, SIP could be used to determine that the party can be reached via H.323 [7], obtain the H.245 [8] gateway and user address and then use H.225.0 [9] to establish the call.

In another example, SIP might be used to determine that the callee is reachable via the PSTN and indicate the phone number to be called, possibly suggesting an Internet-to-PSTN gateway to be used.

SIP does not offer conference control services such as floor control or voting and does not prescribe how a conference is to be managed, but SIP can be used to introduce conference control protocols. SIP does not allocate multicast addresses.

SIP can invite users to sessions with and without resource reservation. SIP does not reserve resources, but can convey to the invited system the information necessary to do this.

1.2 Terminology

In this document, the key words "MUST", "MUST NOT", "REQUIRED", "SHALL", "SHALL NOT", "SHOULD", "SHOULD NOT", "RECOMMENDED", "MAY", and "OPTIONAL" are to be interpreted as described in RFC 2119 [10] and indicate requirement levels for compliant SIP implementations.

1.3 Definitions

This specification uses a number of terms to refer to the roles played by participants in SIP communications. The definitions of client, server and proxy are similar to those used by the Hypertext Transport Protocol (HTTP) (RFC 2068 [11]). The terms and generic syntax of URI and URL are defined in RFC 2396 [12]. The following terms have special significance for SIP.

Call: A call consists of all participants in a conference invited by a common source. A SIP call is identified by a globally unique call-id (Section 6.12). Thus, if a user is, for example, invited to the same multicast session by several people, each of these invitations will be a unique call. A point-to-point Internet telephony conversation maps into a single SIP call. In a multiparty conference unit (MCU) based call-in conference, each participant uses a separate call to invite himself to the MCU.

Call leg: A call leg is identified by the combination of Call-ID, To and From.

Client: An application program that sends SIP requests. Clients may or may not interact directly with a human user. User agents and proxies contain clients (and servers).

Conference: A multimedia session (see below), identified by a common session description. A conference can have zero or more members and includes the cases of a multicast conference, a full-mesh conference and a two-party "telephone call", as well as combinations of these. Any number of calls can be used to create a conference.

Downstream: Requests sent in the direction from the caller to the callee (i.e., user agent client to user agent server).

Final response: A response that terminates a SIP transaction, as opposed to a provisional response that does not. All 2xx, 3xx, 4xx, 5xx and 6xx responses are final.

Initiator, calling party, caller: The party initiating a conference invitation. Note that the calling party does not have to be the same as the one creating the conference.

Invitation: A request sent to a user (or service) requesting participation in a session. A successful SIP invitation consists of two transactions: an INVITE request followed by an ACK request.

Invitee, invited user, called party, callee: The person or service that the calling party is trying to invite to a conference.

Isomorphic request or response: Two requests or responses are defined to be isomorphic for the purposes of this document if they have the same values for the Call-ID, To, From and CSeq header fields. In addition, isomorphic requests have to have the same Request-URI.

Location server: See location service.

Location service: A location service is used by a SIP redirect or proxy server to obtain information about a callee's possible location(s). Location services are offered by location servers. Location servers MAY be co-located with a SIP server, but the manner in which a SIP server requests location services is beyond the scope of this document.

Parallel search: In a parallel search, a proxy issues several requests to possible user locations upon receiving an incoming request. Rather than issuing one request and then waiting for the final response before issuing the next request as in a sequential search , a parallel search issues requests without waiting for the result of previous requests.

Provisional response: A response used by the server to indicate progress, but that does not terminate a SIP transaction. 1xx responses are provisional, other responses are considered final.

Proxy, proxy server: An intermediary program that acts as both a server and a client for the purpose of making requests on behalf of other clients. Requests are serviced internally or by passing them on, possibly after translation, to other servers. A proxy interprets, and, if necessary, rewrites a request message before forwarding it.

Redirect server: A redirect server is a server that accepts a SIP request, maps the address into zero or more new addresses and returns these addresses to the client. Unlike a proxy server , it does not initiate its own SIP request. Unlike a user agent server , it does not accept calls.

Registrar: A registrar is a server that accepts REGISTER requests. A registrar is typically co-located with a proxy or redirect server and MAY offer location services.

Ringback: Ringback is the signaling tone produced by the calling client's application indicating that a called party is being alerted (ringing).

Server: A server is an application program that accepts requests in order to service requests and sends back responses to those requests. Servers are either proxy, redirect or user agent servers or registrars.

Session: From the SDP specification: "A multimedia session is a set of multimedia senders and receivers and the data streams flowing from senders to receivers. A multimedia conference is an example of a multimedia session." (RFC 2327 [6]) (A session as defined for SDP can comprise one or more RTP sessions.) As defined, a callee can be invited several times, by different calls, to the same session. If SDP is used, a session is defined by the concatenation of the user name , session id , network type , address type and address elements in the origin field.

(SIP) transaction: A SIP transaction occurs between a client and a server and comprises all messages from the first request sent from the client to the server up to a final (non-1xx) response sent from the server to the client. A transaction is identified by the CSeq sequence number (Section 6.17) within a single call leg. The ACK request has the same CSeq number as the corresponding INVITE request, but comprises a transaction of its own.

Upstream: Responses sent in the direction from the user agent server to the user agent client.

URL-encoded: A character string encoded according to RFC 1738, Section 2.2 [13].

User agent client (UAC), calling user agent: A user agent client is a client application that initiates the SIP request.

User agent server (UAS), called user agent: A user agent server is a server application that contacts the user when a SIP request is received and that returns a response on behalf of the user. The response accepts, rejects or redirects the request.

User agent (UA): An application which contains both a user agent client and user agent server.

An application program MAY be capable of acting both as a client and a server. For example, a typical multimedia conference control application would act as a user agent client to initiate calls or to invite others to conferences and as a user agent server to accept invitations. The properties of the different SIP server types are summarized in Table 1.

property	redirect server	proxy server	user agent server	registrar
also acts as a SIP client	no	yes	no	no
returns 1xx status	yes	yes	yes	yes
returns 2xx status	no	yes	yes	yes
returns 3xx status	yes	yes	yes	yes
returns 4xx status	yes	yes	yes	yes
returns 5xx status	yes	yes	yes	yes
returns 6xx status	no	yes	yes	yes
inserts Via header	no	yes	no	no
accepts ACK	yes	yes	yes	no

Table 1: Properties of the different SIP server types

1.4 Overview of SIP Operation

This section explains the basic protocol functionality and operation. Callers and callees are identified by SIP addresses, described in Section 1.4.1. When making a SIP call, a caller first locates the appropriate server (Section 1.4.2) and then sends a SIP request (Section 1.4.3). The most common SIP operation is the invitation (Section 1.4.4). Instead of directly reaching the intended callee, a SIP request may be redirected or may trigger a chain of new SIP requests by proxies (Section 1.4.5). Users can register their location(s) with SIP servers (Section 4.2.6).

1.4.1 SIP Addressing

The "objects" addressed by SIP are users at hosts, identified by a SIP URL. The SIP URL takes a form similar to a mailto or telnet URL, i.e., user@host. The user part is a user name or a telephone number. The host part is either a domain name or a numeric network address. See section 2 for a detailed discussion of SIP URL's.

A user's SIP address can be obtained out-of-band, can be learned via existing media agents, can be included in some mailers' message headers, or can be recorded during previous invitation interactions. In many cases, a user's SIP URL can be guessed from their email address.

A SIP URL address can designate an individual (possibly located at one of several end systems), the first available person from a group of individuals or a whole group. The form of the address, for example, sip:sales@example.com , is not sufficient, in general, to determine the intent of the caller.

If a user or service chooses to be reachable at an address that is guessable from the person's name and organizational affiliation, the traditional method of ensuring privacy by having an unlisted "phone" number is compromised. However, unlike traditional telephony, SIP offers authentication and access control mechanisms and can avail itself of lower-layer security mechanisms, so that client software can reject unauthorized or undesired call attempts.

1.4.2 Locating a SIP Server

When a client wishes to send a request, the client either sends it to a locally configured SIP proxy server (as in HTTP), independent of the Request-URI, or sends it to the IP address and port corresponding to the Request-URI.

For the latter case, the client must determine the protocol, port and IP address of a server to which to send the request. A client SHOULD follow the steps below to obtain this information, but MAY follow the alternative, optional procedure defined in Appendix D. At each step, unless stated otherwise, the client SHOULD try to contact a server at the port number listed in the Request-URI. If no port number is present in the Request-URI, the client uses port 5060. If the Request-URI specifies a protocol (TCP or UDP), the client contacts the server using that protocol. If no protocol is specified, the client tries UDP (if UDP is supported). If the attempt fails, or if the client doesn't support UDP but supports TCP, it then tries TCP.

A client SHOULD be able to interpret explicit network notifications (such as ICMP messages) which indicate that a server is not reachable, rather than relying solely on timeouts. (For socket-based programs: For TCP, connect() returns ECONNREFUSED if the client could not connect to a server at that address. For UDP, the socket needs to be bound to the destination address using connect() rather than sendto() or similar so that a second write() fails with ECONNREFUSED if there is no server listening) If the client finds the server is not reachable at a particular address, it SHOULD behave as if it had received a 400-class error response to that request.

The client tries to find one or more addresses for the SIP server by querying DNS. The procedure is as follows:

1. If the host portion of the Request-URI is an IP address, the client contacts the server at the given address. Otherwise, the client proceeds to the next step.

2. The client queries the DNS server for address records for the host portion of the Request-URI. If the DNS server returns no address records, the client stops, as it has been unable to locate a server. By address record, we mean A RR's, AAAA RR's, or other similar address records, chosen according to the client's network protocol capabilities.

There are no mandatory rules on how to select a host name for a SIP server. Users are encouraged to name their SIP servers using the sip.domainname (i.e., sip.example.com) convention, as specified in RFC 2219 [16]. Users may only know an email address instead of a full SIP URL for a callee, however. In that case, implementations may be able to increase the likelihood of reaching a SIP server for that domain by constructing a SIP URL from that email address by prefixing the host name with "sip.". In the future, this mechanism is likely to become unnecessary as better DNS techniques, such as the one in Appendix D, become widely available.

A client MAY cache a successful DNS query result. A successful query is one which contained records in the answer, and a server was contacted at one of the addresses from the answer. When the client wishes to send a request to the same host, it MUST start the search as if it had just received this answer from the name server. The client MUST follow the procedures in RFC1035 [15] regarding DNS cache invalidation when the DNS time-to-live expires.

1.4.3 SIP Transaction

Once the host part has been resolved to a SIP server, the client sends one or more SIP requests to that server and receives one or more responses from the server. A request (and its retransmissions) together with the responses triggered by that request make up a SIP transaction. All responses to a request contain the same values in the Call-ID, CSeq, To, and From fields (with the possible addition of a tag in the To field (section 6.37)). This allows responses to be matched with requests. The ACK request following an INVITE is not part of the transaction since it may traverse a different set of hosts.

If TCP is used, request and responses within a single SIP transaction are carried over the same TCP connection (see Section 10). Several SIP requests from the same client to the same server MAY use the same TCP connection or MAY use a new connection for each request.

If the client sent the request via unicast UDP, the response is sent to the address contained in the next Via header field (Section 6.40) of the response. If the request is sent via multicast UDP, the response is directed to the same multicast address and destination port. For UDP, reliability is achieved using retransmission (Section 10).

The SIP message format and operation is independent of the transport protocol.

1.4.4 SIP Invitation

A successful SIP invitation consists of two requests, INVITE followed by ACK. The INVITE (Section 4.2.1) request asks the callee to join a particular conference or establish a two-party conversation. After the callee has agreed to participate in the call, the caller confirms that it has received that response by sending an ACK (Section 4.2.2) request. If the caller no longer wants to participate in the call, it sends a BYE request instead of an ACK.

The INVITE request typically contains a session description, for example written in SDP (RFC 2327 [6]) format, that provides the called party with enough information to join the session. For multicast sessions, the session description enumerates the media types and formats that are allowed to be distributed to that session. For a unicast session, the session description enumerates the media types and formats that the caller is willing to use and where it wishes the media data to be sent. In either case, if the callee wishes to accept the call, it responds to the invitation by returning a similar description listing the media it wishes to use. For a multicast session, the callee SHOULD only return a session description if it is unable to receive the media indicated in the caller's description or wants to receive data via unicast.

The protocol exchanges for the INVITE method are shown in Fig. 1 for a proxy server and in Fig. 2 for a redirect server. (Note that the messages shown in the figures have been abbreviated slightly.) In Fig. 1, the proxy server accepts the INVITE request (step 1), contacts the location service with all or parts of the address (step 2) and obtains a more precise location (step 3). The proxy server then issues a SIP INVITE request to the address(es) returned by the location service (step 4). The user agent server alerts the user (step 5) and returns a success indication to the proxy server (step

6). The proxy server then returns the success result to the original caller (step 7). The receipt of this message is confirmed by the caller using an ACK request, which is forwarded to the callee (steps 8 and 9). Note that an ACK can also be sent directly to the callee, bypassing the proxy. All requests and responses have the same Call-ID.

```
                                         +....... cs.columbia.edu .......+
                                         :                               :
                                         : (~~~~~~~~~~)                  :
                                         : ( location )                  :
                                         : ( service  )                  :
                                         : (~~~~~~~~~~)                  :
                                         :     ^    |                    :
                                         :     | hgs@lab                 :
                                         :    2|   3|                    :
                                         :     |    |                    :
                                         : henning  |                    :
+.. cs.tu-berlin.de ..+ 1: INVITE        :     |    |                    :
:                     :    henning@cs.col:     |   \/ 4: INVITE  5: ring :
: cz@cs.tu-berlin.de ========================>(~~~~~~)=========>(~~~~~~) :
:                    <........................(      )<.........(      ) :
:                     : 7: 200 OK        :    (      )6: 200 OK (      ) :
:                     :                  :    ( work )          ( lab  ) :
:                     : 8: ACK           :    (      )9: ACK    (      ) :
:                    ========================>(~~~~~~)=========>(~~~~~~) :
+.....................+                  +...............................+

  ====> SIP request
  ....> SIP response

   ^
   |     non-SIP protocols
   |
```

Figure 1: Example of SIP proxy server

The redirect server shown in Fig. 2 accepts the INVITE request (step 1), contacts the location service as before (steps 2 and 3) and, instead of contacting the newly found address itself, returns the address to the caller (step 4), which is then acknowledged via an ACK request (step 5). The caller issues a new request, with the same call-ID but a higher CSeq, to the address returned by the first server (step 6). In the example, the call succeeds (step 7). The caller and callee complete the handshake with an ACK (step 8).

The next section discusses what happens if the location service returns more than one possible alternative.

1.4.5 Locating a User

A callee may move between a number of different end systems over time. These locations can be dynamically registered with the SIP server (Sections 1.4.7, 4.2.6). A location server MAY also use one or more other protocols, such as finger (RFC 1288 [17]), rwhois (RFC 2167 [18]), LDAP (RFC 1777 [19]), multicast-based protocols [20] or operating-system dependent mechanisms to actively determine the end system where a user might be reachable. A location server MAY return several locations because the user is logged in at several hosts simultaneously or because the location server has (temporarily) inaccurate information. The SIP server combines the results to yield a list of a zero or more locations.

The action taken on receiving a list of locations varies with the type of SIP server. A SIP redirect server returns the list to the client as Contact headers (Section 6.13). A SIP proxy server can sequentially or in parallel try the addresses until the call is successful (2xx response) or the callee has declined the call (6xx response). With sequential attempts, a proxy server can implement an "anycast" service.

If a proxy server forwards a SIP request, it MUST add itself to the beginning of the list of forwarders noted in the Via (Section 6.40) headers. The Via trace ensures that replies can take the same path back, ensuring correct operation through compliant firewalls and avoiding request loops. On the response path, each host MUST remove its Via, so that routing internal information is hidden from the callee and outside networks. A proxy server MUST check that it does not generate a request to a host listed in the Via sent-by, via-received or via-maddr parameters (Section 6.40). (Note: If a host has several names or network addresses, this does not always work. Thus, each host also checks if it is part of the Via list.)

A SIP invitation may traverse more than one SIP proxy server. If one of these "forks" the request, i.e., issues more than one request in response to receiving the invitation request, it is possible that a client is reached, independently, by more than one copy of the invitation request. Each of these copies bears the same Call-ID. The user agent MUST return the same status response returned in the first response. Duplicate requests are not an error.

1.4.6 Changing an Existing Session

In some circumstances, it is desirable to change the parameters of an existing session. This is done by re-issuing the INVITE, using the same Call-ID, but a new or different body or header fields to convey the new information. This re INVITE MUST have a higher CSeq than any previous request from the client to the server.

For example, two parties may have been conversing and then want to add a third party, switching to multicast for efficiency. One of the participants invites the third party with the new multicast address and simultaneously sends an INVITE to the second party, with the new multicast session description, but with the old call identifier.

1.4.7 Registration Services

The REGISTER request allows a client to let a proxy or redirect server know at which address(es) it can be reached. A client MAY also use it to install call handling features at the server.

1.5 Protocol Properties

1.5.1 Minimal State

A single conference session or call involves one or more SIP request-response transactions. Proxy servers do not have to keep state for a particular call, however, they MAY maintain state for a single SIP transaction, as discussed in Section 12. For efficiency, a server MAY cache the results of location service requests.

1.5.2 Lower-Layer-Protocol Neutral

SIP makes minimal assumptions about the underlying transport and network-layer protocols. The lower-layer can provide either a packet or a byte stream service, with reliable or unreliable service.

In an Internet context, SIP is able to utilize both UDP and TCP as transport protocols, among others. UDP allows the application to more carefully control the timing of messages and their retransmission, to perform parallel searches without requiring TCP connection state for each outstanding request, and to use multicast. Routers can more readily snoop SIP UDP packets. TCP allows easier passage through existing firewalls.

```
                                         +....... cs.columbia.edu .......+
                                         :                               :
                                         : (~~~~~~~~~~)                  :
                                         : ( location )                  :
                                         : ( service  )                  :
                                         : (~~~~~~~~~~)                  :
                                         :    ^    |                     :
                                         :    | hgs@lab                  :
                                         :   2|   3|                     :
                                         :    |    |                     :
                                         : henning|                      :
+.. cs.tu-berlin.de ..+ 1: INVITE        :    |    |                     :
:                     :    henning@cs.col:    |   \/                     :
: cz@cs.tu-berlin.de ========================>(~~~~~~)                   :
:       | ^ |         <.......................(      )                   :
:       | . |          : 4: 302 Moved     :   (      )                   :
:       | . |          :    hgs@lab       :   ( work )                   :
:       | . |          :                  :   (      )                   :
:       | . |          : 5: ACK           :   (      )                   :
:       | . |         ========================>(~~~~~~)                  :
:       | . |          :                  :                              :
+.......|...|..........+                  :                              :
        | . |                             :                              :
        | . |                             :                              :
        | . |                             :                              :
        | . |                             :                              :
        | . | 6: INVITE hgs@lab.cs.columbia.edu                (~~~~~~)  :
        | . ==================================================> (      ) :
        | ....................................................  (      ) :
        |     7: 200 OK                   :                     ( lab  ) :
        |                                 :                     (      ) :
        |     8: ACK                      :                     (      ) :
        ======================================================> (~~~~~~) :
                                          +..............................+

  ====> SIP request
  ....> SIP response

    ^
    |   non-SIP protocols
    |


   Figure 2: Example of SIP redirect server
```

When TCP is used, SIP can use one or more connections to attempt to contact a user or to modify parameters of an existing conference. Different SIP requests for the same SIP call MAY use different TCP connections or a single persistent connection, as appropriate.

For concreteness, this document will only refer to Internet protocols. However, SIP MAY also be used directly with protocols such as ATM AAL5, IPX, frame relay or X.25. The necessary naming conventions are beyond the scope of this document. User agents SHOULD implement both UDP and TCP transport. Proxy, registrar, and redirect servers MUST implement both UDP and TCP transport.

1.5.3 Text-Based

SIP is text-based, using ISO 10646 in UTF-8 encoding throughout. This allows easy implementation in languages such as Java, Tcl and Perl, allows easy debugging, and most importantly, makes SIP flexible and extensible. As SIP is used for initiating multimedia conferences rather than delivering media data, it is believed that the additional overhead of using a text-based protocol is not significant.

2 SIP Uniform Resource Locators

SIP URLs are used within SIP messages to indicate the originator (From), current destination (Request-URI) and final recipient (To) of a SIP request, and to specify redirection addresses (Contact). A SIP URL can also be embedded in web pages or other hyperlinks to indicate that a particular user or service can be called via SIP. When used as a hyperlink, the SIP URL indicates the use of the INVITE method.

The SIP URL scheme is defined to allow setting SIP request-header fields and the SIP message-body.

> This corresponds to the use of mailto: URLs. It makes it possible, for example, to specify the subject, urgency or media types of calls initiated through a web page or as part of an email message.

A SIP URL follows the guidelines of RFC 2396 [12] and has the syntax shown in Fig. 3. The syntax is described using Augmented Backus-Naur Form (See Section C). Note that reserved characters have to be escaped and that the "set of characters reserved within any given URI component is defined by that component. In general, a character is reserved if the semantics of the URI changes if the character is replaced with its escaped US-ASCII encoding" [12].

```
SIP-URL         = "sip:" [ userinfo "@" ] hostport
                  url-parameters [ headers ]
userinfo        = user [ ":" password ]
user            = *( unreserved | escaped
                | "&" | "=" | "+" | "$" | "," )
password        = *( unreserved | escaped
                | "&" | "=" | "+" | "$" | "," )
hostport        = host [ ":" port ]
host            = hostname | IPv4address
hostname        = *( domainlabel "." ) toplabel [ "." ]
domainlabel     = alphanum | alphanum *( alphanum | "-" ) alphanum
toplabel        = alpha | alpha *( alphanum | "-" ) alphanum
IPv4address     = 1*digit "." 1*digit "." 1*digit "." 1*digit
port            = *digit
url-parameters  = *( ";" url-parameter )
url-parameter   = transport-param | user-param | method-param
                | ttl-param | maddr-param | other-param
transport-param = "transport=" ( "udp" | "tcp" )
ttl-param       = "ttl=" ttl
ttl             = 1*3DIGIT       ; 0 to 255
maddr-param     = "maddr=" host
user-param      = "user=" ( "phone" | "ip" )
method-param    = "method=" Method
tag-param       = "tag=" UUID
UUID            = 1*( hex | "-" )
other-param     = ( token | ( token "=" ( token | quoted-string )))
headers         = "?" header *( "&" header )
header          = hname "=" hvalue
hname           = 1*uric
hvalue          = *uric
uric            = reserved | unreserved | escaped
reserved        = ";" | "/" | "?" | ":" | "@" | "&" | "=" | "+" |
                  "$" | ","
digits          = 1*DIGIT
```

Figure 3: SIP URL syntax

The URI character classes referenced above are described in Appendix C.

The components of the SIP URI have the following meanings.

```
telephone-subscriber  = global-phone-number | local-phone-number
   global-phone-number   = "+" 1*phonedigit [isdn-subaddress]
                            [post-dial]
   local-phone-number    = 1*(phonedigit | dtmf-digit |
                            pause-character) [isdn-subaddress]
                            [post-dial]
   isdn-subaddress       = ";isub=" 1*phonedigit
   post-dial             = ";postd=" 1*(phonedigit | dtmf-digit
                         |  pause-character)
   phonedigit            = DIGIT | visual-separator
   visual-separator      = "-" | "."
   pause-character       = one-second-pause | wait-for-dial-tone
   one-second-pause      = "p"
   wait-for-dial-tone    = "w"
   dtmf-digit            = "*" | "#" | "A" | "B" | "C" | "D"
```

Figure 4: SIP URL syntax; telephone subscriber

user: If the host is an Internet telephony gateway, the user field MAY also encode a telephone number using the notation of telephone-subscriber (Fig. 4). The telephone number is a special case of a user name and cannot be distinguished by a BNF. Thus, a URL parameter, user, is added to distinguish telephone numbers from user names. The phone identifier is to be used when connecting to a telephony gateway. Even without this parameter, recipients of SIP URLs MAY interpret the pre-@ part as a phone number if local restrictions on the name space for user name allow it.

password: The SIP scheme MAY use the format "user:password" in the userinfo field. The use of passwords in the userinfo is NOT RECOMMENDED, because the passing of authentication information in clear text (such as URIs) has proven to be a security risk in almost every case where it has been used.

host: The mailto: URL and RFC 822 email addresses require that numeric host addresses ("host numbers") are enclosed in square brackets (presumably, since host names might be numeric), while host numbers without brackets are used for all other URLs. The SIP URL requires the latter form, without brackets.

The issue of IPv6 literal addresses in URLs is being looked at elsewhere in the IETF. SIP implementers are advised to keep up to date on that activity.

port: The port number to send a request to. If not present, the procedures outlined in Section 1.4.2 are used to determine the port number to send a request to.

URL parameters: SIP URLs can define specific parameters of the request. URL parameters are added after the host component and are separated by semi-colons. The transport parameter determines the the transport mechanism (UDP or TCP). UDP is to be assumed when no explicit transport parameter is included. The maddr parameter provides the server address to be contacted for this user, overriding the address supplied in the host field. This address is typically a multicast address, but could also be the address of a backup server. The ttl parameter determines the time-to-live value of the UDP multicast packet and MUST only be used if maddr is a multicast address and the transport protocol is UDP. The user parameter was described above. For example, to specify to call j.doe@big.com using multicast to 239.255.255.1 with a ttl of 15, the following URL would be used:

```
sip:j.doe@big.com;maddr=239.255.255.1;ttl=15
```

The transport, maddr, and ttl parameters MUST NOT be used in the From and To header fields and the Request-URI; they are ignored if present.

Headers: Headers of the SIP request can be defined with the "?" mechanism within a SIP URL. The special hname "body" indicates that the associated hvalue is the message-body of the SIP INVITE request. Headers MUST NOT be used in the From and To header fields and the Request-URI; they are ignored if present. hname and hvalue are encodings of a SIP header name and value, respectively. All URL reserved characters in the header names and values MUST be escaped.

Method: The method of the SIP request can be specified with the method parameter. This parameter MUST NOT be used in the From and To header fields and the Request-URI; they are ignored if present.

Table 2 summarizes where the components of the SIP URL can be used and what default values they assume if not present.

Examples of SIP URLs are:

	default	Req.-URI	To	From	Contact	external
user	--	x	x	x	x	x
password	--	x	x		x	x
host	mandatory	x	x	x	x	x
port	5060	x	x	x	x	x
user-param	ip	x	x	x	x	x
method	INVITE				x	x
maddr-param	--				x	x
ttl-param	1				x	x
transp.-param	--				x	x
headers	--				x	x

Table 2: Use and default values of URL components for SIP headers, Request-URI and references

```
sip:j.doe@big.com
sip:j.doe:secret@big.com;transport=tcp
sip:j.doe@big.com?subject=project
sip:+1-212-555-1212:1234@gateway.com;user=phone
sip:1212@gateway.com
sip:alice@10.1.2.3
sip:alice@example.com
sip:alice%40example.com@gateway.com
sip:alice@registrar.com;method=REGISTER
```

Within a SIP message, URLs are used to indicate the source and intended destination of a request, redirection addresses and the current destination of a request. Normally all these fields will contain SIP URLs.

SIP URLs are case-insensitive, so that for example the two URLs sip:j.doe@example.com and SIP:J.Doe@Example.com are equivalent. All URL parameters are included when comparing SIP URLs for equality.

SIP header fields MAY contain non-SIP URLs. As an example, if a call from a telephone is relayed to the Internet via SIP, the SIP From header field might contain a phone URL.

3 SIP Message Overview

SIP is a text-based protocol and uses the ISO 10646 character set in UTF-8 encoding (RFC 2279 [21]). Senders MUST terminate lines with a CRLF, but receivers MUST also interpret CR and LF by themselves as line terminators.

Except for the above difference in character sets, much of the message syntax is and header fields are identical to HTTP/1.1; rather than repeating the syntax and semantics here we use [HX.Y] to refer to Section X.Y of the current HTTP/1.1 specification (RFC 2068 [11]). In addition, we describe SIP in both prose and an augmented Backus-Naur form (ABNF). See section C for an overview of ABNF.

Note, however, that SIP is not an extension of HTTP.

Unlike HTTP, SIP MAY use UDP. When sent over TCP or UDP, multiple SIP transactions can be carried in a single TCP connection or UDP datagram. UDP datagrams, including all headers, SHOULD NOT be larger than the path maximum transmission unit (MTU) if the MTU is known, or 1500 bytes if the MTU is unknown.

> The 1500 bytes accommodates encapsulation within the "typical" ethernet MTU without IP fragmentation. Recent studies [22] indicate that an MTU of 1500 bytes is a reasonable assumption. The next lower common MTU values are 1006 bytes for SLIP and 296 for low-delay PPP (RFC 1191 [23]). Thus, another reasonable value would be a message size of 950 bytes, to accommodate packet headers within the SLIP MTU without fragmentation.

A SIP message is either a request from a client to a server, or a response from a server to a client.

```
SIP-message  =  Request | Response
```

Both Request (section 4) and Response (section 5) messages use the generic-message format of RFC 822 [24] for transferring entities (the body of the message). Both types of messages consist of a start-line, one or more header fields (also known as "headers"), an empty line (i.e., a line with nothing preceding the carriage-return line-feed (CRLF)) indicating the end of the header fields, and an optional message-body. To avoid confusion with similar-named headers in HTTP, we refer to the headers describing the message body as entity headers. These components are described in detail in the upcoming sections.

```
generic-message  =  start-line
                    *message-header
```

```
                          CRLF
                          [ message-body ]

     start-line       =   Request-Line |      ;Section 4.1
                          Status-Line         ;Section 5.1


     message-header  =  ( general-header
                        | request-header
                        | response-header
                        | entity-header )
```

In the interest of robustness, any leading empty line(s) MUST be ignored. In other words, if the Request or Response message begins with one or more CRLF, CR, or LFs, these characters MUST be ignored.

4 Request

The Request message format is shown below:

```
     Request  =  Request-Line       ;  Section 4.1
                 *( general-header
                 | request-header
                 | entity-header )
                 CRLF
                 [ message-body ]   ;  Section 8
```

4.1 Request-Line

The Request-Line begins with a method token, followed by the Request-URI and the protocol version, and ending with CRLF. The elements are separated by SP characters. No CR or LF are allowed except in the final CRLF sequence.

```
     Request-Line  =  Method SP Request-URI SP SIP-Version CRLF
```

RFC 2543 26

```
general-header   =  Accept                  ; Section 6.7
                 |  Accept-Encoding         ; Section 6.8
                 |  Accept-Language         ; Section 6.9
                 |  Call-ID                 ; Section 6.12
                 |  Contact                 ; Section 6.13
                 |  CSeq                    ; Section 6.17
                 |  Date                    ; Section 6.18
                 |  Encryption              ; Section 6.19
                 |  Expires                 ; Section 6.20
                 |  From                    ; Section 6.21
                 |  Record-Route            ; Section 6.29
                 |  Timestamp               ; Section 6.36
                 |  To                      ; Section 6.37
                 |  Via                     ; Section 6.40
entity-header    =  Content-Encoding        ; Section 6.14
                 |  Content-Length          ; Section 6.15
                 |  Content-Type            ; Section 6.16
request-header   =  Authorization           ; Section 6.11
                 |  Contact                 ; Section 6.13
                 |  Hide                    ; Section 6.22
                 |  Max-Forwards            ; Section 6.23
                 |  Organization            ; Section 6.24
                 |  Priority                ; Section 6.25
                 |  Proxy-Authorization     ; Section 6.27
                 |  Proxy-Require           ; Section 6.28
                 |  Route                   ; Section 6.33
                 |  Require                 ; Section 6.30
                 |  Response-Key            ; Section 6.31
                 |  Subject                 ; Section 6.35
                 |  User-Agent              ; Section 6.39
response-header  =  Allow                   ; Section 6.10
                 |  Proxy-Authenticate      ; Section 6.26
                 |  Retry-After             ; Section 6.32
                 |  Server                  ; Section 6.34
                 |  Unsupported             ; Section 6.38
                 |  Warning                 ; Section 6.41
                 |  WWW-Authenticate        ; Section 6.42
```

Table 3: SIP headers

4.2 Methods

The methods are defined below. Methods that are not supported by a proxy or redirect server are treated by that server as if they were an OPTIONS method and forwarded accordingly. Methods that are not supported by a user agent server or registrar cause a 501 (Not Implemented) response to be returned (Section 7). As in HTTP, the Method token is case-sensitive.

```
Method  =  "INVITE" | "ACK" | "OPTIONS" | "BYE"
           | "CANCEL" | "REGISTER"
```

4.2.1 INVITE

The INVITE method indicates that the user or service is being invited to participate in a session. The message body contains a description of the session to which the callee is being invited. For two-party calls, the caller indicates the type of media it is able to receive and possibly the media it is willing to send as well as their parameters such as network destination. A success response MUST indicate in its message body which media the callee wishes to receive and MAY indicate the media the callee is going to send.

Not all session description formats have the ability to indicate sending media.

A server MAY automatically respond to an invitation for a conference the user is already participating in, identified either by the SIP Call-ID or a globally unique identifier within the session description, with a 200 (OK) response.

If a user agent receives an INVITE request for an existing call leg with a higher CSeq sequence number than any previous INVITE for the same Call-ID, it MUST check any version identifiers in the session description or, if there are no version identifiers, the content of the session description to see if it has changed. It MUST also inspect any other header fields for changes. If there is a change, the user agent MUST update any internal state or information generated as a result of that header. If the session description has changed, the user agent server MUST adjust the session parameters accordingly, possibly after asking the user for confirmation. (Versioning of the session description can be used to accommodate the capabilities of new arrivals to a conference, add or delete media or change from a unicast to a multicast conference.)

This method MUST be supported by SIP proxy, redirect and user agent servers as well as clients.

4.2.2 ACK

The ACK request confirms that the client has received a final response to an INVITE request. (ACK is used only with INVITE requests.) 2xx responses are acknowledged by client user agents, all other final responses by the first proxy or client user agent to receive the response. The Via is always initialized to the host that originates the ACK request, i.e., the client user agent after a 2xx response or the first proxy to receive a non-2xx final response. The ACK request is forwarded as the corresponding INVITE request, based on its Request-URI. See Section 10 for details.

The ACK request MAY contain a message body with the final session description to be used by the callee. If the ACK message body is empty, the callee uses the session description in the INVITE request.

A proxy server receiving an ACK request after having sent a 3xx, 4xx, 5xx, or 6xx response must make a determination about whether the ACK is for it, or for some user agent or proxy server further downstream. This determination is made by examining the tag in the To field. If the tag in the ACK To header field matches the tag in the To header field of the response, and the From, CSeq and Call-ID header fields in the response match those in the ACK, the ACK is meant for the proxy server. Otherwise, the ACK SHOULD be proxied downstream as any other request.

> It is possible for a user agent client or proxy server to receive multiple 3xx, 4xx, 5xx, and 6xx responses to a request along a single branch. This can happen under various error conditions, typically when a forking proxy transitions from stateful to stateless before receiving all responses. The various responses will all be identical, except for the tag in the To field, which is different for each one. It can therefore be used as a means to disambiguate them.

This method MUST be supported by SIP proxy, redirect and user agent servers as well as clients.

4.2.3 OPTIONS

The server is being queried as to its capabilities. A server that believes it can contact the user, such as a user agent where the user is logged in and has been recently active, MAY respond to this request with a capability set. A called user agent MAY return a status reflecting how it would have responded to an invitation, e.g.,

600 (Busy). Such a server SHOULD return an Allow header field indicating the methods that it supports. Proxy and redirect servers simply forward the request without indicating their capabilities.

This method MUST be supported by SIP proxy, redirect and user agent servers, registrars and clients.

4.2.4 BYE

The user agent client uses BYE to indicate to the server that it wishes to release the call. A BYE request is forwarded like an INVITE request and MAY be issued by either caller or callee. A party to a call SHOULD issue a BYE request before releasing a call ("hanging up"). A party receiving a BYE request MUST cease transmitting media streams specifically directed at the party issuing the BYE request.

If the INVITE request contained a Contact header, the callee SHOULD send a BYE request to that address rather than the From address.

This method MUST be supported by proxy servers and SHOULD be supported by redirect and user agent SIP servers.

4.2.5 CANCEL

The CANCEL request cancels a pending request with the same Call-ID, To, From and CSeq (sequence number only) header field values, but does not affect a completed request. (A request is considered completed if the server has returned a final status response.)

A user agent client or proxy client MAY issue a CANCEL request at any time. A proxy, in particular, MAY choose to send a CANCEL to destinations that have not yet returned a final response after it has received a 2xx or 6xx response for one or more of the parallel-search requests. A proxy that receives a CANCEL request forwards the request to all destinations with pending requests.

The Call-ID, To, the numeric part of CSeq and From headers in the CANCEL request are identical to those in the original request. This allows a CANCEL request to be matched with the request it cancels. However, to allow the client to distinguish responses to the CANCEL from those to the original request, the CSeq Method component is set to CANCEL. The Via header field is initialized to the proxy issuing the CANCEL request. (Thus, responses to this CANCEL request only reach the issuing proxy.)

Once a user agent server has received a CANCEL, it MUST NOT issue a 2xx response for the cancelled original request.

A redirect or user agent server receiving a CANCEL request responds with a status of 200 (OK) if the transaction exists and a status of 481 (Transaction Does Not Exist) if not, but takes no further action. In particular, any existing call is unaffected.

> The BYE request cannot be used to cancel branches of a parallel search, since several branches may, through intermediate proxies, find the same user agent server and then terminate the call. To terminate a call instead of just pending searches, the UAC must use BYE instead of or in addition to CANCEL. While CANCEL can terminate any pending request other than ACK or CANCEL, it is typically useful only for INVITE. 200 responses to INVITE and 200 responses to CANCEL are distinguished by the method in the Cseq header field, so there is no ambiguity.

This method MUST be supported by proxy servers and SHOULD be supported by all other SIP server types.

4.2.6 REGISTER

A client uses the REGISTER method to register the address listed in the To header field with a SIP server.

A user agent MAY register with a local server on startup by sending a REGISTER request to the well-known "all SIP servers" multicast address "sip.mcast.net" (224.0.1.75). This request SHOULD be scoped to ensure it is not forwarded beyond the boundaries of the administrative system. This MAY be done with either TTL or administrative scopes [25], depending on what is implemented in the network. SIP user agents MAY listen to that address and use it to become aware of the location of other local users [20]; however, they do not respond to the request. A user agent MAY also be configured with the address of a registrar server to which it sends a REGISTER request upon startup.

Requests are processed in the order received. Clients SHOULD avoid sending a new registration (as opposed to a retransmission) until they have received the response from the server for the previous one.

> Clients may register from different locations, by necessity using different Call-ID values. Thus, the CSeq value cannot be used to enforce ordering. Since registrations are additive, ordering is less of a problem than if each REGISTER request completely replaced all earlier ones.

The meaning of the REGISTER request-header fields is defined as follows. We define "address-of-record" as the SIP address that the registry knows the registrand, typically of the form "user@domain" rather than "user@host". In third-party registration, the entity issuing the request is different from the entity being registered.

To: The To header field contains the address-of-record whose registration is to be created or updated.

From: The From header field contains the address-of-record of the person responsible for the registration. For first-party registration, it is identical to the To header field value.

Request-URI: The Request-URI names the destination of the registration request, i.e., the domain of the registrar. The user name MUST be empty. Generally, the domains in the Request-URI and the To header field have the same value; however, it is possible to register as a "visitor", while maintaining one's name. For example, a traveler sip:alice@acme.com (To) might register under the Request-URI sip:atlanta.hiayh.org , with the former as the To header field and the latter as the Request-URI. The REGISTER request is no longer forwarded once it has reached the server whose authoritative domain is the one listed in the Request-URI.

Call-ID: All registrations from a client SHOULD use the same Call-ID header value, at least within the same reboot cycle.

Cseq: Registrations with the same Call-ID MUST have increasing CSeq header values. However, the server does not reject out-of-order requests.

Contact: The request MAY contain a Contact header field; future non-REGISTER requests for the URI given in the To header field SHOULD be directed to the address(es) given in the Contact header.

If the request does not contain a Contact header, the registration remains unchanged.

This is useful to obtain the current list of registrations in the response. Registrations using SIP URIs that differ in one or more of host, port, transport-param or maddr-param (see Figure 3) from an existing registration are added to the list of registrations. Other URI types are compared according to the standard URI equivalency rules for the URI schema. If the URIs are equivalent to that of an existing registration, the new registration replaces the old one if it has a higher q value or, for the same value of q, if the ttl value is higher. All current registrations MUST share the same action value. Registrations that have a different action than current registrations for the same user MUST be rejected with status of 409 (Conflict).

A proxy server ignores the q parameter when processing non-REGISTER requests, while a redirect server simply returns that parameter in its Contact response header field.

Having the proxy server interpret the q parameter is not sufficient to guide proxy behavior, as it is not clear, for example, how long it is supposed to wait between trying addresses.

If the registration is changed while a user agent or proxy server processes an invitation, the new information SHOULD be used.

This allows a service known as "directed pick-up". In the telephone network, directed pickup permits a user at a remote station who hears his own phone ringing to pick up at that station, dial an access code, and be connected to the calling user as if he had answered his own phone.

A server MAY choose any duration for the registration lifetime. Registrations not refreshed after this amount of time SHOULD be silently discarded. Responses to a registration SHOULD include an Expires header (Section 6.20) or expires Contact parameters (Section 6.13), indicating the time at which the server will drop the registration. If none is present, one hour is assumed. Clients MAY request a registration lifetime by indicating the time in an Expires header in the request. A server SHOULD NOT use a higher lifetime than the one requested, but MAY use a lower one. A single address (if host-independent) MAY be registered from several different clients.

A client cancels an existing registration by sending a REGISTER request with an expiration time (Expires) of zero seconds for a particular Contact or the wildcard Contact designated by a "*" for all registrations. Registrations are matched based on the user, host, port and maddr parameters.

The server SHOULD return the current list of registrations in the 200 response as Contact header fields.

It is particularly important that REGISTER requests are authenticated since they allow to redirect future requests (see Section 13.2).

Beyond its use as a simple location service, this method is needed if there are several SIP servers on a single host. In that case, only one of the servers can use the default port number.

Support of this method is RECOMMENDED.

4.3 Request-URI

The Request-URI is a SIP URL as described in Section 2 or a general URI. It indicates the user or service to which this request is being addressed. Unlike the To field, the Request-URI MAY be re-written by proxies.

When used as a Request-URI, a SIP-URL MUST NOT contain the transport-param, maddr-param, ttl-param, or headers elements. A server that receives a SIP-URL with these elements removes them before further processing.

> Typically, the UAC sets the Request-URI and To to the same SIP URL, presumed to remain unchanged over long time periods. However, if the UAC has cached a more direct path to the callee, e.g., from the Contact header field of a response to a previous request, the To would still contain the long-term, "public" address, while the Request-URI would be set to the cached address.

Proxy and redirect servers MAY use the information in the Request-URI and request header fields to handle the request and possibly rewrite the Request-URI. For example, a request addressed to the generic address sip:sales@acme.com is proxied to the particular person, e.g., sip:bob@ny.acme.com , with the To field remaining as sip:sales@acme.com. At ny.acme.com , Bob then designates Alice as the temporary substitute.

The host part of the Request-URI typically agrees with one of the host names of the receiving server. If it does not, the server SHOULD proxy the request to the address indicated or return a 404 (Not Found) response if it is unwilling or unable to do so. For example, the Request-URI and server host name can disagree in the case of a firewall proxy that handles outgoing calls. This mode of operation is similar to that of HTTP proxies.

If a SIP server receives a request with a URI indicating a scheme other than SIP which that server does not understand, the server MUST return a 400 (Bad Request) response. It MUST do this even if the To header field contains a scheme it does understand. This is because proxies are responsible for processing the Request-URI; the To field is of end-to-end significance.

4.3.1 SIP Version

Both request and response messages include the version of SIP in use, and follow [H3.1] (with HTTP replaced by SIP, and HTTP/1.1 replaced by SIP/2.0) regarding version ordering, compliance requirements, and upgrading of version numbers. To be compliant with this specification, applications sending SIP messages MUST include a SIP-Version of "SIP/2.0".

4.4 Option Tags

Option tags are unique identifiers used to designate new options in SIP. These tags are used in Require (Section 6.30) and Unsupported (Section 6.38) fields.

Syntax:

```
option-tag  =  token
```

See Section C for a definition of token. The creator of a new SIP option MUST either prefix the option with their reverse domain name or register the new option with the Internet Assigned Numbers Authority (IANA). For example, "com.foo.mynewfeature" is an apt name for a feature whose inventor can be reached at "foo.com". Individual organizations are then responsible for ensuring that option names don't collide. Options registered with IANA have the prefix "org.iana.sip.", options described in RFCs have the prefix "org.ietf.rfc.N", where N is the RFC number. Option tags are case-insensitive.

4.4.1 Registering New Option Tags with IANA

When registering a new SIP option, the following information MUST be provided:

- o Name and description of option. The name MAY be of any length, but SHOULD be no more than twenty characters long. The name MUST consist of alphanum (See Figure 3) characters only;

o Indication of who has change control over the option (for example, IETF, ISO, ITU-T, other international standardization bodies, a consortium or a particular company or group of companies);

o A reference to a further description, if available, for example (in order of preference) an RFC, a published paper, a patent filing, a technical report, documented source code or a computer manual;

o Contact information (postal and email address);

Registrations should be sent to iana@iana.org

This procedure has been borrowed from RTSP [4] and the RTP AVP [26].

5 Response

After receiving and interpreting a request message, the recipient responds with a SIP response message. The response message format is shown below:

```
Response  =  Status-Line         ;  Section 5.1
             *( general-header
             | response-header
             | entity-header )
             CRLF
             [ message-body ]    ;  Section 8
```

SIP's structure of responses is similar to [H6], but is defined explicitly here.

5.1 Status-Line

The first line of a Response message is the Status-Line, consisting of the protocol version (Section 4.3.1) followed by a numeric Status-Code and its associated textual phrase, with each element separated by SP characters. No CR or LF is allowed except in the final CRLF sequence.

```
Status-Line  =  SIP-version SP Status-Code SP Reason-Phrase CRLF
```

5.1.1 Status Codes and Reason Phrases

The Status-Code is a 3-digit integer result code that indicates the outcome of the attempt to understand and satisfy the request. The Reason-Phrase is intended to give a short textual description of the Status-Code. The Status-Code is intended for use by automata, whereas the Reason-Phrase is intended for the human user. The client is not required to examine or display the Reason-Phrase.

```
Status-Code     =  Informational                       ;Fig. 5
                |  Success                             ;Fig. 5
                |  Redirection                         ;Fig. 6
                |  Client-Error                        ;Fig. 7
                |  Server-Error                        ;Fig. 8
                |  Global-Failure                      ;Fig. 9
                |  extension-code
extension-code  =  3DIGIT
Reason-Phrase   =  *<TEXT-UTF8,  excluding CR, LF>
```

We provide an overview of the Status-Code below, and provide full definitions in Section 7. The first digit of the Status-Code defines the class of response. The last two digits do not have any categorization role. SIP/2.0 allows 6 values for the first digit:

1xx: Informational -- request received, continuing to process the request;

2xx: Success -- the action was successfully received, understood, and accepted;

3xx: Redirection -- further action needs to be taken in order to complete the request;

4xx: Client Error -- the request contains bad syntax or cannot be fulfilled at this server;

5xx: Server Error -- the server failed to fulfill an apparently valid request;

6xx: Global Failure -- the request cannot be fulfilled at any server.

Figures 5 through 9 present the individual values of the numeric response codes, and an example set of corresponding reason phrases for SIP/2.0. These reason phrases are only recommended; they may be replaced by local equivalents without affecting the protocol. Note that SIP adopts many HTTP/1.1 response codes. SIP/2.0 adds response codes in the range starting at x80 to avoid conflicts with newly defined HTTP response codes, and adds a new class, 6xx, of response codes.

SIP response codes are extensible. SIP applications are not required to understand the meaning of all registered response codes, though such understanding is obviously desirable. However, applications MUST understand the class of any response code, as indicated by the first digit, and treat any unrecognized response as being equivalent to the x00 response code of that class, with the exception that an unrecognized response MUST NOT be cached. For example, if a client receives an unrecognized response code of 431, it can safely assume that there was something wrong with its request and treat the response as if it had received a 400 (Bad Request) response code. In such cases, user agents SHOULD present to the user the message body returned with the response, since that message body is likely to include human-readable information which will explain the unusual status.

```
Informational  =  "100"  ;  Trying
               |  "180"  ;  Ringing
               |  "181"  ;  Call Is Being Forwarded
               |  "182"  ;  Queued
Success        =  "200"  ;  OK
```

Figure 5: Informational and success status codes

```
Redirection  =  "300"  ;  Multiple Choices
             |  "301"  ;  Moved Permanently
             |  "302"  ;  Moved Temporarily
             |  "303"  ;  See Other
             |  "305"  ;  Use Proxy
             |  "380"  ;  Alternative Service
```

Figure 6: Redirection status codes

```
Client-Error  =  "400"  ;  Bad Request
              |  "401"  ;  Unauthorized
              |  "402"  ;  Payment Required
              |  "403"  ;  Forbidden
              |  "404"  ;  Not Found
              |  "405"  ;  Method Not Allowed
              |  "406"  ;  Not Acceptable
              |  "407"  ;  Proxy Authentication Required
              |  "408"  ;  Request Timeout
              |  "409"  ;  Conflict
              |  "410"  ;  Gone
              |  "411"  ;  Length Required
              |  "413"  ;  Request Entity Too Large
              |  "414"  ;  Request-URI Too Large
              |  "415"  ;  Unsupported Media Type
              |  "420"  ;  Bad Extension
              |  "480"  ;  Temporarily not available
              |  "481"  ;  Call Leg/Transaction Does Not Exist
              |  "482"  ;  Loop Detected
              |  "483"  ;  Too Many Hops
              |  "484"  ;  Address Incomplete
              |  "485"  ;  Ambiguous
              |  "486"  ;  Busy Here
```

Figure 7: Client error status codes

```
Server-Error  =  "500"  ;  Internal Server Error
              |  "501"  ;  Not Implemented
              |  "502"  ;  Bad Gateway
              |  "503"  ;  Service Unavailable
              |  "504"  ;  Gateway Time-out
              |  "505"  ;  SIP Version not supported
```

Figure 8: Server error status codes

6 Header Field Definitions

SIP header fields are similar to HTTP header fields in both syntax and semantics. In particular, SIP header fields follow the syntax for message-header as described in [H4.2]. The rules for extending header fields over multiple lines, and use of multiple message-header fields with the same field-name, described in [H4.2] also apply to SIP. The

```
Global-Failure | "600"  ;  Busy Everywhere
               | "603"  ;  Decline
               | "604"  ;  Does not exist anywhere
               | "606"  ;  Not Acceptable
```

Figure 9: Global failure status codes

rules in [H4.2] regarding ordering of header fields apply to SIP, with the exception of Via fields, see below, whose order matters. Additionally, header fields which are hop-by-hop MUST appear before any header fields which are end-to-end. Proxies SHOULD NOT reorder header fields. Proxies add Via header fields and MAY add other hop-by-hop header fields. They can modify certain header fields, such as Max-Forwards (Section 6.23) and "fix up" the Via header fields with "received" parameters as described in Section 6.40.1. Proxies MUST NOT alter any fields that are authenticated (see Section 13.2).

The header fields required, optional and not applicable for each method are listed in Table 4 and Table 5. The table uses "o" to indicate optional, "m" mandatory and "-" for not applicable. A "*" indicates that the header fields are needed only if message body is not empty. See sections 6.15, 6.16 and 8 for details.

The "where" column describes the request and response types with which the header field can be used. "R" refers to header fields that can be used in requests (that is, request and general header fields). "r" designates a response or general-header field as applicable to all responses, while a list of numeric values indicates the status codes with which the header field can be used. "g" and "e" designate general (Section 6.1) and entity header (Section 6.2) fields, respectively. If a header field is marked "c", it is copied from the request to the response.

The "enc." column describes whether this message header field MAY be encrypted end-to-end. A "n" designates fields that MUST NOT be encrypted, while "c" designates fields that SHOULD be encrypted if encryption is used.

The "e-e" column has a value of "e" for end-to-end and a value of "h" for hop-by-hop header fields.

	where	enc.	e-e	ACK	BYE	CAN	INV	OPT	REG
Accept	R		e	-	-	-	o	o	o
Accept	415		e	-	-	-	o	o	o
Accept-Encoding	R		e	-	-	-	o	o	o
Accept-Encoding	415		e	-	-	-	o	o	o
Accept-Language	R		e	-	o	o	o	o	o
Accept-Language	415		e	-	o	o	o	o	o
Allow	200		e	-	-	-	-	m	-
Allow	405		e	o	o	o	o	o	o
Authorization	R		e	o	o	o	o	o	o
Call-ID	gc	n	e	m	m	m	m	m	m
Contact	R		e	o	-	-	o	o	o
Contact	1xx		e	-	-	-	o	o	-
Contact	2xx		e	-	-	-	o	o	o
Contact	3xx		e	-	o	-	o	o	o
Contact	485		e	-	o	-	o	o	o
Content-Encoding	e		e	o	-	-	o	o	o
Content-Length	e		e	o	-	-	o	o	o
Content-Type	e		e	*	-	-	*	*	*
CSeq	gc	n	e	m	m	m	m	m	m
Date	g		e	o	o	o	o	o	o
Encryption	g	n	e	o	o	o	o	o	o
Expires	g		e	-	-	-	o	-	o
From	gc	n	e	m	m	m	m	m	m
Hide	R	n	h	o	o	o	o	o	o
Max-Forwards	R	n	e	o	o	o	o	o	o
Organization	g	c	h	-	-	-	o	o	o

Table 4: Summary of header fields, A--O

Other header fields can be added as required; a server MUST ignore header fields not defined in this specification that it does not understand. A proxy MUST NOT remove or modify header fields not defined in this specification that it does not understand. A compact form of these header fields is also defined in Section 9 for use over UDP when the request has to fit into a single packet and size is an issue.

Table 6 in Appendix A lists those header fields that different client and server types MUST be able to parse.

6.1 General Header Fields

General header fields apply to both request and response messages. The "general-header" field names can be extended reliably only in combination with a change in the protocol version. However, new or

	where	enc.	e-e	ACK	BYE	CAN	INV	OPT	REG
Proxy-Authenticate	407	n	h	o	o	o	o	o	o
Proxy-Authorization	R	n	h	o	o	o	o	o	o
Proxy-Require	R	n	h	o	o	o	o	o	o
Priority	R	c	e	-	-	-	o	-	-
Require	R		e	o	o	o	o	o	o
Retry-After	R	c	e	-	-	-	-	-	o
Retry-After	404,480,486	c	e	o	o	o	o	o	o
	503	c	e	o	o	o	o	o	o
	600,603	c	e	o	o	o	o	o	o
Response-Key	R	c	e	-	o	o	o	o	o
Record-Route	R		h	o	o	o	o	o	o
Record-Route	2xx		h	o	o	o	o	o	o
Route	R		h	o	o	o	o	o	o
Server	r	c	e	o	o	o	o	o	o
Subject	R	c	e	-	-	-	o	-	-
Timestamp	g		e	o	o	o	o	o	o
To	gc(1)	n	e	m	m	m	m	m	m
Unsupported	420		e	o	o	o	o	o	o
User-Agent	g	c	e	o	o	o	o	o	o
Via	gc(2)	n	e	m	m	m	m	m	m
Warning	r		e	o	o	o	o	o	o
WWW-Authenticate	401	c	e	o	o	o	o	o	o

Table 5: Summary of header fields, P--Z; (1): copied with possible addition of tag; (2): UAS removes first Via header field

experimental header fields MAY be given the semantics of general header fields if all parties in the communication recognize them to be "general-header" fields. Unrecognized header fields are treated as "entity-header" fields.

6.2 Entity Header Fields

The "entity-header" fields define meta-information about the message-body or, if no body is present, about the resource identified by the request. The term "entity header" is an HTTP 1.1 term where the response body can contain a transformed version of the message body. The original message body is referred to as the "entity". We retain the same terminology for header fields but usually refer to the "message body" rather then the entity as the two are the same in SIP.

6.3 Request Header Fields

The "request-header" fields allow the client to pass additional information about the request, and about the client itself, to the server. These fields act as request modifiers, with semantics equivalent to the parameters of a programming language method invocation.

The "request-header" field names can be extended reliably only in combination with a change in the protocol version. However, new or experimental header fields MAY be given the semantics of "request-header" fields if all parties in the communication recognize them to be request-header fields. Unrecognized header fields are treated as "entity-header" fields.

6.4 Response Header Fields

The "response-header" fields allow the server to pass additional information about the response which cannot be placed in the Status-Line. These header fields give information about the server and about further access to the resource identified by the Request-URI.

Response-header field names can be extended reliably only in combination with a change in the protocol version. However, new or experimental header fields MAY be given the semantics of "response-header" fields if all parties in the communication recognize them to be "response-header" fields. Unrecognized header fields are treated as "entity-header" fields.

6.5 End-to-end and Hop-by-hop Headers

End-to-end headers MUST be transmitted unmodified across all proxies, while hop-by-hop headers MAY be modified or added by proxies.

6.6 Header Field Format

Header fields ("general-header", "request-header", "response-header", and "entity-header") follow the same generic header format as that given in Section 3.1 of RFC 822 [24]. Each header field consists of a name followed by a colon (":") and the field value. Field names are case-insensitive. The field value MAY be preceded by any amount of leading white space (LWS), though a single space (SP) is preferred. Header fields can be extended over multiple lines by preceding each extra line with at least one SP or horizontal tab (HT). Applications MUST follow HTTP "common form" when generating these constructs, since there might exist some implementations that fail to accept anything beyond the common forms.

```
message-header  =  field-name ":" [ field-value ] CRLF
field-name      =  token
field-value     =  *( field-content | LWS )
field-content   =  < the OCTETs making up the field-value
                    and consisting of either *TEXT-UTF8
                    or combinations of token,
                    separators, and quoted-string>
```

The relative order of header fields with different field names is not significant. Multiple header fields with the same field-name may be present in a message if and only if the entire field-value for that header field is defined as a comma-separated list (i.e., #(values)). It MUST be possible to combine the multiple header fields into one "field-name: field-value" pair, without changing the semantics of the message, by appending each subsequent field-value to the first, each separated by a comma. The order in which header fields with the same field-name are received is therefore significant to the interpretation of the combined field value, and thus a proxy MUST NOT change the order of these field values when a message is forwarded.

Field names are not case-sensitive, although their values may be.

6.7 Accept

The Accept header follows the syntax defined in [H14.1]. The semantics are also identical, with the exception that if no Accept header is present, the server SHOULD assume a default value of application/sdp.

This request-header field is used only with the INVITE, OPTIONS and REGISTER request methods to indicate what media types are acceptable in the response.

Example:

```
Accept: application/sdp;level=1, application/x-private, text/html
```

6.8 Accept-Encoding

The Accept-Encoding request-header field is similar to Accept, but restricts the content-codings [H3.4.1] that are acceptable in the response. See [H14.3]. The syntax of this header is defined in [H14.3]. The semantics in SIP are identical to those defined in [H14.3].

6.9 Accept-Language

The Accept-Language header follows the syntax defined in [H14.4]. The rules for ordering the languages based on the q parameter apply to SIP as well. When used in SIP, the Accept-Language request-header field can be used to allow the client to indicate to the server in which language it would prefer to receive reason phrases, session descriptions or status responses carried as message bodies. A proxy MAY use this field to help select the destination for the call, for example, a human operator conversant in a language spoken by the caller.

Example:

```
Accept-Language: da, en-gb;q=0.8, en;q=0.7
```

6.10 Allow

The Allow entity-header field lists the set of methods supported by the resource identified by the Request-URI. The purpose of this field is strictly to inform the recipient of valid methods associated with the resource. An Allow header field MUST be present in a 405 (Method Not Allowed) response and SHOULD be present in an OPTIONS response.

```
Allow  =  "Allow" ":" 1#Method
```

6.11 Authorization

A user agent that wishes to authenticate itself with a server -- usually, but not necessarily, after receiving a 401 response -- MAY do so by including an Authorization request-header field with the request. The Authorization field value consists of credentials containing the authentication information of the user agent for the realm of the resource being requested.

Section 13.2 overviews the use of the Authorization header, and section 15 describes the syntax and semantics when used with PGP based authentication.

6.12 Call-ID

The Call-ID general-header field uniquely identifies a particular invitation or all registrations of a particular client. Note that a single multimedia conference can give rise to several calls with different Call-IDs, e.g., if a user invites a single individual several times to the same (long-running) conference.

For an INVITE request, a callee user agent server SHOULD NOT alert the user if the user has responded previously to the Call-ID in the INVITE request. If the user is already a member of the conference and the conference parameters contained in the session description have not changed, a callee user agent server MAY silently accept the call, regardless of the Call-ID. An invitation for an existing Call-ID or session can change the parameters of the conference. A client application MAY decide to simply indicate to the user that the conference parameters have been changed and accept the invitation automatically or it MAY require user confirmation.

A user may be invited to the same conference or call using several different Call-IDs. If desired, the client MAY use identifiers within the session description to detect this duplication. For example, SDP contains a session id and version number in the origin (o) field.

The REGISTER and OPTIONS methods use the Call-ID value to unambiguously match requests and responses. All REGISTER requests issued by a single client SHOULD use the same Call-ID, at least within the same boot cycle.

> Since the Call-ID is generated by and for SIP, there is no reason to deal with the complexity of URL-encoding and case-ignoring string comparison.

```
Call-ID   =  ( "Call-ID" | "i" ) ":" local-id "@" host
local-id  =  1*uric
```

"host" SHOULD be either a fully qualified domain name or a globally routable IP address. If this is the case, the "local-id" SHOULD be an identifier consisting of URI characters that is unique within "host". Use of cryptographically random identifiers [27] is RECOMMENDED. If, however, host is not an FQDN or globally routable IP address (such as a net 10 address), the local-id MUST be globally unique, as opposed to unique within host. These rules guarantee overall global uniqueness of the Call-ID. The value for Call-ID MUST NOT be reused for a different call. Call-IDs are case-sensitive.

> Using cryptographically random identifiers provides some protection against session hijacking. Call-ID, To and From are needed to identify a call leg. The distinction between call and call leg matters in calls with third-party control.

For systems which have tight bandwidth constraints, many of the mandatory SIP headers have a compact form, as discussed in Section 9. These are alternate names for the headers which occupy less space in the message. In the case of Call-ID, the compact form is i.

For example, both of the following are valid:

```
Call-ID: f81d4fae-7dec-11d0-a765-00a0c91e6bf6@foo.bar.com
```

or

```
i:f81d4fae-7dec-11d0-a765-00a0c91e6bf6@foo.bar.com
```

6.13 Contact

The Contact general-header field can appear in INVITE, ACK, and REGISTER requests, and in 1xx, 2xx, 3xx, and 485 responses. In general, it provides a URL where the user can be reached for further communications.

INVITE and ACK requests: INVITE and ACK requests MAY contain Contact headers indicating from which location the request is originating.

> This allows the callee to send future requests, such as BYE, directly to the caller instead of through a series of proxies. The Via header is not sufficient since the desired address may be that of a proxy.

INVITE 2xx responses: A user agent server sending a definitive, positive response (2xx) MAY insert a Contact response header field indicating the SIP address under which it is reachable most directly for future SIP requests, such as ACK, within the same Call-ID. The Contact header field contains the address of the server itself or that of a proxy, e.g., if the host is behind a firewall. The value of this Contact header is copied into the Request-URI of subsequent requests for this call if the response did not also contain a Record-Route header. If the response also contains a Record-Route header field, the address in the Contact header field is added as the last item in the Route header field. See Section 6.29 for details.

The Contact value SHOULD NOT be cached across calls, as it may not represent the most desirable location for a particular destination address.

INVITE 1xx responses: A UAS sending a provisional response (1xx) MAY insert a Contact response header. It has the same semantics in a 1xx response as a 2xx INVITE response. Note that CANCEL requests MUST NOT be sent to that address, but rather follow the same path as the original request.

REGISTER requests: REGISTER requests MAY contain a Contact header field indicating at which locations the user is reachable. The REGISTER request defines a wildcard Contact field, "*", which MUST only be used with Expires: 0 to remove all registrations for a particular user. An optional "expires" parameter indicates the desired expiration time of the registration. If a Contact entry does not have an "expires" parameter, the Expires header field is used as the default value. If neither of these mechanisms is used, SIP URIs are assumed to expire after one hour. Other URI schemes have no expiration times.

REGISTER 2xx responses: A REGISTER response MAY return all locations at which the user is currently reachable. An optional "expires" parameter indicates the expiration time of the registration. If a Contact entry does not have an "expires" parameter, the value of the Expires header field indicates the expiration time. If neither mechanism is used, the expiration time specified in the request, explicitly or by default, is used.

3xx and 485 responses: The Contact response-header field can be used with a 3xx or 485 (Ambiguous) response codes to indicate one or more alternate addresses to try. It can appear in responses to BYE, INVITE and OPTIONS methods. The Contact header field contains URIs giving the new locations or user names to try, or may simply specify additional transport parameters. A 300 (Multiple Choices), 301 (Moved Permanently), 302 (Moved Temporarily) or 485 (Ambiguous) response SHOULD contain a Contact field containing URIs of new addresses to be tried. A

301 or 302 response may also give the same location and username that was being tried but specify additional transport parameters such as a different server or multicast address to try or a change of SIP transport from UDP to TCP or vice versa. The client copies the "user", "password", "host", "port" and "user-param" elements of the Contact URI into the Request-URI of the redirected request and directs the request to the address specified by the "maddr" and "port" parameters, using the transport protocol given in the "transport" parameter. If "maddr" is a multicast address, the value of "ttl" is used as the time-to-live value.

Note that the Contact header field MAY also refer to a different entity than the one originally called. For example, a SIP call connected to GSTN gateway may need to deliver a special information announcement such as "The number you have dialed has been changed."

A Contact response header field can contain any suitable URI indicating where the called party can be reached, not limited to SIP URLs. For example, it could contain URL's for phones, fax, or irc (if they were defined) or a mailto: (RFC 2368, [28]) URL.

The following parameters are defined. Additional parameters may be defined in other specifications.

q: The "qvalue" indicates the relative preference among the locations given. "qvalue" values are decimal numbers from 0 to 1, with higher values indicating higher preference.

action: The "action" parameter is used only when registering with the REGISTER request. It indicates whether the client wishes that the server proxy or redirect future requests intended for the client. If this parameter is not specified the action taken depends on server configuration. In its response, the registrar SHOULD indicate the mode used. This parameter is ignored for other requests.

expires: The "expires" parameter indicates how long the URI is valid. The parameter is either a number indicating seconds or a quoted string containing a SIP-date. If this parameter is not provided, the value of the Expires header field determines how long the URI is valid. Implementations MAY treat values larger than 2**32-1 (4294967295 seconds or 136 years) as equivalent to 2**32-1.

```
Contact = ( "Contact" | "m" ) ":"
          ("*" | (1# (( name-addr | addr-spec )
          [ *( ";" contact-params ) ] [ comment ] )))

name-addr      = [ display-name ] "<" addr-spec ">"
addr-spec      = SIP-URL | URI
display-name   = *token | quoted-string
```

```
contact-params = "q"       "=" qvalue
               | "action"  "=" "proxy" | "redirect"
               | "expires" "=" delta-seconds | <"> SIP-date <">
               | extension-attribute

extension-attribute = extension-name [ "=" extension-value ]
```

only allows one address, unquoted. Since URIs can contain commas and semicolons as reserved characters, they can be mistaken for header or parameter delimiters, respectively. The current syntax corresponds to that for the To and From header, which also allows the use of display names.

Example:

```
  Contact: "Mr. Watson" <sip:watson@worcester.bell-telephone.com>
     ;q=0.7; expires=3600,
     "Mr. Watson" <mailto:watson@bell-telephone.com> ;q=0.1
```

6.14 Content-Encoding

```
Content-Encoding  =  ( "Content-Encoding" | "e" ) ":"
                     1#content-coding
```

The Content-Encoding entity-header field is used as a modifier to the "media-type". When present, its value indicates what additional content codings have been applied to the entity-body, and thus what decoding mechanisms MUST be applied in order to obtain the media-type referenced by the Content-Type header field. Content-Encoding is primarily used to allow a body to be compressed without losing the identity of its underlying media type.

If multiple encodings have been applied to an entity, the content codings MUST be listed in the order in which they were applied.

All content-coding values are case-insensitive. The Internet Assigned Numbers Authority (IANA) acts as a registry for content-coding value tokens. See [3.5] for a definition of the syntax for content-coding.

Clients MAY apply content encodings to the body in requests. If the server is not capable of decoding the body, or does not recognize any of the content-coding values, it MUST send a 415 "Unsupported Media Type" response, listing acceptable encodings in the Accept-Encoding header. A server MAY apply content encodings to the bodies in responses. The server MUST only use encodings listed in the Accept-Encoding header in the request.

6.15 Content-Length

The Content-Length entity-header field indicates the size of the message-body, in decimal number of octets, sent to the recipient.

```
Content-Length  =  ( "Content-Length" | "l" ) ":" 1*DIGIT
```

An example is

```
Content-Length: 3495
```

Applications SHOULD use this field to indicate the size of the message-body to be transferred, regardless of the media type of the entity. Any Content-Length greater than or equal to zero is a valid value. If no body is present in a message, then the Content-Length header field MUST be set to zero. If a server receives a UDP request without Content-Length, it MUST assume that the request encompasses the remainder of the packet. If a server receives a UDP request with a Content-Length, but the value is larger than the size of the body sent in the request, the client SHOULD generate a 400 class response. If there is additional data in the UDP packet after the last byte of the body has been read, the server MUST treat the remaining data as a separate message. This allows several messages to be placed in a single UDP packet.

If a response does not contain a Content-Length, the client assumes that it encompasses the remainder of the UDP packet or the data until the TCP connection is closed, as applicable. Section 8 describes how to determine the length of the message body.

6.16 Content-Type

The Content-Type entity-header field indicates the media type of the message-body sent to the recipient. The "media-type" element is defined in [H3.7].

```
Content-Type  =  ( "Content-Type" | "c" ) ":" media-type
```

Examples of this header field are

```
Content-Type: application/sdp
Content-Type: text/html; charset=ISO-8859-4
```

6.17 CSeq

Clients MUST add the CSeq (command sequence) general-header field to every request. A CSeq header field in a request contains the request method and a single decimal sequence number chosen by the requesting client, unique within a single value of Call-ID. The sequence number MUST be expressible as a 32-bit unsigned integer. The initial value of the sequence number is arbitrary, but MUST be less than 2**31. Consecutive requests that differ in request method, headers or body, but have the same Call-ID MUST contain strictly monotonically increasing and contiguous sequence numbers; sequence numbers do not wrap around. Retransmissions of the same request carry the same sequence number, but an INVITE with a different message body or different header fields (a "re-invitation") acquires a new, higher sequence number. A server MUST echo the CSeq value from the request in its response. If the Method value is missing in the received CSeq header field, the server fills it in appropriately.

The ACK and CANCEL requests MUST contain the same CSeq value as the INVITE request that it refers to, while a BYE request cancelling an invitation MUST have a higher sequence number. A BYE request with a CSeq that is not higher should cause a 400 response to be generated.

A user agent server MUST remember the highest sequence number for any INVITE request with the same Call-ID value. The server MUST respond to, and then discard, any INVITE request with a lower sequence number.

All requests spawned in a parallel search have the same CSeq value as the request triggering the parallel search.

```
CSeq  =  "CSeq" ":" 1*DIGIT Method
```

Strictly speaking, CSeq header fields are needed for any SIP request that can be cancelled by a BYE or CANCEL request or where a client can issue several requests for the same Call-ID in close succession. Without a sequence number, the response to an INVITE could be mistaken for the response to the cancellation (BYE or CANCEL). Also, if the network duplicates packets or if an ACK is delayed until the server has sent an additional response, the client could interpret an old response as the response to a re-invitation issued shortly thereafter. Using CSeq also makes it easy for the server to distinguish different versions of an invitation, without comparing the message body.

The Method value allows the client to distinguish the response to an INVITE request from that of a CANCEL response. CANCEL requests can be generated by proxies; if they were to increase the sequence number, it might conflict with a later request issued by the user agent for the same call.

With a length of 32 bits, a server could generate, within a single call, one request a second for about 136 years before needing to wrap around. The initial value of the sequence number is chosen so that subsequent requests within the same call will not wrap around. A non-zero initial value allows to use a time-based initial sequence number, if the client desires. A client could, for example, choose the 31 most significant bits of a 32-bit second clock as an initial sequence number.

Forked requests MUST have the same CSeq as there would be ambiguity otherwise between these forked requests and later BYE issued by the client user agent.

Example:

```
CSeq: 4711 INVITE
```

6.18 Date

Date is a general-header field. Its syntax is:

```
SIP-date  =  rfc1123-date
```

See [H14.19] for a definition of rfc1123-date. Note that unlike HTTP/1.1, SIP only supports the most recent RFC1123 [29] formatting for dates.

The Date header field reflects the time when the request or response is first sent. Thus, retransmissions have the same Date header field value as the original.

The Date header field can be used by simple end systems without a battery-backed clock to acquire a notion of current time.

6.19 Encryption

The Encryption general-header field specifies that the content has been encrypted. Section 13 describes the overall SIP security architecture and algorithms. This header field is intended for end-to-end encryption of requests and responses. Requests are encrypted based on the public key belonging to the entity named in the To header field. Responses are encrypted based on the public key conveyed in the Response-Key header field. Note that the public keys themselves may not be used for the encryption. This depends on the particular algorithms used.

For any encrypted message, at least the message body and possibly other message header fields are encrypted. An application receiving a request or response containing an Encryption header field decrypts the body and then concatenates the plaintext to the request line and headers of the original message. Message headers in the decrypted part completely replace those with the same field name in the plaintext part. (Note: If only the body of the message is to be encrypted, the body has to be prefixed with CRLF to allow proper concatenation.) Note that the request method and Request-URI cannot be encrypted.

Encryption only provides privacy; the recipient has no guarantee that the request or response came from the party listed in the From message header, only that the sender used the recipient's public key. However, proxies will not be able to modify the request or response.

```
Encryption         =  "Encryption" ":" encryption-scheme 1*SP
                      #encryption-params
encryption-scheme  =  token
encryption-params  =  token "=" ( token | quoted-string )
```

The token indicates the form of encryption used; it is described in section 13.

The example in Figure 10 shows a message encrypted with ASCII-armored PGP that was generated by applying "pgp -ea" to the payload to be encrypted.

```
INVITE sip:watson@boston.bell-telephone.com SIP/2.0
Via: SIP/2.0/UDP 169.130.12.5
From: <sip:a.g.bell@bell-telephone.com>
To: T. A. Watson <sip:watson@bell-telephone.com>
Call-ID: 187602141351@worcester.bell-telephone.com
Content-Length: 885
Encryption: PGP version=2.6.2,encoding=ascii
```


```
hQEMAxkp5GPd+j5xAQf/ZDIfGD/PDOM1wayvwdQAKgGgjmZWe+MTy9NEX8O25Red
h0/pyrd/+DV5C2BYs7yzSOSXaj1C/tTK/4do6rtjhP8QA3vbDdVdaFciwEVAcuXs
ODxlNAVqyDi1RqFC28BJIvQ5KfEkPuACKTK7WlRSBc7vNPEA3nyqZGBTwhxRSbIR
RuFEsHSVojdCam4htcqxGnFwD9sksqs6LIyCFaiTAhWtwcCaN437G7mUYzy2KLcA
zPVGq1VQg83b99zPzIxRdlZ+K7+bAnu8Rtu+ohOCMLV3TPXbyp+err1YiThCZHIu
X9dOVj3CMjCP66RSHa/ea0wYTRRNYA/G+kdP8DSUcqYAAAE/hZPX6nFIqk7AVnf6
IpWHUPTelNUJpzUp5Ou+q/5P7ZAsn+cSAuF2YWtVjCf+SQmBR13p2EYYWHoxlA2/
GgKADYe4M3JSwOtqwU8zUJF3FIfk7vsxmSqtUQrRQaiIhqNyG7KxJt4YjWnEjF5E
WUIPhvyGFMJaeQXIyGRYZAYvKKklyAJcm29zLACxU5alX4M25lHQd9FR9Zmq6Jed
wbWvia6cAIfsvlZ9JGocmQYF7pcuz5pnczqP+/yvRqFJtDGD/v3s++G2R+ViVYJO
z/lxGUZaM4IWBCf+4DUjNanZM0oxAE28NjaIZ0rrldDQmO8V9FtPKdHxkqA5iJP+
6vGOFti1Ak4kmEz0vM/Nsv7kkubTFhRl05OiJIGr9S1UhenlZv9l6RuXsOY/EwH2
z8X9N4MhMyXEVuC9rt8/AUhmVQ==
=bOW+
```


Figure 10: PGP Encryption Example

Since proxies can base their forwarding decision on any combination of SIP header fields, there is no guarantee that an encrypted request "hiding" header fields will reach the same destination as an otherwise identical un-encrypted request.

6.20 Expires

The Expires entity-header field gives the date and time after which the message content expires.

This header field is currently defined only for the REGISTER and INVITE methods. For REGISTER, it is a request and response-header field. In a REGISTER request, the client indicates how long it wishes the registration to be valid. In the response, the server indicates the earliest expiration time of all registrations. The server MAY choose a shorter time interval than that requested by the client, but SHOULD NOT choose a longer one.

For INVITE requests, it is a request and response-header field. In a request, the caller can limit the validity of an invitation, for example, if a client wants to limit the time duration of a search or a conference invitation. A user interface MAY take this as a hint to leave the invitation window on the screen even if the user is not currently at the workstation. This also limits the duration of a search. If the request expires before the search completes, the proxy returns a 408 (Request Timeout) status. In a 302 (Moved Temporarily) response, a server can advise the client of the maximal duration of the redirection.

The value of this field can be either a SIP-date or an integer number of seconds (in decimal), measured from the receipt of the request. The latter approach is preferable for short durations, as it does not depend on clients and servers sharing a synchronized clock. Implementations MAY treat values larger than 2**32-1 (4294967295 or 136 years) as equivalent to 2**32-1.

```
Expires  =  "Expires" ":" ( SIP-date | delta-seconds )
```

Two examples of its use are

```
Expires: Thu, 01 Dec 1994 16:00:00 GMT
Expires: 5
```

6.21 From

Requests and responses MUST contain a From general-header field, indicating the initiator of the request. The From field MAY contain the "tag" parameter. The server copies the From header field from the request to the response. The optional "display-name" is meant to be rendered by a human-user interface. A system SHOULD use the display name "Anonymous" if the identity of the client is to remain hidden.

The SIP-URL MUST NOT contain the "transport-param", "maddr-param", "ttl-param", or "headers" elements. A server that receives a SIP-URL with these elements removes them before further processing.

Even if the "display-name" is empty, the "name-addr" form MUST be used if the "addr-spec" contains a comma, question mark, or semicolon.

```
From        =  ( "From" | "f" ) ":" ( name-addr | addr-spec )
               *( ";" addr-params )
addr-params =  tag-param
tag-param   =  "tag=" UUID
UUID        =  1*( hex | "-" )
```

Examples:

```
From: "A. G. Bell" <sip:agb@bell-telephone.com>
From: sip:+12125551212@server.phone2net.com
From: Anonymous <sip:c8oqz84zk7z@privacy.org>
```

The "tag" MAY appear in the From field of a request. It MUST be present when it is possible that two instances of a user sharing a SIP address can make call invitations with the same Call-ID.

The "tag" value MUST be globally unique and cryptographically random with at least 32 bits of randomness. A single user maintains the same tag throughout the call identified by the Call-ID.

> Call-ID, To and From are needed to identify a call leg. The distinction between call and call leg matters in calls with multiple responses to a forked request. The format is similar to the equivalent RFC 822 [24] header, but with a URI instead of just an email address.

6.22 Hide

A client uses the Hide request header field to indicate that it wants the path comprised of the Via header fields (Section 6.40) to be hidden from subsequent proxies and user agents. It can take two forms: Hide: route and Hide: hop. Hide header fields are typically added by the client user agent, but MAY be added by any proxy along the path.

If a request contains the "Hide: route" header field, all following proxies SHOULD hide their previous hop. If a request contains the "Hide: hop" header field, only the next proxy SHOULD hide the previous hop and then remove the Hide option unless it also wants to remain anonymous.

A server hides the previous hop by encrypting the "host" and "port" parts of the top-most Via header field with an algorithm of its choice. Servers SHOULD add additional "salt" to the "host" and "port" information prior to encryption to prevent malicious downstream proxies from guessing earlier parts of the path based on seeing identical encrypted Via headers. Hidden Via fields are marked with the "hidden" Via option, as described in Section 6.40.

A server that is capable of hiding Via headers MUST attempt to decrypt all Via headers marked as "hidden" to perform loop detection. Servers that are not capable of hiding can ignore hidden Via fields in their loop detection algorithm.

> If hidden headers were not marked, a proxy would have to decrypt all headers to detect loops, just in case one was encrypted, as the Hide: Hop option may have been removed along the way.

A host MUST NOT add such a "Hide: hop" header field unless it can guarantee it will only send a request for this destination to the same next hop. The reason for this is that it is possible that the request will loop back through this same hop from a downstream proxy. The loop will be detected by the next hop if the choice of next hop is fixed, but could loop an arbitrary number of times otherwise.

A client requesting "Hide: route" can only rely on keeping the request path private if it sends the request to a trusted proxy. Hiding the route of a SIP request is of limited value if the request results in data packets being exchanged directly between the calling and called user agent.

The use of Hide header fields is discouraged unless path privacy is truly needed; Hide fields impose extra processing costs and restrictions for proxies and can cause requests to generate 482 (Loop Detected) responses that could otherwise be avoided.

The encryption of Via header fields is described in more detail in Section 13.

The Hide header field has the following syntax:

```
Hide  =  "Hide" ":" ( "route" | "hop" )
```

6.23 Max-Forwards

The Max-Forwards request-header field may be used with any SIP method to limit the number of proxies or gateways that can forward the request to the next downstream server. This can also be useful when the client is attempting to trace a request chain which appears to be failing or looping in mid-chain.

```
Max-Forwards  =  "Max-Forwards" ":" 1*DIGIT
```

The Max-Forwards value is a decimal integer indicating the remaining number of times this request message is allowed to be forwarded.

Each proxy or gateway recipient of a request containing a Max-Forwards header field MUST check and update its value prior to forwarding the request. If the received value is zero (0), the recipient MUST NOT forward the request. Instead, for the OPTIONS and REGISTER methods, it MUST respond as the final recipient. For all other methods, the server returns 483 (Too many hops).

If the received Max-Forwards value is greater than zero, then the forwarded message MUST contain an updated Max-Forwards field with a value decremented by one (1).

Example:

```
Max-Forwards: 6
```

6.24 Organization

The Organization general-header field conveys the name of the organization to which the entity issuing the request or response belongs. It MAY also be inserted by proxies at the boundary of an organization.

The field MAY be used by client software to filter calls.

```
Organization  =  "Organization" ":" *TEXT-UTF8
```

6.25 Priority

The Priority request-header field indicates the urgency of the request as perceived by the client.

```
Priority        =  "Priority" ":" priority-value
priority-value  =  "emergency" | "urgent" | "normal"
                |  "non-urgent"
```

It is RECOMMENDED that the value of "emergency" only be used when life, limb or property are in imminent danger.

Examples:

```
Subject: A tornado is heading our way!
Priority: emergency

Subject: Weekend plans
Priority: non-urgent
```

These are the values of RFC 2076 [30], with the addition of "emergency".

6.26 Proxy-Authenticate

The Proxy-Authenticate response-header field MUST be included as part of a 407 (Proxy Authentication Required) response. The field value consists of a challenge that indicates the authentication scheme and parameters applicable to the proxy for this Request-URI.

Unlike its usage within HTTP, the Proxy-Authenticate header MUST be passed upstream in the response to the UAC. In SIP, only UAC's can authenticate themselves to proxies.

The syntax for this header is defined in [H14.33]. See 14 for further details on its usage.

A client SHOULD cache the credentials used for a particular proxy server and realm for the next request to that server. Credentials are, in general, valid for a specific value of the Request-URI at a particular proxy server. If a client contacts a proxy server that has required authentication in the past, but the client does not have credentials for the particular Request-URI, it MAY attempt to use the most-recently used credential. The server responds with 401 (Unauthorized) if the client guessed wrong.

> This suggested caching behavior is motivated by proxies restricting phone calls to authenticated users. It seems likely that in most cases, all destinations require the same password. Note that end-to-end authentication is likely to be destination-specific.

6.27 Proxy-Authorization

The Proxy-Authorization request-header field allows the client to identify itself (or its user) to a proxy which requires authentication. The Proxy-Authorization field value consists of credentials containing the authentication information of the user agent for the proxy and/or realm of the resource being requested.

Unlike Authorization, the Proxy-Authorization header field applies only to the next outbound proxy that demanded authentication using the Proxy- Authenticate field. When multiple proxies are used in a chain, the Proxy-Authorization header field is consumed by the first outbound proxy that was expecting to receive credentials. A proxy MAY relay the credentials from the client request to the next proxy if that is the mechanism by which the proxies cooperatively authenticate a given request.

See [H14.34] for a definition of the syntax, and section 14 for a discussion of its usage.

6.28 Proxy-Require

The Proxy-Require header field is used to indicate proxy-sensitive features that MUST be supported by the proxy. Any Proxy-Require header field features that are not supported by the proxy MUST be negatively acknowledged by the proxy to the client if not supported. Proxy servers treat this field identically to the Require field.

See Section 6.30 for more details on the mechanics of this message and a usage example.

6.29 Record-Route

The Record-Route request and response header field is added to a request by any proxy that insists on being in the path of subsequent requests for the same call leg. It contains a globally reachable Request-URI that identifies the proxy server. Each proxy server adds its Request-URI to the beginning of the list.

The server copies the Record-Route header field unchanged into the response. (Record-Route is only relevant for 2xx responses.)

The calling user agent client copies the Record-Route header into a Route header field of subsequent requests within the same call leg, reversing the order of requests, so that the first entry is closest to the user agent client. If the response contained a Contact header field, the calling user agent adds its content as the last Route header. Unless this would cause a loop, any client MUST send any subsequent requests for this call leg to the first Request-URI in the Route request header field and remove that entry.

The calling user agent MUST NOT use the Record-Route header field in requests that contain Route header fields.

> Some proxies, such as those controlling firewalls or in an automatic call distribution (ACD) system, need to maintain call state and thus need to receive any BYE and ACK packets for the call.

The Record-Route header field has the following syntax:

```
Record-Route  =  "Record-Route" ":" 1# name-addr
```

Proxy servers SHOULD use the "maddr" URL parameter containing their address to ensure that subsequent requests are guaranteed to reach exactly the same server.

Example for a request that has traversed the hosts ieee.org and bell-telephone.com , in that order:

```
Record-Route: <sip:a.g.bell@bell-telephone.com>,
  <sip:a.bell@ieee.org>
```

6.30 Require

The Require request-header field is used by clients to tell user agent servers about options that the client expects the server to support in order to properly process the request. If a server does not understand the option, it MUST respond by returning status code 420 (Bad Extension) and list those options it does not understand in the Unsupported header.

```
Require  =  "Require" ":" 1#option-tag
```

Example:

```
C->S:   INVITE sip:watson@bell-telephone.com SIP/2.0
        Require: com.example.billing
        Payment: sheep_skins, conch_shells

S->C:   SIP/2.0 420 Bad Extension
        Unsupported: com.example.billing
```

> This is to make sure that the client-server interaction will proceed without delay when all options are understood by both sides, and only slow down if options are not understood (as in the example above). For a well-matched client-server pair, the interaction proceeds quickly, saving a round-trip often required by negotiation mechanisms. In addition, it also removes ambiguity when the client requires features that the server does not understand. Some features, such as call handling fields, are only of interest to end systems.

Proxy and redirect servers MUST ignore features that are not understood. If a particular extension requires that intermediate devices support it, the extension MUST be tagged in the Proxy-Require field as well (see Section 6.28).

6.31 Response-Key

The Response-Key request-header field can be used by a client to request the key that the called user agent SHOULD use to encrypt the response with. The syntax is:

```
Response-Key  =  "Response-Key" ":" key-scheme 1*SP #key-param
key-scheme    =  token
key-param     =  token "=" ( token | quoted-string )
```

The "key-scheme" gives the type of encryption to be used for the response. Section 13 describes security schemes.

If the client insists that the server return an encrypted response, it includes a

```
Require: org.ietf.sip.encrypt-response
```

header field in its request. If the server cannot encrypt for whatever reason, it MUST follow normal Require header field procedures and return a 420 (Bad Extension) response. If this Require header field is not present, a server SHOULD still encrypt if it can.

6.32 Retry-After

The Retry-After general-header field can be used with a 503 (Service Unavailable) response to indicate how long the service is expected to be unavailable to the requesting client and with a 404 (Not Found), 600 (Busy), or 603 (Decline) response to indicate when the called party anticipates being available again. The value of this field can be either an SIP-date or an integer number of seconds (in decimal) after the time of the response.

A REGISTER request MAY include this header field when deleting registrations with "Contact: * ;expires: 0". The Retry-After value then indicates when the user might again be reachable. The registrar MAY then include this information in responses to future calls.

An optional comment can be used to indicate additional information about the time of callback. An optional "duration" parameter indicates how long the called party will be reachable starting at the initial time of availability. If no duration parameter is given, the service is assumed to be available indefinitely.

```
Retry-After  =  "Retry-After" ":" ( SIP-date | delta-seconds )
                [ comment ] [ ";" "duration" "=" delta-seconds ]
```

Examples of its use are

```
Retry-After: Mon, 21 Jul 1997 18:48:34 GMT (I'm in a meeting)
```

```
Retry-After: Mon, 01 Jan 9999 00:00:00 GMT
  (Dear John: Don't call me back, ever)
Retry-After: Fri, 26 Sep 1997 21:00:00 GMT;duration=3600
Retry-After: 120
```

In the third example, the callee is reachable for one hour starting at 21:00 GMT. In the last example, the delay is 2 minutes.

6.33 Route

The Route request-header field determines the route taken by a request. Each host removes the first entry and then proxies the request to the host listed in that entry, also using it as the Request-URI. The operation is further described in Section 6.29.

The Route header field has the following syntax:

```
Route  =  "Route" ":" 1# name-addr
```

6.34 Server

The Server response-header field contains information about the software used by the user agent server to handle the request. The syntax for this field is defined in [H14.39].

6.35 Subject

This is intended to provide a summary, or to indicate the nature, of the call, allowing call filtering without having to parse the session description. (Also, the session description does not have to use the same subject indication as the invitation.)

```
Subject  =  ( "Subject" | "s" ) ":" *TEXT-UTF8
```

Example:

```
Subject: Tune in - they are talking about your work!
```

6.36 Timestamp

The timestamp general-header field describes when the client sent the request to the server. The value of the timestamp is of significance only to the client and it MAY use any timescale. The server MUST echo the exact same value and MAY, if it has accurate information about this, add a floating point number indicating the number of seconds that have elapsed since it has received the request. The timestamp is used by the client to compute the round-trip time to the server so that it can adjust the timeout value for retransmissions.

```
Timestamp  =  "Timestamp" ":" *(DIGIT) [ "." *(DIGIT) ] [ delay ]
delay      =  *(DIGIT) [ "." *(DIGIT) ]
```

Note that there MUST NOT be any LWS between a DIGIT and the decimal point.

6.37 To

The To general-header field specifies recipient of the request, with the same SIP URL syntax as the From field.

```
To  =  ( "To" | "t" ) ":" ( name-addr | addr-spec )
       *( ";" addr-params )
```

Requests and responses MUST contain a To general-header field, indicating the desired recipient of the request. The optional "display-name" is meant to be rendered by a human-user interface. The UAS or redirect server copies the To header field into its response, and MUST add a "tag" parameter if the request contained more than one Via header field.

> If there was more than one Via header field, the request was handled by at least one proxy server. Since the receiver cannot know whether any of the proxy servers forked the request, it is safest to assume that they might have.

The SIP-URL MUST NOT contain the "transport-param", "maddr-param", "ttl-param", or "headers" elements. A server that receives a SIP-URL with these elements removes them before further processing.

The "tag" parameter serves as a general mechanism to distinguish multiple instances of a user identified by a single SIP URL. As proxies can fork requests, the same request can reach multiple instances of a user (mobile and home phones, for example). As each can respond, there needs to be a means to distinguish the responses from each at the caller. The situation also arises with multicast requests. The tag in the To header field serves to distinguish responses at the UAC. It MUST be placed in the To field of the response by each instance when there is a possibility that the request was forked at an intermediate proxy. The "tag" MUST be added by UAS, registrars and redirect servers, but MUST NOT be inserted into responses forwarded upstream by proxies. The "tag" is added for all definitive responses for all methods, and MAY be added for informational responses from a UAS or redirect server. All subsequent transactions between two entities MUST include the "tag" parameter, as described in Section 11.

See Section 6.21 for details of the "tag" parameter.

The "tag" parameter in To headers is ignored when matching responses to requests that did not contain a "tag" in their To header.

A SIP server returns a 400 (Bad Request) response if it receives a request with a To header field containing a URI with a scheme it does not recognize.

Even if the "display-name" is empty, the "name-addr" form MUST be used if the "addr-spec" contains a comma, question mark, or semicolon.

The following are examples of valid To headers:

```
To: The Operator <sip:operator@cs.columbia.edu>;tag=287447
To: sip:+12125551212@server.phone2net.com
```

> Call-ID, To and From are needed to identify a call leg. The distinction between call and call leg matters in calls with multiple responses from a forked request. The "tag" is added to the To header field in the response to allow forking of future requests for the same call by proxies, while addressing only one of the possibly several responding user agent servers. It also allows several instances of the callee to send requests that can be distinguished.

6.38 Unsupported

The Unsupported response-header field lists the features not supported by the server. See Section 6.30 for a usage example and motivation.

Syntax:

```
Unsupported  =  "Unsupported" ":" 1#option-tag
```

6.39 User-Agent

The User-Agent general-header field contains information about the client user agent originating the request. The syntax and semantics are defined in [H14.42].

6.40 Via

The Via field indicates the path taken by the request so far. This prevents request looping and ensures replies take the same path as the requests, which assists in firewall traversal and other unusual routing situations.

6.40.1 Requests

The client originating the request MUST insert into the request a Via field containing its host name or network address and, if not the default port number, the port number at which it wishes to receive responses. (Note that this port number can differ from the UDP source port number of the request.) A fully-qualified domain name is RECOMMENDED. Each subsequent proxy server that sends the request onwards MUST add its own additional Via field before any existing Via fields. A proxy that receives a redirection (3xx) response and then searches recursively, MUST use the same Via headers as on the original proxied request.

A proxy SHOULD check the top-most Via header field to ensure that it contains the sender's correct network address, as seen from that proxy. If the sender's address is incorrect, the proxy MUST add an additional "received" attribute, as described 6.40.2.

> A host behind a network address translator (NAT) or firewall may not be able to insert a network address into the Via header that can be reached by the next hop beyond

the NAT. Use of the received attribute allows SIP requests to traverse NAT's which only modify the source IP address. NAT's which modify port numbers, called Network Address Port Translator's (NAPT) will not properly pass SIP when transported on UDP, in which case an application layer gateway is required. When run over TCP, SIP stands a better chance of traversing NAT's, since its behavior is similar to HTTP in this case (but of course on different ports).

A proxy sending a request to a multicast address MUST add the "maddr" parameter to its Via header field, and SHOULD add the "ttl" parameter. If a server receives a request which contained an "maddr" parameter in the topmost Via field, it SHOULD send the response to the multicast address listed in the "maddr" parameter.

If a proxy server receives a request which contains its own address in the Via header value, it MUST respond with a 482 (Loop Detected) status code.

A proxy server MUST NOT forward a request to a multicast group which already appears in any of the Via headers.

This prevents a malfunctioning proxy server from causing loops. Also, it cannot be guaranteed that a proxy server can always detect that the address returned by a location service refers to a host listed in the Via list, as a single host may have aliases or several network interfaces.

6.40.2 Receiver-tagged Via Header Fields

Normally, every host that sends or forwards a SIP message adds a Via field indicating the path traversed. However, it is possible that Network Address Translators (NATs) changes the source address and port of the request (e.g., from net-10 to a globally routable address), in which case the Via header field cannot be relied on to route replies. To prevent this, a proxy SHOULD check the top-most Via header field to ensure that it contains the sender's correct network address, as seen from that proxy. If the sender's address is incorrect, the proxy MUST add a "received" parameter to the Via header field inserted by the previous hop. Such a modified Via header field is known as a receiver-tagged Via header field. An example is:

```
Via: SIP/2.0/UDP erlang.bell-telephone.com:5060
Via: SIP/2.0/UDP 10.0.0.1:5060 ;received=199.172.136.3
```

In this example, the message originated from 10.0.0.1 and traversed a NAT with the external address border.ieee.org (199.172.136.3) to reach erlang.bell-telephone.com. The latter noticed the mismatch, and added a parameter to the previous hop's Via header field, containing the address that the packet actually came from. (Note that the NAT border.ieee.org is not a SIP server.)

6.40.3 Responses

Via header fields in responses are processed by a proxy or UAC according to the following rules:

1. The first Via header field should indicate the proxy or client processing this response. If it does not, discard the message. Otherwise, remove this Via field.

2. If there is no second Via header field, this response is destined for this client. Otherwise, the processing depends on whether the Via field contains a "maddr" parameter or is a receiver-tagged field:

   - If the second Via header field contains a "maddr" parameter, send the response to the multicast address listed there, using the port indicated in "sent-by", or port 5060 if none is present. The response SHOULD be sent using the TTL indicated in the "ttl" parameter, or with a TTL of 1 if that parameter is not present. For robustness, responses MUST be sent to the address indicated in the "maddr" parameter even if it is not a multicast address.

   - If the second Via header field does not contain a "maddr" parameter and is a receiver-tagged field (Section 6.40.2), send the message to the address in the "received" parameter, using the port indicated in the "sent-by" value, or using port 5060 if none is present.

   - If neither of the previous cases apply, send the message to the address indicated by the "sent-by" value in the second Via header field.

6.40.4 User Agent and Redirect Servers

A UAS or redirect server sends a response based on one of the following rules:

- o If the first Via header field in the request contains a "maddr" parameter, send the response to the multicast address listed there, using the port indicated in "sent-by", or port 5060 if none is present. The response SHOULD be sent using the TTL indicated in the "ttl" parameter, or with a TTL of 1 if that parameter is not present. For robustness, responses MUST be sent to the address indicated in the "maddr" parameter even if it is not a multicast address.

o If the address in the "sent-by" value of the first Via field differs from the source address of the packet, send the response to the actual packet source address, similar to the treatment for receiver-tagged Via header fields (Section 6.40.2).

o If neither of these conditions is true, send the response to the address contained in the "sent-by" value. If the request was sent using TCP, use the existing TCP connection if available.

6.40.5 Syntax

The format for a Via header field is shown in Fig. 11. The defaults for "protocol-name" and "transport" are "SIP" and "UDP", respectively. The "maddr" parameter, designating the multicast address, and the "ttl" parameter, designating the time-to-live (TTL) value, are included only if the request was sent via multicast. The "received" parameter is added only for receiver-added Via fields (Section 6.40.2). For reasons of privacy, a client or proxy may wish to hide its Via information by encrypting it (see Section 6.22). The "hidden" parameter is included if this header field was hidden by the upstream proxy (see 6.22). Note that privacy of the proxy relies on the cooperation of the next hop, as the next-hop proxy will, by necessity, know the IP address and port number of the source host.

The "branch" parameter is included by every forking proxy. The token MUST be unique for each distinct request generated when a proxy forks. CANCEL requests MUST have the same branch value as the corresponding forked request. When a response arrives at the proxy it can use the branch value to figure out which branch the response corresponds to. A proxy which generates a single request (non-forking) MAY also insert the "branch" parameter. The identifier has to be unique only within a set of isomorphic requests.

```
Via: SIP/2.0/UDP first.example.com:4000;ttl=16
  ;maddr=224.2.0.1 ;branch=a7c6a8dlze (Example)
Via: SIP/2.0/UDP adk8
```

```
Via               = ( "Via" | "v") ":" 1#( sent-protocol sent-by
                    *( ";" via-params ) [ comment ] )
via-params        = via-hidden | via-ttl | via-maddr
                  | via-received | via-branch
via-hidden        = "hidden"
via-ttl           = "ttl" "=" ttl
via-maddr         = "maddr" "=" maddr
via-received    = "received" "=" host
via-branch        = "branch" "=" token
sent-protocol     = protocol-name "/" protocol-version "/" transport
protocol-name     = "SIP" | token
protocol-version = token
transport         = "UDP" | "TCP" | token
sent-by           = ( host [ ":" port ] ) | ( concealed-host )
concealed-host    = token
ttl               = 1*3DIGIT     ; 0 to 255
```

Figure 11: Syntax of Via header field

6.41 Warning

The Warning response-header field is used to carry additional information about the status of a response. Warning headers are sent with responses and have the following format:

```
Warning         =  "Warning" ":" 1#warning-value
warning-value   =  warn-code SP warn-agent SP warn-text
warn-code       =  3DIGIT
warn-agent      =  ( host [ ":" port ] ) | pseudonym
                   ;  the name or pseudonym of the server adding
                   ;  the Warning header, for use in debugging
warn-text       =  quoted-string
```

A response MAY carry more than one Warning header.

The "warn-text" should be in a natural language that is most likely to be intelligible to the human user receiving the response. This decision can be based on any available knowledge, such as the location of the cache or user, the Accept-Language field in a request, or the Content-Language field in a response. The default language is i-default [31].

Any server MAY add Warning headers to a response. Proxy servers MUST place additional Warning headers before any Authorization headers. Within that constraint, Warning headers MUST be added after any existing Warning headers not covered by a signature. A proxy server MUST NOT delete any Warning header field that it received with a response.

When multiple Warning headers are attached to a response, the user agent SHOULD display as many of them as possible, in the order that they appear in the response. If it is not possible to display all of the warnings, the user agent first displays warnings that appear early in the response.

The warn-code consists of three digits. A first digit of "3" indicates warnings specific to SIP.

This is a list of the currently-defined "warn-code"s, each with a recommended warn-text in English, and a description of its meaning. Note that these warnings describe failures induced by the session description.

Warnings 300 through 329 are reserved for indicating problems with keywords in the session description, 330 through 339 are warnings related to basic network services requested in the session description, 370 through 379 are warnings related to quantitative QoS parameters requested in the session description, and 390 through 399 are miscellaneous warnings that do not fall into one of the above categories.

300 Incompatible network protocol: One or more network protocols contained in the session description are not available.

301 Incompatible network address formats: One or more network address formats contained in the session description are not available.

302 Incompatible transport protocol: One or more transport protocols described in the session description are not available.

303 Incompatible bandwidth units: One or more bandwidth measurement units contained in the session description were not understood.

304 Media type not available: One or more media types contained in the session description are not available.

305 Incompatible media format: One or more media formats contained in the session description are not available.

306 Attribute not understood: One or more of the media attributes in the session description are not supported.

307 Session description parameter not understood: A parameter other than those listed above was not understood.

330 Multicast not available: The site where the user is located does not support multicast.

331 Unicast not available: The site where the user is located does not support unicast communication (usually due to the presence of a firewall).

370 Insufficient bandwidth: The bandwidth specified in the session description or defined by the media exceeds that known to be available.

399 Miscellaneous warning: The warning text can include arbitrary information to be presented to a human user, or logged. A system receiving this warning MUST NOT take any automated action.

1xx and 2xx have been taken by HTTP/1.1.

Additional "warn-code"s, as in the example below, can be defined through IANA.

Examples:

```
Warning: 307 isi.edu "Session parameter 'foo' not understood"
Warning: 301 isi.edu "Incompatible network address type 'E.164'"
```

6.42 WWW-Authenticate

The WWW-Authenticate response-header field MUST be included in 401 (Unauthorized) response messages. The field value consists of at least one challenge that indicates the authentication scheme(s) and parameters applicable to the Request-URI. See [H14.46] for a definition of the syntax, and section 14 for an overview of usage.

The content of the "realm" parameter SHOULD be displayed to the user. A user agent SHOULD cache the authorization credentials for a given value of the destination (To header) and "realm" and attempt to re-use these values on the next request for that destination.

In addition to the "basic" and "digest" authentication schemes defined in the specifications cited above, SIP defines a new scheme, PGP (RFC 2015, [32]), Section 15. Other schemes, such as S/MIME, are for further study.

7 Status Code Definitions

The response codes are consistent with, and extend, HTTP/1.1 response codes. Not all HTTP/1.1 response codes are appropriate, and only those that are appropriate are given here. Other HTTP/1.1 response codes SHOULD NOT be used. Response codes not defined by HTTP/1.1 have codes x80 upwards to avoid clashes with future HTTP response codes. Also, SIP defines a new class, 6xx. The default behavior for unknown response codes is given for each category of codes.

7.1 Informational 1xx

Informational responses indicate that the server or proxy contacted is performing some further action and does not yet have a definitive response. The client SHOULD wait for a further response from the server, and the server SHOULD send such a response without further prompting. A server SHOULD send a 1xx response if it expects to take more than 200 ms to obtain a final response. A server MAY issue zero or more 1xx responses, with no restriction on their ordering or uniqueness. Note that 1xx responses are not transmitted reliably, that is, they do not cause the client to send an ACK. Servers are free to retransmit informational responses and clients can inquire about the current state of call processing by re-sending the request.

7.1.1 100 Trying

Some unspecified action is being taken on behalf of this call (e.g., a database is being consulted), but the user has not yet been located.

7.1.2 180 Ringing

The called user agent has located a possible location where the user has registered recently and is trying to alert the user.

7.1.3 181 Call Is Being Forwarded

A proxy server MAY use this status code to indicate that the call is being forwarded to a different set of destinations.

7.1.4 182 Queued

The called party is temporarily unavailable, but the callee has decided to queue the call rather than reject it. When the callee becomes available, it will return the appropriate final status response. The reason phrase MAY give further details about the status of the call, e.g., "5 calls queued; expected waiting time is 15 minutes". The server MAY issue several 182 responses to update the caller about the status of the queued call.

7.2 Successful 2xx

The request was successful and MUST terminate a search.

7.2.1 200 OK

The request has succeeded. The information returned with the response depends on the method used in the request, for example:

BYE: The call has been terminated. The message body is empty.

CANCEL: The search has been cancelled. The message body is empty.

INVITE: The callee has agreed to participate; the message body indicates the callee's capabilities.

OPTIONS: The callee has agreed to share its capabilities, included in the message body.

REGISTER: The registration has succeeded. The client treats the message body according to its Content-Type.

7.3 Redirection 3xx

3xx responses give information about the user's new location, or about alternative services that might be able to satisfy the call. They SHOULD terminate an existing search, and MAY cause the initiator to begin a new search if appropriate.

Any redirection (3xx) response MUST NOT suggest any of the addresses in the Via (Section 6.40) path of the request in the Contact header field. (Addresses match if their host and port number match.)

To avoid forwarding loops, a user agent client or proxy MUST check whether the address returned by a redirect server equals an address tried earlier.

7.3.1 300 Multiple Choices

The address in the request resolved to several choices, each with its own specific location, and the user (or user agent) can select a preferred communication end point and redirect its request to that location.

The response SHOULD include an entity containing a list of resource characteristics and location(s) from which the user or user agent can choose the one most appropriate, if allowed by the Accept request header. The entity format is specified by the media type given in the Content-Type header field. The choices SHOULD also be listed as Contact fields (Section 6.13). Unlike HTTP, the SIP response MAY contain several Contact fields or a list of addresses in a Contact field. User agents MAY use the Contact header field value for automatic redirection or MAY ask the user to confirm a choice. However, this specification does not define any standard for such automatic selection.

> This status response is appropriate if the callee can be reached at several different locations and the server cannot or prefers not to proxy the request.

7.3.2 301 Moved Permanently

The user can no longer be found at the address in the Request-URI and the requesting client SHOULD retry at the new address given by the Contact header field (Section 6.13). The caller SHOULD update any local directories, address books and user location caches with this new value and redirect future requests to the address(es) listed.

7.3.3 302 Moved Temporarily

The requesting client SHOULD retry the request at the new address(es) given by the Contact header field (Section 6.13). The duration of the redirection can be indicated through an Expires (Section 6.20) header. If there is no explicit expiration time, the address is only valid for this call and MUST NOT be cached for future calls.

7.3.4 305 Use Proxy

The requested resource MUST be accessed through the proxy given by the Contact field. The Contact field gives the URI of the proxy. The recipient is expected to repeat this single request via the proxy. 305 responses MUST only be generated by user agent servers.

7.3.5 380 Alternative Service

The call was not successful, but alternative services are possible. The alternative services are described in the message body of the response. Formats for such bodies are not defined here, and may be the subject of future standardization.

7.4 Request Failure 4xx

4xx responses are definite failure responses from a particular server. The client SHOULD NOT retry the same request without modification (e.g., adding appropriate authorization). However, the same request to a different server might be successful.

7.4.1 400 Bad Request

The request could not be understood due to malformed syntax.

7.4.2 401 Unauthorized

The request requires user authentication.

7.4.3 402 Payment Required

Reserved for future use.

7.4.4 403 Forbidden

The server understood the request, but is refusing to fulfill it. Authorization will not help, and the request SHOULD NOT be repeated.

7.4.5 404 Not Found

The server has definitive information that the user does not exist at the domain specified in the Request-URI. This status is also returned if the domain in the Request-URI does not match any of the domains handled by the recipient of the request.

7.4.6 405 Method Not Allowed

The method specified in the Request-Line is not allowed for the address identified by the Request-URI. The response MUST include an Allow header field containing a list of valid methods for the indicated address.

7.4.7 406 Not Acceptable

The resource identified by the request is only capable of generating response entities which have content characteristics not acceptable according to the accept headers sent in the request.

7.4.8 407 Proxy Authentication Required

This code is similar to 401 (Unauthorized), but indicates that the client MUST first authenticate itself with the proxy. The proxy MUST return a Proxy-Authenticate header field (section 6.26) containing a challenge applicable to the proxy for the requested resource. The client MAY repeat the request with a suitable Proxy-Authorization header field (section 6.27). SIP access authentication is explained in section 13.2 and 14.

This status code is used for applications where access to the communication channel (e.g., a telephony gateway) rather than the callee requires authentication.

7.4.9 408 Request Timeout

The server could not produce a response, e.g., a user location, within the time indicated in the Expires request-header field. The client MAY repeat the request without modifications at any later time.

7.4.10 409 Conflict

The request could not be completed due to a conflict with the current state of the resource. This response is returned if the action parameter in a REGISTER request conflicts with existing registrations.

7.4.11 410 Gone

The requested resource is no longer available at the server and no forwarding address is known. This condition is expected to be considered permanent. If the server does not know, or has no facility to determine, whether or not the condition is permanent, the status code 404 (Not Found) SHOULD be used instead.

7.4.12 411 Length Required

The server refuses to accept the request without a defined Content-Length. The client MAY repeat the request if it adds a valid Content-Length header field containing the length of the message-body in the request message.

7.4.13 413 Request Entity Too Large

The server is refusing to process a request because the request entity is larger than the server is willing or able to process. The server MAY close the connection to prevent the client from continuing the request.

If the condition is temporary, the server SHOULD include a Retry-After header field to indicate that it is temporary and after what time the client MAY try again.

7.4.14 414 Request-URI Too Long

The server is refusing to service the request because the Request-URI is longer than the server is willing to interpret.

7.4.15 415 Unsupported Media Type

The server is refusing to service the request because the message body of the request is in a format not supported by the requested resource for the requested method. The server SHOULD return a list of acceptable formats using the Accept, Accept-Encoding and Accept-Language header fields.

7.4.16 420 Bad Extension

The server did not understand the protocol extension specified in a Require (Section 6.30) header field.

7.4.17 480 Temporarily Unavailable

The callee's end system was contacted successfully but the callee is currently unavailable (e.g., not logged in or logged in in such a manner as to preclude communication with the callee). The response MAY indicate a better time to call in the Retry-After header. The user could also be available elsewhere (unbeknownst to this host), thus, this response does not terminate any searches. The reason phrase SHOULD indicate a more precise cause as to why the callee is unavailable. This value SHOULD be setable by the user agent. Status 486 (Busy Here) MAY be used to more precisely indicate a particular reason for the call failure.

This status is also returned by a redirect server that recognizes the user identified by the Request-URI, but does not currently have a valid forwarding location for that user.

7.4.18 481 Call Leg/Transaction Does Not Exist

This status is returned under two conditions: The server received a BYE request that does not match any existing call leg or the server received a CANCEL request that does not match any existing transaction. (A server simply discards an ACK referring to an unknown transaction.)

7.4.19 482 Loop Detected

The server received a request with a Via (Section 6.40) path containing itself.

7.4.20 483 Too Many Hops

The server received a request that contains more Via entries (hops) (Section 6.40) than allowed by the Max-Forwards (Section 6.23) header field.

7.4.21 484 Address Incomplete

The server received a request with a To (Section 6.37) address or Request-URI that was incomplete. Additional information SHOULD be provided.

> This status code allows overlapped dialing. With overlapped dialing, the client does not know the length of the dialing string. It sends strings of increasing lengths, prompting the user for more input, until it no longer receives a 484 status response.

7.4.22 485 Ambiguous

The callee address provided in the request was ambiguous. The response MAY contain a listing of possible unambiguous addresses in Contact headers.

Revealing alternatives can infringe on privacy concerns of the user or the organization. It MUST be possible to configure a server to respond with status 404 (Not Found) or to suppress the listing of possible choices if the request address was ambiguous.

Example response to a request with the URL lee@example.com :

```
485 Ambiguous SIP/2.0
Contact: Carol Lee <sip:carol.lee@example.com>
```

Contact: Ping Lee <sip:p.lee@example.com>
Contact: Lee M. Foote <sip:lee.foote@example.com>

> Some email and voice mail systems provide this functionality. A status code separate from 3xx is used since the semantics are different: for 300, it is assumed that the same person or service will be reached by the choices provided. While an automated choice or sequential search makes sense for a 3xx response, user intervention is required for a 485 response.

7.4.23 486 Busy Here

The callee's end system was contacted successfully but the callee is currently not willing or able to take additional calls. The response MAY indicate a better time to call in the Retry-After header. The user could also be available elsewhere, such as through a voice mail service, thus, this response does not terminate any searches. Status 600 (Busy Everywhere) SHOULD be used if the client knows that no other end system will be able to accept this call.

7.5 Server Failure 5xx

5xx responses are failure responses given when a server itself has erred. They are not definitive failures, and MUST NOT terminate a search if other possible locations remain untried.

7.5.1 500 Server Internal Error

The server encountered an unexpected condition that prevented it from fulfilling the request. The client MAY display the specific error condition, and MAY retry the request after several seconds.

7.5.2 501 Not Implemented

The server does not support the functionality required to fulfill the request. This is the appropriate response when the server does not recognize the request method and is not capable of supporting it for any user.

7.5.3 502 Bad Gateway

The server, while acting as a gateway or proxy, received an invalid response from the downstream server it accessed in attempting to fulfill the request.

7.5.4 503 Service Unavailable

The server is currently unable to handle the request due to a temporary overloading or maintenance of the server. The implication is that this is a temporary condition which will be alleviated after some delay. If known, the length of the delay MAY be indicated in a Retry-After header. If no Retry-After is given, the client MUST handle the response as it would for a 500 response.

Note: The existence of the 503 status code does not imply that a server has to use it when becoming overloaded. Some servers MAY wish to simply refuse the connection.

7.5.5 504 Gateway Time-out

The server, while acting as a gateway, did not receive a timely response from the server (e.g., a location server) it accessed in attempting to complete the request.

7.5.6 505 Version Not Supported

The server does not support, or refuses to support, the SIP protocol version that was used in the request message. The server is indicating that it is unable or unwilling to complete the request using the same major version as the client, other than with this error message. The response MAY contain an entity describing why that version is not supported and what other protocols are supported by that server. The format for such an entity is not defined here and may be the subject of future standardization.

7.6 Global Failures 6xx

6xx responses indicate that a server has definitive information about a particular user, not just the particular instance indicated in the Request-URI. All further searches for this user are doomed to failure and pending searches SHOULD be terminated.

7.6.1 600 Busy Everywhere

The callee's end system was contacted successfully but the callee is busy and does not wish to take the call at this time. The response MAY indicate a better time to call in the Retry-After header. If the callee does not wish to reveal the reason for declining the call, the callee uses status code 603 (Decline) instead. This status response is returned only if the client knows that no other end point (such as a voice mail system) will answer the request. Otherwise, 486 (Busy Here) should be returned.

7.6.2 603 Decline

The callee's machine was successfully contacted but the user explicitly does not wish to or cannot participate. The response MAY indicate a better time to call in the Retry-After header.

7.6.3 604 Does Not Exist Anywhere

The server has authoritative information that the user indicated in the To request field does not exist anywhere. Searching for the user elsewhere will not yield any results.

7.6.4 606 Not Acceptable

The user's agent was contacted successfully but some aspects of the session description such as the requested media, bandwidth, or addressing style were not acceptable.

A 606 (Not Acceptable) response means that the user wishes to communicate, but cannot adequately support the session described. The 606 (Not Acceptable) response MAY contain a list of reasons in a Warning header field describing why the session described cannot be supported. Reasons are listed in Section 6.41. It is hoped that negotiation will not frequently be needed, and when a new user is being invited to join an already existing conference, negotiation may not be possible. It is up to the invitation initiator to decide whether or not to act on a 606 (Not Acceptable) response.

8 SIP Message Body

8.1 Body Inclusion

Requests MAY contain message bodies unless otherwise noted. Within this specification, the BYE request MUST NOT contain a message body. For ACK, INVITE and OPTIONS, the message body is always a session description. The use of message bodies for REGISTER requests is for further study.

For response messages, the request method and the response status code determine the type and interpretation of any message body. All responses MAY include a body. Message bodies for 1xx responses contain advisory information about the progress of the request. 2xx responses to INVITE requests contain session descriptions. In 3xx responses, the message body MAY contain the description of alternative destinations or services, as described in Section 7.3. For responses with status 400 or greater, the message body MAY contain additional, human-readable information about the reasons for failure. It is RECOMMENDED that information in 1xx and 300 and greater responses be of type text/plain or text/html

8.2 Message Body Type

The Internet media type of the message body MUST be given by the Content-Type header field. If the body has undergone any encoding (such as compression) then this MUST be indicated by the Content-Encoding header field, otherwise Content-Encoding MUST be omitted. If applicable, the character set of the message body is indicated as part of the Content-Type header-field value.

8.3 Message Body Length

The body length in bytes SHOULD be given by the Content-Length header field. Section 6.15 describes the behavior in detail.

The "chunked" transfer encoding of HTTP/1.1 MUST NOT be used for SIP. (Note: The chunked encoding modifies the body of a message in order to transfer it as a series of chunks, each with its own size indicator.)

9 Compact Form

When SIP is carried over UDP with authentication and a complex session description, it may be possible that the size of a request or response is larger than the MTU. To address this problem, a more compact form of SIP is also defined by using abbreviations for the common header fields listed below:

short field name	long field name	note
c	Content-Type	
e	Content-Encoding	
f	From	
i	Call-ID	
m	Contact	from "moved"
l	Content-Length	
s	Subject	
t	To	
v	Via	

Thus, the message in section 16.2 could also be written:

```
INVITE sip:schooler@vlsi.caltech.edu SIP/2.0
v:SIP/2.0/UDP 131.215.131.131;maddr=239.128.16.254;ttl=16
v:SIP/2.0/UDP 128.16.64.19
f:sip:mjh@isi.edu
t:sip:schoolcr@cs.caltech.edu
i:62729-27@128.16.64.19
c:application/sdp
CSeq: 4711 INVITE
l:187

v=0
o=user1 53655765 2353687637 IN IP4 128.3.4.5
s=Mbone Audio
i=Discussion of Mbone Engineering Issues
e=mbone@somewhere.com
c=IN IP4 224.2.0.1/127
t=0 0
m=audio 3456 RTP/AVP 0
```

Clients MAY mix short field names and long field names within the same request. Servers MUST accept both short and long field names for requests. Proxies MAY change header fields between their long and short forms, but this MUST NOT be done to fields following an Authorization header.

10 Behavior of SIP Clients and Servers

10.1 General Remarks

SIP is defined so it can use either UDP (unicast or multicast) or TCP as a transport protocol; it provides its own reliability mechanism.

10.1.1 Requests

Servers discard isomorphic requests, but first retransmit the appropriate response. (SIP requests are said to be idempotent , i.e., receiving more than one copy of a request does not change the server state.)

After receiving a CANCEL request from an upstream client, a stateful proxy server MAY send a CANCEL on all branches where it has not yet received a final response.

When a user agent receives a request, it checks the Call-ID against those of in-progress calls. If the Call-ID was found, it compares the tag value of To with the user's tag and rejects the request if the two do not match. If the From header, including any tag value, matches the value for an existing call leg, the server compares the CSeq header field value. If less than or equal to the current sequence number, the request is a retransmission. Otherwise, it is a new request. If the From header does not match an existing call leg, a new call leg is created.

If the Call-ID was not found, a new call leg is created, with entries for the To, From and Call-ID headers. In this case, the To header field should not have contained a tag. The server returns a response containing the same To value, but with a unique tag added. The tag MAY be omitted if the request contained only one Via header field.

10.1.2 Responses

A server MAY issue one or more provisional responses at any time before sending a final response. If a stateful proxy, user agent server, redirect server or registrar cannot respond to a request with a final response within 200 ms, it SHOULD issue a provisional (1xx) response as soon as possible. Stateless proxies MUST NOT issue provisional responses on their own.

Responses are mapped to requests by the matching To, From, Call-ID, CSeq headers and the branch parameter of the first Via header. Responses terminate request retransmissions even if they have Via headers that cause them to be delivered to an upstream client.

A stateful proxy may receive a response that it does not have state for, that is, where it has no a record of an associated request. If the Via header field indicates that the upstream server used TCP, the proxy actively opens a TCP connection to that address. Thus, proxies have to be prepared to receive responses on the incoming side of passive TCP connections, even though most responses will arrive on the incoming side of an active connection. (An active connection is a TCP connection initiated by the proxy, a passive connection is one accepted by the proxy, but initiated by another entity.)

100 responses SHOULD NOT be forwarded, other 1xx responses MAY be forwarded, possibly after the server eliminates responses with status codes that had already been sent earlier. 2xx responses are forwarded according to the Via header. Once a stateful proxy has received a 2xx response, it MUST NOT forward non-2xx final responses. Responses with status 300 and higher are retransmitted by each stateful proxy until the next upstream proxy sends an ACK (see below for timing details) or CANCEL.

A stateful proxy SHOULD maintain state for at least 32 seconds after the receipt of the first definitive non-200 response, in order to handle retransmissions of the response.

The 32 second window is given by the maximum retransmission duration of 200-class responses using the default timers, in case the ACK is lost somewhere on the way to the called user agent or the next stateful proxy.

10.2 Source Addresses, Destination Addresses and Connections

10.2.1 Unicast UDP

Responses are returned to the address listed in the Via header field (Section 6.40), not the source address of the request.

Recall that responses are not generated by the next-hop stateless server, but generated by either a proxy server or the user agent server. Thus, the stateless proxy can only use the Via header field to forward the response.

10.2.2 Multicast UDP

Requests MAY be multicast; multicast requests likely feature a host-independent Request-URI. This request SHOULD be scoped to ensure it is not forwarded beyond the boundaries of the administrative system. This MAY be done with either TTL or administrative scopes[25], depending on what is implemented in the network.

A client receiving a multicast query does not have to check whether the host part of the Request-URI matches its own host or domain name. If the request was received via multicast, the response is also returned via multicast. Responses to multicast requests are multicast with the same TTL as the request, where the TTL is derived from the ttl parameter in the Via header (Section 6.40).

To avoid response implosion, servers MUST NOT answer multicast requests with a status code other than 2xx or 6xx. The server delays its response by a random interval uniformly distributed between zero and one second. Servers MAY suppress responses if they hear a lower-numbered or 6xx response from another group member prior to sending. Servers do not respond to CANCEL requests received via multicast to avoid request implosion. A proxy or UAC SHOULD send a CANCEL on receiving the first 2xx or 6xx response to a multicast request.

Server response suppression is a MAY since it requires a server to violate some basic message processing rules. Lets say A sends a multicast request, and it is received by B,C, and D. B sends a 200 response. The topmost Via field in the response will contain the address of A. C will also receive this response, and could use it to suppress its own response. However, C would normally not examine this response, as the topmost Via is not its own. Normally, a response received with an incorrect topmost Via MUST be dropped, but not in this case. To distinguish this packet from a misrouted or multicast looped packet is fairly complex, and for this reason the procedure is a MAY. The CANCEL, instead, provides a simpler and more standard way to perform response suppression. It is for this reason that the use of CANCEL here is a SHOULD

10.3 TCP

A single TCP connection can serve one or more SIP transactions. A transaction contains zero or more provisional responses followed by one or more final responses. (Typically, transactions contain exactly one final response, but there are exceptional circumstances, where, for example, multiple 200 responses can be generated.)

The client SHOULD keep the connection open at least until the first final response arrives. If the client closes or resets the TCP connection prior to receiving the first final response, the server treats this action as equivalent to a CANCEL request.

This behavior makes it less likely that malfunctioning clients cause a proxy server to keep connection state indefinitely.

The server SHOULD NOT close the TCP connection until it has sent its final response, at which point it MAY close the TCP connection if it wishes to. However, normally it is the client's responsibility to close the connection.

If the server leaves the connection open, and if the client so desires it MAY re-use the connection for further SIP requests or for requests from the same family of protocols (such as HTTP or stream control commands).

If a server needs to return a response to a client and no longer has a connection open to that client, it MAY open a connection to the address listed in the Via header. Thus, a proxy or user agent MUST be prepared to receive both requests and responses on a "passive" connection.

10.4 Reliability for BYE, CANCEL, OPTIONS, REGISTER Requests

10.4.1 UDP

A SIP client using UDP SHOULD retransmit a BYE, CANCEL, OPTIONS, or REGISTER request with an exponential backoff, starting at a T1 second interval, doubling the interval for each packet, and capping off at a T2 second interval. This means that after the first packet is sent, the second is sent T1 seconds later, the next 2*T1 seconds after that, the next 4*T1 seconds after that, and so on, until the interval hits T2. Subsequent retransmissions are spaced by T2 seconds. If the client receives a provisional response, it continues to retransmit the request, but with an interval of T2 seconds. Retransmissions cease when the client has sent a total of eleven packets, or receives a definitive response. Default values for T1 and T2 are 500 ms and 4 s, respectively. Clients MAY use larger values, but SHOULD NOT use smaller ones. Servers retransmit the response upon receipt of a request retransmission. After the server sends a final response, it cannot be sure the client has received the response, and thus SHOULD cache the results for at least 10*T2 seconds to avoid having to, for example, contact the user or location server again upon receiving a request retransmission.

> Use of the exponential backoff is for congestion control purposes. However, the back-off must cap off, since request retransmissions are used to trigger response retransmissions at the server. Without a cap, the loss of a single response could significantly increase transaction latencies.

The value of the initial retransmission timer is smaller than that that for TCP since it is expected that network paths suitable for interactive communications have round-trip times smaller than 500 ms. For congestion control purposes, the retransmission count has to be bounded. Given that most transactions are expected to consist of one request and a few responses, round-trip time estimation is not likely to be very useful. If RTT estimation is desired to more quickly discover a missing final response, each request retransmission needs to be labeled with its own Timestamp (Section 6.36), returned in the response. The server caches the result until it can be sure that the client will not retransmit the same request again.

Each server in a proxy chain generates its own final response to a CANCEL request. The server responds immediately upon receipt of the CANCEL request rather than waiting until it has received final responses from the CANCEL requests it generates.

BYE and OPTIONS final responses are generated by redirect and user agent servers; REGISTER final responses are generated by registrars. Note that in contrast to the reliability mechanism described in Section 10.5, responses to these requests are not retransmitted periodically and not acknowledged via ACK.

10.4.2 TCP

Clients using TCP do not need to retransmit requests.

10.5 Reliability for INVITE Requests

Special considerations apply for the INVITE method.

1. After receiving an invitation, considerable time can elapse before the server can determine the outcome. For example, if the called party is "rung" or extensive searches are performed, delays between the request and a definitive response can reach several tens of seconds. If either caller or callee are automated servers not directly controlled by a human being, a call attempt could be unbounded in time.

2. If a telephony user interface is modeled or if we need to interface to the PSTN, the caller's user interface will provide "ringback", a signal that the callee is being alerted. (The status response 180 (Ringing) MAY be used to initiate ringback.) Once the callee picks up, the caller needs to know so that it can enable the voice path and stop ringback. The callee's response to the invitation could get lost. Unless the response is transmitted reliably, the caller will continue to hear ringback while the callee assumes that the call exists.

3. The client has to be able to terminate an on-going request, e.g., because it is no longer willing to wait for the connection or search to succeed. The server will have to wait several retransmission intervals to interpret the lack of request retransmissions as the end of a call. If the call succeeds shortly after the caller has given up, the callee will "pick up the phone" and not be "connected".

10.5.1 UDP

For UDP, A SIP client SHOULD retransmit a SIP INVITE request with an interval that starts at T1 seconds, and doubles after each packet transmission. The client ceases retransmissions if it receives a provisional or definitive response, or once it has sent a total of 7 request packets.

A server which transmits a provisional response should retransmit it upon reception of a duplicate request. A server which transmits a final response should retransmit it with an interval that starts at T1 seconds, and doubles for each subsequent packet. Response retransmissions cease when any one of the following occurs:

1. An ACK request for the same transaction is received;

2. a BYE request for the same call leg is received;

3. a CANCEL request for the same call leg is received and the final response status was equal or greater to 300;

4. the response has been transmitted 7 times.

Only the user agent client generates an ACK for 2xx final responses, If the response contained a Contact header field, the ACK MAY be sent to the address listed in that Contact header field. If the response did not contain a Contact header, the client uses the same To header field and Request-URI as for the INVITE request and sends the ACK to the same destination as the original INVITE request. ACKs for final responses other than 2xx are sent to the same server that the original request was sent to, using the same Request-URI as the original request. Note, however, that the To header field in the ACK is copied from the response being acknowledged, not the request, and thus MAY additionally contain the tag parameter. Also note than unlike 2xx final responses, a proxy generates an ACK for non-2xx final responses.

The ACK request MUST NOT be acknowledged to prevent a response-ACK feedback loop. Fig. 12 and 13 show the client and server state diagram for invitations.

The mechanism in Sec. 10.4 would not work well for INVITE because of the long delays between INVITE and a final response. If the 200 response were to get lost, the callee would believe the call to exist, but the voice path would

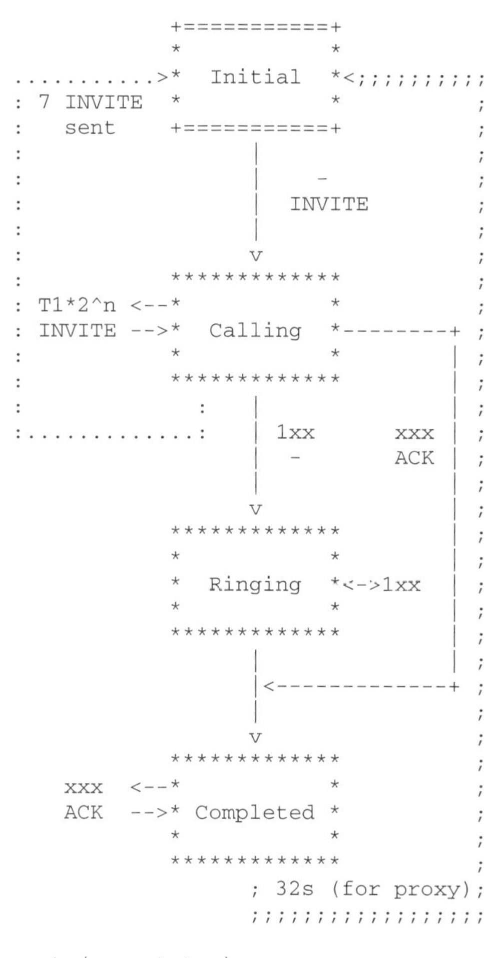

event (xxx=status)
message

Figure 12: State transition diagram of client for INVITE method

```
   7 pkts sent  +===============+
+-------------->*               *
|               *   Initial     *<...............
|;;;;;;;;;;;;;;>*               *               :
|;              +===============+               :
|; CANCEL                !                      :
|;  200                  !  INVITE              :
|;                       !   1xx                :
|;                       !                      :
|;                       v                      :
|;              ****************          BYE   :
|;    INVITE -->*               *         200   :
|;      1xx  <--* Call proceed. *.............>:
|;              *               *               :
|;;;;;;;;;;;;;;;****************                :
|;                    !   !                     :
|:                    !   !                     :
|;         failure    !   !  picks up           :
|;         >= 300     !   !    200              :
|;            +-------+   +-------+             :
|;            v                   v             :
|;       **********          **********         :
|;INVITE<*        *<T1*2^n->*        *>INVITE   :
|;status>* failure *>status<-* success *<status :
|;       *        *         *        *          :
|;;;;;;;;**********          **********         :
|            ! : |           |  !  :            :
|            ! : |           |  !  :            :
+------------!-:-+-----------+  !  :            :
             ! :................!..:.........>:
             !                  !          BYE  :
             +---------+--------+          200  :
  event                ! ACK                    :
message sent           v                        :
                ****************                :
           V---*               *                :
          ACK  *   Confirmed   *                :
           |-->*               *                :
                ****************                .
                        :......................>:
```

Figure 13: State transition diagram of server for INVITE method

be dead since the caller does not know that the callee has picked up. Thus, the INVITE retransmission interval would have to be on the order of a second or two to limit the duration of this state confusion. Retransmitting the response with an exponential back-off helps ensure that the response is received, without placing an undue burden on the network.

10.5.2 TCP

A user agent using TCP MUST NOT retransmit requests, but uses the same algorithm as for UDP (Section 10.5.1) to retransmit responses until it receives an ACK.

It is necessary to retransmit 2xx responses as their reliability is assured end-to-end only. If the chain of proxies has a UDP link in the middle, it could lose the response, with no possibility of recovery. For simplicity, we also retransmit non-2xx responses, although that is not strictly necessary.

10.6 Reliability for ACK Requests

The ACK request does not generate responses. It is only generated when a response to an INVITE request arrives (see Section 10.5). This behavior is independent of the transport protocol. Note that the ACK request MAY take a different path than the original INVITE request, and MAY even cause a new TCP connection to be opened in order to send it.

10.7 ICMP Handling

Handling of ICMP messages in the case of UDP messages is straightforward. For requests, a host, network, port, or protocol unreachable error SHOULD be treated as if a 400-class response was received. For responses, these errors SHOULD cause the server to cease retransmitting the response.

Source quench ICMP messages SHOULD be ignored. TTL exceeded errors SHOULD be ignored. Parameter problem errors SHOULD be treated as if a 400-class response was received.

11 Behavior of SIP User Agents

This section describes the rules for user agent client and servers for generating and processing requests and responses.

11.1 Caller Issues Initial INVITE Request

When a user agent client desires to initiate a call, it formulates an INVITE request. The To field in the request contains the address of the callee. The Request-URI contains the same address. The From field contains the address of the caller. If the From address can appear in requests generated by other user agent clients for the same call, the caller MUST insert the tag parameter in the From field. A UAC MAY optionally add a Contact header containing an address where it would like to be contacted for transactions from the callee back to the caller.

11.2 Callee Issues Response

When the initial INVITE request is received at the callee, the callee can accept, redirect, or reject the call. In all of these cases, it formulates a response. The response MUST copy the To, From, Call-ID, CSeq and Via fields from the request. Additionally, the responding UAS MUST add the tag parameter to the To field in the response if the request contained more than one Via header field. Since a request from a UAC may fork and arrive at multiple hosts, the tag parameter serves to distinguish, at the UAC, multiple responses from different UAS's. The UAS MAY add a Contact header field in the response. It contains an address where the callee would like to be contacted for subsequent transactions, including the ACK for the current INVITE. The UAS stores the values of the To and From field, including any tags. These become the local and remote addresses of the call leg, respectively.

11.3 Caller Receives Response to Initial Request

Multiple responses may arrive at the UAC for a single INVITE request, due to a forking proxy. Each response is distinguished by the "tag" parameter in the To header field, and each represents a distinct call leg. The caller MAY choose to acknowledge or terminate the call with each responding UAS. To acknowledge, it sends an ACK request, and to terminate it sends a BYE request. The To header field in the ACK or BYE MUST be the same as the To field in the 200 response, including any tag. The From header field MUST be the same as the From header field in the 200 (OK) response, including any tag. The Request-URI of the ACK or BYE request MAY be set to whatever address was found in the Contact header field in the 200 (OK) response, if present. Alternately, a UAC may copy the address from the To header field into the Request-URI. The UAC also notes the value of the To and From header fields in each response. For each call leg, the To header field becomes the remote address, and the From header field becomes the local address.

11.4 Caller or Callee Generate Subsequent Requests

Once the call has been established, either the caller or callee MAY generate INVITE or BYE requests to change or terminate the call.

Regardless of whether the caller or callee is generating the new request, the header fields in the request are set as follows. For the desired call leg, the To header field is set to the remote address, and the From header field is set to the local address (both including any tags). The Contact header field MAY be different than the Contact header field sent in a previous response or request. The Request-URI MAY be set to the value of the Contact header field received in a previous request or response from the remote party, or to the value of the remote address.

11.5 Receiving Subsequent Requests

When a request is received subsequently, the following checks are made:

1. If the Call-ID is new, the request is for a new call, regardless of the values of the To and From header fields.

2. If the Call-ID exists, the request is for an existing call. If the To, From, Call-ID, and CSeq values exactly match (including tags) those of any requests received previously, the request is a retransmission.

3. If there was no match to the previous step, the To and From fields are compared against existing call leg local and remote addresses. If there is a match, and the CSeq in the request is higher than the last CSeq received on that leg, the request is a new transaction for an existing call leg.

12 Behavior of SIP Proxy and Redirect Servers

This section describes behavior of SIP redirect and proxy servers in detail. Proxy servers can "fork" connections, i.e., a single incoming request spawns several outgoing (client) requests.

12.1 Redirect Server

A redirect server does not issue any SIP requests of its own. After receiving a request other than CANCEL, the server gathers the list of alternative locations and returns a final response of class 3xx or it refuses the request. For well-formed CANCEL requests, it SHOULD return a 2xx response. This response ends the SIP transaction. The

redirect server maintains transaction state for the whole SIP transaction. It is up to the client to detect forwarding loops between redirect servers.

12.2 User Agent Server

User agent servers behave similarly to redirect servers, except that they also accept requests and can return a response of class 2xx.

12.3 Proxy Server

This section outlines processing rules for proxy servers. A proxy server can either be stateful or stateless. When stateful, a proxy remembers the incoming request which generated outgoing requests, and the outgoing requests. A stateless proxy forgets all information once an outgoing request is generated. A forking proxy SHOULD be stateful. Proxies that accept TCP connections MUST be stateful.

> Otherwise, if the proxy were to lose a request, the TCP client would never retransmit it.

A stateful proxy SHOULD NOT become stateless until after it sends a definitive response upstream, and at least 32 seconds after it received a definitive response.

A stateful proxy acts as a virtual UAS/UAC. It implements the server state machine when receiving requests, and the client state machine for generating outgoing requests, with the exception of receiving a 2xx response to an INVITE. Instead of generating an ACK, the 2xx response is always forwarded upstream towards the caller. Furthermore, ACK's for 200 responses to INVITE's are always proxied downstream towards the UAS, as they would be for a stateless proxy.

A stateless proxy does not act as a virtual UAS/UAC (as this would require state). Rather, a stateless proxy forwards every request it receives downstream, and every response it receives upstream.

12.3.1 Proxying Requests

To prevent loops, a server MUST check if its own address is already contained in the Via header field of the incoming request.

The To, From, Call-ID, and Contact tags are copied exactly from the original request. The proxy SHOULD change the Request-URI to indicate the server where it intends to send the request.

A proxy server always inserts a Via header field containing its own address into those requests that are caused by an incoming request. Each proxy MUST insert a "branch" parameter (Section 6.40).

12.3.2 Proxying Responses

A proxy only processes a response if the topmost Via field matches one of its addresses. A response with a non-matching top Via field MUST be dropped.

12.3.3 Stateless Proxy: Proxying Responses

A stateless proxy removes its own Via field, and checks the address in the next Via field. In the case of UDP, the response is sent to the address listed in the "maddr" tag if present, otherwise to the "received" tag if present, and finally to the address in the "sent-by" field. A proxy MUST remain stateful when handling requests received via TCP.

A stateless proxy MUST NOT generate its own provisional responses.

12.3.4 Stateful Proxy: Receiving Requests

When a stateful proxy receives a request, it checks the To, From (including tags), Call-ID and CSeq against existing request records. If the tuple exists, the request is a retransmission. The provisional or final response sent previously is retransmitted, as per the server state machine. If the tuple does not exist, the request corresponds to a new transaction, and the request should be proxied.

A stateful proxy server MAY generate its own provisional (1xx) responses.

12.3.5 Stateful Proxy: Receiving ACKs

When an ACK request is received, it is either processed locally or proxied. To make this determination, the To, From, CSeq and Call-ID fields are compared against those in previous requests. If there is no match, the ACK request is proxied as if it were an INVITE request. If there is a match, and if the server had ever sent a 200 response upstream, the ACK is proxied. If the server had never sent any responses upstream, the ACK is also proxied. If the server had sent a 3xx, 4xx, 5xx or 6xx response, but no 2xx response, the ACK is processed locally if the tag in the To field of the ACK matches the tag sent by the proxy in the response.

12.3.6 Stateful Proxy: Receiving Responses

When a proxy server receives a response that has passed the Via checks, the proxy server checks the To (without the tag), From (including the tag), Call-ID and CSeq against values seen in previous requests. If there is no match, the response is forwarded upstream to the address listed in the Via field. If there is a match, the "branch" tag in the Via field is examined. If it matches a known branch identifier, the response is for the given branch, and processed by the virtual client for the given branch. Otherwise, the response is dropped.

A stateful proxy should obey the rules in Section 12.4 to determine if the response should be proxied upstream. If it is to be proxied, the same rules for stateless proxies above are followed, with the following addition for TCP. If a request was received via TCP (indicated by the protocol in the top Via header), the proxy checks to see if it has a connection currently open to that address. If so, the response is sent on that connection. Otherwise, a new TCP connection is opened to the address and port in the Via field, and the response is sent there. Note that this implies that a UAC or proxy MUST be prepared to receive responses on the incoming side of a TCP connection. Definitive non 200-class responses MUST be retransmitted by the proxy, even over a TCP connection.

12.3.7 Stateless, Non-Forking Proxy

Proxies in this category issue at most a single unicast request for each incoming SIP request, that is, they do not "fork" requests. However, servers MAY choose to always operate in a mode that allows issuing of several requests, as described in Section 12.4.

The server can forward the request and any responses. It does not have to maintain any state for the SIP transaction. Reliability is assured by the next redirect or stateful proxy server in the server chain.

A proxy server SHOULD cache the result of any address translations and the response to speed forwarding of retransmissions. After the cache entry has been expired, the server cannot tell whether an incoming request is actually a retransmission of an older request. The server will treat it as a new request and commence another search.

12.4 Forking Proxy

The server MUST respond to the request immediately with a 100 (Trying) response.

Successful responses to an INVITE request MAY contain a Contact header field so that the following ACK or BYE bypasses the proxy search mechanism. If the proxy requires future requests to be routed through it, it adds a Record-Route header to the request (Section

6.29).

The following C-code describes the behavior of a proxy server issuing several requests in response to an incoming INVITE request. The function request(r, a, b) sends a SIP request of type r to address a, with branch id b. await_response() waits until a response is received and returns the response. close(a) closes the TCP connection to client with address a. response(r) sends a response to the client. ismulticast() returns 1 if the location is a multicast address and zero otherwise. The variable timeleft indicates the amount of time left until the maximum response time has expired. The variable recurse indicates whether the server will recursively try addresses returned through a 3xx response. A server MAY decide to recursively try only certain addresses, e.g., those which are within the same domain as the proxy server. Thus, an initial multicast request can trigger additional unicast requests.

```
/* request type */
typedef enum {INVITE, ACK, BYE, OPTIONS, CANCEL, REGISTER} Method;

process_request(Method R, int N, address_t address[])
{
  struct {
    int branch;           /* branch id */
    int done;             /* has responded */
  } outgoing[];
  int done[];             /* address has responded */
  char *location[];       /* list of locations */
  int heard = 0;          /* number of sites heard from */
  int class;              /* class of status code */
  int timeleft = 120;     /* sample timeout value */
  int loc = 0;            /* number of locations */
  struct {                /* response */
    int status;           /* response: CANCEL=-1 */
    int locations;        /* number of redirect locations */
    char *location[];     /* redirect locations */
    address_t a;          /* address of respondent */
    int branch;           /* branch identifier */
  } r, best;              /* response, best response */
  int i;

  best.status = 1000;
  for (i = 0; i < N; i++) {
```



```
    request(R, address[i], i);
    outgoing[i].done = 0;
    outgoing[i].branch = i;
  }
```

```
   while (timeleft > 0 && heard < N) {
     r = await_response();
     class = r.status / 100;

     /* If final response, mark branch as done. */
     if (class >= 2) {
       heard++;
       for (i = 0; i < N; i++) {
         if (r.branch == outgoing[i].branch) {
           outgoing[i].done = 1;
           break;
         }
       }
     }
     /* CANCEL: respond, fork and wait for responses */
     else if (class < 0) {
       best.status = 200;
       response(best);
       for (i = 0; i < N; i++) {
         if (!outgoing[i].done)
           request(CANCEL, address[i], outgoing[i].branch);
       }
       best.status = -1;
     }

     /* Send an ACK */

     if (class != 2) {
       if (R == INVITE) request(ACK, r.a, r.branch);
     }


     if (class == 2) {
       if (r.status < best.status) best = r;
       break;
     }
     else if (class == 3) {
       /* A server MAY optionally recurse.  The server MUST check
        * whether it has tried this location before and whether
        * the location is part of the Via path of the incoming
        * request.  This check is omitted here for brevity.
        * Multicast locations MUST NOT be returned to the client if
        * the server is not recursing.
```



```
        */
       if (recurse) {
         multicast = 0;
         N += r.locations;
```

```
          for (i = 0; i < r.locations; i++) {
            request(R, r.location[i]);
          }
        } else if (!ismulticast(r.location)) {
          best = r;
        }
      }
      else if (class == 4) {
        if (best.status >= 400) best = r;
      }
      else if (class == 5) {
        if (best.status >= 500) best = r;
      }
      else if (class == 6) {
        best = r;
        break;
      }
    }

    /* We haven't heard anything useful from anybody. */
    if (best.status == 1000) {
      best.status = 404;
    }
    if (best.status/100 != 3) loc = 0;
    response(best);
  }
```

Responses are processed as follows. The process completes (and state can be freed) when all requests have been answered by final status responses (for unicast) or 60 seconds have elapsed (for multicast). A proxy MAY send a CANCEL to all branches and return a 408 (Timeout) to the client after 60 seconds or more.

1xx: The proxy MAY forward the response upstream towards the client.

2xx: The proxy MUST forward the response upstream towards the client, without sending an ACK downstream. After receiving a 2xx, the server MAY terminate all other pending requests by sending a CANCEL request and closing the TCP connection, if applicable. (Terminating pending requests is advisable as searches consume resources. Also, INVITE requests could "ring" on a number of workstations if the callee is currently logged in more than once.)

3xx: The proxy MUST send an ACK and MAY recurse on the listed Contact addresses. Otherwise, the lowest-numbered response is returned if there were no 2xx responses.

Location lists are not merged as that would prevent forwarding of authenticated responses. Also, responses can have message bodies, so that merging is not feasible.

4xx, 5xx: The proxy MUST send an ACK and remember the response if it has a lower status code than any previous 4xx and 5xx responses. On completion, the lowest-numbered response is returned if there were no 2xx or 3xx responses.

6xx: The proxy MUST forward the response to the client and send an ACK. Other pending requests MAY be terminated with CANCEL as described for 2xx responses.

A proxy server forwards any response for Call-IDs for which it does not have a pending transaction according to the response's Via header. User agent servers respond to BYE requests for unknown call legs with status code 481 (Transaction Does Not Exist); they drop ACK requests with unknown call legs silently.

Special considerations apply for choosing forwarding destinations for ACK and BYE requests. In most cases, these requests will bypass proxies and reach the desired party directly, keeping proxies from having to make forwarding decisions.

A proxy MAY maintain call state for a period of its choosing. If a proxy still has list of destinations that it forwarded the last INVITE to, it SHOULD direct ACK requests only to those downstream servers.

13 Security Considerations

13.1 Confidentiality and Privacy: Encryption

13.1.1 End-to-End Encryption

SIP requests and responses can contain sensitive information about the communication patterns and communication content of individuals. The SIP message body MAY also contain encryption keys for the session itself. SIP supports three complementary forms of encryption to protect privacy:

- o End-to-end encryption of the SIP message body and certain sensitive header fields;

- o hop-by-hop encryption to prevent eavesdropping that tracks who is calling whom;

- o hop-by-hop encryption of Via fields to hide the route a

request has taken.

Not all of the SIP request or response can be encrypted end-to-end because header fields such as To and Via need to be visible to proxies so that the SIP request can be routed correctly. Hop-by-hop encryption encrypts the entire SIP request or response on the wire so that packet sniffers or other eavesdroppers cannot see who is calling whom. Hop-by-hop encryption can also encrypt requests and responses that have been end-to-end encrypted. Note that proxies can still see who is calling whom, and this information is also deducible by performing a network traffic analysis, so this provides a very limited but still worthwhile degree of protection.

SIP Via fields are used to route a response back along the path taken by the request and to prevent infinite request loops. However, the information given by them can also provide useful information to an attacker. Section 6.22 describes how a sender can request that Via fields be encrypted by cooperating proxies without compromising the purpose of the Via field.

End-to-end encryption relies on keys shared by the two user agents involved in the request. Typically, the message is sent encrypted with the public key of the recipient, so that only that recipient can read the message. All implementations SHOULD support PGP-based encryption [33] and MAY implement other schemes.

A SIP request (or response) is end-to-end encrypted by splitting the message to be sent into a part to be encrypted and a short header that will remain in the clear. Some parts of the SIP message, namely the request line, the response line and certain header fields marked with "n" in the "enc." column in Table 4 and 5 need to be read and returned by proxies and thus MUST NOT be encrypted end-to-end. Possibly sensitive information that needs to be made available as plaintext include destination address (To) and the forwarding path (Via) of the call. The Authorization header field MUST remain in the clear if it contains a digital signature as the signature is generated after encryption, but MAY be encrypted if it contains "basic" or "digest" authentication. The From header field SHOULD normally remain in the clear, but MAY be encrypted if required, in which case some proxies MAY return a 401 (Unauthorized) status if they require a From field.

Other header fields MAY be encrypted or MAY travel in the clear as desired by the sender. The Subject, Allow and Content-Type header fields will typically be encrypted. The Accept, Accept-Language, Date, Expires, Priority, Require, Call-ID, Cseq, and Timestamp header fields will remain in the clear.

All fields that will remain in the clear MUST precede those that will be encrypted. The message is encrypted starting with the first character of the first header field that will be encrypted and continuing through to the end of the message body. If no header fields are to be encrypted, encrypting starts with the second CRLF pair after the last header field, as shown below. Carriage return and line feed characters have been made visible as "$", and the encrypted part of the message is outlined.

```
  INVITE sip:watson@boston.bell-telephone.com SIP/2.0$
  Via: SIP/2.0/UDP 169.130.12.5$
  To: T. A. Watson <sip:watson@bell-telephone.com>$
  From: A. Bell <sip:a.g.bell@bell-telephone.com>$
  Encryption: PGP version=5.0$
  Content-Length: 224$
  Call-ID: 187602141351@worcester.bell-telephone.com$
  CSeq: 488$
  $
*******************************************************
* Subject: Mr. Watson, come here.$                    *
* Content-Type: application/sdp$                      *
* $                                                   *
* v=0$                                                *
* o=bell 53655765 2353687637 IN IP4 128.3.4.5$        *
* c=IN IP4 135.180.144.94$                            *
* m=audio 3456 RTP/AVP 0 3 4 5$                       *
*******************************************************
```

An Encryption header field MUST be added to indicate the encryption mechanism used. A Content-Length field is added that indicates the length of the encrypted body. The encrypted body is preceded by a blank line as a normal SIP message body would be.

Upon receipt by the called user agent possessing the correct decryption key, the message body as indicated by the Content-Length field is decrypted, and the now-decrypted body is appended to the clear-text header fields. There is no need for an additional Content-Length header field within the encrypted body because the length of the actual message body is unambiguous after decryption.

Had no SIP header fields required encryption, the message would have been as below. Note that the encrypted body MUST then include a blank line (start with CRLF) to disambiguate between any possible SIP header fields that might have been present and the SIP message body.

```
  INVITE sip:watson@boston.bell-telephone.com SIP/2.0$
  Via: SIP/2.0/UDP 169.130.12.5$
  To: T. A. Watson <sip:watson@bell-telephone.com>$
  From: A. Bell <a.g.bell@bell-telephone.com>$
  Encryption: PGP version=5.0$
  Content-Type: application/sdp$
  Content-Length: 107$
  $
*************************************************
* $                                             *
* v=0$                                          *
* o=bell 53655765 2353687637 IN IP4 128.3.4.5$  *
* c=IN IP4 135.180.144.94$                      *
* m=audio 3456 RTP/AVP 0 3 4 5$                 *
*************************************************
```

13.1.2 Privacy of SIP Responses

SIP requests can be sent securely using end-to-end encryption and authentication to a called user agent that sends an insecure response. This is allowed by the SIP security model, but is not a good idea. However, unless the correct behavior is explicit, it would not always be possible for the called user agent to infer what a reasonable behavior was. Thus when end-to-end encryption is used by the request originator, the encryption key to be used for the response SHOULD be specified in the request. If this were not done, it might be possible for the called user agent to incorrectly infer an appropriate key to use in the response. Thus, to prevent key-guessing becoming an acceptable strategy, we specify that a called user agent receiving a request that does not specify a key to be used for the response SHOULD send that response unencrypted.

Any SIP header fields that were encrypted in a request SHOULD also be encrypted in an encrypted response. Contact response fields MAY be encrypted if the information they contain is sensitive, or MAY be left in the clear to permit proxies more scope for localized searches.

13.1.3 Encryption by Proxies

Normally, proxies are not allowed to alter end-to-end header fields and message bodies. Proxies MAY, however, encrypt an unsigned request or response with the key of the call recipient.

Proxies need to encrypt a SIP request if the end system cannot perform encryption or to enforce organizational security policies.

13.1.4 Hop-by-Hop Encryption

SIP requests and responses MAY also be protected by security mechanisms at the transport or network layer. No particular mechanism is defined or recommended here. Two possibilities are IPSEC [34] or TLS [35]. The use of a particular mechanism will generally need to be specified out of band, through manual configuration, for example.

13.1.5 Via field encryption

When Via header fields are to be hidden, a proxy that receives a request containing an appropriate "Hide: hop" header field (as specified in section 6.22) SHOULD encrypt the header field. As only the proxy that encrypts the field will decrypt it, the algorithm chosen is entirely up to the proxy implementor. Two methods satisfy these requirements:

o The server keeps a cache of Via header fields and the associated To header field, and replaces the Via header field with an index into the cache. On the reverse path, take the Via header field from the cache rather than the message.

This is insufficient to prevent message looping, and so an additional ID MUST be added so that the proxy can detect loops. This SHOULD NOT normally be the address of the proxy as the goal is to hide the route, so instead a sufficiently large random number SHOULD be used by the proxy and maintained in the cache.

It is possible for replies to get directed to the wrong originator if the cache entry gets reused, so great care needs to be taken to ensure this does not happen.

o The server MAY use a secret key to encrypt the Via field, a timestamp and an appropriate checksum in any such message with the same secret key. The checksum is needed to detect whether successful decoding has occurred, and the timestamp is

required to prevent possible replay attacks and to ensure that no two requests from the same previous hop have the same encrypted Via field. This is the preferred solution.

RFC 2543 108

13.2 Message Integrity and Access Control: Authentication

Protective measures need to be taken to prevent an active attacker from modifying and replaying SIP requests and responses. The same cryptographic measures that are used to ensure the authenticity of the SIP message also serve to authenticate the originator of the message. However, the "basic" and "digest" authentication mechanism offer authentication only, without message integrity.

Transport-layer or network-layer authentication MAY be used for hop-by-hop authentication. SIP also extends the HTTP WWW-Authenticate (Section 6.42) and Authorization (Section 6.11) header field and their Proxy counterparts to include cryptographically strong signatures. SIP also supports the HTTP "basic" and "digest" schemes (see Section 14) and other HTTP authentication schemes to be defined that offer a rudimentary mechanism of ascertaining the identity of the caller.

> Since SIP requests are often sent to parties with which no prior communication relationship has existed, we do not specify authentication based on shared secrets.

SIP requests MAY be authenticated using the Authorization header field to include a digital signature of certain header fields, the request method and version number and the payload, none of which are modified between client and called user agent. The Authorization header field is used in requests to authenticate the request originator end-to-end to proxies and the called user agent, and in responses to authenticate the called user agent or proxies returning their own failure codes. If required, hop-by-hop authentication can be provided, for example, by the IPSEC Authentication Header.

SIP does not dictate which digital signature scheme is used for authentication, but does define how to provide authentication using PGP in Section 15. As indicated above, SIP implementations MAY also use "basic" and "digest" authentication and other authentication mechanisms defined for HTTP. Note that "basic" authentication has severe security limitations. The following does not apply to these schemes.

To cryptographically sign a SIP request, the order of the SIP header fields is important. When an Authorization header field is present, it indicates that all header fields following the Authorization

header field have been included in the signature. Therefore, hop-by-hop header fields which MUST or SHOULD be modified by proxies MUST precede the Authorization header field as they will generally be modified or added-to by proxy servers. Hop-by-hop header fields which MAY be modified by a proxy MAY appear before or after the Authorization header. When they appear before, they MAY be modified by a proxy. When they appear after, they MUST NOT be modified by a proxy. To sign a request, a client constructs a message from the request method (in upper case) followed, without LWS, by the SIP version number, followed, again without LWS, by the request headers to be signed and the message body. The message thus constructed is then signed.

For example, if the SIP request is to be:

```
INVITE sip:watson@boston.bell-telephone.com SIP/2.0
Via: SIP/2.0/UDP 169.130.12.5
Authorization: PGP version=5.0, signature=...
From: A. Bell <sip:a.g.bell@bell-telephone.com>
To: T. A. Watson <sip:watson@bell-telephone.com>
Call-ID: 187602141351@worcester.bell-telephone.com
Subject: Mr. Watson, come here.
Content-Type: application/sdp
Content-Length: ...

v=0
o=bell 53655765 2353687637 IN IP4 128.3.4.5
c=IN IP4 135.180.144.94
m=audio 3456 RTP/AVP 0 3 4 5
```

Then the data block that is signed is:

```
INVITESIP/2.0From: A. Bell <sip:a.g.bell@bell-telephone.com>
To: T. A. Watson <sip:watson@bell-telephone.com>
Call-ID: 187602141351@worcester.bell-telephone.com
Subject: Mr. Watson, come here.
Content-Type: application/sdp
Content-Length: ...

v=0
o=bell 53655765 2353687637 IN IP4 128.3.4.5
c=IN IP4 135.180.144.94
m=audio 3456 RTP/AVP 0 3 4 5
```


Clients wishing to authenticate requests MUST construct the portion of the message below the Authorization header using a canonical form. This allows a proxy to parse the message, take it apart, and reconstruct it, without causing an authentication failure due to extra white space, for example. Canonical form consists of the following rules:

- o No short form header fields
- o Header field names are capitalized as shown in this document
- o No white space between the header name and the colon
- o A single space after the colon
- o Line termination with a CRLF
- o No line folding
- o No comma separated lists of header values; each must appear as a separate header
- o Only a single SP between tokens, between tokens and quoted strings, and between quoted strings; no SP after last token or quoted string
- o No LWS between tokens and separators, except as described above for after the colon in header fields

Note that if a message is encrypted and authenticated using a digital signature, when the message is generated encryption is performed before the digital signature is generated. On receipt, the digital signature is checked before decryption.

A client MAY require that a server sign its response by including a Require: org.ietf.sip.signed-response request header field. The client indicates the desired authentication method via the WWW-Authenticate header.

The correct behavior in handling unauthenticated responses to a request that requires authenticated responses is described in section 13.2.1.

13.2.1 Trusting responses

There is the possibility that an eavesdropper listens to requests and then injects unauthenticated responses that terminate, redirect or otherwise interfere with a call. (Even encrypted requests contain enough information to fake a response.)

Clients need to be particularly careful with 3xx redirection responses. Thus a client receiving, for example, a 301 (Moved Permanently) which was not authenticated when the public key of the called user agent is known to the client, and authentication was requested in the request SHOULD be treated as suspicious. The correct behavior in such a case would be for the called-user to form a dated response containing the Contact field to be used, to sign it, and give this signed stub response to the proxy that will provide the redirection. Thus the response can be authenticated correctly. A client SHOULD NOT automatically redirect such a request to the new location without alerting the user to the authentication failure before doing so.

Another problem might be responses such as 6xx failure responses which would simply terminate a search, or "4xx" and "5xx" response failures.

If TCP is being used, a proxy SHOULD treat 4xx and 5xx responses as valid, as they will not terminate a search. However, fake 6xx responses from a rogue proxy terminate a search incorrectly. 6xx responses SHOULD be authenticated if requested by the client, and failure to do so SHOULD cause such a client to ignore the 6xx response and continue a search.

With UDP, the same problem with 6xx responses exists, but also an active eavesdropper can generate 4xx and 5xx responses that might cause a proxy or client to believe a failure occurred when in fact it did not. Typically 4xx and 5xx responses will not be signed by the called user agent, and so there is no simple way to detect these rogue responses. This problem is best prevented by using hop-by-hop encryption of the SIP request, which removes any additional problems that UDP might have over TCP.

These attacks are prevented by having the client require response authentication and dropping unauthenticated responses. A server user agent that cannot perform response authentication responds using the normal Require response of 420 (Bad Extension).

13.3 Callee Privacy

User location and SIP-initiated calls can violate a callee's privacy. An implementation SHOULD be able to restrict, on a per-user basis, what kind of location and availability information is given out to certain classes of callers.

13.4 Known Security Problems

With either TCP or UDP, a denial of service attack exists by a rogue proxy sending 6xx responses. Although a client SHOULD choose to ignore such responses if it requested authentication, a proxy cannot do so. It is obliged to forward the 6xx response back to the client. The client can then ignore the response, but if it repeats the request it will probably reach the same rogue proxy again, and the process will repeat.

14 SIP Authentication using HTTP Basic and Digest Schemes

SIP implementations MAY use HTTP's basic and digest authentication mechanisms to provide a rudimentary form of security. This section overviews usage of these mechanisms in SIP. The basic operation is almost completely identical to that for HTTP [36]. This section outlines this operation, pointing to [36] for details, and noting the differences when used in SIP.

14.1 Framework

The framework for SIP authentication parallels that for HTTP [36]. In particular, the BNF for auth-scheme, auth-param, challenge, realm, realm-value, and credentials is identical. The 401 response is used by user agent servers in SIP to challenge the authorization of a user agent client. Additionally, registrars and redirect servers MAY make use of 401 responses for authorization, but proxies MUST NOT, and instead MAY use the 407 response. The requirements for inclusion of the Proxy-Authenticate, Proxy-Authorization, WWW-Authenticate, and Authorization in the various messages is identical to [36].

Since SIP does not have the concept of a canonical root URL, the notion of protections spaces are interpreted differently for SIP. The realm is a protection domain for all SIP URIs with the same value for the userinfo, host and port part of the SIP Request-URI. For example:

```
INVITE sip:alice.wonderland@example.com SIP/2.0
WWW-Authenticate:  Basic realm="business"
```


and

```
INVITE sip:aw@example.com SIP/2.0
```

WWW-Authenticate: Basic realm="business"

define different protection realms according to this rule.

When a UAC resubmits a request with its credentials after receiving a 401 or 407 response, it MUST increment the CSeq header field as it would normally do when sending an updated request.

14.2 Basic Authentication

The rules for basic authentication follow those defined in [36], but with the words "origin server" replaced with "user agent server, redirect server , or registrar".

Since SIP URIs are not hierarchical, the paragraph in [36] that states that "all paths at or deeper than the depth of the last symbolic element in the path field of the Request-URI also are within the protection space specified by the Basic realm value of the current challenge" does not apply for SIP. SIP clients MAY preemptively send the corresponding Authorization header with requests for SIP URIs within the same protection realm (as defined above) without receipt of another challenge from the server.

14.3 Digest Authentication

The rules for digest authentication follow those defined in [36], with "HTTP 1.1" replaced by "SIP/2.0" in addition to the following differences:

1. The URI included in the challenge has the following BNF:

```
URI  =  SIP-URL
```

2. The BNF for digest-uri-value is:

```
digest-uri-value  =  Request-URI ; a defined in Section
4.3
```


3. The example procedure for choosing a nonce based on Etag does not work for SIP.

4. The Authentication-Info and Proxy-Authentication-Info

fields are not used in SIP.

5. The text in [36] regarding cache operation does not apply to SIP.

6. [36] requires that a server check that the URI in the request line, and the URI included in the Authorization header, point to the same resource. In a SIP context, these two URI's may actually refer to different users, due to forwarding at some proxy. Therefore, in SIP, a server MAY check that the request-uri in the Authorization header corresponds to a user that the server is willing to accept forwarded or direct calls for.

14.4 Proxy-Authentication

The use of the Proxy-Authentication and Proxy-Authorization parallel that as described in [36], with one difference. Proxies MUST NOT add the Proxy-Authorization header. 407 responses MUST be forwarded upstream towards the client following the procedures for any other response. It is the client's responsibility to add the Proxy-Authorization header containing credentials for the proxy which has asked for authentication.

> If a proxy were to resubmit a request with a Proxy-Authorization header field, it would need to increment the CSeq in the new request. However, this would mean that the UAC which submitted the original request would discard a response from the UAS, as the CSeq value would be different.

See sections 6.26 and 6.27 for additional information on usage of these fields as they apply to SIP.

15 SIP Security Using PGP

15.1 PGP Authentication Scheme

The "pgp" authentication scheme is based on the model that the client authenticates itself with a request signed with the client's private key. The server can then ascertain the origin of the request if it has access to the public key, preferably signed by a trusted third party.

15.1.1 The WWW-Authenticate Response Header

```
WWW-Authenticate =  "WWW-Authenticate" ":" "pgp" pgp-challenge
pgp-challenge    =  * (";" pgp-params )
pgp-params       =  realm | pgp-version | pgp-algorithm | nonce
realm            =  "realm" "=" realm-value
realm-value      =  quoted-string
pgp-version      =  "version" "="
                     <"> digit *( "." digit ) *letter <">
pgp-algorithm    =  "algorithm" "=" ( "md5" | "sha1" | token )
nonce            =  "nonce" "=" nonce-value
nonce-value      =  quoted-string
```

The meanings of the values of the parameters used above are as follows:

realm: A string to be displayed to users so they know which identity to use. This string SHOULD contain at least the name of the host performing the authentication and MAY additionally indicate the collection of users who might have access. An example might be " Users with call-out privileges ".

pgp-algorithm: The value of this parameter indicates the PGP message integrity check (MIC) to be used to produce the signature. If this not present it is assumed to be "md5". The currently defined values are "md5" for the MD5 checksum, and "sha1" for the SHA.1 algorithm.

pgp-version: The version of PGP that the client MUST use. Common values are "2.6.2" and "5.0". The default is 5.0.

nonce: A server-specified data string which should be uniquely generated each time a 401 response is made. It is RECOMMENDED that this string be base64 or hexadecimal data. Specifically, since the string is passed in the header lines as a quoted string, the double-quote character is not allowed. The contents of the nonce are implementation dependent. The quality of the implementation depends on a good choice. Since the nonce is used only to prevent replay attacks and is signed, a time stamp in units convenient to the server is sufficient.

Replay attacks within the duration of the call setup are of limited interest, so that timestamps with a resolution of a few seconds are often should be sufficient. In that case, the server does not have to keep a record of the nonces.

Example:

```
WWW-Authenticate: pgp ;version="5.0"
  ;realm="Your Startrek identity, please" ;algorithm=md5
  ;nonce="913082051"
```

15.1.2 The Authorization Request Header

The client is expected to retry the request, passing an Authorization header line, which is defined as follows.

```
Authorization  =  "Authorization" ":" "pgp" *( ";" pgp-response )
pgp-response   =  realm | pgp-version | pgp-signature
                  | signed-by | nonce
pgp-signature  =  "signature" "=" quoted-string
signed-by      =  "signed-by" "=" <"> URI <">
```

The client MUST increment the CSeq header before resubmitting the request. The signature MUST correspond to the From header of the request unless the signed-by parameter is provided.

pgp-signature: The PGP ASCII-armored signature [33], as it appears between the "BEGIN PGP MESSAGE" and "END PGP MESSAGE" delimiters, without the version indication. The signature is included without any linebreaks.

The signature is computed across the nonce (if present), request method, request version and header fields following the Authorization header and the message body, in the same order as they appear in the message. The request method and version are prepended to the header fields without any white space. The signature is computed across the headers as sent, and the terminating CRLF. The CRLF following the Authorization header is NOT included in the signature.

A server MAY be configured not to generate nonces only if replay attacks are not a concern.

Not generating nonces avoids the additional set of request, 401 response and possibly ACK messages and reduces delay by one round-trip time.

Using the ASCII-armored version is about 25% less space-efficient than including the binary signature, but it is significantly easier for the receiver to piece together. Versions of the PGP program always include the full (compressed) signed text in their output unless ASCII-armored mode (-sta) is specified. Typical signatures are about 200 bytes long. -- The PGP signature mechanism allows the client to simply pass the request to an external PGP program. This relies on the requirement that proxy servers are not allowed to reorder or change header fields.

realm: The realm is copied from the corresponding WWW-Authenticate header field parameter.

signed-by: If and only if the request was not signed by the entity listed in the From header, the signed-by header indicates the name of the signing entity, expressed as a URI.

Receivers of signed SIP messages SHOULD discard any end-to-end header fields above the Authorization header, as they may have been maliciously added en route by a proxy.

Example:

```
Authorization: pgp version="5.0"
  ;realm="Your Startrek identity, please"
  ;nonce="913082051"
  ;signature="iQB1AwUBNNJiUaYBnHmiiQh1AQFYsgL/Wt3dk6TWK81/b0gcNDf
  VAUGU4rhEBW972IPxFSOZ94L1qhCLInTPaqhHFw1cb31B01rA0RhpV4t5yCdUt
  SRYBSkOK29o5e1K1FeW23EzYPVUm2T1DAhbcjbMdfC+KLFX
  =aIrx"
```

15.2 PGP Encryption Scheme

The PGP encryption scheme uses the following syntax:

```
Encryption     =  "Encryption" ":" "pgp" pgp-eparams
pgp-eparams    =  1# ( pgp-version | pgp-encoding )
pgp-encoding   =  "encoding" "=" "ascii" | token
```


encoding: Describes the encoding or "armor" used by PGP. The value "ascii" refers to the standard PGP ASCII armor, without the lines containing "BEGIN PGP MESSAGE" and "END PGP MESSAGE" and without the version identifier. By default, the encrypted part is included as binary.

Example:

```
Encryption: pgp version="2.6.2", encoding="ascii"
```

15.3 Response-Key Header Field for PGP

```
Response-Key  =  "Response-Key" ":" "pgp" pgp-eparams
pgp-eparams   =  1# ( pgp-version | pgp-encoding | pgp-key)
pgp-key       =  "key" "=" quoted-string
```

If ASCII encoding has been requested via the encoding parameter, the key parameter contains the user's public key as extracted from the pgp key ring with the "pgp -kxa user ".

Example:

```
Response-Key: pgp version="2.6.2", encoding="ascii",
  key="mQBtAzNWHNYAAAEDAL7QvAdK2utY05wuUG+ItYK5tCF8HNJM60sU4rLaV+eUnkMk
  mOmJWtc2wXcZx1XaXb2lkydTQOesrUR75IwNXBuZXPEIMThEa5WLsT7VLme7njnx
  sE86SgWmAZx5ookIdQAFEbQxSGVubmluZyBTY2h1bHpyaW5uZSA8c2NodWx6cmlu
  bmVAY3MuY29sdW1iaWEuZWR1Pg==
  =+y19"
```

16 Examples

In the following examples, we often omit the message body and the corresponding Content-Length and Content-Type headers for brevity.

16.1 Registration

A user at host saturn.bell-tel.com registers on start-up, via multicast, with the local SIP server named bell-tel.com. In the example, the user agent on saturn expects to receive SIP requests on UDP port 3890.


```
C->S: REGISTER sip:bell-tel.com SIP/2.0
      Via: SIP/2.0/UDP saturn.bell-tel.com
      From: sip:watson@bell-tel.com
      To: sip:watson@bell-tel.com
```

```
       Call-ID: 70710@saturn.bell-tel.com
       CSeq: 1 REGISTER
       Contact: <sip:watson@saturn.bell-tel.com:3890;transport=udp>
       Expires: 7200
```

The registration expires after two hours. Any future invitations for watson@bell-tel.com arriving at sip.bell-tel.com will now be redirected to watson@saturn.bell-tel.com, UDP port 3890.

If Watson wants to be reached elsewhere, say, an on-line service he uses while traveling, he updates his reservation after first cancelling any existing locations:

```
C->S: REGISTER sip:bell-tel.com SIP/2.0
      Via: SIP/2.0/UDP saturn.bell-tel.com
      From: sip:watson@bell-tel.com
      To: sip:watson@bell-tel.com
      Call-ID: 70710@saturn.bell-tel.com
      CSeq: 2 REGISTER
      Contact: *
      Expires: 0

C->S: REGISTER sip:bell-tel.com SIP/2.0
      Via: SIP/2.0/UDP saturn.bell-tel.com
      From: sip:watson@bell-tel.com
      To: sip:watson@bell-tel.com
      Call-ID: 70710@saturn.bell-tel.com
      CSeq: 3 REGISTER
      Contact: sip:tawatson@example.com
```

Now, the server will forward any request for Watson to the server at example.com, using the Request-URI tawatson@example.com. For the server at example.com to reach Watson, he will need to send a REGISTER there, or inform the server of his current location through some other means.

It is possible to use third-party registration. Here, the secretary jon.diligent registers his boss, T. Watson:


```
C->S: REGISTER sip:bell-tel.com SIP/2.0
      Via: SIP/2.0/UDP pluto.bell-tel.com
      From: sip:jon.diligent@bell-tel.com
      To: sip:watson@bell-tel.com
```

```
      Call-ID: 17320@pluto.bell-tel.com
      CSeq: 1 REGISTER
      Contact: sip:tawatson@example.com
```

The request could be sent to either the registrar at bell-tel.com or the server at example.com. In the latter case, the server at example.com would proxy the request to the address indicated in the Request-URI. Then, Max-Forwards header could be used to restrict the registration to that server.

16.2 Invitation to a Multicast Conference

The first example invites schooler@vlsi.cs.caltech.edu to a multicast session. All examples use the Session Description Protocol (SDP) (RFC 2327 [6]) as the session description format.

16.2.1 Request

```
C->S: INVITE sip:schooler@cs.caltech.edu SIP/2.0
      Via: SIP/2.0/UDP csvax.cs.caltech.edu;branch=8348
        ;maddr=239.128.16.254;ttl=16
      Via: SIP/2.0/UDP north.east.isi.edu
      From: Mark Handley <sip:mjh@isi.edu>
      To: Eve Schooler <sip:schooler@caltech.edu>
      Call-ID: 2963313058@north.east.isi.edu
      CSeq: 1 INVITE
      Subject: SIP will be discussed, too
      Content-Type: application/sdp
      Content-Length: 187

      v=0
      o=user1 53655765 2353687637 IN IP4 128.3.4.5
      s=Mbone Audio
      i=Discussion of Mbone Engineering Issues
      e=mbone@somewhere.com
      c=IN IP4 224.2.0.1/127
      t=0 0
      m=audio 3456 RTP/AVP 0
```


The From request header above states that the request was initiated by mjh@isi.edu and addressed to schooler@caltech.edu (From header fields). The Via fields list the hosts along the path from invitation initiator (the last element of the list) towards the callee. In the example above, the message was last multicast to the administratively scoped group 239.128.16.254 with a ttl of 16 from the host csvax.cs.caltech.edu. The second Via header field indicates that it was originally sent from the host north.east.isi.edu. The Request-URI indicates that the request is currently being being addressed to schooler@cs.caltech.edu, the local address that csvax looked up for the callee.

In this case, the session description is using the Session Description Protocol (SDP), as stated in the Content-Type header.

The header is terminated by an empty line and is followed by a message body containing the session description.

16.2.2 Response

The called user agent, directly or indirectly through proxy servers, indicates that it is alerting ("ringing") the called party:

```
S->C: SIP/2.0 180 Ringing
      Via: SIP/2.0/UDP csvax.cs.caltech.edu;branch=8348
        ;maddr=239.128.16.254;ttl=16
      Via: SIP/2.0/UDP north.east.isi.edu
      From: Mark Handley <sip:mjh@isi.edu>
      To: Eve Schooler <sip:schooler@caltech.edu> ;tag=9883472
      Call-ID: 2963313058@north.east.isi.edu
      CSeq: 1 INVITE
```

A sample response to the invitation is given below. The first line of the response states the SIP version number, that it is a 200 (OK) response, which means the request was successful. The Via headers are taken from the request, and entries are removed hop by hop as the response retraces the path of the request. A new authentication field MAY be added by the invited user's agent if required. The Call-ID is taken directly from the original request, along with the remaining fields of the request message. The original sense of From field is preserved (i.e., it is the session initiator).

In addition, the Contact header gives details of the host where the user was located, or alternatively the relevant proxy contact point which should be reachable from the caller's host.


```
S->C: SIP/2.0 200 OK
      Via: SIP/2.0/UDP csvax.cs.caltech.edu;branch=8348
        ;maddr=239.128.16.254;ttl=16
      Via: SIP/2.0/UDP north.east.isi.edu
```

```
      From: Mark Handley <sip:mjh@isi.edu>
      To: Eve Schooler <sip:schooler@caltech.edu> ;tag=9883472
      Call-ID: 2963313058@north.east.isi.edu
      CSeq: 1 INVITE
      Contact: sip:es@jove.cs.caltech.edu
```

The caller confirms the invitation by sending an ACK request to the location named in the Contact header:

```
C->S: ACK sip:es@jove.cs.caltech.edu SIP/2.0
      Via: SIP/2.0/UDP north.east.isi.edu
      From: Mark Handley <sip:mjh@isi.edu>
      To: Eve Schooler <sip:schooler@caltech.edu> ;tag=9883472
      Call-ID: 2963313058@north.east.isi.edu
      CSeq: 1 ACK
```

16.3 Two-party Call

For two-party Internet phone calls, the response must contain a description of where to send the data. In the example below, Bell calls Watson. Bell indicates that he can receive RTP audio codings 0 (PCMU), 3 (GSM), 4 (G.723) and 5 (DVI4).

```
C->S: INVITE sip:watson@boston.bell-tel.com SIP/2.0
      Via: SIP/2.0/UDP kton.bell-tel.com
      From: A. Bell <sip:a.g.bell@bell-tel.com>
      To: T. Watson <sip:watson@bell-tel.com>
      Call-ID: 3298420296@kton.bell-tel.com
      CSeq: 1 INVITE
      Subject: Mr. Watson, come here.
      Content-Type: application/sdp
      Content-Length: ...

      v=0
      o=bell 53655765 2353687637 IN IP4 128.3.4.5
      s=Mr. Watson, come here.
      c=IN IP4 kton.bell-tel.com
      m=audio 3456 RTP/AVP 0 3 4 5
```



```
S->C: SIP/2.0 100 Trying
      Via: SIP/2.0/UDP kton.bell-tel.com
      From: A. Bell <sip:a.g.bell@bell-tel.com>
      To: T. Watson <sip:watson@bell-tel.com> ;tag=37462311
```

```
       Call-ID: 3298420296@kton.bell-tel.com
       CSeq: 1 INVITE
       Content-Length: 0

S->C:  SIP/2.0 180 Ringing
       Via: SIP/2.0/UDP kton.bell-tel.com
       From: A. Bell <sip:a.g.bell@bell-tel.com>
       To: T. Watson <sip:watson@bell-tel.com> ;tag=37462311
       Call-ID: 3298420296@kton.bell-tel.com
       CSeq: 1 INVITE
       Content-Length: 0

S->C:  SIP/2.0 182 Queued, 2 callers ahead
       Via: SIP/2.0/UDP kton.bell-tel.com
       From: A. Bell <sip:a.g.bell@bell-tel.com>
       To: T. Watson <sip:watson@bell-tel.com> ;tag=37462311
       Call-ID: 3298420296@kton.bell-tel.com
       CSeq: 1 INVITE
       Content-Length: 0

S->C:  SIP/2.0 182 Queued, 1 caller ahead
       Via: SIP/2.0/UDP kton.bell-tel.com
       From: A. Bell <sip:a.g.bell@bell-tel.com>
       To: T. Watson <sip:watson@bell-tel.com> ;tag=37462311
       Call-ID: 3298420296@kton.bell-tel.com
       CSeq: 1 INVITE
       Content-Length: 0

S->C:  SIP/2.0 200 OK
       Via: SIP/2.0/UDP kton.bell-tel.com
       From: A. Bell <sip:a.g.bell@bell-tel.com>
       To: <sip:watson@bell-tel.com> ;tag=37462311
       Call-ID: 3298420296@kton.bell-tel.com
       CSeq: 1 INVITE
       Contact: sip:watson@boston.bell-tel.com
       Content-Type: application/sdp
       Content-Length: ...

       v=0
       o=watson 4858949 4858949 IN IP4 192.1.2.3
       s=I'm on my way
       c=IN IP4 boston.bell-tel.com
       m=audio 5004 RTP/AVP 0 3
```


The example illustrates the use of informational status responses. Here, the reception of the call is confirmed immediately (100), then, possibly after some database mapping delay, the call rings (180) and is then queued, with periodic status updates.

Watson can only receive PCMU and GSM. Note that Watson's list of codecs may or may not be a subset of the one offered by Bell, as each party indicates the data types it is willing to receive. Watson will send audio data to port 3456 at c.bell-tel.com, Bell will send to port 5004 at boston.bell-tel.com.

By default, the media session is one RTP session. Watson will receive RTCP packets on port 5005, while Bell will receive them on port 3457.

Since the two sides have agreed on the set of media, Bell confirms the call without enclosing another session description:

```
C->S: ACK sip:watson@boston.bell-tel.com SIP/2.0
      Via: SIP/2.0/UDP kton.bell-tel.com
      From: A. Bell <sip:a.g.bell@bell-tel.com>
      To: T. Watson <sip:watson@bell-tel.com> ;tag=37462311
      Call-ID: 3298420296@kton.bell-tel.com
      CSeq: 1 ACK
```

16.4 Terminating a Call

To terminate a call, caller or callee can send a BYE request:

```
C->S: BYE sip:watson@boston.bell-tel.com SIP/2.0
      Via: SIP/2.0/UDP kton.bell-tel.com
      From: A. Bell <sip:a.g.bell@bell-tel.com>
      To: T. A. Watson <sip:watson@bell-tel.com> ;tag=37462311
      Call-ID: 3298420296@kton.bell-tel.com
      CSeq: 2 BYE
```

If the callee wants to abort the call, it simply reverses the To and From fields. Note that it is unlikely that a BYE from the callee will traverse the same proxies as the original INVITE.

16.5 Forking Proxy

In this example, Bell (a.g.bell@bell-tel.com) (C), currently seated at host c.bell-tel.com wants to call Watson (t.watson@ieee.org). At the time of the call, Watson is logged in at two workstations, t.watson@x.bell-tel.com (X) and watson@y.bell-tel.com (Y), and has registered with the IEEE proxy server (P) called sip.ieee.org. The IEEE server also has a registration for the home machine of Watson, at watson@h.bell-tel.com (H), as well as a permanent registration at watson@acm.org (A). For brevity, the examples omit the session description and Via header fields.

Bell's user agent sends the invitation to the SIP server for the ieee.org domain:

```
C->P: INVITE sip:t.watson@ieee.org SIP/2.0
      Via:     SIP/2.0/UDP c.bell-tel.com
      From:    A. Bell <sip:a.g.bell@bell-tel.com>
      To:      T. Watson <sip:t.watson@ieee.org>
      Call-ID: 31415@c.bell-tel.com
      CSeq:    1 INVITE
```

The SIP server at ieee.org tries the four addresses in parallel. It sends the following message to the home machine:

```
P->H: INVITE sip:watson@h.bell-tel.com SIP/2.0
      Via:     SIP/2.0/UDP sip.ieee.org ;branch=1
      Via:     SIP/2.0/UDP c.bell-tel.com
      From:    A. Bell <sip:a.g.bell@bell-tel.com>
      To:      T. Watson <sip:t.watson@ieee.org>
      Call-ID: 31415@c.bell-tel.com
      CSeq:    1 INVITE
```

This request immediately yields a 404 (Not Found) response, since Watson is not currently logged in at home:

```
H->P: SIP/2.0 404 Not Found
      Via:     SIP/2.0/UDP sip.ieee.org ;branch=1
      Via:     SIP/2.0/UDP c.bell-tel.com
      From:    A. Bell <sip:a.g.bell@bell-tel.com>
      To:      T. Watson <sip:t.watson@ieee.org>;tag=87454273
```



```
      Call-ID: 31415@c.bell-tel.com
      CSeq:    1 INVITE
```

The proxy ACKs the response so that host H can stop retransmitting it:

```
P->H: ACK sip:watson@h.bell-tel.com SIP/2.0
      Via:     SIP/2.0/UDP sip.ieee.org ;branch=1
      From:    A. Bell <sip:a.g.bell@bell-tel.com>
      To:      T. Watson <sip:t.watson@ieee.org>;tag=87454273
      Call-ID: 31415@c.bell-tel.com
      CSeq:    1 ACK
```

Also, P attempts to reach Watson through the ACM server:

```
P->A: INVITE sip:watson@acm.org SIP/2.0
      Via:     SIP/2.0/UDP sip.ieee.org ;branch=2
      Via:     SIP/2.0/UDP c.bell-tel.com
      From:    A. Bell <sip:a.g.bell@bell-tel.com>
      To:      T. Watson <sip:t.watson@ieee.org>
      Call-ID: 31415@c.bell-tel.com
      CSeq:    1 INVITE
```

In parallel, the next attempt proceeds, with an INVITE to X and Y:

```
P->X: INVITE sip:t.watson@x.bell-tel.com SIP/2.0
      Via:     SIP/2.0/UDP sip.ieee.org ;branch=3
      Via:     SIP/2.0/UDP c.bell-tel.com
      From:    A. Bell <sip:a.g.bell@bell-tel.com>
      To:      T. Watson <sip:t.watson@ieee.org>
      Call-ID: 31415@c.bell-tel.com
      CSeq:    1 INVITE

P->Y: INVITE sip:watson@y.bell-tel.com SIP/2.0
      Via:     SIP/2.0/UDP sip.ieee.org ;branch=4
      Via:     SIP/2.0/UDP c.bell-tel.com
      From:    A. Bell <sip:a.g.bell@bell-tel.com>
      To:      T. Watson <sip:t.watson@ieee.org>
      Call-ID: 31415@c.bell-tel.com
      CSeq:    1 INVITE
```


As it happens, both Watson at X and a colleague in the other lab at host Y hear the phones ringing and pick up. Both X and Y return 200s via the proxy to Bell.

```
X->P: SIP/2.0 200 OK
      Via:      SIP/2.0/UDP sip.ieee.org ;branch=3
      Via:      SIP/2.0/UDP c.bell-tel.com
      From:     A. Bell <sip:a.g.bell@bell-tel.com>
      To:       T. Watson <sip:t.watson@ieee.org> ;tag=192137601
      Call-ID:  31415@c.bell-tel.com
      CSeq:     1 INVITE
      Contact:  sip:t.watson@x.bell-tel.com

Y->P: SIP/2.0 200 OK
      Via:      SIP/2.0/UDP sip.ieee.org ;branch=4
      Via:      SIP/2.0/UDP c.bell-tel.com
      Contact:  sip:t.watson@y.bell-tel.com
      From:     A. Bell <sip:a.g.bell@bell-tel.com>
      To:       T. Watson <sip:t.watson@ieee.org> ;tag=35253448
      Call-ID:  31415@c.bell-tel.com
      CSeq:     1 INVITE
```

Both responses are forwarded to Bell, using the Via information. At this point, the ACM server is still searching its database. P can now cancel this attempt:

```
P->A: CANCEL sip:watson@acm.org SIP/2.0
      Via:     SIP/2.0/UDP sip.ieee.org ;branch=2
      From:    A. Bell <sip:a.g.bell@bell-tel.com>
      To:      T. Watson <sip:t.watson@ieee.org>
      Call-ID: 31415@c.bell-tel.com
      CSeq:    1 CANCEL
```

The ACM server gladly stops its neural-network database search and responds with a 200. The 200 will not travel any further, since P is the last Via stop.

```
A->P: SIP/2.0 200 OK
      Via:     SIP/2.0/UDP sip.ieee.org ;branch=2
      From:    A. Bell <sip:a.g.bell@bell-tel.com>
      To:      T. Watson <sip:t.watson@ieee.org>
```



```
      Call-ID: 31415@c.bell-tel.com
      CSeq:    1 CANCEL
```

Bell gets the two 200 responses from X and Y in short order. Bell's reaction now depends on his software. He can either send an ACK to both if human intelligence is needed to determine who he wants to talk to or he can automatically reject one of the two calls. Here, he acknowledges both, separately and directly to the final destination:

```
C->X: ACK sip:t.watson@x.bell-tel.com SIP/2.0
      Via:      SIP/2.0/UDP c.bell-tel.com
      From:     A. Bell <sip:a.g.bell@bell-tel.com>
      To:       T. Watson <sip:t.watson@ieee.org>;tag=192137601
      Call-ID:  31415@c.bell-tel.com
      CSeq:     1 ACK

C->Y: ACK sip:watson@y.bell-tel.com SIP/2.0
      Via:      SIP/2.0/UDP c.bell-tel.com
      From:     A. Bell <sip:a.g.bell@bell-tel.com>
      To:       T. Watson <sip:t.watson@ieee.org>;tag=35253448
      Call-ID:  31415@c.bell-tel.com
      CSeq:     1 ACK
```

After a brief discussion between Bell with X and Y, it becomes clear that Watson is at X. (Note that this is not a three-way call; only Bell can talk to X and Y, but X and Y cannot talk to each other.) Thus, Bell sends a BYE to Y, which is replied to:

```
C->Y: BYE sip:watson@y.bell-tel.com SIP/2.0
      Via:      SIP/2.0/UDP c.bell-tel.com
      From:     A. Bell <sip:a.g.bell@bell-tel.com>
      To:       T. Watson <sip:t.watson@ieee.org>;tag=35253448
      Call-ID:  31415@c.bell-tel.com
      CSeq:     2 BYE

Y->C: SIP/2.0 200 OK
      Via:      SIP/2.0/UDP c.bell-tel.com
      From:     A. Bell <sip:a.g.bell@bell-tel.com>
      To:       T. Watson <sip:t.watson@ieee.org>;tag=35253448
      Call-ID:  31415@c.bell-tel.com
      CSeq:     2 BYE
```


16.6 Redirects

Replies with status codes 301 (Moved Permanently) or 302 (Moved Temporarily) specify another location using the Contact field.

Continuing our earlier example, the server P at ieee.org decides to redirect rather than proxy the request:

```
P->C: SIP/2.0 302 Moved temporarily
      Via:     SIP/2.0/UDP c.bell-tel.com
      From:    A. Bell <sip:a.g.bell@bell-tel.com>
      To:      T. Watson <sip:t.watson@ieee.org>;tag=72538263
      Call-ID: 31415@c.bell-tel.com
      CSeq:    1 INVITE
      Contact: sip:watson@h.bell-tel.com,
               sip:watson@acm.org, sip:t.watson@x.bell-tel.com,
               sip:watson@y.bell-tel.com
      CSeq: 1 INVITE
```

As another example, assume Alice (A) wants to delegate her calls to Bob (B) while she is on vacation until July 29th, 1998. Any calls meant for her will reach Bob with Alice's To field, indicating to him what role he is to play. Charlie (C) calls Alice (A), whose server returns:

```
A->C: SIP/2.0 302 Moved temporarily
      From: Charlie <sip:charlie@caller.com>
      To: Alice <sip:alice@anywhere.com> ;tag=2332462
      Call-ID: 27182@caller.com
      Contact: sip:bob@anywhere.com
      Expires: Wed, 29 Jul 1998 9:00:00 GMT
      CSeq: 1 INVITE
```

Charlie then sends the following request to the SIP server of the anywhere.com domain. Note that the server at anywhere.com forwards the request to Bob based on the Request-URI.

```
C->B: INVITE sip:bob@anywhere.com SIP/2.0
      From: sip:charlie@caller.com
      To: sip:alice@anywhere.com
      Call-ID: 27182@caller.com
      CSeq: 2 INVITE
```


In the third redirection example, we assume that all outgoing requests are directed through a local firewall F at caller.com, with Charlie again inviting Alice:

```
C->F: INVITE sip:alice@anywhere.com SIP/2.0
      From: sip:charlie@caller.com
      To: Alice <sip:alice@anywhere.com>
      Call-ID: 27182@caller.com
      CSeq: 1 INVITE
```

The local firewall at caller.com happens to be overloaded and thus redirects the call from Charlie to a secondary server S:

```
F->C: SIP/2.0 302 Moved temporarily
      From: sip:charlie@caller.com
      To: Alice <sip:alice@anywhere.com>
      Call-ID: 27182@caller.com
      CSeq: 1 INVITE
      Contact: <sip:alice@anywhere.com:5080;maddr=spare.caller.com>
```

Based on this response, Charlie directs the same invitation to the secondary server spare.caller.com at port 5080, but maintains the same Request-URI as before:

```
C->S: INVITE sip:alice@anywhere.com SIP/2.0
      From: sip:charlie@caller.com
      To: Alice <sip:alice@anywhere.com>
      Call-ID: 27182@caller.com
      CSeq: 2 INVITE
```

16.7 Negotiation

An example of a 606 (Not Acceptable) response is:

```
S->C: SIP/2.0 606 Not Acceptable
      From: sip:mjh@isi.edu
      To: <sip:schooler@cs.caltech.edu> ;tag=7434264
      Call-ID: 14142@north.east.isi.edu
```



```
      CSeq: 1 INVITE
      Contact: sip:mjh@north.east.isi.edu
      Warning: 370 "Insufficient bandwidth (only have ISDN)",
        305 "Incompatible media format",
```

```
  330 "Multicast not available"
Content-Type: application/sdp
Content-Length: 50

v=0
s=Let's talk
b=CT:128
c=IN IP4 north.east.isi.edu
m=audio 3456 RTP/AVP 5 0 7
m=video 2232 RTP/AVP 31
```

In this example, the original request specified a bandwidth that was higher than the access link could support, requested multicast, and requested a set of media encodings. The response states that only 128 kb/s is available and that (only) DVI, PCM or LPC audio could be supported in order of preference.

The response also states that multicast is not available. In such a case, it might be appropriate to set up a transcoding gateway and re-invite the user.

16.8 OPTIONS Request

A caller Alice can use an OPTIONS request to find out the capabilities of a potential callee Bob, without "ringing" the designated address. Bob returns a description indicating that he is capable of receiving audio encodings PCM Ulaw (payload type 0), 1016 (payload type 1), GSM (payload type 3), and SX7300/8000 (dynamic payload type 99), and video encodings H.261 (payload type 31) and H.263 (payload type 34).

```
C->S: OPTIONS sip:bob@example.com SIP/2.0
      From: Alice <sip:alice@anywhere.org>
      To: Bob <sip:bob@example.com>
      Call-ID: 6378@host.anywhere.org
      CSeq: 1 OPTIONS
      Accept: application/sdp

S->C: SIP/2.0 200 OK
      From: Alice <sip:alice@anywhere.org>
      To: Bob <sip:bob@example.com> ;tag=376364382
```



```
      Call-ID: 6378@host.anywhere.org
      Content-Length: 81
      Content-Type: application/sdp
```

```
v=0
m=audio 0 RTP/AVP 0 1 3 99
m=video 0 RTP/AVP 31 34
a=rtpmap:99 SX7300/8000
```


A Minimal Implementation

A.1 Client

All clients MUST be able to generate the INVITE and ACK requests. Clients MUST generate and parse the Call-ID, Content-Length, Content-Type, CSeq, From and To headers. Clients MUST also parse the Require header. A minimal implementation MUST understand SDP (RFC 2327, [6]). It MUST be able to recognize the status code classes 1 through 6 and act accordingly.

The following capability sets build on top of the minimal implementation described in the previous paragraph. In general, each capability listed below builds on the ones above it:

Basic: A basic implementation adds support for the BYE method to allow the interruption of a pending call attempt. It includes a User-Agent header in its requests and indicates its preferred language in the Accept-Language header.

Redirection: To support call forwarding, a client needs to be able to understand the Contact header, but only the SIP-URL part, not the parameters.

Firewall-friendly: A firewall-friendly client understands the Route and Record-Route header fields and can be configured to use a local proxy for all outgoing requests.

Negotiation: A client MUST be able to request the OPTIONS method and understand the 380 (Alternative Service) status and the Contact parameters to participate in terminal and media negotiation. It SHOULD be able to parse the Warning response header to provide useful feedback to the caller.

Authentication: If a client wishes to invite callees that require caller authentication, it MUST be able to recognize the 401 (Unauthorized) status code, MUST be able to generate the Authorization request header and MUST understand the WWW-Authenticate response header.

If a client wishes to use proxies that require caller authentication, it MUST be able to recognize the 407 (Proxy Authentication Required) status code, MUST be able to generate the Proxy-Authorization request header and understand the Proxy-Authenticate response header.

A.2 Server

A minimally compliant server implementation MUST understand the INVITE, ACK, OPTIONS and BYE requests. A proxy server MUST also understand CANCEL. It MUST parse and generate, as appropriate, the Call-ID, Content-Length, Content-Type, CSeq, Expires, From, Max-Forwards, Require, To and Via headers. It MUST echo the CSeq and Timestamp headers in the response. It SHOULD include the Server header in its responses.

A.3 Header Processing

Table 6 lists the headers that different implementations support. UAC refers to a user-agent client (calling user agent), UAS to a user-agent server (called user-agent).

The fields in the table have the following meaning. Type is as in Table 4 and 5. "-" indicates the field is not meaningful to this system (although it might be generated by it). "m" indicates the field MUST be understood. "b" indicates the field SHOULD be understood by a Basic implementation. "r" indicates the field SHOULD be understood if the system claims to understand redirection. "a" indicates the field SHOULD be understood if the system claims to support authentication. "e" indicates the field SHOULD be understood if the system claims to support encryption. "o" indicates support of the field is purely optional. Headers whose support is optional for all implementations are not shown.

	type	UAC	proxy	UAS	registrar

Accept	R	-	o	m	m
Accept-Encoding	R	-	-	m	m
Accept-Language	R	-	b	b	b
Allow	405	o	-	-	-
Authorization	R	a	o	a	a
Call-ID	g	m	m	m	m
Content-Encoding	g	m	-	m	m
Content-Length	g	m	m	m	m
Content-Type	g	m	-	m	m
CSeq	g	m	m	m	m
Encryption	g	e	-	e	e
Expires	g	-	o	o	m
From	g	m	o	m	m
Hide	R	-	m	-	-
Contact	R	-	-	-	m
Contact	r	r	r	-	-
Max-Forwards	R	-	b	-	-
Proxy-Authenticate	407	a	-	-	-
Proxy-Authorization	R	-	a	-	-
Proxy-Require	R	-	m	-	-
Require	R	m	-	m	m
Response-Key	R	-	-	e	e
Route	R	-	m	-	-
Timestamp	g	o	o	m	m
To	g	m	m	m	m
Unsupported	r	b	b	-	-
User-Agent	g	b	-	b	-
Via	g	m	m	m	m
WWW-Authenticate	401	a	-	-	-

Table 6: Header Field Processing Requirements

B Usage of the Session Description Protocol (SDP)

This section describes the use of the Session Description Protocol (SDP) (RFC 2327 [6]).

B.1 Configuring Media Streams

The caller and callee align their media descriptions so that the nth media stream ("m=" line) in the caller's session description corresponds to the nth media stream in the callee's description.

All media descriptions SHOULD contain "a=rtpmap" mappings from RTP payload types to encodings.

This allows easier migration away from static payload

types.

If the callee wants to neither send nor receive a stream offered by the caller, the callee sets the port number of that stream to zero in its media description.

There currently is no other way than port zero for the callee to refuse a bidirectional stream offered by the caller. Both caller and callee need to be aware what media tools are to be started.

For example, assume that the caller Alice has included the following description in her INVITE request. It includes an audio stream and two bidirectional video streams, using H.261 (payload type 31) and MPEG (payload type 32).

```
v=0
o=alice 2890844526 2890844526 IN IP4 host.anywhere.com
c=IN IP4 host.anywhere.com
m=audio 49170 RTP/AVP 0
a=rtpmap:0 PCMU/8000
m=video 51372 RTP/AVP 31
a=rtpmap:31 H261/90000
m=video 53000 RTP/AVP 32
a=rtpmap:32 MPV/90000
```

The callee, Bob, does not want to receive or send the first video stream, so it returns the media description below:

```
v=0
o=bob 2890844730 2890844730 IN IP4 host.example.com
c=IN IP4 host.example.com
m=audio 47920 RTP/AVP 0 1
a=rtpmap:0 PCMU/8000
a=rtpmap:1 1016/8000
m=video 0 RTP/AVP 31
m=video 53000 RTP/AVP 32
a=rtpmap:32 MPV/90000
```


B.2 Setting SDP Values for Unicast

If a session description from a caller contains a media stream which is listed as send (receive) only, it means that the caller is only willing to send (receive) this stream, not receive (send). The same is true for the callee.

For receive-only and send-or-receive streams, the port number and address in the session description indicate where the media stream should be sent to by the recipient of the session description, either caller or callee. For send-only streams, the address and port number have no significance and SHOULD be set to zero.

The list of payload types for each media stream conveys two pieces of information, namely the set of codecs that the caller or callee is capable of sending or receiving, and the RTP payload type numbers used to identify those codecs. For receive-only or send-and-receive media streams, a caller SHOULD list all of the codecs it is capable of supporting in the session description in an INVITE or ACK. For send-only streams, the caller SHOULD indicate only those it wishes to send for this session. For receive-only streams, the payload type numbers indicate the value of the payload type field in RTP packets the caller is expecting to receive for that codec type. For send-only streams, the payload type numbers indicate the value of the payload type field in RTP packets the caller is planning to send for that codec type. For send-and-receive streams, the payload type numbers indicate the value of the payload type field the caller expects to both send and receive.

If a media stream is listed as receive-only by the caller, the callee lists, in the response, those codecs it intends to use from among the ones listed in the request. If a media stream is listed as send-only by the caller, the callee lists, in the response, those codecs it is willing to receive among the ones listed in the the request. If the media stream is listed as both send and receive, the callee lists those codecs it is capable of sending or receiving among the ones listed by the caller in the INVITE. The actual payload type numbers in the callee's session description corresponding to a particular codec MUST be the same as the caller's session description.

If caller and callee have no media formats in common for a particular stream, the callee MUST return a session description containing the particular "m=" line, but with the port number set to zero, and no payload types listed.

If there are no media formats in common for all streams, the callee SHOULD return a 400 response, with a 304 Warning header field.

B.3 Multicast Operation

The interpretation of send-only and receive-only for multicast media sessions differs from that for unicast sessions. For multicast, send-only means that the recipient of the session description (caller or callee) SHOULD only send media streams to the address and port indicated. Receive-only means that the recipient of the session description SHOULD only receive media on the address and port indicated.

For multicast, receive and send multicast addresses are the same and all parties use the same port numbers to receive media data. If the session description provided by the caller is acceptable to the callee, the callee can choose not to include a session description or MAY echo the description in the response.

A callee MAY, in the response, return a session description with some of the payload types removed, or port numbers set to zero (but no other value). This indicates to the caller that the callee does not support the given stream or media types which were removed. A callee MUST NOT change whether a given stream is send-only, receive-only, or send-and-receive.

If a callee does not support multicast at all, it SHOULD return a 400 status response and include a 330 Warning.

B.4 Delayed Media Streams

In some cases, a caller may not know the set of media formats which it can support at the time it would like to issue an invitation. This is the case when the caller is actually a gateway to another protocol which performs media format negotiation after call setup. When this occurs, a caller MAY issue an INVITE with a session description that contains no media lines. The callee SHOULD interpret this to mean that the caller wishes to participate in a multimedia session described by the session description, but that the media streams are not yet known. The callee SHOULD return a session description indicating the streams and media formats it is willing to support, however. The caller MAY update the session description either in the ACK request or in a re-INVITE at a later time, once the streams are known.

B.5 Putting Media Streams on Hold

If a party in a call wants to put the other party "on hold", i.e., request that it temporarily stops sending one or more media streams, a party re-invites the other by sending an INVITE request with a modified session description. The session description is the same as

in the original invitation (or response), but the "c" destination addresses for the media streams to be put on hold are set to zero (0.0.0.0).

B.6 Subject and SDP "s=" Line

The SDP "s=" line and the SIP Subject header field have different meanings when inviting to a multicast session. The session description line describes the subject of the multicast session, while the SIP Subject header field describes the reason for the invitation. The example in Section 16.2 illustrates this point. For invitations to two-party sessions, the SDP "s=" line MAY be left empty.

B.7 The SDP "o=" Line

The "o=" line is not strictly necessary for two-party sessions, but MUST be present to allow re-use of SDP-based tools.

C Summary of Augmented BNF

All of the mechanisms specified in this document are described in both prose and an augmented Backus-Naur Form (BNF) similar to that used by RFC 822 [9]. Implementors will need to be familiar with the notation in order to understand this specification. The augmented BNF includes the following constructs:

```
name  =  definition
```

The name of a rule is simply the name itself (without any enclosing "<" and ">") and is separated from its definition by the equal "=" character. White space is only significant in that indentation of continuation lines is used to indicate a rule definition that spans more than one line. Certain basic rules are in uppercase, such as SP, LWS, HT, CRLF, DIGIT, ALPHA, etc. Angle brackets are used within definitions whenever their presence will facilitate discerning the use of rule names.

"literal"

Quotation marks surround literal text. Unless stated otherwise, the text is case-insensitive.

rule1 | rule2

Elements separated by a bar ("|") are alternatives, e.g., "yes | no" will accept yes or no.

(rule1 rule2)

Elements enclosed in parentheses are treated as a single element. Thus, "(elem (foo | bar) elem)" allows the token sequences "elem foo elem" and "elem bar elem".

*rule

The character "*" preceding an element indicates repetition. The full form is "<n>*<m>element" indicating at least <n> and at most <m> occurrences of element. Default values are 0 and infinity so that "*(element)" allows any number, including zero; "1*element" requires at least one; and "1*2element" allows one or two.

[rule]

Square brackets enclose optional elements; "[foo bar]" is equivalent to "*1(foo bar)".

N rule

Specific repetition: "<n>(element)" is equivalent to "<n>*<n>(element)"; that is, exactly <n> occurrences of (element). Thus 2DIGIT is a 2-digit number, and 3ALPHA is a string of three alphabetic characters.

#rule

A construct "#" is defined, similar to "*", for defining lists of elements. The full form is "<n>#<m> element" indicating at least <n> and at most <m> elements, each separated by one or more commas (",") and OPTIONAL linear white space (LWS). This makes the usual form of lists very easy; a rule such as

```
( *LWS element *( *LWS "," *LWS element ))
```

can be shown as 1# element. Wherever this construct is used, null elements are allowed, but do not contribute to the count of elements present. That is, "(element), , (element)" is permitted, but counts as only two elements. Therefore, where at least one element is required, at least one non-null element MUST be present. Default values are 0 and infinity so that "#element" allows any number, including zero; "1#element" requires at least one; and "1#2element" allows one or two.

; comment

A semi-colon, set off some distance to the right of rule text, starts a comment that continues to the end of line. This is a simple way of including useful notes in parallel with the specifications.

implied *LWS

The grammar described by this specification is word-based. Except where noted otherwise, linear white space (LWS) can be included between any two adjacent words (token or quoted-string), and between adjacent tokens and separators, without changing the interpretation of a field. At least one delimiter (LWS and/or separators) MUST exist between any two tokens (for the definition of "token" below), since they would otherwise be interpreted as a single token.

C.1 Basic Rules

The following rules are used throughout this specification to describe basic parsing constructs. The US-ASCII coded character set is defined by ANSI X3.4-1986.

```
OCTET     =  <any 8-bit sequence of data>
CHAR      =  <any US-ASCII character (octets 0 - 127)>
upalpha   =  "A" | "B" | "C" | "D" | "E" | "F" | "G" | "H" | "I" |
             "J" | "K" | "L" | "M" | "N" | "O" | "P" | "Q" | "R" |
             "S" | "T" | "U" | "V" | "W" | "X" | "Y" | "Z"
lowalpha  =  "a" | "b" | "c" | "d" | "e" | "f" | "g" | "h" | "i" |
             "j" | "k" | "l" | "m" | "n" | "o" | "p" | "q" | "r" |
             "s" | "t" | "u" | "v" | "w" | "x" | "y" | "z"
alpha     =  lowalpha | upalpha
digit     =  "0" | "1" | "2" | "3" | "4" | "5" | "6" | "7" |
             "8" | "9"
alphanum  =  alpha | digit
CTL       =  <any US-ASCII control character
             (octets 0 -- 31) and DEL (127)>
CR        =  %d13 ; US-ASCII CR, carriage return character
LF        =  %d10 ; US-ASCII LF, line feed character
SP        =  %d32 ; US-ASCII SP, space character
HT        =  %d09 ; US-ASCII HT, horizontal tab character
CRLF      =  CR LF ; typically the end of a line
```

The following are defined in RFC 2396 [12] for the SIP URI:


```
unreserved  =  alphanum | mark
mark        =  "-" | "_" | "." | "!" | "~" | "*" | "'"
            |  "(" | ")"
escaped     =  "%" hex hex
```

SIP header field values can be folded onto multiple lines if the continuation line begins with a space or horizontal tab. All linear white space, including folding, has the same semantics as SP. A recipient MAY replace any linear white space with a single SP before interpreting the field value or forwarding the message downstream.

```
LWS  =  [CRLF] 1*( SP | HT ) ; linear whitespace
```

The TEXT-UTF8 rule is only used for descriptive field contents and values that are not intended to be interpreted by the message parser. Words of *TEXT-UTF8 contain characters from the UTF-8 character set (RFC 2279 [21]). In this regard, SIP differs from HTTP, which uses the ISO 8859-1 character set.

```
TEXT-UTF8  =  <any UTF-8 character encoding, except CTLs,
              but including LWS>
```

A CRLF is allowed in the definition of TEXT-UTF8 only as part of a header field continuation. It is expected that the folding LWS will be replaced with a single SP before interpretation of the TEXT-UTF8 value.

Hexadecimal numeric characters are used in several protocol elements.

```
hex  =  "A" | "B" | "C" | "D" | "E" | "F"
        | "a" | "b" | "c" | "d" | "e" | "f" | digit
```

Many SIP header field values consist of words separated by LWS or special characters. These special characters MUST be in a quoted string to be used within a parameter value.


```
token        =  1*< any CHAR  except CTL's  or separators>
separators   =  "(" | ")" | "<" | ">" | "@" |
                "," | ";" | ":" | "\" | <"> |
                "/" | "[" | "]" | "?" | "=" |
```

```
                   "{" | "}" | SP | HT
```

Comments can be included in some SIP header fields by surrounding the comment text with parentheses. Comments are only allowed in fields containing "comment" as part of their field value definition. In all other fields, parentheses are considered part of the field value.

```
comment  =  "(" *(ctext | quoted-pair | comment) ")"
ctext    =  < any TEXT-UTF8  excluding "("  and ")">
```

A string of text is parsed as a single word if it is quoted using double-quote marks.

```
quoted-string  =  ( <"> *(qdtext | quoted-pair ) <"> )
qdtext         =  <any TEXT-UTF8 except <">>
```

The backslash character ("\") MAY be used as a single-character quoting mechanism only within quoted-string and comment constructs.

```
quoted-pair  =  " \ " CHAR
```


D Using SRV DNS Records

The following procedure is experimental and relies on DNS SRV records (RFC 2052 [14]). The steps listed below are used in place of the two steps in section 1.4.2.

If a step elicits no addresses, the client continues to the next step. However if a step elicits one or more addresses, but no SIP server at any of those addresses responds, then the client concludes the server is down and doesn't continue on to the next step.

When SRV records are to be used, the protocol to use when querying for the SRV record is "sip". SRV records contain port numbers for servers, in addition to IP addresses; the client always uses this port number when contacting the SIP server. Otherwise, the port number in the SIP URI is used, if present. If there is no port number in the URI, the default port, 5060, is used.

1. If the host portion of the Request-URI is an IP address, the client contacts the server at the given address. If the host portion of the Request-URI is not an IP address, the client proceeds to the next step.

2. The Request-URI is examined. If it contains an explicit port number, the next two steps are skipped.

3. The Request-URI is examined. If it does not specify a protocol (TCP or UDP), the client queries the name server for SRV records for both UDP (if supported by the client) and TCP (if supported by the client) SIP servers. The format of these queries is defined in RFC 2052 [14]. The results of the query or queries are merged together and ordered based on priority. Then, the searching technique outlined in RFC 2052 [14] is used to select servers in order. If DNS doesn't return any records, the user goes to the last step. Otherwise, the user attempts to contact each server in the order listed. If no server is contacted, the user gives up.

4. If the Request-URI specifies a protocol (TCP or UDP) that is supported by the client, the client queries the name server for SRV records for SIP servers of that protocol type only. If the client does not support the protocol specified in the Request-URI, it gives up. The searching technique outlined in RFC 2052 [14] is used to select servers from the DNS response in order. If DNS doesn't

return any records, the user goes to the last step. Otherwise, the user attempts to contact each server in the order listed. If no server is contacted, the user gives up.

5. The client queries the name server for address records for the host portion of the Request-URI. If there were no address records, the client stops, as it has been unable to locate a server. By address record, we mean A RR's, AAAA RR's, or their most modern equivalent.

A client MAY cache a successful DNS query result. A successful query is one which contained records in the answer, and a server was contacted at one of the addresses from the answer. When the client wishes to send a request to the same host, it starts the search as if it had just received this answer from the name server. The server uses the procedures specified in RFC1035 [15] regarding cache invalidation when the time-to-live of the DNS result expires. If the client does not find a SIP server among the addresses listed in the cached answer, it starts the search at the beginning of the sequence described above.

For example, consider a client that wishes to send a SIP request. The Request-URI for the destination is sip:user@company.com. The client only supports UDP. It would follow these steps:

1. The host portion is not an IP address, so the client goes to step 2 above.

2. The client does a DNS query of QNAME="sip.udp.company.com", QCLASS=IN, QTYPE=SRV. Since it doesn't support TCP, it omits the TCP query. There were no addresses in the DNS response, so the client goes to the next step.

3. The client does a DNS query for A records for "company.com". An address is found, so that client attempts to contact a server at that address at port 5060.

E IANA Considerations

Section 4.4 describes a name space and mechanism for registering SIP options.

Section 6.41 describes the name space for registering SIP warn-codes.

F Acknowledgments

We wish to thank the members of the IETF MMUSIC WG for their comments and suggestions. Detailed comments were provided by Anders

Kristensen, Jim Buller, Dave Devanathan, Yaron Goland, Christian Huitema, Gadi Karmi, Jonathan Lennox, Keith Moore, Vern Paxson, Moshe J. Sambol, and Eric Tremblay.

This work is based, inter alia, on [37,38].

G Authors' Addresses

Mark Handley
AT&T Center for Internet Research at ISCI (ACIRI)
1947 Center St., Suite 600
Berkeley, CA 94704-119
USA
Email: mjh@aciri.org

Henning Schulzrinne
Dept. of Computer Science
Columbia University
1214 Amsterdam Avenue
New York, NY 10027
USA
Email: schulzrinne@cs.columbia.edu

Eve Schooler
Computer Science Department 256-80
California Institute of Technology
Pasadena, CA 91125
USA
Email: schooler@cs.caltech.edu

Jonathan Rosenberg
Lucent Technologies, Bell Laboratories
Rm. 4C-526
101 Crawfords Corner Road
Holmdel, NJ 07733
USA
Email: jdrosen@bell-labs.com

H Bibliography

[1] Pandya, R., "Emerging mobile and personal communication systems," IEEE Communications Magazine , vol. 33, pp. 44--52, June 1995.

[2] Braden, B., Zhang, L., Berson, S., Herzog, S. and S. Jamin, "Resource ReSerVation protocol (RSVP) -- version 1 functional specification", RFC 2205, October 1997.

[3] Schulzrinne, H., Casner, S., Frederick, R. and V. Jacobson, "RTP: a transport protocol for real-time applications", RFC 1889, Internet Engineering Task Force, Jan. 1996.

[4] Schulzrinne, H., Lanphier, R. and A. Rao, "Real time streaming protocol (RTSP)", RFC 2326, April 1998.

[5] Handley, M., "SAP: Session announcement protocol," Internet Draft, Internet Engineering Task Force, Nov. 1996. Work in progress.

[6] Handley, M. and V. Jacobson, "SDP: session description protocol", RFC 2327, April 1998.

[7] International Telecommunication Union, "Visual telephone systems and equipment for local area networks which provide a non-guaranteed quality of service," Recommendation H.323, Telecommunication Standardization Sector of ITU, Geneva, Switzerland, May 1996.

[8] International Telecommunication Union, "Control protocol for multimedia communication," Recommendation H.245, Telecommunication Standardization Sector of ITU, Geneva, Switzerland, Feb. 1998.

[9] International Telecommunication Union, "Media stream packetization and synchronization on non-guaranteed quality of service LANs," Recommendation H.225.0, Telecommunication Standardization Sector of ITU, Geneva, Switzerland, Nov. 1996.

[10] Bradner, S., "Key words for use in RFCs to indicate requirement levels", BCP 14, RFC 2119, Mardch 1997.

[11] Fielding, R., Gettys, J., Mogul, J., Nielsen, H. and T. Berners-Lee, "Hypertext transfer protocol -- HTTP/1.1", RFC 2068, January 1997.

[12] Berners-Lee, T., Fielding, R. and L. Masinter, "Uniform resource identifiers (URI): generic syntax", RFC 2396, August 1998.

[13] Berners-Lee, T., Masinter, L. and M. McCahill, "Uniform resource locators (URL)", RFC 1738, December 1994.

[14] Gulbrandsen, A. and P. Vixie, "A DNS RR for specifying the

location of services (DNS SRV)", RFC 2052, October 1996.

[15] Mockapetris, P., "Domain names - implementation and specification", STD 13, RFC 1035, Noveberm 1997.

[16] Hamilton, M. and R. Wright, "Use of DNS aliases for network services", RFC 2219, October 1997.

[17] Zimmerman, D., "The finger user information protocol", RFC 1288, December 1991.

[18] Williamson, S., Kosters, M., Blacka, D., Singh, J. and K. Zeilstra, "Referral whois (rwhois) protocol V1.5", RFC 2167, June 1997.

[19] Yeong, W., Howes, T. and S. Kille, "Lightweight directory access protocol", RFC 1777, March 1995.

[20] Schooler, E., "A multicast user directory service for synchronous rendezvous," Master's Thesis CS-TR-96-18, Department of Computer Science, California Institute of Technology, Pasadena, California, Aug. 1996.

[21] Yergeau, F., "UTF-8, a transformation format of ISO 10646", RFC 2279, January 1998.

[22] Stevens, W., TCP/IP illustrated: the protocols , vol. 1. Reading, Massachusetts: Addison-Wesley, 1994.

[23] Mogul, J. and S. Deering, "Path MTU discovery", RFC 1191, November 1990.

[24] Crocker, D., "Standard for the format of ARPA internet text messages", RFC STD 11, RFC 822, August 1982.

[25] Meyer, D., "Administratively scoped IP multicast", RFC 2365, July 1998.

[26] Schulzrinne, H., "RTP profile for audio and video conferences with minimal control", RFC 1890, January 1996

[27] Eastlake, D., Crocker, S. and J. Schiller, "Randomness recommendations for security", RFC 1750, December 1994.

[28] Hoffman, P., Masinter, L. and J. Zawinski, "The mailto URL scheme", RFC 2368, July 1998.

[29] Braden, B., "Requirements for internet hosts - application and

support", STD 3, RFC 1123, October 1989.

[30] Palme, J., "Common internet message headers", RFC 2076, February 1997.

[31] Alvestrand, H., "IETF policy on character sets and languages", RFC 2277, January 1998.

[32] Elkins, M., "MIME security with pretty good privacy (PGP)", RFC 2015, October 1996.

[33] Atkins, D., Stallings, W. and P. Zimmermann, "PGP message exchange formats", RFC 1991, August 1996.

[34] Atkinson, R., "Security architecture for the internet protocol", RFC 2401, November 1998.

[35] Allen, C. and T. Dierks, "The TLS protocol version 1.0," RFC 2246, January 1999.

[36] Franks, J., Hallam-Baker, P., Hostetler, J., Lawrence, S., Leach, P., Luotonen, A. and L. Stewart, "HTTP authentication: Basic and digest access authentication," Internet Draft, Internet Engineering Task Force, Sept. 1998. Work in progress.

[37] Schooler, E., "Case study: multimedia conference control in a packet-switched teleconferencing system," Journal of Internetworking: Research and Experience , vol. 4, pp. 99--120, June 1993. ISI reprint series ISI/RS-93-359.

[38] Schulzrinne, H., "Personal mobility for multimedia services in the Internet," in European Workshop on Interactive Distributed Multimedia Systems and Services (IDMS) , (Berlin, Germany), Mar. 1996.

Full Copyright Statement

Network Working Group K. McKay
Request for Comments: 2658 QUALCOMM Incorporated
Category: Standards Track August 1999

RTP Payload Format for PureVoice(tm) Audio

Status of this Memo

This document specifies an Internet standards track protocol for the Internet community, and requests discussion and suggestions for improvements. Please refer to the current edition of the "Internet Official Protocol Standards" (STD 1) for the standardization state and status of this protocol. Distribution of this memo is unlimited.

Copyright Notice

ABSTRACT

This document describes the RTP payload format for PureVoice(tm) Audio. The packet format supports variable interleaving to reduce the effect of packet loss on audio quality.

1 Introduction

This document describes how compressed PureVoice audio as produced by the Qualcomm PureVoice CODEC [1] may be formatted for use as an RTP payload type. A method is provided to interleave the output of the compressor to reduce quality degradation due to lost packets. Furthermore, the sender may choose various interleave settings based on the importance of low end-to-end delay versus greater tolerance for lost packets.

The key words "MUST", "MUST NOT", "REQUIRED", "SHALL", "SHALL NOT", "SHOULD", "SHOULD NOT", "RECOMMENDED", "MAY", and "OPTIONAL" in this document are to be interpreted as described in RFC 2119 [3].

2 Background

The Electronic Industries Association (EIA) & Telecommunications Industry Association (TIA) standard IS-733 [1] defines an audio compression algorithm for use in CDMA applications. In addition to being the standard CODEC for all wireless CDMA terminals, the Qualcomm PureVoice CODEC (a.k.a. Qcelp) is used in several Internet applications most notably JFax(tm), Apple(r) QuickTime(tm), and Eudora(r).

The Qcelp CODEC [1] compresses each 20 milliseconds of 8000 Hz, 16-bit sampled input speech into one of four different size output frames: Rate 1 (266 bits), Rate 1/2 (124 bits), Rate 1/4 (54 bits) or Rate 1/8 (20 bits). The CODEC chooses the output frame rate based on analysis of the input speech and the current operating mode (either normal or reduced rate). For typical speech patterns, this results in an average output of 6.8 k bits/sec for normal mode and 4.7 k bits/sec for reduced rate mode.

3 RTP/Qcelp Packet Format

The RTP timestamp is in 1/8000 of a second units. The RTP payload data for the Qcelp CODEC has the following format:

```
 0                   1                   2                   3
 0 1 2 3 4 5 6 7 8 9 0 1 2 3 4 5 6 7 8 9 0 1 2 3 4 5 6 7 8 9 0 1
+-+-+-+-+-+-+-+-+-+-+-+-+-+-+-+-+-+-+-+-+-+-+-+-+-+-+-+-+-+-+-+-+
|                         RTP Header [2]                        |
+=+=+=+=+=+=+=+=+=+=+=+=+=+=+=+=+=+=+=+=+=+=+=+=+=+=+=+=+=+=+=+=+
|RR | LLL | NNN |                                               |
+-+-+-+-+-+-+-+-+      one or more codec data frames            |
|                              ....                             |
+-+-+-+-+-+-+-+-+-+-+-+-+-+-+-+-+-+-+-+-+-+-+-+-+-+-+-+-+-+-+-+-+
```

The RTP header has the expected values as described in [2]. The extension bit is not set and this payload type never sets the marker bit. The codec data frames are aligned on octet boundaries. When interleaving is in use and/or multiple codec data frames are present in a single RTP packet, the timestamp is, as always, that of the oldest data represented in the RTP packet. The other fields have the following meaning:

Reserved (RR): 2 bits
MUST be set to zero by sender, SHOULD be ignored by receiver.

Interleave (LLL): 3 bits
MUST have a value between 0 and 5 inclusive. The remaining two values (6 and 7) MUST not be used by senders. If this field is non-zero, interleaving is enabled. All receivers MUST support interleaving. Senders MAY support interleaving. Senders that do not support interleaving MUST set field LLL and NNN to zero.

Interleave Index (NNN): 3 bits
MUST have a value less than or equal to the value of LLL. Values of NNN greater than the value of LLL are invalid.

3.1 Receiving Invalid Values

On receipt of an RTP packet with an invalid value of the LLL or NNN field, the RTP packet MUST be treated as lost by the receiver for the purpose of generating erasure frames as described in section 4.

3.2 CODEC data frame format

The output of the Qcelp CODEC must be converted into CODEC data frames for inclusion in the RTP payload as follows:

a. Octet 0 of the CODEC data frame indicates the rate and total size of the CODEC data frame as indicated in this table:

OCTET 0	RATE	TOTAL CODEC data frame size (in octets)
0	Blank	1
1	1/8	4
2	1/4	8
3	1/2	17
4	1	35
5	reserved	8 (SHOULD be treated as a reserved value)
14	Erasure	1 (SHOULD NOT be transmitted by sender)
other	n/a	reserved

Receipt of a CODEC data frame with a reserved value in octet 0 MUST be considered invalid data as described in 3.1.

b. The bits as numbered in the standard [1] from highest to lowest are packed into octets. The highest numbered bit (265 for Rate 1, 123 for Rate 1/2, 53 for Rate 1/4 and 19 for Rate 1/8) is placed in the most significant bit (Internet bit 0) of octet 1 of the CODEC data frame. The second highest numbered bit (264 for Rate 1, etc.) is placed in the second most significant bit (Internet bit 1) of octet 1 of the data frame. This continues so that bit 258 from the standard Rate 1 frame is placed in the least significant bit of octet 1. Bit 257 from the standard is placed in the most significant bit of octet 2 and so on until bit 0 from the standard Rate 1 frame is placed in Internet bit 1 of octet 34 of the CODEC data frame. The remaining unused bits of the last octet of the CODEC data frame MUST be set to zero.

Here is a detail of how a Rate 1/8 frame is converted into a CODEC data frame:

```
                           CODEC data frame

 0                   1                   2                   3
 0 1 2 3 4 5 6 7 8 9 0 1 2 3 4 5 6 7 8 9 0 1 2 3 4 5 6 7 8 9 0 1
+-+-+-+-+-+-+-+-+-+-+-+-+-+-+-+-+-+-+-+-+-+-+-+-+-+-+-+-+-+-+-+-+
|               |1|1|1|1|1|1|1|1|1|1| | | | | | | | | | | | | | |
| 1 (Rate 1/8)  |9|8|7|6|5|4|3|2|1|0|9|8|7|6|5|4|3|2|1|0|Z|Z|Z|Z|
+-+-+-+-+-+-+-+-+-+-+-+-+-+-+-+-+-+-+-+-+-+-+-+-+-+-+-+-+-+-+-+-+
```

Octet 0 of the data frame has value 1 (see table above) indicating the total data frame length (including octet 0) is 4 octets. Bits 19 through 0 from the standard Rate 1/8 frame are placed as indicated with bits marked with "Z" being set to zero. The Rate 1, 1/4 and 1/2 standard frames are converted similarly.

3.3 Bundling CODEC data frames

As indicated in section 3, more than one CODEC data frame MAY be included in a single RTP packet by a sender. Receivers MUST handle bundles of up to 10 CODEC data frames in a single RTP packet.

Furthermore, senders have the following additional restrictions:

- o MUST not bundle more CODEC data frames in a single RTP packet than will fit in the MTU of the RTP transport protocol. For the purpose of computing the maximum bundling value, all CODEC data frames should be assumed to have the Rate 1 size.

- o MUST never bundle more than 10 CODEC data frames in a single RTP packet.

- o Once beginning transmission with a given SSRC and given bundling value, MUST NOT increase the bundling value. If the bundling value needs to be increased, a new SSRC number MUST be used.

- o MAY decrease the bundling value only between interleave groups (see section 3.4). If the bundling value is decreased, it MUST NOT be increased (even to the original value), although it may be decreased again at a later time.

3.3.1 Determining the number of bundled CODEC data frames

Since no count is transmitted as part of the RTP payload and the CODEC data frames have differing lengths, the only way to determine how many CODEC data frames are present in the RTP packet is to examine octet 0 of each CODEC data frame in sequence until the end of the RTP packet is reached.

3.4 Interleaving CODEC data frames

Interleaving is meaningful only when more than one CODEC data frame is bundled into a single RTP packet.

All receivers MUST support interleaving. Senders MAY support interleaving.

Given a time-ordered sequence of output frames from the Qcelp CODEC numbered 0..n, a bundling value B, and an interleave value L where n = B * (L+1) - 1, the output frames are placed into RTP packets as follows (the values of the fields LLL and NNN are indicated for each RTP packet):

```
First RTP Packet in Interleave group:
   LLL=L, NNN=0
   Frame 0, Frame L+1, Frame 2(L+1), Frame 3(L+1), ... for a total of
   B frames

Second RTP Packet in Interleave group:
   LLL=L, NNN=1
   Frame 1, Frame 1+L+1, Frame 1+2(L+1), Frame 1+3(L+1), ... for a
   total of B frames

This continues to the last RTP packet in the interleave group:

L+1 RTP Packet in Interleave group:
   LLL=L, NNN=L
   Frame L, Frame L+L+1, Frame L+2(L+1), Frame L+3(L+1), ... for a
   total of B frames
```

Senders MUST transmit in timestamp-increasing order. Furthermore, within each interleave group, the RTP packets making up the interleave group MUST be transmitted in value-increasing order of the NNN field. While this does not guarantee reduced end-to-end delay on the receiving end, when packets are delivered in order by the underlying transport, delay will be reduced to the minimum possible.

Additionally, senders have the following restrictions:

- o Once beginning transmission with a given SSRC and given interleave value, MUST NOT increase the interleave value. If the interleave value needs to be increased, a new SSRC number MUST be used.

- o MAY decrease the interleave value only between interleave groups. If the interleave value is decreased, it MUST NOT be increased (even to the original value), although it may be decreased again at a later time.

3.5 Finding Interleave Group Boundaries

Given an RTP packet with sequence number S, interleave value (field LLL) L, and interleave index value (field NNN) N, the interleave group consists of RTP packets with sequence numbers from S-N to S-N+L inclusive. In other words, the Interleave group always consists of L+1 RTP packets with sequential sequence numbers. The bundling value for all RTP packets in an interleave group MUST be the same.

The receiver determines the expected bundling value for all RTP packets in an interleave group by the number of CODEC data frames bundled in the first RTP packet of the interleave group received. Note that this may not be the first RTP packet of the interleave group sent if packets are delivered out of order by the underlying transport.

On receipt of an RTP packet in an interleave group with other than the expected bundling value, the receiver MAY discard CODEC data frames off the end of the RTP packet or add erasure CODEC data frames to the end of the packet in order to manufacture a substitute packet with the expected bundling value. The receiver MAY instead choose to discard the whole interleave group and play silence.

3.6 Reconstructing Interleaved Audio

Given an RTP sequence number ordered set of RTP packets in an interleave group numbered 0..L, where L is the interleave value and B is the bundling value, and CODEC data frames within each RTP packet that are numbered in order from first to last with the numbers 1..B, the original, time-ordered sequence of output frames from the CODEC may be reconstructed as follows:

```
First L+1 frames:
   Frame 0 from packet 0 of interleave group
   Frame 0 from packet 1 of interleave group
   And so on up to...
   Frame 0 from packet L of interleave group
```

Second L+1 frames:
Frame 1 from packet 0 of interleave group
Frame 1 from packet 1 of interleave group
And so on up to...
Frame 1 from packet L of interleave group

And so on up to...

Bth L+1 frames:
Frame B from packet 0 of interleave group
Frame B from packet 1 of interleave group
And so on up to...
Frame B from packet L of interleave group

3.6.1 Additional Receiver Responsibility

Assume that the receiver has begun playing frames from an interleave group. The time has come to play frame x from packet n of the interleave group. Further assume that packet n of the interleave group has not been received. As described in section 4, an erasure frame will be sent to the Qcelp CODEC.

Now, assume that packet n of the interleave group arrives before frame x+1 of that packet is needed. Receivers SHOULD use frame x+1 of the newly received packet n rather than substituting an erasure frame. In other words, just because packet n wasn't available the first time it was needed to reconstruct the interleaved audio, the receiver SHOULD NOT assume it's not available when it's subsequently needed for interleaved audio reconstruction.

4 Handling lost RTP packets

The Qcelp CODEC supports the notion of erasure frames. These are frames that for whatever reason are not available. When reconstructing interleaved audio or playing back non-interleaved audio, erasure frames MUST be fed to the Qcelp CODEC for all of the missing packets.

Receivers MUST use the timestamp clock to determine how many CODEC data frames are missing. Each CODEC data frame advances the timestamp clock EXACTLY 160 counts.

Since the bundling value may vary (it can only decrease), the timestamp clock is the only reliable way to calculate exactly how many CODEC data frames are missing when a packet is dropped.

Specifically when reconstructing interleaved audio, a missing RTP packet in the interleave group should be treated as containing B erasure CODEC data frames where B is the bundling value for that interleave group.

5 Discussion

The Qcelp CODEC interpolates the missing audio content when given an erasure frame. However, the best quality is perceived by the listener when erasure frames are not consecutive. This makes interleaving desirable as it increases audio quality when dropped packets are more likely.

On the other hand, interleaving can greatly increase the end-to-end delay. Where an interactive session is desired, an interleave (field LLL) value of 0 or 1 and a bundling factor of 4 or less is recommended.

When end-to-end delay is not a concern, a bundling value of at least 4 and an interleave (field LLL) value of 4 or 5 is recommended subject to MTU limitations.

The restrictions on senders set forth in sections 3.3 and 3.4 guarantee that after receipt of the first payload packet from the sender, the receiver can allocate a well-known amount of buffer space that will be sufficient for all future reception from the same SSRC value. Less buffer space may be required at some point in the future if the sender decreases the bundling value or interleave, but never more buffer space. This prevents the possibility of the receiver needing to allocate more buffer space (with the possible result that none is available) should the bundling value or interleave value be increased by the sender. Also, were the interleave or bundling value to increase, the receiver could be forced to pause playback while it receives the additional packets necessary for playback at an increased bundling value or increased interleave.

6 Security Considerations

RTP packets using the payload format defined in this specification are subject to the security considerations discussed in the RTP specification [2], and any appropriate profile (for example [4]). This implies that confidentiality of the media streams is achieved by encryption. Because the data compression used with this payload format is applied end-to-end, encryption may be performed after compression so there is no conflict between the two operations.

A potential denial-of-service threat exists for data encodings using compression techniques that have non-uniform receiver-end computational load. The attacker can inject pathological datagrams into the stream which are complex to decode and cause the receiver to be overloaded. However, this encoding does not exhibit any significant non-uniformity.

As with any IP-based protocol, in some circumstances, a receiver may be overloaded simply by the receipt of too many packets, either desired or undesired. Network-layer authentication may be used to discard packets from undesired sources, but the processing cost of the authentication itself may be too high. In a multicast environment, pruning of specific sources may be implemented in future versions of IGMP [5] and in multicast routing protocols to allow a receiver to select which sources are allowed to reach it.

7 References

[1] TIA/EIA/IS-733. TR45: High Rate Speech Service Option for Wideband Spread Spectrum Communications Systems. Available from Global Engineering +1 800 854 7179 or +1 303 792 2181. May also be ordered online at http://www.eia.org/eng/.

[2] Schulzrinne, H., Casner, S., Frederick, R. and V. Jacobson, "RTP: A Transport Protocol for Real-Time Applications", RFC 1889, January 1996.

[3] Bradner, S., "Key words for use in RFCs to Indicate Requirement Levels", BCP 14, RFC 2119, March 1997.

[4] Schulzrinne, H., "RTP Profile for Audio and Video Conferences with Minimal Control", RFC 1890, January 1996.

[5] Deering, S., "Host Extensions for IP Multicasting", STD 5, RFC 1112, August 1989.

8 Author's Address

Kyle J. McKay
QUALCOMM Incorporated
5775 Morehouse Drive
San Diego, CA 92121-1714
USA

Phone: +1 858 587 1121
EMail: kylem@qualcomm.com

9 Full Copyright Statement

Acknowledgement

Funding for the RFC Editor function is currently provided by the Internet Society.

Network Working Group
Request for Comments: 2705
Category: Informational

M. Arango
RSL COM
A. Dugan
I. Elliott
Level3 Communications
C. Huitema
Telcordia
S. Pickett
Vertical Networks
October 1999

RFC 2705 1

Media Gateway Control Protocol (MGCP) Version 1.0

Status of this Memo

This memo provides information for the Internet community. It does not specify an Internet standard of any kind. Distribution of this memo is unlimited.

Copyright Notice

IESG NOTE:

This document is being published for the information of the community. It describes a protocol that is currently being deployed in a number of products. Implementers should be aware of developments in the IETF Megaco Working Group and ITF-T SG16 who are currently working on a potential successor to this protocol.

Abstract

This document describes an application programming interface and a corresponding protocol (MGCP) for controlling Voice over IP (VoIP) Gateways from external call control elements. MGCP assumes a call control architecture where the call control "intelligence" is outside the gateways and handled by external call control elements.

The document is structured in 6 main sections:

* The introduction presents the basic assumptions and the relation to other protocols such as H.323, RTSP, SAP or SIP.

* The interface section presents a conceptual overview of the MGCP, presenting the naming conventions, the usage of the session description protocol SDP, and the procedures that compose MGCP: Notifications Request, Notification, Create Connection, Modify Connection, Delete Connection, AuditEndpoint, AuditConnection and RestartInProgress.

* The protocol description section presents the MGCP encodings, which are based on simple text formats, and the transmission procedure over UDP.

* The security section presents the security requirement of MGCP, and its usage of IP security services (IPSEC).

* The event packages section provides an initial definition of packages and event names.

* The description of the changes made in combining SGCP 1.1 and IPDC to create MGCP 1.0.

Table of Contents

1. Introduction

This document describes an abstract application programming interface and a corresponding protocol (MGCP) for controlling Telephony Gateways from external call control elements called media gateway controllers or call agents. A telephony gateway is a network element that provides conversion between the audio signals carried on telephone circuits and data packets carried over the Internet or over other packet networks. Example of gateways are:

* Trunking gateways, that interface between the telephone network and a Voice over IP network. Such gateways typically manage a large number of digital circuits.

* Voice over ATM gateways, which operate much the same way as voice over IP trunking gateways, except that they interface to an ATM network.

* Residential gateways, that provide a traditional analog (RJ11) interface to a Voice over IP network. Examples of residential gateways include cable modem/cable set-top boxes, xDSL devices, broad-band wireless devices

* Access gateways, that provide a traditional analog (RJ11) or digital PBX interface to a Voice over IP network. Examples of access gateways include small-scale voice over IP gateways.

* Business gateways, that provide a traditional digital PBX interface or an integrated "soft PBX" interface to a Voice over IP network.

* Network Access Servers, that can attach a "modem" to a telephone circuit and provide data access to the Internet. We expect that, in the future, the same gateways will combine Voice over IP services and Network Access services.

* Circuit switches, or packet switches, which can offer a control interface to an external call control element.

MGCP assumes a call control architecture where the call control "intelligence" is outside the gateways and handled by external call control elements. The MGCP assumes that these call control elements, or Call Agents, will synchronize with each other to send coherent commands to the gateways under their control. MGCP does not define a mechanism for synchronizing Call Agents. MGCP is, in essence, a master/slave protocol, where the gateways are expected to execute commands sent by the Call Agents. In consequence, this document specifies in great detail the expected behavior of the gateways, but only specify those parts of a call agent implementation, such as timer management, that are mandated for proper operation of the protocol.

MGCP assumes a connection model where the basic constructs are endpoints and connections. Endpoints are sources or sinks of data and could be physical or virtual. Examples of physical endpoints are:

* An interface on a gateway that terminates a trunk connected to a PSTN switch (e.g., Class 5, Class 4, etc.). A gateway that terminates trunks is called a trunk gateway.

* An interface on a gateway that terminates an analog POTS connection to a phone, key system, PBX, etc. A gateway that terminates residential POTS lines (to phones) is called a residential gateway.

An example of a virtual endpoint is an audio source in an audio-content server. Creation of physical endpoints requires hardware installation, while creation of virtual endpoints can be done by software.

Connections may be either point to point or multipoint. A point to point connection is an association between two endpoints with the purpose of transmitting data between these endpoints. Once this association is established for both endpoints, data transfer between these endpoints can take place. A multipoint connection is established by connecting the endpoint to a multipoint session.

Connections can be established over several types of bearer networks:

* Transmission of audio packets using RTP and UDP over a TCP/IP network.

* Transmission of audio packets using AAL2, or another adaptation layer, over an ATM network.

* Transmission of packets over an internal connection, for example the TDM backplane or the interconnection bus of a gateway. This is used, in particular, for "hairpin" connections, connections that terminate in a gateway but are immediately rerouted over the telephone network.

For point-to-point connections the endpoints of a connection could be in separate gateways or in the same gateway.

1.1. Relation with the H.323 standards

MGCP is designed as an internal protocol within a distributed system that appears to the outside as a single VoIP gateway. This system is composed of a Call Agent, that may or may not be distributed over several computer platforms, and of a set of gateways, including at least one "media gateway" that perform the conversion of media signals between circuits and packets, and at least one "signalling gateway" when connecting to an SS7 controlled network. In a typical configuration, this distributed gateway system will interface on one side with one or more telephony (i.e. circuit) switches, and on the other side with H.323 conformant systems, as indicated in the following table:

Functional Plane	Phone switch	Terminating Entity	H.323 conformant systems
Signaling Plane	Signaling exchanges through SS7/ISUP	Call agent	Signaling exchanges with the call agent through H.225/RAS and H.225/Q.931.
			Possible negotiation of logical channels and transmission parameters through H.245 with the call agent.
		Internal synchronization through MGCP	
Bearer Data Transport Plane	Connection through high speed trunk groups	Telephony gateways	Transmission of VOIP data using RTP directly between the H.323 station and the gateway.

In the MGCP model, the gateways focus on the audio signal translation function, while the Call Agent handles the signaling and call processing functions. As a consequence, the Call Agent implements the "signaling" layers of the H.323 standard, and presents itself as an "H.323 Gatekeeper" or as one or more "H.323 Endpoints" to the H.323 systems.

1.2. Relation with the IETF standards

While H.323 is the recognized standard for VoIP terminals, the IETF has also produced specifications for other types of multi-media applications. These other specifications include:

* the Session Description Protocol (SDP), RFC 2327,

* the Session Announcement Protocol (SAP),

* the Session Initiation Protocol (SIP),

* the Real Time Streaming Protocol (RTSP), RFC 2326.

The latter three specifications are in fact alternative signaling standards that allow for the transmission of a session description to an interested party. SAP is used by multicast session managers to distribute a multicast session description to a large group of recipients, SIP is used to invite an individual user to take part in a point-to-point or unicast session, RTSP is used to interface a server that provides real time data. In all three cases, the session description is described according to SDP; when audio is transmitted, it is transmitted through the Real-time Transport Protocol, RTP.

The distributed gateway systems and MGCP will enable PSTN telephony users to access sessions set up using SAP, SIP or RTSP. The Call Agent provides for signaling conversion, according to the following table:

Functional Plane	Phone switch	Terminating Entity	IETF conforming systems
Signaling Plane	Signaling exchanges through SS7/ISUP	Call agent	Signaling exchanges with the call agent through SAP, SIP or RTSP.
			Negotiation of session description parameters through SDP (telephony gateway terminated but passed via the call agent to and from the IETF conforming system)
		Internal synchronization through MGCP	
Bearer Data Transport Plane	Connection through high speed trunk groups	Telephony gateways	Transmission of VoIP data using RTP, directly between the remote IP end system and the gateway.

The SDP standard has a pivotal status in this architecture. We will see in the following description that we also use it to carry session descriptions in MGCP.

1.3. Definitions

Trunk: A communication channel between two switching systems. E.g., a DS0 on a T1 or E1 line.

2. Media Gateway Control Interface

The interface functions provide for connection control and endpoint control. Both use the same system model and the same naming conventions.

2.1. Model and naming conventions

The MGCP assumes a connection model where the basic constructs are endpoints and connections. Connections are grouped in calls. One or more connections can belong to one call. Connections and calls are set up at the initiative of one or several Call Agents.

2.1.1. Types of endpoints

In the introduction, we presented several classes of gateways. Such classifications, however, can be misleading. Manufacturers can arbitrarily decide to provide several types of services in a single packaging. A single product could well, for example, provide some trunk connections to telephony switches, some primary rate connections and some analog line interfaces, thus sharing the characteristics of what we described in the introduction as "trunking", "access" and "residential" gateways. MGCP does not make assumptions about such groupings. We simply assume that media gateways support collections of endpoints. The type of the endpoint determines its functionalities. Our analysis, so far, has led us to isolate the following basic endpoint types:

* Digital channel (DS0),

* Analog line,

* Annoucement server access point,

* Interactive Voice Response access point,

* Conference bridge access point,

* Packet relay,

* Wiretap access point,

* ATM "trunk side" interface.

In this section, we will develop the expected behavior of such end points.

This list is not limitative. There may be other types of endpoints defined in the future, for example test endpoint that could be used to check network quality, or frame-relay endpoints that could be used to managed audio channels multiplexed over a frame-relay virtual circuit.

2.1.1.1. Digital channel (DS0)

Digital channels provide an 8Khz*8bit service. Such channels are found in trunk and ISDN interfaces. They are typically part of digital multiplexes, such as T1, E1, T3 or E3 interfaces. Media gateways that support such channels are capable of translating the digital signals received on the channel, which may be encoded according to A or mu-law, using either the complete set of 8 bits or only 7 of these bits, into audio packets. When the media gateway also supports a NAS service, the gateway shall be capable of receiving either audio-encoded data (modem connection) or binary data (ISDN connection) and convert them into data packets.

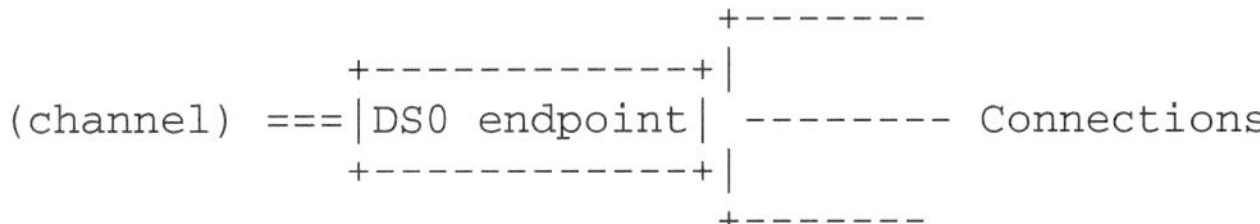

```
                            +-------
               +------------+|
(channel) ===|DS0 endpoint| -------- Connections
               +------------+|
                            +-------
```

Media gateways should be able to establish several connections between the endpoint and the packet networks, or between the endpoint and other endpoints in the same gateway. The signals originating from these connections shall be mixed according to the connection "mode", as specified later in this document. The precise number of connections that an endpoint support is a characteristic of the gateway, and may in fact vary according with the allocation of resource within the gateway.

In some cases, digital channels are used to carry signalling. This is the case for example of SS7 "F" links, or ISDN "D" channels. Media gateways that support these signalling functions shall be able to send and receive the signalling packets to and from a call agent, using the "back haul" procedures defined by the SIGTRAN working group of the IETF. Digital channels are sometimes used in conjunction with channel associated signalling, such as "MF R2". Media gateways that support these signalling functions shall be able to detect and produce the corresponding signals, such as for example "wink" or "A", according to the event signalling and reporting procedures defined in MGCP.

2.1.1.2. Analog line

Analog lines can be used either as a "client" interface, providing service to a classic telephone unit, or as a "service" interface, allowing the gateway to send and receive analog calls. When the media gateway also supports a NAS service, the gateway shall be capable of receiving audio-encoded data (modem connection) and convert them into data packets.

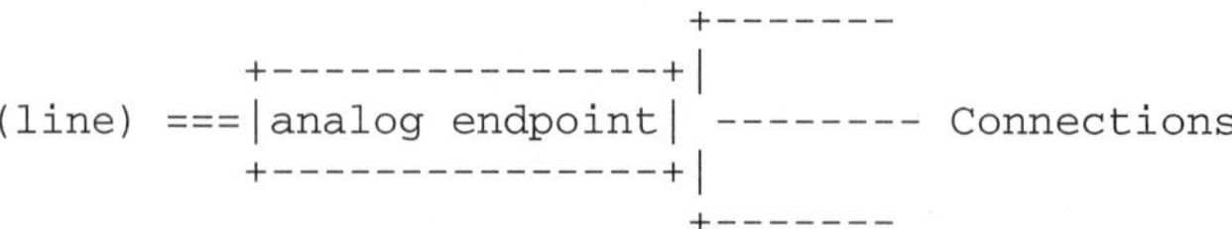

Media gateways should be able to establish several connections between the endpoint and the packet networks, or between the endpoint and other endpoints in the same gateway. The audio signals originating from these connections shall be mixed according to the connection "mode", as specified later in this document. The precise number of connections that an endpoint support is a characteristic of the gateway, and may in fact vary according with the allocation of resource within the gateway. A typical gateway should however be able to support two or three connections per endpoint, in order to provide services such as "call waiting" or "three ways calling".

2.1.1.3. Annoucement server access point

An announcement server endpoint provides acces to an announcement service. Under requests from the call agent, the announcement server will "play" a specified announcement. The requests from the call agent will follow the event signalling and reporting procedures defined in MGCP.

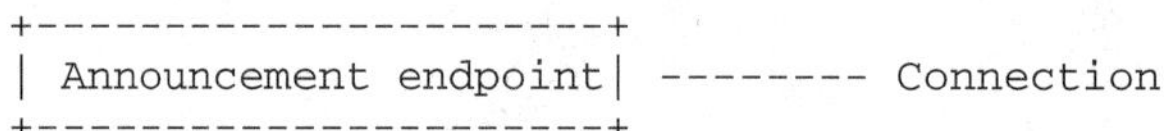

A given announcement endpoint is not supposed to support more than one connection at a time. If several connections were established to the same endpoint, then the same announcements would be played simultaneously over all the connections.

Connections to an announcement server are typically oneway, or "half duplex" -- the announcement server is not expected to listen the audio signals from the connection.

2.1.1.4. Interactive Voice Response access point

An Interactive Voice Response (IVR) endpoint provides acces to an IVR service. Under requests from the call agent, the IVR server will "play" announcements and tones, and will "listen" to responses from the user. The requests from the call agent will follow the event signalling and reporting procedures defined in MGCP.

```
+-------------+
| IVR endpoint| -------- Connection
+-------------+
```

A given IVR endpoint is not supposed to support more than one connection at a time. If several connections were established to the same endpoint, then the same tones and announcements would be played simultaneously over all the connections.

2.1.1.5. Conference bridge access point

A conference bridge endpoint is used to provide access to a specific conference.

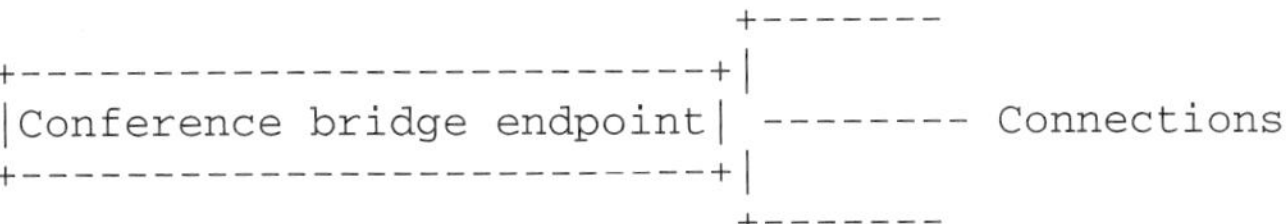

Media gateways should be able to establish several connections between the endpoint and the packet networks, or between the endpoint and other endpoints in the same gateway. The signals originating from these connections shall be mixed according to the connection "mode", as specified later in this document. The precise number of connections that an endpoint support is a characteristic of the gateway, and may in fact vary according with the allocation of resource within the gateway.

2.1.1.6. Packet relay

A packet relay endpoint is a specific form of conference bridge, that typically only supports two connections. Packets relays can be found in firewalls between a protected and an open network, or in transcoding servers used to provide interoperation between incompatible gateways, for example gateways that do not support compatible compression algorithms, or gateways that operate over different transmission networks such as IP and ATM.

2.1.1.7. Wiretap access point

A wiretap access point provides access to a wiretap service, providing either a recording or a life playback of a connection.

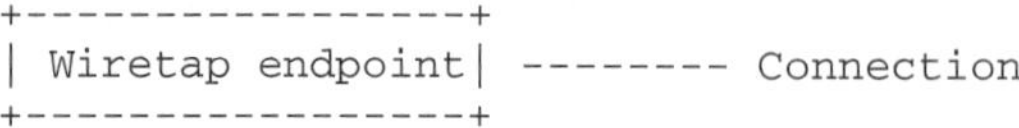

A given wiretap endpoint is not supposed to support more than one connection at a time. If several connections were established to the same endpoint, then the recording or playback would mix the audio signals received on this connections.

Connections to an wiretap endpoint are typically oneway, or "half duplex" -- the wiretap server is not expected to signal its presence in a call.

2.1.1.8. ATM "trunk side" interface.

ATM "trunk side" endpoints are typically found when one or several ATM permanent virtual circuits are used as a replacement for the classic "TDM" trunks linking switches. When ATM/AAL2 is used, several trunks or channels are multiplexed on a single virtual circuit; each of these trunks correspond to a single endpoint.

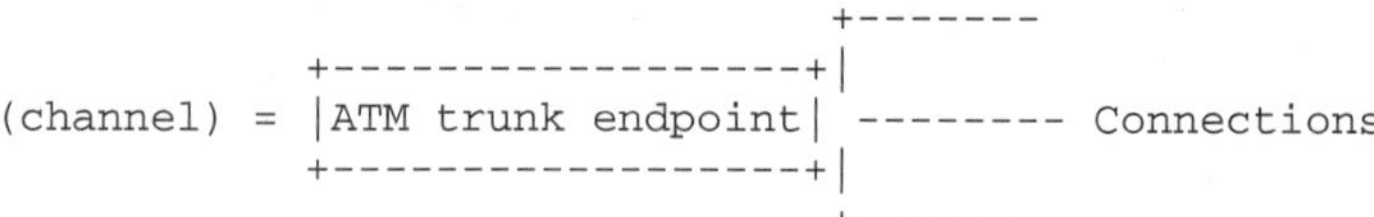

Media gateways should be able to establish several connections between the endpoint and the packet networks, or between the endpoint and other endpoints in the same gateway. The signals originating from these connections shall be mixed according to the connection "mode", as specified later in this document. The precise number of connections that an endpoint support is a characteristic of the gateway, and may in fact vary according with the allocation of resource within the gateway.

2.1.2. Endpoint identifiers

Endpoints identifiers have two components that both are case insensitive:

* the domain name of the gateway that is managing the endpoint,

* a local name within that gateway,

The syntax of the local name depends on the type of endpoint being named. However, the local name for each of these types is naturally hierarchical, beginning with a term which identifies the physical gateway containing the given endpoint and ending in a term which specifies the individual endpoint concerned. With this in mind, the following rules for construction and interpretation of the Entity Name field for these entity types MUST be supported:

1) The individual terms of the naming path MUST be separated by a single slash ("/", ASCII 2F hex).

2) The individual terms are character strings composed of letters, digits or other printable characters, with the exception of characters used as delimitors ("/", "@"), characters used for wildcarding ("*", "$") and white spaces.

3) Wild-carding is represented either by an asterisk ("*") or a dollar sign ("$") for the terms of the naming path which are to be wild-carded. Thus, if the full naming path looks like

```
term1/term2/term3
```

then the Entity Name field looks like this depending on which terms are wild-carded:

```
*/term2/term3 if term1 is wild-carded
term1/*/term3 if term2 is wild-carded
term1/term2/* if term3 is wild-carded
term1/*/* if term2 and term3 are wild-carded,
 etc.
```

In each of these examples a dollar sign could have appeared instead of an asterisk.

4) A term represented by an asterisk is to be interpreted as: "use ALL values of this term known within the scope of the Media Gateway". A term represented by a dollar sign is to be interpreted as: "use ANY ONE value of this term known within the scope of the Media Gateway". The description of a specific command may add further criteria for selection within the general rules given here.

If the Media Gateway controls multiple physical gateways, the first term of the naming MUST identify the physical gateway containing the desired entity. If the Media Gateway controls only a single physical gateway, the first term of the naming string MAY identify that physical gateway, depending on local practice. A local name that is composed of only a wildcard character refers to either all (*) or any ($) endpoints within the media gateway.

In the case of trunking gateways, endpoints are trunk circuits linking a gateway to a telephone switch. These circuits are typically grouped into a digital multiplex, that is connected to the gateway by a physical interface. Such circuits are named in three contexts:

* In the ISUP protocol, trunks are grouped into trunk groups, identified by the SS7 point codes of the switches that the group connects. Circuits within a trunk group are identified by a circuit number (CIC in ISUP).

* In the gateway configuration files, physical interfaces are typically identified by the name of the interface, an arbitrary text string. When the interface multiplexes several circuits, individual circuits are typically identified by a circuit number.

* In MGCP, the endpoints are identified by an endpoint identifier.

The Call Agents use configuration databases to map ranges of circuit numbers within an ISUP trunk group to corresponding ranges of circuits in a multiplex connected to a gateway through a physical interface. The gateway will be identified, in MGCP, by a domain name. The local name will be structured to encode both the name of the physical interface, for example X35V3+A4, and the circuit number within the multiplex connected to the interface, for example 13. The circuit number will be separated from the name of the interface by a fraction bar, as in:

    X35V3+A4/13

Other types of endpoints will use different conventions. For example, in gateways were physical interfaces by construction only control one circuit, the circuit number will be omitted. The exact syntax of such names should be specified in the corresponding server specification.

2.1.3. Calls and connections

Connections are created on the call agent on each endpoint that will be involved in the "call." In the classic example of a connection between two "DS0" endpoints (EP1 and EP2), the call agents controlling the end points will establish two connections (C1 and C2):

```
             +---+                             +---+
(channel1) ===|EP1|--(C1)--...       ...(C2)--|EP2|===(channel2)
             +---+                             +---+
```

Each connection will be designated locally by a connection identifier, and will be characterized by connection attributes.

When the two endpoints are located on gateways that are managed by the same call agent, the creation is done via the three following steps:

1) The call agent asks the first gateway to "create a connection" on the first endpoint. The gateway allocates resources to that connection, and respond to the command by providing a "session description." The session description contains the information necessary for a third party to send packets towards the newly created connection, such as for example IP address, UDP port, and packetization parameters.

2) The call agent then asks the second gateway to "create a connection" on the second endpoint. The command carries the "session description" provided by the first gateway. The gateway allocates resources to that connection, and respond to the command by providing its own "session description."

3) The call agent uses a "modify connection" command to provide this second "session description" to the first endpoint. Once this is done, communication can proceed in both directions.

When the two endpoints are located on gateways that are managed by the different call agents, these two call agents shall exchange information through a call-agent to call-agent signalling protocol, in order to synchronize the creation of the connection on the two endpoints.

Once established, the connection parameters can be modified at any time by a "modify connection" command. The call agent may for example instruct the gateway to change the compression algorithm used on a connection, or to modify the IP address and UDP port to which data should be sent, if a connection is "redirected."

The call agent removes a connection by sending to the gateway a "delete connection" command. The gateway may also, under some circumstances, inform a gateway that a connection could not be sustained.

The following diagram provides a view of the states of a connection, as seen from the gateway:

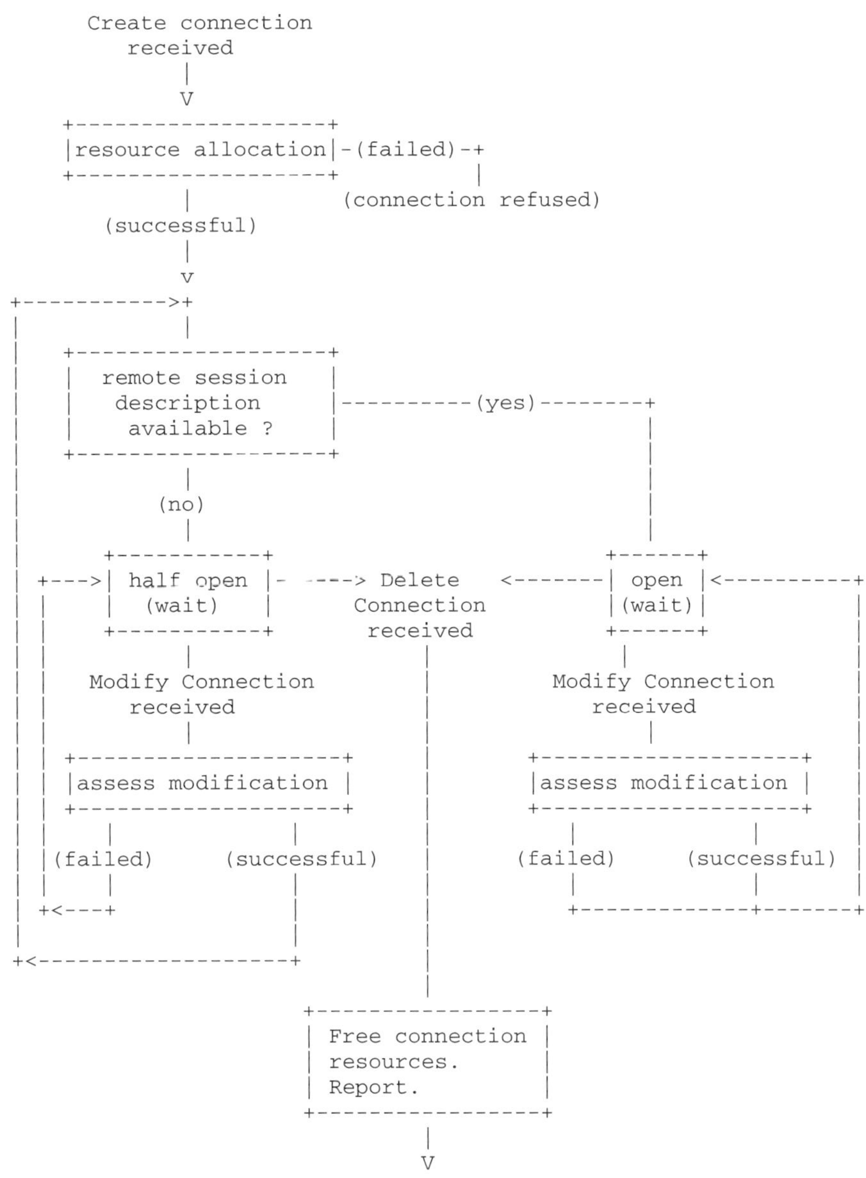
Create connection received
resource allocation
(failed)
(connection refused)
(successful)
remote session description available ?
(yes)
(no)
half open (wait)
Delete Connection received
open (wait)
Modify Connection received
assess modification
(failed)
(successful)
Modify Connection received
assess modification
(failed)
(successful)
Free connection resources. Report.

2.1.3.1. Names of calls

One of the attributes of each connection is the "call identifier."

Calls are identified by unique identifiers, independent of the underlying platforms or agents. These identifiers are created by the Call Agent. They are treated in MGCP as unstructured octet strings.

Call identifiers are expected to be unique within the system, or at a minimum, unique within the collection of Call Agents that control the same gateways. When a Call Agent builds several connections that pertain to the same call, either on the same gateway or in different gateways, these connections that belong to the same call share the same call-id. This identifier can then be used by accounting or management procedures, which are outside the scope of MGCP.

2.1.3.2. Names of connections

Connection identifiers are created by the gateway when it is requested to create a connection. They identify the connection within the context of an endpoint. They are treated in MGCP as unstructured octet strings. The gateway should make sure that a proper waiting period, at least 3 minutes, elapses between the end of a connection that used this identifier and its use in a new connection for the same endpoint. (Gateways may decide to use identifiers that are unique within the context of the gateway.)

2.1.3.3. Management of resources, attributes of connections

Many types of resources will be associated to a connection, such as specific signal processing functions or packetization functions. Generally, these resources fall in two categories:

1) Externally visible resources, that affect the format of "the bits on the network" and must be communicated to the second endpoint involved in the connection.

2) Internal resources, that determine which signal is being sent over the connection and how the received signals are processed by the endpoint.

The resources allocated to a connection, and more generally the handling of the connection, are chosen by the gateway under instructions from the call agent. The call agent will provide these instructions by sending two set of parameters to the gateway:

1) The local directives instruct the gateway on the choice of resources that should be used for a connection,

2) When available, the "session description" provided by the other end of the connection.

The local directives specify such parameters as the mode of the connection (e.g. send only, send-receive), preferred coding or packetization methods, usage of echo cancellation or silence suppression. (A detailed list can be found in the specification of the LocalConnectionOptions parameter of the CreateConnection command.) For each of these parameters, the call agent can either specify a value, a range of value, or no value at all. This allow various implementations to implement various level of control, from a very tight control where the call agent specifies minute details of the connection handling to a very loose control where the call agent only specifies broad guidelines, such as the maximum bandwidth, and let the gateway choose the detailed values.

Based on the value of the local directives, the gateway will determine the resources allocated to the connection. When this is possible, the gateway will choose values that are in line with the remote session description - but there is no absolute requirement that the parameters be exactly the same.

Once the resource have been allocated, the gateway will compose a "session description" that describes the way it intends to receive packets. Note that the session description may in some cases present a range of values. For example, if the gateway is ready to accept one of several compression algorithm, it can provide a list of these accepted algorithms.

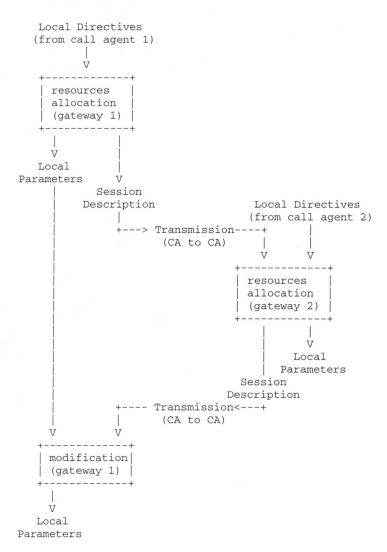

```
                 Local Directives
                (from call agent 1)
                        |
                        V
                 +-------------+
                 | resources   |
                 | allocation  |
                 | (gateway 1) |
                 +-------------+
                   |         |
                   V         |
                 Local       |
              Parameters     V
                   |      Session
                   |    Description               Local Directives
                   |         |                   (from call agent 2)
                   |         +---> Transmission----+      |
                   |                (CA to CA)     |      |
                   |                               V      V
                   |                           +-------------+
                   |                           | resources   |
                   |                           | allocation  |
                   |                           | (gateway 2) |
                   |                           +-------------+
                   |                               |      |
                   |                               |      V
                   |                               |    Local
                   |                               |  Parameters
                   |                            Session
                   |                          Description
                   |         +---- Transmission<---+
                   |         |      (CA to CA)
                   V         V
                 +-------------+
                 | modification|
                 | (gateway 1) |
                 +-------------+
                   |
                   V
                 Local
              Parameters
```

-- Information flow: local directives & session descriptions --

2.1.3.4. Special case of local connections

Large gateways include a large number of endpoints which are often of different types. In some networks, we may often have to set-up connections between endpoints that are located within the same gateway. Examples of such connections may be:

* Connecting a trunk line to a wiretap device,

* Connecting a call to an Interactive Voice-Response unit,

* Connecting a call to a Conferencing unit,

* Routing a call from on endpoint to another, something often described as a "hairpin" connection.

Local connections are much simpler to establish than network connections. In most cases, the connection will be established through some local interconnecting device, such as for example a TDM bus.

When two endpoints are managed by the same gateway, it is possible to specify the connection in a single command that conveys the name of the two endpoints that will be connected. The command is essentially a "Create Connection" command which includes the name of the second endpoint in lieu of the "remote session description."

2.1.4. Names of Call Agents and other entities

The media gateway control protocol has been designed to allow the implementation of redundant Call Agents, for enhanced network reliability. This means that there is no fixed binding between entities and hardware platforms or network interfaces.

Reliability can be improved by the following precautions:

* Entities such as endpoints or Call Agents are identified by their domain name, not their network addresses. Several addresses can be associated with a domain name. If a command or a response cannot be forwarded to one of the network addresses, implementations should retry the transmission using another address.

* Entities may move to another platform. The association between a logical name (domain name) and the actual platform are kept in the domain name service. Call Agents and Gateways should keep track of the time-to-live of the record they read from the DNS. They should query the DNS to refresh the information if the time to live has expired.

In addition to the indirection provided by the use of domain names and the DNS, the concept of "notified entity" is central to reliability and fail-over in MGCP. The "notified entity" for an endpoint is the Call Agent currently controlling that endpoint. At any point in time, an endpoint has one, and only one, "notified entity" associated with it, and when the endpoint needs to send a command to the Call Agent, it MUST send the command to the current "notified entity" for which endpoint(s) the command pertains. Upon startup, the "notified entity" MUST be set to a provisioned value. Most commands sent by the Call Agent include the ability to explicitly name the "notified entity" through the use of a "NotifiedEntity" parameter. The "notified entity" will stay the same until either a new "NotifiedEntity" parameter is received or the endpoint reboots. If the "notified entity" for an endpoint is empty or has not been set explicitly, the "notified entity" will then default to the source address of the last connection handling command or notification request received for the endpoint. Auditing will thus not change the "notified entity."

2.1.5. Digit maps

The Call Agent can ask the gateway to collect digits dialed by the user. This facility is intended to be used with residential gateways to collect the numbers that a user dials; it may also be used with trunking gateways and access gateways alike, to collect the access codes, credit card numbers and other numbers requested by call control services.

An alternative procedure is for the gateway to notify the Call Agent of the dialed digits, as soon as they are dialed. However, such a procedure generates a large number of interactions. It is preferable to accumulate the dialed numbers in a buffer, and to transmit them in a single message.

The problem with this accumulation approach, however, is that it is hard for the gateway to predict how many numbers it needs to accumulate before transmission. For example, using the phone on our desk, we can dial the following numbers:

0	Local operator
00	Long distance operator
xxxx	Local extension number
8xxxxxxx	Local number
#xxxxxxx	Shortcut to local number at other corporate sites
*xx	Star services
91xxxxxxxxxx	Long distance number
9011 + up to 15 digits	International number

The solution to this problem is to load the gateway with a digit map that correspond to the dial plan. This digit map is expressed using a syntax derived from the Unix system command, egrep. For example, the dial plan described above results in the following digit map:

```
(0T| 00T|[1-7]xxx|8xxxxxxx|#xxxxxxx|*xx|91xxxxxxxxxx|9011x.T)
```

The formal syntax of the digit map is described by the DigitMap rule in the formal syntax description of the protocol (section 3.4). A Digit-Map, according to this syntax, is defined either by a "string" or by a list of strings. Each string in the list is an alternative numbering scheme, specified either as a set of digits or timers, or as regular expression. A gateway that detects digits, letters or timers will:

1) Add the event parameter code as a token to the end of an internal state variable called the "current dial string"

2) Apply the current dial string to the digit map table, attempting a match to each regular expression in the Digit Map in lexical order

3) If the result is under-qualified (partially matches at least one entry in the digit map), do nothing further.

If the result matches, or is over-qualified (i.e. no further digits could possibly produce a match), send the current digit string to the Call Agent. A match, in this specification, can be either a "perfect match," exactly matching one of the specified alternatives, or an impossible match, which occur when the dial string does not match any of the alternative. Unexpected timers, for example, can cause "impossible matches." Both perfect matches and impossible matches trigger notification of the accumulated digits.

Digit maps are provided to the gateway by the Call Agent, whenever the Call Agent instructs the gateway to listen for digits.

2.1.6. Names of events

The concept of events and signals is central to MGCP. A Call Agent may ask to be notified about certain events occurring in an endpoint, e.g. off-hook events, and a call agent may request certain signals to be applied to an endpoint, e.g. dial-tone.

Events and signals are grouped in packages within which they share the same namespace which we will refer to as event names in the following. Packages are groupings of the events and signals supported by a particular type of endpoint. For instance, one package may support a certain group of events and signals for analog access lines, and another package may support another group of events and signals for video lines. One or more packages may exist for a given endpoint-type.

Event names are case insensitive and are composed of two logical parts, a package name and an event name. Both names are strings of letters, hyphens and digits, with the restriction that hyphens shall never be the first or last characters in a name. Package or event names are not case sensitive - values such as "hu", "Hu", "HU" or "hU" should be considered equal.

Examples of package names are "D" (DTMF), "M" (MF), "T" (Trunk) or "L" (Line). Examples of event names can be "hu" (off hook or "hang-up" transition), "hf" (flash hook) or "0" (the digit zero).

In textual representations, the package name, when present, is separated from the event name by a slash ("/"). The package name is in fact optional. Each endpoint-type has a default package associated with it, and if the package name is excluded from the event name, the default package name for that endpoint-type is assumed. For example, for an analog access line, the following two event names are equal:

l/dl dial-tone in the line package for an analog access line.

dl dial-tone in the line package (default) for an analog access line.

This document defines a basic set of package names and event names. Additional package names and event names can be registered with the IANA. A package definition shall define the name of the package, and the definition of each event belonging to the package. The event definition shall include the precise name of the event (i.e., the code used in MGCP), a plain text definition of the event, and, when appropriate, the precise definition of the corresponding signals, for example the exact frequencies of audio signal such as dial tones or DTMF tones.

In addition, implementers can gain experience by using experimental packages. The names of experimental packages must start with the two characters "x-"; the IANA shall not register package names that start with these characters.

Digits, or letters, are supported in many packages, notably "DTMF" and "MF". Digits and letters are defined by the rules "Digit" and "Letter" in the definition of digit maps. This definition refers to the digits (0 to 9), to the asterisk or star ("*") and orthotrope, number or pound sign ("#"), and to the letters "A", "B", "C" and "D", as well as the timer indication "T". These letters can be combined in "digit string" that represent the keys that a user punched on a dial. In addition, the letter "X" can be used to represent all digits, and the sign "$" can be used in wildcard notations. The need to easily express the digit strings has a consequence on the form of event names:

> An event name that does not denote a digit should always contain at least one character that is neither a digit, nor one of the letters A, B, C, D, T or X. (Such names should not contain the special signs "*", "#", "/" or "$".)

A Call Agent may often have to ask a gateway to detect a group of events. Two conventions can be used to denote such groups:

* The wildcard convention can be used to detect any event belonging to a package, or a given event in many packages, or event any event in any package supported by the gateway.

* The regular expression Range notation can be used to detect a range of digits.

The star sign (*) can be used as a wildcard instead of a package name, and the keyword "all" can be used as a wildcard instead of an event name:

> A name such as "foo/all" denotes all events in package "foo"
> A name such as "*/bar" denotes the event "bar" in any package supported by the gateway
> The names "*" or "*/all" denote all events supported by the gate way.

The call agent can ask a gateway to detect a set of digits or letters either by individually describing those letters, or by using the "range" notation defined in the syntax of digit strings. For example, the call agent can:

Use the letter "x" to denote "any letter or digit."
Use the notation "[0-9#]" to denote the digits 0 to 9 and the pound sign.

In some cases, Call Agents will request the gateway to generate or detect events on connections rather than on the end point itself. For example, gateways may be asked to provide a ringback tone on a connection. When an event shall be applied on a connection, the name of the connection is added to the name of the event, using an "at" sign (@) as a delimiter, as in:

```
G/rt@0A3F58
```

The wildcard character "*" (star) can be used to denote "all connections". When this convention is used, the gateway will generate or detect the event on all the connections that are connected to the endpoint. An example of this convention could be:

```
R/qa@*
```

The wildcard character "$" can be used to denote "the current connection." It should only be used by the call agent, when the event notification request is "encapsulated" within a command creation or modification command. When this convention is used, the gateway will generate or detect the event on the connection that is currently being created or modified. An example of this convention is:

```
G/rt@$
```

The connection id, or a wildcard replacement, can be used in conjunction with the "all packages" and "all events" conventions. For example, the notation:

```
*/all@*
```

can be used to designate all events on all connections.

Events and signals are described in packages. The package description must provide, for each events, the following informations:

* The description of the event and its purpose, which should mean the actual signal that is generated by the client (i.e., xx ms FSK tone) as well as the resulting user observed result (i.e., MW light on/off).

* The detailed characteristics of the event, such as for example frequencies and amplitude of audio signals, modulations and repetitions,

* The typical and maximum duration of the event.

Signals are divided into different types depending on their behavior:

* On/off (OO) Once applied, these signals last forever until they are turned off. This may happen either as the result of an event or a new SignalRequests (see later).

* Time-out (TO) Once applied, these signals last until they are either turned off (by an event or SignalRequests) or a signal specific period of time has elapsed. Depending on package specifications, a signal that times out may generate an "operation complete" event.

* Brief (BR) The duration of these signals is so short, that they stop on their own. If an event occurs the signal will not stop, however if a new SignalRequests is applied, the signal will stop. (Note: this point should be debated. One could make a case that events such as strings of DTMF digits should in fact be allowed to complete.)

  TO signals are normally used to alert the endpoints' users, to signal them that they are expected to perform a specific action, such as hang down the phone (ringing). Transmission of these signals should typically be interrupted as soon as the first of the requested events has been produced.

  Package descriptions should describe, for all signals, their type (OO, TO, BR). They should also describe the maximum duration of the TO signals.

2.2. Usage of SDP

The Call Agent uses the MGCP to provision the gateways with the description of connection parameters such as IP addresses, UDP port and RTP profiles. These descriptions will follow the conventions delineated in the Session Description Protocol which is now an IETF proposed standard, documented in RFC 2327.

SDP allows for description of multimedia conferences. This version limits SDP usage to the setting of audio circuits and data access circuits. The initial session descriptions contain the description of exactly one media, of type "audio" for audio connections, "nas" for data access.

2.3. Gateway Control Commands

This section describes the commands of the MGCP. The service consists of connection handling and endpoint handling commands. There are nine commands in the protocol:

* The Call Agent can issue an EndpointConfiguration command to a gateway, instructing the gateway about the coding characteristics expected by the "line-side" of the endpoint.

* The Call Agent can issue a NotificationRequest command to a gateway, instructing the gateway to watch for specific events such as hook actions or DTMF tones on a specified endpoint .

* The gateway will then use the Notify command to inform the Call Agent when the requested events occur.

* The Call Agent can use the CreateConnection command to create a connection that terminates in an "endpoint" inside the gateway.

* The Call Agent can use the ModifyConnection command to change the parameters associated to a previously established connection.

* The Call Agent can use the DeleteConnection command to delete an existing connection. The DeleteConnection command may also be used by a gateway to indicate that a connection can no longer be sustained.

* The Call Agent can use the AuditEndpoint and AuditConnection commands to audit the status of an "endpoint" and any connections associated with it. Network management beyond the capabilities provided by these commands are generally desirable, e.g. information about the status of the gateway. Such capabilities are expected to be supported by the use of the Simple Network Management Protocol (SNMP) and definition of a MIB which is outside the scope of this specification.

* The Gateway can use the RestartInProgress command to notify the Call Agent that the gateway, or a group of endpoints managed by the gateway, is being taken out of service or is being placed back in service.

These services allow a controller (normally, the Call Agent) to instruct a gateway on the creation of connections that terminate in an "endpoint" attached to the gateway, and to be informed about events occurring at the endpoint. An endpoint may be for example:

* A specific trunk circuit, within a trunk group terminating in a gateway,

* A specific announcement handled by an announcement server.

Connections are grouped into "calls". Several connections, that may or may not belong to the same call, can terminate in the same endpoint . Each connection is qualified by a "mode" parameter, which can be set to "send only" (sendonly), "receive only" (recvonly), "send/receive" (sendrecv), "conference" (confrnce), "data", "inactive" (inactive), "loopback", "continuity test" (conttest), "network loop back" (netwloop) or "network continuity test" (netwtest).

The handling of the audio signals received on these connections is determined by the mode parameters:

* Audio signals received in data packets through connections in "receive", "conference" or "send/receive" mode are mixed and sent to the endpoint.

* Audio signals originating from the endpoint are transmitted over all the connections whose mode is "send", "conference" or "send/receive."

* In addition to being sent to the endpoint, audio signals received in data packets through connections in "conference" mode are replicated to all the other connections whose mode is "conference."

The "loopback" and "continuity test" modes are used during maintenance and continuity test operations. There are two flavors of continuity test, one specified by ITU and one used in the US. In the first case, the test is a loopback test. The originating switch will send a tone (the go tone) on the bearer circuit and expect the terminating switch to loopback the circuit. If the originating switch sees the same tone returned (the return tone), the COT has passed. If not, the COT has failed. In the second case, the go and return tones are different. The originating switch sends a certain go tone. The terminating switch detects the go tone, it asserts a different return tone in the backwards direction. When the originating switch detects the return tone, the COT is passed. If the originating switch never detects the return tone, the COT has failed.

If the mode is set to "loopback", the gateway is expected to return the incoming signal from the endpoint back into that same endpoint. This procedure will be used, typically, for testing the continuity of trunk circuits according to the ITU specifications.

If the mode is set to "continuity test", the gateway is informed that the other end of the circuit has initiated a continuity test procedure according to the GR specification. The gateway will place the circuit in the transponder mode required for dual-tone continuity tests.

If the mode is set to "network loopback", the audio signals received from the connection will be echoed back on the same connection.

If the mode is set to "network continuity test", the gateway will process the packets received from the connection according to the transponder mode required for dual-tone continuity test, and send the processed signal back on the connection.

2.3.1. EndpointConfiguration

The EndpointConfiguration commands are used to specify the encoding of the signals that will be received by the endpoint. For example, in certain international telephony configurations, some calls will carry mu-law encoded audio signals, while other will use A-law. The Call Agent will use the EndpointConfiguration command to pass this information to the gateway. The configuration may vary on a call by call basis, but can also be used in the absence of any connection.

```
        ReturnCode
        <-- EndpointConfiguration( EndpointId,
                                   BearerInformation)
```

EndpointId is the name for the endpoint in the gateway where EndpointConfiguration executes, as defined in section 2.1.1. The "any of" wildcard convention shall not be used. If the "all of" wildcard convention is used, the command applies to all the endpoint whose name matches the wildcard.

BearerInformation is a parameter defining the coding of the data received from the line side. These information is encoded as a list of sub-parameters. The only sub-parameter defined in this version of the specification is the encoding method, whose values can be set to "A-law" and "mu-law".

ReturnCode is a parameter returned by the gateway. It indicates the outcome of the command and consists of an integer number optionally followed by commentary.

2.3.2. NotificationRequest

The NotificationRequest commands are used to request the gateway to send notifications upon the occurrence of specified events in an endpoint. For example, a notification may be requested for when a gateway detects that an endpoint is receiving tones associated with fax communication. The entity receiving this notification may decide to use a different type of encoding method in the connections bound to this endpoint.

```
ReturnCode
<-- NotificationRequest( EndpointId,
                         [NotifiedEntity,]
                         [RequestedEvents,]
                         RequestIdentifier,
                         [DigitMap,]
                         [SignalRequests,]
                         [QuarantineHandling,]
                         [DetectEvents,]
                         [encapsulated EndpointConfiguration])
```

EndpointId is the name for the endpoint in the gateway where NotificationRequest executes, as defined in section 2.1.1.

NotifiedEntity is an optional parameter that specifies where the notifications should be sent. When this parameter is absent, the notifications should be sent to the originator of the NotificationRequest.

RequestIdentifier is used to correlate this request with the notifications that it triggers.

RequestedEvents is a list of events that the gateway is requested to detect and report. Such events include, for example, fax tones, continuity tones, or on-hook transition. To each event is associated an action, which can be:

* Notify the event immediately, together with the accumulated list of observed events,

* Swap audio,

* Accumulate the event in an event buffer, but don't notify yet,

* Accumulate according to Digit Map,

* Keep Signal(s) active,

* process the Embedded Notification Request,

* Ignore the event.

Some actions can be combined. In particular:

* The "swap audio" action can be combined with "Notify", "Accumulate" and "Ignore."

* The "keep signal active" action can be combined with "Notify", "Accumulate", "Accumulate according to Digit Map", "Ignore" and "Embedded Notification Request."

* The "Embedded Notification Request" can be combined with "Accumulate" and with "Keep signals active." It can also be combined with Notify, if the gateway is allowed to issue several Notify commands in response to a single Notification request.

In addition to the requestedEvents parameter specified in the command, some profiles of MGCP have introduced the concept of "persistent events." According to such profiles, the persistent event list is configured in the endpoint, by means outside the scope of MGCP. The basic MGCP specification does not specify any persistent event.

If a persistent event is not included in the list of RequestedEvents, and the event occurs, the event will be detected anyway, and processed like all other events, as if the persistent event had been requested with a Notify action. Thus, informally, persistent events can be viewed as always being implicitly included in the list of RequestedEvents with an action to Notify, although no glare detection, etc., will be performed.

Non-persistent events are those events explicitly included in the RequestedEvents list. The (possibly empty) list of requested events completely replaces the previous list of requested events. In addition to the persistent events, only the events specified in the requested events list will be detected by the endpoint. If a persistent event is included in the RequestedEvents list, the action specified will then replace the default action associated with the event for the life of the RequestedEvents list, after which the default action is restored. For example, if "Ignore off-hook" was specified, and a new request without any off-hook instructions were received, the default "Notify off-hook" operation then would be restored. A given event MUST NOT appear more than once in a RequestedEvents.

The gateway will detect the union of the persistent events and the requested events. If an event is not specified in either list, it will be ignored.

The Swap Audio action can be used when a gateway handles more than one active connection on an endpoint. This will be the case for three-way calling, call waiting, and possibly other feature scenarios. In order to avoid the round-trip to the Call Agent when just changing which connection is attached to the audio functions of the endpoint, the NotificationRequest can map an event (usually hook flash, but could be some other event) to a local function swap audio, which selects the "next" connection in a round robin fashion. If there is only one connection, this action is effectively a no-op.

If signal(s) are desired to start when an event being looked for occurs, the "Embedded NotificationRequest" action can be used. The embedded NotificationRequest may include a new list of RequestedEvents, SignalRequests and a new digit map as well. The semantics of the embedded NotificationRequest is as if a new NotificationRequest was just received with the same NotifiedEntity, and RequestIdentifier. When the "Embedded NotificationRequest" is activated, the "current dial string" will be cleared; the list of observed events and the quarantine buffer will be unaffected.

MGCP implementations shall be able to support at least one level of embedding. An embedded NotificationRequest that respects this limitation shall not contain another Embedded NotificationRequest.

DigitMap is an optional parameter that allows the Call Agent to provision the gateways with a digit map according to which digits will be accumulated. If this optional parameter is absent, the previously defined value is retained. This parameter must be defined, either explicitly or through a previous command, if the RequestedEvent parameters contain an request to "accumulate according to the digit map." The collection of these digits will result in a digit string. The digit string is initialized to a null string upon reception of the NotificationRequest, so that a subsequent notification only returns the digits that were collected after this request. Digits that were accumulated according to the digit map are reported as any other accumulated event, in the order in which they occur. It is therefore possible that other events be accumulated may be found in between the list of digits.

SignalRequests is a parameter that contains the set of signals that the gateway is asked to apply to the endpoint, such as, for example ringing, or continuity tones. Signals are identified by their name, which is an event name, and may be qualified by parameters.

The action triggered by the SignalRequests is synchronized with the collection of events specified in the RequestedEvents parameter. For example, if the NotificationRequest mandates "ringing" and the event request ask to look for an "off-hook" event, the ringing shall stop as soon as the gateway detect an off hook event. The formal definition is that the generation of all "Time Out" signals shall stop as soon as one of the requested events is detected, unless the "Keep signals active" action is associated to the specified event.

The specific definition of actions that are requested via these SignalRequests, such as the duration of and frequency of a DTMF digit, is out side the scope of MGCP. This definition may vary from location to location and hence from gateway to gateway.

The RequestedEvents and SignalRequests refer to the same event definitions. In one case, the gateway is asked to detect the occurrence of the event, and in the other case it is asked to generate it. The specific events and signals that a given endpoint can detect or perform are determined by the list of event packages that are supported by that end point. Each package specifies a list of events and actions that can be detected or performed. A gateway that is requested to detect or perform an event belonging to a package that is not supported by the specified endpoint shall return an error. When the event name is not qualified by a package name, the default package name for the end point is assumed. If the event name is not registered in this default package, the gateway shall return an error.

The Call Agent can send a NotificationRequest whose requested signal list is empty. It will do so for example when tone generation should stop.

The optional QuarantineHandling parameter specifies the handling of "quarantine" events, i.e. events that have been detected by the gateway before the arrival of this NotificationRequest command, but have not yet been notified to the Call Agent. The parameter provides a set of handling options:

* whether the quarantined events should be processed or discarded (the default is to process them.)

* whether the gateway is expected to generate at most one notification (step by step), or multiple notifications (loop), in response to this request (the default is exactly one.)

When the parameter is absent, the default value is assumed.

We should note that the quarantine-handling parameter also governs the handling of events that were detected but not yet notified when the command is received.

DetectEvents is an optional parameter that specifies a list of events that the gateway is requested to detect during the quarantine period. When this parameter is absent, the events that should be detected in the quarantine period are those listed in the last received DetectEvents list. In addition, the gateway should also detect the events specified in the request list, including those for which the "ignore" action is specified.

Some events and signals, such as the in-line ringback or the quality alert, are performed or detected on connections terminating in the end point rather than on the endpoint itself. The structure of the event names allow the Call Agent to specify the connection (or connections) on which the events should be performed or detected.

The command may carry an encapsulated EndpointConfiguration command, that will apply to the same endpoint. When this command is present, the parameters of the EndpointConfiguration command are inserted after the normal parameters of the NotificationRequest, with the exception of the EndpointId, which is not replicated.

The encapsulated EndpointConfiguration command shares the fate of the NotificationRequest command. If the NotificationRequest is rejected, the EndpointConfiguration is not executed.

ReturnCode is a parameter returned by the gateway. It indicates the outcome of the command and consists of an integer number optionally followed by commentary. .NH 3 Notifications

Notifications are sent via the Notify command and are sent by the gateway when the observed events occur.

```
ReturnCode
<-- Notify( EndpointId,
            [NotifiedEntity,]
            RequestIdentifier,
            ObservedEvents)
```

EndpointId is the name for the endpoint in the gateway which is issuing the Notify command, as defined in section 2.1.1. The identifier should be a fully qualified endpoint identifier, including the domain name of the gateway. The local part of the name shall not use the wildcard convention.

NotifiedEntity is an optional parameter that identifies the entity to which the notifications is sent. This parameter is equal to the last received value of the NotifiedEntity parameter. The parameter is absent if there was no such parameter in the triggering request. The notification is sent to the "current notified entity" or, if no such entity was ever specified, to the address from which the request was received.

RequestIdentifier is parameter that repeats the RequestIdentifier parameter of the NotificationRequest that triggered this notification. It is used to correlate this notification with the request that triggered it.

ObservedEvents is a list of events that the gateway detected. A single notification may report a list of events that will be reported in the order in which they were detected. The list may only contain the identification of events that were requested in the RequestedEvents parameter of the triggering NotificationRequest. It will contain the events that were either accumulated (but not notified) or treated according to digit map (but no match yet), and the final event that triggered the detection or provided a final match in the digit map.

ReturnCode is a parameter returned by the call agent. It indicates the outcome of the command and consists of an integer number optionally followed by commentary.

2.3.3. CreateConnection

This command is used to create a connection between two endpoints.

```
ReturnCode,
ConnectionId,
[SpecificEndPointId,]
[LocalConnectionDescriptor,]
[SecondEndPointId,]
[SecondConnectionId]
<--- CreateConnection(CallId,
                      EndpointId,
                      [NotifiedEntity,]
                      [LocalConnectionOptions,]
                      Mode,
                      [{RemoteConnectionDescriptor |
                        SecondEndpointId}, ]
                      [Encapsulated NotificationRequest,]
                      [Encapsulated EndpointConfiguration])
```

A connection is defined by its endpoints. The input parameters in CreateConnection provide the data necessary to build a gateway's "view" of a connection.

CallId is a globally unique parameter that identifies the call (or session) to which this connection belongs. Connections that belong to the same call share the same call-id. The call-id can be used to identify calls for reporting and accounting purposes. It does not affect the handling of connections by the gateway.

EndpointId is the identifier for the connection endpoint in the gateway where CreateConnection executes. The EndpointId can be fully-specified by assigning a value to the parameter EndpointId in the function call or it may be under-specified by using the "anyone" wildcard convention. If the endpoint is underspecified, the endpoint identifier will be assigned by the gateway and its complete value returned in the SpecificEndPointId parameter of the response.

The NotifiedEntity is an optional parameter that specifies where the Notify or DeleteConnection commands should be sent. If the parameter is absent, the Notify or DeleteConnection commands should be sent to the last received Notified Entity, or to originator of the CreateConnection command if no Notified Entity was ever received for the end point.

LocalConnectionOptions is a parameter used by the Call Agent to direct the handling of the connection by the gateway. The fields contained in LocalConnectionOptions are the following:

* Encoding Method,

* Packetization period,

* Bandwidth,

* Type of Service,

* Usage of echo cancellation,

* Usage of silence suppression or voice activity detection,

* Usage of signal level adaptation and noise level reduction, or "gain control."

* Usage of reservation service,

* Usage of RTP security,

* Type of network used to carry the connection.

This set of field can be completed by vendor specific optional or mandatory extensions. The encoding of the first three fields, when they are present, will be compatible with the SDP and RTP profiles:

* The encoding method shall be specified by using one or several valid encoding names, as defined in the RTP AV Profile or registered with the IANA.

* The packetization period is encoded as either the length of time in milliseconds represented by the media in a packet, as specified in the "ptime" parameter of SDP, or as a range value, specifying both the minimum and maximum acceptable packetization periods.

* The bandwidth is encoded as either a single value or a range, expressed as an integer number of kilobit per seconds.

For each of the first three fields, the Call Agent has three options:

* It may state exactly one value, which the gateway will then use for the connection,

* It may provide a loose specification, such as a list of allowed encoding methods or a range of packetization periods,

* It may simply provide a bandwidth indication, leaving the choice of encoding method and packetization period to the gateway.

The bandwidth specification shall not contradict the specification of encoding methods and packetization period. If an encoding method is specified, then the gateway is authorized to use it, even if it results in the usage of a larger bandwidth than specified.

The LocalConnectionOptions parameter may be absent in the case of a data call.

The Type of Service specifies the class of service that will be used for the connection. When the connection is transmitted over an IP network, the parameters encodes the 8-bit type of service value parameter of the IP header. When the Type of Service is not specified, the gateway shall use a default or configured value.

The gateways can be instructed to perform a reservation, for example using RSVP, on a given connection. When a reservation is needed, the call agent will specify the reservation profile that should be used, which is either "controlled load" or "guaranteed service." The absence of reservation can be indicated by asking for the "best effort" service, which is the default value of this parameter. When reservation has been asked on a connection, the gateway will:

* start emitting RSVP "PATH" messages if the connection is in "send-only", "send-receive", "conference", "network loop back" or "network continuity test" mode (if a remote connection descriptor has been received,)

* start emitting RSVP "RESV" messages as soon as it receives "PATH" messages if the connection is in "receive-only", "send-receive", "conference", "network loop back" or "network continuity test" mode.

The RSVP filters will be deduced from the characteristics of the connection. The RSVP resource profiles will be deduced from the connection's bandwidth and packetization period.

By default, the telephony gateways always perform echo cancellation. However, it is necessary, for some calls, to turn off these operations. The echo cancellation parameter can have two values, "on" (when the echo cancellation is requested) and "off" (when it is turned off.)

The telephony gateways may perform gain control, in order to adapt the level of the signal. However, it is necessary, for example for modem calls, to turn off this function. The gain control parameter may either be specified as "automatic", or as an explicit number of decibels of gain. The default is to not perform gain control, which is equivalent to specifying a gain of 0 decibels.

The telephony gateways may perform voice activity detection, and avoid sending packets during periods of silence. However, it is necessary, for example for modem calls, to turn off this detection. The silence suppression parameter can have two values, "on" (when the detection is requested) and "off" (when it is turned off.) The default is "off."

The Call agent can request the gateway to enable encryption of the audio Packets. It does so by providing an key specification, as specified in RFC 2327. By default, encryption is not used.

The Call Agent may instruct the gateway to prepare the connection on a specified type of network. The type of network is encoded as in the "connection-field" parameter of the SDP standard. Possible values are IN (Internet), ATM and LOCAL. The parameter is optional; if absent, the network is determined by the type of gateway.

RemoteConnectionDescriptor is the connection descriptor for the remote side of a connection, on the other side of the IP network. It includes the same fields as in the LocalConnectionDescriptor, i.e. the fields that describe a session according to the SDP standard. This parameter may have a null value when the information for the remote end is not known yet. This occurs because the entity that builds a connection starts by sending a CreateConnection to one of the two gateways involved in it. For the first CreateConnection issued, there is no information available about the other side of the connection. This information may be provided later via a ModifyConnection call. In the case of data connections (mode=data), this parameter describes the characteristics of the data connection.

The SecondEndpointId can be used instead of the RemoteConnectionDescriptor to establish a connection between two endpoints located on the same gateway. The connection is by definition a local connection. The SecondEndpointId can be fully-specified by assigning a value to the parameter SecondEndpointId in the function call or it may be under-specified by using the "anyone" wildcard convention. If the secondendpoint is underspecified, the second endpoint identifier will be assigned by the gateway and its complete value returned in the SecondEndPointId parameter of the response.

Mode indicates the mode of operation for this side of the connection. The mode are "send", "receive", "send/receive", "conference", "data", "inactive", "loopback", "continuity test", "network loop back" or "network continuity test." The expected handling of these modes is specified in the introduction of the "Gateway Handling Function" section. Some end points may not be capable of supporting all modes. If the command specifies a mode that the endpoint cannot support, and error shall be returned.

The gateway returns a ConnectionId, that uniquely identifies the connection within one endpoint, and a LocalConnectionDescriptor, which is a session description that contains information about addresses and RTP ports, as defined in SDP. The LocalConnectionDescriptor is not returned in the case of data connections. The SpecificEndPointId is an optional parameter that identifies the responding endpoint. It can be used when the EndpointId argument referred to a "any of" wildcard name. When a SpecificEndPointId is returned, the Call Agent should use it as the EndpointId value is successive commands referring to this call.

When a SecondEndpointId is specified, the command really creates two connections that can be manipulated separately through ModifyConnection and DeleteConnection commands. The response to the creation provides a SecondConnectionId parameter that identifies the second connection.

After receiving a "CreateConnection" request that did not include a RemoteConnectionDescriptor parameter, a gateway is in an ambiguous situation. Because it has exported a LocalConnectionDescriptor parameter, it can potentially receive packets. Because it has not yet received the RemoteConnectionDescriptor parameter of the other gateway, it does not know whether the packets that it receives have been authorized by the Call Agent. It must thus navigate between two risks, i.e. clipping some important announcements or listening to insane data. The behavior of the gateway is determined by the value of the Mode parameter:

* If the mode was set to ReceiveOnly, the gateway should accept the voice signals and transmit them through the endpoint.

* If the mode was set to Inactive, Loopback, Continuity Test, the gateway should refuse the voice signals.

* If the mode was set to Network Loopback or Network Continuity Test, the gateway should perform the expected echo or Response.

Note that the mode values SendReceive, Conference, Data and SendOnly don't make sense in this situation. They should be treated as errors, and the command should be rejected (Error code 517).

The command may optionally contain an encapsulated Notification Request command, in which case a RequestIdentifier parameter will be present, as well as, optionally, the RequestedEvents DigitMap, SignalRequests, QuarantineHandling and DetectEvents parameters. The encapsulated NotificationRequest is executed simultaneously with the creation of the connection. For example, when the Call Agent wants to initiate a call to an residential gateway, it should:

* ask the residential gateway to prepare a connection, in order to be sure that the user can start speaking as soon as the phone goes off hook,

* ask the residential gateway to start ringing,

* ask the residential gateway to notify the Call Agent when the phone goes off-hook.

This can be accomplished in a single CreateConnection command, by also transmitting the RequestedEvent parameters for the off hook event, and the SignalRequest parameter for the ringing signal.

When these parameters are present, the creation and the NotificationRequests should be synchronized, which means that bothshould be accepted, or both refused. In our example, the CreateConnection may be refused if the gateway does not have sufficient resources, or cannot get adequate resources from the local network access, and the off-hook Notification-Request can be refused in the glare condition, if the user is already off-hook. In this example, the phone should not ring if the connection cannot be established, and the connection should not be established if the user is already off hook.

The NotifiedEntity parameter, if present, applies to both the CreateConnection and the NotificationRequest command. It defines the new "notified entity" for the endpoint.

The command may carry an encapsulated EndpointConfiguration command, that will apply to the same endpoint. When this command is present, the parameters of the EndpointConfiguration command are inserted after the normal parameters of the CreateConnection with the exception of the EndpointId, which is not replicated. The EndpointConfiguration command may be encapsulated together with an encapsulated NotificationRequest command.

The encapsulated EndpointConfiguration command shares the fate of the CreateConnection command. If the CreateConnection is rejected, the EndpointConfiguration is not executed.

ReturnCode is a parameter returned by the gateway. It indicates the outcome of the command and consists of an integer number optionally followed by commentary.

2.3.4. ModifyConnection

This command is used to modify the characteristics of a gateway's "view" of a connection. This "view" of the call includes both the local connection descriptors as well as the remote connection descriptor.

```
ReturnCode,
[LocalConnectionDescriptor]
 <--- ModifyConnection(CallId,
                       EndpointId,
                       ConnectionId,
                       [NotifiedEntity,]
                       [LocalConnectionOptions,]
                       [Mode,]
                       [RemoteConnectionDescriptor,]
                       [Encapsulated NotificationRequest,]
                       [Encapsulated EndpointConfiguration])
```


The parameters used are the same as in the CreateConnection command, with the addition of a ConnectionId that identifies the connection within the endpoint. This parameter is returned by the CreateConnection function, as part of the local connection descriptor. It uniquely identifies the connection within the context of the endpoint.

The EndpointId should be a fully qualified endpoint identifier. The local name shall not use the wildcard convention.

The ModifyConnection command can be used to affect parameters of a connection in the following ways:

* Provide information about the other end of the connection, through the RemoteConnectionDescriptor.

* Activate or deactivate the connection, by changing the value of the Mode parameter. This can occur at any time during the connection, with arbitrary parameter values.

* Change the sending parameters of the connection, for example by switching to a different coding scheme, changing the packetization period, or modifying the handling of echo cancellation.

Connections can only be activated if the RemoteConnectionDescriptor has been provided to the gateway. The receive only mode, however, can be activated without the provision of this descriptor.

The command will only return a LocalConnectionDescriptor if the local connection parameters, such as RTP ports, were modified. (Usage of this feature is actually for further study.)

The command may optionally contain an encapsulated Notification Request command, in which case a RequestIdentifier parameter will be present, as well as, optionnally, the RequestedEvents DigitMap, SignalRequests, QuarantineHandling and DetectEvents parameters. The encapsulated NotificationRequest is executed simultaneously with the modification of the connection. For example, when a connection is accepted, the calling gateway should be instructed to place the circuit in send-receive mode and to stop providing ringing tones.

This can be accomplished in a single ModifyConnection command, by also transmitting the RequestedEvent parameters, for the on hook event, and an empty SignalRequest parameter, to stop the provision of ringing tones.

When these parameters are present, the modification and the NotificationRequests should be synchronized, which means that both should be accepted, or both refused. The NotifiedEntity parameter, if present, applies to both the ModifyConnection and the NotificationRequest command.

The command may carry an encapsulated EndpointConfiguration command, that will apply to the same endpoint. When this command is present, the parameters of the EndpointConfiguration command are inserted after the normal parameters of the ModifyConnection with the exception of the EndpointId, which is not replicated. The EndpointConfiguration command may be encapsulated together with an encapsulated NotificationRequest command.

The encapsulated EndpointConfiguration command shares the fate of the ModifyConnection command. If the ModifyConnection is rejected, the EndpointConfiguration is not executed.

ReturnCode is a parameter returned by the gateway. It indicates the outcome of the command and consists of an integer number optionally followed by commentary.

2.3.5. DeleteConnection (from the Call Agent)

This command is used to terminate a connection. As a side effect, it collects statistics on the execution of the connection.

```
ReturnCode,
Connection-parameters
<-- DeleteConnection(CallId,
                     EndpointId,
                     ConnectionId,
                     [Encapsulated NotificationRequest,]
                     [Encapsulated EndpointConfiguration])
```

The endpoint identifier, in this form of the DeleteConnection command, shall be fully qualified. Wildcard conventions shall not be used.

In the general case where a connection has two ends, this command has to be sent to both gateways involved in the connection. Some connections, however, may use IP multicast. In this case, they can be deleted individually.

After the connection has been deleted, any loopback that has been requested for the connection should be cancelled. When all connections to an endpoint have been deleted, that endpoint should be placed in inactive mode.

In response to the DeleteConnection command, the gateway returns a list of parameters that describe the status of the connection. These parameters are:

Number of packets sent:

The total number of RTP data packets transmitted by the sender since starting transmission on this connection. The count is not reset if the sender changes its synchronization source identifier (SSRC, as defined in RTP), for example as a result of a Modify command. The value is zero if the connection was set in "receive only" mode.

Number of octets sent:

The total number of payload octets (i.e., not including header or padding) transmitted in RTP data packets by the sender since starting transmission on this connection. The count is not reset if the sender changes its SSRC identifier, for example as a result of a ModifyConnection command. The value is zero if the connection was set in "receive only" mode.

Number of packets received:

The total number of RTP data packets received by the sender since starting reception on this connection. The count includes packets received from different SSRC, if the sender used several values. The value is zero if the connection was set in "send only" mode.

Number of octets received:

The total number of payload octets (i.e., not including header or padding) transmitted in RTP data packets by the sender since starting transmission on this connection. The count includes packets received from different SSRC, if the sender used several values. The value is zero if the connection was set in "send only" mode.

Number of packets lost:

The total number of RTP data packets that have been lost since the beginning of reception. This number is defined to be the number of packets expected less the number of packets actually received, where the number of packets received includes any which are late or duplicates. The count includes packets received from different SSRC, if the sender used several values. Thus packets that arrive late are not counted as lost, and the loss may be negative if there are duplicates. The count includes packets received from different SSRC, if the sender used several values. The number of packets expected is defined to be the extended last sequence number received, as defined next, less the initial sequence number received. The count includes packets received from different SSRC, if the sender used several values. The value is zero if the connection was set in "send only" mode. This parameter is omitted if the connection was set in "data" mode.

Interarrival jitter:

An estimate of the statistical variance of the RTP data packet interarrival time measured in milliseconds and expressed as an unsigned integer. The interarrival jitter J is defined to be the mean deviation (smoothed absolute value) of the difference D in packet spacing at the receiver compared to the sender for a pair of packets. Detailed computation algorithms are found in RFC 1889. The count includes packets received from different SSRC, if the sender used several values. The value is zero if the connection was set in "send only" mode. This parameter is omitted if the connection was set in "data" mode.

Average transmission delay:

An estimate of the network latency, expressed in milliseconds. This is the average value of the difference between the NTP timestamp indicated by the senders of the RTCP messages and the NTP timestamp of the receivers, measured when this messages are received. The average is obtained by summing all the estimates, then dividing by the number of RTCP messages that have been received. This parameter is omitted if the connection was set in "data" mode.
When the gateway's clock is not synchronized by NTP, the latency value can be computed as one half of the round trip delay, as measured through RTCP.
When the gateway cannot compute the one way delay or the round trip delay, the parameter conveys a null value.

For a detailed definition of these variables, refer to RFC 1889.

When the connection was set up over an ATM network, the meaning of these parameters may change:

Number of packets sent: The total number of ATM cells transmitted since starting transmission on this connection.

Number of octets sent:
The total number of payload octets transmitted in ATM cells.

Number of packets received:
The total number of ATM cells received since starting reception on this connection.

Number of octets received:
The total number of payload octets received in ATM cells.

Number of packets lost:
Should be determined as the number of cell losts, or set to zero if the adaptation layer does not enable the gateway to assess losses.

Interarrival jitter:
Should be understood as the interarrival jitter between ATM cells.

Average transmission delay:
The gateway may not be able to assess this parameter over an ATM network. It could simply report a null value.

When the connection was set up over an LOCAL interconnect, the meaning of these parameters is defined as follows:

Number of packets sent:
Not significant.

Number of octets sent:
The total number of payload octets transmitted over the local connection.

Number of packets received:
Not significant.

Number of octets received:
The total number of payload octets received over the connection.

Number of packets lost:
Not significant. A value of zero is assumed.

Interarrival jitter:
Not significant. A value of zero is assumed.

Average transmission delay:
Not significant. A value of zero is assumed.

The standard set of connection parameters can be extended by the creation of extension parameters.

The command may optionally contain an encapsulated Notification Request command, in which case a RequestIdentifier parameter will be present, as well as, optionnally, the RequestedEvents DigitMap, SignalRequests, QuarantineHandling and DetectEvents parameters. The encapsulated NotificationRequest is executed simultaneously with the deletion of the connection. For example, when a user hang-up is notified, the gateway should be instructed to delete the connection and to start looking for an off hook event.

This can be accomplished in a single DeleteConnection command, by also transmitting the RequestedEvent parameters, for the off hook event, and an empty SignalRequest parameter.

When these parameters are present, the DeleteConnection and the NotificationRequests should be synchronized, which means that both should be accepted, or both refused.

The command may carry an encapsulated EndpointConfiguration command, that will apply to the same endpoint. When this command is present, the parameters of the EndpointConfiguration command are inserted after the normal parameters of the DeleteConnection with the exception of the EndpointId, which is not replicated. The EndpointConfiguration command may be encapsulated together with an encapsulated NotificationRequest command.

The encapsulated EndpointConfiguration command shares the fate of the DeleteConnection command. If the DeleteConnection is rejected, the EndpointConfiguration is not executed.

ReturnCode is a parameter returned by the gateway. It indicates the outcome of the command and consists of an integer number optionally followed by commentary.

2.3.6. DeleteConnection (from the VoIP gateway)

In some circumstances, a gateway may have to clear a connection, for example because it has lost the resource associated with the connection, or because it has detected that the endpoint no longer is capable or willing to send or receive voice. The gateway terminates the connection by using a variant of the DeleteConnection command:

```
ReturnCode,
<-- DeleteConnection( CallId,
                      EndpointId,
                      ConnectionId,
                      Reason-code,
                      Connection-parameters)
```

In addition to the call, endpoint and connection identifiers, the gateway will also send the call's parameters that would have been returned to the Call Agent in response to a DeleteConnection command. The reason code indicates the cause of the disconnection.

ReturnCode is a parameter returned by the call agent. It indicates the outcome of the command and consists of an integer number optionally followed by commentary.

2.3.7. DeleteConnection (multiple connections, from the Call Agent)

A variation of the DeleteConnection function can be used by the Call Agent to delete multiple connections at the same time. The command can be used to delete all connections that relate to a Call for an endpoint:

```
ReturnCode,
<-- DeleteConnection( CallId,
                      EndpointId)
```

It can also be used to delete all connections that terminate in a given endpoint:

```
ReturnCode,
<-- DeleteConnection( EndpointId)
```

Finally, Call Agents can take advantage of the hierarchical naming structure of endoints to delete all the connections that belong to a group of endpoints. In this case, the "local name" component of the EndpointID will be specified using the "all value" wildcarding convention. The "any value" convention shall not be used. For example, if endpoints names are structured as the combination of a physical interface name and a circuit number, as in "X35V3+A4/13", the Call Agent may replace the circuit number by a wild card character "*", as in "X35V3+A4/*". This "wildcard" command instructs the gateway to delete all the connections that where attached to circuits connected to the physical interface "X35V3+A4".

After the connections have been deleted, the endpoint should be placed in inactive mode. Any loopback that has been requested for the connections should be cancelled.

This command does not return any individual statistics or call parameters.

ReturnCode is a parameter returned by the gateway. It indicates the outcome of the command and consists of an integer number optionally followed by commentary.

2.3.8. Audit Endpoint

The AuditEndPoint command can be used by the Call Agent to find out the status of a given endpoint.

```
ReturnCode,
  EndPointIdList|{
  [RequestedEvents,]
  [DigitMap,]
  [SignalRequests,]
  [RequestIdentifier,]
  [NotifiedEntity,]
  [ConnectionIdentifiers,]
  [DetectEvents,]
  [ObservedEvents,]
  [EventStates,]
  [BearerInformation,]
  [RestartReason,]
  [RestartDelay,]
  [ReasonCode,]
  [Capabilities]}
          <--- AuditEndPoint(EndpointId,
                                      [RequestedInfo])
```

The EndpointId identifies the endpoint that is being audited. The "all of" wildcard convention can be used to start auditing of a group of endpoints. If this convention is used, the gateway should return the list of endpoint identifiers that match the wildcard in the EndPointIdList parameter. It shall not return any parameter specific to one of these endpoints.

When a non-wildcard EndpointId is specified, the (possibly empty) RequestedInfo parameter describes the information that is requested for the EndpointId specified. The following endpoint info can be audited with this command:

RequestedEvents, DigitMap, SignalRequests, RequestIdentifier, NotifiedEntity, ConnectionIdentifiers, DetectEvents, ObservedEvents, EventStates, RestartReason, RestartDelay, ReasonCode, and Capabilities.

The response will in turn include information about each of the items for which auditing info was requested:

* RequestedEvents: The current value of RequestedEvents the endpoint is using including the action associated with each event. Persistent events are included in the list.

* DigitMap: the digit map the endpoint is currently using.

* SignalRequests: A list of the; Time-Out signals that are currently active, On/Off signals that are currently "on" for the endpoint (with or without parameter), and any pending Brief signals. Time-Out signals that have timed-out, and currently playing Brief signals are not included.

* RequestIdentifier, the RequestIdentifier for the last Notification Request received by this endpoint (includes NotificationRequest encapsulated in Connection handling primitives). If no notification request has been received, the value zero will be returned.

* QuarantineHandling, the QuarantineHandling for the last NotificationRequest received by this endpoint.

* DetectEvents, the list of events that are currently detected in quarantine mode.

* NotifiedEntity, the current notified entity for the endpoint.

* ConnectionIdentifiers, the list of ConnectionIdentifiers for all connections that currently exist for the specified endpoint.

* ObservedEvents: the current list of observed events for the endpoint.

* EventStates: For events that have auditable states associated with them, the event corresponding to the state the endpoint is in, e.g., off-hook if the endpoint is off-hook. The definition of the individual events will state if the event in question has an auditable state associated with it.

* BearerInformation: the value of the last received BearerInformation parameter for this endpoint.

* RestartReason: the value of the restart reason parameter in the last RestartInProgress command issued by the endpoint, "restart" indicating a fully functional endpoint.

* RestartDelay: the value of the restart delay parameter if a RestartInProgress command was issued by the endpoint at the time of the response, or zero if the command would not include this parameter.

* ReasonCode:the value of the Reason-Code parameter in the last RestartInProgress or DeleteConnection command issued by the gateway for the endpoint, or the special value 000 if the endpoint's state is nominal.

* The capabilities for the endpoint similar to the LocalConnectionOptions parameter and including event packages and connection modes. If there is a need to specify that some parameters, such as e.g., silence suppression, are only compatible with some

* codecs, then the gateway will return several capability sets:

  Compression Algorithm: a list of supported codecs. The rest of the parameters will apply to all codecs specified in this list.

  Packetization Period: A single value or a range may be specified.

  Bandwidth: A single value or a range corresponding to the range for packetization periods may be specified (assuming no silence suppression).

  Echo Cancellation: Whether echo cancellation is supported or not.

  Silence Suppression: Whether silence suppression is supported or not.

  Type of Service: Whether type of service is supported or not.

Event Packages: A list of event packages supported. The first event package in the list will be the default package.

Modes: A list of supported connection modes.

The Call Agent may then decide to use the AuditConnection command to obtain further information about the connections.

If no info was requested and the EndpointId refers to a valid endpoint, the gateway simply returns a positive acknowledgement.

If no NotifiedEntity has been specified in the last NotificationRequest, the notified entity defaults to the source address of the last NotificationRequest command received for this connection.

ReturnCode is a parameter returned by the gateway. It indicates the outcome of the command and consists of an integer number optionally followed by commentary.

2.3.9. Audit Connection

The AuditConnection command can be used by the Call Agent to retrieve the parameters attached to a connection:

```
ReturnCode,
[CallId,]
[NotifiedEntity,]
[LocalConnectionOptions,]
[Mode,]
[RemoteConnectionDescriptor,]
[LocalConnectionDescriptor,]
[ConnectionParameters]
          <--- AuditConnection(EndpointId,
                               ConnectionId,
                               RequestedInfo)
```

The EndpointId parameter specifies the endpoint that handles the connection. The wildcard conventions shall not be used.

The ConnectionId parameter is the identifier of the audited connection, within the context of the specified endpoint.

The (possibly empty) RequestedInfo describes the information that is requested for the ConnectionId within the EndpointId specified. The following connection info can be audited with this command:

CallId, NotifiedEntity, LocalConnectionOptions, Mode, RemoteConnectionDescriptor, LocalConnectionDescriptor, ConnectionParameters

The AuditConnectionResponse will in turn include information about each of the items auditing info was requested for:

* CallId, the CallId for the call the connection belongs to.

* NotifiedEntity, the current notified entity for the Connection.

* LocalConnectionOptions, the LocalConnectionOptions that was supplied for the connection.

* Mode, the current mode of the connection.

* RemoteConnectionDescriptor, the RemoteConnectionDescriptor that was supplied to the gateway for the connection.

* LocalConnectionDescriptor, the LocalConnectionDescriptor the gateway supplied for the connection.

* ConnectionParameters, the current value of the connection parameters for the connection.

If no info was requested and the EndpointId is valid, the gateway simply checks that the connection exists, and if so returns a positive acknowledgement.

If no NotifiedEntity has been specified for the connection, the notified entity defaults to the source address of the last connection handling command received for this connection.

ReturnCode is a parameter returned by the gateway. It indicates the outcome of the command and consists of an integer number optionally followed by commentary.

2.3.10. Restart in progress

The RestartInProgress command is used by the gateway to signal that An endpoint, or a group of endpoint, is taken in or out of service.

```
ReturnCode,
[NotifiedEntity]
      <------- RestartInProgress ( EndPointId,
                                   RestartMethod,
                                   [RestartDelay,]
                                   [Reason-code])
```

The EndPointId identifies the endpoint that are taken in or out of service. The "all of" wildcard convention may be used to apply the command to a group of endpoint, such as for example all endpoints that are attached to a specified interface, or even all endpoints that are attached to a given gateway. The "any of" wildcard convention shall not be used.

The RestartMethod parameter specified the type of restart. Three values have been defined:

* A "graceful" restart method indicates that the specified endpoints will Be taken out of service after the specified delay. The established connections are not yet affected, but the Call Agent should refrain to establish new connections, and should try to gracefully tear down the existing connections.

* A "forced" restart method indicates that the specified endpoints are taken abruptely out of service. The established connections, if any, are lost.

* A "restart" method indicates that service will be restored on the endpoints after the specified "restart delay." There are no connections that are currently established on the endpoints.

* A "disconnected" method indicates that the endpoint has become disconnected and is now trying to establish connectivity. The "restart delay" specifies the number of seconds the endpoint has been disconnected. Established connections are not affected.

* A "cancel-graceful" method indicates that a gateway is canceling a previously issued "graceful" restart command.

The optional "restart delay" parameter is expressed as a number of seconds. If the number is absent, the delay value should be considered null. In the case of the "graceful" method, a null delay indicates that the call agent should simply wait for the natural termination of the existing connections, without establishing new connections. The restart delay is always considered null in the case of the "forced" method.

A restart delay of null for the "restart" method indicates that service has already been restored. This typically will occur after gateway startup/reboot.

The optional reason code parameter the cause of the restart.

Gateways SHOULD send a "graceful" or "forced" RestartInProgress message as a courtesy to the Call Agent when they are taken out of service, e.g., by being shutdown, or taken out of service by a network management system, although the Call Agent cannot rely on always receiving such messages. Gateways MUST send a "restart" RestartInProgress message with a null delay to their Call Agent when they are back in service according to the restart procedure specified in Section 4.3.4 - Call Agents can rely on receiving this message. Also, gateways MUST send a "disconnected" RestartInProgress message to their current "notified entity" according to the "disconnected" procedure specified in Section 4.3.5. The "restart delay" parameter MUST NOT be used with the "forced" restart method.

The RestartInProgress message will be sent to the current notified entity for the EndpointId in question. It is expected that a default Call Agent, i.e., notified entity, has been provisioned for each endpoint so, after a reboot, the default Call Agent will be the notified entity for each endpoint. Gateways should take full advantage of wild- carding to minimize the number of RestartInProgress messages generated when multiple endpoints in a gateway restart and the endpoints are managed by the same Call Agent.

ReturnCode is a parameter returned by the gateway. It indicates the outcome of the command and consists of an integer number optionally followed by commentary.

A NotifiedEntity may additionally be returned with the response from the Call Agent:

* If the response indicated success (return code 200 - transaction executed), the restart procedure has completed, and the NotifiedEntity returned is the new "notified entity" for the endpoint(s).

* If the response from the Call Agent indicated an error, the restart procedure is not yet complete, and must therefore be initiated again. If a NotifiedEntity parameter was returned, it then specifies the new "notified entity" for the endpoint(s), which must consequently be used when retrying the restart procedure.

2.4. Return codes and error codes.

All MGCP commands are acknowledged. The acknowledgment carries a return code, which indicates the status of the command. The return code is an integer number, for which four ranges of values have been defined:

* values between 100 and 199 indicate a provisional response,

* values between 200 and 299 indicate a successful completion,

* values between 400 and 499 indicate a transient error,

* values between 500 and 599 indicate a permanent error.

The values that have been already defined are listed in the following list:

100 The transaction is currently being executed. An actual completion message will follow on later.

200 The requested transaction was executed normally.

250 The connection was deleted.

400 The transaction could not be executed, due to a transient error.

401 The phone is already off hook

402 The phone is already on hook

403 The transaction could not be executed, because the endpoint does not have sufficient resources at this time

404 Insufficient bandwidth at this time

500 The transaction could not be executed, because the endpoint is unknown.

01 The transaction could not be executed, because the endpoint is not ready.

502 The transaction could not be executed, because the endpoint does not have sufficient resources

510 The transaction could not be executed, because a protocol error was detected.

11 The transaction could not be executed, because the command contained an unrecognized extension.

512 The transaction could not be executed, because the gateway is not equipped to detect one of the requested events.

513 The transaction could not be executed, because the gateway is not equipped to generate one of the requested signals.

514 The transaction could not be executed, because the gateway cannot send the specified announcement.

515 The transaction refers to an incorrect connection-id (may have been already deleted)

516 The transaction refers to an unknown call-id.

517 Unsupported or invalid mode.

518 Unsupported or unknown package.

519 Endpoint does not have a digit map.

520 The transaction could not be executed, because the endpoint is "restarting".

521 Endpoint redirected to another Call Agent.

522 No such event or signal.

523 Unknown action or illegal combination of actions

524 Internal inconsistency in LocalConnectionOptions

525 Unknown extension in LocalConnectionOptions

526 Insufficient bandwidth

527 Missing RemoteConnectionDescriptor

528 Incompatible protocol version

529 Internal hardware failure

530 CAS signaling protocol error.

531 failure of a grouping of trunks (e.g. facility failure).

2.5. Reason Codes

Reason-codes are used by the gateway when deleting a connection to inform the Call Agent about the reason for deleting the connection. They may also be used in a RestartInProgress command, to inform the gateway of the Restart's reason. The reason code is an integer number, and the following values have been defined:

000 Endpoint state is nominal. (This code is used only in response to audit requests.)

900 Endpoint malfunctioning

901 Endpoint taken out of service

902 Loss of lower layer connectivity (e.g., downstream sync)

3. Media Gateway Control Protocol

The MGCP implements the media gateway control interface as a set of transactions. The transactions are composed of a command and a mandatory response. There are eight types of command:

* CreateConnection
* ModifyConnection
* DeleteConnection
* NotificationRequest
* Notify
* AuditEndpoint
* AuditConnection
* RestartInProgress

The first four commands are sent by the Call Agent to a gateway. The Notify command is sent by the gateway to the Call Agent. The gateway may also send a DeleteConnection as defined in 2.3.6. The Call Agent may send either of the Audit commands to the gateway. The Gateway may send a RestartInProgress command to the Call Agent.

3.1. General description

All commands are composed of a Command header, optionally followed by a session description.

All responses are composed of a Response header, optionally followed by a session description.

Headers and session descriptions are encoded as a set of text lines, separated by a carriage return and line feed character (or, optionnally, a single line-feed character). The headers are separated from the session description by an empty line.

MGCP uses a transaction identifier to correlate commands and responses. The transaction identifier is encoded as a component of the command header and repeated as a component of the response header (see section 3.2.1, 3.2.1.2 and 3.3).

3.2. Command Header

The command header is composed of:

* A command line, identifying the requested action or verb, the transaction identifier, the endpoint towards which the action is requested, and the MGCP protocol version,

* A set of parameter lines, composed of a parameter name followed by a parameter value.

Unless otherwise noted or dictated by other referenced standards, each component in the command header is case insensitive. This goes for verbs as well as parameters and values, and all comparisons MUST treat upper and lower case as well as combinations of these as being equal.

3.2.1. Command line

The command line is composed of:

* The name of the requested verb,

* The identification of the transaction,

* The name of the endpoint that should execute the command (in notifications or restarts, the name of the endpoint that is issuing the command),

* The protocol version.

These four items are encoded as strings of printable ASCII characters, separated by white spaces, i.e. the ASCII space (0x20) or tabulation (0x09) characters. It is recommended to use exactly one ASCII space separator.

3.2.1.1. Coding of the requested verb

The verbs that can be requested are encoded as four letter upper or lower case ASCII codes (comparisons should be case insensitive) as defined in the following table:

Verb	Code
EndpointConfiguration	EPCF
CreateConnection	CRCX
ModifyConnection	MDCX
DeleteConnection	DLCX
NotificationRequest	RQNT
Notify	NTFY
AuditEndpoint	AUEP
AuditConnection	AUCX
RestartInProgress	RSIP

The transaction identifier is encoded as a string of up to 9 decimal digits. In the command lines, it immediately follows the coding of the verb.

New verbs may be defined in further versions of the protocol. It may be necessary, for experimentation purposes, to use new verbs before they are sanctioned in a published version of this protocol. Experimental verbs should be identified by a four letter code starting with the letter X, such as for example XPER.

3.2.1.2. Transaction Identifiers

MGCP uses a transaction identifier to correlate commands and responses. A gateway supports two separate transaction identifier name spaces:

a transaction identifier name space for sending transactions, and

a transaction identifier name space for receiving transactions.

At a minimum, transaction identifiers for commands sent to a given gateway MUST be unique for the maximum lifetime of the transactions within the collection of Call Agents that control that gateway. Thus, regardless of the sending Call Agent, gateways can always detect duplicate transactions by simply examining the transaction identifier. The coordination of these transaction identifiers between Call Agents is outside the scope of this specification though.

Transaction identifiers for all commands sent from a given gateway MUST be unique for the maximum lifetime of the transactions regardless of which Call Agent the command is sent to. Thus, a Call Agent can always detect a duplicate transaction from a gateway by the combination of the domain-name of the endpoint and the transaction identifier.

The transaction identifier is encoded as a string of up to nine decimal digits. In the command lines, it immediately follows the coding of the verb.

Transaction identifiers have values between 1 and 999999999. An MGCP entity MUST NOT reuse a transaction identifier more quickly than three minutes after completion of the previous command in which the identifier was used.

3.2.1.3. Coding of the endpoint identifiers and entity names

The endpoint identifiers and entity names are encoded as case insensitive e-mail addresses, as defined in RFC 821. In these addresses, the domain name identifies the system where the endpoint is attached, while the left side identifies a specific endpoint on that system.

Examples of such addresses can be:

hrd4/56@gw23.example.net	Circuit number 56 in interface "hrd4" of the Gateway 23 of the "Example" network
Call-agent@ca.example.net	Call Agent for the "example" network
Busy-signal@ann12.example.net	The "busy signal" virtual endpoint in the announcement server number 12.

The name of notified entities is expressed with the same syntax, with the possible addition of a port number as in:

```
Call-agent@ca.example.net:5234
```

In case the port number is omitted, the default MGCP port (2427) will be used.

3.2.1.4. Coding of the protocol version

The protocol version is coded as the key word MGCP followed by a white space and the version number, and optionally followed by a profile name.. The version number is composed of a major version, coded by a decimal number, a dot, and a minor version number, coded as a decimal number. The version described in this document is version 1.0.

The profile name, if present, is represented by a white-space separated strings of visible (printable) characters extending to the end of the line. Profile names may be defined for user communities who want to apply restrictions or other profiling to MGCP.

In the initial messages, the version will be coded as:

```
MGCP 1.0
```

3.2.2. Parameter lines

Parameter lines are composed of a parameter name, which in most cases is composed of a single upper case character, followed by a colon, a white space and the parameter value. The parameter that can be present in commands are defined in the following table:

Parameter name	Code	Parameter value
ResponseAck	K	see description
BearerInformation	B	see description
CallId	C	Hexadecimal string, at most 32 chars.
ConnectionId	I	Hexadecimal string, at most 32 chars.
NotifiedEntity	N	An identifier, in RFC 821 format, composed of an arbitrary string and of the domain name of the requesting entity, possibly completed by a port number, as in: Call-agent@ca.example.net:5234
RequestIdentifier	X	Hexadecimal string, at most 32 chars.
LocalConnectionOptions	L	See description
Connection Mode	M	See description
RequestedEvents	R	See description
SignalRequests	S	See description
DigitMap	D	A text encoding of a digit map
ObservedEvents	O	See description
ConnectionParameters	P	See description
ReasonCode	E	An arbitrary character string
SpecificEndpointID	Z	An identifier, in RFC 821 format, composed of an arbitrary string, followed by an "@" followed by the domain name of the gateway to which this endpoint is attached.
Second Endpoint ID	Z2	Endpoint Id.
SecondConnectionId	I2	Connection Id.
RequestedInfo	F	See description
QuarantineHandling	Q	See description
DetectEvents	T	See Description
RestartMethod	RM	See description
RestartDelay	RD	A number of seconds, encoded as a decimal number
EventStates	ES	See description
Capabilities	A	See description
RemoteConnection Descriptor	RC	Session Description
LocalConnection Descriptor	LC	Session Description

The parameters are not necessarily present in all commands. The following table provides the association between parameters and commands. The letter M stands for mandatory, O for optional and F for forbidden.

Parameter name	EP CF	CR CX	MD CX	DL CX	RQ NT	NT FY	AU EP	AU CX	RS IP
ResponseAck	O	O	O	O	O	O	O	O	O
BearerInformation	M	O	O	O	O	F	F	F	F
CallId	F	M	M	O	F	F	F	F	F
ConnectionId	F	F	M	O	F	F	F	M	F
RequestIdentifier	F	O+	O+	O+	M	M	F	F	F
LocalConnection Options	F	O	O	F	F	F	F	F	F
Connection Mode	F	M	M	F	F	F	F	F	F
RequestedEvents	F	O	O	O	O*	F	F	F	F
SignalRequests	F	O	O	O	O*	F	F	F	F
NotifiedEntity	F	O	O	O	O	O	F	F	F
ReasonCode	F	F	F	O	F	F	F	F	O
ObservedEvents	F	F	F	F	F	M	F	F	F
DigitMap	F	O	O	O	O	F	F	F	F
Connection parameters	F	F	F	O	F	F	F	F	F
Specific Endpoint ID	F	F	F	F	F	F	F	F	F
Second Endpoint ID	F	O	F	F	F	F	F	F	F
RequestedInfo	F	F	F	F	F	F	M	M	F
QuarantineHandling	F	O	O	O	O	F	F	F	F
DetectEvents	F	O	O	O	O	F	F	F	F
EventStates	F	F	F	F	F	F	F	F	F
RestartMethod	F	F	F	F	F	F	F	F	M
RestartDelay	F	F	F	F	F	F	F	F	O
SecondConnectionID	F	F	F	F	F	F	F	F	F
Capabilities	F	F	F	F	F	F	F	F	F
RemoteConnection Descriptor	F	O	O	F	F	F	F	F	F
LocalConnection Descriptor	F	F	F	F	F	F	F	F	F

Note (+) that the RequestIdentifier parameter is optional in connection creation, modification and deletion commands, but that it becomes mandatory if the command contains an encapsulated notification request.

Note (*) that the RequestedEvents and SignalRequests parameters are optional in the NotificationRequest. If these parameters are omitted, the corresponding lists will be considered empty.

If implementers need to experiment with new parameters, for example when developing a new application of MGCP, they should identify these parameters by names that start with the string "X-" or "X+", such as for example:

```
X-FlowerOfTheDay: Daisy
```

Parameter names that start with "X+" are critical parameter extensions. An MGCP entity that receives a critical parameter extension that it cannot understand should refuse to execute the command. It should respond with an error code 511 (Unrecognized extension).

Parameter names that start with "X-" are non critical parameter extensions. An MGCP entity that receives a non critical parameter extension that it cannot understand can safely ignore that parameter.

3.2.2.1. Response Acknowledgement

The response acknowledgement attribute is used to managed the "at-most-once" facility described in the "transmission over UDP" section. It contains a comma separated list of "confirmed transaction-id ranges".

Each "confirmed transaction-id ranges" is composed of either one decimal number, when the range includes exactly one transaction, or two decimal numbers separated by a single hyphen, describing the lower and higher transaction identifiers included in the range.

An example of response acknowledgement is:

```
K: 6234-6255, 6257, 19030-19044
```

3.2.2.2. Local connection options

The local connection options describe the operational parameters that the Call Agent suggests to the gateway. These parameters are:

* The packetization period in milliseconds, encoded as the keyword "p", followed by a colon and a decimal number. If the Call Agent specifies a range of values, the range will be specified as two decimal numbers separated by an hyphen.

* The preferred type of compression algorithm, encoded as the keyword "a", followed by a colon and a character string. If the Call Agent specifies a list of values, these values will be separated by a semicolon.

* The bandwidth in kilobits per second (1000 bits per second), encoded as the keyword "b", followed by a colon and a decimal number. If the Call Agent specifies a range of values, the range will be specified as two decimal numbers separated by an hyphen.

* The echo cancellation parameter, encoded as the keyword "e", followed by a colon and the value "on" or "off".

* The gain control parameter, encoded as the keyword "gc", followed by a colon a value which can be either the keyword "auto" or a decimal number (positive or negative) representing the number of decibels of gain.

* The silence suppression parameter, encoded as the keyword "s", followed by a colon and the value "on" or "off".

* The type of service parameter, encoded as the keyword "t", followed by a colon and the value encoded as two hexadecimal digits.

* The resource reservation parameter, encoded as the keyword "r", followed by a colon and the value "g" (guaranteed service), "cl" (controlled load) or "be" (best effort).

* The encryption key, encoded as the keyword "k" followed by a colon and a key specification, as defined for the parameter "K" of SDP (RFC 2327).

* The type of network, encoded as the keyword "nt" followed by a colon and the type of network encoded as the keyword "IN", "ATM" or "LOCAL".

Each of the parameters is optional. When several parameters are present, the values are separated by a comma.

Examples of connection descriptors are:

```
L: p:10, a:PCMU
L: p:10, a:G726-32
L: p:10-20, b:64
L: b:32-64, e:off
```

These set of attributes may be extended by extension attributes.

Extension attributes are composed of an attribute name, followed by a semi-colon and by an attribute value. The attribute name should start by the two characters "x+", for a mandatory extensions, or "x-", for a non mandatory extension. If a gateway receives a mandatory extension attribute that it does not recognize, it should reject the command with an error code 525 (Unknown extension in LocalConnectionOptions).

3.2.2.3. Capabilities

Capabilities inform the Call Agent about endpoints' capabilities when audited. The encoding of capabilities is based on the Local Connection Options encoding for the parameters that are common to both. In addition, capabilities can also contain a list of supported packages, and a list of supported modes.

The parameters used are:

*

A list of supported codecs. The following parameters will apply to all codecs specified in this list. If there is a need to specify that some parameters, such as e.g. silence suppression, are only compatible with some codecs, then the gateway will return several LocalConnectionOptions parameters, one for each set of codecs.

Packetization Period:
A range may be specified.

Bandwidth:
A range corresponding to the range for packetization periods may be specified (assuming no silence suppression). If absent, the values will be deduced from the codec type.

Echo Cancellation:
"on" if echo cancellation is supported for this codec, "off" otherwise. The default is support.

Silence Suppression:
"on" if silence suppression is supported for this codec, "off" otherwise. The default is support.

Gain Control:
"0" if gain control is not supported. The default is support.

Type of Service:
The value "0" indicates no support for type of service, all other values indicate support for type of service. The default is support.

Resource Reservation:
The parameter indicates the reservation services that are supported, in addition to best effort. The value "g" is encoded when the gateway supports both the guaranteed and the controlled load service, "cl" when only the controlled load service is supported. The default is "best effort."

Encryption Key:
Encoding any value indicates support for encryption. Default is no support.

Type of network:
The keyword "nt", followed by a colon and a semicolon separated list of supported network types. This parameter is optional.

Event Packages
The event packages supported by this endpoint encoded as the keyword "v", followed by a colon and a character string. If a list of values is specified, these values will be separated by a semicolon. The first value specified will be the default package for that endpoint.

Modes
The modes supported by this endpoint encoded as the keyword "m", followed by a colon and a semicolon-separated list of supported connection modes for this endpoint.

3.2.2.4. Connection parameters

Connection parameters are encoded as a string of type and value pairs, where the type is a either letter identifier of the parameter or an extension type, and the value a decimal integer. Types are separated from value by an `=' sign. Parameters are encoded from each other by a comma.

The connection parameter types are specified in the following table:

Connection parameter name	Code	Connection parameter value
Packets sent	PS	The number of packets that were sent on the connection.
Octets sent	OS	The number of octets that were sent on the connection.
Packets received	PR	The number of packets that were received on the connection.
Octets received	OR	The number of octets that were received on the connection.
Packets lost	PL	The number of packets that were not received on the connection, as deduced from gaps in the sequence number.
Jitter	JI	The average inter-packet arrival jitter, in milliseconds, expressed as an integer number.
Latency	LA	Average latency, in milliseconds, expressed as an integer number.

Extension parameters names are composed of the string "X-" followed by a two letters extension parameter name. Call agents that received unrecognized extensions shall silently ignore these extensions.

An example of connection parameter encoding is:

```
P: PS=1245, OS=62345, PR=0, OR=0, PL=0, JI=0, LA=48
```

3.2.2.5. Reason Codes

Reason codes are three-digit numeric values. The reason code is optionally followed by a white space and commentary, e.g.:

```
900 Endpoint malfunctioning
```

A list of reason-codes can be found in Section 2.5.

3.2.2.6. Connection mode

The connection mode describes the mode of operation of the connection. The possible values are:

Mode	Meaning
M: sendonly	The gateway should only send packets
M: recvonly	The gateway should only receive packets
M: sendrecv	The gateway should send and receive packets
M: confrnce	The gateway should place the connection in conference mode
M: inactive	The gateway should neither send nor receive packets
M: loopback	The gateway should place the circuit in loopback mode.
M: conttest	The gateway should place the circuit in test mode.
M: netwloop	The gateway should place the connection in network loopback mode.
M: netwtest	The gateway should place the connection in network continuity test mode.
M: data	The gateway should use the circuit for network access for data (e.g., PPP, SLIP, etc.).

3.2.2.7. Coding of event names

Event names are composed of an optional package name, separated by a slash (/) from the name of the actual event. The event name can optionally be followed by an at sign (@) and the identifier of a connection on which the event should be observed. Event names are used in the RequestedEvents, SignalRequests and ObservedEvents parameter.

Each signal has one of the following signal-types associated with: On/Off (OO), Time-out (TO), Brief (BR). (These signal types are specified in the package definitions, and are not present in the messages.) On/Off signals can be parameterized with a "+" to turn the signal on, or a "-" to turn the signal off. If an on/off signal is not parameterized, the signal is turned on. Both of the following will turn the vmwi signal on:

```
vmwi(+), vmwi
```

The following are valid examples of event names:

L/hu	on-hook transition, in the line package
F/0	digit 0 in the MF package
fh	Flash-hook, assuming that the line package is a default package for the end point.
G/rt@0A3F58	Ring back signal on connection "0A3F58".

In addition, the range and wildcard notation of events can be used, instead of individual names, in the RequestedEvents and DetectEvents parameters. The star sign can be used to denote "all connections", and the dollar sign can be used to denote the "current" connection. The following are valid examples of such notations:

M/[0-9]	Digits 0 to 9 in the MF package
fh	Flash-hook, assuming that the line package is a default package for the end point.
[0-9*#A-D]	All digits and letters in the DTMF packages (default for endpoint).
T/$	All events in the trunk packages.
R/qa@*	The quality alert event in all connections
R/rt@$	Ringback on current connection

3.2.2.8. RequestedEvents

The RequestedEvent parameter provides the list of events that have been requested. The event codes are described in the previous section.

Each event can be qualified by a requested action, or by a list of actions. The actions, when specified, are encoded as a list of keywords, enclosed in parenthesis and separated by commas. The codes for the various actions are:

Action	Code
Notify immediately	N
Accumulate	A
Treat according to digit map	D
Swap	S
Ignore	I
Keep Signal(s) active	K
Embedded Notification Request	E

When no action is specified, the default action is to notify the event. This means that, for example, ft and ft(N) are equivalent. Events that are not listed are ignored.

The digit-map action can only be specified for the digits, letters and interdigit timers in the MF and DTMF packages, or in other packages that would define the encoding of digits and timers.

The requested list is encoded on a single line, with event/action groups separated by commas. Examples of RequestedEvents encoding are:

```
R: hu(N), hf(S,N)
R: hu(N), [0-9#T](D)
```

In the case of the "enable" action, the embedded notification request parameters are encoded as a list of up to three parameter groups, separated by commas. Each group start by a one letter identifier, followed by a list of parameters enclosed between parenthesis. The first optional parameter group, identified by the letter "R", is the enabled value of the RequestedEvents parameter. The second optional group, identified by the letter "S", is the enabled value of the SignalRequests parameter. The third optional group, identified by the letter "D", is the enabled value of the DigitMap. (Note that some existing implementation may encode these three components in a different order.)

If the RequestedEvents is not present, the parameter will be set to a null value. If the SignalRequest is not present, the parameter will be set to a null value. If the DigitMap is absent, the current value should be used. The following are valid examples of embedded requests:

```
R: hd(E(R([0-9#T](D),hu(N)),S(dl),D([0-9].[#T])))
R: hd(E(R([0-9#T](D),hu(N)),S(dl)))
```

3.2.2.9. SignalRequests

The SignalRequests parameter provides the name of the signals that have been requested. Each signal is identified by a name, as indicated in the previous section.

Several signals, such as for example announcement or ADSI display, can be qualified by additional parameters:

* the name and parameters of the announcement,

* the string that should be displayed.

These parameters will be encoded as a set of UTF8 character strings, speárated by comams and enclosed within parenthesis, as in:

```
S: adsi("123456 Francois Gerard")
S: ann(no-such-number, 1234567)
```

When several signals are requested, their codes are separated by a comma, as in:

```
S: asdi(123456 Your friend), rg
```


3.2.2.10. ObservedEvent

The observed event parameters provides the list of events that have been observed. The event codes are the same as those used in the NotificationRequest. Events that have been accumulated according to the digit map may be grouped in a single string; they should be reported as lists of isolated events if other events where detected during the digit accumulation. Examples of observed actions are:

```
O: L/hu
O: 8295555T
O: 8,2,9,5,5,L/hf,5,5,T
O: L/hf, L/hf, L/hu
```

3.2.2.11. RequestedInfo

The RequestedInfo parameter contains a comma separated list of parameter codes, as defined in the "Parameter lines" section. For example, if one wants to audit the value of the NotifiedEntity, RequestIdentifier, RequestedEvents, SignalRequests, DigitMap, QuarantineHandling and DetectEvents parameters, The value of the RequestedInfo parameter will be:

```
F:N,X,R,S,D,Q,T
```

The capabilities request, in the AuditEndPoint command, is encoded by the keyword "A", as in:

```
F:A
```

3.2.2.12. QuarantineHandling

The quarantine handling parameter contains a list of comma separated keywords:

* The keyword "process" or "discard" to indicate the treatment of quarantined events. If neither process or discard is present, process is assumed.

* The keyword "step" or "loop" to indicate whether exactly at most one notification is expected, or whether multiple notifications are allowed. If neither step or loop is present, step is assumed. The following values are valid examples:

```
Q:loop
Q:process
Q:discard,loop
```

3.2.2.13. DetectEvents

The DetectEvent parameter is encoded as a comma separated list of events, such as for example:

```
T: hu,hd,hf,[0-9#*]
```

It should be noted, that no actions can be associated with the events.

3.2.2.14. EventStates

The EventStates parameter is encoded as a comma separated list of events, such as for example:

```
ES: hu
```

It should be noted, that no actions can be associated with the events.

3.2.2.15. RestartMethod

The RestartMethod parameter is encoded as one of the keywords "graceful", "forced", "restart", "disconnected" or "cancel-graceful" as for example:

```
RM:restart
```

3.2.2.16. Bearer Information

The values of the bearer informations are encoded as a comma separated list of attributes, represented by an attribute name, separated by a colon from an attribute value.

The only attribute that is defined is the "encoding" (code "e"), whose defined values are "A" (A-law) and "mu" (mu-law).

An example of bearer information encoding is:

```
B: e:mu
```


3.3. Format of response headers

The response header is composed of a response line, optionally followed by headers that encode the response parameters.

An example of response header could be:

```
200 1203 OK
```

The response line starts with the response code, which is a three digit numeric value. The code is followed by a white space, the transaction identifier, and an optional commentary preceded by a white space.

The following table describe the parameters whose presence is mandatory or optional in a response header, as a function of the command that triggered the response. The letter M stands for mandatory, O for optional and F for forbidden.

Parameter name	EP CF	CR CX	MD CX	DL CX	RQ NT	NT FY	AU EP	AU CX	RS IP
ResponseAck	F	F	F	F	F	F	F	F	F
BearerInformation	F	F	F	F	F	F	O	F	F
CallId	F	F	F	F	F	F	F	O	F
ConnectionId	F	O*	F	F	F	F	F	F	F
RequestIdentifier	F	F	F	F	F	F	O	F	F
LocalConnection Options	F	F	F	F	F	F	O	O	F
Connection Mode	F	F	F	F	F	F	F	O	F
RequestedEvents	F	F	F	F	F	F	O	F	F
SignalRequests	F	F	F	F	F	F	O	F	F
NotifiedEntity	F	F	F	F	F	F	F	F	O
ReasonCode	F	F	F	F	F	F	O	F	F
ObservedEvents	F	F	F	F	F	F	O	F	F
DigitMap	F	F	F	F	F	F	O	F	F
Connection Parameters	F	F	F	O	F	F	F	O	F
Specific Endpoint ID	F	O	F	F	F	F	F	F	F
RequestedInfo	F	F	F	F	F	F	F	F	F
QuarantineHandling	F	F	F	F	F	F	O	F	F
DetectEvents	F	F	F	F	F	F	O	F	F
EventStates	F	F	F	F	F	F	O	F	F
RestartMethod	F	F	F	F	F	F	O	F	F
RestartDelay	F	F	F	F	F	F	O	F	F
Capabilities	F	F	F	F	F	F	O	F	F
SecondConnectionId	F	O	F	F	F	F	F	F	F
SecondEndpointID	F	O	F	F	F	F	F	F	F
LocalConnection Descriptor	F	M	O	F	F	F	F	O*	F
RemoteConnection Descriptor	F	F	F	F	F	F	F	O*	F

In the case of a CreateConnection message, the response line is followed by a Connection-Id parameter. It may also be followed a Specific-Endpoint-Id parameter, if the creation request was sent to a wildcarded Endpoint-Id. The connection-Id parameter is marked as optional in the Table. In fact, it is mandatory with all positive responses, when a connection was created, and forbidden when the response is negative, when no connection as created.

In the case of a DeleteConnection message, the response line is followed by a Connection Parameters parameter, as defined in section 3.2.2.2.

A LocalConnectionDescriptor should be transmitted with a positive response (code 200) to a CreateConnection. It may be transmitted in response to a ModifyConnection command, if the modification resulted in a modification of the session parameters. The LocalConnectionDescriptor is encoded as a "session description," as defined in section 3.4. It is separated from the response header by an empty line.

When several session descriptors are encoded in the same response, they are encoded one after each other, separated by an empty line. This is the case for example when the response to an audit connection request carries both a local session description and a remote session description, as in:


```
200 1203 OK
C: A3C47F21456789F0
N: [128.96.41.12]
L: p:10, a:PCMU;G726-32
M: sendrecv
P: PS=1245, OS=62345, PR=780, OR=45123, PL=10, JI=27,LA=48

v=0
c=IN IP4 128.96.41.1
m=audio 1296 RTP/AVP 0

v=0
c=IN IP4 128.96.63.25
m=audio 1296 RTP/AVP 0 96
a=rtpmap:96 G726-32/8000
```

In this example, according to the SDP syntax, each description starts with a "version" line, (v=...). The local description is always transmitted before the remote description. If a connection descriptor is requested, but it does not exist for the connection audited, that connection descriptor will appear with the SDP protocol version field only.

3.4. Formal syntax description of the protocol

In this section, we provided a formal description of the protocol syntax, following the "Augmented BNF for Syntax Specifications" defined in RFC 2234.

```
MGCPMessage = MGCPCommand / MGCPResponse

MGCPCommand = MGCPCommandLine 0*(MGCPParameter) [EOL *SDPinformation]

MGCPCommandLine = MGCPVerb 1*(WSP) <transaction-id> 1*(WSP)
                        <endpointName> 1*(WSP) MGCPversion EOL

MGCPVerb = "EPCF" / "CRCX" / "MDCX" / "DLCX" / "RQNT"
         / "NTFY" / "AUEP" / "AUCX" / "RSIP" / extensionVerb

extensionVerb = "X" 3(ALPHA / DIGIT)

transaction-id = 1*9(DIGIT)

endpointName =  localEndpointName "@" DomainName
LocalEndpointName = LocalNamePart 0*("/" LocalNamePart)
LocalNamePart = AnyName / AllName / NameString
AnyName = "$"
AllNames = "*"
NameString = 1*(range-of-allowed-characters)
DomainName = 1*256(ALPHA / DIGIT / "." / "-") ; as defined in RFC 821

MGCPversion = "MGCP" 1*(WSP) 1*(DIGIT) "." 1*(DIGIT)
              [1*(WSP) ProfileName]
ProfileName = 1*(range-of-allowed-characters)

MGCPParameter = ParameterValue EOL

ParameterValue = ("K" ":" 0*WSP <ResponseAck>) /
                 ("B" ":" 0*WSP <BearerInformation>) /
                 ("C" ":" 0*WSP <CallId>) /
                 ("I" ":" 0*WSP <ConnectionId>) /
                 ("N" ":" 0*WSP <NotifiedEntity>) /
                 ("X" ":" 0*WSP <RequestIdentifier>) /
                 ("L" ":" 0*WSP <LocalConnectionOptions>) /
                 ("M" ":" 0*WSP <ConnectionMode>) /
                 ("R" ":" 0*WSP <RequestedEvents>) /
                 ("S" ":" 0*WSP <SignalRequests>) /
                 ("D" ":" 0*WSP <DigitMap>) /
                 ("O" ":" 0*WSP <ObservedEvents>) /
                 ("P" ":" 0*WSP <ConnectionParameters>) /
                 ("E" ":" 0*WSP <ReasonCode>) /
```

```
                  ("Z" ":" 0*WSP <SpecificEndpointID>) /
                  ("Z2" ":" 0*WSP <SecondEndpointID>) /
                  ("I2" ":" 0*WSP <SecondConnectionID>) /
                  ("F" ":" 0*WSP <RequestedInfo>) /
                  ("Q" ":" 0*WSP <QuarantineHandling>) /
                  ("T" ":" 0*WSP <DetectEvents>) /
                  ("RM" ":" 0*WSP <RestartMethod>) /
                  ("RD" ":" 0*WSP <RestartDelay>) /
                  ("A" ":" 0*WSP <Capabilities>) /
                  ("ES" ":" 0*WSP <EventStates>) /
                      (extensionParameter ":" 0*WSP <parameterString>)

ResponseAck =  confirmedTransactionIdRange
               *[ ","  confirmedTransactionIdRange ]

confirmedTransactionIdRange = 1*9DIGIT [ "-" 1*9DIGIT ]

BearerInformation = BearerAttribute 0*("," 0*WSP BearerAttribute)
BearerAttribute = ("e" ":" <BearerEncoding>)
BearerEncoding = "A" / "mu"

CallId = 1*32(HEXDIG)

// The audit request response may include a list of identifiers
ConnectionId = 1*32(HEXDIG) 0*("," 1*32(HEXDIG))
SecondConnectionID = ConnectionId

NotifiedEntity = [LocalName "@"] DomainName [":" portNumber]
LocalName = 1*32(suitableCharacter)
portNumber = 1*5(DIGIT)

RequestIdentifier = 1*32(HEXDIG)

LocalConnectionOptions = [ LocalOptionValue 0*(WSP)
                 0*("," 0*(WSP) LocalOptionValue 0*(WSP)) ]
LocalOptionValue = ("p" ":" <packetizationPeriod> )
                 / ("a" ":" <compressionAlgorithm> )
                 / ("b" ":" <bandwidth> )
                 / ("e" ":" <echoCancellation> )
                 / ("gc" ":" <gainControl> )
                 / ("s" ":" <silenceSuppression> )
                 / ("t" ":" <typeOfService> )
                 / ("r" ":" <resourceReservation> )
                 / ("k" ":" <encryptionmethod>[":"<encryptionKey>])
                 / ("nt" ":" <typeOfNetwork> )
                 / (localOptionExtensionName ":"
                 / localOptionExtensionValue)
```

```
Capabilities = [ CapabilityValue 0*(WSP)
                 0*("," 0*(WSP) CapabilityValue 0*(WSP)) ]


CapabilityValue = LocalOptionValue
                / ("v" ":" <supportedPackages>)
                / ("m" ":" <supportedModes> )


packetizationPeriod = 1*4(DIGIT)["-" 1*4(DIGIT)]
compressionAlgorithm = algorithmName 0*(";" algorithmName)
algorithmName = 1*32(SuitableCharacter)
bandwidth = 1*4(DIGIT)["-" 1*4(DIGIT)]
echoCancellation = "on" / "off"
gainControl = "auto" / ["-"]1*4(DIGIT)
silenceSuppression = "on" / "off"
typeOfService = 2HEXDIG
resourceReservation = "g" / "cl" / "be"

;encryption parameters are coded as in SDP (RFC 2327)
encryptiondata = ( "clear" ":" <encryptionKey> )
               / ( "base64" ":" <encodedEncryptionKey> )
               / ( "uri" ":" <URItoObtainKey> )
               / ( "prompt" ) ; defined in SDP, not usable in MGCP!
encryptionKey = 1*(SuitableCharacter / SP)
encodedEncryptionKey = 1*(ALPHA / DIGIT / "+" / "/" / "=")
URItoObtainKey = 1*(SuitableCharacter) / quotedString

typeOfNetwork = "IN" / "ATM" / "LOCAL"
supportedModes= ConnectionMode 0*(";" ConnectionMode)
supportedPackages = packageName 0*(";" packageName)

localOptionExtensionName = "x" ("+"/"-") 1*32(SuitableCharacter)
localOptionExtensionValue = 1*32(SuitableCharacter) / quotedString


ConnectionMode = "sendonly" / "recvonly" / "sendrecv" /
                 "confrnce" / "inactive" / "loopback" /
                 "conttest" / "netwloop" / "netwtest" / "data"

RequestedEvents = [requestedEvent 0*("," 0*(WSP) requestedEvent)]
requestedEvent = eventName [ "(" requestedActions ")" ]

eventName = [ (packageName / "*") "/" ] (eventId / "all" / eventRange)
            [ "@" (ConnectionId / "$" / "*") ]
packageName = 1*(ALPHA / DIGIT / HYPHEN)
eventId = 1*(SuitableCharacter)
eventRange = "[" 1*(DIGIT / DTMFLetter / "*" / "#" /
```

```
                         (DIGIT "-" DIGIT)/(DTMFLetter "-"
                          DTMFLetter)) "]"

requestedActions = requestedAction 0*("," 0*(WSP) requestedAction)
requestedAction = "N" / "A" / "D" / "S" / "I" / "K" /
                  "E" "(" EmbeddedRequest ")"

EmbeddedRequest =    (       "R" "(" EmbeddedRequestList ")"
                       ["," "S" "(" EmbeddedSignalRequest ")" ]
                       ["," "D" "(" EmbeddedDigitMap ")" ] )
                 /   (       "S" "(" EmbeddedSignalRequest ")"
                       ["," "D" "(" EmbeddedDigitMap ")" ] )
                 /   (       "D" "(" EmbeddedDigitMap ")" )

EmbeddedRequestList = RequestedEvents
EmbeddedSignalRequest = SignalRequests
EmbeddedDigitMap = DigitMap

SignalRequests = [ SignalRequest 0*("," 0*(WSP) SignalRequest ) ]
SignalRequest = eventName [ "(" eventParameters ")" ]
eventParameters = eventParameter 0*("," 0*(WSP) eventParameter)
eventParameter = eventParameterString / quotedString
eventParameterString = 1*(SuitableCharacter)

DigitMap = DigitString  / "(" DigitStringList ")"
DigitStringList = DigitString 0*( "|" DigitString )
DigitString = 1*(DigitStringElement)
DigitStringElement = DigitPosition ["."]
DigitPosition = DigitMapLetter / DigitMapRange
DigitMapLetter = DIGIT / "#" / "*" / "A" / "B" / "C" / "D" / "T"
DigitMapRange =  "x" / "[" 1*DigitLetter "]"
DigitLetter ::= *((DIGIT "-" DIGIT ) / DigitMapLetter)

ObservedEvents = SignalRequests
EventStates = SignalRequests

ConnectionParameters = [ConnectionParameter
                        0*( "," 0*(WSP) ConnectionParameter )
ConnectionParameter = ( "PS" "=" packetsSent )
                    / ( "OS" "=" octetsSent )
                    / ( "PR" "=" packetsReceived )
                    / ( "OR" "=" octetsReceived )
                    / ( "PL" "=" packetsLost )
                    / ( "JI" "=" jitter )
                    / ( "LA" "=" averageLatency )
                    / ( ConnectionParameterExtensionName "="
                        ConnectionParameterExtensionValue )
packetsSent = 1*9(DIGIT)
```

```
octetsSent = 1*9(DIGIT)
packetsReceived = 1*9(DIGIT)
octetsReceived = 1*9(DIGIT)
packetsLost = 1*9(DIGIT)
jitter = 1*9(DIGIT)
averageLatency = 1*9(DIGIT)
ConnectionParameterExtensionName = "X" "-" 2*ALPHA
ConnectionParameterExtensionValue = 1*9(DIGIT)

ReasonCode = 3DIGIT [SPACE 1*(%x20-7E)]

SpecificEndpointID = endpointName
SecondEndpointID = endpointName

RequestedInfo = [infoCode 0*("," infoCode)]

infoCode = "B" / "C" / "I" / "N" / "X" / "L" / "M" /
           "R" / "S" / "D" / "O" / "P" / "E" / "Z" /
           "Q" / "T" / "RC" / "LC" / "A" / "ES" / "RM" / "RD"

QuarantineHandling = loopControl / processControl /
              (loopControl "," processControl )
loopControl = "step" / "loop"
processControl = "process" / "discard"

DetectEvents = [eventName 0*("," eventName)]

RestartMethod = "graceful" / "forced" / "restart" / "disconnected"

RestartDelay = 1*6(DIGIT)

extensionParameter = "X" ("-"/"+") 1*6(ALPHA / DIGIT)
parameterString = 1*(%x20-7F)

MGCPResponse = MGCPResponseLine 0*(MGCPParameter)
                [EOL *SDPinformation]

MGCPResponseLine = (<responseCode> 1*(WSP) <transaction-id>
                          [1*(WSP) <responseString>] EOL)
responseCode = 3DIGIT
responseString = *(%x20-7E)

SuitableCharacter= DIGIT / ALPHA / "+" / "-" / "_" / "&" /
                   "!" / "'" / "|" / "=" / "#" / "?" / "/" /
                   "." / "$" / "*" / ";" / "@" / "[" / "]" /
                   "^" / "`" / "{" / "}" / "~"

quotedString = DQUOTE visibleString
```

```
               0*(quoteEscape visibleString) DQUOTE
quoteEscape = DQUOTE DQUOTE
visibleString = (%x00-21 / %x23-FF)
EOL = CRLF / LF

SDPinformation = ;See RFC 2327
```


3.5. Encoding of the session description

The session description is encoded in conformance with the session description protocol, SDP. MGCP implementations are expected to be fully capable of parsing any conformant SDP message, and should send session descriptions that strictly conform to the SDP standard. The usage of SDP actually depends on the type of session that is being, as specified in the "mode" parameter:

* if the mode is set to "data", the session description describes the configuration of a data access service.

* if the mode is set to any other value, the session description is for an audio service.

For an audio service, the gateway will consider the information provided in SDP for the "audio" media. For a data service, the gateway will consider the information provided for the "network-access" media.

3.5.1. Usage of SDP for an audio service

In a telephony gateway, we only have to describe sessions that use exactly one media, audio. The parameters of SDP that are relevant for the telephony application are:

At the session description level:

* The IP address of the remote gateway (in commands) or of the local gateway (in responses), or multicast address of the audio conference, encoded as an SDP "connection data" parameter. This parameter specifies the IP address that will be used to exchange RTP packets.

For the audio media:

* Media description field (m) specifying the audio media, the transport port used for receiving RTP packets by the remote gateway (commands) or by the local gateway (responses), the

RTP/AVP transport, and the list of formats that the gateway will accept. This list should normally always include the code 0 (reserved for PCMU).

* Optionally, RTPMAP attributes that define the encoding of dynamic audio formats,

* Optionally, a packetization period (packet time) attribute (Ptime) defining the duration of the packet,

* Optionally, an attribute defining the type of connection (sendonly, recvonly, sendrecv, inactive). Note that this attribute does not have a direct relation with the "Mode" parameter of MGCP. In fact, the SDP type of connection will most of the time be set to "sendrecv", regardless of the value used by MGCP. Other values will only be used rarely, for example in the case of information or announcement servers that need to establish one way connections.

* The IP address of the remote gateway (in commands) or of the local gateway (in responses), if it is not present at the session level.

An example of SDP specification for an audio connection could be:

```
v=0
c=IN IP4 128.96.41.1
m=audio 3456 RTP/AVP 0 96
a=rtpmap:96 G726-32/8000
```

There is a request, in some environments, to use the MGCP to negotiate connections that will use other transmission channels than RTP over UDP and IP. This will be detailed in an extension to this document.

3.5.2. Usage of SDP in a network access service

The parameters of SDP that are relevant for a data network access application are:

For the data media:

* Media description field (m) specifying the network access media, identified by the code "m=nas/xxxx", where "xxxx" describes the access control method that should be used for parametrizing the network access, as specified below. The field may also specify the port that should be used for contacting the server, as specified in the SDP syntax.

* Connection address parameter (c=) specifying the address, or the domain name, of the server that implement the access control method. This parameter may also be specified at the session level.

* Optionally, a bearer type attribute (a=bearer:) describing the type of data connection to be used, including the modem type.

* Optionally, a framing type attribue (a=framing:) describing the type of framing that will be used on the channel.

* Optionally, attributes describing the called number (a=dialed:), the number to which the call was delivered (a=called:) and the calling number (a=dialing:).

* Optionally, attributes describing the range of addresses that could be used by the dialup client on its LAN (a=subnet:).

* Optionally, an encryption key, encoded as specified in the SDP protocol(k=).

The connection address shall be encoded as specified in the SDP standard. It will be used in conjunction with the port specified in the media line to access a server, whose type will one of:

Method name	Method description
radius	Authentication according to the Radius protocol.
tacacs	Authentication according to the TACACS+ protocol.
diameter	Authentication according to the Diameter protocol.
l2tp	Level 2 tunneling protocol. The address and port are those of the LNS.
login	Local login. (There is normally no server for that method.)
none	No authentication required. (The call was probably vetted by the Call Agent.)

If needed, the gateway may use the key specified in the announcement to access the service. That key, in particular, may be used for the establishment of an L2TP tunnel.

The bearer attribute is composed of a bearer name and an optional extension. The bearer type specifies the type of modulation (modem name) or, in the case of digital connections, the type of ISDN service (8 bits, 7 bits). When an extension is present, it is separated from the bearer name by a single slash (/). The valid values of the bearer attribute are defined in the following table:

Type of bearer description	Example of values
ITU modem standard	V.32, V.34, V.90.
ITU modem standard qualified by a manufacturer name	v.90/3com, v.90/rockwell, v.90/xxx
Well known modem types	X2, K56flex
ISDN transparent access, 64 kbps	ISDN64
ISDN64 + V.110	ISDN64/V.110
ISDN64 + V.120	ISDN64/V.120
ISDN transparent access, 56 kbps	ISDN56
Informal identification	(Requires coordination between the Call Agent and the gateway)

The valid values of the framing attribute are defined in the following table:

Type of framing description	Example of values
PPP, asynchronous framing	ppp-asynch
PPP, HDLC framing	ppp-hdlc
SLIP, asynchronous	slip
Asynchronous, no framing	asynch

The network access authentication parameter provides instructions on the access control that should be exercized for the data call. This optional attribute is encoded as:

```
"a=subnet:" <network type> <address type>
   <connection address> "/" <prefix length>
```

Where the parameters "network type", "address type", and "connection address" are formatted as defined for the connection address parameter (c=) in SDP, and where the "prefix length" is a decimal representation of the number of bits in the prefix.

Examples of SDP announcement for the network access service could be:

```
v=0
m=nas/radius
c=IN IP4 radius.example.net
a=bearer:v.34
a=framing:ppp-asynch
a=dialed:18001234567
a=called:12345678901
a=dialing:12340567890

v=0
m=nas/none
c=IN IP4 128.96.41.1
a=subnet:IN IP4 123.45.67.64/26
a=bearer:isdn64
a=framing:ppp-sync
a=dialed:18001234567
a=dialing:2345678901

v=0
c=IN IP4 access.example.net
m=nas/l2tp
k=clear:some-shared-secret
a=bearer:v.32
a=framing:ppp-asynch
a=dialed:18001234567
a=dialing:2345678901
```

3.5.3. Usage of SDP for ATM connections

The specification of the SDP payload for ATM connections will be described in a companion document, "Usage of MGCP to control Voice over ATM gateways." The following text is indicative.

The SDP payload will specify:

* That the connection is to be established over an ATM interface, using the "c=" parameter of SDP to specify an address in the ATM family, the ATM addressing variant (NSAP, UNI, E.164) and the ATM address.

* The "m=audio" parameter will specify the audio encoding and, if needed, the VPI and VCI.

* Additional attributes parameters (a=) will be used to specify the ATM coding variants, such as the type of adaptation layer and the error correction or loss compenmsation algorithms.

An example of SDP payload for an ATM connection could be:

```
v=0 c=ATM NSAP
47.0091.8100.0000.0060.3e64.fd01.0060.3e64.fd01.fe m=audio
5/1002 ATM/AVP PCMU a=connection_type:AAL2
```

3.5.4. Usage of SDP for local connections

When MGCP is used to set up internal connections within a single gateway, the SDP format is used to encode the parameters of that connection. The following parameters will be used:

* The connection parameter (C=) will specify that the connection is local, using the keyword "LOCAL" as network type space, the keyword "EPN" (endpoint name) as address type, and the name of the endpoint as the connection-address.

* The "m=audio" parameter will specify a port number, which will always be set to 0, the type of protocol, always set to the keyword LOCAL, and the type of encoding, using the same conventions used for RTP (RTP payload numbers.) The type of encoding should normally be set to 0 (PCMU).

An example of local SDP payload could be:

```
v=0
c=LOCAL EPN X35V3+A4/13
m=audio 0 LOCAL 0
```

3.6. Transmission over UDP

MGCP messages are transmitted over UDP. Commands are sent to one of the IP addresses defined in the DNS for the specified endpoint . The responses are sent back to the source address of the commands.

When no port is specified for the endpoint, the commands should be sent:

* by the Call Agents, to the default MGCP port for gateways, 2427.

* by the Gateways, to the default MGCP port for Call Agents, 2727.

3.6.1. Providing the At-Most-Once functionality

MGCP messages, being carried over UDP, may be subject to losses. In the absence of a timely response, commands are repeated. Most MGCP commands are not idempotent. The state of the gateway would become unpredictable if, for example, CreateConnection commands were executed several times. The transmission procedures must thus provide an "At-Most-Once" functionality.

MGCP entities are expected to keep in memory a list of the responses that they sent to recent transactions and a list of the transactions that are currently being executed. The transaction identifiers of incoming commands are compared to the transaction identifiers of the recent responses. If a match is found, the MGCP entity does not execute the transaction, but simply repeats the response. The remaining commands will be compared to the list of current transaction. If a match is found, the MGCP entity does not execute the transaction, which is simply ignored.

The procedure use a long timer value, noted LONG-TIMER in the following. The timer should be set larger than the maximum duration of a transaction, which should take into account the maximum number of repetitions, the maximum value of the repetition timer and the maximum propagation delay of a packet in the network. A suggested value is 30 seconds.

The copy of the responses can be destroyed either LONG-TIMER seconds after the response is issued, or when the gateway (or the call agent) receives a confirmation that the response has been received, through the "Response Acknowledgement attribute". For transactions that are acknowledged through this attribute, the gateway shall keep a copy of the transaction-id for LONG-TIMER seconds after the response is issued, in order to detect and ignore duplicate copies of the transaction request that could be produced by the network.

3.6.2. Transaction identifiers and three ways handshake

Transaction identifiers are integer numbers in the range from 0 to 999,999,999. Call-agents may decide to use a specific number space for each of the gateways that they manage, or to use the same number space for all gateways that belong to some arbitrary group. Call agents may decide to share the load of managing a large gateway between several independent processes. These processes will share the same transaction number space. There are multiple possible implementations of this sharing, such as having a centralized allocation of transaction identifiers, or pre-allocating non-overlapping ranges of identifiers to different processes. The implementations must guarantee that unique transaction identifiers are allocated to all transactions that originate from a logical call agent, as defined in the "states, failover and race conditions" section. Gateways can simply detect duplicate transactions by looking at the transaction identifier only.

The Response Acknowledgement Attribute can be found in any command. It carries a set of "confirmed transaction-id ranges."

MGCP gateways may choose to delete the copies of the responses to transactions whose id is included in "confirmed transaction-id ranges" received in the Response Confirmation messages. They should silently discard further commands from that Call Agent when the transaction-id falls within these ranges.

The "confirmed transaction-id ranges" values shall not be used if more than LONG-TIMER seconds have elapsed since the gateway issued its last response to that call agent, or when a gateway resumes operation. In this situation, commands should be accepted and processed, without any test on the transaction-id.

Commands that carry the "Response Acknowledgement attribute" may be transmitted in disorder. The gateway shall retain the union of the "confirmed transaction-id ranges" received in recent commands.

3.6.3. Computing retransmission timers

It is the responsibility of the requesting entity to provide suitable time outs for all outstanding commands, and to retry commands when time outs have been exceeded. Furthermore, when repeated commands fail to be acknowledged, it is the responsibility of the requesting entity to seek redundant services and/or clear existing or pending connections.

The specification purposely avoids specifying any value for the retransmission timers. These values are typically network dependent. The retransmission timers should normally estimate the timer by measuring the time spent between the sending of a command and the return of a response. One possibility is to use the algorithm implemented in TCP-IP, which uses two variables:

* the average acknowledgement delay, AAD, estimated through an exponentially smoothed average of the observed delays,

* the average deviation, ADEV, estimated through an exponentially smoothed average of the absolute value of the difference between the observed delay and the current average

The retransmission timer, in TCP, is set to the sum of the average delay plus N times the average deviation. In MGCP, the maximum value of the timer should however be bounded, in order to guarantee that no repeated packet will be received by the gateways after LONG-TIMER seconds. A suggested maximum value is 4 seconds.

After any retransmission, the MGCP entity should do the following:

* It should double the estimated value of the average delay, AAD

* It should compute a random value, uniformly distributed between 0.5 AAD and AAD

* It should set the retransmission timer to the sum of that random value and N times the average deviation.

This procedure has two effects. Because it includes an exponentially increasing component, it will automatically slow down the stream of messages in case of congestion. Because it includes a random component, it will break the potential synchronization between notifications triggered by the same external event.

3.6.4. Piggy backing

There are cases when a Call Agent will want to send several messages at the same time to the same gateways. When several MGCP messages have to be sent in the same UDP packets, they should be separated by a line of text that contain a single dot, as in for example:

```
200 2005 OK
DLCX 1244 card23/21@trgw-7.example.net MGCP 1.0
C: A3C47F21456789F0
I: FDE234C8
```

The piggy-backed messages should be processed exactly has if they had been received in several simultaneous messages.

3.6.5. Provisional responses

Executing some transactions may require a long time. Long execution times may interact with the timer based retransmission procedure. This may result either in an inordinate number of retransmissions, or in timer values that become too long to be efficient.

Gateways that can predict that a transaction will require a long execution time may send a provisional response, with response code 100. They should send this response if they receive a repetition of a transaction that is still being executed.

MGCP entities that receive a provisional response shall switch to a longer repetition timer for that transaction.

4. States, failover and race conditions.

In order to implement proper call signalling, the Call Agent must keep track of the state of the endpoint, and the gateway must make sure that events are properly notified to the call agent. Special conditions exist when the gateway or the call agent are restarted: the gateway must be redirected to a new call agent during "failover" procedures, the call agent must take special action when the gateway is taken offline, or restarted.

4.1. Basic Asumptions

The support of "failover" is based on the following assumptions:

* Call Agents are identified by their domain name, not their network addresses, and several addresses can be associated with a domain name.

* An endpoint has one NotifiedEntity associated with it any given point in time.

* The NotifiedEntity is the last value of the "NotifiedEntity" parameter received for this endpoint (including wild-carded end-point-names). If no explicit "NotifiedEntity" parameter has been received, the "NotifiedEntity" defaults to the provisioned NotifiedEntity value, or if no value was provisioned to the source address of the last command received for the endpoint,

* Responses to commands are always sent to the source address of the command, regardless of the NotifiedEntity.

* When the "notified entity" refers to a domain name that resolves to multiple IP- address, endpoints are capable of switching between different interfaces on the same logical call agent, however they cannot switch to other (backup) call agent(s) on their own. A backup call agent can however instruct them to switch, either directly or indirectly.

* If an entire call agent becomes unavailable, the endpoints managed by that call agent will eventually become "disconnected". The only way for these endpoints to become connected again is either for the failed call agent to become available, or for a backup call agent to contact the affected endpoints.

* When a backup call agent has taken over control of a group of endpoints, it is assumed that the failed call agent will communicate and synchronize with the backup call agent in order to

transfer control of the affected endpoints back to the original call agent (if that's even desired - maybe the failed call agent should simply become the backup call agent now).

We should note that handover conflict resolution between separate CA's is not in place - we are relying strictly on the CA's knowing what they are doing and communicating with each other (although AuditEndpoint can be used to learn about the current NotifiedEntity).

4.2. Security, Retransmission, and Detection of Lost Associations:

The media gateway control protocol is organized as a set of transactions, each of which is composed of a command and a response, commonly referred to as an acknowledgement. The MGCP messages, being carried over UDP, may be subject to losses. In the absence of a timely response, commands are repeated. MGCP entities are expected to keep in memory a list of the responses that they sent to recent transactions, i.e. a list of all the responses they sent over the last LONG-TIMER seconds, and a list of the transactions that are currently being executed.

The transaction identifiers of incoming commands are compared to the transaction identifiers of the recent responses. If a match is found, the MGCP entity does not execute the transaction, but simply repeats the response. The remaining commands will be compared to the list of current transaction. If a match is found, the MGCP entity does not execute the transaction, which is simply ignored - a response will be provided when the execution of the command is complete.

The repetition mechanism is used to guard against four types of possible errors:

* transmission errors, when for example a packet is lost due to noise on a line or congestion in a queue,

* component failure, when for example an interface to a call agent becomes unavailable,

* call agent failure, when for example an entire call agent becomes unavailable,

* failover, when a new call agent is "taking over" transparently.

The elements should be able to derive from the past history an estimate of the packet loss rate due to transmission errors. In a properly configured system, this loss rate should be kept very low, typically less than 1%. If a call agent or a gateway has to repeat a message more than a few times, it is very legitimate to assume that something else than a transmission error is occurring. For example, given a loss rate of 1%, the probability that 5 consecutive transmission attempts fail is 1 in 100 billion, an event that should occur less than once every 10 days for a call agent that processes 1,000 transactions per second. (Indeed, the number of repetition that is considered excessive should be a function of the prevailing packet loss rate.) We should note that the "suspicion threshold", which we will call "Max1", is normally lower than the "disconnection threshold", which should be set to a larger value.

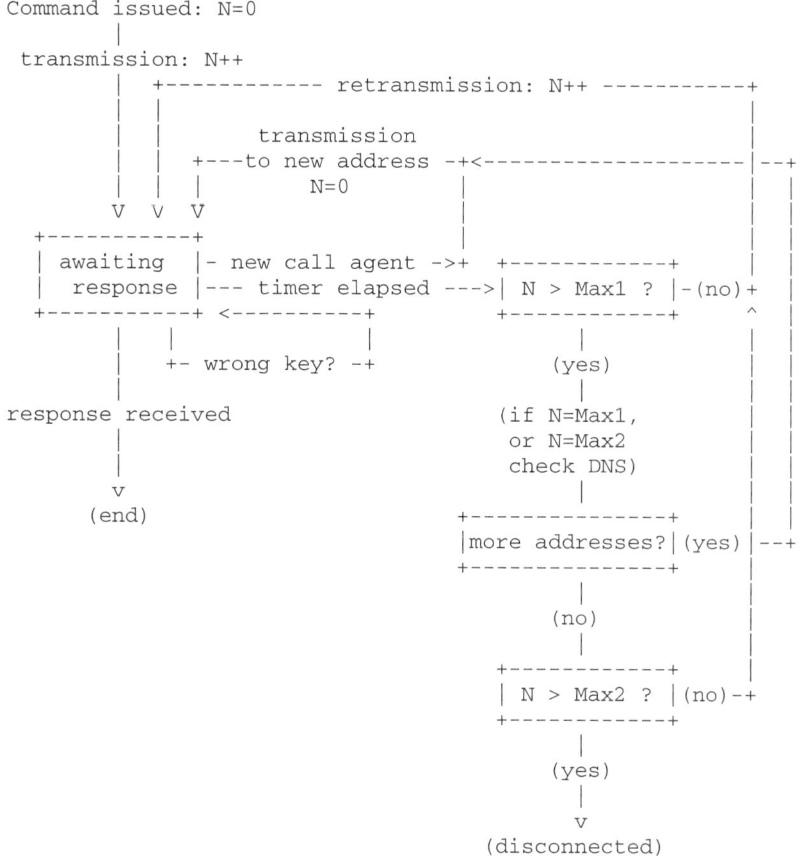

A classic retransmission algorithm would simply count the number of successive repetitions, and conclude that the association is broken after re-transmitting the packet an excessive number of times (typically between 7 and 11 times.) In order to account for the possibility of an undetected or in-progress "failover", we modify the classic algorithm as follows:

* We request that the gateway always checks for the presence of a new call agent. It can be noticed either by

  - receiving a valid multicast message announcing a failover, or

  - receiving a command where the NotifiedEntity points to the new call agent, or

  - receiving a redirection response pointing to a new Call Agent.

  If a new call agent is detected, the gateway starts transmitting outstanding commands to that new agent. Responses to commands are still transmitted to the source address of the command.

* we request that if the number of repetitions for this Call Agent is larger than "Max1", that the gateway actively queries the name server in order to detect the possible change of the call agent interfaces.

* The gateway may have learned several IP addresses for the call agent. If the number of repetitions is larger than "Max1" and lower than "Max2", and there are more interfaces that have not been tried, then the gateway should direct the retransmissions to alternate addresses.

* If there are no more interfaces to try, and the number of repetitions is Max2, then the gateway contacts the DNS one more time to see if any other interface should have become available. If not, the gateway is now disconnected.

The procedure will maximize the chances of detecting an ongoing failover. It poses indeed two very specific problems, the potentially long delays of a timer based procedure and the risk of confusion caused by the use of cryptographic protections.

In order to automatically adapt to network load, MGCP specifies exponentially increasing timers. If the initial timer is set to 200 milliseconds, the loss of a fifth retransmission will be detected after about 6 seconds. This is probably an acceptable waiting delay to detect a failover. The repetitions should continue after that delay not only in order to perhaps overcome a transient connectivity problem, but also in order to allow some more time for the execution of a failover - waiting a total delay of 30 seconds is probably acceptable.

It is however important that the maximum delay of retransmissions be bounded. Prior to any retransmission, it is checked that the time elapsed since the sending of the initial datagram is no greater than T- MAX. If more than T-MAX time has elapsed, the endpoint becomes disconnected. The value T-MAX is related to the LONG-TIMER value: the LONG-TIMER value is obtained by adding to T-MAX the maximum propagation delay in the network.

Another potential cause of connection failure would be the reception of a "wrong key" message, sent by a call agent that could not authenticate the command, presumably because it had lost the security parameters of the association. Such messages are actually not authorized in IPSEC, and they should in fact not be taken at face value: an attacker could easily forge "wrong key" messages in order to precipitate the loss of a control connection. The current algorithm ignores these messages, which translates into a strict reliance on timers. The algorithm could in fact be improved, maybe by executing a check with the key server of the call agent after "Max1" repetitions.

4.3. Race conditions

MGCP deals with race conditions through the notion of a "quarantine list" and through explicit detection of desynchronization.

MGCP does not assume that the transport mechanism will maintain the order of command and responses. This may cause race conditions, that may be obviated through a proper behavior of the call agent. (Note that some race conditions are inherent to distributed systems; they would still occur, even if the commands were transmitted in strict order.)

In some cases, many gateways may decide to restart operation at the same time. This may occur, for example, if an area loses power or transmission capability during an earthquake or an ice storm. When power and transmission are reestablished, many gateways may decide to send "RestartInProgress" commands simultaneously, leading to very unstable operation.

4.3.1. Quarantine list

MGCP controlled gateways will receive "notification requests" that ask them to watch for a list of "events." The protocol elements that determine the handling of these events are the "Requested Events" list, the "Digit Map" and the "Detect Events" list.

When the endpoint is initialized, the requested events list and the digit map are empty. After reception of a command, the gateway starts observing the endpoint for occurrences of the events mentioned in the list.

The events are examined as they occur. The action that follows is determined by the "action" parameter associated to the event in the list of requested events, and also by the digit map. The events that are defined as "accumulate" or "treat according to digit map" are accumulated in a list of events, the events that are marked as "treated according to the digit map" will additionally be accumulated in the dialed string. This will go on until one event is encountered that triggers a Notification to the "notified entity."

The gateway, at this point, will transmit the notification command and will place the endpoint in a "notification" state. As long as the endpoint is in this notification state, the events that are to be detected on the endpoint are stored in a "quarantine" buffer for later processing. The events are, in a sense, "quarantined." All events that are specified by the union of the RequestedEvents parameter and the most recently received DetectEvent parameter or, in the absence of the latter, all events that are referred to in the RequestedEvents, should be detected and quarantined, regardless of the action associated to the event.

The endpoint exits the "notification state" when the acknowledgement of the Notify command is received. The Notify command may be retransmitted in the "notification state", as specified in section 3.5. When the endpoint exits the "notification state" it resets the list of observed events and the "current dial string" of the endpoint to a null value.

Following that point, the behavior of the gateway depends on the value of The QuarantineHandling parameter in the notification request. If the Call Agent specified that it expected at most one notification in response to the notification request command, then the gateway should simply keep on accumulating events in the quarantine list until it receives the next notification request command.

If the gateway is authorized to send multiple successive Notify commands, it will proceed as follows. When the gateway exits the "notification state", it resets the list of observed events and the "current dial string" of the endpoint to a null value and starts processing the list of quarantined events, using the already received list of requested events and digit map. When processing these events, the gateway may encounter an event which requires a Notify command to be sent. If that is the case, the gateway can adopt one of the two following behaviors:

* it can immediately transmit a Notify command that will report all events that were accumulated in the list of observed events until the triggering event, included, leaving the unprocessed events in the quarantine list,

* or it can attempt to empty the quarantined list and transmit a single Notify command reporting several sets of events and possibly several dial strings. The dial string is reset to a null value after each triggering event. The events that follow the last triggering event are left in the quarantine list.

If the gateway transmits a Notify command, the end point will remain in the "notification state" until the acknowledgement is received. If the gateway does not find a quarantined event that requests a Notify command, it places the end point in a normal state. Events are then processed as they come, in exactly the same way as if a Notification Request command had just been received.

A gateway may receive at any time a new Notification Request command for the end point. When a new notification request is received in the notification state, the gateway shall ensure that the pending notification is received by the Call Agent prior to a successful response to the new NotificationRequest. It does so by using the "piggy-backing" functionality of the protocol. The messages will then be sent in a single packetto the source of the new NotificationRequest, regardless of respectively the source and "notified entity" for the old and new command. The steps involved are the following:

a) the gateway builds a message that carries in a single packet a repetition of the old pending Notify command and the acknowledgement of the new notification request.

b) the endpoint is then taken out of the "notification state" without waiting for the acknowledgement of the notification command.

c) a copy of the unacknowledged Notify command command is kept until an acknowledgement is received. If a timer elapses, the notification will be repeated, in a packet that will also carry a repetition of the acknowledgement of the notification request.

d) if the acknowledgement is lost, the Call Agent will retransmit the Notification Request. The gateway will reply to this repetition by retransmitting in a single packet the unacknowledged Notify and the acknowledgement of the notification request.

e) if the gateway has to transmit a Notify before the previous Notify is acknowledged, it should construct a packet that piggybacks a repetition of the old Notify, a repetition of the acknowledgement of the last notification request and the new Notify.

f) Gateways that cannot piggyback several packets in the same message should elect to leave the endpoint in the "notification" state as long as the last notification is not acknowledged.

After receiving the Notification Request command, the requested events list and digit map (if a new one was provided) are replaced by the newly received parameters, and the list of observed events and accumulated dial string are reset to a null value. The behavior is conditioned by the value of the QuarantineHandling parameter. The parameter may specify that quarantined events, or previously observed events, should be discarded, in which case they will be. If the parameter specifies that the quarantined events should be processed, the gateway will start processing the list of quarantined events or previously observed events, using the newly received list of requested events and digit map. When processing these events, the gateway may encounter an event which requires a Notify command to be sent. If that is the case, the gateway will immediately transmit a Notify command that will report all events that were accumulated in the list of observed events until the triggering event, included, leaving the unprocessed events in the quarantine buffer, and will enter the "notification state".

A new notification request may be received while the gateway has accumulated events according to the previous notification requests, but has not yet detected a notification-triggering events. The handling of not-yet-notified events is determined, as with the quarantined events, by the quarantine handling parameters:

* If the quarantine-handling parameter specifies that quarantined events shall be ignored, the observed event list is simply reset.

* If the quarantine-handling parameter specifies that quarantined events shall be processed, the observed event list is transferred to the quarantined event list. The observed event list is then reset, and the quarantined event list is processed.

Call Agents SHOULD provide the response to a successful Notify message and the new NotificationRequest in the same datagram using the piggy-backing mechanism.

4.3.2. Explicit detection

A key element of the state of several endpoints is the position of the hook. A race condition may occur when the user decides to go off-hook before the Call Agent has the time to ask the gateway to notify an off hook event (the "glare" condition well known in telephony), or if the user goes on-hook before the Call Agent has the time to request the event's notification.

To avoid this race condition, the gateway should check the condition of the endpoint before acknowledging a NotificationRequest. It should return an error:

1- If the gateway is requested to notify an "off hook" transition while the phone is already off hook,

2- If the gateway is requested to notify an "on hook" or "flash hook" condition while the phone is already on hook.

It should be noted, that the condition check is performed at the time the notification request is received, where as the actual event that caused the current condition may have either been reported, or ignored earlier, or it may currently be quarantined.

The other state variables of the gateway, such as the list of RequestedEvent or list of requested signals, are entirely replaced after each successful NotificationRequest, which prevents any long term discrepancy between the Call Agent and the gateway.

When a NotificationRequest is unsuccessful, whether it is included in a connection-handling command or not, the gateway will simply continue as if the command had never been received. As all other transactions, the NotificationRequest should operate as an atomic transaction, thus any changes initiated as a result of the command should be reverted.

Another race condition may occur when a Notify is issued shortly before the reception by the gateway of a NotificationRequest. The RequestIdentifier is used to correlate Notify commands with NotificationRequest commands.

4.3.3. Ordering of commands, and treatment of disorder

MGCP does not mandate that the underlying transport protocol guarantees the sequencing of commands sent to a gateway or an endpoint. This property tends to maximize the timeliness of actions, but it has a few draw backs. For example:

* Notify commands may be delayed and arrive to the call agent after the transmission of a new Notification Request command,

* If a new NotificationRequest is transmitted before a previous one is acknowledged, there is no guarantee that the previous one will not be received in second position.

Call Agents that want to guarantee consistent operation of the end points can use the following rules:

1) When a gateway handles several endpoints, commands pertaining to the different endpoints can be sent in parallel, for example following a model where each endpoint is controlled by its own process or its own thread.

2) When several connections are created on the same endpoint, commands pertaining to different connections can be sent in parallel.

3) On a given connection, there should normally be only one outstanding command (create or modify). However, a DeleteConnection command can be issued at any time. In consequence, a gateway may sometimes receive a ModifyConnection command that applies to a previously deleted connection. Such commands should be ignored, and an error code should be returned.

4) On a given endpoint, there should normally be only one outstanding NotificationRequest command at any time. The RequestId parameter should be used to correlate Notify commands with the triggering notification request.

5) In some cases, an implicitly or explicitly wildcarded DeleteConnection command that applies to a group of endpoints can step in front of a pending CreateConnection command. The Call Agent should individually delete all connections whose completion was pending at the time of the global DeleteConnection command. Also, new CreateConnection commands for endpoints named by the wild-carding cannot be sent until the wild-carded DeleteConnection command is acknowledged.

6) When commands are embedded within each other, sequencing requirements for all commands must be adhered to. For example a Create Connection command with a Notification Request in it must adhere to the sequencing for CreateConnection and NotificationRequest at the same time.

7) AuditEndpoint and AuditConnection is not subject to any sequencing.

8) RestartInProgress must always be the first command sent by an endpoint as defined by the restart procedure. Any other command or response must be delivered after this RestartInProgress command (piggy-backing allowed).

9) When multiple messages are piggy-backed in a single packet, the messages are always processed in order.

These rules do not affect the gateway, which should always respond to commands.

4.3.4. Fighting the restart avalanche

Let's suppose that a large number of gateways are powered on simultaneously. If they were to all initiate a RestartInProgress transaction, the call agent would very likely be swamped, leading to message losses and network congestion during the critical period of service restoration. In order to prevent such avalanches, the following behavior is suggested:

1) When a gateway is powered on, it should initiate a restart timer to a random value, uniformly distributed between 0 and a maximum waiting delay (MWD). Care should be taken to avoid synchronicity of the random number generation between multiple gateways that would use the same algorithm.

2) The gateway should then wait for either the end of this timer, the reception of a command from the call agent, or the detection of a local user activity, such as for example an off-hook transition on a residential gateway.

3) When the timer elapses, when a command is received, or when an activity is detected, the gateway should initiate the restart procedure.

The restart procedure simply requires the endpoint to guarantee that the first message (command or response) that the Call Agent sees from this endpoint is a RestartInProgress message informing the Call Agent about the restart. The endpoint is free to take full advantage of piggy-backing to achieve this.

It is expected that each endpoint in a gateway will have a provisionable Call Agent, i.e., "notified entity", to direct the initial restart message towards. When the collection of endpoints in a gateway is managed by more than one Call Agent, the above procedure must be performed for each collection of endpoints managed by a given Call Agent. The gateway MUST take full advantage of wild-carding to minimize the number of RestartInProgress messages generated when multiple endpoints in a gateway restart and the endpoints are managed by the same Call Agent.

The value of MWD is a configuration parameter that depends on the type of the gateway. The following]reasoning can be used to determine the value of this delay on residential gateways.

Call agents are typically dimensioned to handle the peak hour traffic load, during which, in average, 10% of the lines will be busy, placing calls whose average duration is typically 3 minutes. The processing of a call typically involves 5 to 6 MGCP transactions between each end point and the call agent. This simple calculation shows that the call agent is expected to handle 5 to 6 transactions for each end point, every 30 minutes on average, or, to put it otherwise, about one transaction per end point every 5 to 6 minutes on average. This suggest that a reasonable value of MWD for a residential gateway would be 10 to 12 minutes. In the absence of explicit configuration, residential gateways should adopt a value of 600 seconds for MWD.

The same reasoning suggests that the value of MWD should be much shorter for trunking gateways or for business gateways, because they handle a large number of endpoints, and also because the usage rate of these endpoints is much higher than 10% during the peak busy hour, a typical value being 60%. These endpoints, during the peak hour, are this expected to contribute about one transaction per minute to the call agent load. A reasonable algorithm is to make the value of MWD per "trunk" endpoint six times shorter than the MWD per residential gateway, and also inversely proportional to the number of endpoints that are being restarted. for example MWD should be set to 2.5 seconds for a gateway that handles a T1 line, or to 60 milliseconds for a gateway that handles a T3 line.

4.3.5. Disconnected Endpoints

In addition to the restart procedure, gateways also have a "disconnected" procedure, which is initiated when an endpoint becomes "disconnected" as described in Section 3.4.2. It should here be noted, that endpoints can only become disconnected when they attempt to communicate with the Call Agent. The following steps are followed by an endpoint that becomes "disconnected":

1. A "disconnected" timer is initialized to a random value, uniformly distributed between 0 and a provisionable "disconnected" initial waiting delay (Tdinit), e.g., 15 seconds. Care MUST be taken to avoid synchronicity of the random number generation between multiple gateways and endpoints that would use the same algorithm.

2. The gateway then waits for either the end of this timer, the reception of a command from the call agent, or the detection of a local user activity for the endpoint, such as for example an off-hook transition.

3. When the "disconnected" timer elapses, when a command is received, or when a local user activity is detected, the gateway initiates the "disconnected" procedure for the endpoint. In the case of local user activity, a provisionable "disconnected" minimum waiting delay (Tdmin) must furthermore have elapsed since the gateway became disconnected or the last time it initiated the "disconnected" procedure in order to limit the rate at which the procedure is performed.

4. If the "disconnected" procedure still left the endpoint disconnected, the "disconnected" timer is then doubled, subject to a provisionable "disconnected" maximum waiting delay (Tdmax), e.g., 600 seconds, and the gateway proceeds with step 2 again.

The "disconnected" procedure is similar to the restart procedure in that it now simply states that the endpoint MUST send a RestartInProgress command to the Call Agent informing it that the endpoint was disconnected and furthermore guarantee that the first message (command or response) that the Call Agent now sees from this endpoint MUST be this RestartInProgress command. The endpoint MUST take full advantage of piggy-backing in achieving this. The Call Agent may then for instance decide to audit the endpoint, or simply clear all connections for the endpoint.

This specification purposely does not specify any additional behavior for a disconnected endpoint. Vendors MAY for instance choose to provide silence, play reorder tone, or even enable a downloaded wav file to be played.

The default value for Tdinit is 15 seconds, the default value for Tdmin, is 15 seconds, and the default value for Tdmax is 600 seconds.

5. Security requirements

If unauthorized entities could use the MGCP, they would be able to set-up unauthorized calls, or to interfere with authorized calls. We expect that MGCP messages will always be carried over secure Internet connections, as defined in the IP security architecture as defined in RFC 2401, using either the IP Authentication Header, defined in RFC 2402, or the IP Encapsulating Security Payload, defined in RFC 2406. The complete MGCP protocol stack would thus include the following layers:

```
 _________________________________
|             MGCP                |
|_________________________________|
|             UDP                 |
|_________________________________|
|          IP security            |
| (authentication or encryption)  |
|_________________________________|
|             IP                  |
|_________________________________|
|     transmission media          |
|_________________________________|
```

Adequate protection of the connections will be achieved if the gateways and the Call Agents only accept messages for which IP security provided an authentication service. An encryption service will provide additional protection against eavesdropping, thus forbidding third parties from monitoring the connections set up by a given endpoint

The encryption service will also be requested if the session descriptions are used to carry session keys, as defined in SDP.

These procedures do not necessarily protect against denial of service attacks by misbehaving gateways or misbehaving call agents. However, they will provide an identification of these misbehaving entities, which should then be deprived of their authorization through maintenance procedures.

5.1. Protection of media connections

MGCP allows call agent to provide gateways with "session keys" that can be used to encrypt the audio messages, protecting against eavesdropping.

A specific problem of packet networks is "uncontrolled barge-in." This attack can be performed by directing media packets to the IP address and UDP port used by a connection. If no protection is implemented, the packets will be decompressed and the signals will be played on the "line side".

A basic protection against this attack is to only accept packets from known sources, checking for example that the IP source address and UDP source port match the values announced in the "remote session description." But this has two inconveniences: it slows down connection establishment and it can be fooled by source spoofing:

* To enable the address-based protection, the call agent must obtain the remote session description of the e-gress gateway and pass it to the in-gress gateway. This requires at least one network round trip, and leaves us with a dilemma: either allow the call to proceed without waiting for the round trip to complete, and risk for example "clipping" a remote announcement, or wait for the full round trip and settle for slower call-set-up procedures.

* Source spoofing is only effective if the attacker can obtain valid pairs of source destination addresses and ports, for example by listening to a fraction of the traffic. To fight source spoofing, one could try to control all access points to the network. But this is in practice very hard to achieve.

An alternative to checking the source address is to encrypt and authenticate the packets, using a secret key that is conveyed during the call set-up procedure. This will no slow down the call set-up, and provides strong protection against address spoofing.

6. Event packages and end point types

This section provides an initial definition of packages and event names. More packages can be defined in additional documents.

6.1. Basic packages

The list of basic packages includes the following:

Package	name
Generic Media Package	G
DTMF package	D
MF Package	M
Trunk Package	T
Line Package	L
Handset Package	H
RTP Package	R
Network Access Server Package	N
Announcement Server Package	A
Script Package	Script

In the tables of events for each package, there are five columns:

Symbol: the unique symbol used for the event
Definition: a short description of the event

R: an x appears in this column is the event can be Requested by the call agent.

S: if nothing appears in this column for an event, then the event cannot be signaled on command by the call agent. Otherwise, the following symbols identify the type of event:

OO On/Off signal. The signal is turned on until commanded by the call agent to turn it off, and vice versa.

TO Timeout signal. The signal lasts for a given duration unless it is superseded by a new signal.

BR Brief signal. The event has a short, known duration.

Duration: specifies the duration of TO signals.

6.1.1. Generic Media Package

Package Name: G

The generic media package group the events and signals that can be observed on several types of endpoints, such as trunking gateways, access gateways or residential gateways.

Symbol	Definition	R	S	Duration
mt	Modem detected	x		
ft	Fax tone detected	x		
ld	Long duration connection	x		
pat(###)	Pattern ### detected	x	OO	
rt	Ringback tone		TO	
rbk(###)	ring back on connection		TO	180 seconds
cf	Confirm tone		BR	
cg	Network Congestion tone		TO	
it	Intercept tone		OO	
pt	Preemption tone		OO	
of	report failure	x		

The signals are defined as follows:

The pattern definition can be used for specific algorithms such as answering machine detection, tone detection, and the like.

Ring back tone (rt)
an Audible Ring Tone, a combination of two AC tones with frequencies of 440 and 480 Hertz and levels of -19 dBm each, to give a combined level of -16 dBm. The cadence for Audible Ring Tone is 2 seconds on followed by 4 seconds off. See GR- 506-CORE - LSSGR: SIGNALING, Section 17.2.5.

Ring back on connection
A ring back tone, applied to the connection whose identifier is passed as a parameter.

The "long duration connection" is detected when a connection has been established for more than 1 hour.

6.1.2. DTMF package

Package name: D

Symbol	Definition	R	S	Duration
0	DTMF 0	x	BR	
1	DTMF 1	x	BR	
2	DTMF 2	x	BR	
3	DTMF 3	x	BR	
4	DTMF 4	x	BR	
5	DTMF 5	x	BR	
6	DTMF 6	x	BR	
7	DTMF 7	x	BR	
8	DTMF 8	x	BR	
9	DTMF 9	x	BR	
#	DTMF #	x	BR	
*	DTMF *	x	BR	
A	DTMF A	x	BR	
B	DTMF B	x	BR	
C	DTMF C	x	BR	
D	DTMF D	x	BR	
L	long duration indicator	x		2 seconds
X	Wildcard, match any digit 0-9	x		
T	Interdigit timer	x		4 seconds
of	report failure	x		

The "interdigit timer" T is a digit input timer that can be used in two ways:

* When timer T is used with a digit map, the timer is not started until the first digit is entered, and the timer is restarted after each new digit is entered until either a digit map match or mismatch occurs. In this case, timer T functions as an inter-digit timer.

* When timer T is used without a digit map, the timer is started immediately and simply cancelled (but not restarted) as soon as a digit is entered. In this case, timer T can be used as an interdigit timer when overlap sending is used.

  When used with a digit map, timer T takes on one of two values, T(partial) or T(critical). When at least one more digit is required for the digit string to match any of the patterns in the digit map, timer T takes on the value T(partial), corresponding to partial dial timing. If a timer is all that is required to produce a match, timer T takes on the value T(critical) corresponding to critical timing. When timer T is used without a digit map, timer T takes on the value T(critical). The default value for T(partial) is 16 seconds and the default value for T(critical) is 4 seconds. The provisioning process may alter both of these.

The "long duration indicator" is observed when a DTMF signal is produced for a duration larger than two seconds. In this case, the gateway will detect two successive events: first, when the signal has been recognized, the DTMF signal, and then, 2 seconds later, the long duration signal.

6.1.3. MF Package

Package Name: M

Symbol	Definition	R	S	Duration
0	MF 0	x	BR	
1	MF 1	x	BR	
2	MF 2	x	BR	
3	MF 3	x	BR	
4	MF 4	x	BR	
5	MF 5	x	BR	
6	MF 6	x	BR	
7	MF 7	x	BR	
8	MF 8	x	BR	
9	MF 9	x	BR	
X	Wildcard, match any digit 0-9	x		
T	Interdigit timer	x		4 seconds
K0	MF K0 or KP	x	BR	
K1	MF K1	x	BR	
K2	MF K2	x	BR	
S0	MF S0 or ST	x	BR	
S1	MF S1	x	BR	
S2	MF S2	x	BR	
S3	MF S3	x	BR	
wk	Wink	x	BR	
wko	Wink off	x	BR	
is	Incoming seizure	x	OO	
rs	Return seizure	x	OO	
us	Unseize circuit	x	OO	
of	report failure	x		

The definition of the MF package events is as follows:

Wink
A transition from unseized to seized to unseized trunk states within a specified period. Typical seizure period is 100-350 msec.)

Incoming seizure
Incoming indication of call attempt.

Return seizure:
Seizure in response to outgoing seizure.

Unseize circuit:
Unseizure of a circuit at the end of a call.

Wink off:
A signal used in operator services trunks. A transition from seized to unseized to seized trunk states within a specified period of 100-350 ms. (To be checked)

6.1.4. Trunk Package

Package Name: T

Symbol	Definition	R	S	Duration
co1	Continuity tone (single tone, or return tone)	x	OO	
co2	Continuity test (go tone, in dual tone procedures)	x	OO	
lb	Loopback		OO	
om	Old Milliwatt Tone (1000 Hz)	x	OO	
nm	New Milliwatt Tone (1004 Hz)	x	OO	
tl	Test Line	x	OO	
zz	No circuit	x	OO	
as	Answer Supervision	x	OO	
ro	Reorder Tone	x	TO	30 seconds
of	report failure	x		
bl	Blocking		OO	

The definition of the trunk package signal events is as follows:

Continuity Tone (co1):
A tone at 2010 + or - 30 Hz.

Continuity Test (co2):
A tone at the 1780 + or - 30 Hz.

Milliwatt Tones:
Old Milliwatt Tone (1000 Hz), New Milliwatt Tone (1004 Hz)

Line Test:
105 Test Line test progress tone (2225 Hz + or - 25 Hz at -10 dBm0 + or -- 0.5dB).

No circuit:
(that annoying tri-tone, low to high)

Answer Supervision:

Reorder Tone:
Reorder tone is a combination of two AC tones with frequencies of 480 and 620 Hertz and levels of -24 dBm each, to give a combined level of -21 dBm. The cadence for Station Busy Tone is 0.25 seconds on followed by 0.25 seconds off, repeating continuously. See GR-506-CORE - LSSGR: SIGNALING, Section 17.2.7.

Blocking:
The call agent can place the circuit in a blocked state by applying the "bl(+)" signal to the endpoint. It can unblock it by applying the "bl(-)" signal.

The continuity tones are used when the call agent wants to initiate a continuity test. There are two types of tests, single tone and dual tone. The Call agent is expected to know, through provisioning information, which test should be applied to a given endpoint. For example, the call agent that wants to initiate a single frequency test will send to the gateway a command of the form:

```
RQNT 1234 epx-t1/17@tgw2.example.net
X: AB123FE0
S: co1
R: co1
```

If it wanted instead to initiate a dual-tone test, it would send the command:

```
RQNT 1234 epx-t1/17@tgw2.example.net
X: AB123FE0
S: co2
R: co1
```

The gateway would send the requested signal, and in both cases would look for the return of the 2010 Hz tone (co1). When it detects that tone, it will send the corresponding notification.

The tones are of type OO: the gateway will keep sending them until it receives a new notification request.

6.1.5. Line Package

Package Name: L

Symbol	Definition	R	S	Duration
adsi(string)	adsi display		BR	
vmwi	visual message waiting indicator		OO	
hd	Off hook transition	x		
hu	On hook transition	x		
hf	Flash hook	x		
aw	Answer tone	x	OO	
bz	Busy tone		TO	30 seconds
ci(ti,nu,na)	Caller-id		BR	
wt	Call Waiting tone		TO	30 seconds
wt1, wt2, wt3, wt4	Alternative call waiting tones			
dl	Dial tone		TO	16 seconds
mwi	Message waiting ind.		TO	16 seconds
nbz	Network busy (fast cycle busy)	x	OO	
ro	Reorder tone		TO	30 seconds
rg	Ringing		TO	180 seconds
r0, r1, r2, r3, r4, r5, r6 or r7	Distinctive ringing		TO	180 seconds
rs	Ringsplash		BR	
p	Prompt tone	x	BR	
e	Error tone	x	BR	
sl	Stutter dialtone		TO	16 seconds
v	Alerting Tone		OO	
y	Recorder Warning Tone		OO	
sit	SIT tone			
z	Calling Card Service Tone		OO	
oc	Report on completion	x		
ot	Off hook warning tone		TO	indefinite
s(###)	Distinctive tone pattern	x	BR	
of	report failure	x		

The definition of the tones is as follows:

Dial tone:
A combined 350 + 440 Hz tone.

Visual Message Waiting Indicator
The transmission of the VMWI messages will conform to the requirements in Section 2.3.2, "On-hook Data Transmission Not Associated with Ringing" in TR-H-000030 and the CPE guidelines in SR-TSV-002476. VMWI messages will only be sent from the SPCS when the line is idle. If new messages arrive while the line is busy, the VMWI indicator message will be delayed until the line goes back to the idle state. The CA should periodically refresh the CPE's visual indicator. See TR-NWT-001401 - Visual Message Waiting Indicator Generic Requirements; and GR- 30-CORE - Voiceband Data Transmission Interface.

Message waiting Indicator
See GR-506-CORE, 17.2.3.

Alerting Tone:
a 440 Hz Tone of 2 second duration followed by 1/2 second of tone every 10 seconds.

Ring splash
Ringsplash, also known as "Reminder ring" is a burst of ringing that may be applied to the physical forwarding line (when idle) to indicate that a call has been forwarded and to remind the user that a CF subfeature is active. In the US, it is defined to be a 0.5(-0,+0.1) second burst of power ringing. See TR-TSY-000586 - Call Forwarding Subfeatures.

Call waiting tone
Call Waiting tone is defined in GR-506-CORE, 14.2. Call Waiting feature is defined in TR-TSY-000571. By defining "wt" as a TO signal you are really defining the feature which seems wrong to me (given the spirit of MGCP), hence the definition of "wt" as a BR signal in ECS, per GR-506-CORE. Also, it turns out that there is actually four different call waiting tone patterns (see GR-506-CORE, 14.2) so we have wt1, wt2, wt3, wt4.

Caller Id (ci(time, number, name)):
The caller-id event carries three parameters, the time of the call, the calling number and the calling name. Each of the three fields are optional, however each of the commas will always be included. See TR-NWT-001188, GR-30-CORE, and TR-NWT-000031.

Recorder Warning Tone:
1400 Hz of Tone of 0.5 second duration every 15 seconds.

SIT tone:
used for indicating a line is out of service.

Calling Card Service Tone:
60 ms of 941 + 1477 Hz and 940 ms of 350 + 440 Hz (dial tone), decaying exponentially with a time constant of 200 ms.

Distinctive tone pattern:
where ### is any number between 000 and 999, inclusive. Can be used for distinctive ringing, customized dial tone, etc.

Report on completion
The report on completion event is detected when the gateway was asked to perform one or several signals of type TO on the endpoint, and when these signals were completed without being stopped by the detection of a requested event such as off-hook transition or dialed digit. The completion report may carry as parameter the name of the signal that came to the end of its live time, as in:

```
O: L/oc(L/dl)
```

Ring back on connection
A ring back tone, applied to the connection wghose identifier is passed as a parameter.

We should note that many of these definitions vary from country to country. The frequencies listed above are the one in use in North America. There is a need to accommodate different tone sets in different countries, and there is still an ongoing debate on the best way to meet that requirement:

* One solution is to define different event packages specifying for example the German dialtone as "L-DE/DL".

* Another solution is to use a management interface to specify on an endpoint basis which frequency shall be associated to what tone.

6.1.6. Handset emulation package

Package Name: H

Symbol	Definition	R	S	Duration
adsi(string)	adsi display	x	BR	
tdd				
vmwi				
hd	Off hook transition	x	OO	
hu	On hook transition	x	OO	
hf	Flash hook	x	BR	
aw	Answer tone	x	OO	
bz	Busy tone	x	OO	
wt	Call Waiting tone	x	TO	30 seconds
dl	Dial tone (350 + 440 Hz)	x	TO	120 seconds
nbz	Network busy (fast cycle busy)	x	OO	
rg	Ringing	x	TO	30 seconds
r0, r1, r2, r3, r4, r5, r6 or r7	Distinctive ringing	x	TO	30 seconds
p	Prompt tone	x	BR	
e	Error tone	x	BR	
sdl	Stutter dialtone	x	TO	16 seconds
v	Alerting Tone	x	OO	
y	Recorder Warning Tone	x	OO	
t	SIT tone	x		
z	Calling Card Service Tone	x	OO	
oc	Report on completion	x		
ot	Off hook warning tone	x	OO	
s(###)	Distinctive tone pattern	x	BR	
of	report failure	x		

The handset emulation package is an extension of the line package, to be used when the gateway is capable of emulating a handset. The difference with the line package is that events such as "off hook" can be signalled as well as detected.

6.1.7. RTP Package

Package Name: R

Symbol	Definition	R	S	Duration
UC	Used codec changed	x		
SR(###)	Sampling rate changed	x		
JI(###)	Jitter buffer size changed	x		
PL(###)	Packet loss exceeded	x		
qa	Quality alert	x		
co1	Continuity tone (single tone, or return tone)	x	OO	
co2	Continuity test (go tone, in dual tone procedures)	x	OO	
of	report failure	x		

Codec Changed:

Codec changed to hexadecimal codec number enclosed in parenthesis, as in UC(15), to indicate the codec was changed to PCM mu-law. Codec Numbers are specified in RFC 1890, or in a new definition of the audio profiles for RTP that replaces this RFC. Some implementations of media gateways may not allow the codec to be changed upon command from the call agent. codec changed to codec hexadecimal ##.

Sampling Rate Changed:

Sampling rate changed to decimal number in milliseconds enclosed in parenthesis, as in SR(20), to indicate the sampling rate was changed to 20 milliseconds. Some implementations of media gateways may not allow the sampling rate to be changed upon command from a call agent.

Jitter Buffer Size Changed:

When the media gateway has the ability to automatically adjust the depth of the jitter buffer for received RTP streams, it is useful for the media gateway controller to receive notification that the media gateway has automatically increased its jitter buffer size to accomodate increased or decreased variability in network latency. The syntax for requesting notification is "JI", which tells the media gateway that the controller wants notification of any jitter buffer size changes. The syntax for notification from the media gateway to the controller is "JI(####)", where the #### is the new size of the jitter buffer, in milliseconds.

Packet Loss Exceeded:
Packet loss rate exceed the threshold of the specified decimal number of packets per 100,000 packets, where the packet loss number is contained in parenthesis. For example, PL(10) indicates packets are being dropped at a rate of 1 in 10,000 packets.

Quality alert
The packet loss rate or the combination of delay and jitter exceed a specified quality threshold.

The continuity tones are the same as those defined in the Trunk package. They can be use in conjunction with the Network LoopBack or Network Continuity Test modes to test the continuity of an RTP circuit.

The "operation failure" code can be used to report problems such as the loss of underlying connectivity. The observed event can include as parameter the reason code of the failure.

6.1.8. Network Access Server Package

Package Name: N

Symbol	Definition	R	S	Duration
pa	Packet arrival	x		
cbk	Call back request	x		
cl	Carrier lost	x		
au	Authorization succeeded	x		
ax	Authorization denied	x		
of	Report failure	x		

The packet arrival event is used to notify that at least one packet was recently sent to an Internet address that is observed by an endpoint. The event report includes the Internet address, in standard ASCII encoding, between parenthesis:

```
O: pa(192.96.41.1)
```

The call back event is used to notify that a call back has been requested during the initial phase of a data connection. The event report includes the identification of the user that should be called back, between parenthesis:

```
O: cbk(user25)
```

6.1.9. Announcement Server Package

Package Name: A

Symbol	Definition	R	S	Duration
ann(url,parms)	Play an announcement		TO	variable
oc	Report on completion	x		
of	Report failure	x		

The announcement action is qualified by an URL name and by a set of initial parameters as in for example:

```
S: ann(http://scripts.example.net/all-lines-busy.au)
```

The "operation complete" event will be detected when the announcement is played out. If the announcement cannot be played out, an operation failure event can be returned. The failure may be explained by a commentary, as in:

```
O: A/of(file not found)
```

6.1.10. Script Package

Package Name: Script

Symbol	Definition	R	S	Duration
java(url)	Load a java script		TO	variable
perl(url)	Load a perl script		TO	variable
tcl(url)	Load a TCL script		TO	variable
xml(url)	Load an XML script		TO	variable
oc	Report on completion	x		
of	Report failure	x		

The "language" action define is qualified by an URL name and by a set of initial parameters as in for example:

```
S: script/java(http://scripts.example.net/credit-
   card.java,long,1234)
```

The current definition defines keywords for the most common languages. More languages may be defined in further version of this documents. For each language, an API specification will describe how the scripts can issue local "notificationRequest" commands, and receive the corresponding notifications.

The script produces an output which consists of one or several text string, separated by commas. The text string are reported as a commentary in the report on completion, as in for example:

```
O: script/oc(21223456794567,9738234567)
```

The failure report may also return a string, as in:

```
O: script/oc(21223456794567,9738234567)
```

The definition of the script environment and the specific actions in that environment are for further study.

6.2. Basic endpoint types and profiles

We define the following basic endpoint types and profiles:

* Trunk gateway (ISUP)

* Trunk gateway (MF)

* Network Access Server (NAS)

* Combined NAS/VOIP gateway

* Access Gateway

* Residential Gateway

* Announcement servers

These gateways are supposed to implement the following packages

Gateway	Supported packages
Trunk gateway (ISUP)	GM, DTMF, TK, RTP
Trunk gateway (MF)	GM, MF, DTMF, TK, RTP
Network Access Server (NAS)	GM, MF, TK, NAS
Combined NAS/VOIP gateway	GM, MF, DTMF, TK, NAS, RTP
Access Gateway (VOIP)	GM, DTMF, MF, RTP
Access Gateway (VOIP+NAS)	GM, DTMF, MF, NAS, RTP
Residential Gateway	GM, DTMF, Line, RTP
Announcement Server	ANN, RTP

Advanced announcement servers may also support the Script package.

Advanced trunking servers may support the ANN package, the Script package, and in some cases the Line and Handset package as well.

7. Versions and compatibility

7.1. Differences between version 1.0 and draft 0.5

Draft 0-5 was issued in February 1999, as the last update of draft version 0.1. Version 1.0 benefits from implementation experience, and also aligns as much as possible with the CableLabs' NCS project. The main differences between the February draft and version 1.0 are:

* Specified more clearly that the encoding of three LocalConnectionOptions parameters, Encoding Method, Packetization Period and Bandwidth, shall follow the conventions laid out in SDP.

* Specified how the quarantine handling parameter governs the handling of detected but not yet specified events.

* Specified that unexpected timers or digits should trigger transmission of the dialed string.

* Removed the digit map syntax description from section 2.1.5 (it was redundant with section 3.4.)

* Corrected miscellaneous bugs in the formal syntax description.

* Aligned specification of commands with the CableLabs NCS specification. This mostly affects the AuditEndpoint and

RestartInProgress commands.

* Aligned the handling of retransmission with the CableLabs NCS specification.

* Added the provisional response return code and corresponding behavior description.

* Added an optional reason code parameter to restart in progress.

* Added the possibility to audit the restart method, restart delay and reason code.

7.2. Differences between draft-04 and draft-05

Differences are minor: corrected the copyright statement, and corrected a bug in the formal description.

7.3. Differences between draft-03 and draft-04

Draft 04 corrects a number of minor editing mistakes that were pointed out during the review of draft 03, issued on February 1.

7.4. Differences between draft-02 and draft-03

The main differences between draft-02, issued in January 22 1998, and draft 03 are:

* Introduced a discussion on endpoint types,

* Introduced a discussion of the connection set-up procedure, and of the role of connection parameters,

* Introduced a notation of the connection identifier within event names,

* Documented the extension procedure for the LocalConnectionOptions parameter and for the ConnectionParameters parameter,

* Introduced a three-way handshake procedure, using a ResponseAck parameter, in order to allow gateways to delete copies of old responses without waiting for a 30 seconds timer,

* Expanded the security section to include a discussion of "uncontrolled barge-in."

* Propsed a "create two connections" command, as an appendix.

7.5. Differences between draft-01 and draft-02

The main differences between draft-01, issued in November 1998, and draft 02 are:

* Added an ABNF description of the protocol.

* Specification of an EndpointConfiguration command,

* Addition of a "two endpoints" mode in the create connection command,

* Modification of the package wildcards from "$/$" to "*/all" at the Request of early implementors,

* Revision of some package definitions to better align with external specifications.

* Addition of a specification for the handling of "failover."

* Revision of the section on race conditions.

7.6. The making of MGCP from IPDC and SGCP

MGCP version 0.1 results from the fusion of the SGCP and IPDC proposals.

7.7. Changes between MGCP and initial versions of SGCP

MGCP version 0.1 (which subsumes SGCP version 1.2) introduces the following changes from SGCP version 1.1:

* Protocol name changed to MGCP.

* Introduce a formal wildcarding structure in the name of endpoints, inspired from IPDC, and detailed the usage of wildcard names in each operation.

* Naming scheme for events, introducing a package structure inspired from IPDC.

* New operations for audit endpoint, audit connection (requested by the Cablelabs) and restart (inspired from IPDC).

* New parameter to control the behavior of the notification request.

* Improved text on the detection and handling of race conditions.

* Syntax modification for event reporting, to incorporate package names.

* Definition of basic event packages (inspired from IPDC).

* Incorporation of mandatory and optional extension parameters, inspired by IPDC.

SGCP version 1.1 introduces the following changes from version SGCP 1.0:

* Extension parameters (X-??:)

* Error Code 511 (Unrecognized extension).

* All event codes can be used in RequestEvent, SignalRequest and ObservedEvent parameters.

* Error Code 512 (Not equipped to detect requested event).

* Error Code 513 (Not equipped to generate requested signal).

* Error Code 514 (Unrecognized announcement).

* Specific Endpoint-ID can be returned in creation commands.

* Changed the code for the ASDI display from "ad" to "asdi" to avoid conflict with the digits A and D.

* Changed the code for the answer tone from "at" to "aw" to avoid conflict with the digit A and the timer mark T

* Changed the code for the busy tone from "bt" to "bz" to avoid conflict with the digit B and the timer mark T

* Specified that the continuity tone value is "co" (CT was incorrectly used in several instances; CT conflicts with .)

* Changed the code for the dial tone from "dt" to "dl" to avoid conflict with the digit D and the timer mark T

* Added a code point for announcement requests.

* Added a code point for the "wink" event.

* Set the "octet received" code in the "Connection Parameters" to "OR" (was set to RO, but then "OR" was used throughout all examples.)

* Added a "data" mode.

* Added a description of SDP parameters for the network access mode (NAS).

* Added four flow diagrams for the network access mode.

* Incorporated numerous editing suggestions to make the description easier to understand. In particular, cleared the confusion between requests, queries, functions and commands.

* Defined the continuity test mode as specifying a dual-tone transponder, while the loopback mode can be used for a single tone test.

* Added event code "OC", operation completed.

* Added the specification of the "quarantine list", which clarifies the expected handling of events and notifications.

* Added the specification of a "wildcard delete" operation.

8. Security Considerations

Security issues are discussed in section 5.

9. Acknowledgements

We want to thank here the many reviewers who provided us with advice on the design of SGCP and then MGCP, notably Flemming Andreasen, Sankar Ardhanari, Francois Berard, David Auerbach, Bob Biskner, David Bukovinsky, Jerry Kamitses, Oren Kudevitzki, Barry Hoffner, Troy Morley, Dave Oran, Jeff Orwick, John Pickens, Lou Rubin, Chip Sharp, Paul Sijben, Kurt Steinbrenner, Joe Stone and Stuart Wray.

The version 0.1 of MGCP is heavily inspired by the "Internet Protocol Device Control" (IPDC) designed by the Technical Advisory Committee set up by Level 3 Communications. Whole sets of text have been retrieved from the IP Connection Control protocol, IP Media Control protocol, and IP Device Management. The authors wish to acknowledge the contribution to these protocols made by Ilya Akramovich, Bob Bell, Dan Brendes, Peter Chung, John Clark, Russ Dehlinger, Andrew Dugan, Isaac Elliott, Cary FitzGerald, Jan Gronski, Tom Hess, Geoff Jordan, Tony Lam, Shawn Lewis, Dave Mazik, Alan Mikhak, Pete O'Connell, Scott Pickett, Shyamal Prasad, Eric Presworsky, Paul Richards, Dale Skran, Louise Spergel, David Sprague, Raj Srinivasan, Tom Taylor and Michael Thomas.

10. References

* Schulzrinne, H., Casner, S., Frederick, R. and V. Jacobson, "RTP: A Transport Protocol for Real-Time Applications", RFC 1889, January 1996.

* Schulzrinne, H., "RTP Profile for Audio and Video Conferences with Minimal Control", RFC 1890, January 1996.

* Handley, M and V. Jacobson, "SDP: Session Description Protocol", RFC 2327, April 1998.

* Handley, M., "SAP - Session Announcement Protocol", Work in Progress.

* Handley, M., Schulzrinne, H. and E. Schooler, "Session Initiation Protocol (SIP)", RFC 2543, March 1999.

* Schulzrinne, H., Rao, A. and R. Lanphier, "Real Time Streaming Protocol (RTSP)", RFC 2326, April 1998.

* ITU-T, Recommendation Q.761, "FUNCTIONAL DESCRIPTION OF THE ISDN USER PART OF SIGNALLING SYSTEM No. 7", (Malaga-Torremolinos, 1984; modified at Helsinki, 1993)

* ITU-T, Recommendation Q.762, "GENERAL FUNCTION OF MESSAGES AND SIGNALS OF THE ISDN USER PART OF SIGNALLING SYSTEM No. 7", (MalagaTorremolinos, 1984; modified at Helsinki, 1993)

* ITU-T, Recommendation H.323 (02/98), "PACKET-BASED MULTIMEDIA COMMUNICATIONS SYSTEMS."

* ITU-T, Recommendation H.225, "Call Signaling Protocols and Media Stream Packetization for Packet Based Multimedia Communications Systems."

* ITU-T, Recommendation H.245 (02/98), "CONTROL PROTOCOL FOR MULTIMEDIA COMMUNICATION."

* Kent, S. and R. Atkinson, "Security Architecture for the Internet Protocol", RFC 2401, November 1998.

* Kent, S. and R. Atkinson, "IP Authentication Header", RFC 2402, November 1998.

* Kent, S. and R. Atkinson, "IP Encapsulating Security Payload (ESP)", RFC 2406, November 1998.

* Crocker, D. and P. Overell, "Augmented BNF for Syntax Specifications: ABNF", RFC 2234, November 1997.

11. Authors' Addresses

Mauricio Arango
RSL COM Latin America
6300 N.W. 5th Way, Suite 100
Ft. Lauderdale, FL 33309

Phone: (954) 492-0913
EMail: marango@rslcom.com

Andrew Dugan
Level3 Communications
1450 Infinite Drive
Louisville, CO 80027

Phone: (303)926 3123
EMail: andrew.dugan@l3.com

Isaac Elliott
Level3 Communications
1450 Infinite Drive
Louisville, CO 80027

Phone: (303)926 3123
EMail: ike.elliott@l3.com

Christian Huitema
Telcordia Technologies
MCC 1J236B
445 South Street
Morristown, NJ 07960
U.S.A.

Phone: +1 973-829-4266
EMail: huitema@research.telcordia.com

Scott Pickett
Vertical Networks
1148 East Arques Ave
Sunnyvale, CA 94086

Phone: (408) 523-9700 extension 200
EMail: ScottP@vertical.com

Further information is available on the SGCP web site:

http://www.argreenhouse.com/SGCP/

12. Appendix A: Proposed "MoveConnection" command

It has been proposed to create a new command, that would move an existing connection from one endpoint to another, on the same gateway. This command would be specially useful for handling certain call services, such as call forwarding between endpoints served by the same gateway.

```
[SecondEndPointId,]
[ConnectionId,]
[LocalConnectionDescriptor]
 <--- ModifyConnection(CallId,
                       EndpointId,
                       ConnectionId,
                       SecondEndPointId,
                       [NotifiedEntity,]
                       [LocalConnectionOptions,]
                       [Mode,]
                       [RemoteConnectionDescriptor,]
                       [Encapsulated NotificationRequest,]
                       [Encapsulated EndpointConfiguration])
```

The parameters used are the same as in the ModifyConnection command, with the addition of a SecondEndpointId that identifies the endpoint towards which the connection is moved.

The EndpointId should be the fully qualified endpoint identifier of the endpoint on which the connection has been created. The local name shall not use the wildcard convention.

The SecondEndpointId shall be the endpoint identifier of the endpoint towards which the connection has been created. The "any of" wildcard convention can be used, but not the "all of" convention. If the SecondEndpointId parameter is unqualified, the gateway will choose a value, that will be returned to the call agent as a response parameter.

The command will result in the "move" of the existing connection to the second endpoint. Depending on gateway implementations, the connection identifier of the connection after the move may or may not be the same as the connection identifier before the move. If it is not the same, the new value is returned as a response parameter.

The intent of the command is to effect a local relocation of the connection, without having to modify such transmission parameters as IP addresses and port, and thus without forcing the call agent to signal the change of parameters to the remote gateway, at the other end of the connection. However, gateway architectures may not always allow such transparent moves. For example, some architectures could allow specific IP addresses to different boards that handles specific group of endpoints. If for any reason the transmission parameters have to be changed as a result of the move, the new LocalConnectionDescriptor is returned as a response parameter.

The LocalConnectionOptions, Mode, and RemoteConnectionDescriptor, when present, are applied after the move.

The RequestedEvents, RequestIdentifier, DigitMap, SignalRequests, QuarantineHandling and DetectEvents parameters are optional. They can be used by the Call Agent to transmit a NotificationRequest that is executed simultaneously with the move of the connection. When these parameters are present, the NotificationRequest applies to the second endpoint.

When these parameters are present, the move and the NotificationRequests should be synchronized, which means that both should be accepted, or both refused. The NotifiedEntity parameter, if present, applies to both the ModifyConnection and the NotificationRequest command.

The command may carry an encapsulated EndpointConfiguration command, that will also apply to the second endpoint. When this command is present, the parameters of the EndpointConfiguration command are inserted after the normal parameters of the MoveConnection with the exception of the SecondEndpointId, which is not replicated. The EndpointConfiguration command may be encapsulated together with an encapsulated NotificationRequest command.

The encapsulated EndpointConfiguration command shares the fate of the MoveConnection command. If the MoveConnection is rejected, the EndpointConfiguration is not executed.

12.1. Proposed syntax modification

The only syntax modification necessary for the addition of the moveConnection command is the addition of the keyword MOVE to the authorized values in the MGCPVerb clause of the formal syntax.

Acknowledgement

Funding for the RFC Editor function is currently provided by the Internet Society.

Network Working Group
Request for Comments: 2719
Category: Informational

L. Ong
Nortel Networks
I. Rytina
M. Garcia
Ericsson
H. Schwarzbauer
L. Coene
Siemens
H. Lin
Telcordia
I. Juhasz
Telia
M. Holdrege
Lucent
C. Sharp
Cisco Systems
October 1999

Framework Architecture for Signaling Transport

Status of this Memo

This memo provides information for the Internet community. It does not specify an Internet standard of any kind. Distribution of this memo is unlimited.

Copyright Notice

Abstract

This document defines an architecture framework and functional requirements for transport of signaling information over IP. The framework describes relationships between functional and physical entities exchanging signaling information, such as Signaling Gateways and Media Gateway Controllers. It identifies interfaces where signaling transport may be used and the functional and performance requirements that apply from existing Switched Circuit Network (SCN) signaling protocols.

Table of Contents

1. Introduction

1.1 Overview

This document defines an architecture framework for transport of message-based signaling protocols over IP networks. The scope of this work includes definition of encapsulation methods, end-to-end protocol mechanisms and use of existing IP capabilities to support the functional and performance requirements for signaling transport.

The framework portion describes the relationships between functional and physical entities used in signaling transport, including the framework for control of Media Gateways, and other scenarios where signaling transport may be required.

The requirements portion describes functional and performance requirements for signaling transport such as flow control, in-sequence delivery and other functions that may be required for specific SCN signaling protocols.

1.2 Terminology

The following are general terms are used in this document:

Backhaul:

Backhaul refers to the transport of signaling from the point of interface for the associated data stream (i.e., SG function in the MGU) back to the point of call processing (i.e., the MGCU), if this is not local.

Signaling Transport (SIG):

SIG refers to a protocol stack for transport of SCN signaling protocols over an IP network. It will support standard primitives to interface with an unmodified SCN signaling application being transported, and supplements a standard IP transport protocol underneath with functions designed to meet transport requirements for SCN signaling.

Switched Circuit Network (SCN):

The term SCN is used to refer to a network that carries traffic within channelized bearers of pre-defined sizes. Examples include Public Switched Telephone Networks (PSTNs) and Public Land Mobile Networks (PLMNs). Examples of signaling protocols used in SCN include Q.931, SS7 MTP Level 3 and SS7 Application/User parts.

The following are terms for functional entities relating to signaling transport in a distributed gateway model.

Media Gateway (MG):

A MG terminates SCN media streams, packetizes the media data,, if it is not already packetized, and delivers packetized traffic to the packet network. It performs these functions in reverse order for media streams flowing from the packet network to the SCN.

Media Gateway Controller (MGC):

An MGC handles the registration and management of resources at the MG. The MGC may have the ability to authorize resource usage based on local policy. For signaling transport purposes, the MGC serves as a possible termination and origination point for SCN application protocols, such as SS7 ISDN User Part and Q.931/DSS1.

Signaling Gateway (SG):

An SG is a signaling agent that receives/sends SCN native signaling at the edge of the IP network. The SG function may relay, translate or terminate SS7 signaling in an SS7-Internet Gateway. The SG function may also be co-resident with the MG function to process SCN signaling associated with line or trunk terminations controlled by the MG (e.g., signaling backhaul).

The following are terms for physical entities relating to signaling transport in a distributed gateway model:

Media Gateway Unit (MGU)

An MG-Unit is a physical entity that contains the MG function. It may contain other functions, esp. an SG function for handling facility-associated signaling.

Media Gateway Control Unit (MGCU)

An MGC-Unit is a physical entity containing the MGC function.

Signaling Gateway Unit (SGU)

An SG-Unit is a physical entity containing the SG function.

Signaling End Point (SEP):

This is a node in an SS7 network that originates or terminates signaling messages. One example is a central office switch.

Signal Transfer Point (STP):

This is a node in an SS7 network that routes signaling messages based on their destination point code in the SS7 network.

1.3 Scope

Signaling transport provides transparent transport of message-based signaling protocols over IP networks. The scope of this work includes definition of encapsulation methods, end-to-end protocol mechanisms and use of IP capabilities to support the functional and performance requirements for signaling.

Signaling transport shall be used for transporting SCN signaling between a Signaling Gateway Unit and Media Gateway Controller Unit. Signaling transport may also be used for transport of message-based signaling between a Media Gateway Unit and Media Gateway Controller Unit, between dispersed Media Gateway Controller Units, and between two Signaling Gateway Units connecting signaling endpoints or signal transfer points in the SCN.

Signaling transport will be defined in such a way as to support encapsulation and carriage of a variety of SCN protocols. It is defined in such a way as to be independent of any SCN protocol translation functions taking place at the endpoints of the signaling transport, since its function is limited to the transport of the SCN protocol.

Since the function being provided is transparent transport, the following areas are considered outside the scope of the signaling transport work:

- definition of the SCN protocols themselves.
- signaling interworking such as conversion from Channel Associated Signaling (CAS) to message signaling protocols.
- specification of the functions taking place within the SGU or MGU
- in particular, this work does not address whether the SGU provides mediation/interworking, as this is transparent to the transport function.
- similarly, some management and addressing functions taking place within the SGU or MGU are also considered out of scope, such as determination of the destination IP address for signaling, or specific procedures for assessing the performance of the transport session (i.e., testing and proving functions).

2. Signaling Transport Architecture

2.1 Gateway Component Functions

Figure 1 defines a commonly defined functional model that separates out the functions of SG, MGC and MG. This model may be implemented in a number of ways, with functions implemented in separate devices or combined in single physical units.

Where physical separation exists between functional entities, Signaling Transport can be applied to ensure that SCN signaling information is transported between entities with the required functionality and performance.

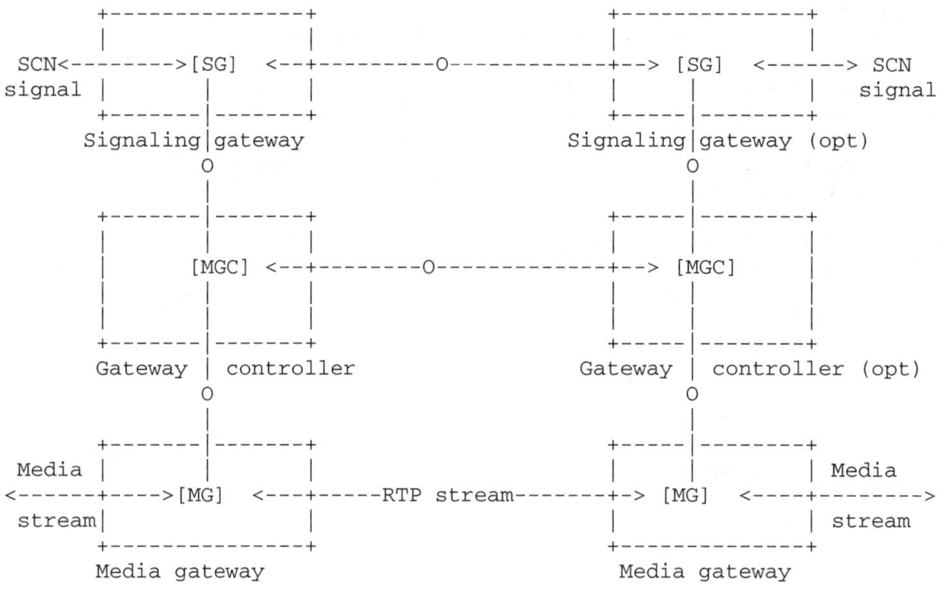

Figure 1: Sigtran Functional Model

As discussed above, the interfaces pertaining to signaling transport include SG to MGC, SG to SG. Signaling transport may potentially be applied to the MGC to MGC or MG to MGC interfaces as well, depending on requirements for transport of the associated signaling protocol.

2.2 SS7 Interworking for Connection Control

Figure 2 below shows some example implementations of these functions in physical entities as used for interworking of SS7 and IP networks for Voice over IP, Voice over ATM, Network Access Servers, etc. No recommendation is made as to functional distribution and many other examples are possible but are not shown to be concise. The use of signaling transport is independent of the implementation.

For interworking with SS7-controlled SCN networks, the SG terminates the SS7 link and transfers the signaling information to the MGC using signaling transport. The MG terminates the interswitch trunk and controls the trunk based on the control signaling it receives from the MGC. As shown below in case (a), the SG, MGC and MG may be implemented in separate physical units, or as in case (b), the MGC and MG may be implemented in a single physical unit.

In alternative case (c), a facility-associated SS7 link is terminated by the same device (i.e., the MGU) that terminates the interswitch trunk. In this case, the SG function is co-located with the MG function, as shown below, and signaling transport is used to "backhaul" control signaling to the MGCU.

Note: SS7 links may also be terminated directly on the MGCU by cross-connecting at the physical level before or at the MGU.

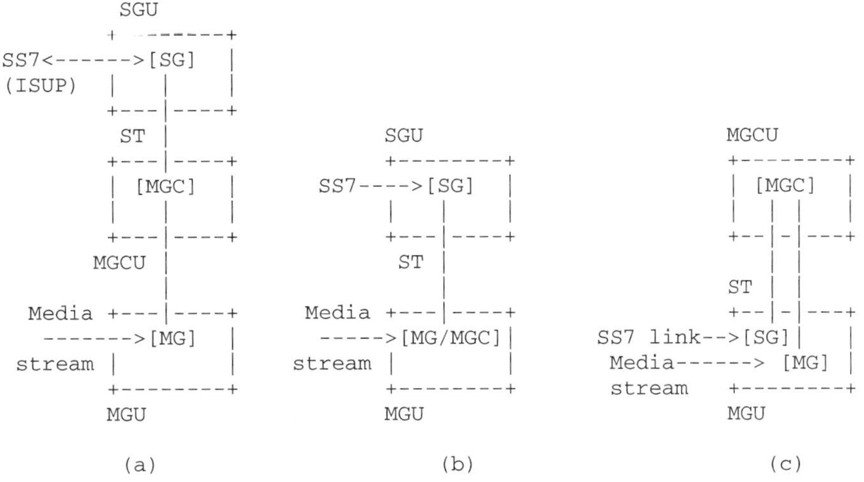

Notes: ST = Signaling Transport used to carry SCN signaling

Figure 2: Example Implementations

RFC 2719 7

In some implementations, the function of the SG may be divided into multiple physical entities to support scaling, signaling network management and addressing concerns. Thus, Signaling Transport can be used between SGs as well as from SG to MGC. This is shown in Figure 3 below.

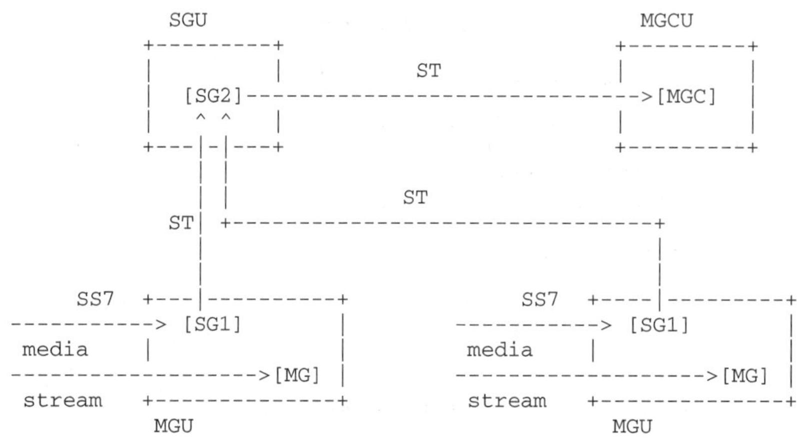

Figure 3: Multiple SG Case

In this configuration, there may be more than one MGU handling facility associated signaling (i.e. more than one containing it's own SG function), and only a single SGU. It will therefore be possible to transport one SS7 layer between SG1 and SG2, and another SS7 layer between SG2 and MGC. For example, SG1 could transport MTP3 to SG2, and SG2 could transport ISUP to MGC.

2.3 ISDN Interworking for Connection Control

In ISDN access signaling, the signaling channel is carried along with data channels, so that the SG function for handling Q.931 signaling is co-located with the MG function for handling the data stream. Where Q.931 is then transported to the MGC for call processing, signaling transport would be used between the SG function and MGC. This is shown in Figure 3 below.

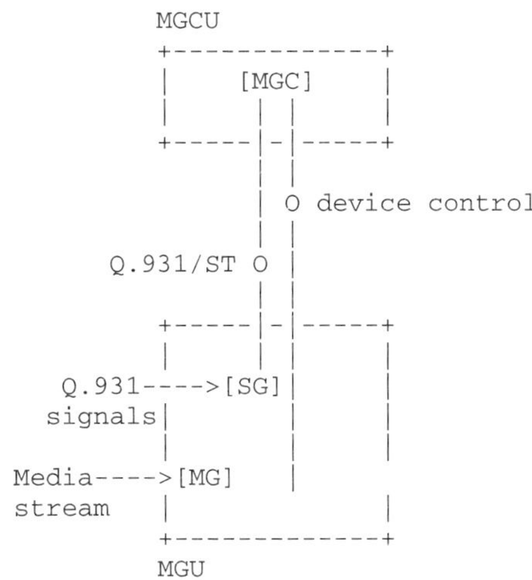

Figure 4: Q.931 transport model

2.4 Architecture for Database Access

Transaction Capabilities (TCAP) is the application part within SS7 that is used for non-circuit-related signaling.

TCAP signaling within IP networks may be used for cross-access between entities in the SS7 domain and the IP domain, such as, for example:

- access from an SS7 network to a Service Control Point (SCP) in IP.
- access from an SS7 network to an MGC.
- access from an MGC to an SS7 network element.
- access from an IP SCP to an SS7 network element.

A basic functional model for TCAP over IP is shown in Figure 5.

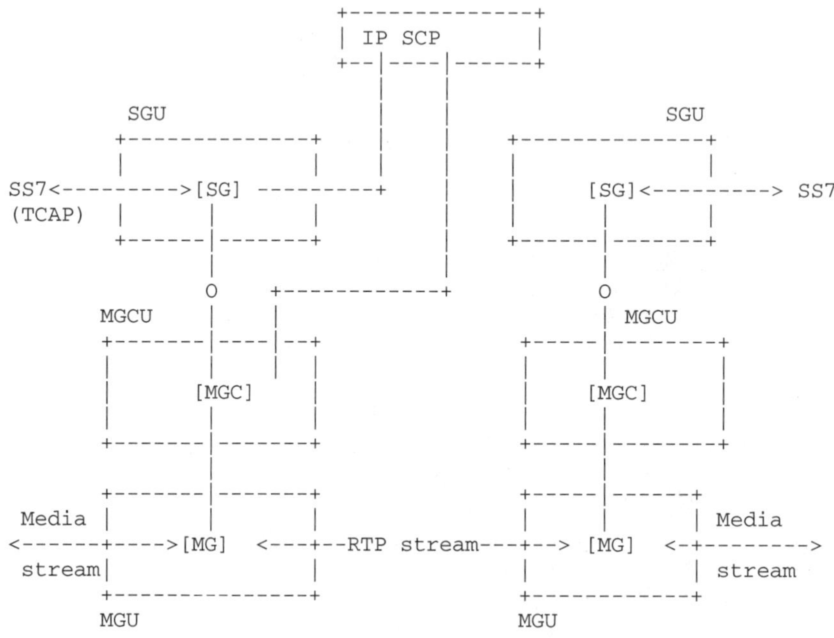

Figure 5: TCAP Signaling over IP

3. Protocol Architecture

This section provides a series of examples of protocol architecture for the use of Signaling Transport (SIG).

3.1 Signaling Transport Components

Signaling Transport in the protocol architecture figures below is assumed to consist of three components (see Figure 6):

1) an adaptation sub-layer that supports specific primitives, e.g., management indications, required by a particular SCN signaling application protocol.
2) a Common Signaling Transport Protocol that supports a common set of reliable transport functions for signaling transport.
3) a standard, unmodified IP transport protocol.

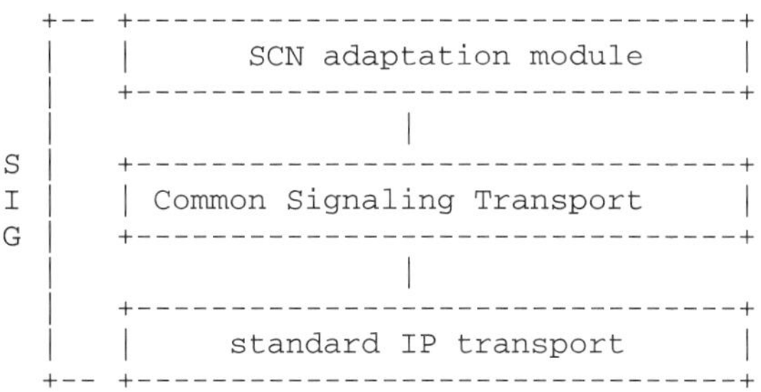

Figure 6: Signaling Transport Components

3.2. SS7 access for Media Gateway Control

This section provides a protocol architecture for signaling transport supporting SS7 access for Media Gateway Control.

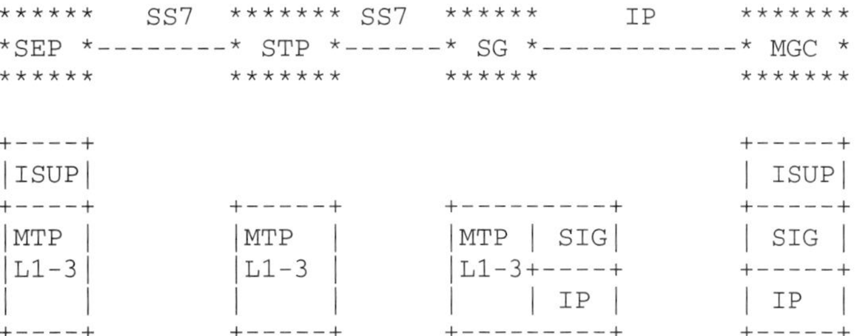

STP - Signal Transfer Point   SEP - Signaling End Point
SG - Signaling Gateway   SIG - Signaling Transport
MGC - Media Gateway Controller

Figure 7: SS7 Access to MGC

3.3. Q.931 Access to MGC

This section provides a protocol architecture for signaling transport supporting ISDN point-to-point access (Q.931) for Media Gateway Control.

```
     ******    ISDN      *********     IP      *******
     * EP *--------------* SG/MG *------------* MGC *
     ******              *********             *******

     +----+                                    +-----+
     |Q931|                                    | Q931|
     +----+              +---------+           +-----+
     |Q921|              |Q921| SIG|           | SIG |
     +    +              +    +----+           +-----+
     |    |              |    | IP |           | IP  |
     +----+              +---------+           +-----+

     MG/SG - Media Gateway with SG function for backhaul
     EP - ISDN End Point
```

Figure 8: ISDN Access

3.4. SS7 Access to IP/SCP

This section provides a protocol architecture for database access, for example providing signaling between two IN nodes or two mobile network nodes. There are a number of scenarios for the protocol stacks and the functionality contained in the SIG, depending on the SS7 application.

In the diagrams, SS7 Application Part (S7AP) is used for generality to cover all Application Parts (e.g. MAP, IS-41, INAP, etc). Depending on the protocol being transported, S7AP may or may not include TCAP. The interface to the SS7 layer below S7AP can be either the TC-user interface or the SCCP-user interface.

Figure 9a shows the scenario where SCCP is the signaling protocol being transported between the SG and an IP Signaling Endpoint (ISEP), that is, an IP destination supporting some SS7 application protocols.

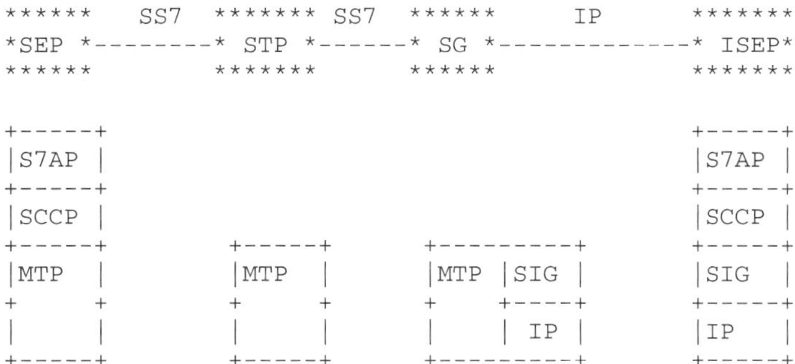

```
******   SS7  ******* SS7  ******     IP      *******
*SEP *--------* STP *------* SG *-------------* ISEP*
******        *******      ******             *******

+-----+                                       +-----+
|S7AP |                                       |S7AP |
+-----+                                       +-----+
|SCCP |                                       |SCCP |
+-----+       +-----+      +----------+       +-----+
|MTP  |       |MTP  |      |MTP |SIG  |       |SIG  |
+     +       +     +      +    +-----+       +-----+
|     |       |     |      |    | IP  |       |IP   |
+-----+       +-----+      +----------+       +-----+
```

Figure 9a: SS7 Access to IP node - SCCP being transported

Figure 9b shows the scenario where S7AP is the signaling protocol being transported between SG and ISEP. Depending on the protocol being transported, S7AP may or may not include TCAP, which implies that SIG must be able to support both the TC-user and the SCCP-user interfaces.

```
******   SS7  ******* SS7  ******     IP      *******
*SEP *--------* STP *------* SG *-------------* ISEP*
******        *******      ******             *******

+-----+                                       +-----+
|S7AP |                                       |S7AP |
+-----+                    +----+-----+       +-----+
|SCCP |                    |SCCP|     |       |     |
+-----+       +-----+      +----|SIG  |       |SIG  |
|MTP  |       |MTP  |      |MTP |     |       |     |
+     +       +     +      +    +-----+       +-----+
|     |       |     |      |    |IP   |       |IP   |
+-----+       +-----+      +----------+       +-----+
```

Figure 9b: SS7 Access to IP node - S7AP being transported

3.5. SG to SG

This section identifies a protocol architecture for support of signaling between two endpoints in an SCN signaling network, using signaling transport directly between two SGs.

The following figure describes protocol architecture for a scenario with two SGs providing different levels of function for interworking of SS7 and IP. This corresponds to the scenario given in Figure 3.

The SS7 User Part (S7UP) shown is an SS7 protocol using MTP directly for transport within the SS7 network, for example, ISUP.

In this scenario, there are two different usage cases of SIG, one which transports MTP3 signaling, the other which transports ISUP signaling.

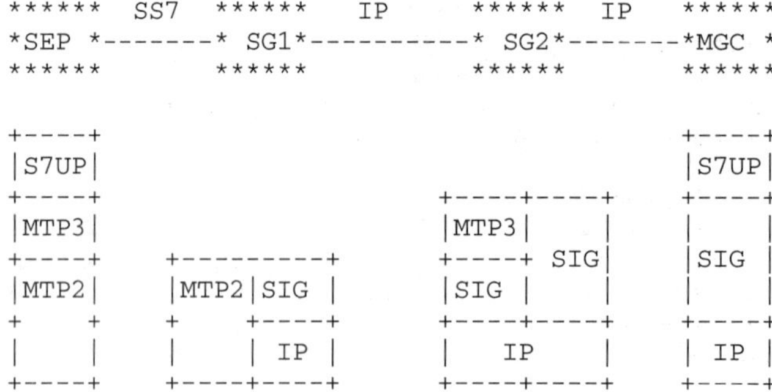

S7UP - SS7 User Part

Figure 10: SG to SG Case 1

The following figure describes a more generic use of SS7-IP interworking for transport of SS7 upper layer signaling across an IP network, where the endpoints are both SS7 SEPs.

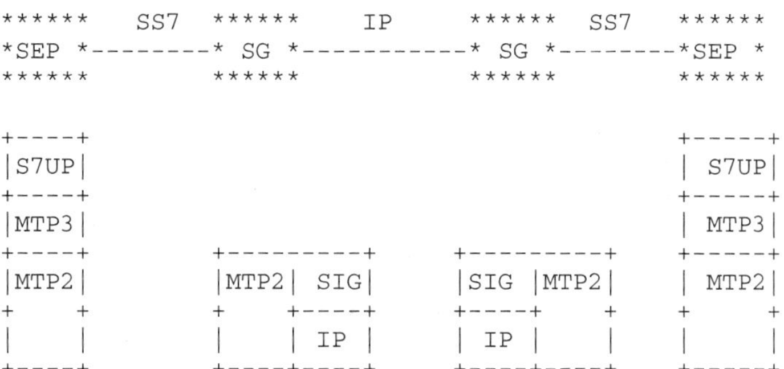

Figure 11: SG to SG Case 2

4. Functional Requirements

4.1 Transport of SCN Signaling Protocols

Signaling transport provides for the transport of native SCN protocol messages over a packet switched network.

Signaling transport shall:

1) Transport of a variety of SCN protocol types, such as the application and user parts of SS7 (including MTP Level 3, ISUP, SCCP, TCAP, MAP, INAP, IS-41, etc.) and layer 3 of the DSS1/PSS1 protocols (i.e. Q.931 and QSIG).

2) Provide a means to identify the particular SCN protocol being transported.

3) Provide a common base protocol defining header formats, security extensions and procedures for signaling transport, and support extensions as necessary to add individual SCN protocols if and when required.

4) In conjunction with the underlying network protocol (IP), provide the relevant functionality as defined by the appropriate SCN lower layer.

Relevant functionality may include (according to the protocol being transported):

- flow control
- in sequence delivery of signaling messages within a control stream

- logical identification of the entities on which the signaling messages originate or terminate
- logical identification of the physical interface controlled by the signaling message
- error detection
- recovery from failure of components in the transit path
- retransmission and other error correcting methods
- detection of unavailability of peer entities.

For example:

- if the native SCN protocol is ISUP or SCCP, the relevant functionality provided by MTP2/3 shall be provided.
- if the native SCN protocol is TCAP, the relevant functionality provided by SCCP connectionless classes and MTP 2/3 shall be supported.
- if the native SCN protocol is Q.931, the relevant functionality provided by Q.921 shall be supported.
- if the native SCN protocol is MTP3, the relevant functionality of MTP2 shall be supported.

5) Support the ability to multiplex several higher layer SCN sessions on one underlying signaling transport session. This allows, for example, several DSS1 D-Channel sessions to be carried in one signaling transport session.

In general, in-sequence delivery is required for signaling messages within a single control stream, but is not necessarily required for messages that belong to different control streams. The protocol should if possible take advantage of this property to avoid blocking delivery of messages in one control stream due to sequence error within another control stream. The protocol should also allow the SG to send different control streams to different destination ports if desired.

6) Be able to transport complete messages of greater length than the underlying SCN segmentation/reassembly limitations. For example, signaling transport should not be constrained by the length limitations defined for SS7 lower layer protocol (e.g. 272 bytes in the case of narrowband SS7) but should be capable of carrying longer messages without requiring segmentation.

7) Allow for a range of suitably robust security schemes to protect signaling information being carried across networks. For example, signaling transport shall be able to operate over proxyable sessions, and be able to be transported through firewalls.

8) Provide for congestion avoidance on the Internet, by supporting appropriate controls on signaling traffic generation (including signaling generated in SCN) and reaction to network congestion.

4.2 Performance of SCN Signaling Protocols

This section provides basic values regarding performance requirements of key SCN protocols to be transported. Currently only message-based SCN protocols are considered. Failure to meet these requirements is likely to result in adverse and undesirable signaling and call behavior.

4.2.1 SS7 MTP requirements

The performance requirements below have been specified for transport of MTP Level 3 network management messages. The requirements given here are only applicable if all MTP Level 3 messages are to be transported over the IP network.

- Message Delay
  - MTP Level 3 peer-to-peer procedures require response within 500 to 1200 ms. This value includes round trip time and processing at the remote end.
    Failure to meet this limitation will result in the initiation of error procedures for specific timers, e.g., timer T4 of ITU-T Recommendation Q.704.

4.2.2 SS7 MTP Level 3 requirements

The performance requirements below have been specified for transport of MTP Level 3 user part messages as part of ITU-T SS7 Recommendations [SS7].

- Message Loss
  - no more than 1 in 10E+7 messages will be lost due to transport failure

- Sequence Error
  - no more than 1 in 10E+10 messages will be delivered out-of-sequence (including duplicated messages) due to transport failure

- Message Errors
  - no more than 1 in 10E+10 messages will contain an error that is undetected by the transport protocol (requirement is 10E+9 for ANSI specifications)

RFC 2719 17

- Availability
  - availability of any signaling route set is 99.9998% or better, i.e., downtime 10 min/year or less. A signaling route set is the complete set of allowed signaling paths from a given signaling point towards a specific destination.

- Message length (payload accepted from SS7 user parts)
  - 272 bytes for narrowband SS7, 4091 bytes for broadband SS7

4.2.3 SS7 User Part Requirements

More detailed analysis of SS7 User Part Requirements can be found in [Lin].

ISUP Message Delay - Protocol Timer Requirements

- one example of ISUP timer requirements is the Continuity Test procedure, which requires that a tone generated at the sending end be returned from the receiving end within 2 seconds of sending an IAM indicating continuity test. This implies that one way signaling message transport, plus accompanying nodal functions need to be accomplished within 2 seconds.

ISUP Message Delay - End-to-End Requirements

- the requirement for end-to-end call setup delay in ISUP is that an end-to-end response message be received within 20-30 seconds of the sending of the IAM. Note: while this is the protocol guard timer value, users will generally expect faster response time.

TCAP Requirements - Delay Requirements

- TCAP does not itself define a set of delay requirements. Some work has been done [Lin2] to identify application-based delay requirements for TCAP applications.

4.2.4 ISDN Signaling Requirements

Q.931 Message Delay

- round-trip delay should not exceed 4 seconds. A Timer of this length is used for a number of procedures, esp. RELASE/RELEASE COMPLETE and CONNECT/CONNECT ACK where excessive delay may result in management action on the channel, or release of a call being set up. Note: while this value is indicated by protocol timer specifications, faster response time is normally expected by the user.

- 12 sec. timer (T309) is used to maintain an active call in case of loss of the data link, pending re-establishment. The related ETSI documents specify a maximum value of 4 seconds while ANSI specifications [T1.607] default to 90 seconds.

5. Management

Operations, Administration & Management (OA&M) of IP networks or SCN networks is outside the scope of SIGTRAN. Examples of OA&M include legacy telephony management systems or IETF SNMP managers. OA&M implementors and users should be aware of the functional interactions of the SG, MGC and MG and the physical units they occupy.

6. Security Considerations

6.1 Security Requirements

When SCN related signaling is transported over an IP network two possible network scenarios can be distinguished:

- Signaling transported only within an Intranet;
  Security measures are applied at the discretion of the network owner.

- Signaling transported, at least to some extent, in the public Internet;
  The public Internet should be regarded generally as an "insecure" network and usage of security measures is required.

Generally security comprises several aspects

- Authentication:
  It is required to ensure that the information is sent to/from a known and trusted partner.

- Integrity:
  It is required to ensure that the information hasn't been modified while in transit.

- Confidentiality:
  It might be sometimes required to ensure that the transported information is encrypted to avoid illegal use.

- Availability:
  It is required that the communicating endpoints remain in service for authorized use even if under attack.

6.2 Security Mechanisms Currently Available in IP Networks

Several security mechanisms are currently available for use in IP networks.

- IPSEC ([RFC2401]):
  IPSEC provides security services at the IP layer that address the above mentioned requirements. It defines the two protocols AH and ESP respectively that essentially provide data integrity and data confidentiality services.

  The ESP mechanism can be used in two different modes:
  - Transport mode;
  - Tunnel mode.

In Transport mode IPSEC protects the higher layer protocol data portion of an IP packet, while in Tunnel mode a complete IP packet is encapsulated in a secure IP tunnel.

If the SIG embeds any IP addresses outside of the SA/DA in the IP header, passage through a NAT function will cause problems. The same is true for using IPsec in general, unless an IPsec ready RSIP function is used as described in RFC 2663 [NAT].

The use of IPSEC does not hamper the use of TCP or UDP as the underlying basis of SIG. If automated distribution of keys is required the IKE protocol ([RFC2409]) can be applied.

- SSL, TLS ([RFC2246]):
  SSL and TLS also provide appropriate security services but operate on top of TCP/IP only.

It is not required to define new security mechanisms in SIG, as the use of currently available mechanisms is sufficient to provide the necessary security. It is recommended that IPSEC or some equivalent method be used, especially when transporting SCN signaling over public Internet.

7. Abbreviations

CAS	Channel-Associated Signaling
DSS1	Digital Subscriber Signaling
INAP	Intelligent Network Application Part
ISEP	IP Signaling End Point
ISUP	Signaling System 7 ISDN User Part
MAP	Mobile Application Part
MG	Media Gateway
MGU	Media Gateway Unit
MGC	Media Gateway Controller
MGCU	Media Gateway Controller Unit
MTP	Signaling System 7 Message Transfer Part
PLMN	Public Land Mobile Network
PSTN	Public Switched Telephone Network
S7AP	SS7 Application Part
S7UP	SS7 User Part
SCCP	SS7 Signaling Connection Control Part
SCN	Switched Circuit Network
SEP	Signaling End Point
SG	Signaling Gateway
SIG	Signaling Transport protocol stack
SS7	Signaling System No. 7
TCAP	Signaling System 7 Transaction Capabilities Part

8. Acknowledgements

The authors would like to thank K. Chong, I. Elliott, Ian Spiers, Al Varney, Goutam Shaw, C. Huitema, Mike McGrew and Greg Sidebottom for their valuable comments and suggestions.

9. References

[NAT] Srisuresh P. and M. Holdrege, "IP Network Address Translator (NAT) Terminology and Considerations", RFC 2663, August 1999.

[PSS1/QSIG] ISO/IEC 11572 Ed. 2 (1997-06), "Information technology - Telecommunications and information exchange between systems - Private Integrated Services Network - Circuit mode bearer services - Inter-exchange signalling procedures and protocol"

[Q.931/DSS1] ITU-T Recommendation Q.931, ISDN user-network interface layer 3 specification (5/98)

[SS7] ITU-T Recommendations Q.700-775, Signalling System No. 7

[SS7 MTP] ITU-T Recommendations Q.701-6, Message Transfer Part of SS7

[T1.607] ANSI T1.607-1998, Digital Subscriber Signaling System Number 1 (DSS1) - Layer 3 Signaling Specification for Circuit-Switched Bearer Services

[Lin] Lin, H., Seth, T., et al., "Performance Requirements for Signaling in Internet Telephony", Work in Progress.

[Lin2] Lin, H., et al., "Performance Requirements for TCAP Signaling in Internet Telephony", Work in Progress.

[RFC2246] Dierks, T. and C. Allen, "The TLS Protocol Version 1.0", RFC 2246, January 1999.

[RFC2409] Harkins, D. and C. Carrel, "The Internet Key Exchange (IKE)", RFC 2409, November 1998.

[RFC2401] Kent, S. and R. Atkinson, "Security Architecture for the Internet Protocol", RFC 2401, November 1998.

Authors' Addresses

Lyndon Ong
Nortel Networks
4401 Great America Parkway
Santa Clara, CA 95054, USA

EMail: long@nortelnetworks.com

Ian Rytina
Ericsson Australia
37/360 Elizabeth Street
Melbourne, Victoria 3000, Australia

EMail: ian.rytina@ericsson.com

Matt Holdrege
Lucent Technologies
1701 Harbor Bay Parkway
Alameda, CA 94502 USA

EMail: holdrege@lucent.com

Lode Coene
Siemens Atea
Atealaan 34
Herentals, Belgium

EMail: lode.coene@siemens.atea.be

Miguel-Angel Garcia
Ericsson Espana
Retama 7
28005 Madrid, Spain

EMail: Miguel.A.Garcia@ericsson.com

Chip Sharp
Cisco Systems
7025 Kit Creek Road
Res Triangle Pk, NC 27709, USA

EMail: chsharp@cisco.com

Imre Juhasz
Telia
Sweden

EMail: imre.i.juhasz@telia.se

Haui-an Paul Lin
Telcordia Technologies
Piscataway, NJ, USA

EMail: hlin@research.telcordia.com

HannsJuergen Schwarzbauer
SIEMENS AG
Hofmannstr. 51
81359 Munich, Germany

EMail: HannsJuergen.Schwarzbauer@icn.siemens.de

Acknowledgement

Funding for the RFC Editor function is currently provided by the Internet Society.

Network Working Group
Request for Comments: 2804
Category: Informational

IAB
IESG
May 2000

IETF Policy on Wiretapping

Status of this Memo

This memo provides information for the Internet community. It does not specify an Internet standard of any kind. Distribution of this memo is unlimited.

Copyright Notice

Abstract

The Internet Engineering Task Force (IETF) has been asked to take a position on the inclusion into IETF standards-track documents of functionality designed to facilitate wiretapping.

This memo explains what the IETF thinks the question means, why its answer is "no", and what that answer means.

1. Summary position

The IETF has decided not to consider requirements for wiretapping as part of the process for creating and maintaining IETF standards.

It takes this position for the following basic reasons:

- The IETF, an international standards body, believes itself to be the wrong forum for designing protocol or equipment features that address needs arising from the laws of individual countries, because these laws vary widely across the areas that IETF standards are deployed in. Bodies whose scope of authority correspond to a single regime of jurisdiction are more appropriate for this task.

- The IETF sets standards for communications that pass across networks that may be owned, operated and maintained by people from numerous jurisdictions with numerous requirements for privacy. In light of these potentially divergent requirements, the IETF believes that the operation of the Internet and the needs of its users are best served by making sure the security properties of connections across the Internet are as well known as possible. At the present stage of our ignorance this means making them as free from security loopholes as possible.

- The IETF believes that in the case of traffic that is today going across the Internet without being protected by the end systems (by encryption or other means), the use of existing network features, if deployed intelligently, provides extensive opportunities for wiretapping, and should be sufficient under presently seen requirements for many cases. The IETF does not see an engineering solution that allows such wiretapping when the end systems take adequate measures to protect their communications.

- The IETF believes that adding a requirement for wiretapping will make affected protocol designs considerably more complex. Experience has shown that complexity almost inevitably jeopardizes the security of communications even when it is not being tapped by any legal means; there are also obvious risks raised by having to protect the access to the wiretap. This is in conflict with the goal of freedom from security loopholes.

- The IETF restates its strongly held belief, stated at greater length in [RFC 1984], that both commercial development of the Internet and adequate privacy for its users against illegal intrusion requires the wide availability of strong cryptographic technology.

- On the other hand, the IETF believes that mechanisms designed to facilitate or enable wiretapping, or methods of using other facilities for such purposes, should be openly described, so as to ensure the maximum review of the mechanisms and ensure that they adhere as closely as possible to their design constraints. The IETF believes that the publication of such mechanisms, and the publication of known weaknesses in such mechanisms, is a Good Thing.

2. The Raven process

The issue of the IETF doing work on legal intercept technologies came up as a byproduct of the extensive work that the IETF is now doing in the area if IP-based telephony.

In the telephony world, there has been a tradition of cooperation (often mandated by law) between law enforcement agencies and telephone equipment operators on wiretapping, leading to companies that build telephone equipment adding wiretapping features to their telephony-related equipment, and an emerging consensus in the industry of how to build and manage such features. Some traditional telephony standards organizations have supported this by adding intercept features to their telephony-related standards.

Since the future of the telephone seems to be intertwined with the Internet it is inevitable that the primary Internet standards organization would be faced with the issue sooner or later.

In this case, some of the participants of one of the IETF working groups working on a new standard for communication between components of a distributed phone switch brought up the issue. Since adding features of this type would be something the IETF had never done before, the IETF management decided to have a public discussion before deciding if the working group should go ahead. A new mailing list was created (the Raven mailing list, see http://www.ietf.org/mailman/listinfo/raven) for this discussion. Close to 500 people subscribed to the list and about 10% of those sent at least one message to the list. The discussion on this list was a precursor to a discussion held during the IETF plenary in Washington, D.C.

Twenty-nine people spoke during the plenary session. Opinions ranged from libertarian: 'governments have no right to wiretap' - to pragmatic: 'it will be done somewhere, best have it done where the technology was developed'. At the end of the discussion there was a show of hands to indicate opinions: should the IETF add special features, not do this or abstain. Very few people spoke out strongly in support for adding the intercept features, while many spoke out against it, but a sizable portion of the audience refused to state an opinion (raised their hands when asked for "abstain" in the show of hands).

This is the background on the basis of which the Internet Engineering Steering Group (IESG) and the Internet Architecture Board (IAB) was asked to formulate a policy.

3. A definition of wiretapping

The various legal statutes defining wiretapping do not give adequate definitions to distinguish between wiretapping and various other activities at the technical level. For the purposes of this memo, the following definition of wiretapping is used:

Wiretapping is what occurs when information passed across the Internet from one party to one or more other parties is delivered to a third party:

1. Without the sending party knowing about the third party

2. Without any of the recipient parties knowing about the delivery to the third party

3. When the normal expectation of the sender is that the transmitted information will only be seen by the recipient parties or parties obliged to keep the information in confidence

4. When the third party acts deliberately to target the transmission of the first party, either because he is of interest, or because the second party's reception is of interest.

The term "party", as used here, can refer to one person, a group of persons, or equipment acting on behalf of persons; the term "party" is used for brevity.

Of course, many wiretaps will be bidirectional, monitoring traffic sent by two or more parties to each other.

Thus, for instance, monitoring public newsgroups is not wiretapping (condition 3 violated), random monitoring of a large population is not wiretapping (condition 4 violated), a recipient passing on private email is not wiretapping (condition 2 violated).

An Internet equivalent of call tracing by means of accounting logs (sometimes called "pen registers") that is a feature of the telephone network is also wiretapping by this definition, since the normal expectation of the sender is that the company doing the accounting will keep this information in confidence.

Wiretapping may logically be thought of as 3 distinct steps:

- Capture - getting information off the wire that contains the information wanted.

- Filtering - selecting the information wanted from information gathered by accident.

- Delivery - transmitting the information wanted to the ones who want it.

The term applies to the whole process; for instance, random monitoring followed by filtering to extract information about a smaller group of parties would be wiretapping by this definition.

In all these stages, the possibility of using or abusing mechanisms defined for this purpose for other purposes exists.

This definition deliberately does not include considerations of:

- Whether the wiretap is legal or not, since that is a legal, not a technical matter.

- Whether the wiretap occurs in real time, or can be performed after the fact by looking at information recorded for other purposes (such as the accounting example given above).

- What the medium targeted by the wiretap is - whether it is email, IP telephony, Web browsing or EDI transfers.

These questions are believed to be irrelevant to the policy outlined in this memo.

Wiretapping is also sometimes called "interception", but that term is also used in a sense that is considerably wider than the monitoring of data crossing networks, and is therefore not used here.

4. Why the IETF does not take a moral position

Much of the debate about wiretapping has centered around the question of whether wiretapping is morally evil, no matter who does it, necessary in any civilized society, or an effective tool for catching criminals that has been abused in the past and will be abused again.

The IETF has decided not to take a position in this matter, since:

- There is no clear consensus around a single position in the IETF.

- There is no means of detecting the morality of an act "on the wire". Since the IETF deals with protocol standardization, not protocol deployment, it is not in a position to dictate that its product is only used in moral or legal ways.

However, a few observations can be made:

- Experience shows that tools which are effective for a purpose tend to be used for that purpose.

- Experience shows that tools designed for one purpose that are effective for another tend to be used for that other purpose too, no matter what its designers intended.

- Experience shows that if a vulnerability exists in a security system, it is likely that someone will take advantage of it sooner or later.

- Experience shows that human factors, not technology per se, is the biggest single source of such vulnerabilities.

What this boils down to is that if effective tools for wiretapping exist, it is likely that they will be used as designed, for purposes legal in their jurisdiction, and also in ways they were not intended for, in ways that are not legal in that jurisdiction. When weighing the development or deployment of such tools, this should be borne in mind.

5. Utility considerations

When designing any communications function, it is a relevant question to ask if such functions efficiently perform the task they are designed for, or whether the work spent in developing them is not, in fact, worth the benefit gained.

Given that there are no specific proposals being developed in the IETF, the IETF cannot weigh proposals for wiretapping directly in this manner.

However, as above, a few general observations can be made:

- Wiretapping by copying the bytes passed between two users of the Internet with known, static points of attachment is not hard. Standard functions designed for diagnostic purposes can accomplish this.

- Correlating users' identities with their points of attachment to the Internet can be significantly harder, but not impossible, if the user uses standard means of identification. However, this means linking into multiple Internet subsystems used for address assignment, name resolution and so on; this is not trivial.

- An adversary has several simple countermeasures available to defeat wiretapping attempts, even without resorting to encryption. This includes Internet cafes and anonymous dialups, anonymous remailers, multi-hop login sessions and use of obscure communications media; these are well known tools in the cracker community.

- Of course, communications where the content is protected by strong encryption can be easily recorded, but the content is still not available to the wiretapper, defeating all information gathering apart from traffic analysis. Since Internet data is already in digital form, encrypting it is very simple for the end-user.

These things taken together mean that while wiretapping is an efficient tool for use in situations where the target of a wiretap is either ignorant or believes himself innocent of wrongdoing, Internet-based wiretapping is a less useful tool than might be imagined against an alerted and technically competent adversary.

6. Security Considerations

Wiretapping, by definition (see above), releases information that the information sender did not expect to be released.

This means that a system that allows wiretapping has to contain a function that can be exercised without alerting the information sender to the fact that his desires for privacy are not being met.

This, in turn, means that one has to design the system in such a way that it cannot guarantee any level of privacy; at the maximum, it can only guarantee it as long as the function for wiretapping is not exercised.

For instance, encrypted telephone conferences have to be designed in such a way that the participants cannot know to whom any shared keying material is being revealed.

This means:

- The system is less secure than it could be had this function not been present.

- The system is more complex than it could be had this function not been present.

- Being more complex, the risk of unintended security flaws in the system is larger.

Wiretapping, even when it is not being exercised, therefore lowers the security of the system.

7. Acknowledgements

This memo is endorsed by the IAB and the IESG.

Their membership is:

IAB:

Harald Alvestrand
Randall Atkinson
Rob Austein
Brian Carpenter
Steve Bellovin
Jon Crowcroft
Steve Deering
Ned Freed
Tony Hain
Tim Howes
Geoff Huston
John Klensin

IESG:

Fred Baker
Keith Moore
Patrik Falstrom
Erik Nordmark
Thomas Narten
Randy Bush
Bert Wijnen
Rob Coltun
Dave Oran
Jeff Schiller
Marcus Leech
Scott Bradner
Vern Paxson
April Marine

The number of contributors to the discussion are too numerous to list.

8. Author's Address

This memo is authored by the IAB and the IESG.

The chairs are:

Fred Baker, IETF Chair
519 Lado Drive
Santa Barbara California 93111

Phone: +1-408-526-4257
EMail: fred@cisco.com

Brian E. Carpenter, IAB Chair
IBM
c/o iCAIR
Suite 150
1890 Maple Avenue
Evanston IL 60201
USA

EMail: brian@icair.org

9. References

[RFC 1984] IAB and IESG, "IAB and IESG Statement on Cryptographic Technology and the Internet", RFC 1984, August 1996.

9. Full Copyright Statement

Acknowledgement

Funding for the RFC Editor function is currently provided by the Internet Society.

Network Working Group
Request for Comments: 2805
Category: Informational

N. Greene
Nortel Networks
M. Ramalho
Cisco Systems
B. Rosen
Marconi
April 2000

Media Gateway Control Protocol Architecture and Requirements

Status of this Memo

This memo provides information for the Internet community. It does not specify an Internet standard of any kind. Distribution of this memo is unlimited.

Copyright Notice

Abstract

This document describes protocol requirements for the Media Gateway Control Protocol between a Media Gateway Controller and a Media Gateway.

Table of Contents

1. Introduction

This document describes requirements to be placed on the Media Gateway Control Protocol. When the word protocol is used on its own in this document it implicitly means the Media Gateway Control Protocol.

2. Terminology

In this document, the key words "MUST", "MUST NOT", "REQUIRED", "SHALL", "SHALL NOT", "SHOULD", "SHOULD NOT", "RECOMMENDED", "MAY", and "OPTIONAL" are to be interpreted as described in RFC 2119 [1] and indicate requirement levels for the protocol.

3. Definitions

* Connection

Under the control of a Media Gateway Controller (MGC), the Media Gateway (MG) realizes connections. In this document, connections are associations of resources hosted by the MG. They typically involve two terminations, but may involve more.

* Line or Loop

An analogue or digital access connection from a user terminal which carries user media content and telephony access signalling (DP, DTMF, BRI, proprietary business set).

* Media Gateway (MG) function

A Media Gateway (MG) function provides the media mapping and/or transcoding functions between potentially dissimilar networks, one of which is presumed to be a packet, frame or cell network. For example, an MG might terminate switched circuit network (SCN) facilities (trunks, loops), packetize the media stream, if it is not already packetized, and deliver packetized traffic to a packet network. It would perform these functions in the reverse order for media streams flowing from the packet network to the SCN.

Media Gateways are not limited to SCN <-> packet/frame/cell functions: A conference bridge with all packet interfaces could be an MG, as well as an (IVR) interactive voice recognition unit, an audio resource function, or a voice recognition system with a cell interface.

* Media Gateway unit (MG-unit)

An MG-unit is a physical entity that contains an MG function and may also contain other functions, e.g. an SG function.

* Media Gateway Controller (MGC) function

A Media Gateway Controller (MGC) function controls a MG.

* Media Resource

Examples of media resources are codecs, announcements, tones, and modems, interactive voice response (IVR) units, bridges, etc.

* Signaling Gateway (SG) function

An SG function receives/sends SCN native signalling at the edge of a data network. For example the SG function may relay, translate or terminate SS7 signaling in an SS7-Internet Gateway. The SG function may also be co-resident with the MG function to process SCN signalling associated with line or trunk terminations controlled by the MG, such as the "D" channel of an ISDN PRI trunk.

* Termination

A termination is a point of entry and/or exit of media flows relative to the MG. When an MG is asked to connect two or more terminations, it understands how the flows entering and leaving each termination are related to each other.

Terminations are, for instance, DS0's, ATM VCs and RTP ports. Another word for this is bearer point.

* Trunk

An analog or digital connection from a circuit switch which carries user media content and may carry telephony signalling (MF, R2, etc.). Digital trunks may be transported and may appear at the Media Gateway as channels within a framed bit stream, or as an ATM cell stream. Trunks are typically provisioned in groups, each member of which provides equivalent routing and service.

* Type of Bearer

A Type of Bearer definition provides the detailed requirements for its particular application/bearer type. A particular class of Media Gateway, for example, would support a particular set of Bearer types.

4. Specific functions assumed within the MG

This section provides an environment for the definition of the general Media Gateway Control Protocol requirements.

MGs can be architected in many different ways depending where the media conversions and transcoding (if required) are performed, the level of programmability of resources, how conferences are supported, and how associated signalling is treated. The functions assumed to be within the MG must not be biased towards a particular architecture.

For instance, announcements in a MG could be provided by media resources or by the bearer point resource or termination itself. Further, this difference must not be visible to MGC: The MGC must be able to issue the identical request to two different implementations and achieve the identical functionality.

Depending on the application of the MG (e.g., trunking, residential), some functions listed below will be more prominent than others, and in some cases, functions may even disappear.

Although media adaptation is the essence of the MG, it is not necessary for it to be involved every time. An MG may join two terminations/resources of the same type (i.e., the MG behaves as a switch). The required media conversion depends on the media type supported by the resources being joined together.

In addition to media adaptation function, resources have a number of unique properties, for instance:

* certain types of resources have associated signalling capabilities (e.g., PRI signalling, DTMF),

* some resources perform maintenance functions (e.g., continuity tests),

* the MGC needs to know the state changes of resources (e.g., a trunk group going out of service),

* the MG retains some control over the allocation and control of some resources (e.g., resource name space: RTP port numbers).

Therefore, an MG realizes point-to-point connections and conferences, and supports several resource functions. These functions include media conversion, resource allocation and management, and event notifications. Handling termination associated signalling is either done using event notifications, or is handled by the signalling backhaul part of a MG-unit (i.e. NOT directly handled by the MG).

MGs must also support some level of system related functions, such as establishing and maintaining some kind of MG-MGC association. This is essential for MGC redundancy, fail-over and resource sharing.

Therefore, an MG is assumed to contain these functions:

* Reservation and release, of resources

* Ability to provide state of resources

* Maintenance of resources - It must be possible to make maintenance operations independent of other termination functions, for instance, some maintenance states should not affect the resources associated with that resource . Examples of maintenance functions are loopbacks and continuity tests.

* Connection management, including connection state.

* Media processing, using media resources: these provide services such as transcoding, conferencing, interactive voice recognition units, audio resource function units. Media resources may or may not be directly part of other resources.

* Incoming digit analysis for terminations, interpretation of scripts for terminations

* Event detection and signal insertion for per-channel signalling

* Ability to configure signalling backhauls (for example, a Sigtran backhaul)

* Management of the association between the MGC and MG, or between the MGC and MG resources.

5. Per-Call Requirements

5.1. Resource Reservation

The protocol must:

a. Support reservation of bearer terminations and media resources for use by a particular call and support their subsequent release (which may be implicit or explicit).

b. Allow release in a single exchange of messages, of all resources associated with a particular set of connectivity and/or associations between a given number terminations.

c. The MG is not required (or allowed) by the protocol to maintain a sense of future time: a reservation remains in effect until explicitly released by the MGC.

5.2. Connection Requirements

The protocol must:

a. Support connections involving packet and circuit bearer terminations in any combination, including "hairpin" connections (connections between two circuit connections within the same MG).

b. Support connections involving TDM, Analogue, ATM, IP or FR transport in any combination.

c. Allow the specification of bearer plane (e.g. Frame Relay, IP, etc.) on a call by call basis.

d. Support unidirectional, symmetric bi-directional, and asymmetric bi-directional flows of media.

e. Support multiple media types (e.g. audio, text, video, T.120).

f. Support point-to-point and point-to-multipoint connections.

g. Support creation and modification of more complex flow topologies e.g. conference bridge capabilities. Be able to add or delete media streams during a call or session, and be able to add or subtract participants to/from a call or session.

h. Support inclusion of media resources into call or session as required. Depending on the protocol and resource type, media resources may be implicitly included, class-assigned, or individually assigned.

i. Provide unambiguous specification of which media flows pass through a point and which are blocked at a given point in time, if the protocol permits multiple flows to pass through the same point.

j. Allow modifications of an existing termination, for example, use of higher compression to compensate for insufficient bandwidth or changing transport network connections.

k. Allow the MGC to specify that a given connection has higher priority than other connections.

l. Allow a reference to a port/termination on the MG to be a logical identifier,

with a one-to-one mapping between a logical identifier and a physical port.

m. Allow the MG to report events such as resource reservation and connection completion.

5.3. Media Transformations

The Protocol must:

a. Support mediation/adaptation of flows between different types of transport

b. Support invocation of additional processing such as echo cancellation.

c. Support mediation of flows between different content encoding (codecs, encryption/decryption)

d. Allow the MGC to specify whether text telephony/FAX/data modem traffic is to be terminated at the MG, modulated/demodulated, and converted to packets or forwarded by the MG in the media flow as voice band traffic.

e. Allow the MGC to specify that Dual-Tone MultiFrequency (DTMF) digits or other line and trunk signals and general Multi-Frequency (MF) tones are to be processed in the MG and how these digits/signals/tones are to be handled. The MGC must be able to specify any of the following handling of such digits/signals/tones:

1. The digits/signals/tones are to be encoded normally in the audio RTP stream (e.g., no analysis of the digits/signals/tones).

2. Analyzed and sent to the MGC.

3. Received from the MGC and inserted in the line-side audio stream.

4. Analyzed and sent as part of a separate RTP stream (e.g., DTMF digits sent via a RTP payload separate from the audio RTP stream).

5. Taken from a separate RTP stream and inserted in the line-side audio stream.

6. Handled according to a script of instructions. For all but the first case, an option to mute the digits/signals/tones with silence, comfort noise, or other means (e.g., notch filtering of some telephony tones) must be provided. As detection of these events may take up to tens of milliseconds, the first few milliseconds of such digit/signal/tone may be encoded and sent in the audio RTP stream before the digit/signal/tone can be verified. Therefore muting of such digits/signals/tones in the audio RTP stream with silence or comfort noise is understood to occur at the earliest opportunity after the digit/signal/tone is verified.

f. Allow the MGC to specify signalled flow characteristics on circuit as well as on packet bearer connections, e.g. u-law/a-law.

g. Allow for packet/cell transport adaptation only (no media adaptation) e.g. mid-stream (packet-to-packet) transpacketization/transcoding, or ATM AAL5 to and from ATM AAL2 adaptation.

h. Allow the transport of audio normalization levels as a setup parameter, e.g., for conference bridging.

i. Allow conversion to take place between media types e.g., text to speech and speech to text.

5.4. Signal/Event Processing and Scripting

The Protocol must:

a. Allow the MGC to enable/disable monitoring for specific supervision events at specific circuit terminations

b. Allow the MGC to enable/disable monitoring for specific events within specified media streams

c. Allow reporting of detected events on the MG to the MGC. The protocol should provide the means to minimize the messaging required to report commonly-occurring event sequences.

d. Allow the MGC to specify other actions (besides reporting) that the MG should take upon detection of specified events.

e. Allow the MGC to enable and/or mask events.

f. Provide a way for MGC to positively acknowledge event notification.

g. Allow the MGC to specify signals (e.g., supervision, ringing) to be applied at circuit terminations.

h. Allow the MGC to specify content of extended duration (announcements, continuous tones) to be inserted into specified media flows.

i. Allow the MGC to specify alternative conditions (detection of specific events, timeouts) under which the insertion of extended-duration signals should cease.

j. Allow the MGC to download, and specify a script to be invoked on the occurrence of an event.

k. Specify common events and signals to maximize MG/MGC interworking.

l. Provide an extension mechanism for implementation defined events and signals with, for example, IANA registration procedures. It may be useful to have an Organizational Identifier (i.e. ITU, ETSI, ANSI,) as part of the registration mechanism.

m. The protocol shall allow the MGC to request the arming of a mid-call trigger even after the call has been set up.

5.5. QoS/CoS

The Protocol must:

a. Support the establishment of a bearer channel with a specified QoS/CoS.

b. Support the ability to specify QoS for the connection between MGs, and by direction.

c. Support a means to change QoS during a connection, as a whole and by direction.

d. Allow the MGC to set QOS thresholds and receive notification when such thresholds cannot be maintained.

e. Allow the jitter buffer parameters on RTP channels to be specified at connection setup.

5.6. Test Support

The protocol must:

a. Support of the different types of PSTN Continuity Testing (COT) for both the originating and terminating ends of the circuit connection (2-wire and 4- wire).

b. Specifically support test line operation (e.g. 103, 105, 108).

5.7. Accounting

The protocol must:

a. Support a common identifier to mark resources related to one connection.

b. Support collection of specified accounting information from MGs.

c. Provide the mechanism for the MGC to specify that the MG report accounting information automatically at end of call, in mid-call upon request, at specific time intervals as specified by the MGC and at unit usage thresholds as specified by the MGC.

d. Specifically support collection of:

* start and stop time, by media flow,

* volume of content carried (e.g. number of packets/cells transmitted, number received with and without error, inter-arrival jitter), by media flow,

* QOS statistics, by media flow.

e. Allow the MGC to have some control over which statistics are reported, to enable it to manage the amount of information transferred.

5.8. Signalling Control

Establishment and provisioning of signalling backhaul channels (via SIGTRAN for example) is out of scope. However, the MG must be capable of supporting detection of events, and application of signals associated with basic analogue line, and CAS type signalling. The protocol must:

a. Support the signalling requirements of analogue lines and Channel Associated Signaling (CAS).

b. Support national variations of such signalling.

c. Provide mechanisms to support signalling without requiring MG-MGC timing constraints beyond that specified in this document.

d. Must not create a situation where the MGC and the MG must be homologated together as a mandatory requirement of using the protocol;

i.e. it must be possible to optionally conceal signaling type variation from the MGC.

6. Resource Control

6.1. Resource Status Management

The protocol must:

a. Allow the MG to report changes in status of physical entities supporting bearer terminations, media resources, and facility-associated signalling channels, due to failures, recovery, or administrative action. It must be able to report whether a termination is in service or out of service.

b. Support administrative blocking and release of TDM circuit terminations.

Note: as the above point only relates to ISUP-controlled circuits, it may be unnecessary to require this since the MGC controls their use. However, it may be meaningful for MF and R2-signalled trunks, where supervisory states are set to make the trunks unavailable at the far end.

c. Provide a method for the MGC to request that the MG release all resources under the control of a particular MGC currently in use, or reserved, for any or all connections.

d. Provide an MG Resource Discovery mechanism which must allow an MGC to discover what resources the MG has. Expressing resources can be an arbitrarily difficult problem and the initial release of the protocol may have a simplistic view of resource discovery.

At a minimum, resource discovery must enumerate the names of available circuit terminations and the allowed values for parameters supported by terminations.

The protocol should be defined so that simple gateways could respond with a relatively short, pre-stored response to the discovery request mechanism. In general, if the protocol defines a mechanism that allows the MGC to specify a setting or parameter for a resource or connection in the MG, and MGs are not required to support all possible values for that setting or parameter, then the discovery mechanism should provide the MGC with a method to determine what possible values such settings or parameters are supported in a particular MG.

e. Provide a mechanism to discover the current available resources in the MG, where resources are dynamically consumed by connections and the MGC cannot reasonably or reliably track the consumption of such resources. It should also be possible to discover resources currently in use, in order to reconcile inconsistencies between the MGC and the MG.

f. Not require an MGC to implement an SNMP manager function in order to discover capabilities of an MG that may be specified during context establishment.

6.2. Resource Assignment

The protocol must:

a. Provide a way for the MG to indicate that it was unable to perform a requested action because of resource exhaustion, or because of temporary resource unavailability.

b. Provide an ability for the MGC to indicate to an MG the resource to use for a call (e.g. DS0) exactly, or indicate a set of resources (e.g. pick a DS0 on a T1 line or a list of codec types) via a "wild card" mechanism from which the MG can select a specific resource for a call (e.g. the 16th timeslot, or G.723).

c. Allow the use of DNS names and IP addresses to identify MGs and MGCs. This shall not preclude using other identifiers for MGs or MGCs when other non IP transport technologies for the protocol are used.

7. Operational/Management Requirements

7.1. Assurance of Control/Connectivity

To provide assurance of control and connectivity, the protocol must provide the means to minimize duration of loss of control due to loss of contact, or state mismatches.

The protocol must:

a. Support detection and recovery from loss of contact due to failure/congestion of communication links or due to MG or MGC failure.

Note that failover arrangements are one of the mechanisms which could be used to meet this requirement.

b. Support detection and recovery from loss of synchronized view of resource and connection states between MGCs and MGs. (e.g. through the use of audits).

c. Provide a means for MGC and MG to provide each other with booting and reboot indications, and what the MG's configuration is.

d. Permit more than one backup MGC and provide an orderly way for the MG to contact one of its backups.

e. Provide for an orderly switchback to the primary MGC after it recovers. How MGCs coordinate resources between themselves is outside the scope of the protocol.

f. Provide a mechanism so that when an MGC fails, connections already established can be maintained. The protocol does not have to provide a capability to maintain connections in the process of being connected, but not actually connected when the failure occurs.

g. The Protocol must allow the recovery or redistribution of traffic without call loss.

7.2. Error Control

The protocol must:

a. Allow for the MG to report reasons for abnormal failure of lower layer connections e.g. TDM circuit failure, ATM VCC failure.

b. Allow for the MG to report Usage Parameter Control (UPC) events.

c. Provide means to ameliorate potential synchronization or focused overload of supervisory/signaling events that can be detrimental to either MG or MGC operation. Power restoration or signaling transport re-establishment are typical sources of potentially detrimental signaling showers from MG to MGC or vice-versa.

d. Allow the MG to notify the MGC that a termination was terminated and communicate a reason when a terminations is taken out-of-service unilaterally by the MG due to abnormal events.

e. Allow the MGC to acknowledge that a termination has been taken out-of-service.

f. Allow the MG to request the MGC to release a termination and communicate a reason.

g. Allow the MGC to specify, as a result of such a request its decision to take termination down, leave it as is or modify it.

7.3. MIB Requirements

The Protocol must define a common MG MIB, which must be extensible, but must:

a. Provide information on:

* mapping between resources and supporting physical entities.

* statistics on quality of service on the control and signalling backhaul interfaces.

* statistics required for traffic engineering within the MG.

b. The protocol must allow the MG to provide to the MGC all information the MGC needs to provide in its MIB.

c. MG MIB must support implementation of H.341 by either the MG, MGC, or both acting together.

8. General Protocol Requirements

The protocol must:

a. Support multiple operations to be invoked in one message and treated as a single transaction.

b. Be both modular and extensible. Not all implementations may wish to support all of the possible extensions for the protocol. This will permit lightweight implementations for specialized tasks where processing resources are constrained. This could be accomplished by defining particular profiles for particular uses of the protocol.

c. Be flexible in allocation of intelligence between MG and MGC. For example, an MGC may want to allow the MG to assign particular MG resources in some implementations, while in others, the MGC may want to be the one to assign MG resources for use.

d. Support scalability from very small to very large MGs: The protocol must support MGs with capacities ranging from one to millions of terminations.

e. Support scalability from very small to very large MGC span of control: The protocol should support MGCs that control from one MG to a few tens of thousands of MGs.

f. Support the needs of a residential gateway that supports one to a few lines, and the needs of a large PSTN gateway supporting tens of thousands of lines. Protocol mechanisms favoring one extreme or the other should be minimized in favor of more general purpose mechanism applicable to a wide range of MGs. Where special purpose mechanisms are proposed to optimize a subset of implementations, such mechanisms should be defined as optional, and should have minimal impact on the rest of the protocol.

g. Facilitate MG and MGC version upgrades independently of one another. The protocol must include a version identifier in the initial message exchange.

h. Facilitate the discovery of the protocol capabilities of the one entity to the other.

i. Specify commands as optional (they can be ignored) or mandatory (the command must be rejected), and within a command, to specify parameters as optional (they can be ignored) or mandatory (the command must be rejected).

8.1. MG-MGC Association Requirements

The Protocol must:

a. Support the establishment of a control relationship between an MGC and an MG.

b. Allow multiple MGCs to send control messages to an MG. Thus, the protocol must allow control messages from multiple signalling addresses to a single MG.

c. Provide a method for the MG to tell an MGC that the MG received a command for a resource that is under the control of a different MGC.

d. Support a method for the MG to control the rate of requests it receives from the MGC (e.g. windowing techniques, exponential back-off).

e. Support a method for the MG to tell an MGC that it cannot handle any more requests.

8.2. Performance Requirements

The protocol must:

a. Minimize message exchanges between MG and MGC, for example during boot/reboot, and during continuity tests.

b. Support Continuity test constraints which are a maximum of 200ms cross-MGC IAM (IAM is the name given to an SS7 connection setup msg) propagation delay, and a maximum of 200ms from end of dialing to IAM emission.

c. Make efficient use of the underlying transport mechanism. For example, protocol PDU sizes vs. transport MTU sizes needs to be considered in designing the protocol.

d. Not contain inherent architectural or signaling constraints that would prohibit peak calling rates on the order of 140 calls/second on a moderately loaded network.

e. Allow for default/provisioned settings so that commands need only contain non-default parameters.

9. Transport

9.1. Assumptions made for underlying network

The protocol must assume that the underlying network:

a. May be over large shared networks: proximity assumptions are not allowed.

b. Does not assure reliable delivery of messages.

c. Does not guarantee ordering of messages: Sequenced delivery of messages associated with the same source of events is not assumed.

d. Does not prevent duplicate transmissions.

9.2. Transport Requirements

The protocol must:

a. Provide the ability to abort delivery of obsolete messages at the sending end if their transmission has not been successfully completed. For example, aborting a command that has been overtaken by events.

b. Support priority messages: The protocol shall allow a command precedence to allow priority messages to supercede non-priority messages.

c. Support of large fan-out at the MGC.

d. Provide a way for one entity to correlate commands and responses with the other entity.

e. Provide a reason for any command failure.

f. Provide that loss of a packet not stall messages not related to the message(s) contained in the packet lost.

Note that there may be enough protocol reliability requirements here to warrant a separate reliable transport layer be written apart from the Media Gateway Control Protocol. Also need to compare Megaco reliable transport requirements with similar Sigtran requirements.

10. Security Requirements

Security mechanisms may be specified as provided in underlying transport mechanisms, such as IPSEC. The protocol, or such mechanisms, must:

a. Allow for mutual authentication at the start of an MGC-MG association

b. Allow for preservation of the of control messages once the association has been established.

c. Allow for optional confidentiality protection of control messages. The mechanism should allow a choice in the algorithm to be used.

d. Operate across untrusted domains in a secure fashion.

e. Support non-repudiation for a customer-located MG talking to a network operator's MGC.

f. Define mechanisms to mitigate denial of service attacks

Note: the protocol document will need to include an extended discussion of security requirements, offering more precision on each threat and giving a complete picture of the defense including non-protocol measures such as configuration.

g. It would be desirable for the protocol to be able to pass through commonly-used firewalls.

11. Requirements specific to particular bearer types

The bearer types listed in Table 1 can be packaged into different types of MGs. Examples are listed in the following sections. How they are packaged is outside the scope of the general Media Gateway control protocol. The protocol must support all types of bearer types listed in Table 1.

Table 1: Bearer Types and Applications

Bearer Type	Applications	Transit Network
Trunk+ISUP	trunking/access Voice,Fax,NAS, Multimedia	IP, ATM, FR
Trunk+MF	trunking/access Voice,Fax,NAS, Multimedia	IP, ATM, FR
ISDN	trunking/access Voice,Fax,NAS, Multimedia	IP, ATM, FR
Analogue	Voice,Fax, Text Telephony	IP, ATM, FR
Termination in a Restricted Capability Gateway	Voice,Fax, Text Telephony	IP, ATM, FR
Application Termination	IVR,ARF, Announcement Server, Voice Recognition Server,...	
Multimedia H.323	H.323 Multimedia Gateway and MCU	IP, ATM, FR
Multimedia H.320	H.323 GW and MCU	ISDN, IP, ATM, FR

11.1. Media-specific Bearer Types

This section describes requirements for handling terminations attached to specific types of networks.

11.1.1. Requirements for TDM PSTN (Circuit)

This bearer type is applicable to a Trunking GW, Access GW, ...

The protocol must allow:

a. the MGC to specify the encoding to use on the attached circuit.

b. In general, if something is set by a global signalling protocol (e.g. ISUP allows mu-Law or A-Law to be signaled using ISUP) then it must be settable by the protocol.

c. TDM attributes:

* Echo cancellation,

* PCM encoding or other voice compression (e.g. mu-law or A-law),

* encryption,

* rate adaptation (e.g. V.110, or V.120).

d. for incoming calls, identification of a specific TDM circuit (timeslot and facility).

e. for calls outgoing to the circuit network, identification of a specific circuit or identification of a circuit group with the indication that the MG must select and return the identification of an available member of that group.

f. specification of the default encoding of content passing to and from a given circuit, possibly on a logical or physical circuit group basis.

g. specification at any point during the life of a connection of variable aspects of the content encoding, particularly including channel information capacity.

h. specification at any point during the life of a connection of loss padding to be applied to incoming and outgoing media streams at the circuit termination.

i. specification at any point during the life of a connection of the applicability of echo cancellation to the outgoing media stream.

j. Multi-rate calls to/from the SCN.

k. H-channel (n x 64K) calls to/from the SCN.

l. B channel aggregation protocols for creating high speed channels for multimedia over the SCN.

m. Modem terminations and negotiations.

The protocol may also allow:

n. specification of sub-channel media streams,

o. specification of multi-channel media streams.

11.1.2. Packet Bearer Type

The protocol must be able to specify:

a. ingress and egress coding (i.e. the way packets coming in and out are encoded) (including encryption).

b. near and far-end ports and other session parameters for RTP and RTCP.

The protocol must support reporting of:

c. re-negotiation of codec for cause - for further study

d. on Trunking and Access Gateways, resources capable of more than one active connection at a time must also be capable of mixing and packet duplication.

The protocol must allow:

e. specification of parameters for outgoing and incoming packet flows at separate points in the life of the connection (because far-end port addresses are typically obtained through a separate signalling exchange before or after the near-end port addresses are assigned).

f. the possibility for each Media Gateway to allocate the ports on which it will receive packet flows (including RTCP as well as media streams) and report its allocations to the Media Gateway Controller for signalling to the far end. Note that support of different IP backbone providers on a per call basis would require that the ports on which packets flow be selected by the MGC. (but only if the IP address of the MG is different for each backbone provider).

g. the specification at any point during the life of a connection of RTP payload type and RTP session number for each RTP-encapsulated media flow.

h. the ability to specify whether outgoing flows are to be uni-cast or multi-cast. Note that on an IP network this information is implicit in the destination address, but in other networks this is a connection parameter.

i. invoking of encryption/decryption on media flows and specification of the associated algorithm and key.

The protocol should also allow:

j. the MGC to configure non-RTP (proprietary or other) encapsulated packet flows.

11.1.3. Bearer type requirements for ATM

This bearer type is applicable to Trunking GW, Access GW, ...

11.1.3.1. Addressing

a. The protocol must be able to specify the following termination attributes:

* VC identifier,

* VC identifier plus AAL2 slot, and variant of these allowing the gateway to choose (part of) the identifier,

* remote termination network address, remote MG name.

b. Allow specification of an ATM termination which is to be assigned to an MG connection as a VC identifier, a VC identifier plus AAL2 slot, a wild-carded variant of either of these. A remote termination network address, or a remote MG name could also be used when the MG can select the VC and change the VC during the life of the connection by using ATM signalling.

c. Provide an indication by the MG of the VC identifier and possibly AAL2 slot of the termination actually assigned to a connection.

d. Provide a means to refer subsequently to that termination.

e. Refer to an existing VCC as the physical interface + Virtual Path Identifier (VPI) + Virtual Circuit Identifier (VCI).

f. Where the VCC is locally established (SVCs signalled by the Gateway through UNI or PNNI signalling or similar), the VCC must be indirectly referred to in terms which are of significance to both ends of the VCC. For example, a global name or the ATM address of the ATM devices at each end of the VCC. However, it is possible/probable that there may be several VCCs between a given pair of ATM devices. Therefore the ATM address pair must be further resolved by a VCC identifier unambiguous within the context of the ATM address pair.

g. refer to a VCC as the Remote GW ATM End System Address + VCCI.

h. allow the VCCI to be selected by the MG or imposed on the MG.

i. support all ATM addressing variants (e.g. ATM End System Address (AESA) and E.164).

11.1.3.2. Connection related requirements

The protocol must:

a. Allow for the de-coupling of creation/deletion of the narrow-band connection from the creation/deletion of the underlying VCC.

b. Allow for efficient disconnection of all connections associated with a physical port or VCC. As an example, this could aggregate disconnections across a broadband circuit which experienced a physical error.

c. Allow the connection established using this protocol to be carried over a VCC, which may be a:

* PVC or SPVC,

* an SVC established on demand, either by the MGC itself or by a broker acting on its behalf or,

* an SVC originated as required by the local MG, or by the remote end to the local MG through UNI or PNNI signalling.

d. Allow ATM transport parameters and QoS parameters to be passed to the MG.

e. Allow blocking and unblocking of a physical interface, a VCC or an AAL1/AAL2 channel.

The protocol should:

f. Where a VCC is required to be established on a per narrow-band call basis, allow all necessary information to be passed in one message.

11.1.3.3. Media adaptation

The protocol must:

a. Allow AAL parameters to be passed to the MG.

b. Allow AAL1/AAL2 multiple narrow-band calls to be mapped to a single VCC. For AAL2, these calls are differentiated within each VCC by a AAL2 channel identifier. An AAL2 connection may span more than 1 VCC and transit AAL2 switching devices. ITU Q.2630.1 [2] defines an end-to-end identifier called the Served User Generated Reference (SUGR). It carries information from the originating user of the AAL2 signalling protocol to the terminating user transparently and unmodified.

c. Allow unambiguous binding of a narrow band call to an AAL2 connection identifier, or AAL1 channel, within the specified VCC.

d. Allow the AAL2 connection identifier, or AAL1 channel, to be selected by the MG or imposed on the MG.

e. Allow the use of the AAL2 channel identifier (cid) instead of the AAL2 connection identifier.

f. Allow the AAL2 voice profile to be imposed or negotiated before the start of the connection. AAL2 allows for variable length packets and varying packet rates, with multiple codecs possible within a given profile. Thus a given call may upgrade or downgrade the codec within the lifetime of the call. Idle channels may generate zero bandwidth. Thus an AAL2 VCC may vary in bandwidth and possibly exceed its contract. Congestion controls within a gateway may react to congestion by modifying codec rates/types.

g. Allow the MGC to instruct the MG on how individual narrow-band calls behave under congestion.

h. Allow for the MGC to specify an AAL5 bearer, with the following choices:

* Per ATM Forum standard AF-VTOA-0083 [4],

* RTP with IP/UDP,

* RTP without IP/IDP per H.323v2 Annex C [5],

* Compressed RTP per ATM Forum AF-SAA-0124.000 [6].

i. Allow unambiguous binding of a narrow band call to an AAL1 channel within the specified VCC. (In AAL1, multiple narrow-band calls may be mapped to a single VCC.)

11.1.3.4. Reporting requirements

The protocol should:

a. Allow any end-of-call statistics to show loss/restoration of underlying VCC within the calls duration, together with duration of loss.

b. Allow notification, as requested by MGC, of any congestion avoidance actions taken by the MG.

The protocol must:

c. Allow for ATM VCCs or AAL2 channels to be audited by the MGC.

d. Allow changes in status of ATM VCCs or AAL2 channels to be notified as requested by the MGC.

e. Allow the MGC to query the resource and endpoint availability. Resources may include VCCs, and DSPs. VCCs may be up or down. End-points may be connection-free, connected or unavailable.

11.1.3.5. Functional requirements

The protocol must:

a. Allow an MGC to reserve a bearer, and specify a route for it through the network.

11.2. Application-Specific Requirements

11.2.1. Trunking Gateway

A Trunking Gateway is an interface between SCN networks and Voice over IP or Voice over ATM networks. Such gateways typically interface to SS7 or other NNI signalling on the SCN and manage a large number of digital circuits.

The protocol must:

a. Provide circuit and packet-side loopback.

b. Provide circuit-side n x 64kbs connections.

c. Provide subrate and multirate connections for further study.

d. Provide the capability to support Reporting/generation of per-trunk CAS signalling (DP, DTMF, MF, R2, J2, and national variants).

e. Provide the capability to support reporting of detected DTMF events either digit-by-digit, as a sequence of detected digits with a flexible mechanism For the MG to determine the likely end of dial string, or in a separate RTP stream.

f. Provide the capability to support ANI and DNIS generation and reception.

11.2.2. Access Gateway

An Access Gateway connects UNI interfaces like ISDN (PRI and BRI) or traditional analog voice terminal interfaces, to a Voice over IP or Voice over ATM network, or Voice over Frame Relay network.

The Protocol must:

a. Support detection and generation of analog line signaling (hook-state, ring generation).

b. Provide the capability to support reporting of detected DTMF events either digit-by-digit, as a sequence of detected digits with a flexible mechanism For the MG to determine the likely end of dial string, or in a separate RTP stream.

c. Not require scripting mechanisms, event buffering, digit map storage when implementing restricted function (1-2 line) gateways with very limited capabilities.

d. Provide the capability to support CallerID generation and reception.

Proxying of the protocol is for further study.

11.2.3. Trunking/Access Gateway with fax ports

a. the protocol must be able to indicate detection of fax media.

b. the protocol must be able to specify T.38 for the transport of the fax.

c. the protocol must be able to specify G.711 encoding for transport of fax tones across a packet network.

11.2.4. Trunking/Access Gateway with text telephone access ports

An access gateway with ports capable of text telephone communication, must provide communication between text telephones in the SCN and text conversation channels in the packet network.

Text telephone capability of ports is assumed to be possible to combine with other options for calls as described in section 11.2.6 (e.) on "Adaptable NASes".

The port is assumed to adjust for the differences in the supported text telephone protocols, so that the text media stream can be communicated T.140 coded in the packet network without further transcoding [7].

The protocol must be capable of reporting the type of text telephone that is connected to the SCN port. The foreseen types are the same as the ones supported by ITU-T V.18: DTMF, EDT, Baudot-45, Baudot-50, Bell, V.21, Minitel and V.18. It should be possible to control which protocols are supported. The SCN port is assumed to contain ITU-T V.18 functionality [8].

The protocol must be able to control the following functionality levels of text telephone support:

a. Simple text-only support: The call is set into text mode from the beginning of the call, in order to conduct a text-only conversation.

b. Alternating text-voice support: The call may begin in voice mode or text mode and, at any moment during the call, change mode on request by the SCN user. On the packet side, the two media streams for voice and text must be opened, and it must be possible to control the feeding of each stream by the protocol.

c. Simultaneous text and voice support: The call is performed in a mode when simultaneous text and voice streams are supported. The call may start in voice mode and during the call change state to a text-and-voice call.

A port may implement only level a, or any level combination of a, b and c, always including level a.

The protocol must support:

d. A text based alternative to the interactive voice response, or audio resource functionality of the gateway when the port is used in text telephone mode.

e. Selection of what national translation table to be used between the Unicode based T.140 and the 5-7 bit based text telephone protocols.

f. Control of the V.18 probe message to be used on incoming calls.

11.2.5. Network Access Server

A NAS is an access gateway, or Media Gateway (MG), which terminates modem signals or synchronous HDLC connections from a network (e.g. SCN or xDSL network) and provides data access to the packet network. Only those requirements specific to a NAS are described here.

Figure 1 provides a reference architecture for a Network Access Server (NAS). Signaling comes into the MGC and the MGC controls the NAS.

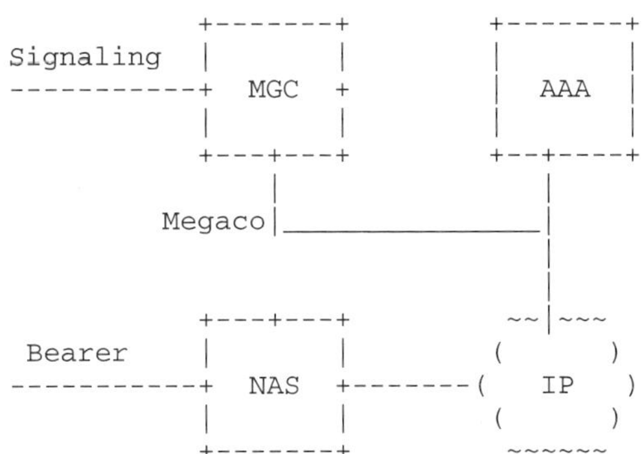

Figure 1: NAS reference architecture

The Protocol must support:

a. Callback capabilities:

* Callback

b. Modem calls. The protocol must be able to specify the modem type(s) to be used for the call.

c. Carriage of bearer information. The protocol must be able to specify the data rate of the TDM connection (e.g., 64 kbit/s, 56 kbit/s, 384 kbit/s), if this is available from the SCN.

d. Rate Adaptation: The protocol must be able to specify the type of rate adaptation to be used for the call including indicating the subrate, if this is available from the SCN (e.g. 56K, or V.110 signaled in Bearer capabilities with subrate connection of 19.2kbit/s).

e. Adaptable NASes: The protocol must be able to support multiple options for an incoming call to allow the NAS to dynamically select the proper type of call. For example, an incoming ISDN call coded for "Speech" Bearer Capability could actually be a voice, modem, fax, text telephone, or 56 kbit/s synchronous call. The protocol should allow the NAS to report back to the MGC the actual type of call once it is detected.

The 4 basic types of bearer for a NAS are:

1. Circuit Mode, 64-kbps, 8-khz structured, Speech

2. Circuit Mode, 64-kbps, 8-khz structured, 3.1-khz, Audio

3. Circuit Mode, 64-kbps, 8-khz structured, Unrestricted Digital Transmission-Rate Adapted from 56-kbps

4. Circuit Mode, 64-kbps, 8-khz structure, Unrestricted Digital Transmission

f. Passage of Called and Calling Party Number information to the NAS from the MGC. Also, passage of Charge Number/Billing Number, Redirecting Number, and Original Call Number, if known, to the NAS from the MGC. If there are other Q.931 fields that need to be passed from the MGC to the MG, then it should be possible to pass them [9].

g. Ability for the MGC to direct the NAS to connect to a specific tunnel, for example to an LNS, or to an AAA server.

h. When asked by the MGC, be able to report capability information, for example, connection types (V.34/V90/Synch ISDN..), AAA mechanism (RADIUS/DIAMETER/..), access type (PPP/SLIP/..) after restart or upgrade.

11.2.6. Restricted Capability Gateway

The requirements here may also be applied to small analog gateways, and to cable/xDSL modems. See also the section on access gateways.

The Protocol must support:

a. The ability to provide a scaled down version of the protocol. When features of the protocol are not supported, an appropriate error message must be sent. Appropriate default action must be defined. Where this is defined may be outside the scope of the protocol.

b. The ability to provide device capability information to the MGC with respect to the use of the protocol.

11.2.7. Multimedia Gateway

The protocol must have sufficient capability to support a multimedia gateway. H.320 and H.324 are characterized by a single data stream with multiple media streams multiplexed on it.

If the mapping is from H.320 or H.324 on the circuit side, and H.323 on the packet side, it is assumed that the MG knows how to map respective subchannels from H.320/H.324 side to streams on packet side. If extra information is required when connecting two terminations, then it must be supplied so that the connections are not ambiguous.

The Multimedia Gateway:

1) should support Bonding Bearer channel aggregation,

2) must support 2xB (and possibly higher rates) aggregation via H.221,

3) must be able to dynamically change the size of audio, video and data channels within the h.320 multiplex,

4) must react to changes in the H.320 multiplex on 20 msec boundaries,

5) must support TCS4/IIS BAS commands,

6) must support detection and creation of DTMF tones,

7) should support SNMP MIBS as specified in H.341 [3]

a. If some of the above cannot be handled by the MGC to MG protocol due to timing constraints, then it is likely that the H.245 to H.242 processing must take place in the MG. Otherwise, support for this functionality in the multimedia gateway are protocol requirements.

b. It must be possible on a call by call basis for the protocol to specify different applications. Thus, one call might be PSTN to PSTN under SS7 control, while the next might be ISDN/H.320 under SS7 control to H.323. This is only one example; the key requirement is that the protocol not prevent such applications.

11.2.8. Audio Resource Function

An Audio Resource Function (ARF) consists of one or more functional modules which can be deployed on an stand alone media gateway server IVR, Intelligent Peripheral, speech/speaker recognition unit, etc. or a traditional media gateway. Such a media gateway is known as an Audio Enabled Gateway (AEG) if it performs tasks defined in one or more of the following ARF functional modules:

Play Audio,
DTMF Collect,
Record Audio,
Speech Recognition,
Speaker Verification/Identification,
Auditory Feature Extraction/Recognition, or
Audio Conferencing.

Additional ARF function modules that support human to machine communications through the use of telephony tones (e.g., DTMF) or auditory means (e.g. speech) may be appended to the AEG definition in future versions of these requirements.

Generic scripting packages for any module must support all the requirements for that module. Any package extension for a given module must include, by inheritance or explicit reference, the requirements for that given module.

The protocol requirements for each of the ARF modules are provided in the following subsections.

11.2.8.1. Play Audio Module

a. Be able to provide the following basic operation:

- request an ARF MG to play an announcement.

b. Be able to specify these play characteristics:

- Play volume

- Play speed

- Play iterations

- Interval between play iterations

- Play duration

c. Permit the specification of voice variables such as DN, number, date, time, etc. The protocol must allow specification of both the value (eg 234-3456), and well as the type (Directory number).

d. Using the terminology that a segment is a unit of playable speech, or is an abstraction that is resolvable to a unit of playable speech, permit specification of the following segment types:

- A provisioned recording.

- A block of text to be converted to speech.

- A block of text to be displayed on a device.

- A length of silence qualified by duration.

- An algorithmically generated tone.

- A voice variable, specified by type and value. Given a variable type and value, the IVR/ARF unit would dynamically assemble the phrases required for its playback.

- An abstraction that represents a sequence of audio segments. Nesting of these abstractions must also be permitted.

An example of this abstraction is a sequence of audio segments, the first of which is a recording of the words "The number you have dialed", followed by a Directory Number variable, followed by a recording of the words "is no longer in service".

- An abstraction that represents a set of audio segments and which is resolved to a single segment by a qualifier. Nesting of these abstractions must be permitted.

For example take a set of audio segments recorded in different languages all of which express the semantic concept "The number you have dialed is no longer in service". The set is resolved by a language qualifier. If the qualifier is "French", the set resolves to the French version of this announcement.

In the case of a nested abstraction consisting of a set qualified by language at one level and and a set qualified by gender at another level, it would be possible to specify that an announcement be played in French and spoken by a female voice.

e. Provide two different methods of audio specification:

- Direct specification of the audio components to be played by specifying the sequence of segments in the command itself.

- Indirect specification of the audio components to be played by reference to a single identifier that resolves to a provisioned sequence of audio segments.

11.2.8.2. DTMF Collect Module

The DTMF Collect Module must support all of the requirements in the Play Module in addition to the following requirements:

a. Be able to provide the following basic operation:

- request an AEG to play an announcement, which may optionally terminated by DTMF, and then collect DTMF

b. Be able to specify these event collection characteristics:

- The number of attempts to give the user to enter a valid DTMF pattern.

c. With respect to digit timers, allow the specification of:

- Time allowed to enter the first digit.

- Time allowed for user to enter each digit subsequent to the first digit.

- Time allowed for user to enter a digit once the maximum expected number of digits has been entered.

d. To be able to allow multiple prompt operations DTMF digit collection, voice recording (if supported), and/or speech recognition analysis (if supported) provide the following types of prompts:

- Initial Prompt

- Reprompt

- Error prompt

- Failure announcement

- Success announcement.

e. To allow digit pattern matching, allow the specification of:

- maximum number of digits to collect.

- minimum number of digits to collect.

- a digit pattern using a regular expression.

f. To allow digit buffer control, allow the specification of:

- Ability to clear digit buffer prior to playing initial prompt (default is not to clear buffer).

- Default clearing of buffer following playing of un-interruptible announcement segment.

- Default clearing of buffer before playing a re-prompt in response to previous invalid input.

g. Provide a method to specify DTMF interruptibility on a per audio segment basis.

h. Allow the specification of definable key sequences for DTMF digit collection to:

- Discard collected digits in progress, replay the prompt, and resume DTMF digit collection.

- Discard collected digits in progress and resume DTMF digit collection.

- Terminate the current operation and return the terminating key sequence to the MGC.

i. Provide a way to ask the ARF MG to support the following definable keys for digit collection and recording. These keys would then be able to be acted upon by the ARF MG:

- A key to terminate playing of an announcement in progress.

- A set of one or more keys that can be accepted as the first digit to be collected.

- A key that signals the end of user input. The key may or may not be returned to the MGC along with the input already collected.

- Keys to stop playing the current announcement and resume playing at the beginning of the first segment of the announcement, last segment of the announcement, previous segment of the announcement, next segment of the announcement, or the current announcement segment.

11.2.8.3. Record Audio Module

The Record Module must support all of the requirements in the Play Module as in addition to the following requirements:

a. Be able to provide the following basic operation:

- request an AEG to play an announcement and then record voice.

b. Be able to specify these event collection characteristics:

- The number of attempts to give the user to make a recording.

c. With respect to recording timers, allow the specification of:

- Time to wait for the user to initially speak.

- The amount of silence necessary following the last speech segment for the recording to be considered complete.

- The maximum allowable length of the recording (not including pre- and post- speech silence).

d. To be able to allow multiple prompt operations for DTMF digit collection (if supported), voice recording (if supported), speech recognition analysis (if supported) and/or speech verification/identification (if supported) and then to provide the following types of prompts:

- Initial Prompt

- Reprompt

- Error prompt

- Failure announcement

- Success announcement.

e. Allow the specification of definable key sequences for digit recording or speech recognition analysis (if supported) to:

- Discard recording in progress, replay the prompt, and resume recording.

- Discard recording in progress and resume recording.

- Terminate the current operation and return the terminating key sequence to the MGC.

f. Provide a way to ask the ARF MG to support the following definable keys for recording. These keys would then be able to be acted upon by the ARF MG:

- A key to terminate playing of an announcement in progress.

- A key that signals the end of user input. The key may or may not be returned to the MGC along with the input already collected.

- Keys to stop playing the current announcement and resume playing at the beginning of the first segment of the announcement, last segment of the announcement, previous segment of the announcement, next segment of the announcement, or the current announcement segment.

g. While audio prompts are usually provisioned in IVR/ARF MGs, support changing the provisioned prompts in a voice session rather than a data session. In particular, with respect to audio management:

- A method to replace provisioned audio with audio recorded during a call. The newly recorded audio must be accessible using the identifier of the audio it replaces.

- A method to revert from replaced audio to the original provisioned audio.

- A method to take audio recorded during a call and store it such that it is accessible to the current call only through its own newly created unique identifier.

- A method to take audio recorded during a call and store it such that it is accessible to any subsequent call through its own newly created identifier.

11.2.8.4. Speech Recognition Module

The speech recognition module can be used for a number of speech recognition applications, such as:

- Limited Vocabulary Isolated Speech Recognition (e.g., "yes", "no", the number "four"),

- Limited Vocabulary Continuous Speech Feature Recognition (e.g., the utterance "four hundred twenty-three dollars"),and/or

- Continuous Speech Recognition (e.g., unconstrained speech recognition tasks).

The Speech Recognition Module must support all of the requirements in the Play Module as in addition to the following requirements:

a. Be able to provide the following basic operation: request an AEG to play an announcement and then perform speech recognition analysis.

b. Be able to specify these event collection characteristics:

- The number of attempts to give to perform speech recognition task.

c. With respect to speech recognition analysis timers, allow the specification of:

- Time to wait for the user to initially speak.

- The amount of silence necessary following the last speech segment for the speech recognition analysis segment to be considered complete.

- The maximum allowable length of the speech recognition analysis (not including pre- and post- speech silence).

d. To be able to allow multiple prompt operations for DTMF digit collection (if supported), voice recording (if supported), and/or speech recognition analysis and then to provide the following types of prompts:

- Initial Prompt

- Reprompt

- Error prompt

- Failure announcement

- Success announcement.

e. Allow the specification of definable key sequences for digit recording (if supported) or speech recognition analysis to:

- Discard in process analysis, replay the prompt, and resume analysis.

- Discard recording in progress and resume analysis.

- Terminate the current operation and return the terminating key sequence to the MGC.

f. Provide a way to ask the ARF MG to support the following definable keys for speech recognition analysis. These keys would then be able to be acted upon by the ARF MG:

- A key to terminate playing of an announcement in progress.

- A key that signals the end of user input. The key may or may not be returned to the MGC along with the input already collected.

- Keys to stop playing the current announcement and resume playing at the beginning of the first segment of the announcement, last segment of the announcement, previous segment of the announcement, next segment of the announcement, or the current announcement segment.

11.2.8.5. Speaker Verification/Identification Module

The speech verification/identification module returns parameters that indicate either the likelihood of the speaker to be the person that they claim to be (verification task) or the likelihood of the speaker being one of the persons contained in a set of previously characterized speakers (identification task).

The Speaker Verification/Identification Module must support all of the requirements in the Play Module in addition to the following requirements:

a. Be able to download parameters, such as speaker templates (verification task) or sets of potential speaker templates (identification task), either prior to the session or in mid-session.

b. Be able to download application specific software to the ARF either prior to the session or in mid-session.

c. Be able to return parameters indicating either the likelihood of the speaker to be the person that they claim to be (verification task) or the likelihood of the speaker being one of the persons contained in a set of previously characterized speakers (identification task).

d. Be able to provide the following basic operation: request an AEG to play an announcement and then perform speech verification/identification analysis.

e. Be able to specify these event collection characteristics: The number of attempts to give to perform speech verification/identification task.

f. With respect to speech verification/identification analysis timers, allow the specification of:

- Time to wait for the user to initially speak.

- The amount of silence necessary following the last speech segment for the speech verification/identification analysis segment to be considered complete.

- The maximum allowable length of the speech verification/identification analysis (not including pre- and post- speech silence).

g. To be able to allow multiple prompt operations for DTMF digit collection (if supported), voice recording, (if supported), speech recognition analysis (if supported) and/or speech verification/identification and provide the following types of prompts:

- Initial Prompt

- Reprompt

- Error prompt

- Failure announcement

- Success announcement.

h. Allow the specification of definable key sequences for digit recording (if supported) or speech recognition (if supported) in the speech verification/identification analysis to:

- Discard speech verification/identification in analysis, replay the prompt, and resume analysis.

- Discard speech verification/identification analysis in progress and resume analysis.

- Terminate the current operation and return the terminating key sequence to the MGC.

i. Provide a way to ask the ARF MG to support the following definable keys for speech verification/identification analysis. These keys would then be able to be acted upon by the ARF MG:

- A key to terminate playing of an announcement in progress.

- A key that signals the end of user input. The key may or may not be returned to the MGC along with the input already collected.

- Keys to stop playing the current announcement and resume speech verification/identification at the beginning of the first segment of the announcement, last segment of the announcement, previous segment of the announcement, next segment of the announcement, or the current announcement segment.

11.2.8.6. Auditory Feature Extraction/Recognition Module

The auditory feature extraction/recognition module is engineered to continuously monitor the auditory stream for the appearance of particular auditory signals or speech utterances of interest and to report these events (and optionally a signal feature representation of these events) to network servers or MGCs.

The Auditory Feature Extraction/Recognition Module must support the following requirements:

a. Be able to download application specific software to the ARF either prior to the session or in mid-session.

b. Be able to download parameters, such as a representation of the auditory feature to extract/recognize, for prior to the session or in mid-session.

c. Be able to return parameters indicating the auditory event found or a representation of the feature found (i.e., auditory feature).

11.2.8.7. Audio Conferencing Module

The protocol must support:

a. a mechanism to create multi-point conferences of audio only and multimedia conferences in the MG.

b. audio mixing; mixing multiple audio streams into a new composite audio stream

c. audio switching; selection of incoming audio stream to be sent out to all conference participants.

11.2.9. Multipoint Control Units

The protocol must support:

a. a mechanism to create multi-point conferences of audio only and multimedia conferences in the MG.

b. audio mixing; mixing multiple audio streams into a new composite audio stream

c. audio switching; selection of incoming audio stream to be sent out to all conference participants.

d. video switching; selection of video stream to be sent out to all conference participants

e. lecture video mode; a video selection option where on video source is sent out to all conference users

f. multi-point of T.120 data conferencing.

g. The ability for the MG to function as an H.323 MP, and for the MGC to function as an H.323 MC, connected by this protocol (MEGACOP/H.248). It should be possible for audio, data, and video MG/MPs to be physically separate while being under the control of a single MGC/H.323 MC.

12. References

[1] Bradner, S., "Key words for use in RFCs to Indicate Requirement Levels", BCP 14, RFC 2119, March 1997.

[2] ITU-T Recommendation Q.2630.1, AAL type 2 Signalling Protocol (Capability Set 1), December 1999.

[3] ITU-T Recommendation H.341, Line Transmission of Non-Telephone Signals, May 1999.

[4] ATM Forum Technical Committee, af-vtoa-0083.001, Voice and Telephony Over ATM to the Desktop Specification, March 1999.

[5] ITU-T Recommendation H.323v3, Packet-based Multimedia Communications Systems (includes Annex C - H.323 on ATM), September 1999.

[6] ATM Forum Technical Committee, af-saa-0124.000, Gateway for H.323 Media Transport Over ATM, May 1999.

[7] ITU-T Recommendation T.140, Protocol for Multimedia Application Text Conversation, February 1998.

[8] ITU-T Recommendation V.18, Operational and Interworking Requirements for DCEs Operating in Text Telephone Mode, February 1998.

[9] ITU-T Recommendation Q.931, Digital Subscriber Signalling System No. 1 (DSS 1) - ISDN User - Network Interface Layer 3 Specification for Basic Call Control, May 1998.

14. Acknowledgements

The authors would like to acknowledge the many contributors who debated the Media Gateway Control Architecture and Requirements on the IETF Megaco and Sigtran mailing lists. Contributions to this document have also been made through internet-drafts and discussion with members of ETSI Tiphon, ITU-T SG16, TIA TR41.3.4, the ATM Forum, and the Multiservice Switching Forum.

15. Authors' Addresses

Nancy Greene
Nortel Networks
P.O. Box 3511 Stn C
Ottawa, ON, Canada K1Y 4H7

Phone: (514) 271-7221
EMail: ngreene@nortelnetworks.com

Michael A. Ramalho
Cisco Systems
1802 Rue de la Port
Wall Township, NJ

Phone: +1.732.449.5762
EMail: mramalho@cisco.com

Brian Rosen
Marconi
1000 FORE Drive, Warrendale, PA 15086

Phone: (724) 742-6826
EMail: brosen@eng.fore.com

16. Full Copyright Statement

Acknowledgement

Funding for the RFC Editor function is currently provided by the Internet Society.

Network Working Group A. Vaha-Sipila
Request for Comments: 2806 Nokia
Category: Standards Track April 2000

URLs for Telephone Calls

Status of this Memo

This document specifies an Internet standards track protocol for the Internet community, and requests discussion and suggestions for improvements. Please refer to the current edition of the "Internet Official Protocol Standards" (STD 1) for the standardization state and status of this protocol. Distribution of this memo is unlimited.

Copyright Notice

Abstract

This document specifies URL (Uniform Resource Locator) schemes "tel", "fax" and "modem" for specifying the location of a terminal in the phone network and the connection types (modes of operation) that can be used to connect to that entity. This specification covers voice calls (normal phone calls, answering machines and voice messaging systems), facsimile (telefax) calls and data calls, both for POTS and digital/mobile subscribers.

Table of Contents

RFC 2806 1

1. Introduction

1.1 New URL schemes

This specification defines three new URL schemes: "tel", "fax" and "modem". They are intended for describing a terminal that can be contacted using the telephone network. The description includes the subscriber (telephone) number of the terminal and the necessary parameters to be able to successfully connect to that terminal.

The "tel" scheme describes a connection to a terminal that handles normal voice telephone calls, a voice mailbox or another voice messaging system or a service that can be operated using DTMF tones.

The "fax" scheme describes a connection to a terminal that can handle telefaxes (facsimiles). The name (scheme specifier) for the URL is "fax" as recommended by [E.123].

The "modem" scheme describes a connection to a terminal that can handle incoming data calls. The term "modem" refers to a device that does digital-to-analog and analog-to-digital conversions; in addition to these, a "modem" scheme can describe a fully digital connection.

The notation for phone numbers is the same which is specified in [RFC2303] and [RFC2304]. However, the syntax definition is a bit different due to the fact that this document specifies URLs whereas [RFC2303] and [RFC2304] specify electronic mail addresses. For example, "/" (used in URLs to separate parts in a hierarchical URL [RFC2396]) has been replaced by ";". In addition, this URL scheme has been synchronized with [RFC2543].

When these URLs are used, the number of parameters should be kept to the minimum, unless this would make the context of use unclear. Having a short URL is especially important if the URL is intended to be shown to the end user, printed, or otherwise distributed so that it is visible.

1.2 Formal definitions

The ABNF (augmented Backus-Naur form) notation used in formal definitions follows [RFC2234]. This specification uses elements from the 'core' definitions (Appendix A of [RFC2234]). Some elements have been defined in previous RFCs. If this is the case, the RFC in question has been referenced in comments.

Note on non-unreserved characters [RFC2396] in URLs: the ABNF in this document specifies strings of raw, unescaped characters. If those characters are present in a URL, and are not unreserved [RFC2396], they MUST be escaped as explained in [RFC2396] prior to using the URL. In addition, when parsing a URL, it must be noted that some characters may have been escaped.

An example: ABNF notation "%x20" means a single octet with a hexadecimal value of "20" (in US-ASCII, a space character). This must be escaped in a URL, and it becomes "%20".

In addition, the ABNF in this document only uses lower case. The URLs are case-insensitive (except for the <future-extension> parameter, whose case-sensitivity is application-specific).

1.3 Requirements

The key words "MUST", "MUST NOT", "REQUIRED", "SHALL", "SHALL NOT", "SHOULD", "SHOULD NOT", "RECOMMENDED", "MAY", and "OPTIONAL" in this document are to be interpreted as described in [RFC2119].

Compliant software MUST follow this specification.

2. URL schemes for telephone calls

2.1 Applicability

In this document, "local entity" means software and hardware that can detect and parse one or more of these URLs and possibly place a call to a remote entity, or otherwise utilize the contents of the URL.

These URL schemes are used to direct the local entity to place a call using the telephone network, or as a method to transfer or store a phone number plus other relevant data. The network in question may be a landline or mobile phone network, or a combination of these. If the phone network differentiates between (for example) voice and data calls, or if the local entity has several different telecommunications equipment at its disposal, it is possible to specify which kind of call (voice/fax/data) is requested. The URL can also contain information about the capabilities of the remote entity, so that the connection can be established successfully.

The "tel", "fax" and "modem" URL schemes defined here do not use the hierarchical URL syntax; there are no applicable relative URL forms. The URLs are always case-insensitive, except for the <future-extension> parameter (see below), whose case-sensitivity is application specific. Characters in the URL MUST be escaped when needed as explained in [RFC2396].

2.2 "tel" URL scheme

The URL syntax is formally described as follows. For the basis of this syntax, see [RFC2303].

```
telephone-url         = telephone-scheme ":"
                        telephone-subscriber
telephone-scheme      = "tel"
telephone-subscriber  = global-phone-number / local-phone-number
global-phone-number   = "+" base-phone-number [isdn-subaddress]
                        [post-dial] *(area-specifier /
                        service-provider / future-extension)
base-phone-number     = 1*phonedigit
local-phone-number    = 1*(phonedigit / dtmf-digit /
                        pause-character) [isdn-subaddress]
                        [post-dial] area-specifier
                        *(area-specifier / service-provider /
                        future-extension)
isdn-subaddress       = ";isub=" 1*phonedigit
post-dial             = ";postd=" 1*(phonedigit /
                        dtmf-digit / pause-character)
area-specifier        = ";" phone-context-tag "=" phone-context-ident
phone-context-tag     = "phone-context"
phone-context-ident   = network-prefix / private-prefix
network-prefix        = global-network-prefix / local-network-prefix
global-network-prefix = "+" 1*phonedigit
local-network-prefix  = 1*(phonedigit / dtmf-digit / pause-character)
private-prefix        = (%x21-22 / %x24-27 / %x2C / %x2F / %x3A /
                        %x3C-40 / %x45-4F / %x51-56 / %x58-60 /
                        %x65-6F / %x71-76 / %x78-7E)
                        *(%x21-3A / %x3C-7E)
                        ; Characters in URLs must follow escaping rules
                        ; as explained in [RFC2396]
```

```
                         ; See sections 1.2 and 2.5.2
service-provider       = ";" provider-tag "=" provider-hostname
provider-tag           = "tsp"
provider-hostname      = domain ; <domain> is defined in [RFC1035]
                         ; See section 2.5.10
future-extension       = ";" 1*(token-char) ["=" ((1*(token-char)
                         ["?" 1*(token-char)]) / quoted-string )]
                         ; See section 2.5.11 and [RFC2543]
token-char             = (%x21 / %x23-27 / %x2A-2B / %x2D-2E / %x30-39
                         / %x41-5A / %x5E-7A / %x7C / %x7E)
                         ; Characters in URLs must follow escaping rules
                         ; as explained in [RFC2396]
                         ; See sections 1.2 and 2.5.11
quoted-string          = %x22 *( "\" CHAR / (%x20-21 / %x23-7E
                         / %x80-FF )) %x22
                         ; Characters in URLs must follow escaping rules
                         ; as explained in [RFC2396]
                         ; See sections 1.2 and 2.5.11
phonedigit             = DIGIT / visual-separator
visual-separator       = "-" / "." / "(" / ")"
pause-character        = one-second-pause / wait-for-dial-tone
one-second-pause       = "p"
wait-for-dial-tone     = "w"
dtmf-digit             = "*" / "#" / "A" / "B" / "C" / "D"
```


The URL starts with <telephone-scheme>, which tells the local entity that what follows is a URL that should be parsed as described in this document. After that, the URL contains the phone number of the remote entity. Phone numbers can also contain subaddresses, which are used to identify different remote entities under the same phone number. If a subaddress is present, it is appended to the phone number after ";isub=". Phone numbers can also contain a post-dial sequence. This is what is often used with voice mailboxes and other services that are controlled by dialing numbers from your phone keypad while the call is in progress. The <post-dial> sequence describes what and when the local entity should send to the phone line.

Phone numbers can be either "global" or "local". Global numbers are unambiguous everywhere. Local numbers are usable only within a certain area, which is called "context", see section 2.5.2.

Local numbers always have an <area-specifier>, which specifies the context in which the number is usable (the same number may have different interpretation in different network areas). The context can be indicated with three different prefixes. A <global-network-prefix> indicates that the number is valid within a numbering area whose global numbers start with <global-network-prefix>. Similarly, <local-network-prefix> means that the number is valid within a numbering area whose numbers (or dial strings) start with it. A <private-prefix> is a name of a context. The local entity must have knowledge of this private context to be able to deduce whether it can use the number, see section 2.5.2. Additional information about the phone number's usage can be included by adding the name of the telephony services provider in <service-provider>, see section 2.5.10.

The <future-extension> mechanism makes it possible to add new parameters to this URL scheme. See section 2.5.11.

The <private-prefix>, <token-char> and <quoted-string> nonterminals may seem a bit complex at first, but they simply describe the set of octets that are legal in those nonterminals. Some octets may have to be escaped, see [RFC2396].

2.3 "fax" URL scheme

The URL syntax is formally described as follows (the definition reuses nonterminals from the above definition). For the basis of this syntax, see [RFC2303] and [RFC2304].

```
fax-url          = fax-scheme ":" fax-subscriber
fax-scheme       = "fax"
fax-subscriber   = fax-global-phone / fax-local-phone
fax-global-phone = "+" base-phone-number [isdn-subaddress]
                   [t33-subaddress] [post-dial]
                   *(area-specifier / service-provider /
                   future-extension)
fax-local-phone  = 1*(phonedigit / dtmf-digit /
                   pause-character) [isdn-subaddress]
                   [t33-subaddress] [post-dial]
                   area-specifier
                   *(area-specifier / service-provider /
                   future-extension)
t33-subaddress   = ";tsub=" 1*phonedigit
```

The fax: URL is very similar to the tel: URL. The main difference is that in addition to ISDN subaddresses, telefaxes also have an another type of subaddress, see section 2.5.8.

2.4 "modem" URL scheme

The URL syntax is formally described as follows (the definition reuses nonterminals from the above definitions). For the basis of this syntax, see [RFC2303].

```
modem-url          = modem-scheme ":" remote-host
modem-scheme       = "modem"
remote-host        = telephone-subscriber *(modem-params
                     / recommended-params)
modem-params       = ";type=" data-capabilities
recommended-params = ";rec=" data-capabilities
data-capabilities  = accepted-modem ["?" data-bits parity
                     stop-bits]
accepted-modem     = "V21" / "V22" / "V22b" /
                     "V23" / "V26t" / "V32" /
                     "V32b" / "V34" / "V90" /
                     "V110" / "V120" / "B103" /
                     "B212" / "X75" /
                     "vnd." vendor-name "." modem-type
data-bits          = "7" / "8"
parity             = "n" / "e" / "o" / "m" / "s"
stop-bits          = "1" / "2"
vendor-name        = 1*(ALPHA / DIGIT / "-" / "+")
modem-type         = 1*(ALPHA / DIGIT / "-" / "+")
```

The modem: URL scheme is also very similar to both the tel: and fax: schemes, but it adds the description of the capabilities of the remote entity. Minimum required compliance is listed in <modem-params> and recommended compliance is listed in <recommended-params>. For details, see section 2.5.9.

2.5 Parsing telephone, fax and modem URLs

2.5.1 Call type

The type of call is specified by the scheme specifier. "Tel" means that a voice call is opened. "Fax" indicates that the call should be a facsimile (telefax) call. "Modem" means that it should be a data call. Not all networks differentiate between the types of call; in this case, the scheme specifier indicates the telecommunications equipment type to use.

2.5.2 Phone numbers and their scope

<telephone-subscriber> and <fax-subscriber> indicate the phone number to be dialed. The phone number can be written in either international or local notation. All phone numbers SHOULD always be written in the international form if there is no good reason to use the local form.

Not all numbers are valid within all numbering areas. The <area-specifier> parameter, which is mandatory for local numbers, is used to indicate the locale within which this number is valid, or to qualify the phone number so that it may be used unambiguously. The

<area-specifier> can take three forms: <global-network-prefix>, <local-network-prefix> or <private-prefix>. These are used to describe the validity area of the phone number either in global numbering plan, local numbering plan, or in a private numbering plan, respectively.

If <area-specifier> is present, the local entity MUST NOT attempt to call out using the phone number if it cannot originate the call within the specified locale. If a <local-phone-number> is used, an <area-specifier> MUST be included as well.

There can be multiple instances of <area-specifier>. In this case, the number is valid in all of the given numbering areas.

The global prefix form is intended to act as the outermost context for a phone number, so it will start with a "+", followed by some part of an E.164 number. It also specifies the region in which the phone number is valid. For example, if <global-network-prefix> is "+358", the given number is valid only within Finland (country code 358) - even if it is a <global-phone-number>.

The local prefix form is intended to act as an intermediate context in those situations where the outermost context for a phone number is given by another means. One example of use is where the local entity is known to originate calls only within the North American Number Plan Area, so an "outermost" phone context can be assumed. The local context could, for example, be used to indicate the area code within which an associated phone number is situated. Thus "tel:456-7890;phone-context=213" would suffice to deliver a call to the telephone number "+1-213-456-7890". Note that the version including the <phone-context> implies further that the call can only be originated within the "area code 213" region.

The <private-prefix> form is intended for use in those situations where the context cannot be expressed with a start of a global phone number or a dialing string. The <private-prefix> is actually a name of a private context. The creator of the URL and the local entity have been configured to recognize this name, and as such they can interpret the number and know how they can utilize the number. For example, a private network numbering plan may be indicated by the name "X-COMPANY-NET", but the private dialling plan from the locales of the sender of the telephony URL and the local entity are different. The syntax of these tokens will be left for future specification. The ABNF above specifies the accepted characters that can be a part of <private-prefix>.

Unless the sender is absolutely sure that they share the same private network access digit string with the local entity, then they MUST NOT use a dialling plan number (a local phone number, or one qualified by a local context), as the result may be incorrect. Instead, they SHOULD use a global number, or if that is not possible, a private context as the last resort. If the local entity does not support dialling into the private network indicated by that context, then the request MUST be rejected. If it does, then it will use the access digit string appropriate for its locale.

Note that the use of <area-specifier> is orthogonal to use of the telephony service provider parameter (see 2.5.10); it qualifies the phone number, whilst the <service-provider> parameter indicates the carrier to be used for the call attempt.

For example, a large company may have private network interconnections between its sites, as well as connections to the Global Switched Telephone Network. A phone number may be given in "public network" form, but with a <service-provider> indicating that the call should be carried over the corporate network.

Conversely, it would be possible to represent a phone number in private network form, with a private context to indicate this, but indicate a public telephony service provider. This would request that the user agent convert the private network number plan address into a form that can be carried using the selected service provider.

Any telephone number MUST contain at least one <phonedigit> or <dtmf-digit>, that is, subscriber numbers consisting only of pause characters are not allowed.

International numbers MUST begin with the "+" character. Local numbers MUST NOT contain that character. International numbers MUST be written with the country (CC) and national (NSN) numbers as specified in [E.123] and [E.164]. International numbers have the property of being totally unambiguous everywhere in the world if the local entity is properly configured.

Local numbers MAY be used if the number only works from inside a certain geographical area or a network. Note that some numbers may work from several networks but not from the whole world - these SHOULD be written in international form, with a set of <area-specifier> tags and optional <service-provider> parameters. URLs containing local phone numbers should only appear in an environment where all local entities can get the call successfully set up by passing the number to the dialing entity "as is". An example could be a company intranet, where all local entities are located under a the same private telephone exchange. If local phone numbers are used, the document in which they are present SHOULD contain an indication of the context in which they are intended to be used, and an appropriate <area-specifier> SHOULD be present in the URL.

In some regions, it is popular to write phone numbers using alphabetic characters which correspond to certain numbers on the telephone keypad. Letters in <dtmf-digit> characters do not have anything to do with this, nor is this method supported by these URL schemes.

It should also be noted that implementations MUST NOT assume that telephone numbers have a maximum, minimum or fixed length, or that they would always begin with a certain number. Implementors are encouraged to familiarize themselves with the international standards.

2.5.3 Separators in phone numbers

All <visual-separator> characters MUST be ignored by the local entity when using the URL. These characters are present only to aid readability: they MUST NOT have any other meaning. Note that although [E.123] recommends the use of space (SP) characters as the separators in printed telephone numbers, spaces MUST NOT be used in phone numbers in URLs as the space character cannot be used in URLs without escaping it.

2.5.4 Converting the number to the local numbering scheme

After the telephone number has been extracted, it can be converted to the local dialing convention. (For example, the "+" character might be replaced by the international call prefix, or the international and trunk prefixes might be removed to place a local call.) Numbers that have been specified using <local-phone> or <fax-local-phone> MUST be used by the local entity "as is", without any conversions, unless the local entity decides to utilize the information in an optional <service-provider> parameter.

2.5.5 Sending post-dial sequence after call setup

The number may contain a <post-dial> sequence, which MUST be dialled using Dual Tone Multifrequency (DTMF) in-band signalling or pulse dialing after the call setup is complete. If the user agent does not support DTMF or pulse dialing after the call has been set up, <post-dial> MUST be ignored. In that case, the user SHOULD be notified.

2.5.6 Pauses in dialing and post-dial sequence

A local phone number or a post-dial sequence may contain <pause-character> characters which indicate a pause while dialing ("p"), or a wait for dial tone ("w").

Local entities MAY support this method of dialing, and the final interpretation of these characters is left to the local entity. It is RECOMMENDED that the length of each pause is about one second.

If it is not supported, local entities MUST ignore everything in the dial string after the first <pause-character> and the user SHOULD be notified. The user or the local entity MAY opt not to place a call if this feature is not supported and these characters are present in the URL.

Any <dtmf-digit> characters and all dial string characters after the first <pause-character> or <dtmf-digit> SHOULD be sent to line using DTMF (Dual Tone Multifrequency) in-band signaling, even if dialing is done using direct network signaling (a digital subscriber loop or a mobile phone). If the local infrastructure does not support DTMF codes, the local entity MAY opt to use pulse dialing. However, it should be noted that certain services which are controlled using DTMF tones cannot be controlled with pulse dialing. If pulse dialing is used, the user SHOULD be notified.

2.5.7 ISDN subaddresses

A phone number MAY also contain an <isdn-subaddress> which indicates an ISDN subaddress. The local entity SHOULD support ISDN subaddresses. These addresses are sent to the network by using a method available to the local entity (typically, ISDN subscribers send the address with the call setup signalling). If ISDN subaddressing is not supported by the caller, <isdn-subaddress> MUST be ignored and the user SHOULD be notified. The user or the local entity MAY opt not to place a call if this feature is not supported.

2.5.8 T.33 subaddresses

A fax number MAY also contain a <t33-subaddress>, which indicates the start of a T.33 subaddress [T.33]. Local entities SHOULD support this. Otherwise <t33-subaddress> MUST be ignored and the user SHOULD be notified. The user or the local entity MAY opt not to place a call if this feature is not supported.

2.5.9 Data call parameters

<modem-params> indicate the minimum compliance required from the local entity to be able to connect to the remote entity. The minimum compliance is defined as being equal to or a superset of the capabilities of the listed modem type. There can be several <modem-param> parameters, in which case compliance to any one of them will be accepted. <recommended-params> indicates the recommended compliance required from the local entity. This is typically the fastest and/or the most reliable modem type supported by the modem pool. The local entity can use this information to select the best number from a group of modem URLs. There can be several recommended modem types, which are equally desirable from the modem pool's point of view. <recommended-params> MAY NOT conflict with <modem-params>. If they do, the local entity MUST ignore the <recommended-params>.

The local entity MUST call out using compatible hardware, or request that the network provides such a service.

For example, if the local entity only has access to a V.22bis modem and the URL indicates that the minimum acceptable connection is V.32bis, the local entity MUST NOT try to connect to the remote host since V.22bis is a subset of V.32bis. However, if the URL lists V.32 as the minimum acceptable connection, the local entity can use V.32bis to create a connection since V.32bis is a superset of V.32.

This feature is present because modem pools often have separate numbers for slow modems and fast modems, or have different numbers for analog and ISDN connections, or may use proprietary modems that are incompatible with standards. It is somewhat analogous to the connection type specifier (typecode) in FTP URLs [RFC1738]: it provides the local entity with information that can not be deduced from the scheme specifier, but is helpful for successful operation.

This also means that the number of data and stop bits and parity MUST be set according to the information given in the URL, or to default values given in this document, if the information is not present.

The capability tokens are listed below. If capabilities suggest that it is impossible to create a connection, the connection MUST NOT be created.

If new modem types are standardized by ITU-T, this list can be extended with those capability tokens. Tokens are formed by taking the number of the standard and joining together the first letter (for example, "V"), number (for example, 22) and the first letter of the postfix (for example "bis" would become "b").

Proprietary modem types MUST be specified using the 'vendor naming tree', which takes the form "vnd.x.y", in which "x" is the name of the entity from which the specifications for the modem type can be acquired and "y" is the type or model of the modem. Vendor names MUST share the same name space with vendor names used in MIME types [RFC2048]. Submitting the modem types to ietf-types list for review is strongly recommended.

New capabilities MUST always be documented in an RFC, and they MUST refer to this document or a newer version of it. The documentation SHOULD also list the existing modem types with which the newly defined modem type is compatible with.

Capability	Explanation
V21	ITU-T V.21
V22	ITU-T V.22
V22b	ITU-T V.22bis
V23	ITU-T V.23
V26t	ITU-T V.26ter
V32	ITU-T V.32
V32b	ITU-T V.32bis
V34	ITU-T V.34
V90	ITU-T V.90
V110	ITU-T V.110
V120	ITU-T V.120
X75	ITU-T X.75
B103	Bell 103
B212	Bell 212
Data bits: "8" or "7"	The number of data bits. If not specified, defaults to "8".
Parity: "n", "e", "o", "m", "s"	Parity. None, even, odd, mark or space parity, respectively. If not specified, defaults to "n".
Stop bits: "1" or "2"	The number of stop bits. If not specified, defaults to "1".

2.5.10 Telephony service provider identification

It is possible to indicate the identity of the telephony service provider for the given phone number. <service-provider> MAY be used by the user-agent to place the call using this network, to enhance the user interface, for billing estimates or to otherwise optimize its functionality. It MAY also be ignored by the user-agent. <service-provider> consists of a fully qualified Internet domain name of the telephony service provider, for example ";tsp=terrifictelecom.com". The syntax of the domain name follows Internet domain name rules and is defined in [RFC1035].

2.5.11 Additional parameters

In addition to T.33 and ISDN subaddresses, modem types and area specifiers, future extensions to this URL scheme may add other additional parameters (<future-extension> in the BNF) to these URLs. These parameters are added to the URL after a semicolon (";"). Implementations MUST be prepared to handle additional and/or unknown parameters gracefully. Implementations MUST NOT use the URL if it contains unknown parameters, as they may be vital for the correct interpretation of the URL. Instead, the implementation SHOULD report an error.

For example, <future-extension> can be used to store application-specific additional data about the phone number, its intended use, or any conversions that have been applied to the number. Whenever a <future-extension> is used in an open environment, its syntax and usage MUST be properly documented in an RFC.

<future-extension> nonterminal a rephrased version of, and compatible with the <other-param> as defined in [RFC2543] (which actually borrows BNF from an earlier version of this specification).

2.6 Examples of Use

```
tel:+358-555-1234567
```

This URL points to a phone number in Finland capable of receiving voice calls. The hyphens are included to make the number more human-readable: country and area codes have been separated from the subscriber number.

```
fax:+358.555.1234567
```

The above URL describes a phone number which can receive fax calls. It uses dots instead of hyphens as separators, but they have no effect on the functionality.

```
modem:+3585551234567;type=v32b?7e1;type=v110
```

This phone number belongs to an entity which is able to receive data calls. The local entity may opt to use either a ITU-T V.32bis modem (or a faster one, which is compatible with V.32bis), using settings of 7 data bits, even parity and one stop bit, or an ISDN connection using ITU-T V.110 protocol.

```
tel:+358-555-1234567;postd=pp22
```

The above URL instructs the local entity to place a voice call to +358-555-1234567, then wait for an implementation-dependent time (for example, two seconds) and emit two DTMF dialing tones "2" on the line (for example, to choose a particular extension number, or to invoke a particular service).

```
tel:0w003585551234567;phone-context=+3585551234
```

This URL places a voice call to the given number. The number format is intended for local use: the first zero opens an outside line, the "w" character waits for a second dial tone, and the number already has the international access code appended to it ("00"). This kind of phone number MUST NOT be used in an environment where all users of this URL might not be able to successfully dial out by using this number directly. However, this might be appropriate for pages in a company intranet. The <area-specifier> which is present hints that the number is usable only in an environment where the local entity's phone number starts with the given string (perhaps singling out a company-wide block of telephone numbers).

```
tel:+1234567890;phone-context=+1234;vnd.company.option=foo
```

The URL describes a phone number which, even if it is written in its international form, is only usable within the numbering area where phone numbers start with +1234. There is also a proprietary extension "vnd.company.option", which has the value "foo". The meaning of this extension is application-specific. Note that the order of these parameters (phone-context and vnd.company.option) is irrelevant.

2.7 Rationale behind the syntax

2.7.1 Why distinguish between call types?

URLs locate resources, which in this case is some telecommunications equipment at a given phone number. However, it is not necessarily enough to know the subscriber number in order to successfully communicate with that equipment. Digital phone networks distinguish between voice, fax and data calls (and possibly other types of calls, not discussed in this specification). To be able to successfully connect to, say, a fax machine, the caller may have to specify that a fax call is being made. Otherwise the call might be routed to the voice number of the subscriber. In this sense, the call type is an integral part of the 'location' of the target resource.

The reason to have the call type in the scheme specifier is to make the URL simple to remember and use. Making it a parameter, much like the way modem parameters are handled now, will substantially reduce the human readability of this URL.

2.7.2 Why "tel" is "tel"?

There has been discussion on whether the scheme name "tel" is appropriate. To summarize, these are the points made against the other proposals.

callto	URL schemes locate a resource and do not specify an action to be taken.
telephone	Too long. Also, "tel" considered to be a more international form.
phone	Was countered on the basis that "tel" is more internationally acceptable.

2.7.3 Why to use E.164-style numbering?

E.164 refers to international telephone numbers, and the string of digits after the country code is usually a national matter. In any case, phone numbers are usually written as a simple string of numbers everywhere. Because of this, the syntax in this specification is intuitively clear to most people. This is the usual way to write phone numbers in business cards, advertisements, telephone books and so on.

It should be noted that phone numbers may have 'hierarchical' characteristics, so that one could build a 'forest' of phone numbers with country codes as roots, area codes as branches and subscriber numbers as leaves. However, this is not always the case. Not all areas have area codes; some areas may have different area codes depending on how one wants to route the call; some numbers must always be dialled "as is", without prepending area or country codes (notably emergency numbers); and area codes can and do change.

Usually, if something has a hierarchical structure, the URL syntax should reflect that fact. These URLs are an exception.

Also, when writing the phone number in the form described in this specification, the writer does not need to know which part of the number is the country code and which part is the area code. If a hierarchical URL would be used (with a "/" character separating the parts of the phone numbers), the writer of the URL would have to know which parts are which.

Finally, when phone numbers are written in the international form as specified here, they are unambiguous and can always be converted to the local dialing convention, given that the user agent has the knowledge of the local country and area codes.

2.7.4 Not everyone has the same equipment as you

There are several ways for the subscriber to dial a phone number:

- By pulse dialing. Typically old telephone exchanges. Usually this dialing method has only to be used to set up the call; after connecting to the remote entity, <post-dial> can be sent to the line using DTMF, because it will typically be processed by the remote entity, not the telephone network.

- By DTMF. These are the 'beeps' that you hear when you dial on most phones.

- By direct network signalling. ISDN subscribers and mobile phone users usually have this. There is no dial tone (or if there is, it is generated locally by the equipment), and the number of the called party is communicated to the telephone network using some network signalling method. After setting up the call, <post-dial> sequences are usually sent using DTMF codes.

2.7.5 Do not confuse numbers with how they are dialled

As an example, +123456789 will be dialled in many countries as 00123456789, where the leading "00" is a prefix for international calls. However, if a URL contains a local phone number 00123456789, the user-agent MUST NOT assume that this number is equal to a global phone number +123456789. If a user-agent received a telephony URL with a local number in it, it MUST make sure that it knows the context in which the local phone number is to be processed, or else the number MUST NOT be used. Equally, anyone sending a telephony URL MUST take into consideration that the recipient may have insufficient information about the phone number's context.

3. Comments on usage

These are examples of the recommended usage of this URL in HTML documents.

First of all, the number SHOULD be visible to the end user, if it is conceivable that the user might not have a local entity which is able to use these URLs.

```
Telephone: <a href="tel:+3585551234567">+358-555-1234567</a>
```

Second, on a public HTML page, the telephone number in the URL SHOULD always be in the international form, even if the text of the link uses some local format.

Telephone: <a href="tel:+3585551234567">(0555) 1234567</a>

or even

For more info, call <a href="tel:+15554383785965">1-555-IETF-RULZ-OK</a>.

Moreover, if the number is a <local-phone-number>, and the scope of the number is not clear from the context in which the URL is displayed, a human-readable explanation SHOULD be included.

For customer service, dial <a href="tel:1234;phone-context=+358555">1234</a> (only from Terrific Telecom mobile phones).

4. References

[RFC1035] Mockapetris, P., "Domain Names - Implementation and Specification", STD 13, RFC 1035, November 1987.

[RFC1738] Berners-Lee, T., et al., "Uniform Resource Locators (URL)", RFC 1738, December 1994.

[RFC1866] Berners-Lee, T. and D. Connolly, "Hypertext Markup Language - 2.0", RFC 1866, November 1995.

[RFC2048] Freed, N., Klensin, J. and J. Postel, "Multipurpose Internet Mail Extensions (MIME) Part Four: Registration Procedures", RFC 2048, November 1996.

[RFC2119] Bradner, S., "Key Words for Use in RFCs to Indicate Requirement Levels", BCP 14, RFC 2119, March 1997.

[RFC2234] Crocker, D. and P. Overall, "Augmented BNF for Syntax Specifications: ABNF", RFC 2234, November 1997.

[RFC2303] Allocchio, C., "Minimal PSTN Address Format in Internet Mail", RFC 2303, March 1998.

[RFC2304] Allocchio, C., "Minimal FAX Address Format in Internet Mail", RFC 2304, March 1998.

[RFC2396] Berners-Lee, T., R. Fielding and L. Manister, "Uniform Resource Identifiers (URI): Generic Syntax", RFC 2396, August 1998.

[RFC2543] Handley, M., Schulzrinne, H., Schooler, E. and J. Rosenberg, "SIP: Session Initiation Protocol", RFC 2543, March 1999.

[E.123] ITU-T Recommendation E.123: Telephone Network and ISDN Operation, Numbering, Routing and Mobile Service: Notation for National and International Telephone Numbers. 1993.

[E.164] ITU-T Recommendation E.164/I.331 (05/97): The International Public Telecommunication Numbering Plan. 1997.

[T.33] ITU-T Recommendation T.33: Facsimile Routing Utilizing the Subaddress. 1996.

5. Security Considerations

It should be noted that the local entity SHOULD NOT call out without the knowledge of the user because of associated risks, which include

- call costs (including long calls, long distance calls, international calls and premium rate calls, or calls which do not terminate due to <post-dial> sequences that have been left out by the local entity)

- wrong numbers inserted on web pages by malicious users, or sent via e-mail, perhaps in direct advertising

- making the user's phone line unavailable (off-hook) for a malicious purpose

- opening a data call to a remote host, thus possibly opening a back door to the user's computer

- revealing the user's (possibly unlisted) phone number to the remote host in the caller identification data, and correlating the local entity's phone number with other information such as the e-mail or IP address

- using the same local number in different contexts, in which the number may have a different meaning

All of these risks MUST be taken into consideration when designing the local entity.

The local entity SHOULD have some mechanism that the user can use to filter out unwanted numbers. The local entity SHOULD NOT use rapid redialing of the number if it is busy to avoid the congestion of the (signaling) network. Also, the local entity SHOULD detect if the number is unavailable or if the call is terminated before the dialing string has been completely processed (for example, the call is terminated while waiting for user input) and not try to call again, unless instructed by the user.

6. Acknowledgements

Writing this specification would not have been possible without extensive support from many people.

Contributors include numerous people from IETF FAX, PINT, URI and URLREG mailing lists, as well as from World Wide Web Consortium and several companies, plus several individuals. Thanks to all people who offered criticism, corrections and feedback.

All phone numbers and company names used in the examples of this specification are fictional. Any similarities to real entities are coincidental.

7. Author's Address

Antti Vaha-Sipila
(quoted-printable: Antti V=E4h=E4-Sipil=E4)
Nokia Mobile Phones
P. O. Box 68
FIN-33721 Tampere
Finland

EMail: avs@iki.fi
antti.vaha-sipila@nokia.com

8. Full Copyright Statement

Acknowledgement

Funding for the RFC Editor function is currently provided by the Internet Society.

Network Working Group
Request for Comments: 2824
Category: Informational

J. Lennox
H. Schulzrinne
Columbia University

May 2000

Call Processing Language Framework and Requirements

Status of this Memo

Copyright Notice

Abstract

A large number of the services we wish to make possible for Internet telephony require fairly elaborate combinations of signalling operations, often in network devices, to complete. We want a simple and standardized way to create such services to make them easier to implement and deploy. This document describes an architectural framework for such a mechanism, which we call a call processing language. It also outlines requirements for such a language.

Table of Contents

1 Introduction

Recently, several protocols have been created to allow telephone calls to be made over IP networks, notably SIP [1] and H.323 [2]. These emerging standards have opened up the possibility of a broad and dramatic decentralization of the provisioning of telephone services so they can be under the user's control.

Many Internet telephony services can, and should, be implemented entirely on end devices. Multi-party calls, for instance, or call waiting alert tones, or camp-on services, depend heavily on end-system state and on the specific content of media streams, information which often is only available to the end system. A variety of services, however -- those involving user location, call distribution, behavior when end systems are busy, and the like -- are independent of a particular end device, or need to be operational even when an end device is unavailable. These services are still best located in a network device, rather than in an end system.

Traditionally, network-based services have been created only by service providers. Service creation typically involved using proprietary or restricted tools, and there was little range for customization or enhancement by end users. In the Internet environment, however, this changes. Global connectivity and open protocols allow end users or third parties to design and implement new or customized services, and to deploy and modify their services dynamically without requiring a service provider to act as an intermediary.

A number of Internet applications have such customization environments -- the web has CGI [3], for instance, and e-mail has Sieve [4] or procmail. To create such an open customization environment for Internet telephony, we need a standardized, safe way for these new service creators to describe the desired behavior of network servers.

This document describes an architecture in which network devices respond to call signalling events by triggering user-created programs written in a simple, static, non-expressively-complete language. We call this language a call processing language.

The development of this document has been substantially informed by the development of a particular call processing language, as described in [5]. In general, when this document refers to "a call processing language," it is referring to a generic language that fills this role; "the call processing language" or "the CPL" refers to this particular language.

2 Terminology

In this section we define some of the terminology used in this document.

SIP [1] terminology used includes:

invitation: The initial INVITE request of a SIP transaction, by which one party initiates a call with another.

redirect server: A SIP device which responds to invitations and other requests by informing the request originator of an alternate address to which the request should be sent.

proxy server: A SIP device which receives invitations and other requests, and forwards them to other SIP devices. It then receives the responses to the requests it forwarded, and forwards them back to the sender of the initial request.

user agent: A SIP device which creates and receives requests, so as to set up or otherwise affect the state of a call. This may be, for example, a telephone or a voicemail system.

user agent client: The portion of a user agent which initiates requests.

user agent server: The portion of a user agent which responds to requests.

H.323 [2] terminology used includes:

terminal: An H.323 device which originates and receives calls, and their associated media.

gatekeeper: An H.323 entity on the network that provides address translation and controls access to the network for H.323 terminals and other endpoints. The gatekeeper may also provide other services to the endpoints such as bandwidth management and locating gateways.

gateway: A device which translates calls between an H.323 network and another network, typically the public-switched telephone network.

RAS: The Registration, Admission and Status messages communicated between two H.323 entities, for example between an endpoint and a gatekeeper.

General terminology used in this document includes:

user location: The process by which an Internet telephony device determines where a user named by a particular address can be found.

CPL: A Call Processing Language, a simple language to describe how Internet telephony call invitations should be processed.

script: A particular instance of a CPL, describing a particular set of services desired.

end system: A device from which and to which calls are established. It creates and receives the call's media (audio, video, or the like). This may be a SIP user agent or an H.323 terminal.

signalling server: A device which handles the routing of call invitations. It does not process or interact with the media of a call. It may be a SIP proxy or redirect server, or an H.323 gatekeeper.

3 Example services

To motivate the subsequent discussion, this section gives some specific examples of services which we want users to be able to create programmatically. Note that some of these examples are deliberately somewhat complicated, so as to demonstrate the level of decision logic that should be possible.

- Call forward on busy/no answer

  When a new call comes in, the call should ring at the user's desk telephone. If it is busy, the call should always be redirected to the user's voicemail box. If, instead, there's no answer after four rings, it should also be redirected to his or her voicemail, unless it's from a supervisor, in which case it should be proxied to the user's cell phone if it is currently registered.

- Information address

  A company advertises a general "information" address for prospective customers. When a call comes in to this address, if it's currently working hours, the caller should be given a list of the people currently willing to accept general information calls. If it's outside of working hours, the caller should get a webpage indicating what times they can call.

- Intelligent user location

  When a call comes in, the list of locations where the user has registered should be consulted. Depending on the type of call (work, personal, etc.), the call should ring at an appropriate subset of the registered locations, depending on information in the registrations. If the user picks up from more than one station, the pick-ups should be reported back separately to the calling party.

- Intelligent user location with media knowledge

  When a call comes in, the call should be proxied to the station the user has registered from whose media capabilities best match those specified in the call request. If the user does not pick up from that station within four rings, the call should be proxied to the other stations from which he or she has registered, sequentially, in order of decreasing closeness of match.

- Client billing allocation -- lawyer's office

  When a call comes in, the calling address is correlated with the corresponding client, and client's name, address, and the time of the call is logged. If no corresponding client is found, the call is forwarded to the lawyer's secretary.

4 Usage scenarios

A CPL would be useful for implementing services in a number of different scenarios.

- Script creation by end user

  In the most direct approach for creating a service with a CPL, an end user simply creates a script describing their service. He or she simply decides what service he or she wants, describes it using a CPL script, and then uploads it to a server.

- Third party outsourcing

  Because a CPL is a standardized language, it can also be used to allow third parties to create or customize services for clients. These scripts can then be run on servers owned by the end user or the user's service provider.

- Administrator service definition

  A CPL can also be used by server administrators to create simple services or describe policy for servers they control. If a server is implementing CPL services in any case, extending the service architecture to allow administrators as well as users to create scripts is a simple extension.

- Web middleware

  Finally, there have been a number of proposals for service creation or customization using web interfaces. A CPL could be used as the back-end to such environments: a web application could create a CPL script on behalf of a user, and the telephony server could then implement the services without either component having to be aware of the specifics of the other.

5 CPL creation

There are also a number of means by which CPL scripts could be created. Like HTML, which can be created in a number of different manners, we envision multiple creation styles for a CPL script.

- o Hand authoring

  Most directly, CPL scripts can be created by hand, by knowledgeable users. The CPL described in [5] has a text format with an uncomplicated syntax, so hand authoring will be straightforward.

- o Automated scripts

  CPL features can be created by automated means, such as in the example of the web middleware described in the previous section. With a simple, text-based syntax, standard text-processing languages will be able to create and edit CPL scripts easily.

- o GUI tools

  Finally, users will be able to use GUI tools to create and edit CPL scripts. We expect that most average-experience users will take this approach once the CPL gains popularity. The CPL will be designed with this application in mind, so that the full expressive power of scripts can be represented simply and straightforwardly in a graphical manner.

6 Network model

The Call Processing Language operates on a generalized model of an Internet telephony network. While the details of various protocols differ, on an abstract level all major Internet telephony architectures are sufficiently similar that their major features can be described commonly. This document generally uses SIP terminology, as its authors' experience has mainly been with that protocol.

6.1 Model components

In the Call Processing Language's network model, an Internet telephony network contains two types of components.

6.1.1 End systems

End systems are devices which originate and/or receive signalling information and media. These include simple and complex telephone devices, PC telephony clients, and automated voice systems. The CPL abstracts away the details of the capabilities of these devices. An end system can originate a call; and it can accept, reject, or forward incoming calls. The details of this process (ringing, multi-line telephones, and so forth) are not important for the CPL.

For the purposes of the CPL, gateways -- for example, a device which connects calls between an IP telephony network and the PSTN -- are also considered to be end systems. Other devices, such as mixers or firewalls, are not directly dealt with by the CPL, and they will not be discussed here.

6.1.2 Signalling servers

Signalling servers are devices which relay or control signalling information. In SIP, they are proxy servers, redirect servers, or registrars; in H.323, they are gatekeepers.

Signalling servers can perform three types of actions on call setup information. They can:

proxy it: forward it on to one or more other network or end systems, returning one of the responses received.

redirect it: return a response informing the sending system of a different address to which it should send the request.

reject it: inform the sending system that the setup request could not be completed.

RFC 2543 [1] has illustrations of proxy and redirect functionality. End systems may also be able to perform some of these actions: almost certainly rejection, and possibly redirection.

Signalling servers also normally maintain information about user location. Whether by means of registrations (SIP REGISTER or H.323 RAS messages), static configuration, or dynamic searches, signalling servers must have some means by which they can determine where a user is currently located, in order to make intelligent choices about their proxying or redirection behavior.

Signalling servers are also usually able to keep logs of transactions that pass through them, and to send e-mail to destinations on the Internet, under programmatic control.

6.2 Component interactions

When an end system places a call, the call establishment request can proceed by a variety of routes through components of the network. To begin with, the originating end system must decide where to send its requests. There are two possibilities here: the originator may be configured so that all its requests go to a single local server; or it may resolve the destination address to locate a remote signalling server or end system to which it can send the request directly.

Once the request arrives at a signalling server, that server uses its user location database, its local policy, DNS resolution, or other methods, to determine the next signalling server or end system to which the request should be sent. A request may pass through any number of signalling servers: from zero (in the case when end systems communicate directly) to, in principle, every server on the network. What's more, any end system or signalling server can (in principle) receive requests from or send them to any other.

For example, in figure 1, there are two paths the call establishment request information may take. For Route 1, the originator knows only a user address for the user it is trying to contact, and it is configured to send outgoing calls through a local outgoing proxy server. Therefore, it forwards the request to its local server, which finds the server of record for that address, and forwards it on to that server.

In this case, the organization the destination user belongs to uses a multi-stage setup to find users. The corporate server identifies which department a user is part of, then forwards the request to the appropriate departmental server, which actually locates the user. (This is similar to the way e-mail forwarding is often configured.) The response to the request will travel back along the same path.

For Route 2, however, the originator knows the specific device address it is trying to contact, and it is not configured to use a local outgoing proxy. In this case, the originator can directly contact the destination without having to communicate with any network servers at all.

We see, then, that in Internet telephony signalling servers cannot in general know the state of end systems they "control," since signalling information may have bypassed them. This architectural limitation implies a number of restrictions on how some services can be implemented. For instance, a network system cannot reliably know if an end system is currently busy or not; a call may have been placed to the end system without traversing that network system. Thus, signalling messages must explicitly travel to end systems to find out their state; in the example, the end system must explicitly return a "busy" indication.

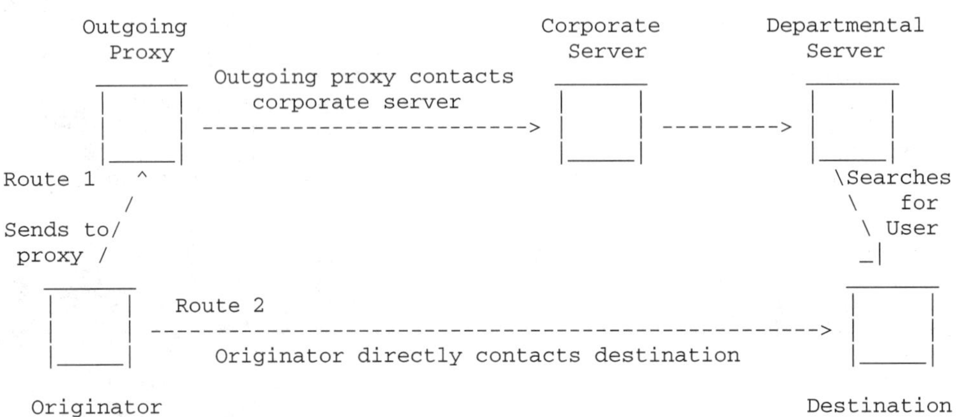

Figure 1: Possible paths of call setup messages

7 Interaction of CPL with network model

7.1 What a script does

A CPL script runs in a signalling server, and controls that system's proxy, redirect, or rejection actions for the set-up of a particular call. It does not attempt to coordinate the behavior of multiple signalling servers, or to describe features on a "Global Functional Plane" as in the Intelligent Network architecture [6].

More specifically, a script replaces the user location functionality of a signalling server. As described in section 6.1.2, a signalling server typically maintains a database of locations where a user can be reached; it makes its proxy, redirect, and rejection decisions based on the contents of that database. A CPL script replaces this basic database lookup functionality; it takes the registration information, the specifics of a call request, and other external information it wants to reference, and chooses the signalling actions to perform.

Abstractly, a script can be considered as a list of condition/action pairs; if some attribute of the registration, request, and external information matches a given condition, then the corresponding action (or more properly set of actions) is taken. In some circumstances, additional actions can be taken based on the consequences of the first action and additional conditions. If no condition matches the invitation, the signalling server's standard action -- its location database lookup, for example -- is taken.

7.2 Which script is executed

CPL scripts are usually associated with a particular Internet telephony address. When a call establishment request arrives at a signalling server which is a CPL server, that server associates the source and destination addresses specified in the request with its database of CPL scripts; if one matches, the corresponding script is executed.

Once the script has executed, if it has chosen to perform a proxy action, a new Internet telephony address will result as the destination of that proxying. Once this has occurred, the server again checks its database of scripts to see if any of them are associated with the new address; if one is, that script as well is executed (assuming that a script has not attempted to proxy to an address which the server has already tried). For more details of this recursion process, and a description of what happens when a server has scripts that correspond both to a scripts origination address and its destination address, see section 9.2.

In general, in an Internet telephony network, an address will denote one of two things: either a user, or a device. A user address refers to a particular individual, for example sip:joe@example.com, regardless of where that user actually is or what kind of device he or she is using. A device address, by contrast, refers to a particular physical device, such as sip:x26063@phones.example.com. Other, intermediate sorts of addresses are also possible, and have some use (such as an address for "my cell phone, wherever it currently happens to be registered"), but we expect them to be less common. A CPL script is agnostic to the type of address it is associated with; while scripts associated with user addresses are probably the most useful for most services, there is no reason that a script could not be associated with any other type of address as well. The recursion process described above allows scripts to be associated with several of a user's addresses; thus, a user script could specify an action "try me at my cell phone," whereas a device script could say "I don't want to accept cell phone calls while I'm out of my home area."

It is also possible for a CPL script to be associated not with one specific Internet telephony address, but rather with all addresses handled by a signalling server, or a large set of them. For instance, an administrator might configure a system to prevent calls from or to a list of banned incoming or outgoing addresses; these should presumably be configured for everyone, but users should still to be able to have their own custom scripts as well. Exactly when such scripts should be executed in the recursion process depends on the precise nature of the administrative script. See section 9.2 for further discussion of this.

7.3 Where a script runs

Users can have CPL scripts on any network server which their call establishment requests pass through and with which they have a trust relationship. For instance, in the example in figure 1, the originating user could have a script on the outgoing proxy, and the destination user could have scripts on both the corporate server and the departmental server. These scripts would typically perform different functions, related to the role of the server on which they reside; a script on the corporate-wide server could be used to customize which department the user wishes to be found at, for instance, whereas a script at the departmental server could be used for more fine-grained location customization. Some services, such as filtering out unwanted calls, could be located at either server. See section 9.3 for some implications of a scenario like this.

This model does not specify the means by which users locate a CPL-capable network server. In general, this will be through the same means by which they locate a local Internet telephony server to register themselves with; this may be through manual configuration, or through automated means such as the Service Location Protocol [7]. It has been proposed that automated means of locating such servers should include a field to indicate whether the server allows users to upload CPLs.

8 Creation and transport of a call processing language script

Users create call processing language scripts, typically on end devices, and transmit them through the network to signalling servers. Scripts persist in signalling servers until changed or deleted, unless they are specifically given an expiration time; a network system which supports CPL scripting will need stable storage.

The end device on which the user creates the CPL script need not bear any relationship to the end devices to which calls are actually placed. For example, a CPL script might be created on a PC, whereas calls might be intended to be received on a simple audio-only telephone. Indeed, the device on which the script is created may not be an "end device" in the sense described in section 6.1.1 at all; for instance, a user could create and upload a CPL script from a non-multimedia-capable web terminal.

The CPL also might not necessarily be created on a device near either the end device or the signalling server in network terms. For example, a user might decide to forward his or her calls to a remote location only after arriving at that location.

The exact means by which the end device transmits the script to the server remains to be determined; it is likely that many solutions will be able to co-exist. This method will need to be authenticated in almost all cases. The methods that have been suggested include web file upload, SIP REGISTER message payloads, remote method invocation, SNMP, ACAP, LDAP, and remote file systems such as NFS.

Users can also retrieve their current script from the network to an end system so it can be edited. The signalling server should also be able to report errors related to the script to the user, both static errors that could be detected at upload time, and any run-time errors that occur.

If a user has trust relationships with multiple signalling servers (as discussed in section 7.3), the user may choose to upload scripts to any or all of those servers. These scripts can be entirely independent.

9 Feature interaction behavior

Feature interaction is the term used in telephony systems when two or more requested features produce ambiguous or conflicting behavior [8]. Feature interaction issues for features implemented with a call processing language can be roughly divided into three categories: feature-to-feature in one server, script-to-script in one server, and server-to-server.

9.1 Feature-to-feature interactions

Due to the explicit nature of event conditions discussed in the previous section, feature-to-feature interaction is not likely to be a problem in a call processing language environment. Whereas a subscriber to traditional telephone features might unthinkingly subscribe to both "call waiting" and "call forward on busy," a user creating a CPL script would only be able to trigger one action in response to the condition "a call arrives while the line is busy." Given a good user interface for creation, or a CPL server which can check for unreachable code in an uploaded script, contradictory condition/action pairs can be avoided.

9.2 Script-to-script interactions

Script-to-script interactions arise when a server invokes multiple scripts for a single call, as described in section 7.2. This can occur in a number of cases: if both the call originator and the destination have scripts specified on a single server; if a script forwards a request to another address which also has a script; or if an administrative script is specified as well as a user's individual script.

The solution to this interaction is to determine an ordering among the scripts to be executed. In this ordering, the "first" script is executed first; if this script allows or permits the call to be proxied, the script corresponding to the next address is executed. When the first script says to forward the request to some other address, those actions are considered as new requests which arrive at the second script. When the second script sends back a final response, that response arrives at the first script in the same manner as if a request arrived over the network. Note that in some cases, forwarding can be recursive; a CPL server must be careful to prevent forwarding loops.

Abstractly, this can be viewed as equivalent to having each script execute on a separate signalling server. Since the CPL architecture is designed to allow scripts to be executed on multiple signalling servers in the course of locating a user, we can conceptually transform script-to-script interactions into the server-to-server interactions described in the next section, reducing the number of types of interactions we need to concern ourselves with.

The question, then, is to determine the correct ordering of the scripts. For the case of a script forwarding to an address which also has a script, the ordering is obvious; the other two cases are somewhat more subtle. When both originator and destination scripts exist, the originator's script should be executed before the destination script; this allows the originator to perform address translation, call filtering, etc., before a destination address is determined and a corresponding script is chosen.

Even more complicated is the case of the ordering of administrative scripts. Many administrative scripts, such as ones that restrict source and destination addresses, need to be run after originator scripts, but before destination scripts, to avoid a user's script evading administrative restrictions through clever forwarding; however, others, such as a global address book translation function, would need to be run earlier or later. Servers which allow administrative scripts to be run will need to allow the administrator to configure when in the script execution process a particular administrative script should fall.

9.3 Server-to-server interactions

The third case of feature interactions, server-to-server interactions, is the most complex of these three. The canonical example of this type of interaction is the combination of Originating Call Screening and Call Forwarding: a user (or administrator) may wish to prevent calls from being placed to a particular address, but the local script has no way of knowing if a call placed to some other, legitimate address will be proxied, by a remote server, to the banned address. This type of problem is unsolvable in an administratively heterogeneous network, even a "lightly" heterogeneous network such as current telephone systems. CPL does not claim to solve it, but the problem is not any worse for CPL scripts than for any other means of deploying services.

Another class of server-to-server interactions are best resolved by the underlying signalling protocol, since they can arise whether the signalling servers are being controlled by a call processing language or by some entirely different means. One example of this is forwarding loops, where user X may have calls forwarded to Y, who has calls forwarded back to X. SIP has a mechanism to detect such loops. A call processing language server thus does not need to define any special mechanisms to prevent such occurrences; it should, however, be possible to trigger a different set of call processing actions in the event that a loop is detected, and/or to report back an error to the owner of the script through some standardized run-time error reporting mechanism.

9.4 Signalling ambiguity

As an aside, [8] discusses a fourth type of feature interaction for traditional telephone networks, signalling ambiguity. This can arise when several features overload the same operation in the limited signal path from an end station to the network: for example, flashing the switch-hook can mean both "add a party to a three-way call" and "switch to call waiting." Because of the explicit nature of signalling in both the Internet telephony protocols discussed here, this issue does not arise.

10 Relationship with existing languages

This document's description of the CPL as a "language" is not intended to imply that a new language necessarily needs to be implemented from scratch. A server could potentially implement all the functionality described here as a library or set of extensions for an existing language; Java, or the various freely-available scripting languages (Tcl, Perl, Python, Guile), are obvious possibilities.

However, there are motivations for creating a new language. All the existing languages are, naturally, expressively complete; this has two inherent disadvantages. The first is that any function implemented in them can take an arbitrarily long time, use an arbitrarily large amount of memory, and may never terminate. For call processing, this sort of resource usage is probably not necessary, and as described in section 12.1, may in fact be undesirable. One model for this is the electronic mail filtering language Sieve [4], which deliberately restricts itself from being Turing-complete.

Similar levels of safety and protection (though not automatic generation and parsing) could also be achieved through the use of a "sandbox" such as is used by Java applets, where strict bounds are imposed on the amount of memory, cpu time, stack space, etc., that a program can use. The difficulty with this approach is primarily in its lack of transparency and portability: unless the levels of these bounds are imposed by the standard, a bad idea so long as available resources are increasing exponentially with Moore's Law, a user can never be sure whether a particular program can successfully be executed on a given server without running into the server's resource limits, and a program which executes successfully on one server may fail unexpectedly on another. Non-expressively-complete languages, on the other hand, allow an implicit contract between the script writer and the server: so long as the script stays within the rules of the language, the server will guarantee that it will execute the script.

The second disadvantage with expressively complete languages is that they make automatic generation and parsing of scripts very difficult, as every parsing tool must be a full interpreter for the language. An analogy can be drawn from the document-creation world: while text markup languages like HTML or XML can be, and are, easily manipulated by smart editors, powerful document programming languages such as LaTeX or Postscript usually cannot be. While there are word processors that can save their documents in LaTeX form, they cannot accept as input arbitrary LaTeX documents, let alone preserve the structure of the original document in an edited form. By contrast, essentially any HTML editor can edit any HTML document from the web, and the high-quality ones preserve the structure of the original documents in the course of editing them.

11 Related work

11.1 IN service creation environments

The ITU's IN series describe, on an abstract level, service creation environments [6]. These describe services in a traditional circuit-switched telephone network as a series of decisions and actions arranged in a directed acyclic graph. Many vendors of IN services use modified and extended versions of this for their proprietary service creation environments.

11.2 SIP CGI

SIP CGI [9] is an interface for implementing services on SIP servers. Unlike a CPL, it is a very low-level interface, and would not be appropriate for services written by non-trusted users.

The paper "Programming Internet Telephony Services" [10] discusses the similarities and contrasts between SIP CGI and CPL in more detail.

12 Necessary language features

This section lists those properties of a call processing language which we believe to be necessary to have in order to implement the motivating examples, in line with the described architecture.

12.1 Language characteristics

These are some abstract attributes which any proposed call processing language should possess.

- Light-weight, efficient, easy to implement

  In addition to the general reasons why this is desirable, a network server might conceivably handle very large call volumes, and we don't want CPL execution to be a major bottleneck. One way to achieve this might be to compile scripts before execution.

- Easily verifiable for correctness

  For a script which runs in a server, mis-configurations can result in a user becoming unreachable, making it difficult to indicate run-time errors to a user (though a second-channel error reporting mechanism such as e-mail could ameliorate this). Thus, it should be possible to verify, when the script is committed to the server, that it is at least syntactically correct, does not have any obvious loops or other failure modes, and does not use too many server resources.

o Executable in a safe manner

No action the CPL script takes should be able to subvert anything about the server which the user shouldn't have access to, or affect the state of other users without permission. Additionally, since CPL scripts will typically run on a server on which users cannot normally run code, either the language or its execution environment must be designed so that scripts cannot use unlimited amounts of network resources, server CPU time, storage, or memory.

o Easily writeable and parsable by both humans and machines.

For maximum flexibility, we want to allow humans to write their own scripts, or to use and customize script libraries provided by others. However, most users will want to have a more intuitive user-interface for the same functionality, and so will have a program which creates scripts for them. Both cases should be easy; in particular, it should be easy for script editors to read human-generated scripts, and vice-versa.

o Extensible

It should be possible to add additional features to a language in a way that existing scripts continue to work, and existing servers can easily recognize features they don't understand and safely inform the user of this fact.

o Independent of underlying signalling details

The same scripts should be usable whether the underlying protocol is SIP, H.323, a traditional telephone network, or any other means of setting up calls. It should also be agnostic to address formats. (We use SIP terminology in our descriptions of requirements, but this should map fairly easily to other systems.) It may also be useful to have the language extend to processing of other sorts of communication, such as e-mail or fax.

12.2 Base features -- call signalling

To be useful, a call processing language obviously should be able to react to and initiate call signalling events.

o Should execute actions when a call request arrives

  See section 7, particularly 7.1.

o Should be able to make decisions based on event properties

  A number of properties of a call event are relevant for a script's decision process. These include, roughly in order of importance:

  - Destination address

    We want to be able to do destination-based routing or screening. Note that in SIP we want to be able to filter on either or both of the addresses in the To header and the Request-URI.

  - Originator address

    Similarly, we want to be able to do originator-based screening or routing.

  - Caller Preferences

    In SIP, a caller can express preferences about the type of device to be reached -- see [11]. The script should be able to make decisions based on this information.

  - Information about caller or call

    SIP has textual fields such as Subject, Organization, Priority, etc., and a display name for addresses; users can also add non-standard additional headers. H.323 has a single Display field. The script should be able to make decisions based on these parameters.

  - Media description

    Call invitations specify the types of media that will flow, their bandwidth usage, their network destination addresses, etc. The script should be able to make decisions based on these media characteristics.

- Authentication/encryption status

  Call invitations can be authenticated. Many properties of the authentication are relevant: the method of authentication/encryption, who performed the authentication, which specific fields were encrypted, etc. The script should be able to make decisions based on these security parameters.

o Should be able to take action based on a call invitation

  There are a number of actions we can take in response to an incoming call setup request. We can:

  - reject it

    We should be able to indicate that the call is not acceptable or not able to be completed. We should also be able to send more specific rejection codes (including, for SIP, the associated textual string, warning codes, or message payload).

  - redirect it

    We should be able to tell the call initiator sender to try a different location.

  - proxy it

    We should be able to send the call invitation on to another location, or to several other locations ("forking" the invitation), and await the responses. It should also be possible to specify a timeout value after which we give up on receiving any definitive responses.

o Should be able to take action based a response to a proxied or forked call invitation

  Once we have proxied an invitation, we need to be able to make decisions based on the responses we receive to that invitation (or the lack thereof). We should be able to:

  - consider its message fields

    We should be able to consider the same fields of a response as we consider in the initial invitation.

- relay it on to the call originator

  If the response is satisfactory, it should be returned to the sender.

- for a fork, choose one of several responses to relay back

  If we forked an invitation, we obviously expect to receive several responses. There are several issues here -- choosing among the responses, and how long to wait if we've received responses from some but not all destinations.

- initiate other actions

  If we didn't get a response, or any we liked, we should be able to try something else instead (e.g., call forward on busy).

12.3 Base features -- non-signalling

A number of other features that a call processing language should have do not refer to call signalling per se; however, they are still extremely desirable to implement many useful features.

The servers which provide these features might reside in other Internet devices, or might be local to the server (or other possibilities). The language should be independent of the location of these servers, at least at a high level.

o Logging

In addition to the CPL server's natural logging of events, the user will also want to be able to log arbitrary other items. The actual storage for this logging information might live either locally or remotely.

o Error reporting

If an unexpected error occurs, the script should be able to report the error to the script's owner. This may use the same mechanism as the script server uses to report language errors to the user (see section 12.5).

o Access to user-location info

Proxies will often collect information on users' current location, either through SIP REGISTER messages, the H.323 RRQ family of RAS messages, or some other mechanism (see section

6.2). The CPL should be able to refer to this information so a call can be forwarded to the registered locations or some subset of them.

o Database access

Much information for CPL control might be stored in external databases, for example a wide-area address database, or authorization information, for a CPL under administrative control. The language could specify some specific database access protocols (such as SQL or LDAP), or could be more generic.

o Other external information

Other external information a script could access includes web pages, which could be sent back in a SIP message body; or a clean interface to remote procedure calls such as Corba, RMI, or DCOM, for instance to access an external billing database. However, for simplicity, these interfaces may not be in the initial version of the protocol.

12.4 Language features

Some features do not involve any operations external to the CPL's execution environment, but are still necessary to allow some standard services to be implemented. (This list is not exhaustive.)

o Pattern-matching

It should be possible to give special treatment to addresses and other text strings based not only on the full string but also on more general or complex sub-patterns of them.

o Address filtering

Once a set of addresses has been retrieved through one of the methods in section 12.3, the user needs to be able to choose a sub-set of them, based on their address components or other parameters.

o Randomization

Some forms of call distribution are randomized as to where they actually end up.

o Date/time information

Users may wish to condition some services (e.g., call forwarding, call distribution) on the current time of day, day of the week, etc.

12.5 Control

As described in section 8, we must have a mechanism to send and retrieve CPL scripts, and associated data, to and from a signalling server. This method should support reporting upload-time errors to users; we also need some mechanism to report errors to users at script execution time. Authentication is vital, and encryption is very useful. The specification of this mechanism can be (and probably ought to be) a separate specification from that of the call processing language itself.

13 Security Considerations

The security considerations of transferring CPL scripts are discussed in sections 8 and 12.5. Some considerations about the execution of the language are discussed in section 12.1.

14 Acknowledgments

We would like to thank Tom La Porta and Jonathan Rosenberg for their comments and suggestions.

15 Authors' Addresses

Jonathan Lennox
Dept. of Computer Science
Columbia University
1214 Amsterdam Avenue, MC 0401
New York, NY 10027
USA

EMail: lennox@cs.columbia.edu

Henning Schulzrinne
Dept. of Computer Science
Columbia University
1214 Amsterdam Avenue, MC 0401
New York, NY 10027
USA

EMail: schulzrinne@cs.columbia.edu

16 Bibliography

[1] Handley, M., Schulzrinne, H., Schooler, E. and J. Rosenberg, "SIP: Session Initiation Protocol", RFC 2543, March 1999.

[2] International Telecommunication Union, "Packet based multimedia communication systems," Recommendation H.323, Telecommunication Standardization Sector of ITU, Geneva, Switzerland, Feb. 1998.

[3] K. Coar and D. Robinson, "The WWW common gateway interface version 1.1", Work in Progress.

[4] T. Showalter, "Sieve: A mail filtering language", Work in Progress.

[5] J. Lennox and H. Schulzrinne, "CPL: a language for user control of internet telephony services", Work in Progress.

[6] International Telecommunication Union, "General recommendations on telephone switching and signaling -- intelligent network: Introduction to intelligent network capability set 1," Recommendation Q.1211, Telecommunication Standardization Sector of ITU, Geneva, Switzerland, Mar. 1993.

[7] Guttman, E., Perkins, C., Veizades, J. and M. Day, "Service Location Protocol, Version 2", RFC 2608, June 1999.

[8] E. J. Cameron, N. D. Griffeth, Y.-J. Lin, M. E. Nilson, W. K. Schure, and H. Velthuijsen, "A feature interaction benchmark for IN and beyond," Feature Interactions in Telecommunications Systems, IOS Press, pp. 1-23, 1994.

[9] J. Lennox, J. Rosenberg, and H. Schulzrinne, "Common gateway interface for SIP", Work in Progress.

[10] J. Rosenberg, J. Lennox, and H. Schulzrinne, "Programming internet telephony services," Technical Report CUCS-010-99, Columbia University, New York, New York, Mar. 1999.

[11] H. Schulzrinne and J. Rosenberg, "SIP caller preferences and callee capabilities", Work in Progress.

17 Full Copyright Statement

Acknowledgement

Funding for the RFC Editor function is currently provided by the Internet Society.

Network Working Group H. Schulzrinne
Request for Comments: 2833 Columbia University
Category: Standards Track S. Petrack
MetaTel
May 2000

RTP Payload for DTMF Digits, Telephony Tones and Telephony Signals

Status of this Memo

This document specifies an Internet standards track protocol for the Internet community, and requests discussion and suggestions for improvements. Please refer to the current edition of the "Internet Official Protocol Standards" (STD 1) for the standardization state and status of this protocol. Distribution of this memo is unlimited.

Copyright Notice

Abstract

This memo describes how to carry dual-tone multifrequency (DTMF) signaling, other tone signals and telephony events in RTP packets.

1 Introduction

This memo defines two payload formats, one for carrying dual-tone multifrequency (DTMF) digits, other line and trunk signals (Section 3), and a second one for general multi-frequency tones in RTP [1] packets (Section 4). Separate RTP payload formats are desirable since low-rate voice codecs cannot be guaranteed to reproduce these tone signals accurately enough for automatic recognition. Defining separate payload formats also permits higher redundancy while maintaining a low bit rate.

The payload formats described here may be useful in at least three applications: DTMF handling for gateways and end systems, as well as "RTP trunks". In the first application, the Internet telephony gateway detects DTMF on the incoming circuits and sends the RTP payload described here instead of regular audio packets. The gateway likely has the necessary digital signal processors and algorithms, as it often needs to detect DTMF, e.g., for two-stage dialing. Having the gateway detect tones relieves the receiving Internet end system from having to do this work and also avoids that low bit-rate codecs like G.723.1 render DTMF tones unintelligible. Secondly, an Internet end system such as an "Internet phone" can emulate DTMF functionality without concerning itself with generating precise tone pairs and without imposing the burden of tone recognition on the receiver.

In the "RTP trunk" application, RTP is used to replace a normal circuit-switched trunk between two nodes. This is particularly of interest in a telephone network that is still mostly circuit-switched. In this case, each end of the RTP trunk encodes audio channels into the appropriate encoding, such as G.723.1 or G.729. However, this encoding process destroys in-band signaling information which is carried using the least-significant bit ("robbed bit signaling") and may also interfere with in-band signaling tones, such as the MF digit tones. In addition, tone properties such as the phase reversals in the ANSam tone, will not survive speech coding. Thus, the gateway needs to remove the in-band signaling information from the bit stream. It can now either carry it out-of-band in a signaling transport mechanism yet to be defined, or it can use the mechanism described in this memorandum. (If the two trunk end points are within reach of the same media gateway controller, the media gateway controller can also handle the signaling.) Carrying it in-band may simplify the time synchronization between audio packets and the tone or signal information. This is particularly relevant where duration and timing matter, as in the carriage of DTMF signals.

1.1 Terminology

In this document, the key words "MUST", "MUST NOT", "REQUIRED", "SHALL", "SHALL NOT", "SHOULD", "SHOULD NOT", "RECOMMENDED", "MAY", and "OPTIONAL" are to be interpreted as described in RFC 2119 [2] and indicate requirement levels for compliant implementations.

2 Events vs. Tones

A gateway has two options for handling DTMF digits and events. First, it can simply measure the frequency components of the voice band signals and transmit this information to the RTP receiver (Section 4). In this mode, the gateway makes no attempt to discern the meaning of the tones, but simply distinguishes tones from speech signals.

All tone signals in use in the PSTN and meant for human consumption are sequences of simple combinations of sine waves, either added or modulated. (There is at least one tone, the ANSam tone [3] used for indicating data transmission over voice lines, that makes use of periodic phase reversals.)

As a second option, a gateway can recognize the tones and translate them into a name, such as ringing or busy tone. The receiver then produces a tone signal or other indication appropriate to the signal.

Generally, since the recognition of signals often depends on their on/off pattern or the sequence of several tones, this recognition can take several seconds. On the other hand, the gateway may have access to the actual signaling information that generates the tones and thus can generate the RTP packet immediately, without the detour through acoustic signals.

In the phone network, tones are generated at different places, depending on the switching technology and the nature of the tone. This determines, for example, whether a person making a call to a foreign country hears her local tones she is familiar with or the tones as used in the country called.

For analog lines, dial tone is always generated by the local switch. ISDN terminals may generate dial tone locally and then send a Q.931 SETUP message containing the dialed digits. If the terminal just sends a SETUP message without any Called Party digits, then the switch does digit collection, provided by the terminal as KEYPAD messages, and provides dial tone over the B-channel. The terminal can either use the audio signal on the B-channel or can use the Q.931 messages to trigger locally generated dial tone.

Ringing tone (also called ringback tone) is generated by the local switch at the callee, with a one-way voice path opened up as soon as the callee's phone rings. (This reduces the chance of clipping the called party's response just after answer. It also permits pre-answer announcements or in-band call-progress indications to reach the caller before or in lieu of a ringing tone.) Congestion tone and special information tones can be generated by any of the switches along the way, and may be generated by the caller's switch based on ISUP messages received. Busy tone is generated by the caller's switch, triggered by the appropriate ISUP message, for analog instruments, or the ISDN terminal.

Gateways which send signaling events via RTP MAY send both named signals (Section 3) and the tone representation (Section 4) as a single RTP session, using the redundancy mechanism defined in Section 3.7 to interleave the two representations. It is generally a good idea to send both, since it allows the receiver to choose the appropriate rendering.

If a gateway cannot present a tone representation, it SHOULD send the audio tones as regular RTP audio packets (e.g., as payload format PCMU), in addition to the named signals.

3 RTP Payload Format for Named Telephone Events

3.1 Introduction

The payload format for named telephone events described below is suitable for both gateway and end-to-end scenarios. In the gateway scenario, an Internet telephony gateway connecting a packet voice network to the PSTN recreates the DTMF tones or other telephony events and injects them into the PSTN. Since, for example, DTMF digit recognition takes several tens of milliseconds, the first few milliseconds of a digit will arrive as regular audio packets. Thus, careful time and power (volume) alignment between the audio samples and the events is needed to avoid generating spurious digits at the receiver.

DTMF digits and named telephone events are carried as part of the audio stream, and MUST use the same sequence number and time-stamp base as the regular audio channel to simplify the generation of audio waveforms at a gateway. The default clock frequency is 8,000 Hz, but the clock frequency can be redefined when assigning the dynamic payload type.

The payload format described here achieves a higher redundancy even in the case of sustained packet loss than the method proposed for the Voice over Frame Relay Implementation Agreement [4].

If an end system is directly connected to the Internet and does not need to generate tone signals again, time alignment and power levels are not relevant. These systems rely on PSTN gateways or Internet end systems to generate DTMF events and do not perform their own audio waveform analysis. An example of such a system is an Internet interactive voice-response (IVR) system.

In circumstances where exact timing alignment between the audio stream and the DTMF digits or other events is not important and data is sent unicast, such as the IVR example mentioned earlier, it may be preferable to use a reliable control protocol rather than RTP packets. In those circumstances, this payload format would not be used.

3.2 Simultaneous Generation of Audio and Events

A source MAY send events and coded audio packets for the same time instants, using events as the redundant encoding for the audio stream, or it MAY block outgoing audio while event tones are active and only send named events as both the primary and redundant encodings.

Note that a period covered by an encoded tone may overlap in time with a period of audio encoded by other means. This is likely to occur at the onset of a tone and is necessary to avoid possible errors in the interpretation of the reproduced tone at the remote end. Implementations supporting this payload format must be prepared to handle the overlap. It is RECOMMENDED that gateways only render the encoded tone since the audio may contain spurious tones introduced by the audio compression algorithm. However, it is anticipated that these extra tones in general should not interfere with recognition at the far end.

3.3 Event Types

This payload format is used for five different types of signals:

- o DTMF tones (Section 3.10);
- o fax-related tones (Section 3.11);
- o standard subscriber line tones (Section 3.12);
- o country-specific subscriber line tones (Section 3.13) and;
- o trunk events (Section 3.14).

A compliant implementation MUST support the events listed in Table 1 with the exception of "flash". If it uses some other, out-of-band mechanism for signaling line conditions, it does not have to implement the other events.

In some cases, an implementation may simply ignore certain events, such as fax tones, that do not make sense in a particular environment. Section 3.9 specifies how an implementation can use the SDP "fmtp" parameter within an SDP description to indicate its inability to understand a particular event or range of events.

Depending on the available user interfaces, an implementation MAY render all tones in Table 5 the same or, preferably, use the tones conveyed by the concurrent "tone" payload or other RTP audio payload. Alternatively, it could provide a textual representation.

Note that end systems that emulate telephones only need to support the events described in Sections 3.10 and 3.12, while systems that receive trunk signaling need to implement those in Sections 3.10, 3.11, 3.12 and 3.14, since MF trunks also carry most of the "line" signals. Systems that do not support fax or modem functionality do not need to render fax-related events described in Section 3.11.

The RTP payload format is designated as "telephone-event", the MIME type as "audio/telephone-event". The default timestamp rate is 8000 Hz, but other rates may be defined. In accordance with current practice, this payload format does not have a static payload type number, but uses a RTP payload type number established dynamically and out-of-band.

3.4 Use of RTP Header Fields

Timestamp: The RTP timestamp reflects the measurement point for the current packet. The event duration described in Section 3.5 extends forwards from that time. The receiver calculates jitter for RTCP receiver reports based on all packets with a given timestamp. Note: The jitter value should primarily be used as a means for comparing the reception quality between two users or two time-periods, not as an absolute measure.

Marker bit: The RTP marker bit indicates the beginning of a new event.

3.5 Payload Format

The payload format is shown in Fig. 1.

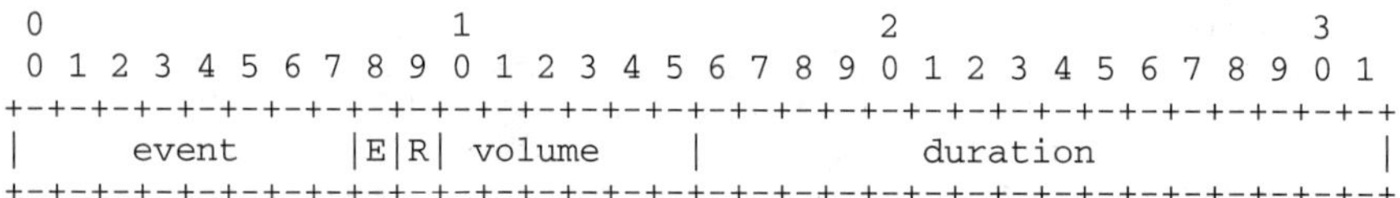

Figure 1: Payload Format for Named Events

events: The events are encoded as shown in Sections 3.10 through 3.14.

volume: For DTMF digits and other events representable as tones, this field describes the power level of the tone, expressed in dBm0 after dropping the sign. Power levels range from 0 to -63 dBm0. The range of valid DTMF is from 0 to -36 dBm0 (must accept); lower than -55 dBm0 must be rejected (TR-TSY-000181, ITU-T Q.24A). Thus, larger values denote lower volume. This value is defined only for DTMF digits. For other events, it is set to zero by the sender and is ignored by the receiver.

duration: Duration of this digit, in timestamp units. Thus, the event began at the instant identified by the RTP timestamp and has so far lasted as long as indicated by this parameter. The event may or may not have ended.

For a sampling rate of 8000 Hz, this field is sufficient to express event durations of up to approximately 8 seconds.

E: If set to a value of one, the "end" bit indicates that this packet contains the end of the event. Thus, the duration parameter above measures the complete duration of the event.

A sender MAY delay setting the end bit until retransmitting the last packet for a tone, rather than on its first transmission. This avoids having to wait to detect whether the tone has indeed ended.

Receiver implementations MAY use different algorithms to create tones, including the two described here. In the first, the receiver simply places a tone of the given duration in the audio playout buffer at the location indicated by the timestamp. As additional packets are received that extend the same tone, the waveform in the playout buffer is extended accordingly. (Care has to be taken if audio is mixed, i.e., summed, in the playout buffer rather than simply copied.) Thus, if a packet in a tone lasting longer than the packet interarrival time gets lost and the playout delay is short, a gap in the tone may occur. Alternatively, the receiver can start a tone and play it until it receives a packet with the "E" bit set, the next tone, distinguished by a different timestamp value or a given time period elapses. This is more robust against packet loss, but may extend the tone if all retransmissions of the last packet in an event are lost. Limiting the time period of extending the tone is necessary to avoid that a tone "gets stuck". Regardless of the algorithm used, the tone SHOULD NOT be extended by more than three packet interarrival times. A slight extension of tone durations and shortening of pauses is generally harmless.

R: This field is reserved for future use. The sender MUST set it to zero, the receiver MUST ignore it.

3.6 Sending Event Packets

An audio source SHOULD start transmitting event packets as soon as it recognizes an event and every 50 ms thereafter or the packet interval for the audio codec used for this session, if known. (The sender does not need to maintain precise time intervals between event packets in order to maintain precise inter-event times, since the timing information is contained in the timestamp.)

> Q.24 [5], Table A-1, indicates that all administrations surveyed use a minimum signal duration of 40 ms, with signaling velocity (tone and pause) of no less than 93 ms.

If an event continues for more than one period, the source generating the events should send a new event packet with the RTP timestamp value corresponding to the beginning of the event and the duration of the event increased correspondingly. (The RTP sequence number is incremented by one for each packet.) If there has been no new event in the last interval, the event SHOULD be retransmitted three times or until the next event is recognized. This ensures that the duration of the event can be recognized correctly even if the last packet for an event is lost.

> DTMF digits and events are sent incrementally to avoid having the receiver wait for the completion of the event. Since some tones are two seconds long, this would incur a substantial delay. The transmitter does not know if event length is important and thus needs to transmit immediately and incrementally. If the receiver application does not care about event length, the incremental transmission mechanism avoids delay. Some applications, such as gateways into the PSTN, care about both delays and event duration.

3.7 Reliability

During an event, the RTP event payload format provides incremental updates on the event. The error resiliency depends on the playout delay at the receiver. For example, for a playout delay of 120 ms and a packet gap of 50 ms, two packets in a row can get lost without causing a gap in the tones generated at the receiver.

The audio redundancy mechanism described in RFC 2198 [6] MAY be used to recover from packet loss across events. The effective data rate is r times 64 bits (32 bits for the redundancy header and 32 bits for the telephone-event payload) every 50 ms or r times 1280 bits/second, where r is the number of redundant events carried in each packet. The value of r is an implementation trade-off, with a value of 5 suggested.

The timestamp offset in this redundancy scheme has 14 bits, so that it allows a single packet to "cover" 2.048 seconds of telephone events at a sampling rate of 8000 Hz. Including the starting time of previous events allows precise reconstruction of the tone sequence at a gateway. The scheme is resilient to consecutive packet losses spanning this interval of 2.048 seconds or r digits, whichever is less. Note that for previous digits, only an average loudness can be represented.

An encoder MAY treat the event payload as a highly-compressed version of the current audio frame. In that mode, each RTP packet during an event would contain the current audio codec rendition (say, G.723.1 or G.729) of this digit as well as the representation described in Section 3.5, plus any previous events seen earlier.

This approach allows dumb gateways that do not understand this format to function. See also the discussion in Section 1.

3.8 Example

A typical RTP packet, where the user is just dialing the last digit of the DTMF sequence "911". The first digit was 200 ms long (1600 timestamp units) and started at time 0, the second digit lasted 250 ms (2000 timestamp units) and started at time 800 ms (6400 timestamp units), the third digit was pressed at time 1.4 s (11,200 timestamp units) and the packet shown was sent at 1.45 s (11,600 timestamp units). The frame duration is 50 ms. To make the parts recognizable, the figure below ignores byte alignment. Timestamp and sequence number are assumed to have been zero at the beginning of the first digit. In this example, the dynamic payload types 96 and 97 have been assigned for the redundancy mechanism and the telephone event payload, respectively.

3.9 Indication of Receiver Capabilities using SDP

```
 0                   1                   2                   3
 0 1 2 3 4 5 6 7 8 9 0 1 2 3 4 5 6 7 8 9 0 1 2 3 4 5 6 7 8 9 0 1
+-+-+-+-+-+-+-+-+-+-+-+-+-+-+-+-+-+-+-+-+-+-+-+-+-+-+-+-+-+-+-+-+
|V=2|P|X|  CC   |M|     PT      |       sequence number         |
| 2 |0|0|   0   |0|     96      |              28               |
+-+-+-+-+-+-+-+-+-+-+-+-+-+-+-+-+-+-+-+-+-+-+-+-+-+-+-+-+-+-+-+-+
|                           timestamp                           |
|                             11200                             |
+-+-+-+-+-+-+-+-+-+-+-+-+-+-+-+-+-+-+-+-+-+-+-+-+-+-+-+-+-+-+-+-+
|           synchronization source (SSRC) identifier            |
|                            0x5234a8                           |
+-+-+-+-+-+-+-+-+-+-+-+-+-+-+-+-+-+-+-+-+-+-+-+-+-+-+-+-+-+-+-+-+
|F|   block PT  |     timestamp offset      |   block length    |
|1|     97      |           11200           |         4         |
+-+-+-+-+-+-+-+-+-+-+-+-+-+-+-+-+-+-+-+-+-+-+-+-+-+-+-+-+-+-+-+-+
|F|   block PT  |     timestamp offset      |   block length    |
|1|     97      |   11200 - 6400 = 4800     |         4         |
+-+-+-+-+-+-+-+-+-+-+-+-+-+-+-+-+-+-+-+-+-+-+-+-+-+-+-+-+-+-+-+-+
|F|   Block PT  |
|0|     97      |
+-+-+-+-+-+-+-+-+-+-+-+-+-+-+-+-+-+-+-+-+-+-+-+-+-+-+-+-+-+-+-+-+
|     digit     |E R| volume    |          duration             |
|       9       |1 0|     7     |            1600               |
+-+-+-+-+-+-+-+-+-+-+-+-+-+-+-+-+-+-+-+-+-+-+-+-+-+-+-+-+-+-+-+-+
|     digit     |E R| volume    |          duration             |
|       1       |1 0|    10     |            2000               |
+-+-+-+-+-+-+-+-+-+-+-+-+-+-+-+-+-+-+-+-+-+-+-+-+-+-+-+-+-+-+-+-+
|     digit     |E R| volume    |          duration             |
|       1       |0 0|    20     |             400               |
+-+-+-+-+-+-+-+-+-+-+-+-+-+-+-+-+-+-+-+-+-+-+-+-+-+-+-+-+-+-+-+-+
```

Figure 2: Example RTP packet after dialing "911"

Receivers MAY indicate which named events they can handle, for example, by using the Session Description Protocol (RFC 2327 [7]). The payload formats use the following fmtp format to list the event values that they can receive:

a=fmtp:<format> <list of values>

The list of values consists of comma-separated elements, which can be either a single decimal number or two decimal numbers separated by a hyphen (dash), where the second number is larger than the first. No whitespace is allowed between numbers or hyphens. The list does not have to be sorted.

For example, if the payload format uses the payload type number 100, and the implementation can handle the DTMF tones (events 0 through 15) and the dial and ringing tones, it would include the following description in its SDP message:

```
a=fmtp:100 0-15,66,70
```

Since all implementations MUST be able to receive events 0 through 15, listing these events in the a=fmtp line is OPTIONAL.

The corresponding MIME parameter is "events", so that the following sample media type definition corresponds to the SDP example above:

```
audio/telephone-event;events="0-11,66,67";rate="8000"
```

3.10 DTMF Events

Table 1 summarizes the DTMF-related named events within the telephone-event payload format.

Event	encoding (decimal)
0--9	0--9
*	10
#	11
A--D	12--15
Flash	16

Table 1: DTMF named events

3.11 Data Modem and Fax Events

Table 3.11 summarizes the events and tones that can appear on a subscriber line serving a fax machine or modem. The tones are described below, with additional detail in Table 7.

ANS: This 2100 +/- 15 Hz tone is used to disable echo suppression for data transmission [8,9]. For fax machines, Recommendation T.30 [9] refers to this tone as called terminal identification (CED) answer tone.

/ANS: This is the same signal as ANS, except that it reverses phase at an interval of 450 +/- 25 ms. It disables both echo cancellers and echo suppressors. (In the ITU Recommendation V.25 [8], this signal is rendered as ANS with a bar on top.)

ANSam: The modified answer tone (ANSam) [3] is a sinewave signal at 2100 +/- 1 Hz without phase reversals, amplitude-modulated by a sinewave at 15 +/- 0.1 Hz. This tone is sent by modems if network echo canceller disabling is not required.

/ANSam: The modified answer tone with phase reversals (ANSam) [3] is a sinewave signal at 2100 +/- 1 Hz with phase reversals at intervals of 450 +/- 25 ms, amplitude-modulated by a sinewave at 15 +/- 0.1 Hz. This tone [10,8] is sent by modems [11] and faxes to disable echo suppressors.

CNG: After dialing the called fax machine's telephone number (and before it answers), the calling Group III fax machine (optionally) begins sending a CalliNG tone (CNG) consisting of an interrupted tone of 1100 Hz. [9]

CRdi: Capabilities Request (CRd), initiating side, [12] is a dual-tone signal with tones at 1375 Hz and 2002 Hz for 400 ms, followed by a single tone at 1900 Hz for 100 ms. "This signal requests the remote station transition from telephony mode to an information transfer mode and requests the transmission of a capabilities list message by the remote station. In particular, CRdi is sent by the initiating station during the course of a call, or by the calling station at call establishment in response to a CRe or MRe."

CRdr: CRdr is the response tone to CRdi (see above). It consists of a dual-tone signal with tones at 1529 Hz and 2225 Hz for 400 ms, followed by a single tone at 1900 Hz for 100 ms.

CRe: Capabilities Request (CRe) [12] is a dual-tone signal with tones at tones at 1375 Hz and 2002 Hz for 400 ms, followed by a single tone at 400 Hz for 100 ms. "This signal requests the remote station transition from telephony mode to an information transfer mode and requests the transmission of a capabilities list message by the remote station. In particular, CRe is sent by an automatic answering station at call establishment."

CT: "The calling tone [8] consists of a series of interrupted bursts of binary 1 signal or 1300 Hz, on for a duration of not less than 0.5 s and not more than 0.7 s and off for a duration of not less than 1.5 s and not more than 2.0 s." Modems not starting with the V.8 call initiation tone often use this tone.

ESi: Escape Signal (ESi) [12] is a dual-tone signal with tones at 1375 Hz and 2002 Hz for 400 ms, followed by a single tone at 980 Hz for 100 ms. "This signal requests the remote station transition from telephony mode to an information transfer mode. signal ESi is sent by the initiating station."

ESr: Escape Signal (ESr) [12] is a dual-tone signal with tones at 1529 Hz and 2225 Hz for 400 ms, followed by a single tone at 1650 Hz for 100 ms. Same as ESi, but sent by the responding station.

MRdi: Mode Request (MRd), initiating side, [12] is a dual-tone signal with tones at 1375 Hz and 2002 Hz for 400 ms followed by a single tone at 1150 Hz for 100 ms. "This signal requests the remote station transition from telephony mode to an information transfer mode and requests the transmission of a mode select message by the remote station. In particular, signal MRd is sent by the initiating station during the course of a call, or by the calling station at call establishment in response to an MRe." [12]

MRdr: MRdr is the response tone to MRdi (see above). It consists of a dual-tone signal with tones at 1529 Hz and 2225 Hz for 400 ms, followed by a single tone at 1150 Hz for 100 ms.

MRe: Mode Request (MRe) [12] is a dual-tone signal with tones at 1375 Hz and 2002 Hz for 400 ms, followed by a single tone at 650 Hz for 100 ms. "This signal requests the remote station transition from telephony mode to an information transfer mode and requests the transmission of a mode select message by the remote station. In particular, signal MRe is sent by an automatic answering station at call establishment." [12]

V.21: V.21 describes a 300 b/s full-duplex modem that employs frequency shift keying (FSK). It is used by Group 3 fax machines to exchange T.30 information. The calling transmits on channel 1 and receives on channel 2; the answering modem transmits on channel 2 and receives on channel 1. Each bit value has a distinct tone, so that V.21 signaling comprises a total of four distinct tones.

In summary, procedures in Table 2 are used.

Procedure	indications
V.25 and V.8	ANS
V.25, echo canceller disabled	ANS, /ANS, ANS, /ANS
V.8	ANSam
V.8, echo canceller disabled	/ANSam

Table 2: Use of ANS, ANSam and /ANSam in V.x recommendations

Event	encoding (decimal)
Answer tone (ANS)	32
/ANS	33
ANSam	34
/ANSam	35
Calling tone (CNG)	36
V.21 channel 1, "0" bit	37
V.21 channel 1, "1" bit	38
V.21 channel 2, "0" bit	39
V.21 channel 2, "1" bit	40
CRdi	41
CRdr	42
CRe	43
ESi	44
ESr	45
MRdi	46
MRdr	47
MRe	48
CT	49

Table 3: Data and fax named events

3.12 Line Events

Table 4 summarizes the events and tones that can appear on a subscriber line.

ITU Recommendation E.182 [13] defines when certain tones should be used. It defines the following standard tones that are heard by the caller:

Dial tone: The exchange is ready to receive address information.

PABX internal dial tone: The PABX is ready to receive address information.

Special dial tone: Same as dial tone, but the caller's line is subject to a specific condition, such as call diversion or a voice mail is available (e.g., "stutter dial tone").

Second dial tone: The network has accepted the address information, but additional information is required.

Ring: This named signal event causes the recipient to generate an alerting signal ("ring"). The actual tone or other indication used to render this named event is left up to the receiver. (This differs from the ringing tone, below, heard by the caller

Ringing tone: The call has been placed to the callee and a calling signal (ringing) is being transmitted to the callee. This tone is also called "ringback".

Special ringing tone: A special service, such as call forwarding or call waiting, is active at the called number.

Busy tone: The called telephone number is busy.

Congestion tone: Facilities necessary for the call are temporarily unavailable.

Calling card service tone: The calling card service tone consists of 60 ms of the sum of 941 Hz and 1477 Hz tones (DTMF '#'), followed by 940 ms of 350 Hz and 440 Hz (U.S. dial tone), decaying exponentially with a time constant of 200 ms.

Special information tone: The callee cannot be reached, but the reason is neither "busy" nor "congestion". This tone should be used before all call failure announcements, for the benefit of automatic equipment.

Comfort tone: The call is being processed. This tone may be used during long post-dial delays, e.g., in international connections.

Hold tone: The caller has been placed on hold.

Record tone: The caller has been connected to an automatic answering device and is requested to begin speaking.

Caller waiting tone: The called station is busy, but has call waiting service.

Pay tone: The caller, at a payphone, is reminded to deposit additional coins.

Positive indication tone: The supplementary service has been activated.

Negative indication tone: The supplementary service could not be activated.

Off-hook warning tone: The caller has left the instrument off-hook for an extended period of time.

The following tones can be heard by either calling or called party during a conversation:

Call waiting tone: Another party wants to reach the subscriber.

Warning tone: The call is being recorded. This tone is not required in all jurisdictions.

Intrusion tone: The call is being monitored, e.g., by an operator.

CPE alerting signal: A tone used to alert a device to an arriving in-band FSK data transmission. A CPE alerting signal is a combined 2130 and 2750 Hz tone, both with tolerances of 0.5% and a duration of 80 to. 80 ms. The CPE alerting signal is used with ADSI services and Call Waiting ID services [14].

The following tones are heard by operators:

Payphone recognition tone: The person making the call or being called is using a payphone (and thus it is ill-advised to allow collect calls to such a person).

Event	encoding (decimal)
Off Hook	64
On Hook	65
Dial tone	66
PABX internal dial tone	67
Special dial tone	68
Second dial tone	69
Ringing tone	70
Special ringing tone	71
Busy tone	72
Congestion tone	73
Special information tone	74
Comfort tone	75
Hold tone	76
Record tone	77
Caller waiting tone	78
Call waiting tone	79
Pay tone	80
Positive indication tone	81
Negative indication tone	82
Warning tone	83
Intrusion tone	84
Calling card service tone	85
Payphone recognition tone	86
CPE alerting signal (CAS)	87
Off-hook warning tone	88
Ring	89

Table 4: E.182 line events

3.13 Extended Line Events

Table 5 summarizes country-specific events and tones that can appear on a subscriber line.

3.14 Trunk Events

Table 6 summarizes the events and tones that can appear on a trunk. Note that trunk can also carry line events (Section 3.12), as MF signaling does not include backward signals [15].

ABCD transitional: 4-bit signaling used by digital trunks. For N-state signaling, the first N values are used.

Event	encoding (decimal)
Acceptance tone	96
Confirmation tone	97
Dial tone, recall	98
End of three party service tone	99
Facilities tone	100
Line lockout tone	101
Number unobtainable tone	102
Offering tone	103
Permanent signal tone	104
Preemption tone	105
Queue tone	106
Refusal tone	107
Route tone	108
Valid tone	109
Waiting tone	110
Warning tone (end of period)	111
Warning Tone (PIP tone)	112

Table 5: Country-specific Line events

The T1 ESF (extended super frame format) allows 2, 4, and 16 state signaling bit options. These signaling bits are named A, B, C, and D. Signaling information is sent as robbed bits in frames 6, 12, 18, and 24 when using ESF T1 framing. A D4 superframe only transmits 4-state signaling with A and B bits. On the CEPT E1 frame, all signaling is carried in timeslot 16, and two channels of 16-state (ABCD) signaling are sent per frame.

Since this information is a state rather than a changing signal, implementations SHOULD use the following triple-redundancy mechanism, similar to the one specified in ITU-T Rec. I.366.2 [16], Annex L. At the time of a transition, the same ABCD information is sent 3 times at an interval of 5 ms. If another transition occurs during this time, then this continues. After a period of no change, the ABCD information is sent every 5 seconds.

Wink: A brief transition, typically 120-290 ms, from on-hook (unseized) to off-hook (seized) and back to onhook, used by the incoming exchange to signal that the call address signaling can proceed.

Incoming seizure: Incoming indication of call attempt (off-hook).

Event	encoding (decimal)
MF 0... 9	128...137
MF K0 or KP (start-of-pulsing)	138
MF K1	139
MF K2	140
MF S0 to ST (end-of-pulsing)	141
MF S1... S3	142...143
ABCD signaling (see below)	144...159
Wink	160
Wink off	161
Incoming seizure	162
Seizure	163
Unseize circuit	164
Continuity test	165
Default continuity tone	166
Continuity tone (single tone)	167
Continuity test send	168
Continuity verified	170
Loopback	171
Old milliwatt tone (1000 Hz)	172
New milliwatt tone (1004 Hz)	173

Table 6: Trunk events

Seizure: Seizure by answering exchange, in response to outgoing seizure.

Unseize circuit: Transition of circuit from off-hook to on-hook at the end of a call.

Wink off: A brief transition, typically 100-350 ms, from off-hook (seized) to on-hook (unseized) and back to off-hook (seized). Used in operator services trunks.

Continuity tone send: A tone of 2010 Hz.

Continuity tone detect: A tone of 2010 Hz.

Continuity test send: A tone of 1780 Hz is sent by the calling exchange. If received by the called exchange, it returns a "continuity verified" tone.

Continuity verified: A tone of 2010 Hz. This is a response tone, used in dual-tone procedures.

4 RTP Payload Format for Telephony Tones

4.1 Introduction

As an alternative to describing tones and events by name, as described in Section 3, it is sometimes preferable to describe them by their waveform properties. In particular, recognition is faster than for naming signals since it does not depend on recognizing durations or pauses.

There is no single international standard for telephone tones such as dial tone, ringing (ringback), busy, congestion ("fast-busy"), special announcement tones or some of the other special tones, such as payphone recognition, call waiting or record tone. However, across all countries, these tones share a number of characteristics [17]:

- o Telephony tones consist of either a single tone, the addition of two or three tones or the modulation of two tones. (Almost all tones use two frequencies; only the Hungarian "special dial tone" has three.) Tones that are mixed have the same amplitude and do not decay.

- o Tones for telephony events are in the range of 25 (ringing tone in Angola) to 1800 Hz. CED is the highest used tone at 2100 Hz. The telephone frequency range is limited to 3,400 Hz. (The piano has a range from 27.5 to 4186 Hz.)

- o Modulation frequencies range between 15 (ANSam tone) to 480 Hz (Jamaica). Non-integer frequencies are used only for frequencies of 16 2/3 and 33 1/3 Hz. (These fractional frequencies appear to be derived from older AC power grid frequencies.)

- o Tones that are not continuous have durations of less than four seconds.

- o ITU Recommendation E.180 [18] notes that different telephone companies require a tone accuracy of between 0.5 and 1.5%. The Recommendation suggests a frequency tolerance of 1%.

4.2 Examples of Common Telephone Tone Signals

As an aid to the implementor, Table 7 summarizes some common tones. The rows labeled "ITU ..." refer to the general recommendation of Recommendation E.180 [18]. Note that there are no specific guidelines for these tones. In the table, the symbol "+" indicates addition of the tones, without modulation, while "*" indicates amplitude modulation. The meaning of some of the tones is described in Section 3.12 or Section 3.11 (for V.21).

Tone name	frequency	on period	off period
CNG	1100	0.5	3.0
V.25 CT	1300	0.5	2.0
CED	2100	3.3	--
ANS	2100	3.3	--
ANSam	2100*15	3.3	--
V.21 "0" bit, ch. 1	1180	0.00333	
V.21 "1" bit, ch. 1	980	0.00333	
V.21 "0" bit, ch. 2	1850	0.00333	
V.21 "1" bit, ch. 2	1650	0.00333	
ITU dial tone	425	--	--
U.S. dial tone	350+440	--	--
ITU ringing tone	425	0.67--1.5	3--5
U.S. ringing tone	440+480	2.0	4.0
ITU busy tone	425		
U.S. busy tone	480+620	0.5	0.5
ITU congestion tone	425		
U.S. congestion tone	480+620	0.25	0.25

Table 7: Examples of telephony tones

4.3 Use of RTP Header Fields

Timestamp: The RTP timestamp reflects the measurement point for the current packet. The event duration described in Section 3.5 extends forwards from that time.

4.4 Payload Format

Based on the characteristics described above, this document defines an RTP payload format called "tone" that can represent tones consisting of one or more frequencies. (The corresponding MIME type is "audio/tone".) The default timestamp rate is 8,000 Hz, but other rates may be defined. Note that the timestamp rate does not affect the interpretation of the frequency, just the durations.

In accordance with current practice, this payload format does not have a static payload type number, but uses a RTP payload type number established dynamically and out-of-band.

It is shown in Fig. 3.

```
 0                   1                   2                   3
 0 1 2 3 4 5 6 7 8 9 0 1 2 3 4 5 6 7 8 9 0 1 2 3 4 5 6 7 8 9 0 1
+-+-+-+-+-+-+-+-+-+-+-+-+-+-+-+-+-+-+-+-+-+-+-+-+-+-+-+-+-+-+-+-+
|    modulation   |T|  volume   |          duration             |
+-+-+-+-+-+-+-+-+-+-+-+-+-+-+-+-+-+-+-+-+-+-+-+-+-+-+-+-+-+-+-+-+
|R R R R|       frequency       |R R R R|       frequency       |
+-+-+-+-+-+-+-+-+-+-+-+-+-+-+-+-+-+-+-+-+-+-+-+-+-+-+-+-+-+-+-+-+
|R R R R|       frequency       |R R R R|       frequency       |
+-+-+-+-+-+-+-+-+-+-+-+-+-+-+-+-+-+-+-+-+-+-+-+-+-+-+-+-+-+-+-+-+
......

+-+-+-+-+-+-+-+-+-+-+-+-+-+-+-+-+-+-+-+-+-+-+-+-+-+-+-+-+-+-+-+-+
|R R R R|       frequency       |R R R R|      frequency        |
+-+-+-+-+-+-+-+-+-+-+-+-+-+-+-+-+-+-+-+-+-+-+-+-+-+-+-+-+-+-+-+-+
```

Figure 3: Payload format for tones

The payload contains the following fields:

modulation: The modulation frequency, in Hz. The field is a 9-bit unsigned integer, allowing modulation frequencies up to 511 Hz. If there is no modulation, this field has a value of zero.

T: If the "T" bit is set (one), the modulation frequency is to be divided by three. Otherwise, the modulation frequency is taken as is.

This bit allows frequencies accurate to 1/3 Hz, since modulation frequencies such as 16 2/3 Hz are in practical use.

volume: The power level of the tone, expressed in dBm0 after dropping the sign, with range from 0 to -63 dBm0. (Note: A preferred level range for digital tone generators is -8 dBm0 to -3 dBm0.)

duration: The duration of the tone, measured in timestamp units. The tone begins at the instant identified by the RTP timestamp and lasts for the duration value.

The definition of duration corresponds to that for sample-based codecs, where the timestamp represents the sampling point for the first sample.

frequency: The frequencies of the tones to be added, measured in Hz and represented as a 12-bit unsigned integer. The field size is sufficient to represent frequencies up to 4095 Hz, which exceeds the range of telephone systems. A value of zero indicates silence. A single tone can contain any number of frequencies.

R: This field is reserved for future use. The sender MUST set it to zero, the receiver MUST ignore it.

4.5 Reliability

This payload format uses the reliability mechanism described in Section 3.7.

5 Combining Tones and Named Events

The payload formats in Sections 3 and 4 can be combined into a single payload using the method specified in RFC 2198. Fig. 4 shows an example. In that example, the RTP packet combines two "tone" and one "telephone-event" payloads. The payload types are chosen arbitrarily as 97 and 98, respectively, with a sample rate of 8000 Hz. Here, the redundancy format has the dynamic payload type 96.

The packet represents a snapshot of U.S. ringing tone, 1.5 seconds (12,000 timestamp units) into the second "on" part of the 2.0/4.0 second cadence, i.e., a total of 7.5 seconds (60,000 timestamp units) into the ring cycle. The 440 + 480 Hz tone of this second cadence started at RTP timestamp 48,000. Four seconds of silence preceded it, but since RFC 2198 only has a fourteen-bit offset, only 2.05 seconds (16383 timestamp units) can be represented. Even though the tone sequence is not complete, the sender was able to determine that this is indeed ringback, and thus includes the corresponding named event.

6 MIME Registration

6.1 audio/telephone-event

MIME media type name: audio

MIME subtype name: telephone-event

Required parameters: none.

```
  0                   1                   2                   3
  0 1 2 3 4 5 6 7 8 9 0 1 2 3 4 5 6 7 8 9 0 1 2 3 4 5 6 7 8 9 0 1
 +-+-+-+-+-+-+-+-+-+-+-+-+-+-+-+-+-+-+-+-+-+-+-+-+-+-+-+-+-+-+-+-+
 | V |P|X|  CC   |M|     PT      |       sequence number         |
 | 2 |0|0|   0   |0|     96      |              31               |
 +-+-+-+-+-+-+-+-+-+-+-+-+-+-+-+-+-+-+-+-+-+-+-+-+-+-+-+-+-+-+-+-+
 |                           timestamp                           |
 |                             48000                             |
 +-+-+-+-+-+-+-+-+-+-+-+-+-+-+-+-+-+-+-+-+-+-+-+-+-+-+-+-+-+-+-+-+
 |           synchronization source (SSRC) identifier            |
 |                            0x5234a8                           |
 +-+-+-+-+-+-+-+-+-+-+-+-+-+-+-+-+-+-+-+-+-+-+-+-+-+-+-+-+-+-+-+-+
 |F|   block PT  |     timestamp offset      |   block length    |
 |1|     98      |           16383           |         4         |
 +-+-+-+-+-+-+-+-+-+-+-+-+-+-+-+-+-+-+-+-+-+-+-+-+-+-+-+-+-+-+-+-+
 |F|   block PT  |     timestamp offset      |   block length    |
 |1|     97      |           16383           |         8         |
 +-+-+-+-+-+-+-+-+-+-+-+-+-+-+-+-+-+-+-+-+-+-+-+-+-+-+-+-+-+-+-+-+
 |F|   Block PT  |
 |0|     97      |
 +-+-+-+-+-+-+-+-+-+-+-+-+-+-+-+-+-+-+-+-+-+-+-+-+-+-+-+-+-+-+-+-+
 |  event=ring   |0|0| volume=0  |      duration=28383           |
 +-+-+-+-+-+-+-+-+-+-+-+-+-+-+-+-+-+-+-+-+-+-+-+-+-+-+-+-+-+-+-+-+

 +-+-+-+-+-+-+-+-+-+-+-+-+-+-+-+-+-+-+-+-+-+-+-+-+-+-+-+-+-+-+-+-+
 | modulation=0    |0| volume=63 |      duration=16383           |
 +-+-+-+-+-+-+-+-+-+-+-+-+-+-+-+-+-+-+-+-+-+-+-+-+-+-+-+-+-+-+-+-+
 |0 0 0 0|     frequency=0       |0 0 0 0|     frequency=0       |
 +-+-+-+-+-+-+-+-+-+-+-+-+-+-+-+-+-+-+-+-+-+-+-+-+-+-+-+-+-+-+-+-+

 +-+-+-+-+-+-+-+-+-+-+-+-+-+-+-+-+-+-+-+-+-+-+-+-+-+-+-+-+-+-+-+-+
 | modulation=0    |0| volume=5  |      duration=12000           |
 +-+-+-+-+-+-+-+-+-+-+-+-+-+-+-+-+-+-+-+-+-+-+-+-+-+-+-+-+-+-+-+-+
 |0 0 0 0|     frequency=440     |0 0 0 0|     frequency=480     |
 +-+-+-+-+-+-+-+-+-+-+-+-+-+-+-+-+-+-+-+-+-+-+-+-+-+-+-+-+-+-+-+-+
```

Figure 4: Combining tones and events in a single RTP packet

Optional parameters: The "events" parameter lists the events supported by the implementation. Events are listed as one or more comma-separated elements. Each element can either be a single integer or two integers separated by a hyphen. No white space is allowed in the argument. The integers designate the event numbers supported by the implementation. All implementations MUST support events 0 through 15, so that the parameter can be omitted if the implementation only supports these events.

The "rate" parameter describes the sampling rate, in Hertz. The number is written as a floating point number or as an integer. If omitted, the default value is 8000 Hz.

Encoding considerations: This type is only defined for transfer via RTP [1].

Security considerations: See the "Security Considerations" (Section 7) section in this document.

Interoperability considerations: none

Published specification: This document.

Applications which use this media: The telephone-event audio subtype supports the transport of events occurring in telephone systems over the Internet.

Additional information:

1. Magic number(s): N/A

2. File extension(s): N/A

3. Macintosh file type code: N/A

6.2 audio/tone

MIME media type name: audio

MIME subtype name: tone

Required parameters: none

Optional parameters: The "rate" parameter describes the sampling rate, in Hertz. The number is written as a floating point number or as an integer. If omitted, the default value is 8000 Hz.

Encoding considerations: This type is only defined for transfer via RTP [1].

Security considerations: See the "Security Considerations" (Section 7) section in this document.

Interoperability considerations: none

Published specification: This document.

Applications which use this media: The tone audio subtype supports the transport of pure composite tones, for example those commonly used in the current telephone system to signal call progress.

Additional information:

1. Magic number(s): N/A

2. File extension(s): N/A

3. Macintosh file type code: N/A

7 Security Considerations

RTP packets using the payload format defined in this specification are subject to the security considerations discussed in the RTP specification (RFC 1889 [1]), and any appropriate RTP profile (for example RFC 1890 [19]).This implies that confidentiality of the media streams is achieved by encryption. Because the data compression used with this payload format is applied end-to-end, encryption may be performed after compression so there is no conflict between the two operations.

This payload type does not exhibit any significant non-uniformity in the receiver side computational complexity for packet processing to cause a potential denial-of-service threat.

In older networks employing in-band signaling and lacking appropriate tone filters, the tones in Section 3.14 may be used to commit toll fraud.

Additional security considerations are described in RFC 2198 [6].

8 IANA Considerations

This document defines two new RTP payload formats, named telephone-event and tone, and associated Internet media (MIME) types, audio/telephone-event and audio/tone.

Within the audio/telephone-event type, additional events MUST be registered with IANA. Registrations are subject to approval by the current chair of the IETF audio/video transport working group, or by an expert designated by the transport area director if the AVT group has closed.

The meaning of new events MUST be documented either as an RFC or an equivalent standards document produced by another standardization body, such as ITU-T.

9 Acknowledgements

The suggestions of the Megaco working group are gratefully acknowledged. Detailed advice and comments were provided by Fred Burg, Steve Casner, Fatih Erdin, Bill Foster, Mike Fox, Gunnar Hellstrom, Terry Lyons, Steve Magnell, Vern Paxson and Colin Perkins.

10 Authors' Addresses

Henning Schulzrinne
Dept. of Computer Science
Columbia University
1214 Amsterdam Avenue
New York, NY 10027
USA

EMail: schulzrinne@cs.columbia.edu

Scott Petrack
MetaTel
45 Rumford Avenue
Waltham, MA 02453
USA

EMail: scott.petrack@metatel.com

11 Bibliography

[1] Schulzrinne, H., Casner, S., Frederick, R. and V. Jacobson, "RTP: A Transport Protocol for Real-Time Applications", RFC 1889, January 1996.

[2] Bradner, S., "Key words for use in RFCs to Indicate Requirement Levels", BCP 14, RFC 2119, March 1997.

[3] International Telecommunication Union, "Procedures for starting sessions of data transmission over the public switched telephone network," Recommendation V.8, Telecommunication Standardization Sector of ITU, Geneva, Switzerland, Feb. 1998.

[4] R. Kocen and T. Hatala, "Voice over frame relay implementation agreement", Implementation Agreement FRF.11, Frame Relay Forum, Foster City, California, Jan. 1997.

[5] International Telecommunication Union, "Multifrequency push-button signal reception," Recommendation Q.24, Telecommunication Standardization Sector of ITU, Geneva, Switzerland, 1988.

[6] Perkins, C., Kouvelas, I., Hodson, O., Hardman, V., Handley, M., Bolot, J., Vega-Garcia, A. and S. Fosse-Parisis, "RTP Payload for Redundant Audio Data", RFC 2198, September 1997.

[7] Handley M. and V. Jacobson, "SDP: Session Description Protocol", RFC 2327, April 1998.

[8] International Telecommunication Union, "Automatic answering equipment and general procedures for automatic calling equipment on the general switched telephone network including procedures for disabling of echo control devices for both manually and automatically established calls," Recommendation V.25, Telecommunication Standardization Sector of ITU, Geneva, Switzerland, Oct. 1996.

[9] International Telecommunication Union, "Procedures for document facsimile transmission in the general switched telephone network," Recommendation T.30, Telecommunication Standardization Sector of ITU, Geneva, Switzerland, July 1996.

[10] International Telecommunication Union, "Echo cancellers," Recommendation G.165, Telecommunication Standardization Sector of ITU, Geneva, Switzerland, Mar. 1993.

[11] International Telecommunication Union, "A modem operating at data signaling rates of up to 33 600 bit/s for use on the general switched telephone network and on leased point-to-point 2-wire telephone-type circuits," Recommendation V.34, Telecommunication Standardization Sector of ITU, Geneva, Switzerland, Feb. 1998.

[12] International Telecommunication Union, "Procedures for the identification and selection of common modes of operation between data circuit-terminating equipments (DCEs) and between data terminal equipments (DTEs) over the public switched telephone network and on leased point-to-point telephone-type circuits," Recommendation V.8bis, Telecommunication Standardization Sector of ITU, Geneva, Switzerland, Sept. 1998.

[13] International Telecommunication Union, "Application of tones and recorded announcements in telephone services," Recommendation E.182, Telecommunication Standardization Sector of ITU, Geneva, Switzerland, Mar. 1998.

[14] Bellcore, "Functional criteria for digital loop carrier systems," Technical Requirement TR-NWT-000057, Telcordia (formerly Bellcore), Morristown, New Jersey, Jan. 1993.

[15] J. G. van Bosse, Signaling in Telecommunications Networks Telecommunications and Signal Processing, New York, New York: Wiley, 1998.

[16] International Telecommunication Union, "AAL type 2 service specific convergence sublayer for trunking," Recommendation I.366.2, Telecommunication Standardization Sector of ITU, Geneva, Switzerland, Feb. 1999.

[17] International Telecommunication Union, "Various tones used in national networks," Recommendation Supplement 2 to Recommendation E.180, Telecommunication Standardization Sector of ITU, Geneva, Switzerland, Jan. 1994.

[18] International Telecommunication Union, "Technical characteristics of tones for telephone service," Recommendation Supplement 2 to Recommendation E.180, Telecommunication Standardization Sector of ITU, Geneva, Switzerland, Jan. 1994.

[19] Schulzrinne, H., "RTP Profile for Audio and Video Conferences with Minimal Control", RFC 1890, January 1996.

12 Full Copyright Statement

Acknowledgement

Funding for the RFC Editor function is currently provided by the Internet Society.

Network Working Group
Request for Comments: 2846
Category: Standards Track

C. Allocchio
GARR-Italy
June 2000

GSTN Address Element Extensions in E-mail Services

Status of this Memo

This document specifies an Internet standards track protocol for the Internet community, and requests discussion and suggestions for improvements. Please refer to the current edition of the "Internet Official Protocol Standards" (STD 1) for the standardization state and status of this protocol. Distribution of this memo is unlimited.

Copyright Notice

Abstract

There are numerous applications where there is a need for interaction between the GSTN addressing and Internet addressing. This memo defines a full syntax for one specific case, where there is a need to represent GSTN addresses within Internet e-mail addresses. This full syntax is a superset of a minimal syntax which has been defined in [1].

1. Introduction

The possible elements composing a "Global Switched Telephone Network (GSTN) address in e-mail" (also known as the Public Switched Telephone Network - PSTN) can vary from a minimum number up to a really large and complex collection. As noted the minimal format and general address syntax have been defined in [1], along with the mechanism needed to define additional address elements. This memo uses this extension mechanism to complete the syntax for representing GSTN addresses within e-mail addresses and contains the IANA registrations for all newly defined elements.

In particular, the following additional address elements shall be defined:

- the detailed definition of GSTN number formats, in order to cover various alternative standard GSTN numbering schemes, (i.e. gstn-phone, sub-addr-spec and post-dial)

- the message originator and/or recipient specification (pstn-recipient)

GSTN addresses in e-mail MAY contain additional elements defined and registered in other specifications (see for example "T33S" element in [2]), but they MUST use definitions contained in this memo for those elements specified here.

In particular, "service-selector" names and "qualif-type1" elements MUST be registered with IANA, and published within the "ASSIGNED NUMBERS" document. This provides a standard mechanism for extending the element sets and should avoid unnecessary duplication. IANA Registration form templates for the purpouse of registering new elements are provided in Appendix B. In addition the IANA consideration section of this document defines the procedures required to proceed with new registrations.

A collection of forms for already defined "service-selector" and "qualif-type1" elements is listed in appendix C and appendix D respectively.

In particular, efforts have been made to maintain compatibility with elements defined in existing e-mail gateway services and standard specifications. For example, to the extent possible, compatibility has been maintained with the MIXER [3] gateways specifications.

1.1 Relationship with Internet addressing other than e-mail

Even if in this memo we focus on e-mail addresses, a number of elements defined in this specification can also be used for other specifications dealing with embedding GSTN addresses into other addresses: for example there is some work in progress about URLs specification which adopts similar definitions, with slight changes in the global syntax due to specific URL format.

1.2 Terminology and Syntax conventions

In this document the formal definitions are described using ABNF syntax, as defined into [4]. We will also use some of the "CORE DEFINITIONS" defined in "APPENDIX A - CORE" of that document. The exact meaning of the capitalised words

"MUST", "MUST NOT", "REQUIRED", "SHALL", "SHALL NOT", "SHOULD", "SHOULD NOT", "RECOMMENDED", "MAY", "OPTIONAL"

is defined in reference [5].

2. GSTN extended number and pstn-mbox extended format

In reference [1], section 2, the minimal definition of pstn-mbox includes the global-phone element, and further details are defined in [1] section 2.1.

However other non global-phone numbering schemes are also possible. Thus, the minimal set syntax defined in [1] shall be extended to enable support for local-phone elements. Therefore, the gstn-phone format is defined as follows:

```
gstn-phone = ( global-phone / local-phone )
```

The complexity of the GSTN system includes also the optional use of subaddresses and post dialling sequences. As a consequence, there is a need to extend the definition of pstn-mbox per [1] to include support for both the minimal set definition and an extended syntax.

The expanded definition of pstn-mbox is as follows:

```
pstn-mbox = service-selector "=" global-phone

pstn-mbox =/ service-selector "=" gstn-phone
             [ sub-addr-spec ] [post-sep post-dial]
```

NOTE: see section 4 in the event multiple "sub-addr-spec" elements per pstn-mbox need to be specified.

2.1 The local-phone syntax

The local-phone element is intended to represent the set of possible cases where the global-phone numbering schema does not apply. Given the different and complex conventions currently being used in the GSTN system, the local-phone definition supports a large number of elements.

The detailed syntax for local-phone elements follows:

```
local-phone = [ exit-code ] [ dial-number ]

exit-code = phone-string
            ; this will include elements such as the digit to
            ; access outside line, the long distance carrier
            ; access code, the access password to the service,
            ; etc...
```

```
dial-number = phone-string
            ; this is in many cases composed of different elements
            ; such as the local phone number, the area code
            ; (if needed), the international country code
            ; (if needed), etc...
```

Note:
the "+" character is reserved for use in global-phone addresses per [7] and MUST NOT be used as the starting character in a local-phone string.

```
phone-string = 1*( DTMF / pause / tonewait / written-sep )

DTMF = ( DIGIT / "#" / "*" / "A" / "B" / "C" / "D" )
               ; special DTMF codes like "*", "#", "A", "B",
               ; "C", "D" are defined in [6]
               ; Important Note: these elements only apply for
               ; alphabetic strings used in DTMF operations.
               ; They are NOT applicable for the alphabetic
               ; characters that are mapped to digits on phone
               ; keypads in some countries.

pause = "p"

tonewait = "w"
```

The written-sep element is defined in [1], section 2.1.

Note:
"pause" and "tonewait" character interpretation in local-phone numbers depends on the specific MTA implementation. Thus its exact meaning is not defined here. Both "pause" and "tonewait" are case insensitive.

Important Note:
A local-phone specification is a sequence which should be used only by the destination MTA specified by mta-I-pstn (see [1], section 3). Per [12], other MTAs should transfer the message without modifying the LHS.

2.2 The sub-addr-spec element

In GSTN service there are cases where a sub-addr-spec is required to specify the final destination. In particular there are ISDN subaddresses [7], which apply for various services, whereas other subaddress types may be service specific (see the fax service T.33 subaddress [8], [2]).

Within actual telephone operations there may be cases where different types of subaddresses are used as part of a single complete address. Therefore, the sub-addr-spec syntax definition which follows defines the subaddress element for the context of ISDN use; the T.33 subaddress element is defined in [2], section 2.

The definition of sub-addr-spec is:

```
sub-addr-spec = [ isdn-sep isub-addr ]
```

In detail:

```
isdn-sep = "/ISUB="
           ; note that "/ISUB=" is case INSENSITIVE

isub-addr = 1*( DIGIT )

isub-addr =/ 1*( DIGIT / written-sep )
```

The IANA registration form for sub-addr-spec is given in appendix D.2

2.3 The post-sep and post-dial elements

In some cases, after the connection with the destination GSTN device has been established, a further dialling sequence is required to access further services. A typical example is an automated menu-driven service using DTMF sequences. These cases may be handled using "post-sep" and "post-dial" elements as defined below:

```
post-sep =  "/POSTD="
            ; note that "/POSTD=" is case INSENSITIVE

post-dial = phone-string
```

The IANA registration form for post-sep and post-dial are given in appendix D.3

3. The pstn-recipient

There are some application where it is valuable to supplement the pstn-mbox element with additional details. Common examples include the use of originator and/or recipient names and physical addresses, particularly in the context of onramp and/or offramp gateways.

The optional pstn-recipient element provides support for such details.

As an example, when an offramp fax gateway is involved, the pstn-recipient element could be used to specify the intended recipient on a fax cover page, and the fax cover page headers could be qualified using the originator pstn-recipient information.

In the interest of a compact syntax, the pstn-recipient element may be used to support both originator and recipient addresses. For all cases within the ABNF definitions to follow, the elements labelled with "recipient" may also be used for originator information.

The pstn-recipient is a sequence of qualif-type1 elements as defined below:

```
pstn-recipient = [ recipient-name ]
                 [ 1*( recipient-qualifier ) ]
```

As a consequence, the extended definition of pstn-address becomes:

```
pstn-address = pstn-mbox  [ qualif-type1 ]

pstn-address =/ pstn-mbox [ pstn-recipient ] [ qualif-type1 ]
```

The definition for qualif-type1 elements is contained in [1] section 2.

3.1 The recipient-name

The recipient-name specifies the personal name of the originator and/or recipient:

```
recipient-name = "/ATTN=" pers-name

pers-name = [ givenname "." ]
            [ initials "." ]
            surname
```

The following definitions come directly from the MIXER specification [3]:

```
surname = printablestring

givenname = 1*( DIGIT /  ALPHA / SP / "'" / "+" /
                "," / "-" / "/" / ":" / "=" / "?" )

initials = 1*ALPHA
```

Note:
the "initials" element can specify the middle initial which is common in some countries; however it is also possible to support multiple initials, which may be commonly used in other countries. This allows the complete set of givennames initials in any possible combination. See examples at section 5.2

It is essential to remember that the "pstn-address" element (in all its components and extensions) MUST strictly follow the "quoting rules" specified in the relevant e-mail standards [11], [12].

The IANA registration form for recipient-name is given in appendix D.4.

3.2 The extensible recipient-qualifier

The recipient-name is sometimes not enough to specify completely the originator and/or recipient. An additional set of optional elements, whose specific definition is in most cases application dependent, is thus defined:

```
recipient-qualifier = ( qualif-type1 / qualif-type2 )
```

The recipient-qualifier is a qualif-type1 element, and contains a qualif-type1 element in a recursive definition which allows an extensible format. The purpouse of qualif-type2 element is to permit additional extensibility for items which go beyond the scope of those defined for use with the qualif-type1 element.

A series of qualif-type2 elements are defined below:

```
qualif-type2 = "/" qual2-label "=" string

qual2-label = "ORG" / "OFNO" / "OFNA" / "STR" / "ADDR"
              "ADDU" / "ADDL" / "POB" / "ZIP" / "CO"

string = PCHAR
         ; note that printable characters are %x20-7E

printablestring = 1*( DIGIT / ALPHA / SP /
                      "'" / "(" / ")" / "+" / "," / "-" /
                      "." / "/" / ":" / "=" / "?" )
                  ; this definition comes from ITU F.401 [9]
                  ; and MIXER [3]
```

Table 1 includes short definition of qual2-label fields:

Table 1 - qual2-label

qual2-label	Description
"ORG"	Organization Name for Physical Delivery (example: ACME Inc)
"OFNO"	Office Number for physical delivery (example: BLD2-44)
"OFNA"	Office Name for physical delivery (example: Sales)
"STR"	Street address for physical delivery (example: 45, Main Street)
"ADDR"	Unformatted postal address for physical delivery (example: HWY 14, Km 94.5 - Loc. Redhill)
"ADDU"	Unique postal name for physical delivery (example: ACMETELEX)
"ADDL"	Local postal attributes for physical delivery (example: Entrance 3, 3rd floor, Suite 296)
"POB"	Post Office Box for physical delivery
"ZIP"	Postal ZIP code for physical delivery
"CO"	Country Name for physical delivery

One or a combination of some of the above elements is usually enough to exactly specify the originator and/or recipient of the message. The use of a large number of these elements could in fact create a very long recipient-qualifier. Thus, only the strictly needed elements SHOULD be used. The maximum total length of the pstn-email MUST in fact not exceed the limits specified in the relevant e-mail standards [11] [12].

IMPORTANT NOTE: Although the meaning of the above elements is derived directly from similar elements available in F.401 specification [9], the naming convention used in this document is explicitly different. In this way a conflict is avoided with related X.400 addressing rules. Other specification which use the extension mechanism of this document to define new qualif-type1 elements which overlap with F.401 are cautioned to create new labels which are different than those used in F.401.

The IANA registration form for these elements is given in appendix D.5 to D.14.

4. Multiple sub-addr-spec cases

There are some instances in GSTN applications where multiple subaddresses are used: T.33 subaddresses in fax service are one of these cases. In e-mail practice a separate and unique e-mail address is always used for each recipient; as such, if multiple subaddresses are present, the use of multiple "pstn-email" elements [1] is REQUIRED.

Implementors' note:

> The UA MAY accept multiple subaddress elements for the same global-phone, but it MUST generate multiple "pstn-mbox" elements when submitting the message to the MTA.

5. Examples

In order to clarify the specification we present here a limited set of examples. Many of the examples refer to the fax service, but also additional possible services are included. Check also the examples in [1] and [2] for additional information. Please note that all the examples are for illustration purpouses, only.

5.1 pstn-mbox examples

A pstn-mbox address in Italy for the fax service, dialled from U.S.A., using local-phone, without sub-addr-spec and without written-sep:

```
FAX=0103940226338
```

A pstn-mbox address in Germany for an hypothetical XYZ service, using global-phone, with ISDN sub-addr-spec 1234 and written-sep ".":

```
XYZ=+49.81.7856345/ISUB=1234
```

A pstn-mbox address in U.S.A. for fax service, using global-phone, with T.33 sub-addr-spec 8745, with written-sep "-" and post-dial sequence p1w7005393w373

```
FAX=+1-202-455-7622/T33S=8745/PostD=p1w7005393w373
```

A pstn-mbox address in Italy for fax service, using local-phone, dialed from an MTA in Germany, (international access code "00", with ISDN subaddress 9823, with T.33 subaddress "4312" and without pause or written-sep:

```
FAX=003940226338/Isub=9823/T33S=4312
```

The same pstn-mbox address in Italy, using local-phone dialed from an MTA in Italy (long distance call), with long distant access "0", with exit-code "9", T.33 subaddress "4312", pause "p" and written-sep ".":

```
FAX=9p040p22.63.38/t33s=4312
```

A pstn-mbox address in North America for hypothetical service XYZ, using global-phone, without sub-addr-spec and written-sep "-" and ".":

```
XYZ=+1.202.344-5723
```

A pstn-mbox address for fax service in France, using local-phone dialed from an MTA in France (long distance call), with exit-code "0", T.33 subaddress "3345" and pause "p":

```
FAX=0p0134782289/T33s=3345
```

A pstn-mbox address for fax service in North America, using local-phone, without sub-addr-spec, without local-number, using only post-dial sequences to reach numbers stored in a locally defined short-dial numbers database, where 6743 is an access password, and 99p51 is the sequence to access the local short-dial number:

```
FAX=/postd=w6743w99p51
```

5.2 pstn-recipient examples

Here are a number of pstn-recipient examples. Please note that pstn-recipient is just an optional element, and thus a pstn-mbox element also is required in a pstn-address.

A pstn-recipient using only recipient-name, with givenname initials and surname:

```
/ATTN=Tom.J.Smiths
```

A pstn-recipient using only recipient-name, with givenname, a complete set of initials (including the first name initial "C") and surname (where the "real life" givennames are "Carlo Maria Luis Santo" and the surname is "Nascimento"):

```
/ATTN=Carlo.CMLS.Nascimento
```

A pstn-recipient using only recipient-name, with givenname and surname:

```
/ATTN=Mark.Collins
```

A pstn-recipient using only recipient-name, with surname only:

```
/ATTN=Smiths
```

A pstn-recipient using recipient-name, and one recipient-qualifier element:

```
/ATTN=J.Smiths/OFNA=Quaility-control
```

A pstn-recipient using two recipient-qualifier extension, only:

```
/OFNO=T2-33A/OFNA=Quality-Ccontrol
```

A fax-recipient using some recipient-qualifier for physical delivery:

```
/STR=45, Main.Street/OFNA=Sales.dept
```

5.3 pstn-address examples

Some pstn-address examples, obtained combining elements from previous examples. There are complete addresses which can be used as "local part" (LHS) element of an e-mail address.

Without optional pstn-recipient (fax service):

```
FAX=+12023445723
```

With pstn-recipient (XYZ service):

```
XYZ=+3940226338/ATTN=Mark.Collins
```

With pstn-recipient made of two recipient-qualifier extensions (fax service):

```
FAX=9p040p22.63.38/t33s=4312/ofno=T2-33A/OFNA=Q-C
```

5.4 pstn-email examples

Here are the same addresses as before, where "faxgw" is the mta-I-pstn field for the fax service.

```
FAX=+12023445723@faxgw

FAX=+39-40-226338/ATTN=Mark.Collins@faxgw

FAX=9p040p226338/T33S=4312/OFNO=T2-33A/OFNA=Q-C@faxgw
```

```
FAX=+39040226338/ATTN=Mark.Collins/@faxgw
```

NOTE: the optional "/" in front for the "@" sign can be generated by gateways to other services, like MIXER [3].

5.5 A complete SMTP transaction example:

Here is an example of complete SMTP transaction.

```
S: <listening on SMTP port>
C: <opens connection to SMTP port>
S: 220 foo.domain.com ESMTP service ready
C: EHLO pc.mailfax.com
S: 250 foo.domain.com says hello
C: MAIL FROM:<tom@mailfax.com>
S: 250 <tom@mailfax.com> Sender ok
C: RCPT TO:<FAX=+3940226338@foo.mailfax.com>
S: 250 <FAX=+3940226338> recipient ok
C: DATA
S: 354 Enter your data
C: From: Thomas Blake <tom@mailfax.com>
C: To: Jim Burton <FAX=+3940226338@foo.mailfax.com>
C: Subject: Hello there
C: MIME-version: 1.0
C: Date: Mon, 01 Sep 1997 18:14:23 -0700
C: Content-Type: multipart/mixed; boundary=16820115-1435684603#2306
C:
C: This is a MIME message. It contains a
C: TIFF fax bodypart
C:
C: --16820115-1435684603#2306
C: Content-Type: image/TIFF
C: Content-Transfer-Encoding: BASE64
C: Content-Description: FAX
C:
C: ABAA745HDKLSW932ALSDL3ANCVSASDFLALSDFA
C: 87AASS2999499ASDANASDF0000ASDFASDFNANN
C: 87BBHDXBADS00288SADFNAZBZNNDNNSNNA11A0
C: H8V73KS0C8JS6BFJEH78CDWWDUJEDF7JKES8==
C: --16820115-1435684603#2306--
C: .
S: 250 Okay
C: QUIT
S: 221 Goodbye
```

6. Conclusion

This proposal creates a standard set of extensions for GSTN addresses, enriching the existing minimal specification [1]. The proposal is consistent with existing e-mail standards, but allows a more detailed GSTN address specification, including per originator and/or recipient specific elements. The IANA registration mechanism to permit the addition of new services and qualifiers using the GSTN addresses is also provided.

7. Security Considerations

This document specifies a means by which GSTN addresses and more can be encoded into e-mail addresses. Since e-mail routing is determined by Domain Name System (DNS) data, a successful attack to DNS could disseminate tampered information, which causes e-mail messages to be diverted via some MTA or Gateway where the security of the software has been compromised.

There are several means by which an attacker might be able to deliver incorrect mail routing information to a client. These include: (a) compromise of a DNS server, (b) generating a counterfeit response to a client's DNS query, (c) returning incorrect "additional information" in response to an unrelated query. Clients SHOULD ensure that mail routing are based only on authoritative answers. Once DNS Security mechanisms [7] become more widely deployed, clients SHOULD employ those mechanisms to verify the authenticity and integrity of mail routing records.

Some GSTN service require dialing of private codes, like Personal Identification Numbers, to dial a G3 fax recipient or to access special services. As e-mail addresses are transmitted without encoding over the MTAs transport service, this could allow unauthorized people to gain access to these codes when used inside local-phone. More over these codes might appear in some cases in the originator and/or recipient addresses on cover pages delivered via offramp gateways to G3 fax recipients. Senders SHOULD be provided methods to prevent this disclosure, like code encryption, or masquerading techniques: out-of-band communication of authorization information or use of encrypted data in special fields are the available non-standard techniques.

8. Appendix A: Collected ABNF Syntax

In this section we provide a summary of ABNF specifications defining both the minimal [1] and the extended elements of pstn-address.

```
pstn-email =  ["/"] pstn-address ["/"] "@" mta-I-pstn

mta-I-pstn = domain

pstn-address = pstn-mbox  [ qualif-type1 ]

pstn-address =/ pstn-mbox [ pstn-recipient ] [ qualif-type1 ]

pstn-mbox = service-selector "=" global-phone

pstn-mbox =/ service-selector "=" gstn-phone
             [ sub-addr-spec ] [post-sep post-dial]

service-selector = 1*( DIGIT / ALPHA / "-" )

qualif-type1 = "/" keyword "=" string

keyword = 1*( DIGIT / ALPHA / "-" )

string = PCHAR

gstn-phone = ( global-phone / local-phone )

global-phone = "+" 1*( DIGIT , written-sep )

local-phone = [ exit-code ] [ dial-number ]

exit-code = phone-string

dial-number = phone-string

phone-string = 1*( DTMF / pause / tonewait / written-sep )

DTMF = ( DIGIT / "#" / "*" / "A" / "B" / "C" / "D" )

written-sep = ( "-" / "." )

pause = "p"

tonewait = "w"

sub-addr-spec = [ isdn-sep isub-addr ]
```

```
isdn-sep = "/ISUB="

isub-addr = 1*( DIGIT )

isub-addr =/ 1*( DIGIT / written-sep )

post-sep =  "/POSTD="

post-dial = phone-string

pstn-recipient = [ recipient-name ]
                 [ 1*( recipient-qualifier ) ]

recipient-name = "/ATTN=" pers-name

pers-name = [ givenname "." ]
            [ initials "." ]
            surname

surname = printablestring

givenname = 1*( DIGIT /  ALPHA / SP / "'" / "+" /
              "," / "-" / "/" / ":" / "=" / "?" )

initials = 1*ALPHA

recipient-qualifier = ( qualif-type1 / qualif-type2 )

qualif-type2 = "/" qual2-label "=" string

qual2-label = "ORG" / "OFNO" / "OFNA" / "STR" / "ADDR"
              "ADDU" / "ADDL" / "POB" / "ZIP" / "CO"

printablestring = 1*( DIGIT / ALPHA / SP /
                      "'" / "(" / ")" / "+" / "," / "-" /
                      "." / "/" / ":" / "=" / "?" )
```

10. Appendix B: IANA Considerations

As the service-selector and qualif-type1 elements values are extensible ones, they MUST be registered with IANA.

To register a service-selector or a qualif-type1 element, the registration form templates given in B.1 and B.2 MUST be used. Any new registration MUST fulfill the "Specification Required" criterion, as defined in RFC 2434, section 2 [13]:

"Specification Required - Values and their meaning MUST be documented in an RFC or other permanent and readily available reference, in sufficient detail so that interoperability between independent implementations is possible."

IANA MUST NOT accept registrations which are not supplemented by a Specification as defined above and which are not fully specified according to the template forms given in B.1 and B.2. In case of need for further consultation about accepting a new registration, IANA SHOULD refer to the Application Area Director to be directed to the appropriate "expert" individual or IETF Working Group.

After successful registration, IANA should publish the registered new element in the appropriate on-line IANA WEB site, and include it into the updates of the "Assigned Numbers" RFC series.

B.1: IANA Registration form template for new values of GSTN address service-selector

```
To: IANA@isi.edu
Subject: Registration of new values for the GSTN address
         service-selector specifier "foo"

service-selector name:

   foo

Description of Use:

   foo - ("foo" is a fictional new service-selector used in this
   template as an example, it is to be replaced with the new value
   being registered. Include a short description of the use of the
   new value here. This MUST include reference to Standard Track RFCs
   and eventually to other Standard Bodies documents for the complete
   description;  the use of the value must be defined completely
   enough for independent implementation).

Security Considerations:

   (Any additional security considerations that may be introduced by
   use of the new service-selector parameter should be defined here
   or in the reference Standards Track RFCs)

Person & email address to contact for further information:

   (fill in contact information)
```

INFORMATION TO THE SUBMITTER:

The accepted registrations will be listed in the "Assigned Numbers" series of RFCs. The information in the registration form is freely distributable.

B.2: IANA Registration form template for new values of GSTN address qualif-type1 keyword and value

To: IANA@isi.edu
Subject: Registration of new values for the GSTN address
         qualif-type1 element "bar"

qualif-type1 "keyword" name:

bar

qualif-type1 "value" ABNF definition:

abnf - ("abnf" MUST define the ABNF form of the qualif-type1 value. The ABNF specification MUST be self-contained, using as basic elements the tokens given in specification [4]. To avoid any duplication (when appropriate), it MUST also use as building non-basic tokens any already registered non-basic token from other qualif-type1 elements, i.e. it MUST use the same non-basic token name and then repeat its identical ABNF definition from basic tokens; see appendix E for examples).

Description of Use:

bar - ("bar" is a fictional description for a new qualif-type1 element used in this template as an example. It is to be replaced by the real description of qualif-type1 element being registered. Include a short description of the use of the new qualif-type1 here. This MUST include reference to Standards Track RFCs and eventually to other Standard Bodies documents for the complete description; the use of the value MUST be defined completely enough for independent implementation.)

Use Restriction:

(If the new qualif-type1 elements is meaningful only for a specific set of service-element, you MUST specify here the list of allowed service-element types. If there is no restriction, then specify the keyword "none")

Security Considerations:

(Any additional security considerations that may be introduced by use of the new service-selector parameter should be defined here or in the reference Standards Track RFCs)

Person & email address to contact for further information:

(fill in contact information)

INFORMATION TO THE SUBMITTER:

The accepted registrations will be listed in the "Assigned Numbers" series of RFCs. The information in the registration form is freely distributable.

11. Appendix C: IANA Registration form for new value of GSTN address service-selector "FAX"

To: IANA@isi.edu
Subject: Registration of new values for the GSTN address
         service-selector specifier "FAX"

service-selector name:

FAX

Description of Use:

FAX - specify that the GSTN address refers either to an Internet Fax device, or an onramp/offramp Fax gateway.

For a complete description refer to RFC 2304 and RFC 2303

Security Considerations:

See the Security Consideration section of RFC 2304.

Person & email address to contact for further information:

Claudio Allocchio
INFN-GARR
c/o Sincrotrone Trieste
SS 14 Km 163.5 Basovizza
I 34012 Trieste
Italy

RFC822: Claudio.Allocchio@elettra.trieste.it
X.400: C=it;A=garr;P=Trieste;O=Elettra;
S=Allocchio;G=Claudio;
Phone: +39 040 3758523
Fax: +39 040 3758565

12. Appendix D: IANA Registration forms for new values of GSTN address qualit-type1 keyword and value

D.1 - T33S

To: IANA@isi.edu
Subject: Registration of new values for the GSTN address
qualif-type1 element "T33S"

qualif-type1 "keyword" name:

T33S

qualif-type1 "value" ABNF definition:

```
sub-addr = 1*( DIGIT )
```

Description of Use:

T33S is used to specify the numeric only optional fax sub-address element described in "ITU T.33 - Facsimile routing utilizing the subaddress; recommendation T.33 (July, 1996)". Further detailed description is available in RFC 2304.

Use Restriction:

The use of "T33S" is restricted to "FAX" service-selector, is it has no meaning outside the fax service.

Security Considerations:

See the Security Consideration section of RFC 2304.

Person & email address to contact for further information:

Claudio Allocchio
INFN-GARR
c/o Sincrotrone Trieste
SS 14 Km 163.5 Basovizza
I 34012 Trieste
Italy

RFC822: Claudio.Allocchio@elettra.trieste.it
X.400: C=it;A=garr;P=Trieste;O=Elettra;
S=Allocchio;G=Claudio;
Phone: +39 040 3758523
Fax: +39 040 3758565

D.2 - ISUB

To: IANA@isi.edu
Subject: Registration of new values for the GSTN address qualif-type1 element "ISUB"

qualif-type1 "keyword" name:

ISUB

qualif-type1 "value" ABNF definition:

```
isub-addr = 1*( DIGIT )

isub-addr =/ 1*( DIGIT / written-sep )

written-sep = ( "-" / "." )
```

Description of Use:

"ISUB" is used to specify the optional ISDN sub-address elements used in ISDN service to reach specific objects on the ISDN service. It can eventually embed written separator elements for the only scope to enhance human readability. See RFC 2846 for further details.

Use Restriction:

none.

Security Considerations:

See the Security Consideration section of RFC 2846.

Person & email address to contact for further information:

Claudio Allocchio
INFN-GARR
c/o Sincrotrone Trieste
SS 14 Km 163.5 Basovizza
I 34012 Trieste
Italy

RFC822: Claudio.Allocchio@elettra.trieste.it
X.400: C=it;A=garr;P=Trieste;O=Elettra;
S=Allocchio;G=Claudio;
Phone: +39 040 3758523
Fax: +39 040 3758565

D.3 - POSTD

To: IANA@isi.edu
Subject: Registration of new values for the GSTN address
qualif-type1 element "POSTD"

qualif-type1 "keyword" name:

POSTD

qualif-type1 "value" ABNF definition:

```
phone-string = 1*( DTMF / pause / tonewait / written-sep )

DTMF = ( DIGIT / "#" / "*" / "A" / "B" / "C" / "D" )

pause = "p"

tonewait = "w"

written-sep = ( "-" / "." )
```

Description of Use:

POSTD is the optional further dialling sequence needed to access additional services (for example a menu' driven interface) available after the service site has been accessed using gstn-phone. See RFC 2846 for further details.

Use Restriction:

none.

Security Considerations:

See the Security Consideration section of RFC 2846.

Person & email address to contact for further information:

Claudio Allocchio
INFN-GARR
c/o Sincrotrone Trieste
SS 14 Km 163.5 Basovizza
I 34012 Trieste
Italy

RFC822: Claudio.Allocchio@elettra.trieste.it
X.400: C=it;A=garr;P=Trieste;O=Elettra;
S=Allocchio;G=Claudio;
Phone: +39 040 3758523
Fax: +39 040 3758565

D.4 - ATTN

To: IANA@isi.edu
Subject: Registration of new values for the GSTN address
qualif-type1 element "ATTN"

qualif-type1 "keyword" name:

ATTN

qualif-type1 "value" ABNF definition:

```
pers-name = [ givenname "." ] [ initials "." ] surname

surname = printablestring

givenname = 1*( DIGIT /  ALPHA / SP / "'" / "+" /
             "," / "-" / "/" / ":" / "=" / "?" )

initials = 1*ALPHA

printablestring = 1*( DIGIT / ALPHA / SP /
                      "'" / "(" / ")" / "+" / "," / "-" /
                      "." / "/" / ":" / "=" / "?" )
```

Description of Use:

To specify the personal name of the individual intended as the originator or the recipient of the message. See RFC 2846 for further details.

Use Restriction:

none.

Security Considerations:

See the Security Consideration section of RFC 2846.

Person & email address to contact for further information:

Claudio Allocchio
INFN-GARR
c/o Sincrotrone Trieste
SS 14 Km 163.5 Basovizza
I 34012 Trieste
Italy

RFC822: Claudio.Allocchio@elettra.trieste.it
X.400: C=it;A=garr;P=Trieste;O=Elettra;
S=Allocchio;G=Claudio;
Phone: +39 040 3758523
Fax: +39 040 3758565

D.5 - ORG

To: IANA@isi.edu
Subject: Registration of new values for the GSTN address qualif-type1 element "ORG"

qualif-type1 "keyword" name:

ORG

qualif-type1 "value" ABNF definition:

string = PCHAR

Description of Use:

To specify the Organization Name (example: ACME Inc.) See RFC 2846 for further details.

Use Restriction:

none.

Security Considerations:

See the Security Consideration section of RFC 2846.

Person & email address to contact for further information:

Claudio Allocchio
INFN-GARR
c/o Sincrotrone Trieste
SS 14 Km 163.5 Basovizza
I 34012 Trieste
Italy

RFC822: Claudio.Allocchio@elettra.trieste.it
X.400: C=it;A=garr;P=Trieste;O=Elettra;
S=Allocchio;G=Claudio;
Phone: +39 040 3758523
Fax: +39 040 3758565

D.6 - OFNO

To: IANA@isi.edu
Subject: Registration of new values for the GSTN address
qualif-type1 element "OFNO"

qualif-type1 "keyword" name:

OFNO

qualif-type1 "value" ABNF definition:

string = PCHAR

Description of Use:

To specify the Office Number (example: BLD2-44) See RFC 2846 for further details.

Use Restriction:

none.

Security Considerations:

See the Security Consideration section of RFC 2846.

Person & email address to contact for further information:

Claudio Allocchio
INFN-GARR
c/o Sincrotrone Trieste
SS 14 Km 163.5 Basovizza
I 34012 Trieste
Italy

RFC822: Claudio.Allocchio@elettra.trieste.it
X.400: C=it;A=garr;P=Trieste;O=Elettra;
S=Allocchio;G=Claudio;
Phone: +39 040 3758523
Fax: +39 040 3758565

D.7 - OFNA

To: IANA@isi.edu
Subject: Registration of new values for the GSTN address
qualif-type1 element "OFNA"

qualif-type1 "keyword" name:

OFNA

qualif-type1 "value" ABNF definition:

string = PCHAR

Description of Use:

To specify the Office Name (example: Sales) See RFC 2846 for further details.

Use Restriction:

none.

Security Considerations:

See the Security Consideration section of RFC 2846.

Person & email address to contact for further information:

Claudio Allocchio
INFN-GARR
c/o Sincrotrone Trieste
SS 14 Km 163.5 Basovizza
I 34012 Trieste
Italy

RFC822: Claudio.Allocchio@elettra.trieste.it
X.400: C=it;A=garr;P=Trieste;O=Elettra;
S=Allocchio;G=Claudio;
Phone: +39 040 3758523
Fax: +39 040 3758565

D.8 - STR

To: IANA@isi.edu
Subject: Registration of new values for the GSTN address
qualif-type1 element "STR"

qualif-type1 "keyword" name:

STR

qualif-type1 "value" ABNF definition:

string = PCHAR

Description of Use:

To specify the Street Address (example: 45, Main Street).
See RFC 2846 for further details.

Use Restriction:

none.

Security Considerations:

See the Security Consideration section of RFC 2846.

Person & email address to contact for further information:

Claudio Allocchio
INFN-GARR
c/o Sincrotrone Trieste
SS 14 Km 163.5 Basovizza
I 34012 Trieste
Italy

RFC822: Claudio.Allocchio@elettra.trieste.it
X.400: C=it;A=garr;P=Trieste;O=Elettra;
S=Allocchio;G=Claudio;
Phone: +39 040 3758523
Fax: +39 040 3758565

D.9 - ADDR

To: IANA@isi.edu
Subject: Registration of new values for the GSTN address qualif-type1 element "ADDR"

qualif-type1 "keyword" name:

ADDR

qualif-type1 "value" ABNF definition:

string = PCHAR

Description of Use:

To specify the Unformatted Postal Address (example: HWY 14, Km 94.5 - Loc. Redhill). See RFC 2846 for further details.

Use Restriction:

none.

Security Considerations:

See the Security Consideration section of RFC 2846.

Person & email address to contact for further information:

Claudio Allocchio
INFN-GARR
c/o Sincrotrone Trieste
SS 14 Km 163.5 Basovizza
I 34012 Trieste
Italy

RFC822: Claudio.Allocchio@elettra.trieste.it
X.400: C=it;A=garr;P=Trieste;O=Elettra;
S=Allocchio;G=Claudio;
Phone: +39 040 3758523
Fax: +39 040 3758565

D.10 - ADDU

To: IANA@isi.edu
Subject: Registration of new values for the GSTN address
qualif-type1 element "ADDU"

qualif-type1 "keyword" name:

ADDU

qualif-type1 "value" ABNF definition:

string = PCHAR

Description of Use:

To specify the Unique Postal Name (example: ACMETELEX). See RFC 2846 for further details.

Use Restriction:

none.

Security Considerations:

See the Security Consideration section of RFC 2846.

Person & email address to contact for further information:

Claudio Allocchio
INFN-GARR
c/o Sincrotrone Trieste
SS 14 Km 163.5 Basovizza
I 34012 Trieste
Italy

RFC822: Claudio.Allocchio@elettra.trieste.it
X.400: C=it;A=garr;P=Trieste;O=Elettra;
S=Allocchio;G=Claudio;
Phone: +39 040 3758523
Fax: +39 040 3758565

D.11 - ADDL

To: IANA@isi.edu
Subject: Registration of new values for the GSTN address
qualif-type1 element "ADDL"

qualif-type1 "keyword" name:

ADDL

qualif-type1 "value" ABNF definition:

string = PCHAR

Description of Use:

To specify the Local Postal Attributes (example: Entrance 3, 3rd floor, Suite 296). See RFC 2846 for further details.

Use Restriction:

none.

Security Considerations:

See the Security Consideration section of RFC 2846.

Person & email address to contact for further information:

Claudio Allocchio
INFN-GARR
c/o Sincrotrone Trieste
SS 14 Km 163.5 Basovizza
I 34012 Trieste
Italy

RFC822: Claudio.Allocchio@elettra.trieste.it
X.400: C=it;A=garr;P=Trieste;O=Elettra;
S=Allocchio;G=Claudio;
Phone: +39 040 3758523
Fax: +39 040 3758565

D.12 - POB

To: IANA@isi.edu
Subject: Registration of new values for the GSTN address
qualif-type1 element "POB"

qualif-type1 "keyword" name:

POB

qualif-type1 "value" ABNF definition:

string = PCHAR

Description of Use:

To specify the Post Office Box (example: CP 1374). See RFC 2846 for further details.

Use Restriction:

none.

Security Considerations:

See the Security Consideration section of RFC 2846.

Person & email address to contact for further information:

Claudio Allocchio
INFN-GARR
c/o Sincrotrone Trieste
SS 14 Km 163.5 Basovizza
I 34012 Trieste
Italy

RFC822: Claudio.Allocchio@elettra.trieste.it
X.400: C=it;A=garr;P=Trieste;O=Elettra;
S=Allocchio;G=Claudio;
Phone: +39 040 3758523
Fax: +39 040 3758565

D.13 - ZIP

To: IANA@isi.edu
Subject: Registration of new values for the GSTN address qualif-type1 element "ZIP"

qualif-type1 "keyword" name:

ZIP

qualif-type1 "value" ABNF definition:

string = PCHAR

Description of Use:

To specify Postal ZIP code (example: I 34012). See RFC 2846 for further details.

Use Restriction:

none.

Security Considerations:

See the Security Consideration section of RFC 2846.

Person & email address to contact for further information:

Claudio Allocchio
INFN-GARR
c/o Sincrotrone Trieste
SS 14 Km 163.5 Basovizza
I 34012 Trieste
Italy

RFC822: Claudio.Allocchio@elettra.trieste.it
X.400: C=it;A=garr;P=Trieste;O=Elettra;
S=Allocchio;G=Claudio;
Phone: +39 040 3758523
Fax: +39 040 3758565

D.14 - CO

To: IANA@isi.edu
Subject: Registration of new values for the GSTN address
qualif-type1 element "CO"

qualif-type1 "keyword" name:

CO

qualif-type1 "value" ABNF definition:

string = PCHAR

Description of Use:

To specify the Country Name (example: Belgium) See RFC 2846
for further details.

Use Restriction:

none.

Security Considerations:

See the Security Consideration section of RFC 2846.

Person & email address to contact for further information:

Claudio Allocchio
INFN-GARR
c/o Sincrotrone Trieste
SS 14 Km 163.5 Basovizza
I 34012 Trieste
Italy

RFC822: Claudio.Allocchio@elettra.trieste.it
X.400: C=it;A=garr;P=Trieste;O=Elettra;
S=Allocchio;G=Claudio;
Phone: +39 040 3758523
Fax: +39 040 3758565

13. Author's Address

Claudio Allocchio
INFN-GARR
c/o Sincrotrone Trieste
SS 14 Km 163.5 Basovizza
I 34012 Trieste
Italy

RFC822: Claudio.Allocchio@elettra.trieste.it
X.400: C=it;A=garr;P=Trieste;O=Elettra;
S=Allocchio;G=Claudio;
Phone: +39 040 3758523
Fax: +39 040 3758565

14. References

[1] Allocchio, C., "Minimal PSTN address format in Internet Mail", RFC 2303, March 1998.

[2] Allocchio, C., "Minimal FAX address format in Internet Mail", RFC 2304, March 1998.

[3] Kille, S., "MIXER (Mime Internet X.400 Enhanced Relay): Mapping between X.400 and RFC 822/MIME", RFC 2156, January 1998.

[4] Crocker, D. and P. Overell, "Augmented BNF for Syntax Specifications", RFC 2234, November 1997.

[5] Bradner, S., "Key words for use in RFCs to Indicate Requirement Levels", BCP 14, RFC 2119, March 1997.

[6] ETSI I-ETS 300,380 - Universal Personal Telecommunication (UPT): Access Devices Dual Tone Multi Frequency (DTMF) sender for acoustical coupling to the microphone of a handset telephone (March 1995)

[7] ITU E.164 - The International Public Telecommunication Numbering Plan E.164/I.331 (May 1997)

[8] ITU T.33 - Facsimile routing utilizing the subaddress; recommendation T.33 (July, 1996)

[9] ITU F.401 - Message Handling Services: Naming and Addressing for Public Massage Handling Service; recommendation F.401 (August 1992)

[10] ITU F.423 - Message Handling Services: Intercommunication Between the Interpersonal Messaging Service and the Telefax Service; recommendation F.423 (August 1992)

[11] Crocker, D., "Standard for the format of ARPA Internet text messages", STD 11, RFC 822, August 1982.

[12] Braden, R., "Requirements for Internet hosts - application and support", STD 3, RFC 1123, October 1989.

[13] Narten, T. and H. Alvestrand, "Guidelines for Writing an IANA Considerations Section in RFCs", BCP 26, RFC 2434, October 1998.

15. Full Copyright Statement

Acknowledgement

Funding for the RFC Editor function is currently provided by the Internet Society.

Network Working Group   S. Petrack
Request for Comments: 2848   MetaTel
Category: Standards Track   L. Conroy
                                          Siemens Roke Manor Research
                                                            June 2000

RFC 2848 1

The PINT Service Protocol:
Extensions to SIP and SDP for IP Access to Telephone Call Services

Status of this Memo

This document specifies an Internet standards track protocol for the Internet community, and requests discussion and suggestions for improvements. Please refer to the current edition of the "Internet Official Protocol Standards" (STD 1) for the standardization state and status of this protocol. Distribution of this memo is unlimited.

Copyright Notice

Abstract

This document contains the specification of the PINT Service Protocol 1.0, which defines a protocol for invoking certain telephone services from an IP network. These services include placing basic calls, sending and receiving faxes, and receiving content over the telephone. The protocol is specified as a set of enhancements and additions to the SIP 2.0 and SDP protocols.

Table of Contents

1. Introduction

The desire to invoke certain telephone call services from the Internet has been identified by many different groups (users, public and private network operators, call center service providers, equipment vendors, see [7]). The generic scenario is as follows (when the invocation is successful):

1. an IP host sends a request to a server on an IP network;
2. the server relays the request into a telephone network;
3. the telephone network performs the requested call service.

As examples, consider a user who wishes to have a callback placed to his/her telephone. It may be that a customer wants someone in the support department of some business to call them back. Similarly, a user may want to hear some announcement of a weather warning sent from a remote automatic weather service in the event of a storm.

We use the term "PSTN/Internet Interworking (PINT) Service" to denote such a complete transaction, starting with the sending of a request from an IP client and including the telephone call itself. PINT services are distinguished by the fact that they always involve two separate networks:

> an IP network to request the placement of a call, and the Global Switched Telephone Network (GSTN) to execute the actual call. It is understood that Intelligent Network systems, private PBXs, cellular phone networks, and the ISDN can all be used to deliver PINT services. Also, the request for service might come from within a private IP network that is disconnected from the whole Internet.

The requirements for the PINT protocol were deliberately restricted to providing the ability to invoke a small number of fixed telephone call services. These "Milestone PINT services" are specified in section 2. Great care has been taken, however, to develop a protocol that is aligned with other Internet protocols where possible, so that future extensions to PINT could develop along with Internet conferencing.

Within the Internet conference architecture, establishing media calls is done via a combination of protocols. SIP [1] is used to establish the association between the participants within the call (this association between participants within the call is called a "session"), and SDP [2] is used to describe the media to be exchanged within the session. The PINT protocol uses these two protocols together, providing some extensions and enhancements to enable SIP clients and servers to become PINT clients and servers.

A PINT user who wishes to invoke a service within the telephone network uses SIP to invite a remote PINT server into a session. The invitation contains an SDP description of the media session that the user would like to take place. This might be a "sending a fax session" or a "telephone call session", for example. In a PINT service execution session the media is transported over the phone system, while in a SIP session the media is normally transported over an internet.

When used to invoke a PINT service, SIP establishes an association between a requesting PINT client and the PINT server that is responsible for invoking the service within the telephone network. These two entities are not the same entities as the telephone network entities involved in the telephone network service. The SIP messages carry within their SDP payloads a description of the telephone network media session.

Note that the fact that a PINT server accepts an invitation and a session is established is no guarantee that the media will be successfully transported. (This is analogous to the fact that if a SIP invitation is accepted successfully, this is no guarantee against a subsequent failure of audio hardware).

The particular requirements of PINT users lead to some new messages. When a PINT server agrees to send a fax to telephone B, it may be that the fax transmission fails after part of the fax is sent. Therefore, the PINT client may wish to receive information about the status of the actual telephone call session that was invoked as a result of the established PINT session. Three new requests, SUBSCRIBE, UNSUBSCRIBE, and NOTIFY, are added here to vanilla SIP to allow this.

The enhancements and additions specified here are not intended to alter the behaviour of baseline SIP or SDP in any way. The purpose of PINT extensions is to extend the usual SIP/SDP services to the telephone world. Apart from integrating well into existing protocols and architectures, and the advantages of reuse, this means that the protocol specified here can handle a rather wider class of call services than just the Milestone services.

The rest of this document is organised as follows: Section 2 describes the PINT Milestone services; section 3 specifies the PINT functional and protocol architecture; section 4 gives examples of the PINT 1.0 extensions of SIP and SDP; section 5 contains some security considerations for PINT. The final section contains descriptions of how the PINT protocol may be used to provide service over the GSTN.

For a summary of the extensions to SIP and SDP specified in this document, Section 3.2 gives an combined list, plus one each describing the extensions to SIP and SDP respectively.

The key words "MUST", "MUST NOT", "REQUIRED", "SHALL", "SHALL NOT", "SHOULD", "SHOULD NOT", "RECOMMENDED", "MAY", and "OPTIONAL" in this document are to be interpreted as described in RFC 2119. In addition, the construct "MUST .... OR ...." implies that it is an absolute requirement of this specification to implement one of the two possibilities stated (represented by dots in the above phrase). An implementation MUST be able to interoperate with another implementation that chooses either of the two possibilities.

1.1 Glossary

Requestor - An Internet host from which a request for service originates

PINT Service - A service invoked within a phone system in response to a request received from an PINT client.

PINT Client - An Internet host that sends requests for invocation of a PINT Service, in accordance with this document.

PINT Gateway - An Internet host that accepts requests for PINT Service and dispatches them onwards towards a telephone network.

Executive System - A system that interfaces to a PINT Server and to a telephone network that executes a PINT service. It need not be directly associated with the Internet, and is represented by the PINT Server in transactions with Internet entities.

Requesting User - The initiator of a request for service. This role may be distinct from that of the "party" to any telephone network call that results from the request.

(Service Call) Party - A person who is involved in a telephone network call that results from the execution of a PINT service request, or a telephone network-based resource that is involved (such as an automatic Fax Sender or a Text-to-Speech Unit).

2. PINT Milestone Services

The original motivation for defining this protocol was the desire to invoke the following three telephone network services from within an IP network:

2.1 Request to Call

A request is sent from an IP host that causes a phone call to be made, connecting party A to some remote party B.

2.2 Request to Fax Content

A request is sent from an IP host that causes a fax to be sent to fax machine B. The request MAY contain a pointer to the fax data (that could reside in the IP network or in the Telephone Network), OR the fax data itself. The content of the fax MAY be text OR some other more general image data. The details of the fax transmission are not accessible to the IP network, but remain entirely within the telephone network.

Note that this service does not relate to "Fax over IP": the IP network is only used to send the request that a certain fax be sent. Of course, it is possible that the resulting telephone network fax call happens to use a real-time IP fax solution, but this is completely transparent to the PINT transaction.

2.3 Request to Speak/Send/Play Content

A request is sent from an IP host that causes a phone call to be made to user A, and for some sort of content to be spoken out. The request MUST EITHER contain a URL pointing to the content, OR include the content itself. The content MAY be text OR some other more general application data. The details of the content transmission are not accessible to the IP network, but remain entirely within the telephone network. This service could equally be called "Request to Hear Content"; the user's goal is to hear the content spoken to them. The mechanism by which the request is formulated is outside the scope of this document; however, an example might be that a Web page has a button that when pressed causes a PINT request to be passed to the PSTN, resulting in the content of the page (or other details) being spoken to the person.

2.4 Relation between PINT milestone services and traditional telephone services

There are many different versions and variations of each telephone call service invoked by a PINT request. Consider as an example what happens when a user requests to call 1-800-2255-287 via the PINT Request-to-Call service.

There may be thousands of agents in the call center, and there may be any number of sophisticated algorithms and pieces of equipment that are used to decide exactly which agent will return the call. And once this choice is made, there may be many different ways to set up the call: the agent's phone might ring first, and only then the original user will be called; or perhaps the user might be called first, and hear some horrible music or pre-recorded message while the agent is located.

Similarly, when a PINT request causes a fax to be sent, there are hundreds of fax protocol details to be negotiated, as well as transmission details within the telephone networks used.

PINT requests do not specify too precisely the exact telephone-side service. Operational details of individual events within the telephone network that executes the request are outside the scope of PINT. This does not preclude certain high-level details of the telephone network session from being expressed within a PINT request. For example, it is possible to use the SDP "lang" attribute to express a language preference for the Request-to-Hear-Content Service. If a particular PINT system wishes to allow requests to contain details of the telephone-network-side service, it uses the SDP attribute mechanism (see section 3.4.2).

3. PINT Functional and Protocol Architecture

3.1. PINT Functional Architecture

Familiarity is assumed with SIP 2.0 [1] and with SDP [2].

PINT clients and servers are SIP clients and servers. SIP is used to carry the request over the IP network to the correct PINT server in a secure and reliable manner, and SDP is used to describe the telephone network session that is to be invoked or whose status is to be returned.

A PINT system uses SIP proxy servers and redirect servers for their usual purpose, but at some point there must be a PINT server with the means to relay received requests into a telephone system and to receive acknowledgement of these relayed requests. A PINT server with this capability is called a "PINT gateway". A PINT gateway appears to a SIP system as a User Agent Server. Notice that a PINT gateway appears to the PINT infrastructure as if it represents a "user", while in fact it really represents an entire telephone network infrastructure that can provide a set of telephone network services.

So the PINT system might appear to an individual PINT client as follows:

Figure 1: PINT Functional Architecture

The system of PINT servers is represented as a cloud to emphasise that a single PINT request might pass through a series of location servers, proxy servers, and redirect servers, before finally reaching the correct PINT gateway that can actually process the request by passing it to the Telephone Network Cloud.

The PINT gateway might have a true telephone network interface, or it might be connected via some other protocol or API to an "Executive System" that is capable of invoking services within the telephone cloud.

As an example, within an I.N. (Intelligent Network) system, the PINT gateway might appear to realise the Service Control Gateway Function. In an office environment, it might be a server adjunct to the office PBX, connected to both the office LAN and the office PBX.

The Executive System that lies beyond the PINT gateway is outside the scope of PINT.

3.2. PINT Protocol Architecture

This section explains how SIP and SDP work in combination to convey the information necessary to invoke telephone network sessions.

The following list summarises the extension features used in PINT 1.0. Following on from this the features are considered separately for SDP and then for SIP:

1) Telephony URLs in SDP Contact Fields
2) Refinement of SIP/SDP Telephony URLs
   * Inclusion of private dialling plans
3) Specification of Telephone Service Provider (TSP) and/or phone-context URL-parameters
4) Data Objects as session media

4a) Protocol Transport formats to indicate the treatment of the media within the GSTN
5) Implicit (Indirect) media streams and opaque arguments
6) In-line data objects using multipart/mime
7) Refinement/Clarification of Opaque arguments passed onwards to Executive Systems
    * Framework for Presentation Restriction Indication
    * Framework for Q.763 arguments
8) An extension mechanism for SDP to specify strictures and force failure when a recipient does NOT support the specified extensions, using "require" headers.
9) Mandatory support for "Warning" headers to give more detailed information on request disposition.
10) Mechanism to register interest in the disposition of a requested service, and to receive indications on that disposition.

Both PINT and SIP rely on features of MIME[4]. The use of SIP 2.0 is implied by PINT 1.0, and this also implies compliance with version 1.0 of MIME.

3.2.1. SDP operation in PINT

The SDP payload contains a description of the particular telephone network session that the requestor wishes to occur in the GSTN. This information includes such things as the telephone network address (i.e. the "telephone number") of the terminal(s) involved in the call, an indication of the media type to be transported (e.g. audio, text, image or application data), and an indication if the information is to be transported over the telephone network via voice, fax, or pager transport. An indication of the content to be sent to the remote telephone terminal (if there is any) is also included.

SDP is flexible enough to convey these parameters independently. For example, a request to send some text via voice transport will be fulfilled by invoking some text-to-speech-over-the-phone service, and a request to send text via fax will be fulfilled by invoking some text-to-fax service.

The following is a list of PINT 1.0 enhancements and additions to SDP.

a. A new network type "TN" and address types "RFC2543" and "X-..." (section 3.4.1)
b. New media types "text", "image", and "application", new protocol transport keywords "voice", "fax" and "pager" and the associated format types and attribute tags (section 3.4.2)

c. New format specific attributes for included content data (section 3.4.2.4)
d. New attribute tags, used to pass information to the telephone network (section 3.4.3)
e. A new attribute tag "require", used by a client to indicate that some attribute is required to be supported in the server (section 3.4.4)

3.2.2. SIP Operation in PINT

SIP is used to carry the request for telephone service from the PINT client to the PINT gateway, and may include a telephone number if needed for the particular service. The following is a complete list of PINT enhancements and additions to SIP:

f. The multipart MIME payloads (section 3.5.1)
g. Mandatory support for "Warning:" headers (section 3.5.2)
h. The SUBSCRIBE and NOTIFY, and UNSUBSCRIBE requests (section 3.5.3)
i. Require: headers (section 3.5.4)
j. A format for PINT URLS within a PINT request (section 3.5.5)
k. Telephone Network Parameters within PINT URLs (section 3.5.6)

Section 3.5.8 contains remarks about how BYE requests are used within PINT. This is not an extension to baseline SIP; it is included here only for clarification of the semantics when used with telephone network sessions.

3.3. REQUIRED and OPTIONAL elements for PINT compliance

Of these, only the TN network type (with its associated RFC2543 address type) and the "require" attribute MUST be supported by PINT 1.0 clients and servers. In practice, most PINT service requests will use other changes, of which references to Data Objects in requests are most likely to appear in PINT requests.

Each of the other new PINT constructs enables a different function, and a client or server that wishes to enable that particular function MUST do so by the construct specified in this document. For example, building a PINT client and server that provide only the Request-to-Call telephone call service, without support for the other Milestone services, is allowed.

The "Require:" SIP header and the "require" attribute provide a mechanism that can be used by clients and servers to signal their need and/or ability to support specific "new" PINT protocol elements.

It should be noted that many optional features of SIP and SDP make sense as specified in the PINT context. One example is the SDP a=lang: attribute, which can be used to describe the preferred language of the callee. Another example is the use of the "t=" parameter to indicate that the time at which the PINT service is to be invoked. This is the normal use of the "t=" field. A third example is the quality attributes. Any SIP or SDP option or facility is available to PINT clients and servers without change.

Conversely, support for Data Objects within Internet Conference sessions may be useful, even if the aim is not to provide a GSTN service request. In this case, the extensions covering these items may be incorporated into an otherwise "plain" SIP/SDP invitation. Likewise, support for SDP "require" may be useful, as a framework for addition of features to a "traditional" SIP/SDP infrastructure. Again, these may be convenient to incorporate into SIP/SDP implementations that would not be used for PINT service requests. Such additions are beyond the scope of this document, however.

3.4. PINT Extensions to SDP

PINT 1.0 adds to SDP the possibility to describe audio, fax, and pager telephone sessions. It is deliberately designed to hide the underlying technical details and complexity of the telephone network. The only network type defined for PINT is the generic "TN" (Telephone Network). More precise tags such as "ISDN", "GSM", are not defined. Similarly, the transport protocols are designated simply as "fax", "voice", and "pager"; there are no more specific identifiers for the various telephone network voice, fax, or pager protocols. Similarly, the data to be transported are identified only by a MIME content type, such as "text" data, "image" data, or some more general "application" data. An important example of transporting "application" data is the milestone service "Voice Access to Web Content". In this case the data to be transported are pointed to by a URI, the data content type is application/URI, and the transport protocol would be "voice". Some sort of speech-synthesis facility, speaking out to a Phone, will have to be invoked to perform this service.

This section gives details of the new SDP keywords.

3.4.1. Network Type "TN" and Address Type "RFC2543"

The TN ("Telephone Network") network type is used to indicate that the terminal is connected to a telephone network.

The address types allowed for network type TN are "RFC2543" and private address types, which MUST begin with an "X-".

Address type RFC2543 is followed by a string conforming to a subset of the "telephone-subscriber" BNF specified in figure 4 of SIP [1]). Note that this BNF is NOT identical to the BNF that defines the "phone-number" within the "p=" field of SDP.

Examples:

```
c= TN  RFC2543  +1-201-406-4090

c= TN  RFC2543  12014064090
```

A telephone-subscriber string is of one of two types: global-phone-number or local-phone-number. These are distinguished by preceeding a global-phone-number with a "plus" sign ("+"). A global-phone-number is by default to be interpreted as an internationally significant E.164 Number Plan Address, as defined by [6], whilst a local-phone-number is a number specified in the default dialling plan within the context of the recipient PINT Gateway.

An implementation MAY use private addressing types, which can be useful within a local domain. These address types MUST begin with an "X-", and SHOULD contain a domain name after the X-, e.g. "X-mytype.mydomain.com". An example of such a connection line is as follows:

```
c= TN X-mytype.mydomain.com  A*8-HELEN
```

where "X-mytype.mydomain.com" identifies this private address type, and "A*8-HELEN" is the number in this format. Such a format is defined as an "OtherAddr" in the ABNF of Appendix A. Note that most dialable telephone numbers are expressable as local-phone-numbers within address RFC2543; new address types SHOULD only be used for formats which cannot be so written.

3.4.2. Support for Data Objects within PINT

One significant change over traditional SIP/SDP Internet Conference sessions with PINT is that a PINT service request may refer to a Data Object to be used as source information in that request. For example, a PINT service request may specify a document to be processed as part of a GSTN service by which a Fax is sent. Similarly, a GSTN service may be take a Web page and result in a vocoder processing that page and speaking the contents over a telephone.

The SDP specification does not have explicit support for reference to or carriage of Data Objects within requests. In order to use SDP for PINT, there is a need to describe such media sessions as "a telephone call to a certain number during which such-and-such an image is sent as a fax".

To support this, two extensions to the session description format are specified. These are some new allowed values for the Media Field, and a description of the "fmtp" parameter when used with the Media Field values (within the context of the Contact Field Network type "TN").

An addition is also made to the SIP message format to allow the inclusion of data objects as sub-parts within the request message itself. The original SDP syntax (from [2]) for media-field is given as:


```
media-field =          "m=" media space port ["/" integer]
                       space proto 1*(space fmt) CRLF
```

When used within PINT requests, the definition of the sub-fields is expanded slightly. The Media sub-field definition is relaxed to accept all of the discrete "top-level" media types defined in [4]. In the milestone services the discrete type "video" is not used, and the extra types "data" and "control" are likewise not needed. The use of these types is not precluded, but the behaviour expected of a PINT Gateway receiving a request including such a type is not defined here.

The Port sub-field has no meaning in PINT requests as the destination terminals are specified using "TN" addressing, so the value of the port sub-field in PINT requests is normally set to "1". A value of "0" may be used as in SDP to indicate that the terminal is not receiving media. This is useful to indicate that a telephone terminal has gone "on hold" temporarily. Likewise, the optional integer sub-field is not used in PINT.

As mentioned in [2], the Transport Protocol sub-field is specific to the associated Address Type. In the case that the Address Type in the preceeding Contact field is one of those defined for use with the Network Type "TN", the following values are defined for the Transport Protocol sub-field:

"voice", "fax", and "pager".

The interpretation of this sub-field within PINT requests is the treatment or disposition of the resulting GSTN service. Thus, for transport protocol "voice", the intent is that the service will result in a GSTN voice call, whilst for protocol "fax" the result will be a GSTN fax transmission, and protocol "pager" will result in a pager message being sent.

Note that this sub-field does not necessarily dictate the media type and subtype of any source data; for example, one of the milestone services calls for a textual source to be vocoded and spoken in a resulting telephone service call. The transport protocol value in this case would be "voice", whilst the media type would be "text".

The Fmt sub-field is described in [2] as being transport protocol-specific. When used within PINT requests having one of the above protocol values, this sub-field consists of a list of one or more values, each of which is a defined MIME sub-type of the associated Media sub-field value. The special value "-" is allowed, meaning that there is no MIME sub-type. This sub-field retains (from [2]) its meaning that the list will contain a set of alternative sub-types, with the first being the preferred value.

For experimental purposes and by mutual consent of the sender and recipient, a sub-type value may be specified as an <X-token>, i.e. a character string starting with "X-". The use of such values is discouraged, and if such a value is expected to find common use then it SHOULD be registered with IANA using the standard content type registration process (see Appendix C).

When the Fmt parameter is the single character "-" (a dash), this is interpreted as meaning that a unspecified or default sub-type can be used for this service. Thus, the media field value "m=audio 1 voice -<CRLF>" is taken to mean that a voice call is requested, using whatever audio sub type is deemed appropriate by the Executive System. PINT service is a special case, in that the request comes from the IP network but the service call is provided within the GSTN. Thus the service request will not normally be able to define the particular codec used for the resulting GSTN service call. If such an intent IS required, then the quality attribute may be used (see "Suggested Attributes" section of [2]).

3.4.2.1. Use of fmtp attributes in PINT requests

For each element of the Fmt sub-field, there MUST be a following fmtp attribute. When used within PINT requests, the fmtp attribute has a general structure as defined here:

```
    "a=fmtp:" <subtype> <space> resolution
                        *(<space> resolution)
                        (<space> ";" 1(<attribute>)
                                     *(<space> <attribute>))
where:
    <resolution> := (<uri-ref> | <opaque-ref> | <sub-part-ref>)
```

A fmtp attribute describes the sources used with a given Fmt entry in the Media field. The entries in a Fmt sub-field are alternatives (with the preferred one first in the list). Each entry will have a matching fmtp attribute. The list of resolutions in a fmtp attribute describes the set of sources that resolve the matching Fmt choice; all elements of this set will be used.

It should be noted that, for use in PINT services, the elements in such a set will be sent as a sequence; it is unlikely that trying to send them in parallel would be successful.

A fmtp attribute can contain a mixture of different kinds of element. Thus an attribute might contain a sub-part-ref indicating included data held in a sub-part of the current message, followed by an opaque-ref referring to some content on the GSTN, followed by a uri-ref pointing to some data held externally on the IP network.

To indicate which form each resolution element takes, each of them starts with its own literal tag. The detailed syntax of each form is described in the following sub-sections.

3.4.2.2. Support for Remote Data Object References in PINT

Where data objects stored elsewhere on the IP Network are to be used as sources for processing within a PINT service, they may be referred to using the uri-ref form. This is simply a Uniform Resource Identifier (URI), as described in [9].

Note that the reference SHOULD be an absolute URI, as there may not be enough contextual information for the recipient server to resolve a relative reference; any use of relative references requires some private agreement between the sender and recipient of the message, and SHOULD be avoided unless the sender can be sure that the recipient is the one intended and the reference is unambiguous in context.

This also holds for partial URIs (such as"uri:http://aNode/index.htm") as these will need to be resolved in the context of the eventual recipient of the message.

The general syntax of a reference to an Internet-based external data object in a fmtp line within a PINT session description is:

```
<uri-ref> := ("uri:" URI-reference)
```

where URI-reference is as defined in Appendix A of [9]

For example:

```
      c= TN RFC2543 +1-201-406-4090
      m= text 1  fax plain
      a=fmtp:plain  uri:ftp://ftp.isi.edu/in-notes/rfc2468.txt
or:
      c= TN RFC2543 +1-201-406-4090
      m= text 1  fax plain
      a=fmtp:plain
uri:http://www.ietf.org/meetings/glance_minneapolis.txt
```

means get this data object from the Internet and use it as a source for the requested GSTN Fax service.

3.4.2.3. Support for GSTN-based Data Objects in PINT

PINT services may refer to data that are held not on the IP Network but instead within the GSTN. The way in which these items are indicated need have no meaning within the context of the Requestor or the PINT Gateway; the reference is merely some data that may be used by the Executive System to indicate the content intended as part of the request. These data form an opaque reference, in that they are sent "untouched" through the PINT infrastructure.

A reference to some data object held on the GSTN has the general definition:

```
    <opaque-ref> := ("opr:" *uric)
```

where uric is as defined in Appendix A of [9].

For example:

```
      c= TN RFC2543 +1-201-406-4090
      m= text 1  fax plain
      a=fmtp:plain  opr:APPL.123.456
```

means send the data that is indexed ON THE GSTN by the reference value "APPL.123.456" to the fax machine on +1-201-406-4090. The Executive System may also take the Telephone URL held in the To: field of the enclosing SIP message into account when deciding the context to be used for the data object dereference.

Of course, an opaque reference may also be used for other purposes; it could, for example, be needed to authorise access to a document held on the GSTN rather than being required merely to disambiguate the data object. The purpose to which an opaque reference is put, however, is out of scope for this document. It is merely an indicator carried within a PINT Request.

An opaque reference may have no value in the case where the value to be used is implicit in the rest of the request. For example, suppose some company wishes to use PINT to implement a "fax-back service". In their current implementation, the image(s) to be faxed are entirely defined by the telephone number dialled. Within the PINT request, this telephone number would appear within the "To:" field of the PINT request, and so there is no need for an opaque reference value.

If there are several resolutions for a PINT Service Request, and one of these is an opaque reference with no value, then that opaque reference MUST be included in the attribute line, but with an empty value field.

For example:

```
c= TN RFC2543 +1-201-406-4090
m= text 1  fax plain
a=fmtp:plain  uri:http://www.sun.com/index.html opr:
```

might be used to precede some data to be faxed with a covering note.

In the special case where an opaque reference is the sole resolution of a PINT Service Request, AND that reference needs no value, there is no need for a Fmt list at all; the intent of the service is unambiguous without any further resolution.

For example:

```
c= TN RFC2543 +1-201-406-4090
m= text 1  fax -
```

means that there is an implied content stored on the GSTN, and that this is uniquely identified by the combination of SIP To-URI and the Contact field of the session description.

3.4.2.4. Session Description support for included Data Objects

As an alternative to pointing to the data via a URI or an opaque reference to a data item held on the GSTN, it is possible to include the content data within the SIP request itself. This is done by using multipart MIME for the SIP payload. The first MIME part contains the SDP description of the telephone network session to be executed. The other MIME parts contain the content data to be transported.

Format specific attribute lines within the session description are used to indicate which other MIME part within the request contains the content data. Instead of a URI or opaque reference, the format-specific attribute indicates the Content-ID of the MIME part of the request that contains the actual data, and is defined as:

```
<sub-part-ref> := ("spr:" Content-ID)
```

where Content-ID is as defined in Appendix A of [3] and in [10]).

For example:

```
c= TN RFC2543 +1-201-406-4090
m= text 1  fax plain
a=fmtp:plain  spr:<Content-ID>
```

The <Content-ID> parameter is the Content-ID of one of the MIME parts inside the message, and this fragment means that the requesting user would like the data object held in the sub-part of this message labelled <Content-ID> to be faxed to the machine at phone number +1-201-406-4090.

See also section 3.5.1 for a discussion on the support needed in the enclosing SIP request for included data objects.

3.4.3. Attribute Tags to pass information into the Telephone Network

It may be desired to include within the PINT request service parameters that can be understood only by some entity in the "Telephone Network Cloud". SDP attribute parameters are used for this purpose. They MAY appear within a particular media description or outside of a media description.

These attributes may also appear as parameters within PINT URLS (see section 3.5.6) as part of a SIP request.

This is necessary so that telephone terminals that require the attributes to be defined can appear within the To: line of a PINT request as well as within PINT session descriptions.

The purpose of these attributes is to allow the client to specify extra context within which a particular telephone number is to be interpreted. There are many reasons why extra context might be necessary to interpret a given telephone number:

a. The telephone number might be reachable in many different ways (such as via competing telephone service providers), and the PINT client wishes to indicate its selection of service provider.
b. The telephone number might be reachable only from a limited number of networks (such as an '800' freephone number).
c. The telephone number might be reachable only within a single telephone network (such as the '152' customer service number of BT). Similarly, the number might be an internal corporate extension reachable only within the PBX.

However, as noted above, it is not usually necessary to use SDP attributes to specify the phone context. URLs such as 152@pint.bt.co.il within the To: and From: headers and/or Request-URI, normally offer sufficient context to resolve telephone numbers.

If the client wishes the request to fail if the attributes are not supported, these attributes SHOULD be used in conjunction with the "require" attribute (section 3.4.4) and the "Require:org.ietf.sdp.require" header (section 3.5.4).

It is not possible to standardise every possible internal telephone network parameter. PINT 1.0 attributes have been chosen for specification because they are common enough that many different PINT systems will want to use them, and therefore interoperability will be increased by having a single specification.

Proprietary attribute "a=" lines, that by definition are not interoperable, may be nonetheless useful when it is necessary to transport some proprietary internal telephone network variables over the IP network, for example to identify the order in which service call legs are to be be made. These private attributes SHOULD BE, however, subject to the same IANA registration procedures mentioned in the SDP specification[2] (see also this Appendix C).

3.4.3.1. The phone-context attribute

An attribute is specified to enable "remote local dialling". This is the service that allows a PINT client to reach a number from far outside the area or network that can usually reach the number. It is useful when the sending or receiving address is only dialable within some local context, which may be remote to the origin of the PINT client.

For example, if Alice wanted to report a problem with her telephone, she might then dial a "network wide" customer care number; within the British Telecom network in the U.K., this is "152". Note that in this case she doesn't dial any trunk prefix - this is the whole dialable number. If dialled from another operator's network, it will not connect to British Telecom's Engineering Enquiries service; and dialling "+44 152" will not normally succeed. Such numbers are called Network-Specific Service Numbers.

Within the telephone network, the "local context" is provided by the physical connection between the subscriber's terminal and the central office. An analogous association between the PINT client and the PINT server that first receives the request may not exist, which is why it may be necessary to supply this missing "telephone network context". This attribute is defined as follows:

```
a=phone-context: <phone-context-ident>
phone-context-ident     =  network-prefix / private-prefix
network-prefix          =  intl-network-prefix / local-network-prefix
intl-network-prefix     =  "+" 1*DIGIT
local-network-prefix    =  1*DIGIT
excldigandplus          =  (0x21-0x2d,0x2f,0x40-0x7d))
private-prefix          =  1*excldigandplus 0*uric
```

An intl-network-prefix and local-network-prefix MUST be a bona fide network prefix, and a network-prefix that is an intl-network-prefix MUST begin with an E.164 service code ("country code").

It is possible to register new private-prefixes with IANA so as to avoid collisions. Prefixes that are not so registered MUST begin with an "X-" to indicate their private, non-standard nature (see Appendix C).

Example 1:

```
c= TN   RFC2543  1-800-765-4321
a=phone-context:+972
```

This describes an terminal whose address in Israel (E.164 country code 972) is 1-800-765-4321.

Example 2:

```
c= TN   RFC2543  1-800-765-4321
a=phone-context:+1
```

This describes an terminal whose address in North America (E.164 country code 1) is 1-800-765-4321.

The two telephone terminals described by examples 1 and 2 are different; in fact they are located in different countries.

Example 3:

```
c=TN RFC2543  123
a=phone-context:+97252
```

This describes a terminal whose address when dialled from within the network identified by +97252 is the string "123". It so happens that +97252 defines one of the Israeli cell phone providers, and 123 reaches customer service when dialled within that network.

It may well be useful or necessary to use the SDP "require" parameter in conjunction with the phone-context attribute.

Example 4:

```
c= TN  RFC2543  321
a=phone-context:X-acme.com-23
```

This might describe the telephone terminal that is at extension 321 of PBX number 23 within the acme.com private PBX network. It is expected that such a description would be understandable by the acme.com PINT server that receives the request.

Note that if the PINT server receiving the request is inside the acme.com network, the same terminal might be addressable as follows:

```
c= TN  RFC2543 7-23-321
```

(assuming that "7" is dialled in order to reach the private PBX network from within acme.com)

3.4.3.2. Presentation Restriction attribute

Although it has no affect on the transport of the service request through the IP Network, there may be a requirement to allow originators of a PINT service request to indicate whether or not they wish the "B party" in the resulting service call to be presented with the "A party's" calling telephone number. It is a legal requirement in some jurisdictions that a caller be able to select whether or not their correspondent can find out the calling telephone number (using Automatic Number Indication or Caller Display or Calling Line Identity Presentation equipment). Thus an attribute may be needed to indicate the originator's preference.

Whether or not the default behaviour of the Executive System is to present or not present a party's telephone number to the correspondent GSTN terminal is not specified, and it is not mandatory in all territories for a PINT Gateway or Executive System to act on this attribute. It is, however, defined here for use where there are regulatory restrictions on GSTN operation, and in that case the Executive System can use it to honour the originator's request.

The attribute is specified as follows:
    a=clir:<"true" | "false">

This boolean value is needed within the attribute as it may be that the GSTN address is, by default, set to NOT present its identity to correspondents, and the originator wants to do so for this particular call. It is in keeping with the aim of this attribute to allow the originator to specify what treatment they want for the requested service call.

The expected interpretation of this attribute is that, if it is present and the value is "false" then the Calling Line Identity CAN be presented to the correspondent terminal, whilst if it is "true" then if possible the Executive System is requested to NOT present the Calling Line Identity.

3.4.3.3. ITU-T CalledPartyAddress attributes parameters

These attributes correspond to fields that appear within the ITU-T Q.763 "CalledPartyAddress" field (see [8] ,section 3.9). PINT clients use these attributes in order to specify further parameters relating to Terminal Addresses, in the case when the address indicates a "local-phone-number". In the case that the PINT request contains a reference to a GSTN terminal, the parameters may be required to correctly identify that remote terminal.

The general form of this attribute is: "a=Q763-<token>((":" <value>) |"")". Three of the possible elements and their use in SDP attributes are described here. Where other Q763 elements are to be used, then these should be the subject of further specification to define the syntax of the attribute mapping. It is recommended that any such specification maintains the value sets shown in Q.763.

The defined attributes are:

a=Q763-nature: - indicates the "nature of address indicator".
    The value MAY be any number between 0 and 127.
    The following values are specified:

"1" a subscriber number
"2" unknown
"3" a nationally significant number
"4" an internationally significant number

The values have been chosen to coincide with the values in Q.763. Note that other values are possible, according to national rules or future expansion of Q.763.

a=Q763-plan: - indicates the numbering plan to which the address belongs. The value MAY be any number between 0 and 7. The following values are specified:

"1" Telephone numbering plan (ITU-T E.164)
"3" Data numbering plan (ITU-T X.121)
"4" Telex numbering plan (ITU-T F.69)

The values have been chosen to coincide with the values in Q.763. Other values are allowed, according to national rules or future expansion of Q.763.

a=Q763-INN - indicates if routing to the Internal Network Number is allowed. The value MUST be ONE of:

"0" routing to internal network number allowed
"1" routing to internal network number not allowed

The values have been chosen to coincide with the values in Q.763. Note that it is possible to use a local-phone-number and indicate via attributes that the number is in fact an internationally significant E.164 number. Normally this SHOULD NOT be done; an internationally significant E.164 number is indicated by using a "global-phone-number" for the address string.

3.4.4. The "require" attribute

According to the SDP specification, a PINT server is allowed simply to ignore attribute parameters that it does not understand. In order to force a server to decline a request if it does not understand one of the PINT attributes, a client SHOULD use the "require" attribute, specified as follows:

```
a=require:<attribute-list>
```

where the attribute-list is a comma-separated list of attributes that appear elsewhere in the session description.

In order to process the request successfully the PINT server must BOTH understand the attribute AND ALSO fulfill the request implied by the presence of the attribute, for each attribute appearing within the attribute-list of the require attribute.

If the server does not recognise the attribute listed, the PINT server MUST return an error status code (such as 420 (Bad Extension) or 400 (Bad Request)), and SHOULD return suitable Warning: lines explaining the problem or an Unsupported: header containing the attribute it does not understand. If the server recognizes the attribute listed, but cannot fulfill the request implied by the presence of the attribute, the request MUST be rejected with a status code of (606 Not Acceptable), along with a suitable Unsupported: header or Warning: line.

The "require" attribute may appear anywhere in the session description, and any number of times, but it MUST appear before the use of the attribute marked as required.

Since the "require" attribute is itself an attribute, the SIP specification allows a server that does not understand the require attribute to ignore it. In order to ensure that the PINT server will comply with the "require" attribute, a PINT client SHOULD include a Require: header with the tag "org.ietf.sdp.require" (section 3.5.4)

Note that the majority of the PINT extensions are "tagged" and these tags can be included in Require strictures. The exception is the use of phone numbers in SDP parts. However, these are defined as a new network and address type, so that a receiving SIP/SDP server should be able to detect whether or not it supports these forms. The default behaviour for any SDP recipient is that it will fail a PINT request if it does not recognise or support the TN and RFC2543 or X-token network and address types, as without the contents being recognised no media session could be created. Thus a separate stricture is not required in this case.

3.5. PINT Extensions to SIP 2.0

PINT requests are SIP requests; Many of the specifications within this document merely explain how to use existing SIP facilities for the purposes of PINT.

3.5.1. Multi-part MIME (sending data along with SIP request)

A PINT request can contain a payload which is multipart MIME. In this case the first part MUST contain an SDP session description that includes at least one of the format specific attribute tags for "included content data" specified above in section 3.4.3. Subsequent parts contain content data that may be transferred to the requested Telephone Call Service. As discussed earlier, within a single PINT request, some of the data MAY be pointed to by a URI within the request, and some of the data MAY be included within the request.

Where included data is carried within a PINT service request, the Content Type entity header of the enclosing SIP message MUST indicate this. To do so, the media type value within this entity header MUST be set to a value of "multipart". There is a content sub-type that is intended for situations like this in which sub-parts are to be handled together. This is the multipart/related type (defined in [19]), and it's use is recommended.

The enclosed body parts SHOULD include the part-specific Content Type headers as appropriate ("application/sdp" for the first body part holding the session description, with an appropriate content type for each of the subsequent, "included data object" parts). This matches the standard syntax of MIME multipart messages as defined in [4].

For example, in a multipart message where the string

"------next-------" is the boundary, the first two parts might be as follows:

```
------next-------
Content-Type: application/sdp
....
c= TN RFC2543 +1-201-406-4090
m= text 1 pager plain
a=fmtp:plain spr:17@mymessage.acme.com

----------next-------
Content-Type: text/plain
Content-ID:  17@mymessage.acme.com

This is the text that is to be paged to +1-201-406-4090

----------next-----------
```

The ability to indicate different alternatives for the content to be transported is useful, even when the alternatives are included within the request. For example, a request to send a short message to a pager might include the message in Unicode [5] and an alternative version of the same content in text/plain, should the PINT server or telephone network not be able to process the unicode.

PINT clients should be extremely careful when sending included data within a PINT request. Such requests SHOULD be sent via TCP, to avoid fragmentation and to transmit the data reliably. It is possible that the PINT server is a proxy server that will replicate and fork the request, which could be disastrous if the request contains a large amount of application data. PINT proxy servers should be careful not to create many copies of a request with large amounts of data in it.

If the client does not know the actual location of the PINT gateway, and is using the SIP location services to find it, and the included data makes the PINT request likely to be transported in several IP datagrams, it is RECOMMENDED that the initial PINT request not include the data object but instead hold a reference to it.

3.5.2. Warning header

A PINT server MUST support the SIP "Warning:" header so that it can signal lack of support for individual PINT features. As an example, suppose the PINT request is to send a jpeg picture to a fax machine, but the server cannot retrieve and/or translate jpeg pictures from the Internet into fax transmissions.

In such a case the server fails the request and includes a Warning such as the following:

```
Warning:  305  pint.acme.com  Incompatible media format:  jpeg
```

SIP servers that do not understand the PINT extensions at all are strongly encouraged to implement Warning: headers to indicate that PINT extensions are not understood.

Also, Warning: headers may be included within NOTIFY requests if it is necessary to notify the client about some condition concerning the invocation of the PINT service (see next).

3.5.3. Mechanism to register interest in the disposition of a PINT service, and to receive indications on that disposition

It can be very useful to find out whether or not a requested service has completed, and if so whether or not it was successful. This is especially true for PINT service, where the person requesting the service is not (necessarily) a party to it, and so may not have an easy way of finding out the disposition of that service. Equally, it may be useful to indicate when the service has changed state, for example when the service call has started.

Arranging a flexible system to provide extensive monitoring and control during a service is non-trivial (see section 6.4 for some issues); PINT 1.0 uses a simple scheme that should nevertheless provide useful information. It is possible to expand the scheme in a "backwards compatible" manner, so if required it can be enhanced at a later date.

The PINT 1.0 status registration and indication scheme uses three new methods; SUBSCRIBE, UNSUBSCRIBE, and NOTIFY. These are used to allow a PINT client to register an interest in (or "subscribe" to) the status of a service request, to indicate that a prior interest has lapsed (i.e "unsubscribe" from the status), and for the server to return service indications. The state machine of SUBSCRIBE/UNSUBSCRIBE is identical to that of INVITE/BYE; just as INVITE signals the beginning and BYE signals the end of participation in a media session, SUBSCRIBE signals the beginning and UNSUBSCRIBE signals the end of participation in a monitoring session. During the monitoring session, NOTIFY messages are sent to inform the subscriber of a change in session state or disposition.

3.5.3.1. Opening a monitoring session with a SUBSCRIBE request

When a SUBSCRIBE request is sent to a PINT Server, it indicates that a user wishes to receive information about the status of a service session. The request identifies the session of interest by including the original session description along with the request, using the SDP global-session-id that forms part of the origin-field to identify the service session uniquely.

The SUBSCRIBE request (like any other SIP request about an ongoing session) is sent to the same server as was sent the original INVITE, or to a server which was specified in the Contact: field within a subsequent response (this might well be the PINT gateway for the session).

Whilst there are situations in which re-use of the Call-ID used in the original INVITE that initiated the session of interest is possible, there are other situations in which it is not. In detail, where the subscription is being made by the user who initiated the original service request, the Call-ID may be used as it will be known to the receiver to refer to a previously established session. However, when the request comes from a user other than the original requesting user, the SUBSCRIBE request constitutes a new SIP call leg, so the Call-ID SHOULD NOT be used; the only common identifier is the origin-field of the session description enclosed within the original service request, and so this MUST be used.

Rather than have two different methods of identifying the "session of interest" the choice is to use the origin-field of the SDP sub-part included both in the original INVITE and in this SUBSCRIBE request.

Note that the request MUST NOT include any sub-parts other than the session description, even if these others were present in the original INVITE request. A server MUST ignore whatever sub-parts are included within a SUBSCRIBE request with the sole exception of the enclosed session description.

The request MAY contain a "Contact:" header, specifying the PINT User Agent Server to which such information should be sent.

In addition, it SHOULD contain an Expires: header, which indicates for how long the PINT Requestor wishes to receive notification of the session status. We refer to the period of time before the expiration of the SUBSCRIBE request as the "subscription period". See section 5.1.4. for security considerations, particularly privacy implications.

A value of 0 within the Expires: header indicates a desire to receive one single immediate response (i.e. the request expires immediately). It is possible for a sequence of monitoring sessions to be opened, exist, and complete, all relating to the same service session.

A successful response to the SUBSCRIBE request includes the session description, according to the Gateway. Normally this will be identical to the last cached response that the Gateway returned to any request concerning the same SDP global session id (see [2], section 6, o= field). The t= line may be altered to indicate the actual start or stop time, however. The Gateway might add an i= line to the session description to indicate such information as how many fax pages were sent. The Gateway SHOULD include an Expires: header indicating how long it is willing to maintain the monitoring session. If this is unacceptable to the PINT Requestor, then it can close the session by sending an immediate UNSUBSCRIBE message (see 3.5.3.3).

In principle, a user might send a SUBSCRIBE request after the telephone network service has completed. This allows, for example, checking up "the morning after" to see if the fax was successfully transmitted. However, a PINT gateway is only required to keep state about a call for as long as it indicated previously in an Expires: header sent within the response to the original INVITE message that triggered the service session, within the response to the SUBSCRIBE message, within the response to any UNSUBSCRIBE message, or within its own UNSUBSCRIBE message (but see section 3.5.8, point 3).

If the Server no longer has a record of the session to which a Requestor has SUBSCRIBEd, it returns "606 Not Acceptable", along with the appropriate Warning: 307 header indicating that the SDP session ID is no longer valid. This means that a requesting Client that knows that it will want information about the status of a session after the session terminates SHOULD send a SUBSCRIBE request before the session terminates.

3.5.3.2. Sending Status Indications with a NOTIFY request

During the subscription period, the Gateway may, from time to time, send a spontaneous NOTIFY request to the entity indicated in the Contact: header of the "opening" SUBSCRIBE request. Normally this will happen as a result of any change in the status of the service session for which the Requestor has subscribed.

The receiving user agent server MUST acknowledge this by returning a final response (normally a "200 OK"). In this version of the PINT extensions, the Gateway is not required to support redirects (3xx codes), and so may treat them as a failure.

Thus, if the response code class is above 2xx then this may be treated by the Gateway as a failure of the monitoring session, and in that situation it will immediately attempt to close the session (see next).

The NOTIFY request contains the modified session description. For example, the Gateway may be able to indicate a more accurate start or stop time.

The Gateway may include a Warning: header to describe some problem with the invocation of the service, and may indicate within an i= line some information about the telephone network session itself.

Example:

```
NOTIFY  sip:petrack@pager.com SIP/2.0
To: sip:petrack@pager.com
From: sip:R2F.pint.com@service.com
Call-ID: 19971205T234505.56.78@pager.com
CSeq: 4711 SUBSCRIBE
Warning: xxx  fax aborted, will try for the next hour.
Content-Type:application/sdp

c=...
i=3 pages of 5 sent
t=...
```

3.5.3.3. Closing a monitoring session with an UNSUBSCRIBE request

At some point, either the Client's representative User Agent Server or the Gateway may decide to terminate the monitoring session. This is achieved by sending an UNSUBSCRIBE request to the correspondent server. Such a request indicates that the sender intends to close the monitoring session immediately, and, on receipt of the final response from the receiving server, the session is deemed over.

Note that unlike the SUBSCRIBE request, which is never sent by a PINT gateway, an UNSUBSCRIBE request can be sent by a PINT gateway to the User Agent Server to indicate that the monitoring session is closed. (This is analogous to the fact that a gateway never sends an INVITE, although it can send a BYE to indicate that a telephone call has ended.)

If the Gateway initiates closure of the monitoring session by sending an UNSUBSCRIBE message, it SHOULD include an "Expires:" header showing for how much longer after this monitoring session is closed it is willing to store information on the service session. This acts as a minimum time within which the Client can send a new SUBSCRIBE message to open another monitoring session; after the time indicated in the Expires: header the Gateway is free to dispose of any record of the service session, so that subsequent SUBSCRIBE requests can be rejected with a "606" response.

If the subscription period specified by the Client has expired, then the Gateway may send an immediate UNSUBSCRIBE request to the Client's representative User Agent Server. This ensures that the monitoring session always completes with a UNSUBSCRIBE/response exchange, and that the representative User Agent Server can avoid maintaining state in certain circumstances.

3.5.3.4. Timing of SUBSCRIBE requests

As it relies on the Gateway having a copy of the INVITEd session description, the SUBSCRIBE message is limited in when it can be issued. The Gateway must have received the service request to which this monitoring session is to be associated, which from the Client's perspective happens as soon as the Gateway has sent a 1xx response back to it.

However, once this has been done, there is no reason why the Client should not send a monitoring request. It does not have to wait for the final response from the Gateway, and it can certainly send the SUBSCRIBE request before sending the ACK for the Service request final response. Beyond this point, the Client is free to send a SUBSCRIBE request when it decides, unless the Gateway's final response to the initial service request indicated a short Expires: time.

However, there are good reasons (see 6.4) why it may be appropriate to start a monitoring session immediately before the service is confirmed by the PINT Client sending an ACK. At this point the Gateway will have decided whether or not it can handle the service request, but will not have passed the request on to the Executive System. It is therefore in a good position to ask the Executive

System to enable monitoring when it sends the service request onwards. In practical implementations, it is likely that more information on transient service status will be available if this is indicated as being important BEFORE or AS the service execution phase starts; once execution has begun the level of information that can be returned may be difficult to change.

Thus, whilst it is free to send a SUBSCRIBE request at any point after receiving an Interim response from the Gateway to its service request, it is recommended that the Client should send such a monitoring request immediately prior to sending an ACK message confirming the service if it is interested in transient service status messages.

3.5.4. The "Require:" header for PINT

PINT clients use the Require: header to signal to the PINT server that a certain PINT extension of SIP is required. PINT 1.0 defines two strings that can go into the Require header:

```
org.ietf.sip.subscribe  -- the server can fulfill SUBSCRIBE requests
                           and associated methods (see section 3.5.3)

org.ietf.sdp.require    -- the PINT server (or the SDP parser
                           associated to it) understands the "require"
                           attribute defined in (section 3.4.4)
```

Example:

```
      Require:org.ietf.sip.subscribe,org.ietf.sdp.require
```

A client SHOULD only include a Require: header where it truly requires the server to reject the request if the option is not supported.

3.5.5. PINT URLs within PINT requests

Normally the hostnames and domain names that appear in the PINT URLs are the internal affair of each individual PINT system. A client uses the appropriate SDP payload to indicate the particular service it wishes to invoke; it is not necessary to use a particular URL to identify the service.

A PINT URL is used in two different ways within PINT requests: within the Request-URI, and within the To: and From: headers. Use within the Request-URI requires clarification in order to ensure smooth interworking with the Telephone Network serviced by the PINT infrastructure, and this is covered next.

3.5.5.1. PINT URLS within Request-URIs

There are some occasions when it may be useful to indicate service information within the URL in a standardized way:

a. it may not be possible to use SDP information to route the request if it is encrypted;
b. it allows implementation that make use of I.N. "service indicators";
c. It enables multiple competing PINT gateways to REGISTER with a single "broker" server (proxy or redirect) (see section 6.3)

For these reasons, the following conventions for URLs are offered for use in PINT requests:

1. The user portion of a sip URL indicates the service to be requested. At present the following services are defined:

```
R2C   (for Request-to-Call)
R2F   (for Request-to-Fax)
R2HC  (for Request-to-Hear-Content)
```

The user portions "R2C", "R2F", and "R2HC" are reserved for the PINT milestone services. Other user portions MUST be used in case the requested service is not one of the Milestone services. See section 6.2 for some related considerations concerning registrations by competing PINT systems to a single PINT proxy server acting as a service broker.

2. The host portion of a sip URL contains the domain name of the PINT service provider.

3. A new url-parameter is defined to be "tsp" (for "telephone service provider"). This can be used to indicate the actual telephone network provider to be used to fulfill the PINT request.

Thus, for example:-

```
INVITE sip:R2C@pint.pintservice.com SIP/2.0
INVITE sip:R2F@pint.pintservice.com;tsp=telco.com SIP/2.0
INVITE sip:R2HC@pint.mycom.com;tsp=pbx23.mycom.com SIP/2.0
INVITE sip:13@pint.telco.com SIP/2.0
```

3.5.6. Telephony Network Parameters within PINT URLs

Any legal SIP URL can appear as a PINT URL within the Request-URI or To: header of a PINT request. But if the address is a telephone address, we indicated in section 3.4.3 that it may be necessary to include more information in order correctly to identify the remote telephone terminal or service. PINT clients MAY include these attribute tags within PINT URLs if they are necessary or a useful complement to the telephone number within the SIP URL. These attribute tags MUST be included as URL parameters as defined in [1] (i.e. in the semi-colon separated manner).

The following is an example of a PINT URL containing extra attribute tags:

```
sip:+9725228808@pint.br.com;user=phone;require=Q763-plan;a=Q763-plan:4
```

As we noted in section 3.4.3, these extra attribute parameters will not normally be needed within a URL, because there is a great deal of context available to help the server interpret the phone number correctly. In particular, there is the SIP URL within the To: header, and there is also the Request-URI. In most cases this provides sufficient information for the telephone network.

The SDP attributes defined in section 3 above will normally only be used when they are needed to supply necessary context to identify a telephone terminal.

3.5.7. REGISTER requests within PINT

A PINT gateway is a SIP user agent server. A User Agent Server uses the REGISTER request to tell a proxy or redirect server that it is available to "receive calls" (i.e. to service requests). Thus a PINT Gateway registers with a proxy or redirect server the service that is accessible via itself, whilst in SIP, a user is registering his/her presence at a particular SIP Server.

There may be competing PINT servers that can offer the same PINT service trying to register at a single PINT server. The PINT server might act as a "broker" among the various PINT gateways that can fulfill a request. A format for PINT URLs was specified in section 3.5.5 that enables independent PINT systems to REGISTER an offer to provide the same service. The registrar can apply its own mechanisms and policies to decide how to respond to INVITEs from clients seeking service (See section 6.3 for some possible deployment options). There is no change between SIP and PINT REGISTER semantics or syntax.

Of course, the information in the PINT URLs within the REGISTER request may not be sufficient to completely define the service that a gateway can offer. The use of SIP and SDP within PINT REGISTER requests to enable a gateway to specify in more detail the services it can offer is the subject of future study.

3.5.8. BYE Requests in PINT

The semantics of BYE requests within PINT requires some extra precision. One issue concerns conferences that "cannot be left", and the other concerns keeping call state after the BYE.

The BYE request [1] is normally used to indicate that the originating entity no longer wishes to be involved in the specified call. The request terminates the call and the media session. Applying this model to PINT, if a PINT client makes a request that results in invocation of a telephone call from A to B, a BYE request from the client, if accepted, should result in a termination of the phone call.

One might expect this to be the case if the telephone call has not started when the BYE request is received. For example, if a request to fax is sent with a t= line indicating that the fax is to be sent tomorrow at 4 AM, the requestor might wish to cancel the request before the specified time.

However, even if the call has yet to start, it may not be possible to terminate the media session on the telephone system side. For example, the fax call may be in progress when the BYE arrives, and perhaps it is just not possible to cancel the fax in session. Another possibility is that the entire telephone-side service might be completed before the BYE is received. In the above Request-to-Fax example, the BYE might be sent the following morning, and the entire fax has been sent before the BYE was received. It is too late to send the BYE.

In the case where the telephone network cannot terminate the call, the server MUST return a "606 Not Acceptable" response to the BYE, along with a session description that indicates the telephone network session that is causing the problem.

Thus, in PINT, a "Not Acceptable" response MAY be returned both to INVITE and BYE requests. It indicates that some aspect of the session description makes the request unacceptable.

By allowing a server to return a "Not Acceptable" response to BYE requests, we are not changing its semantics, just enlarging its use.

A combination of Warning: headers and i= lines within the session description can be used to indicate the precise nature of the problem.

Example:

```
SIP/2.0 606 Not Acceptable
From: ...
To: .......
.....
Warning: 399 pint.mycom.com Fax in progress, service cannot be
   aborted
Content-Type: application/sdp
Content-Length: ...

v=0
...
...
i=3 of 5 pages sent OK
c=TN  RFC2543  +12014064090
m=image 1 fax tif
a=fmtp:tif uri:http://tifsRus.com/yyyyyy.tif
```


Note that the server might return an updated session description within a successful response to a BYE as well. This can be used, for example, to indicate the actual start times and stop times of the telephone session, or how many pages were sent in the fax transmission.

The second issue concerns how long must a server keep call state after receiving a BYE. A question arises because other clients might still wish to send queries about the telephone network session that was the subject of the PINT transaction. Ordinary SIP semantics have three important implications for this situation:

1. A BYE indicates that the requesting client will clear out all call state as soon as it receives a successful response. A client SHOULD NOT send a SUBSCRIBE request after it has sent a BYE.

2. A server may return an Expires: header within a successful response to a BYE request. This indicates for how long the server will retain session state about the telephone network session. At any point during this time, a client may send a SUBSCRIBE request to the server to learn about the session state (although as explained in the previous paragraph, a client that has sent a BYE will not normally send a SUBSCRIBE).

3. When engaged in a SUBSCRIBE/NOTIFY monitoring session, PINT servers that send UNSUBSCRIBE to a URL listed in the Contact: header of a client request SHOULD not clear session state until after the successful response to the UNSUBSCRIBE message is received. For example, it may be that the requesting client host is turned off (or

in a low power mode) when the telephone service is executed (and is therefore not available at the location previously specified in the Contact: attribute) to receive the PINT server's UNSUBSCRIBE. Of course, it is possible that the UNSUBSCRIBE request will simply time out.

4. Examples of PINT Requests and Responses

4.1. A request to a call center from an anonymous user to receive a phone call.

```
C->S: INVITE  sip:R2C@pint.mailorder.com  SIP/2.0
      Via: SIP/2.0/UDP 169.130.12.5
      From: sip:anon-1827631872@chinet.net
      To: sip:+1-201-456-7890@iron.org;user=phone
      Call-ID: 19971205T234505.56.78@pager.com
      CSeq: 4711 INVITE
      Subject: Sale on Ironing Boards
      Content-type: application/sdp
      Content-Length: 174

      v=0
      o=- 2353687637 2353687637 IN IP4 128.3.4.5
      s=R2C
      i=Ironing Board Promotion
      e=anon-1827631872@chinet.net
      t=2353687637 0
      m=audio 1  voice -
      c=TN  RFC2543  +1-201-406-4090
```

In this example, the context that is required to interpret the To: address as a telephone number is not given explicitly; it is implicitly known to the R2C@pint.mailorder.com server. But the telephone of the person who wishes to receive the call is explicitly identified as an internationally significant E.164 number that falls within the North American numbering plan (because of the "+1" within the c= line).

4.2. A request from a non anonymous customer (John Jones) to receive a phone call from a particular sales agent (Mary James) concerning the defective ironing board that was purchased

```
C->S: INVITE  sip:marketing@pint.mailorder.com  SIP/2.0
      Via: SIP/2.0/UDP 169.130.12.5
      From: sip:john.jones.3@chinet.net
      To: sip:mary.james@mailorder.com
      Call-ID: 19971205T234505.56.78@pager.com
      CSeq: 4712 INVITE
```

```
Subject: Defective Ironing Board - want refund
Content-type: application/sdp
Content-Length: 150

v=0
o=- 2353687640 2353687640 IN IP4 128.3.4.5
s=marketing
e=john.jones.3@chinet.net
c= TN RFC2543  +1-201-406-4090
t=2353687640 0
m=audio 1  voice -
```


The To: line might include the Mary James's phone number instead of a email-like address. An implementation that cannot accept email-like URLs in the "To:" header must decline the request with a 606 Not Acceptable. Note that the sending PINT client "knows" that the PINT Gateway contacted with the "marketing@pint.mailorder.com" Request-URI is capable of processing the client request as expected. (see 3.5.5.1 for a discussion on this).

Note also that such a telephone call service could be implemented on the phone side with different details. For example, it might be that first the agent's phone rings, and then the customer's phone rings, or it might be that first the customer's phone rings and he hears silly music until the agent comes on line. If necessary, such service parameter details might be indicated in "a=" attribute lines within the session description. The specification of such attribute lines for service consistency is beyond the scope of the PINT 1.0 specifications.

4.3. A request from the same user to get a fax back on how to assemble the Ironing Board

```
C->S: INVITE  sip:faxback@pint.mailorder.com  SIP/2.0
      Via: SIP/2.0/UDP 169.130.12.5
      From: sip:john.jones.3@chinet.net
      To: sip:1-800-3292225@steam.edu;user=phone;phone-context=+1
      Call-ID: 19971205T234505.66.79@chinet.net
      CSeq: 4713 INVITE
      Content-type: application/sdp
      Content-Length: 218

      v=0
      o=- 2353687660 2353687660 IN IP4 128.3.4.5
      s=faxback
      e=john.jones.3@chinet.net
      t=2353687660 0
      m=application 1 fax URI
```

```
c=TN  RFC2543  1-201-406-4091
a=fmtp:URI uri:http://localstore/Products/IroningBoards/2344.html
```

In this example, the fax to be sent is stored on some local server (localstore), whose name may be only resolvable, or that may only be reachable, from within the IP network on which the PINT server sits. The phone number to be dialled is a "local phone number" as well. There is no "phone-context" attribute, so the context (in this case, for which nation the number is "nationally significant") must be supplied by the faxback@pint.mailorder.com PINT server.

If the server that receives it does not understand the number, it SHOULD decline the request and include a "Network Address Not Understood" warning. Note that no "require" attribute was used here, since it is very likely that the request can be serviced even by a server that does not support the "require" attribute.

4.4. A request from same user to have that same information read out over the phone

```
C->S: INVITE  sip:faxback@pint.mailorder.com  SIP/2.0
      Via: SIP/2.0/UDP 169.130.12.5
      From: sip:john.jones.3@chinet.net
      To: sip:1-800-3292225@steam.edu;user=phone;phone-context=+1
      Call-ID: 19971205T234505.66.79@chinet.net
      CSeq: 4713 INVITE
      Content-type: application/sdp
      Content-Length: 220

      v=0
      o=- 2353687660 2353687660 IN IP4 128.3.4.5
      s=faxback
      e=john.jones.3@chinet.net
      t=2353687660 0
      m=application 1 voice URI
      c=TN  RFC2543  1-201-406-4090
      a=fmtp:URI uri:http://localstore/Products/IroningBoards/2344.html
```

4.5. A request to send an included text page to a friend's pager.

In this example, the text to be paged out is included in the request.

```
C->S: INVITE  sip:R2F@pint.pager.com  SIP/2.0
      Via: SIP/2.0/UDP 169.130.12.5
      From: sip:scott.petrack@chinet.net
      To: sip:R2F@pint.pager.com
      Call-ID: 19974505.66.79@chinet.net
      CSeq: 4714 INVITE
```

```
      Content-Type: multipart/related; boundary=--next

      ----next
      Content-Type: application/sdp
      Content-Length: 236
      v=0
      o=- 2353687680 2353687680 IN IP4 128.3.4.5
      s=R2F
      e=scott.petrack@chinet.net
      t=2353687680 0
      m=text 1 pager plain
      c= TN  RFC2543  +972-9-956-1867
      a=fmtp:plain spr:2@53655768


      ----next
      Content-Type: text/plain
      Content-ID: 2@53655768
      Content-Length:50

      Hi Joe! Please call me asap at 555-1234.

      ----next--
```


4.6. A request to send an image as a fax to phone number +972-9-956-1867

```
C->S: INVITE  sip:faxserver@pint.vocaltec.com  SIP/2.0
      Via: SIP/2.0/UDP 169.130.12.5
      From: sip:scott.petrack@chinet.net
      To: sip:faxserver@pint.vocaltec.com
      Call-ID: 19971205T234505.66.79@chinet.net
      CSeq: 4715 INVITE
      Content-type: application/sdp
      Content-Length: 267

      v=0
      o=- 2353687700 2353687700 IN IP4 128.3.4.5
      s=faxserver
      e=scott.petrack@chinet.net
      t=2353687700 0
      m=image  1 fax  tif gif
      c= TN  RFC2543  +972-9-956-1867
      a=fmtp:tif  uri:http://petrack/images/tif/picture1.tif
      a=fmtp:gif  uri:http://petrack/images/gif/picture1.gif
```

The image is available as tif or as gif. The tif is the preferred format. Note that the http server where the pictures reside is local, and the PINT server is also local (because it can resolve machine name "petrack")

4.7. A request to read out over the phone two pieces of content in sequence.

First some included text is read out by text-to-speech. Then some text that is stored at some URI on the internet is read out.

```
C->S: INVITE  sip:R2HC@pint.acme.com  SIP/2.0
      Via: SIP/2.0/UDP 169.130.12.5
      From: sip:scott.petrack@chinet.net
      To: sip:R2HC@pint.acme.com
      Call-ID: 19974505.66.79@chinet.net
      CSeq: 4716 INVITE
      Content-Type: multipart/related; boundary=next

      --next
      Content-Type: application/sdp
      Content-Length: 316
      v=0
      o=- 2353687720 2353687720 IN IP4 128.3.4.5
      s=R2HC
      e=scott.petrack@chinet.net

      c= TN  RFC2543  +1-201-406-4091
      t=2353687720 0
      m=text  1  voice  plain
      a=fmtp:plain   spr:2@53655768
      m=text  1 voice plain
      a=fmtp:plain  uri:http://www.your.com/texts/stuff.doc

      --next
      Content-Type: text/plain
      Content-ID: 2@53655768
      Content-Length: 172

      Hello!! I am about to read out to you the document you
      requested, "uri:http://www.your.com/texts/stuff.doc".
      We hope you like acme.com's new speech synthesis server.
      --next--
```

4.8. Request for the prices for ISDN to be sent to my fax machine

```
INVITE sip:R2FB@pint.bt.co.uk  SIP/2.0
Via: SIP/2.0/UDP 169.130.12.5
To: sip:0345-12347-01@pint.bt.co.uk;user=phone;phone-context=+44
From: sip:hank.wangford@newts.demon.co.uk
Call-ID: 19981204T201505.56.78@demon.co.uk
CSeq: 4716 INVITE
Subject: Price List
Content-type: application/sdp
Content-Length: 169

v=0
o=- 2353687740 2353687740 IN IP4 128.3.4.5
s=R2FB
i=ISDN Price List
e=hank.wangford@newts.demon.co.uk
t=2353687740 0
m=text 1  fax -
c=TN  RFC2543  +44-1794-8331010
```

4.9. Request for a callback

```
INVITE sip:R2C@pint.bt.co.uk  SIP/2.0
Via: SIP/2.0/UDP 169.130.12.5
To: sip:0345-123456@pint.bt.co.uk;user=phone;phone-context=+44
From: sip:hank.wangford@newts.demon.co.uk
Call-ID: 19981204T234505.56.78@demon.co.uk
CSeq: 4717 INVITE
Subject: It costs HOW much?
Content-type: application/sdp
Content-Length: 176

v=0
o=- 2353687760 2353687760 IN IP4 128.3.4.5
s=R2C
i=ISDN pre-sales query
e=hank.wangford@newts.demon.co.uk
c=TN  RFC2543  +44-1794-8331013
t=2353687760 0
m=audio 1  voice -
```

4.10. Sending a set of information in response to an enquiry

```
INVITE sip:R2FB@pint.bt.co.uk  SIP/2.0
Via: SIP/2.0/UDP 169.130.12.5
To: sip:0345-12347-01@pint.bt.co.uk;user=phone;phone-context=+44
From: sip:colin.masterton@sales.hh.bt.co.uk
Call-ID: 19981205T234505.56.78@sales.hh.bt.co.uk
CSeq: 1147 INVITE
Subject: Price Info, as requested
Content-Type: multipart/related; boundary=next

--next
Content-type: application/sdp
Content-Length: 325
v=0
o=- 2353687780 2353687780 IN IP4 128.3.4.5
s=R2FB
i=Your documents
e=colin.masterton@sales.hh.bt.co.uk
t=2353687780 0
m=application 1  fax octet-stream
c=TN  RFC2543  +44-1794-8331010
a=fmtp:octet-stream uri:http://www.bt.co.uk/imgs/pipr.gif opr:
  spr:2@53655768

--next
Content-Type: text/plain
Content-ID: 2@53655768
Content-Length: 352

Dear Sir,
  Thank you for your enquiry. I have checked availability in your
area, and we can provide service to your cottage. I enclose a
quote for the costs of installation, together with the ongoing
rental costs for the line. If you want to proceed with this,
please quote job reference isdn/hh/123.45.9901.
Yours Sincerely,
   Colin Masterton
--next--
```

Note that the "implicit" faxback content is given by an EMPTY opaque reference in the middle of the fmtp line in this example.

4.11. Sportsline "headlines" message sent to your phone/pager/fax

(i) phone

```
      INVITE sip:R2FB@pint.wwos.skynet.com  SIP/2.0
      Via: SIP/2.0/UDP 169.130.12.5
      To:
sip:1-900-123-456-7@wwos.skynet.com;user=phone;phone-context=+1
      From: sip:fred.football.fan@skynet.com
      Call-ID: 19971205T234505.56.78@chinet.net
      CSeq: 4721 INVITE
      Subject: Wonderful World Of Sports NFL Final Scores
      Content-type: application/sdp
      Content-Length: 220

      v=0
      o=- 2353687800 2353687800 IN IP4 128.3.4.5
      s=R2FB
      i=NFL Final Scores
      e=fred.football.fan@skynet.com
      c=TN  RFC2543 +44-1794-8331013
      t=2353687800 0
      m=audio 1 voice x-pay
      a=fmtp:x-pay opr:mci.com/md5:<crypto signature>
```

(ii) fax

```
      INVITE sip:R2FB@pint.wwos.skynet.com  SIP/2.0
      Via: SIP/2.0/UDP 169.130.12.5
      To: sip:1-900-123-456-7@wwos.skynet.com;user=phone;
          phone-context=+1
      From: sip:fred.football.fan@skynet.com
      Call-ID: 19971205T234505.56.78@chinet.net
      CSeq: 4722 INVITE
      Subject: Wonderful World Of Sports NFL Final Scores
      Content-type: application/sdp
      Content-Length: 217

      v=0
      o=- 2353687820 2353687820 IN IP4 128.3.4.5
      s=R2FB
      i=NFL Final Scores
      e=fred.football.fan@skynet.com
      c=TN  RFC2543 +44-1794-8331010
      t=2353687820 0
      m=text 1 fax x-pay
      a=fmtp:x-pay opr:mci.com/md5:<crypto signature>
```

(iii) pager

```
INVITE sip:R2FB@pint.wwos.skynet.com  SIP/2.0
Via: SIP/2.0/UDP 169.130.12.5
To: sip:1-900-123-456-7@wwos.skynet.com;user=phone;
    phone-context=+1
From: sip:fred.football.fan@skynet.com
Call-ID: 19971205T234505.56.78@chinet.net
CSeq: 4723 INVITE
Subject: Wonderful World Of Sports NFL Final Scores
Content-type: application/sdp
Content-Length: 219

v=0
o=- 2353687840 2353687840 IN IP4 128.3.4.5
s=R2FB
i=NFL Final Scores
e=fred.football.fan@skynet.com
c=TN  RFC2543 +44-1794-8331015
t=2353687840 0
m=text 1 pager x-pay
a=fmtp:x-pay opr:mci.com/md5:<crypto signature>
```

Note that these are all VERY similar.

4.12. Automatically giving someone a fax copy of your phone bill

```
INVITE sip:BillsRUs@pint.sprint.com SIP/2.0
Via: SIP/2.0/UDP 169.130.12.5
To: sip:+1-555-888-1234@fbi.gov;user=phone
From: sip:agent.mulder@fbi.gov
Call-ID: 19991231T234505.56.78@fbi.gov
CSeq: 911 INVITE
Subject: Itemised Bill for January 98
Content-type: application/sdp
Content-Length: 247

v=0
o=- 2353687860 2353687860 IN IP4 128.3.4.5
s=BillsRUs
i=Joe Pendleton's Phone Bill
e=agent.mulder@fbi.gov
c=TN  RFC2543  +1-202-833-1010
t=2353687860 0
m=text 1  fax x-files-id
a=fmtp:x-files-id opr:fbi.gov/jdcn-123@45:3des;base64,<signature>
```

Note: in this case the opaque reference is a collection of data used to convince the Executive System that the requester has the right to get this information, rather than selecting the particular content (the A party in the To: field of the SIP "wrapper" does that alone).

5. Security Considerations

5.1. Basic Principles for PINT Use

A PINT Gateway, and the Executive System(s) with which that Gateway is associated, exist to provide service to PINT Requestors. The aim of the PINT protocol is to pass requests from those users on to a PINT Gateway so an associated Executive System can service those requests.

5.1.1. Responsibility for service requests

The facility of making a GSTN-based call to numbers specified in the PINT request, however, comes with some risks. The request can specify an incorrect telephone of fax number. It is also possible that the Requestor has purposely entered the telephone number of an innocent third party. Finally, the request may have been intercepted on its way through any intervening PINT or SIP infrastructure, and the request may have been altered.

In any of these cases, the result may be that a call is placed incorrectly. Where there is intent or negligence, this may be construed as harassment of the person incorrectly receiving the call. Whilst the regulatory framework for misuse of Internet connections differs throughout the world and is not always mature, the rules under which GSTN calls are made are much more settled. Someone may be liable for mistaken or incorrect calls.

Understandably, the GSTN Operators would prefer that this someone is not them, so they will need to ensure that any PINT Gateway and Executive System combination does not generate incorrect calls through some error in the Gateway or Executive system implementation or GSTN-internal communications fault. Equally, it is important that the Operator can show that they act only on requests that they have good reason to believe are correct. This means that the Gateway must not pass on requests unless it is sure that they have not been corrupted in transit from the Requestor.

If a request can be shown to have come from a particular Requestor and to have been acted on in good faith by the PINT service provider, then responsibility for making requests may well fall to the Requestor rather than the Operator who executed these requests.

Finally, it may be important for the PINT service provider to be able to show that they act only on requests for which they have some degree of assurance of origin. In many jurisdictions, it is a requirement on GSTN Operators that they place calls only when they can, if required, identify the parties to the call (such as when required to carry out a Malicious Call Trace). It is at least likely that the provider of PINT services will have a similar responsibility placed on them.

It follows that the PINT service provider may require that the identity of the Requestor be confirmed. If such confirmation is not available, then they may be forced (or choose) not to provide service. This identification may require personal authentication of the Requesting User.

5.1.2. Authority to make requests

Where GSTN resources are used to provide a PINT service, it is at least possible that someone will have to pay for it. This person may not be the Requestor, as, for example, in the case of existing GSTN split-charging services like free phone in which the recipient of a call rather than the originator is responsible for the call cost.

This is not, of course, the only possibility; for example, PINT service may be provided on a subscription basis, and there are a number of other models. However, whichever model is chosen, there may be a requirement that the authority of a Requestor to make a PINT request is confirmed.

If such confirmation is not available, then, again, the PINT Gateway and associated Executive System may choose not to provide service.

5.1.3. Privacy

Even if the identity of the Requesting User and the Authority under which they make their request is known, there remains the possibility that the request is either corrupted, maliciously altered, or even replaced whilst in transit between the Requestor and the PINT Gateway.

Similarly, information on the Authority under which a request is made may well be carried within that request. This can be sensitive information, as an eavesdropper might steal this and use it within their own requests. Such authority SHOULD be treated as if it were financial information (such as a credit card number or PIN).

The data authorizing a Requesting User to make a PINT request should be known only to them and the service provider. However, this information may be in a form that does not match the schemes normally used within the Internet. For example, X.509 certificates[14] are commonly used for secured transactions on the Internet both in the IP Security Architecture[12] and in the TLS protocol[13], but the GSTN provider may only store an account code and PIN (i.e. a fixed string of numbers).

A Requesting User has a reasonable expectation that their requests for service are confidential. For some PINT services, no content is carried over the Internet; however, the telephone or fax numbers of the parties to a resulting service calls may be considered sensitive. As a result, it is likely that the Requestor (and their PINT service provider) will require that any request that is sent across the Internet be protected against eavesdroppers; in short, the requests SHOULD to be encrypted.

5.1.4. Privacy Implications of SUBSCRIBE/NOTIFY

Some special considerations relate to monitoring sessions using the SUBSCRIBE and NOTIFY messages. The SUBSCRIBE message that is used to register an interest in the disposition of a PINT service transaction uses the original Session Description carried in the related INVITE message. This current specification does not restrict the source of such a SUBSCRIBE message, so it is possible for an eavesdropper to capture an unprotected session description and use this in a subsequent SUBSCRIBE request. In this way it is possible to find out details on that transaction that may well be considered sensitive.

The initial solution to this risk is to recommend that a session description that may be used within a subsequent SUBSCRIBE message SHOULD be protected.

However, there is a further risk; if the origin-field used is "guessable" then it might be possible for an attacker to reconstruct the session description and use this reconstruction within a SUBSCRIBE message.

SDP (see section 6 of [2], "o=" field) does not specify the mechanism used to generate the sess-id field, and suggests that a method based on timestamps produced by Network Time Protocol [16] can be used. This is sufficient to guarantee uniqueness, but may allow the value to be guessed, particularly if other unprotected requests from the same originator are available.

Thus, to ensure that the session identifier is not guessable the techniques described in section 6.3 of [17] can be used when generating the origin-field for a session description to be used inside a PINT INVITE message. If all requests from (and responses to) a particular PINT requesting entity are protected, then this is not needed. Where such a situation is not assured, AND where session monitoring is supported, then a method by which an origin-field within a session description is not guessable SHOULD be used.

5.2. Registration Procedures

Any number of PINT Gateways may register to provide the same service; this is indicated by the Gateways specifying the same "userinfo" part in the To: header field of the REGISTER request. Whilst such ambiguity would be unlikely to occur with the scenarios covered by "core" SIP, it is very likely for PINT; there could be any number of service providers all willing to support a "Request-To-Fax" service, for example.

Unless a request specifies the Gateway name explicitly, an intervening Proxy that acts on a registration database to which several Gateways have all registered is in a position to select from the registrands using whatever algorithm it chooses; in principle, any Gateway that has registered as "R2F" would be appropriate.

However, this opens up an avenue for attack, and this is one in which a "rogue" Gateway operator stands to make a significant gain. The standard SIP procedure for releasing a registration is to send a REGISTER request with a Contact field having a wildcard value and an expires parameter with a value of 0. It is important that a PINT Registrar uses authentication of the Registrand, as otherwise one PINT service provider would be able to "spoof" another and remove their registration. As this would stop the Proxy passing any requests to that provider, this would both increase requests being sent to the rogue and stop requests going to the victim.

Another variant on this attack would be to register a Gateway using a name that has been registered by another provider; thus a rogue Operator might register its Gateway as "R2C@pint.att.com", thereby hijacking requests.

The solution is the same; all registrations by PINT Gateways MUST be authenticated; this includes both new or apparent replacement registrations, and any cancellation of current registrations. This recommendation is also made in the SIP specification, but for the correct operation of PINT, it is very important indeed.

5.3. Security mechanisms and implications on PINT service

PINT is a set of extensions to SIP[1] and SDP[2], and will use the security procedures described in SIP. There are several implications of this, and these are covered here.

For several of the PINT services, the To: header field of SIP is used to identify one of the parties to the resulting service call. The PINT Request-To-Call service is an example. As mentioned in the SIP specification, this field is used to route SIP messages through an infrastructure of Redirect and Proxy server between the corresponding User Agent Servers, and so cannot be encrypted. This means that, although the majority of personal or sensitive data can be protected whilst in transit, the telephone (or fax) number of one of the parties to a PINT service call cannot, and will be "visible" to any interception. For the PINT milestone services this may be acceptable, since the caller named in the To: service is typically a "well known" provider address, such as a Call Center.

Another aspect of this is that, even if the Requesting User does not consider the telephone or fax numbers of the parties to a PINT service to be private, those parties might. Where PINT servers have reason to believe this might be the case they SHOULD encrypt the request, even if the Requestor has not done so. This could happen, for example, if a Requesting User within a company placed a PINT request and this was carried via the company's Intranet to their Proxy/firewall and thence over the Internet to a PINT Gateway at another location.

If a request carries data that can be reused by an eavesdropper either to "spoof" the Requestor or to obtain PINT service by inserting the Requestor's authorization token into an eavesdropper's request, then this data MUST be protected. This is particularly important if the authorization token consists of static text (such as an account code and/or PIN).

One approach is to encrypt the whole of the request, using the methods described in the SIP specification. As an alternative, it may be acceptable for the authorization token to be held as an opaque reference (see section 3.4.2.3 and examples 4.11 and 4.12), using some proprietary scheme agreed between the Requestor and the PINT service provider, as long as this is resistant to interception and re-use. Also, it may be that the authorization token cannot be used outside of a request cryptographically signed by the Requestor; if so then this requirement can be relaxed, as in this case the token cannot be re-used by another. However, unless both the Requestor and the Gateway are assured that this is the case, any authorization token MUST be treated as sensitive, and so MUST be encrypted.

A PINT request may contain data within the SDP message body that can be used more efficiently to route that request. For example, it may be that one Gateway and Executive System combination cannot handle a request that specifies one of the parties as a pager, whilst another can. Both gateways may have registered with a PINT/SIP Registrar, and this information may be available to intervening PINT/SIP Proxies. However, if the message body is encrypted, then the request cannot be decoded at the Proxy server, and so Gateway selection based on contained information cannot be made there.

The result is that the Proxy may deliver the request to a Gateway that cannot handle it; the implication is that a PINT/SIP Proxy SHOULD consider its choice for the appropriate Gateway subject to correction, and, on receiving a 501 or 415 rejection from the first gateway chosen, try another. In this way, the request will succeed if at all possible, even though it may be delayed (and tie up resources in the inappropriate Gateways).

This opens up an interesting avenue for Denial Of Service; sending a valid request that appears to be suitable for a number of different Gateways, and simply occupying those Gateways in decrypting a message requesting a service they cannot provide. As mentioned in section 3.5.5.1, the choice of service name to be passed in the userinfo portion of the SIP Request-URI is flexible, and it is RECOMMENDED that names be chosen that allow a Proxy to select an appropriate Gateway without having to examine the SDP body part. Thus, in the example given here, the service might be called "Request-To-Page" or "R2P" rather than the more general use of "R2F", if there is a possibility of the SDP body part being protected during transit.

A variation on this attack is to provide a request that is syntactically invalid but that, due to the encryption, cannot be detected without expending resources in decoding it. The effects of this form of attack can be minimised in the same way as for any SIP Invitation; the Proxy should detect the 400 rejection returned from the initial Gateway, and not pass the request onwards to another.

Finally, note that the Requesting User may not have a prior relationship with a PINT Gateway, whilst still having a prior relationship with the Operator of the Executive System that fulfills their request. Thus there may be two levels of authentication and authorization; one carried out using the techniques described in the SIP specification (for use between the Requestor and the Gateway), with another being used between the Requesting User or the Requestor and the Executive System.

For example, the Requesting User may have an account with the PINT service provider. That provider might require that requests include this identity before they will be convinced to provide service. In addition, to counter attacks on the request whilst it is in transit across the Internet, the Gateway may require a separate X.509-based certification of the request. These are two separate procedures, and data needed for the former would normally be expected to be held in opaque references inside the SDP body part of the request.

The detailed operation of this mechanism is, by definition, outside the scope of an Internet Protocol, and so must be considered a private matter. However, one approach to indicating to the Requestor that such "second level" authentication or authorization is required by their Service Provider would be to ask for this inside the textual description carried with a 401 response returned from the PINT Gateway.

5.4. Summary of Security Implications

From the above discussion, PINT always carries data items that are sensitive, and there may be financial considerations as well as the more normal privacy concerns. As a result, the transactions MUST be protected from interception, modification and replay in transit.

PINT is based on SIP and SDP, and can use the security procedures outlined in [1] (sections 13 and 15). However, in the case of PINT, the SIP recommendation that requests and responses MAY be protected is not enough. PINT messages MUST be protected, so PINT Implementations MUST support SIP Security (as described in [1], sections 13 & 15), and be capable of handling such received messages.

In some configurations, PINT Clients, Servers, and Gateways can be sure that they operate using the services of network level security [13], transport layer security [12], or physical security for all communications between them. In these cases messages MAY be exchanged without SIP security, since all traffic is protected already. Clients and servers SHOULD support manual configuration to use such lower layer security facilities.

When using network layer security [13], the Security Policy Database MUST be configured to provide appropriate protection to PINT traffic. When using TLS, a port configured MUST NOT also be configured for non-TLS traffic. When TLS is used, basic authentication MUST be supported, and client-side certificates MAY be supported.

Authentication of the Client making the request is required, however, so if this is not provided by the underlying mechanism used, then it MUST be included within the PINT messages using SIP authentication techniques. In contrast with SIP, PINT requests are often sent to parties with which a prior communications relationship exists (such as a Telephone Carrier). In this case, there may be a shared secret between the client and the PINT Gateway. Such PINT systems MAY use authentication based on shared secrets, with HTTP "basic authentication". When this is done, the message integrity and privacy must be guaranteed by some lower layer mechanism.

There are implications on the operation of PINT here though. If a PINT proxy or redirect server is used, then it must be able to examine the contents of the IP datagrams carried. It follows that an end-to-end approach using network-layer security between the PINT Client and a PINT Gateway precludes the use of an intervening proxy; communication between the Client and Gateway is carried via a tunnel to which any intervening entity cannot gain access, even if the IP datagrams are carried via this node. Conversely, if a "hop-by-hop" approach is used, then any intervening PINT proxies (or redirect servers) are, by implication, trusted entities.

However, if there is any doubt that there is an underlying network or transport layer security association in place, then the players in a PINT protocol exchange MUST use encryption and authentication techniques within the protocol itself. The techniques described in section 15 of RFC2543 MUST be used, unless there is an alternative protection scheme that is agreed between the parties. In either case, the content of any message body (or bodies) carried within a PINT request or response MUST be protected; this has implications on the options for routing requests via Proxies (see 5.3).

Using SIP techniques for protection, the Request-URI and To: fields headers within PINT requests cannot be protected. In the baseline PINT services these fields may contain sensitive information. This is a consideration, and if these data ARE considered sensitive, then this will preclude the sole use of SIP techniques; in such a situation, transport [12] or network layer [13] protection mechanisms MUST be used.

As a final point, this choice will in turn have an influence on the choice of transport layer protocol that can be used; if a TLS association is available between two nodes, then TCP will have to be used. This is different from the default behaviour of SIP (try UDP, then try TCP if that fails).

6. Deployment considerations and the Relationship PINT to I.N. (Informative)

6.1. Web Front End to PINT Infrastructure

It is possible that some other protocol may be used to communicate a Requesting User's requirements. Due to the high numbers of available Web Browsers and servers it seems likely that some PINT systems will use HTML/HTTP as a "front end". In this scenario, HTTP will be used over a connection from the Requesting User's Web Browser (WC) to an Intermediate Web Server (WS). This will be closely associated with a PINT Client (using some unspecified mechanism to transfer the data from the Web Server to the PINT Client). The PINT Client will represent the Requesting User to the PINT Gateway, and thus to the Executive System that carries out the required action.

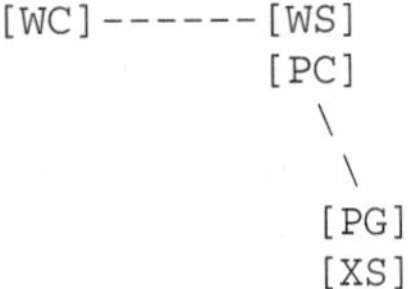

Figure 2: Basic "Web-fronted" Configuration

6.2. Redirects to Multiple Gateways

It is quite possible that a given PINT Gateway is associated with an Executive System (or systems) that can connect to the GSTN at different places. Equally, if there is a chain of PINT Servers, then each of these intermediate or proxy servers (PP) may be able to route PINT requests to Executive Systems that connect at specific points to the GSTN. The result of this is that there may be more than one PINT Gateway or Executive System that can deal with a given request. The mechanisms by which the choice on where to deliver a request are outside the scope of this document.

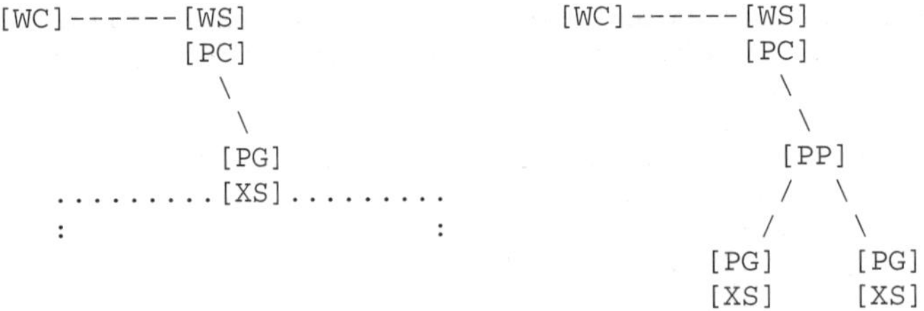

Figure 3: Multiple Access Configurations

However, there do seem to be two approaches. Either a Server that acts as a proxy or redirect will select the appropriate Gateway itself and will cause the request to be sent on accordingly, or a list of possible Locations will be returned to the Requesting User from which they can select their choice.

In SIP, the implication is that, if a proxy cannot resolve to a single unique match for a request destination, then a response containing a list of the choices should be returned to the Requesting User for selection. This is not too likely a scenario within the normal use of SIP.

However, within PINT, such ambiguity may be quite common; it implies that there are a number of possible providers of a given service.

6.3. Competing PINT Gateways REGISTERing to offer the same service

With PINT, the registration is not for an individual but instead for a service that can be handled by a service provider. Thus, one can envisage a registration by the PINT Server of the domain telcoA.com of its ability to support the service R2C as "R2C@telcoA.com", sent to an intermediary server that acts as registrar for the "broker.telcos.com" domain from "R2C@pint.telcoA.com" as follows:

```
REGISTER sip:registrar@broker.telcos.com SIP/2.0
To: sip:R2C@pint.telcoA.com
From: sip:R2C@pint.telcoA.com
...
```

This is the standard SIP registration service.

However, what happens if there are a number of different Service Providers, all of whom support the "R2C" service? Suppose there is a PINT system at domain "broker.com". PINT clients requesting a Request-to-Call service from broker.com might be very willing to be redirected or proxied to any one of the various service providers that had previously registered with the registrar. PINT servers might also be interested in providing service for requests that did not specify the service provider explicitly, as well as those requests that were directed "at them".

To enable such service, PINT servers would REGISTER at the broker PINT server registrations of the form:

```
REGISTER sip:registrar@broker.com SIP/2.0
To: sip:R2C@broker.com
From: sip:R2C@pint.telcoA.com
```

When several such REGISTER messages appear at the registrar, each differing only in the URL in the From: line, the registrar has many possibilities, e.g.:

(i) it overwrites the prior registration for "R2C@broker.telcos.com" when the next comes in;

(ii) it rejects the subsequent registration for "R2C@broker.telcos.com";

(iii) it maintains all such registrations.

In this last case, on receiving an Invitation for the "general" service, either:

(iii.1) it passes on the invitation to all registered service providers, returning a collated response with all acceptances, using multiple Location: headers,

or

(iii.2) it silently selects one of the registrations (using, for example, a "round robin" approach) and routes the Invitation and response onwards without further comment.

As an alternative to all of the above approaches, it:

(iv) may choose to not allow registrations for the "general" service, rejecting all such REGISTER requests.

The algorithm by which such a choice is made will be implementation-dependent, and is outside the scope of PINT. Where a behaviour is to be defined by requesting users, then some sort of call processing language might be used to allow those clients, as a pre-service operation, to download the behaviour they expect to the server making such decisions. This, however, is a topic for other protocols, not for PINT.

6.4. Limitations on Available Information and Request Timing for SUBSCRIBE

A reference configuration for PINT is that service requests are sent, via a PINT Gateway, to an Executive System that fulfills the Service Control Function (SCF) of an Intelligent Network (see [11]). The success or failure of the resulting service call may be information available to the SCF and so may potentially be made available to the PINT Gateway. In terms of historical record of whether or not a service succeeded, a large SCF may be dealing with a million call attempts per hour. Given that volume of service transactions, there are finite limits beyond which it cannot store service disposition records; expecting to find out if a Fax was sent last month from a busy SCF is unrealistic.

Other status changes, such as that on completion of a successful service call, require the SCF to arrange monitoring of the service call in a way that the service may not do normally, for performance reasons. In most implementations, it is difficult efficiently to interrupt a service to change it once it has begun execution, so it may be necessary to have two different services; one that sets GSTN resources to monitor service call termination, and one that doesn't. It is unlikely to be possible to decide that monitoring is required once the service has started.

These factors can have implications both on the information that is potentially available at the PINT Gateway, and when a request to register interest in the status of a PINT service can succeed. The alternative to using a general SCF is to provide a dedicated Service Node just for PINT services. As this node is involved in placing all service calls, it is in a position to collect the information needed. However, it may well still not be able to respond successfully to a registration of interest in call state changes once a service logic program instance is running.

Thus, although a Requesting User may register an interest in the status of a service request, the PINT Gateway may not be in a position to comply with that request. Although this does not affect the protocol used between the Requestor and the PINT Gateway, it may influence the response returned. To avoid the problem of changing service logic once running, any registration of interest in status changes should be made at or before the time at which the service request is made.

Conversely, if a historical request is made on the disposition of a service, this should be done within a short time after the service has completed; the Executive System is unlikely to store the results of service requests for long; these will have been processed as AMA (Automatic Message Accounting) records quickly, after which the Executive System has no reason to keep them, and so they may be discarded.

Where the PINT Gateway and the Executive System are intimately linked, the Gateway can respond to status subscription requests that occur while a service is running. It may accept these requests and simply not even try to query the Executive System until it has information that a service has completed, merely returning the final status. Thus the PINT Requestor may be in what it believes is a monitoring state, whilst the PINT Gateway has not even informed the

Executive System that a request has been made. This will increase the internal complexity of the PINT Gateway in that it will have a complex set of interlocking state machines, but does mean that status registration and indication CAN be provided in conjunction with an I.N. system.

6.5. Parameters needed for invoking traditional GSTN Services within PINT

This section describes how parameters needed to specify certain traditional GSTN services can be carried within PINT requests.

6.5.1. Service Identifier

When a Requesting User asks for a service to be performed, he or she will, of course, have to specify in some way which service. This can be done in the URLs within the To: header and the Request-URI (see section 3.5.5.1).

6.5.2. A and B parties

With the Request-to-Call service, they will also need to specify the A and B parties they want to be engaged in the resulting service call. The A party could identify, for example, the Call Center from which they want a call back, whilst the B party is their telephone number (i.e. who the Call Center agent is to call).

The Request-to-Fax and Request-to-Hear-Content services require the B party to be specified (respectively the telephone number of the destination Fax machine or the telephone to which spoken content is to be delivered), but the A party is a Telephone Network based resource (either a Fax or speech transcoder/sender), and is implicit; the Requesting User does not (and cannot) specify it.

With the "Fax-Back" variant of the Request-to-Fax service, (i.e. where the content to be delivered resides on the GSTN) they will also have specify two parties. As before, the B party is the telephone number of the fax machine to which they want a fax to be sent. However, within this variant the A party identifies the "document context" for the GSTN-based document store from which a particular document is to be retrieved; the analogy here is to a GSTN user dialling a particular telephone number and then entering the document number to be returned using "touch tone" digits. The telephone number they dial is that of the document store or A party, with the "touch tone" digits selecting the document within that store.

6.5.3. Other Service Parameters

In terms of the extra parameters to the request, the services again differ. The Request-to-Call service needs only the A and B parties. Also it is convenient to assert that the resulting service call will carry voice, as the Executive System within the destination GSTN may be able to check that assertion against the A and B party numbers specified and may treat the call differently.

With the Request-to-Fax and Request-to-Hear-Content services, the source information to be transcoded is held on the Internet. That means either that this information is carried along with the request itself, or that a reference to the source of this information is given.

In addition, it is convenient to assert that the service call will carry fax or voice, and, where possible, to specify the format for the source information.

The GSTN-based content or "Fax-Back" variant of the Request-to-Fax service needs to specify the Document Store number and the Fax machine number to which the information is to be delivered. It is convenient to assert that the call will carry Fax data, as the destination Executive System may be able to check that assertion against the document store number and that of the destination Fax machine.

In addition, the document number may also need to be sent. This parameter is an opaque reference that is carried through the Internet but has significance only within the GSTN. The document store number and document number together uniquely specify the actual content to be faxed.

6.5.4. Service Parameter Summary

The following table summarises the information needed in order to specify fully the intent of a GSTN service request. Note that it excludes any other parameters (such as authentication or authorisation tokens, or Expires: or CallId: headers) that may be used in a request.

Service	ServiceID	AParty	BParty	CallFmt	Source	SourceFmt
R2C	x	x	x	voice	-	-
R2F	x	-	x	fax	URI/IL	ISF/ILSF
R2FB	x	x	x	fax	OR	-
R2HC	x	-	x	voice	URI/IL	ISF/ILSF

In this table, "x" means that the parameter is required, whilst "-" means that the parameter is not required.

The Services listed are Request-to-Call (R2C), Request-to-Fax (R2F), the GSTN-based content or "Fax-back" Variant of Request-to-Fax (R2FB), and Request-to-Hear-Content (R2HC).

The Call Format parameter values "voice" or "fax" indicate the kind of service call that results.

The Source Indicator "URI/IL" implies that the information is either an Internet source reference (a Universal Resource Identifier, or URI) or is carried "in-line" with the message. The Source indicator "OR" means that the value passed is an Opaque Reference that should be carried along with the rest of the message but is to be interpreted only within the destination (GSTN) context. As an alternative, it could be given as a "local" reference with the "file" style, or even using a partial reference with the "http" style. However, the way in which such a reference is interpreted is a matter for the receiving PINT Server and Executive System; it remains, in effect, an opaque reference.

The Source Format value "ISF/ILSF" means that the format of the source is specified either in terms of the URI or that it is carried "in-line". Note that, for some data, the format either can be detected by inspection or, if all else fails, can be assumed from the URI (for example, by assuming that the file extension part of a URL indicates the data type). For an opaque reference, the Source Format is not available on the Internet, and so is not given.

6.6. Parameter Mapping to PINT Extensions

This section describes the way in which the parameters needed to specify a GSTN service request fully might be carried within a "PINT extended" message. There are other choices, and these are not precluded. However, in order to ensure that the Requesting User receives the service that they expect, it is necessary to have some shared understanding of the parameters passed and the behaviour expected of the PINT Server and its attendant Executive System.

The Service Identifier can be sent as the userinfo element of the Request-URI. Thus, the first line of a PINT Invitation would be of the form:

```
INVITE <serviceID>@<pint-server>.<domain>  SIP/2.0
```

The A Party for the Request-to-Call and "Fax-back" variant of Request-to-Fax service can be held in the "To:" header field. In this case the "To:" header value will be different from the Request-URI. In the services where the A party is not specified, the "To:" field is free to repeat the value held in the Request-URI. This is the case for Request-to-Fax and Request-to-Hear-Content services.

The B party is needed in all these milestone services, and can be held in the enclosed SDP sub-part, as the value of the "c=" field.

The call format parameter can be held as part of the "m=" field value. It maps to the "transport protocol" element as described in section 3.4.2 of this document.

The source format specifier is held in the "m=", as a type and either "-" or sub-type. The latter is normally required for all services except Request-to-Call or "Faxback", where the "-" form may be used. As shown earlier, the source format and source are not always required when generating requests for services. However, the inclusion in all requests of a source format specifier can make parsing the request simpler and allows for other services to be specified in the future, and so values are always given. The source format parameter is covered in section 3.4.2 as the "media type" element.

The source itself is identified by an "a=fmtp:" field value, where needed. With the exception of the Request-to-Call service, all invitations will normally include such a field. From the perspective of the SDP extensions, it can be considered as qualifying the media sub-type, as if to say, for example, "when I say jpeg, what I mean is the following".

In summary, the parameters needed by the different services are carried in fields as shown in the following table:

Service	Svc Param	PINT/SIP or SDP field used	Example value
R2C			
	ServiceID:	<SIP Request-URI userinfo>	R2C
	AParty:	<SIP To: field>	sip:123@p.com
	BParty:	<SDP c= field>	TN RFC2543 4567
	CallFormat:	<SDP transport protocol sub-field of m= field>	voice
	SourceFmt:	<SDP media type sub-field of m= field>	audio
		(--- only "-" sub-type sub-field value used)	---
	Source:	(--- No source specified)	---

```
R2F
        ServiceID:    <SIP Request-URI userinfo>      R2F
        AParty:       (--- SIP To: field not used) sip:R2F@pint.xxx.net
        BParty:       <SDP c= field>               TN RFCxxx +441213553
        CallFormat:   <SDP transport protocol
                           sub-field of m= field>     fax
        SourceFmt:    <SDP media type sub-field
                           of m= field>               image
                      <SDP media sub-type sub-field
                           of m= field>               jpeg
        Source:       <SDP a=fmtp: field qualifying
                           preceding m= field>    a=fmtp:jpeg<uri-ref>

R2FB
        ServiceID:    <SIP Request-URI userinfo>      R2FB
        AParty:       <SIP To: field>              sip:1-730-1234@p.com
        BParty:       <SDP c= field>               TN RFCxxx +441213553
        CallFormat:   <SDP transport protocol
                           sub-field of m= field>     fax
        SourceFmt:    <SDP media type sub-field
                           of m= field>               image
                      <SDP media sub-type sub-field
                           of m= field>               jpeg
        Source:       <SDP a=fmtp: field qualifying
                           preceding m= field>     a=fmtp:jpeg opr:1234

R2HC
        ServiceID:    <SIP Request-URI userinfo>      R2HC
        AParty:       (--- SIP To: field not used) sip:R2HC@pint.ita.il
        BParty:       <SDP c= field>               TN RFCxxx +441213554
        CallFormat:   <SDP transport protocol
                           sub-field of m= field>     voice
        SourceFmt:    <SDP media type sub-field
                           of m= field>               text
                      <SDP media sub-type sub-field
                           of m= field>               html
        Source:       <SDP a=fmtp: field qualifying
                           preceding m= field>     a=fmtp:html<uri-ref>
```

7. References

[1] Handley, M., Schooler, E., Schulzrinne, H. and J. Rosenberg, "SIP: Session Initiation Protocol", RFC 2543, March 1999.

[2] Handley, M. and V. Jacobsen, "SDP: Session Description Protocol", RFC 2327, April 1998.

[3] Freed, N. and N. Borenstein, "Multipurpose Internet Mail Extensions (MIME) Part One: Format of Internet Message Bodies", RFC 2045, November 1996.

[4] Freed, N. and N. Borenstein, "Multipurpose Internet Mail Extensions (MIME) Part Two: Media Types", RFC 2046, November 1996.

[5] The Unicode Consortium, "The Unicode Standard -- Version 2.0", Addison-Wesley, 1996.

[6] ITU-T Study Group 2, "E.164 - The International Public Network Numbering Plan", ITU-T, June 1997.

[7] Lu, H., Krishnaswamy, M., Conroy, L., Bellovin, S., Burg, F., DeSimone, A., Tewani, K., Davidson, P., Schulzrinne, H. and K. Vishwanathan "Toward the PSTN/Internet Inter-Networking--Pre-PINT Implementations", RFC 2458, November 1998.

[8] ITU-T Study Group XI, "Q.763 - Formats and Codes for the ISDN User Part of SS No7" ITU-T, August 1994.

[9] Berners-Lee, T., Fielding, R. and L. Masinter, "Uniform Resource Identifiers (URI): Generic Syntax", RFC 2396, August 1998.

[10] Crocker, D., "Standard for the format of ARPA Internet text messages", STD 11, RFC 822, August 1982.

[11] ITU-T Study Group XI, "Q.1204 - IN Distributed Functional Plane Architecture", ITU-T, February 1994.

[12] Dierks, T. and C. Allen, "The TLS Protocol Version 1.0", RFC 2246, January 1999.

[13] Kent, S. and R. Atkinson, "Security Architecture for the Internet Protocol", RFC 2401, November 1998.

[14] Housley, R., Ford, W., Polk W. and D. Solo, "Internet X.509 Public Key Infrastructure Certificate and CRL Profile", RFC 2459, January 1999.

[15] Crocker, D. and P. Overall, "Augmented BNF for Syntax Specifications: ABNF", RFC 2234, November 1997.

[16] Mills, D., "Network Time Protocol (version 3) specification and implementation", RFC 1305, March 1992.

[17] Eastlake, D., Crocker, S. and J.Schiller, "Randomness Recommendations for Security", RFC 1750, December 1994.

[18] Mockapetris, P., "Domain Names - Implementation and Specification", STD 13, RFC 1035, November 1987.

[19] Levinson, E., "The MIME Multipart/Related Content-type" RFC 2387, August 1998.

8. Acknowledgements

The authors wish to thank the members of the PINT working group for comments that were helpful to the preparation of this specification. Ian Elz's comments were extremely useful to our understanding of internal PSTN operations. The SUBSCRIBE and NOTIFY requests were first suggested by Henning Schulzrinne and Jonathan Rosenberg. The suggestion to use an audio port of 0 to express that the phone is "on hold" (i.e. not receiving voice) is due to Ray Zibman. Finally, thanks to Bernie Hoeneisen for his close proofreading.

Appendix A: Collected ABNF for PINT Extensions

```
;; --(ABNF is specified in RFC 2234 [15])

;; --Variations on SDP definitions

connection-field    = ["c=" nettype space addrtype space
                        connection-address CRLF]
; -- this is the original definition from SDP, included for completeness
; -- the following are PINT interpretations and modifications

nettype = ("IN"/"TN")
; -- redefined as a superset of the SDP definition

addrtype = (INAddrType / TNAddrType)
; -- redefined as a superset of the SDP definition

INAddrType = ("IP4"/"IP6")
; -- this non-terminal added to hold original SDP address types

TNAddrType = ("RFC2543"/OtherAddrType)

OtherAddrType = (<X-Token>)
; -- X-token is as defined in RFC2045

addr = (<FQDN> / <unicast-address> / TNAddr)
; -- redefined as a superset of the original SDP definition
; -- FQDN and unicast address as specified in SDP

TNAddr = (RFC2543Addr/OtherAddr)
; -- TNAddr defined only in context of nettype == "TN"

RFC2543Addr = (INPAddr/LDPAddr)

INPAddr = "+" <POS-DIGIT> 0*(("-" <DIGIT>)/<DIGIT>)
; -- POS-DIGIT and DIGIT as defined in SDP

LDPAddr = <DIGIT> 0*(("-" <DIGIT>)/<DIGIT>)

OtherAddr = 1*<uric>
; -- OtherAdd defined in the context of OtherAddrType
; -- uric is as defined in RFC2396

media-field = "m=" media <space> port <space> proto
                   1*(<space> fmt) <CRLF>
; -- NOTE redefined as subset/relaxation of original SDP definition
; -- space and CRLF as defined in SDP
```

```
media = ("application"/"audio"/"image"/"text")
; -- NOTE redefined as a subset of the original SDP definition
; -- This could be any MIME discrete type; Only those listed are
; --  used in PINT 1.0

port = ("0" / "1")
; -- NOTE redefined from the original SDP definition;
; -- 0 retains usual sdp meaning of "temporarily no media"
; -- (i.e. "line is on hold")
; -- (1 means there is media)

proto = (INProto/TNProto)
; -- redefined as a superset of the original SDP definition

INProto = 1* (<alpha-numeric>)
; -- this is the "classic" SDP protocol, defined if nettype == "IN"
; -- alpha-numeric is as defined in SDP
TNProto = ("voice"/"fax"/"pager")
; -- this is the PINT protocol, defined if nettype == "TN"

fmt = (<subtype> / "-")
; -- NOTE redefined as a subset of the original SDP definition
; -- subtype as defined in RFC2046, or "-". MUST be a subtype of type
held
; --  in associated media sub-field or the special value "-".

attribute-fields = *("a=" attribute-list <CRLF>)
; -- redefined as a superset of the definition given in SDP
; -- CRLF is as defined in SDP

attribute-list = 1(PINT-attribute / <attribute>)
; -- attribute is as defined in SDP

PINT-attribute = (clir-attribute / q763-nature-attribute /
                   q763plan-attribute / q763-INN-attribute /
                   phone-context-attribute / tsp-attribute /
                   pint-fmtp-attribute / strict-attribute)

clir-attribute = clir-tag ":" ("true" / "false")

clir-tag = "clir"

q763-nature-attribute = Q763-nature-tag ":" q763-natures

q763-nature-tag = "Q763-nature"

q763-natures = ("1" / "2" / "3" / "4")
```

```
q763-plan-attribute = Q763-plan-tag ":" q763-plans

q763-plan-tag = "Q763-plan"

q763-plans = ("1" / "2" / "3" / "4" / "5" / "6" / "7")
; -- of these, the meanings of 1, 3, and 4 are defined in the text

q763-INN-attribute = Q763-INN-tag ":" q763-INNs

q763-INN-tag = "Q763-INN"

q763-INNs = ("0" / "1")

phone-context-attribute = phone-context-tag ":" phone-context-ident

phone-context-tag = "phone-context"

phone-context-ident = network-prefix / private-prefix

network-prefix = intl-network-prefix / local-network-prefix

intl-network-prefix = "+" 1*<DIGIT>

local-network-prefix = 1*<DIGIT>

private-prefix = 1*excldigandplus 0*<uric>

excldigandplus = (0x21-0x2d,0x2f,0x40-0x7d))
tsp-attribute = tsp-tag "=" provider-domainname

tsp-tag = "tsp"

provider-domainname = <domain>
; -- domain is defined in RFC1035

; -- NOTE the following is redefined relative to the normal use in SDP
pint-fmtp-attribute = "fmtp:" <subtype> <space> resolution
                      *(<space> resolution)
                      (<space> ";" 1(<attribute>) *(<space>
<attribute>))
; -- subtype as defined in RFC2046.
; -- NOTE that this value MUST match a fmt on the ultimately preceeding
; --  media-field
; -- attribute is as defined in SDP

resolution = (uri-ref / opaque-ref / sub-part-ref)

uri-ref = uri-tag ":" <URI-Reference>
```

RFC 2848 67

```
; -- URI-Reference defined in RFC2396

uritag = "uri"

opaque-ref = opr-tag ":" 0*<uric>

opr-tag = "opr"

sub-part-ref = spr-tag ":" <Content-ID>
; -- Content-ID is as defined in RFC2046 and RFC822

spr-tag = "spr"

strict-attribute = "require:" att-tag-list

att-tag-list = 1(PINT-att-tag-list / <att-field> /
                    pint-fmtp-tag-list)
                  *(","
                    (PINT-att-tag-list / <att-field> /
                      pint-fmtp-tag-list)
                   )
; -- att-field as defined in SDP

PINT-att-tag-list = (phone-context-tag / clir-tag /
                        q763-nature-tag / q763-plan-tag /
                        q763-INN-tag)

pint-fmtp-tag-list = (uri-tag / opr-tag / spr-tag)

;; --Variations on SIP definitions

clir-parameter = clir-tag "=" ("true" / "false")

q763-nature-parameter = Q763-nature-tag "=" Q763-natures

q763plan-parameter = Q763-plan-tag "=" q763plans

q763-INN-parameter = Q763-INN-tag "=" q763-INNs

tsp-parameter = tsp-tag "=" provider-domainname

phone-context-parameter = phone-context-tag "=" phone-context-ident

SIP-param = ( <transport-param> / <user-param> / <method-param> /
                <ttl-param> / <maddr-param> / <other-param> )
; -- the values in this list are all as defined in SIP

PINT-param = ( clir-parameter / q763-nature-parameter /
```

```
                q763plan-parameter / q763-INN-parameter/
                tsp-parameter / phone-context-parameter )

URL-parameter = (SIP-param / PINT-param)
; -- redefined SIP's URL-parameter to include ones defined in PINT

Require-header = "require:" 1(required-extensions)
                             *("," required-extensions)
; -- NOTE this is redefined as a subset of the SIP definition
; -- (from RFC2543/section 6.30)

required-extensions = ("org.ietf.sip.subscribe" /
                       "org.ietf.sdp.require")
```


Appendix B: IANA Considerations

There are three kinds of identifier used in PINT extensions that SHOULD be registered with IANA, if a new value is specified. These are:

* Media Format sub-types, as described in section 3.4.2 of this document.
* Private Attributes as mentioned in section 3.4.3
* Private Phone Context values, as described in section 3.4.3.1.

It should be noted that private Address Types (in section 3.4.1) have been explicitly excluded from this process, as they must be in the form of an X-Token.

B.1. Media Format Sub-types

Taking these in turn, the media format sub-types are used within the PINT extensions to SDP to specify the attribute line that holds the data source definitions. In normal use, the values in this field are sub-types of MIME discrete types[4]. If a value other than an IANA-registered sub-type is to be used, then it should either be an X-Token (i.e. start with "X-") or it should be registered with IANA. if the intention is to describe a new MIME sub-type, then the procedures specified in RFC 2048 should be used. It is ASSUMED that any new MIME sub-type would follow the syntactic rules for interpretation of associated PINT fmtp lines defined in this document.

Note that, in keeping with the SDP description, such registrations SHOULD include the "proto" field values within which they are defined; however, it is appropriate to specify only that they can be used with "all values of TNProto".

Conversely, if the intent is to define a new way of including data source definitions within PINT, then it will be necessary to specify, in the documentation supporting any such new "PINT Media Format Sub-type" registration, the syntax of the associated "fmtp" attribute line, as the identifier serves to indicate the interpretation that should be made of format specific attribute lines "tagged" with such a sub-type.

If the fmtp interpretation follows the PINT default, then it is adequate to mention this in the defining document rather than repeating the syntax definition given here (although, in this case, it is unclear why such a new registration would be required). As before, the Media Format sub-type SHOULD specify the values of "proto" field within which it is defined, but this can be "all values of TNProto".

B.2. Private Attributes

Any proprietary attribute lines that are added may be registered with IANA using the procedures mentioned in [2]; the mechanism is the same as that used in SDP. If the attribute is defined for use only within PINT, then it may be appropriate to mention this in the supporting documentation. Note that, in the PINT 1.0 specification covered here, there is no mechanism to add such freshly registered attribute lines to a "require:" clause.

B.3. Private phone-contexts

Within the session description used for PINT requests, a phone-context attribute may be used to specify the prefix or context within which an associated telephone-number (in a connection line) should be interpreted.

For "public" phone contexts the prefix to be used MUST start with either a DIGIT or a "+". Private phone contexts may be registered with IANA that do NOT start with either of these characters. Such a prefix may be useful to identify a private network, potentially with an associated numeric ID (see example 4 in section 3.4.3.1). In the example, the prefix acts as the context for X-acme.com's private network numbering plan.

It is recommended that any private context to be registered have the general form of a token including a domain name, optionally followed by a digit string or other token. The appropriate form of the initial token name space will be similar to that used for private or vendor registrations for sub-types (e.g. vnd.acme.com). However, note that the registration will be used to specify a customer's private network numbering plan format rather than being used generally for all of their equipment vendor's customer's; thus, fbi.gov would be appropriate, but lucent.com would not (unless the private network were to be that used by Lucent internally).

In addition, the supporting documentation MUST either declare that there is no associated token, or define the syntax by which that token can be parsed (e.g. vnd.fbi.gov <space> 1*DIGIT). Note that the registration describes a format, not a value range; it is sufficient that the private context can be parsed, without the value being interpreted.

In detail, the registration request SHOULD include:

* Kind of registration (i.e. private phone-context attribute to be used within the service description of PINT service requests)
* Contact details for the person responsible for the registration request (name, organisation, e-mail address, public telephone number)
* Private Prefix initial token name (e.g. vnd.fbi.gov)
* syntax for private context (e.g. "vnd.fbi.gov" <space> 1*DIGIT, or "vnd.gtn.gov.uk")
* Description of use (e.g. "This phone context declares an associated telephone number to be within the 'government telecommunications network'; the number is in an internal or private number plan form)
* Network Type and Address Type with which this private context is associated; If the "normal" telephone types (as specified in this document) are used, then the values would be shown as: "nettype=TN" , addrtype="RFC2543Addr". If, however, this context were to be used with another address type, then a reference to that address type name and the syntax of that address value would be required.

In short, this context is the telephone equivalent of a "Net 10" address space behind a NAT, and the initial name (and contact information) shows the context within which that address is valid. It also specifies the format for the network and address types (and address value syntax) with which this context is associated.

Of course, IANA may refer the requested registration to the IESG or an appropriate IETF working group for review, and may require revisions to be made before the registration is accepted.

Authors' Addresses

Scott Petrack
MetaTel, Inc.
45 Rumford Ave.
Waltham MA 02453-3844

Phone: +1 (781)-891-9000
EMail: scott.petrack@metatel.com

Lawrence Conroy
Siemens Roke Manor Research
Roke Manor
Old Salisbury Lane
Romsey, Hampshire
U.K. SO51 0ZN

Phone: +44 (1794) 833666
EMail: lwc@roke.co.uk

Full Copyright Statement

Acknowledgement

Funding for the RFC Editor function is currently provided by the Internet Society.

Network Working Group
Request for Comments: 2871
Category: Informational

J. Rosenberg
dynamicsoft
H. Schulzrinne
Columbia University

June 2000

A Framework for Telephony Routing over IP

Status of this Memo

This memo provides information for the Internet community. It does not specify an Internet standard of any kind. Distribution of this memo is unlimited.

Copyright Notice

Abstract

This document serves as a framework for Telephony Routing over IP (TRIP), which supports the discovery and exchange of IP telephony gateway routing tables between providers. The document defines the problem of telephony routing exchange, and motivates the need for the protocol. It presents an architectural framework for TRIP, defines terminology, specifies the various protocol elements and their functions, overviews the services provided by the protocol, and discusses how it fits into the broader context of Internet telephony.

Table of Contents

RFC 2871 1

1 Introduction

This document serves as a framework for Telephony Routing over IP (TRIP), which supports the discovery and exchange of IP telephony gateway routing tables between providers. The document defines the problem of telephony routing exchange, and motivates the need for the protocol. It presents an architectural framework for TRIP, defines terminology, specifies the various protocol elements and their functions, overviews the services provided by the protocol, and discusses how it fits into the broader context of Internet telephony.

2 Terminology

We define the following terms. Note that there are other definitions for these terms, outside of the context of gateway location. Our definitions aren't general, but refer to the specific meaning here:

Gateway: A device with some sort of circuit switched network connectivity and IP connectivity, capable of initiating and terminating IP telephony signaling protocols, and capable of initiating and terminating telephone network signaling protocols.

End User: The end user is usually (but not necessarily) a human being, and is the party who is the ultimate initiator or recipient of calls.

Calling Device: The calling device is a physical entity which has IP connectivity. It is under the direction of an end user who wishes to place a call. The end user may or may not be directly controlling the calling device. If the calling device is a PC, the end user is directly controlling it. If, however, the calling device is a telephony gateway, the end user may be accessing it through a telephone.

Gatekeeper: The H.323 gatekeeper element, defined in [1].

SIP Server: The Session Initiation Protocol proxy or redirect server defined in [2].

Call Agent: The MGCP call agent, defined in [3].

GSTN: The Global Switched Telephone Network, which is the worldwide circuit switched network.

Signaling Server: A signaling server is an entity which is capable of receiving and sending signaling messages for some IP telephony signaling protocol, such as H.323 or SIP. Generally speaking, a signaling server is a gatekeeper, SIP server, or call agent.

Location Server (LS): A logical entity with IP connectivity which has knowledge of gateways that can be used to terminate calls towards the GSTN. The LS is the main entity that participates in Telephony Routing over IP. The LS is generally a point of contact for end users for completing calls to the telephony network. An LS may also be responsible for propagation of gateway information to other LS's. An LS may be coresident with an H.323 gatekeeper or SIP server, but this is not required.

Internet Telephony Administrative Domain (ITAD): The set of resources (gateways and Location Servers) under the control of a single administrative authority. End users are customers of an ITAD.

Provider: The administrator of an ITAD.

Location Server Policy: The set of rules which dictate how a location server processes information it sends and receives via TRIP. This includes rules for aggregating, propagating, generating, and accepting information.

End User Policy: Preferences that an end user has about how a call towards the GSTN should be routed.

Peers: Two LS's are peers when they have a persistent association between them over which gateway information is exchanged.

Internal peers: Peers that both reside within the same ITAD.

External peers: Peers that reside within different ITADs.

Originating Location Server: A Location Server which first generates a route to a gateway in its ITAD.

Telephony Routing Information Base (TRIB): The database of gateways an LS builds up as a result of participation in TRIP.

3 Motivation and Problem Definition

As IP telephony gateways grow in terms of numbers and usage, managing their operation will become increasingly complex. One of the difficult tasks is that of gateway location, also known as gateway selection, path selection, gateway discovery, and gateway routing. The problem occurs when a calling device (such as a telephony gateway or a PC with IP telephony software) on an IP network needs to complete a call to a phone number that represents a terminal on a circuit switched telephone network. Since the intended target of the call resides in a circuit switched network, and the caller is initiating the call from an IP host, a telephony gateway must be used. The gateway functions as a conversion point for media and signaling, converting between the protocols used on the IP network, and those used in the circuit switched network.

The gateway is, in essence, a relaying point for an application layer signaling protocol. There may be many gateways which could possibly complete the call from the calling device on the IP network to the called party on the circuit switched network. Choosing such a gateway is a non-trivial process. It is complicated because of the following issues:

Number of Candidate Gateways: It is anticipated that as IP telephony becomes widely deployed, the number of telephony gateways connecting the Internet to the GSTN will become large. Attachment to the GSTN means that the gateway will have connectivity to the nearly one billion terminals reachable on this network. This means that every gateway could theoretically complete a call to any terminal on the GSTN. As such, the number of candidate gateways for completing a call may be very large.

Business Relationships: In reality, the owner of a gateway is unlikely to make the gateway available to any user who wishes to connect to it. The gateway provides a useful service, and incurs cost when completing calls towards the circuit switched network. As a result, providers of gateways will, in many cases, wish to charge for use of these gateways. This may restrict usage of the gateway to those users who have, in some fashion, an established relationship with the gateway provider.

Provider Policy: In all likelihood, an end user who wishes to make use of a gateway service will not compensate the gateway provider directly. The end user may have a relationship with an IP telephony service provider which acts as an intermediary to providers of gateways. The IP telephony service provider may have gateways of its own as well. In this case, the IP telephony service provider may have policies regarding the usage of various gateways from other providers by its customers. These policies must figure into the selection process.

End User Policy: In some cases, the end user may have specific requirements regarding the gateway selection. The end user may need a specific feature, or have a preference for a certain provider. These need to be taken into account as well.

Capacity: All gateways are not created equal. Some are large, capable of supporting hundreds or even thousands of simultaneous calls. Others, such as residential gateways, may only support one or two calls. The process for selecting gateways should allow gateway capacity to play a role. It is particularly desirable to support some form of load balancing across gateways based on their capacities.

Protocol and Feature Compatibilities: The calling party may be using a specific signaling or media protocol that is not supported by all gateways.

From these issues, it becomes evident that the selection of a gateway is driven in large part by the policies of various parties, and by the relationships established between these parties. As such, there cannot be a global "directory of gateways" in which users look up phone numbers. Rather, information on availability of gateways must be exchanged by providers, and subject to policy, made available locally and then propagated to other providers. This would allow each provider to build up its own local database of available gateways - such a database being very different for each provider depending on policy.

From this, we can conclude that a protocol is needed between administrative domains for exchange of gateway routing information. The protocol that provides these functions is Telephony Routing over IP (TRIP). TRIP provides a specific set of functions:

- o Establishment and maintenance of peering relationships between providers;
- o Exchange and synchronization of telephony gateway routing information between providers;
- o Prevention of stable routing loops for IP telephony signaling protocols;
- o Propagation of learned gateway routing information to other providers in a timely and scalable fashion;
- o Definition of the syntax and semantics of the data which describe telephony gateway routes.

TRIP can be generally summarized as an inter-domain IP telephony gateway routing protocol.

4 Related Problems

At a high level, the problem TRIP solves appears to be a mapping problem: given an input telephone number, determine, based on some criteria, the address of a telephony gateway. For this reason, the gateway location problem is often called a "phone number to IP address translation problem". This is an over-simplification, however. There are at least three separate problems, all of which can be classified as a "phone number to IP address translation problem", and only one of which is addressed by TRIP:

- o Given a phone number that corresponds to a terminal on a circuit switched network, determine the IP address of a gateway capable of completing a call to that phone number.
- o Given a phone number that corresponds to a specific host on the Internet (this host may have a phone number in order to facilitate calls to it from the circuit switched network), determine the IP address of this host.
- o Given a phone number that corresponds to a user of a terminal on a circuit switched network, determine the IP address of an IP terminal which is owned by the same user.

The last of these three mapping functions is useful for services where the PC serves as an interface for the phone. One such service is the delivery of an instant message to a PC when the user's phone rings. To deliver this service, a switch in the GSTN is routing a call towards a phone number. It wishes to send an Instant Message to the PC for this user. This switch must somehow have access to the IP network, in order to determine the IP address of the PC corresponding to the user with the given phone number. The mapping function is a name to address translation problem, where the name happens to be represented by a string of digits. Such a translation function is best supported by directory protocols. This problem is not addressed by TRIP.

The second of these mappings is needed to facilitate calls from traditional phones to IP terminals. When a user on the GSTN wishes to call a user with a terminal on the IP network, they need to dial a number identifying that terminal. This number could be an IP address. However, IP addresses are often ephemeral, assigned on demand by DHCP [4] or by dialup network access servers using PPP [5]. The number could be a hostname, obtained through some translation of groups of numbers to letters. However, this is cumbersome. It has been proposed instead to assign phone numbers to IP telephony terminals. A caller on the GSTN would then dial this number as they would any other. This number serves as an alternate name for the IP terminal, in much the same way its hostname serves as a name. A switch in the GSTN must then access the IP network, and obtain the mapping from this number to an IP address for the PC. Like the previous case, this problem is a name to address translation problem, and is best handled by a directory protocol. It is not addressed by TRIP.

The first mapping function, however, is fundamentally an address to route translation problem. It is this problem which is considered by TRIP. As discussed in Section 3, this mapping depends on local factors such as policies and provider relationships. As a result, the database of available gateways is substantially different for each provider, and needs to be built up through specific inter-provider relationships. It is for this reason that a directory protocol is not appropriate for TRIP, whereas it is appropriate for the others.

5 Relationship with BGP

TRIP can be classified as a close cousin of inter-domain IP routing protocols, such as BGP [6]. However, there are important differences between BGP and TRIP:

- o TRIP runs at the application layer, not the network layer, where BGP resides.
- o TRIP runs between servers which may be separated by many intermediate networks and IP service providers. BGP runs between routers that are usually adjacent.

- o The information exchanged between TRIP peers describes routes to application layer devices, not IP routers, as is done with BGP.

- o TRIP assumes the existence of an underlying IP transport network. This means that servers which exchange TRIP routing information need not act as forwarders of signaling messages that are routed based on this information. This is not true in BGP, where the peers must also act as forwarding points (or name an adjacent forwarding hop) for IP packets.

- o The purpose of TRIP is not to establish global connectivity across all ITADs. It is perfectly reasonable for there to be many small islands of TRIP connectivity. Each island represents a closed set of administrative relationships. Furthermore, each island can still have complete connectivity to the entire GSTN. This is in sharp contrast to BGP, where the goal is complete connectivity across the Internet. If a set of AS's are isolated from some other set because of a BGP disconnect, no IP network connectivity exists between them.

- o Gateway routes are far more complex than IP routes (since they reside at the application, not the network layer), with many more parameters which may describe them.

- o BGP exchanges prefixes which represent a portion of the IP name space. TRIP exchanges phone number ranges, representing a portion of the GSTN numbering space. The organization and hierarchies in these two namespaces are different.

These differences means that TRIP borrows many of the concepts from BGP, but that it is still a different protocol with its own specific set of functions.

6 Example Applications of TRIP

TRIP is a general purpose tool for exchanging IP telephony routes between providers. TRIP does not, in any way, dictate the structure or nature of the relationships between those providers. As a result, TRIP has applications for a number of common cases for IP telephony.

6.1 Clearinghouses

A clearinghouse is a provider that serves as an exchange point between a number of other providers, called the members of the clearinghouse. Each member signs on with the clearinghouse. As part of the agreement, the member makes their gateways available to the other members of the clearinghouse. In exchange, the members have access to the gateways owned by the other members of the clearinghouse. When a gateway belonging to one member makes a call, the clearinghouse plays a key role in determining which member terminates the call.

TRIP can be applied here as the tool for exchanging routes between the members and the clearinghouse. This is shown in Figure 1.

There are 6 member companies, M1 through M6. Each uses TRIP to send and receive gateway routes with the clearinghouse provider.

6.2 Confederations

We refer to a confederation as a group of providers which all agree to share gateways with each other in a full mesh, without using a central clearinghouse. Such a configuration is shown in Figure 2. TRIP would run between each pair of providers.

6.3 Gateway Wholesalers

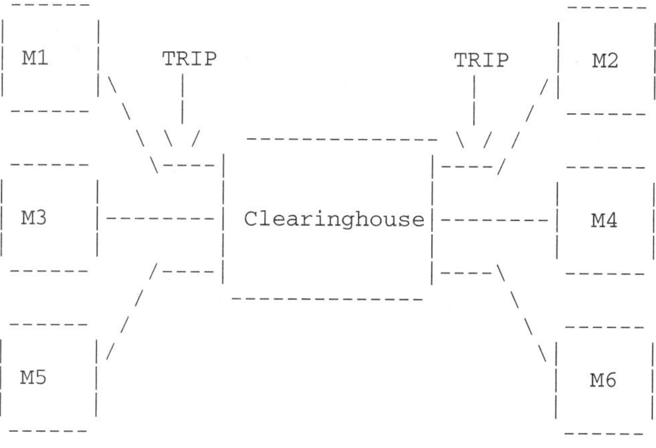

Figure 1: TRIP in the Clearinghouse Application

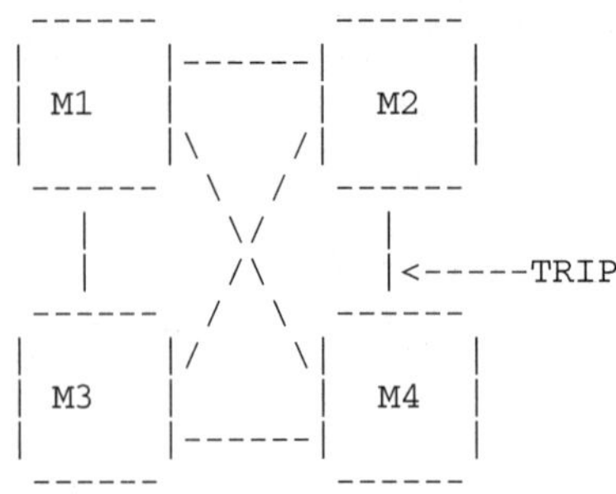

Figure 2: TRIP for Confederations

In this application, there are a number of large providers of telephony gateways. Each of these resells its gateway services to medium sized providers. These, in turn, resell to local providers who sell directly to consumers. This is effectively a pyramidal relationship, as shown in Figure 3.

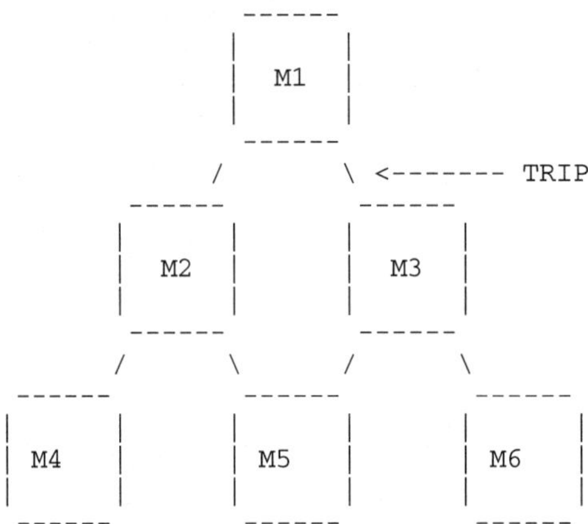

Figure 3: TRIP for Wholesalers

Note that in this example, provider M5 resells gateways from both M2 and M3.

7 Architecture

Figure 4 gives the overall architecture of TRIP.

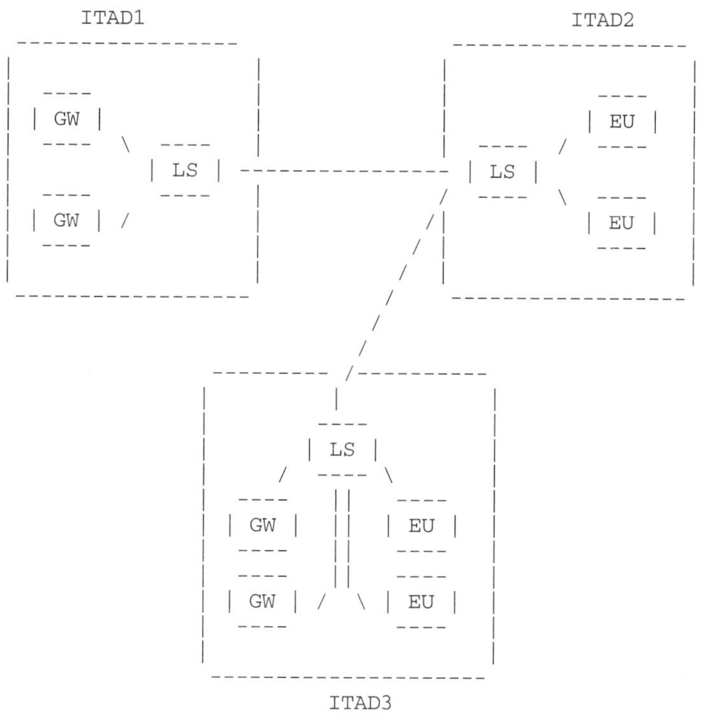

Figure 4: TRIP Architecture

There are a number of Internet Telephony administrative domains (ITAD's), each of which has at least one Location Server (LS). The LS's, through an out-of-band means, called the intra-domain protocol, learn about the gateways in their domain. The intra-domain protocol is represented by the lines between the GW and LS elements in ITAD1 in the Figure. The LS's have associations with other LS's, over which they exchange gateway information. These associations are established administratively, and are set up when the IT administrative domains have some kind of agreements in place regarding exchange of gateway information. In the figure, the LS in ITAD1 is connected to the LS in ITAD2, which is in turn connected to the LS in ITAD3. Through Telephony Routing over IP (TRIP), the LS in ITAD2 learns about the two gateways in ITAD1. This information is accessed by end users

(EUs) in ITAD2 through the front-end. The front-end is a non-TRIP protocol or mechanism by which the LS databases are accessed. In ITAD3, there are both EUs and gateways. The LS in ITAD3 learns about the gateways in ITAD1 through a potentially aggregated advertisement from the LS in ITAD2.

8 Elements

The architecture in Figure 4 consists of a number of elements. These include the IT administrative domain, end user, gateway, and location server.

8.1 IT Administrative Domain

An IT administrative domain consists of zero or more gateways, at least one Location Server, and zero or more end users. The gateways and LS's are those which are under the administrative control of a single authority. This means that there is one authority responsible for dictating the policies and configuration of the gateways and LS's.

An IT administrative domain need not be the same as an autonomous system. While an AS represents a set of physically connected networks, an IT administrative domain may consist of elements on disparate networks, and even within disparate autonomous systems.

The end users within an IT administrative domain are effectively the customers of that IT administrative domain. They are interested in completing calls towards the telephone network, and thus need access to gateways. An end user may be a customer of one IT administrative domain for one call, and then a customer of a different one for the next call.

An IT administrative domain need not have any gateways. In this case, its LS learns about gateways in other domains, and makes these available to the end users within its domain. In this case, the IT administrative domain is effectively a virtual IP telephony gateway provider. This is because it provides gateway service, but may not actually own or administer any gateways.

An IT administrative domain need not have any end users. In this case, it provides "wholesale" gateway service, making its gateways available to customers in other IT administrative domains.

An IT administrative domain need not have gateways nor end users. In this case, the ITAD only has LS's. The ITAD acts as a reseller, learning about other gateways, and then aggregating and propagating this information to other ITAD's which do have customers.

8.2 Gateway

A gateway is a logical device which has both IP connectivity and connectivity to some other network, usually a public or private telephone network. The function of the gateway is to translate the media and signaling protocols from one network technology to the other, achieving a transparent connection for the users of the system.

A gateway has a number of attributes which characterize the service it provides. Most fundamental among these are the range of phone numbers to which it is willing to provide service. This range may be broken into subranges, and associated with each, some cost metric or cost token. This token indicates some notion of cost or preference for completing calls for this part of the telephone number range.

A gateway has attributes which characterize the volume of service which it can provide. These include the number of ports it has (i.e., the number of simultaneous phone calls it can support), and the access link speed. These two together represent some notion of the capacity of the gateway. The metric is useful for allowing Location Servers to decide to route calls to gateways in proportion to the value of the metric, thus achieving a simple form of load balancing.

A gateway also has attributes which characterize the type of service it provides. This includes, but is not limited to, signaling protocols supported, telephony features provided, speech codecs understood, and encryption algorithms which are implemented. These attributes may be important in selecting a gateway. In the absence of baseline required features across all gateways (an admirable, but difficult goal), such a set of attributes is required in order to select a gateway with which communications can be established. End users which have specific requirements for the call (such as a user requesting a business class call, in which case certain call features may need to be supported) may wish to make use of such information as well.

Some of these attributes are transported in TRIP to describe gateways, and others are not. This depends on whether the metric can be reasonably aggregated, and whether it is something which must be conveyed in TRIP before the call is set up (as opposed to negotiated or exchanged by the signaling protocols themselves). The philosophy of TRIP is to keep it simple, and to favor scalability above abundance of information. TRIP's attribute set is readily extensible. Flags provide information that allow unknown attributes to be reasonably processed by an LS.

8.3 End Users

An end user is an entity (usually a human being) which wishes to complete a call through a gateway from an IP network to a terminal on a telephone network. An end user may be a user logged on at a PC with some Internet telephony software. The end user may also be connected to the IP network through an ingress telephone gateway, which the user accessed from telephone handset. This is the case for what is referred to as "phone to phone" service with the IP network used for interexchange transport.

End users may, or may not be aware that there is a telephony routing service running when they complete a call towards the telephone network. In cases where they are aware, end users may have preferences for how a call is completed. These preferences might include call features which must be supported, quality metrics, owner or administrator, and cost preferences.

TRIP does not dictate how these preferences are combined with those of the provider to yield the final gateway selection. Nor does TRIP support the transport of these preferences to the LS. This transport can be accomplished using the front end, or by some non-protocol means.

8.4 Location Server

The Location Server (LS) is the main functional entity of TRIP. It is a logical device which has access to a database of gateways, called the Telephony Routing Information Base (TRIB). This database of gateways is constructed by combining the set of locally available gateways and the set of remote gateways (learned through TRIP) based on policy. The LS also exports a set of gateways to its peer LS's in other ITAD's. The set of exported gateways is constructed from the set of local gateways and the set of remote gateways (learned through TRIP) based on policy. As such, policy plays a central role in the LS operation. This flow of information is shown in Figure 5.

```
                           |
                           |Intra-domain protocol
                         \ /
                        Local
                       Gateways


   TRIP-->  Gateways    POLICY     Gateways -->TRIP
               IN                     Out
                             |
                            \ /
                      Telephony Routing
                      Information Base
```

Figure 5: Flow of Information in TRIP

The TRIB built up in the LS allows it to make decisions about IP telephony call routing. When a signaling message arrives at a signaling server, destined for a telephone network address, the LS's database can provide information which is useful for determining a gateway or an additional signaling server to forward the signaling message to. For this reason, an LS may be coresident with a signaling server. When they are not coresident, some means of communication between the LS and the signaling server is needed. This communication is not specifically addressed by TRIP, although it is possible that TRIP might meet the needs of such a protocol.

An ITAD must have at least one LS in order to participate in TRIP. An ITAD may have more than one LS, for purposes of load balancing, ease of management, or any other reason. In that case, communications between these LS's may need to take place in order to synchronize databases and share information learned from external peers. This is often referred to as the interior component of an inter-domain protocol. TRIP includes such a function.

Figure 5 shows an LS learning about gateways within the ITAD by means of an intra-domain protocol. There need not be an intra-domain protocol. An LS may operate without knowledge of any locally run gateways. Or, it may know of locally run gateways, but through static configuration. An LS may also be co-resident with a gateway, in which case it would know about the gateway that it is co-resident with.

9 Element Interactions

9.1 Gateways and Location Servers

Gateways must somehow propagate information about their characteristics to an LS within the same ITAD. This LS may, in turn, further propagate this information outside of the ITAD by means of TRIP. This LS is called an originating LS for that gateway. When an LS nis not coresident with the gateway, the means by which the information gets propagated is not within the scope of TRIP. The protocol used to accomplish this is generally called an intra-domain protocol.

One way in which the information can be propagated is with the Service Location Protocol (SLP) [7]. The gateway can contain a Service Agent (SA), and the LS can act as a Directory Agent (DA). SLP defines procedures by which service information is automatically propagated to DA's from SA's. In this fashion, an LS can learn about gateways in the ITAD.

An alternate mechanism for the intra-domain protocol is via the registration procedures of SIP or H.323. The registration procedures provide a means by which users inform a gatekeeper or SIP server about their address. Such a registration procedure could be extended to allow a gateway to effectively register as well.

LDAP [8] might also be used for the intra-domain protocol. A gateway can use LDAP to add an entry for itself into the database. If the LS also plays the role of the LDAP server, it will be able to learn about all those gateways in its ITAD.

The intra-domain protocol which is used may be different from IT administrative domain to IT administrative domain, and is a matter of local configuration. There may also be more than one intra-domain protocol in a particular ITAD. An LS can also function without an intra-domain protocol. It may learn about gateways through static configuration, or may not know of any local gateways.

9.2 Location Server to Location Server

The interaction between LS's is what is defined by TRIP. LS's within the same ITAD use TRIP to synchronize information amongst themselves. LS's within different ITADs use TRIP to exchange gateway information according to policy. In the former case the LS's are referred to as internal peers, and in the latter case, external peers.

LS's communicate with each other through persistent associations. An LS may be connected to one or more other LS's. LS's need not be physically adjacent or part of the same autonomous system. The association between a pair of LS's is normally set up administratively. Two LS's are configured to communicate with each other when their administrators have an agreement in place to exchange gateway information. While TRIP does not provide an autodiscovery procedure for peer LS's to discover each other, one could possibly be used. Such a procedure might be useful for finding a backup peer LS when a crash occurs. Alternatively, in an environment where the business relationships between peers become more standardized, peers might be allowed to discover each other through protocols like the Service Location Protocol (SLP) [9]. Determination about whether autodiscovery should or should not be used is at the discretion of the administrator.

The syntax and semantics of the messages exchanged over the association between LS's are dictated by TRIP. The protocol does not dictate the nature of the agreements which must be in place. TRIP merely provides a transport means to exchange whatever gateway routing information is deemed appropriate by the administrators of the system. Details are provided in the TRIP protocol specification itself.

The rules which govern which gateway information is generated, propagated, and accepted by a gateway is called a location server policy. TRIP does not dictate or mandate any specific policy.

9.2.1 Nature of Exchanged Information

The information exchanged by the LS's is a set of routing objects. Each routing object minimally consists of a range of telephone numbers which are reachable, and an IP address or host name which is the application-layer "next hop" towards a gateway which can reach that range. Routing objects are learned from the intra-domain protocol, static configuration, or from LS's in remote ITAD's. An LS may aggregate these routing objects together (merging ranges of telephone numbers, and replacing the IP address with its own IP address, or with the IP address of a signaling server with which the LS is communicating) and then propagate them to another LS. The decision about which objects to aggregate and propagate is known as a route selection operation. The administrator has great latitude in selecting which objects to aggregate and propagate, so long as they are within the bounds of correct protocol operation (i.e., no loops are formed). The selection can be made based on information learned through TRIP, or through any out of band means.

A routing object may have additional information which characterizes the service at the gateway. These attributes include things like protocols, features supported, and capacity. Greater numbers of attributes can provide useful information, however, they come at a cost. Aggregation becomes difficult with more and more information, impacting the scalability of the protocol.

Aggregation plays a central role in TRIP. In order to facilitate scalability, routing objects can be combined into larger aggregates before being propagated. The mechanisms by which this is done are specified in TRIP. Aggregation of application layer routes to gateways is a non-trivial problem. There is a fundamental tradeoff between aggregatability and verbosity. The more information that is present in a TRIP routing object, the more difficult it is to aggregate.

Consider a simple example of two gateways, A and B, capable of reaching some set of telephone numbers, X and Y, respectively. C is an LS for the ITAD in which A and B are resident. C learns of A and B through some other means. As it turns out, X and Y can be combined into a single address range, Z. C has several options. It can propagate just the advertisement for A, just the advertisement for B, propagate both, or combine them and propagate the aggregate advertisement. In this case C chooses the latter approach, and sends a single routing object to one of its peers, D, containing address range Z and its own address, since it is also a signaling server. D is also a signaling server.

Some calling device, E, wishes to place a phone call to telephone number T, which happens to be in the address range X. E is configured to use D as its default H.323 gatekeeper. So, E sends a call setup message to D, containing destination address T. D determines that the address T is within the range Z. As D had received a routing object from C containing address range Z, it forwards the call setup message to C. C, in turn, sees that T is within range X, and so it forwards the call setup to A, which terminates the call signaling and initiates a call towards the telephone network.

RFC 2871 18

9.2.2 Quality of Service

One of the factors which is useful to consider when selecting a gateway is "QoS" - will a call through this gateway suffer sufficiently low loss, delay, and jitter? The quality of a call depends on two components - the QoS on the path between the caller and gateway, and the capacity of the gateway itself (measured in terms of number of circuits available, link capacity, DSP resources, etc.). Determination of the latter requires intricate knowledge of underlying network topologies, and of where the caller is located. This is something handled by QoS routing protocols, and is outside the scope of TRIP.

However, gateway capacity is not dependent on the caller location or path characteristics. For this reason, a capacity metric of some form is supported by TRIP. This metric represents the static capacity of the gateway, not the dynamic available capacity which varies continuously during the gateways operation. LS's can use this metric as a means of load balancing of calls among gateways. It can also be used as an input to any other policy decision.

9.2.3 Cost Information

Another useful attribute to propagate is a pricing metric. This might represent the amount a particular gateway might charge for a call. The metric can be an index into a table that defines a pricing structure according to a pre-existing business arrangement, or it can contain a representation of the price itself. TRIP itself does not define a pricing metric, but one can and should be defined as an extension. Using an extension for pricing means more than one such metric can be defined.

10 The Front End

As a result of TRIP, the LS builds up a database (the TRIB) of gateway routes. This information is made available to various entities within the ITAD. The way in which this information is made available is called the front end. It is the visible means by which TRIP services are exposed outside of the protocol.

10.1 Front End Customers

There are several entities which might use the front end to access the TRIB. These include, but are not limited to:

Signaling Servers: Signaling servers receive signaling messages (such as H.323 or SIP messages) whose purpose is the initiation of IP telephony calls. The destination address of these calls may be a phone number corresponding to a terminal on the GSTN. In order to route these calls to an appropriate gateway, the signaling server will need access to the database built up in the LS.

End Users: End users can directly query the LS to get routing information. This allows them to provide detailed information on their requirements. They can then go and contact the next hop signaling server or gateway towards that phone number.

Administrators: Administrators may need to access the TRIB for maintenance and management functions.

When a signaling server contacts the LS to route a phone number, it is usually doing so because a calling device (on behalf of an end user) has attempted to set up a call. As a result, signaling servers effectively act as proxies for end users when accessing the LS database. The communication between the calling devices and their proxies (the signaling servers) is through the signaling protocol.

The advantage of this proxy approach is that the actual LS interaction is hidden from the calling device. Therefore, whether the call is to a phone number or IP address is irrelevant. The routing in the case of phone numbers takes place transparently. Proxy mode is also advantageous for thin clients (such as standalone IP telephones) which do not have the interfaces or processing power for a direct query of the LS.

The disadvantage of the proxy approach is the same as its advantage - the LS interaction is hidden from the calling device (and thus the end user). In some cases, the end user may have requirements as to how they would like the call to be routed. These include preferences about cost, quality, administrator, or call services and protocols. These requirements are called the end user policy. In the proxy approach, the user effectively accesses the service through the signaling protocol. The signaling protocol is not likely to be able to support expression of complex call routing preferences from end users (note however, that SIP does support some forms of caller preferences for call routing [10]). Therefore, direct access from the end user to the LS can provide much richer call routing services.

When the end user policy is presented to the LS (either directly or through the signaling protocol), it is at the discretion of the LS how to make use of it. The location server may have its own policies regarding how end user preferences are handled.

10.2 Front End Protocols

There are numerous protocols that can be used in the front end to access the LS database. TRIP does not specify or restrict the possibilities for the front end. It is not clear that it is necessary or even desirable for there to be a single standard for the front end. The various protocols have their strengths and weaknesses. One may be the right solution in some cases, and another in different cases.

Some of the possible protocols for the front end are:

Service Location Protocol (SLP): SLP has been designed to fit exactly this kind of function. SLP is ideal for locating servers described by a set of attributes. In this case, the server is a gateway (or next hop towards the gateway), and the attributes are the end user policy. The end user is an SLP UA, and the LS is an SLP DA. The Service Query is used to ask for a gateway with a particular set of attributes.

Open Settlements Protocol (OSP): OSP [11] is a client server protocol. It allows the client to query a server with a phone number, and get back the address of a next hop, along with authorization tokens to use for the call. In this case, the server can be an LS. The routing table it uses to respond to OSP queries is the one built up using TRIP.

Lightweight Directory Access Protocol (LDAP): LDAP is used for accessing distributed databases. Since the LS server contains a database, LDAP could be used to query it.

Web Page: The LS could have a web front end. Users could enter queries into a form, and the matching gateways returned in the response. This access mechanism is more appropriate for human access, however. A signaling server would not likely access the front end through a web page.

TRIP: The protocols discussed above are all of the query-response type. There is no reason why the LS access must be of this form. It is perfectly acceptable for the access to be through complete database synchronization, so that the entity accessing the LS database effectively has a full copy of it. If this approach were desired, TRIP itself is an appropriate mechanism. This approach has obvious drawbacks, but nothing precludes it from being done.

11 Number Translations

The model for TRIP is that of many gateways, each of which is willing to terminate calls towards some set of phone numbers. Often, this set will be based on the set of telephone numbers which are in close geographic proximity to the gateway. For example, a gateway in New York might be willing to terminate calls to the 212 and 718 area codes. Of course, it is up to the administrator to decide on what phone numbers the gateway is willing to call.

However, certain phone numbers don't represent GSTN terminals at all, but rather they represent services or virtual addresses. An example of such numbers are freephone and LNP numbers. In the telephone network, these are actually mapped to routable telephone numbers, often based on complex formulae. A classic example is time-of-day-based translation.

While nothing prevents a gateway from advertising reachability to these kinds of numbers, this usage is highly discouraged. Since TRIP is a routing protocol, the routes it propagates should be to routable numbers, not to names which are eventually translated to routable numbers. Numerous problems arise when TRIP is used to propagate routes to these numbers:

- o Often, these numbers have only local significance. Calls to a freephone number made from New York might terminate in a New York office of a company, while calls made from California will terminate in a California branch. If this freephone number is injected into TRIP by a gateway in New York, it could be propagated to other LS's with end users in California. If this route is used, calls may be not be routed as intended.

- o The call signaling paths might be very suboptimal. Consider a gateway in New York that advertises a ported number that maps to a phone in California. This number is propagated by TRIP, eventually being learned by an LS with end users in California. When one of them dials this number, the call is routed over the IP network towards New York, where it hits the gateway, and then is routed over the GSTN back to California. This is a waste of resources. Had the ported number been translated before the gateway routing function was invoked, a California gateway could have been accessed directly.

As a result, it is more efficient to perform translations of these special numbers before the LS routing databases are accessed. How this translation is done is outside the scope of TRIP. It can be accomplished by the calling device before making the call, or by a signaling server before it accesses the LS database.

12 Security Considerations

Security is an important component in TRIP. The TRIP model assumes a level of trust between peer LS's that exchange information. This information is used to propagate information which determines where calls will be routed. If this information were incorrect, it could cause complete misrouting of calls. This enables a significant denial of service attack. The information might also be propagated to other

ITADs, causing the problem to potentially spread. As a result, mutual authentication of peer LS's is critical. Furthermore, message integrity is required.

TRIP messages may contain potentially sensitive information. They represent the routing capabilities of an ITAD. Such information might be used by corporate competitors to determine the network topology and capacity of the ITAD. As a result, encryption of messages is also supported in TRIP.

As routing objects can be passed via one LS to another, there is a need for some sort of end to end authentication as well. However, aggregation will cause the routing objects to be modified, and therefore authentication can only take place from the point of last aggregation to the receiving LS's.

13 Acknowledgments

The authors would like to thank Randy Bush, Mark Foster, Dave Oran, Hussein Salama, and Matt Squire for their useful comments on this document.

14 Bibliography

[1] International Telecommunication Union, "Visual telephone systems and equipment for local area networks which provide a non-guaranteed quality of service," Recommendation H.323, Telecommunication Standardization Sector of ITU, Geneva, Switzerland, May 1996.

[2] Handley, M., Schulzrinne, H., Schooler, E. and J. Rosenberg, "SIP: Session Initiation Protocol", RFC 2543, March 1999.

[3] Arango, M., Dugan, A., Elliott, I., Huitema, C. and S. Pickett, "Media Gateway Control Protocol (MGCP) Version 1.0", RFC 2705, October 1999.

[4] Droms, R., "Dynamic Host Configuration Protocol", RFC 2131, March 1997.

[5] Simpson, W., "The Point-to-Point Protocol (PPP)," STD 51, RFC 1661, July 1994.

[6] Rekhter Y. and T. Li, "A Border Gateway Protocol 4 (BGP-4)", RFC 1771, March 1995.

[7] Veizades, J., Guttman, E., Perkins, C. and S. Kaplan, "Service Location Protocol", RFC 2165, June 1997.

[8] Yeong, W., Howes, T. and S. Kille, "Lightweight Directory Access Protocol", RFC 1777, March 1995.

[9] Guttman, E., Perkins, C., Veizades, J. and M. Day, "Service Location Protocol, Version 2", RFC 2608, June 1999.

[10] Schulzrinne H. and J. Rosenberg, "SIP caller preferences and callee capabilities", Work in progress.

[11] European Telecommunications Standards Institute (ETSI), Telecommunications and Internet Protocol Harmonization Over Networks (TIPHON), "Inter-domain pricing, authorization, and usage exchange," Technical Specification 101 321 version 1.4.2, ETSI, 1998.

15 Authors' Addresses

Jonathan Rosenberg
dynamicsoft
72 Eagle Rock Avenue
First Floor
East Hanover, NJ 07936

Email: jdrosen@dynamicsoft.com

Henning Schulzrinne
Columbia University
M/S 0401
1214 Amsterdam Ave.
New York, NY 10027-7003

Email: schulzrinne@cs.columbia.edu

16. Full Copyright Statement

Acknowledgement

Funding for the RFC Editor function is currently provided by the Internet Society.

Network Working Group S. Donovan
Request for Comments: 2976 dynamicsoft
Category: Standards Track October 2000

The SIP INFO Method

Status of this Memo

This document specifies an Internet standards track protocol for the Internet community, and requests discussion and suggestions for improvements. Please refer to the current edition of the "Internet Official Protocol Standards" (STD 1) for the standardization state and status of this protocol. Distribution of this memo is unlimited.

Copyright Notice

Abstract

This document proposes an extension to the Session Initiation Protocol (SIP). This extension adds the INFO method to the SIP protocol. The intent of the INFO method is to allow for the carrying of session related control information that is generated during a session. One example of such session control information is ISUP and ISDN signaling messages used to control telephony call services.

This and other example uses of the INFO method may be standardized in the future.

Table of Contents

1. Introduction

The SIP protocol described in [1] defines session control messages used during the setup and tear down stages of a SIP controlled session.

In addition, the SIP re-INVITE can be used during a session to change the characteristics of the session. This is generally to change the properties of media flows related to the session or to update the SIP session timer.

However, there is no general-purpose mechanism to carry session control information along the SIP signaling path during the session.

The purpose of the INFO message is to carry application level information along the SIP signaling path.

The INFO method is not used to change the state of SIP calls, or the parameters of the sessions SIP initiates. It merely sends optional application layer information, generally related to the session.

It is necessary that the mid-session signaling information traverse the post session setup SIP signaling path. This is the path taken by SIP re-INVITEs, BYEs and other SIP requests that are tied to an individual session. This allows SIP proxy servers to receive, and potentially act on, the mid-session signaling information.

This document proposes an extension to SIP by defining the new INFO method. The INFO method would be used for the carrying of mid-call signaling information along the session signaling path.

1.1 Example Uses

The following are a few of the potential uses of the INFO message:

- Carrying mid-call PSTN signaling messages between PSTN gateways.

- Carrying DTMF digits generated during a SIP session.

- Carrying wireless signal strength information in support of wireless mobility applications.

- Carrying account balance information.

- Carrying images or other non streaming information between the participants of a session.

These are just potential uses; this document does not specify such uses nor does it necessarily recommend them.

It can also be envisioned that there will be other telephony and non-telephony uses of the INFO method.

2. INFO Method

The INFO method is used for communicating mid-session signaling information along the signaling path for the call.

The INFO method is not used to change the state of SIP calls, nor does it change the state of sessions initiated by SIP. Rather, it provides additional optional information which can further enhance the application using SIP.

The signaling path for the INFO method is the signaling path established as a result of the call setup. This can be either direct signaling between the calling and called user agents or a signaling path involving SIP proxy servers that were involved in the call setup and added themselves to the Record-Route header on the initial INVITE message.

The mid-session information can be communicated in either an INFO message header or as part of a message body. The definition of the message body and/or message headers used to carry the mid-session information is outside the scope of this document.

There are no specific semantics associated with INFO. The semantics are derived from the body or new headers defined for usage in INFO.

2.1 Header Field Support for INFO Method

Tables 1 and 2 add a column to tables 4 and 5 in the [1]. Refer to Section 6 of [1] for a description of the content of the tables. Note that the rules defined in the enc. and e-e columns in tables 4 and 5 in [1] also apply to use of the headers in the INFO request and responses to the INFO request.

2.2 Responses to the INFO Request Method

If a server receives an INFO request it MUST send a final response.

A 200 OK response MUST be sent by a UAS for an INFO request with no message body if the INFO request was successfully received for an existing call. Beyond that, no additional operations are required.

Header	Where	INFO
Accept	R	o
Accept-Encoding	R	o
Accept-Language	R	o
Allow	200	-
Allow	405	o
Authorization	R	o
Call-ID	gc	m
Contact	R	o
Contact	1xx	-
Contact	2xx	-
Contact	3xx	-
Contact	485	-
Content-Encoding	e	o
Content-Length	e	o
Content-Type	e	*
CSeq	gc	m
Date	g	o
Encryption	g	o
Expires	g	o
From	gc	m
Hide	R	o
Max-Forwards	R	o
Organization	g	o

Table 1 Summary of header fields, A-0

Handling of INFO messages that contain message bodies is outside the scope of this document. The documents defining the message bodies will also need to define the SIP protocol rules associated with those message bodies.

A 481 Call Leg/Transaction Does Not Exist message MUST be sent by a UAS if the INFO request does not match any existing call leg.

If a server receives an INFO request with a body it understands, but it has no knowledge of INFO associated processing rules for the body, the body MAY be rendered and displayed to the user. The INFO is responded to with a 200 OK.

If the INFO request contains a body that the server does not understand then, in the absence of INFO associated processing rules for the body, the server MUST respond with a 415 Unsupported Media Type message.

Header	Where	INFO
Priority	R	o
Proxy-Authenticate	407	o
Proxy-Authorization	R	o
Proxy-Require	R	o
Require	R	o
Retry-After	R	-
Retry-After	404,480,486	o
Retry-After	503	o
Retry-After	600,603	o
Response-Key	R	o
Record-Route	R	o
Record-Route	2xx	o
Route	R	o
Server	r	o
Subject	R	o
Timestamp	g	o
To	gc(1)	m
Unsupported	420	o
User-Agent	g	o
Via	gc(2)	m
Warning	r	o
WWW-Authenticate	401	o

Table 2 Summary of header fields, P-Z

Bodies which imply a change in the SIP call state or the sessions initiated by SIP MUST NOT be sent in an INFO message.

Other request failure (4xx), Server Failure (5xx) and Global Failure (6xx) responses MAY be sent for the INFO Request.

2.3 Message Body Inclusion

The INFO request MAY contain a message body.

2.4 Behavior of SIP User Agents

Unless stated otherwise, the protocol rules for the INFO request governing the usage of tags, Route and Record-Route, retransmission and reliability, CSeq incrementing and message formatting follow those in [1] as defined for the BYE request.

An INFO request MAY be cancelled. A UAS receiving a CANCEL for an INFO request SHOULD respond to the INFO with a "487 Request Cancelled" response if a final response has not been sent to the INFO and then behave as if the request were never received.

However, the INFO message MUST NOT change the state of the SIP call, or the sessions initiated by SIP.

2.5 Behavior of SIP Proxy and Redirect Servers

2.5.1 Proxy Server

Unless stated otherwise, the protocol rules for the INFO request at a proxy are identical to those for a BYE request as specified in [1].

2.5.2 Forking Proxy Server

Unless stated otherwise, the protocol rules for the INFO request at a proxy are identical to those for a BYE request as specified in [1].

2.5.3 Redirection Server

Unless stated otherwise, the protocol rules for the INFO request at a proxy are identical to those for a BYE request as specified in [1].

3. INFO Message Bodies

The purpose of the INFO message is to carry mid-session information between SIP user agents. This information will generally be carried in message bodies, although it can be carried in headers in the INFO message.

The definition of the message bodies or any new headers created for the INFO method is outside the scope of this document. It is expected that separate documents will be created to address definition of these entities.

In addition, the INFO method does not define additional mechanisms for ensuring in-order delivery. While the CSeq header will be incremented upon the transmission of new INFO messages, this should not be used to determine the sequence of INFO information. This is due to the fact that there could be gaps in the INFO message CSeq count caused by a user agent sending re-INVITES or other SIP messages.

4. Guidelines for extensions making use of INFO

The following are considerations that should be taken into account when defining SIP extensions that make use of the INFO method.

- Consideration should be taken on the size of message bodies to be carried by INFO messages. The message bodies should be kept small due to the potential for the message to be carried over UDP and the potential for fragmentation of larger messages.

- There is potential that INFO messages could be forked by a SIP Proxy Server. The implications of this forking of the information in the INFO message need to be taken into account.

- The use of multi-part message bodies may be helpful when defining the message bodies to be carried by the INFO message.

- The extensions that use the INFO message MUST NOT rely on the INFO message to do anything that effects the SIP call state or the state of related sessions.

- The INFO extension defined in this document does not depend on the use of the Require or Proxy-Require headers. Extensions using the INFO message may need the use of these mechanisms. However, the use of Require and Proxy-Require should be avoided, if possible, in order to improve interoperability between SIP entities.

5. Security Considerations

If the contents of the message body are private then end-to-end encryption of the message body can be used to prevent unauthorized access to the content.

There are no other security issues specific to the INFO method. The security requirements specified in the SIP specification apply to the INFO method.

6. References

[1] Handley, M., Schulzrinne, H., Schooler, E. and J. Rosenberg, "SIP: Session Initiation Protocol", RFC 2543, March 1999.

7. Acknowledgements

The author would like to thank Matthew Cannon for his contributions to this document. In addition, the author would like to thank the members of the MMUSIC and SIP working groups, especially Jonathan Rosenberg, for comments and suggestions on how to improve the document.

8. Author's Address

Steve Donovan
dynamicsoft
5100 Tennyson Parkway, Suite 200
Plano, Texas 75024

Email: sdonovan@dynamicsoft.com

9. Full Copyright Statement

Acknowledgement

Funding for the RFC Editor function is currently provided by the Internet Society.

Index

Related Titles from Morgan Kaufmann

http://www.mkp.com

- **Big Book of IPsec RFC's: Internet Security Architecture**
  Pete Loshin
  ISBN: - 0-12-455839-9; $34.95

- **Big Book of Border Gateway Protocol (BGP) RFCs**
  Pete Loshin
  ISBN: - 0-12-455846-1; $34.95

- **Big Book of Internet File Transfer RFCs**
  Pete Loshin
  ISBN: - 0-12-455845-3; $34.95

- **Big Book of Internet Host Standards RFCs**
  Pete Loshin
  ISBN: - 0-12-455844-5; $34.95

- **Big Book of IPv6 Addressing RFCs**
  Peter Salus
  ISBN: 0-12-616770-2; $34.95

- **Big Book of Lightweight Directory Access Protocol (LDAP) RFCs**
  Pete Loshin
  ISBN: - 0-12-455843-7; $34.95

- **Big Book of Terminal Emulation RFCs**
  Pete Loshin
  ISBN: - 0-12-455842-9; $34.95

- **Big Book of World Wide Web RFCs**
  Pete Loshin
  ISBN: - 0-12-455841-0; $34.95

- **Big Book of Best Current Practices (BCP) RFCs**
  Pete Loshin
  ISBN: - 0-12-455847-X; $34.95

- **Big Book of FYI RFCs**
  Pete Loshin
  ISBN: - 0-12-455848-8; $34.95